ETHICAL THEORY AND BUSINESS

Edited by

TOM L. BEAUCHAMP
NORMAN E. BOWIE

PRENTICE-HALL, INC., *Englewood Cliffs, New Jersey 07632*

Library of Congress Cataloging in Publication Data
Main entry under title:

Ethical theory and business.

  Includes bibliographies.
  1. Business ethics—Addresses, essays, lectures.
2. Business—Moral and religious aspects—Addresses,
essays, lectures.   3. Corporations—Moral and religious
aspects—Addresses, essays, lectures.   4. Industry—
Social aspects—Addresses, essays, lectures.
I. Beauchamp, Tom L.   II. Bowie, Norman E., date
HF5387.E82   174'.4   78-20875
ISBN 0-13-290460-8

Editorial/production supervision and interior
  design by Teru Uyeyama
Cover design by Edsal Enterprises
Manufacturing buyer: John Hall

©1979 by Prentice-Hall, Inc.
Englewood Cliffs, N.J. 07632

Printed in the United States of America

10   9   8   7   6   5   4   3   2

Prentice-Hall International, Inc., *London*
Prentice-Hall of Australia Pty. Limited, *Sydney*
Prentice-Hall of Canada, Ltd., *Toronto*
Prentice-Hall of India Private Limited, *New Delhi*
Prentice-Hall of Japan, Inc., *Tokyo*
Prentice-Hall of Southeast Asia Pte. Ltd., *Singapore*
Whitehall Books Limited, *Wellington, New Zealand*

CONTENTS

PREFACE

Recent work in applied ethics should have convinced many philosophers and nonphilosophers that ethical theory is relevant to the insightful discussion and resolution of moral problems. The sensational growth of courses and research in biomedical ethics, for example, has demonstrated that many problems in medicine, nursing, and the biological sciences are subject to ethical scrutiny. A similar movement is underway in legal ethics. It seems appropriate, then, that philosophers should also turn their attention to ethical issues in business.

This anthology is intended as a text for courses in this growing field. It provides a set of interrelated readings presenting different sides of important contemporary controversies. In every chapter we have attempted to provide articles that are free of technical jargon and yet contain depth of ethical and conceptual reflection. The articles have been selected on the basis of their teachability, clarity, and significance for ongoing controversies in both moral philosophy and business. Throughout the book the articles have been arranged to reflect a controversy between authors, in order that the strengths and weaknesses of alternative positions may be readily confronted. At the end of each chapter, suggested additional readings have been appended. These lists are to be interpreted as recommended readings, not as exhaustive bibliographies.

We have been able neither to address all the important questions nor to represent all points of view on the issues under discussion. We have tried, however, to provide the essentials of ethical theory and to distinguish questions about the enterprise of business itself from questions of ethics that arise within business. The main part of the anthology is directed to the latter type of question, and all chapters following the first two contain case studies, legal opinions, and contributions from both philosophers and persons in business.

Our special appreciation is owed to James Blandford for his helpful research and critical analysis, to William Pitt for comprehensive biblio-graphical searches, and to Bud Therien and Teru Uyeyama for profes-sionally shepherding the manuscript through its editorial stages. Both Mary Baker and Marguerite Baker endured retyping draft after draft of portions of this book—always with patience and good humor. Finally, we are grateful to those who agreed to produce the original essays prepared for this volume; thus, special thanks go to Jan Narveson, Carl Cohen, Joseph Margolis, Robert L. Holmes, Alex Michalos, Norman Gillespie, Peter A. French, Michael Hoffman and James Fisher.

TOM L. BEAUCHAMP

NORMAN E. BOWIE

Chapter 1

ETHICAL THEORY AND ITS APPLICATION TO BUSINESS

This book is about moral problems in business. It is not a traditional business text designed either to describe the nature of business or to give business advice to persons engaged in business, although we would of course not be unhappy if our discussions influenced how business people resolve their moral problems. In order to understand these special problems in business, one should have some acquaintance with ethical theory and how ethical theory helps resolve moral problems in general. This first chapter provides the fundamentals of ethical theory, while later chapters apply these fundamentals to moral problems in business.

An ethical theory is not something we are born with; it must be developed. When we are growing up, we learn that there are certain things we ought not to do and certain things we ought to do. For example, we are told: "Don't touch the hot stove." "Don't cross the street without looking both ways." "Brush your teeth after meals." "Eat your vegetables." Most of these oughts and ought nots are instructions which are in our self-interest. They are instructions in *prudence*. However, we are later given oughts or ought nots of a different kind. We are told either by our parents, teachers, or peers that there are certain things we ought or ought not to do because these actions affect the interests of other people. "Don't pull your sister's hair." "Don't take money from your Mother's pocketbook." "Share your toys." "Write a thank-you note to Grandma for the Christmas gift she sent you." As we grow up, we learn what society expects of us in terms of taking the interests of other people into account. We thus learn what society expects of us in the way of *moral* behavior.

Many people go through life with an understanding of morality not much different from that portrayed above; they have a view that might be called the checklist conception of conventional social morality. Other persons, however, are not satisfied simply to conform to the morality of society. Such individuals want difficult questions answered: Is what our society forbids really *wrong?* Is what our society values *really* good? What is the point of morality? Do the moral rules of society fit together in a unified whole, or are there conflicts and inconsistencies in society's moral rules? If there are conflicts and inconsistencies, how should they be resolved? What should we do when we face a moral problem for which society has as yet provided no instruction? One who raises questions such as these and works at answering them is engaged in ethical inquiry. To put it more formally, philosophical ethics is inquiry into theories of what is good and evil and into what is right and wrong (and thus is inquiry into what we ought and ought not to do). Persons actively engaged in normative ethics examine the theoretical basis of a society's morality and, where appropriate, make suggestions for improving it. Their reflection eventuates in systematic ethical theories, which provide rules that help us determine what ought to be done in situations of moral choice.

It is common to hear people say that ethics is of little concern to business persons. It is said that ethics is ethics and business is business. The implication is that ethical issues do not matter in business. Such a view is so fundamentally mistaken that one might wonder why it is widely held. First, the practice of business depends for its very existence on the moral behavior of the vast majority of citizens. Imagine trying to practice business in a society where lying, stealing, and other immoral actions were permitted. Business could not be practiced in such a society, for, at a minimum, business requires a society where contracts are honored and where private property is respected. Bribery, kickbacks, fraud, and monopolistic activities in the restraint of trade have all been judged inappropriate, because they are immoral practices. Second, there are and always have been special moral norms for business activity itself. These norms are usually devised by business persons. There are, for example, standards of good business practice. Sometimes these standards are written into special business codes of ethics.

Recently certain business practices have come under intense moral scrutiny. Many actions long acceptable in the business community are now widely condemned as immoral—e.g., the discharge of waste into the air and water, large political contributions to those who support business interests, and the payment of bribes by multinational corporations in countries where such payments are prevalent. Many persons in society are claiming that some business practices traditionally considered morally acceptable are no longer so considered. These persons are raising questions of ethical theory with respect to business practices and are thus challenging persons in business to respond. Since business activity takes place within a larger social framework, business persons will probably be forced to reflect on the moral judgments of their critics, and in turn they will be called upon to engage in ethical theory.

UTILITARIAN THEORIES

In contemporary philosophy, ethical theories are commonly divided into two fundamental types, teleological and deontological. Presumably these two approaches provide radically different perspectives on the moral life and entail different conclusions about what ought to be done. However, the two theories have never been demonstrated to be inconsistent, and their exact differences remain in question.

Teleological theories hold that the moral worth of actions or practices is determined solely by the consequences of the actions or practices. The most widely studied example of a teleological theory is utilitarianism. To understand utilitarianism, consider a person trying to decide whether or not he should give $50 to charity or spend it on gifts for a friend. The counsel of a utilitarian would be that one ought to make one's choice on the basis of that action which would lead to the production of the best consequences for all affected. Or, consider a debate in Congress concerning whether the minimum wage should be raised. The utilitarian would again urge that the decision be made on the basis of the greatest good for the greatest number. If a raise in the minimum wage would provide the greatest increment of good throughout society, then it should be approved. Otherwise it should not be approved. Utilitarianism, then, is the view that an action or practice is right (when compared to any alternative action or practice) if it leads to the greatest possible balance of good consequences and that the concepts of duty and right are subordinated to or determined by that which is good.

Although utilitarian views were espoused throughout the early history of ethical theory, the first developed utilitarian philosophical writings were those of David Hume (1711–1776), Jeremy Bentham (1748–1832), and John Stuart Mill (1806–1873). Bentham provides an especially appropriate example because he came to his utilitarian views as a result of his unhappiness with the British legal system and the writings of its chief apologist, William Blackstone. Bentham thought the British system for classifying crimes was outdated, because it was based on an abstract moral theory concerning the gravity of offenses. As an alternative, Bentham suggested that crimes be classified according to the unhappiness and misery a crime caused to the victims and to society. His revisions in the classification scheme were intended to bring about revisions in views on how severely certain crimes should be punished. Bentham's fundamental rule was that while the punishment for any crime should exceed the advantage gained by committing the crime, the punishment should not be any greater than that necessary to ensure that the crime is in the end disadvantageous for the criminal. Bentham thought that one should calculate the social benefits of rehabilitating and deterring criminals and should subtract from that figure the pain that punishment causes. One should punish up to, but should not exceed, that point where the infliction of pain brings about the greatest benefits in rehabilitation and deterrence. Prisons, then, should make sure that crime does not pay, but they should not go overboard.

Essential Features of Utilitarianism

Maximization of the Good. Several essential features of utilitarianism may be extracted from the reasoning of Bentham and other utilitarians. First, utilitarianism is committed to the maximization of the good, for it asserts that we ought always to produce the greatest possible balance of value for all persons affected. The obvious means to maximization is efficiency, a goal with which business executives are certainly sympathetic since efficiency is highly prized in the entire economic sector of society. Efficiency is a means to higher profits and to lower prices, and the struggle to be maximally profitable is what enables the free enterprise system as a whole to squeeze maximum production from limited economic resources. These produced goods and services are presumably intended to promote the greatest good of the greatest number. The utilitarian commitment to the principle of optimal productivity through efficiency is thus an essential part of the traditional business conception of society and a standard part of business practice. We could correctly say that the enterprise of business harbors a fundamentally utilitarian conception of the good society.

Intrinsic Goodness. There is more to utilitarianism than efficiency, however, and hence a second essential feature must be considered. Efficiency is simply an instrumental good. That is, efficiency is valuable strictly as a means to something else. In the corporation, efficiency is valuable as a means to maximizing profit. Within the free enterprise system of competing firms, efficiency is valuable as a means toward maximizing the production of goods and services. Within utilitarian moral theory, efficiency is the means for maximizing the good. But what things are "good" for the utilitarian? Utilitarians are in disagreement as to what constitutes the complete range of things that are good. Bentham is a hedonist, i.e., one who believes that pleasure or happiness (which are synonymous terms in this context) is the only thing good in and for itself. Everything besides pleasure is merely instrumentally good, i.e., good as a means to the end of pleasure. *Hedonistic* utilitarianism, then, believes that any act or practice which maximizes pleasure (when compared with any alternative act or practice) is right. Hedonistic utilitarians insist that "pleasure" covers a broad range of experiences and states of affairs, including most satisfactions we find in life. Nonetheless, later utilitarian philosophers have argued that other values besides pleasure possess intrinsic worth—e.g., values such as friendship, knowledge, courage, health, and beauty. Those utilitarians who believe in many intrinsic values are referred to as *pluralistic* utilitarians.

What, however, does it mean to say that something is intrinsically valuable rather than extrinsically valuable? That is, what does it mean to assert that some things are good in themselves and not merely good as a means to something else? We can begin to frame an answer to this question by considering, as an illustration, the procedure of abortion. Neither undergoing nor performing an abortion is considered by anyone to be something intrinsically good. However, many people would consider it sometimes extrinsically good as a means to another end, such as the restoration of an ill woman to a state of health, or the alleviation of an impossible financial burden from an already overwhelmed widow. Utilitarians believe that what we really ought to seek in life are certain experiences and conditions that are good in themselves without reference to their further consequences, and that all values are ultimately to be gauged in terms of these intrinsic goods. Health, friendship, and freedom from pain—but certainly not undergoing an abortion—would be included among such values by most pluralistic utilitarians. An intrinsic value, then, is a value in life that we wish to possess and enjoy just for its own sake and not for something else that it brings. Without such values, the things we pursue as means to other ends (extrinsic goods) would probably lose their value. If, for example, a surgical procedure such as an abortion technique is employed to restore a person to a state of health, but the health is not itself valued, then it is hard to understand what the value of the surgical procedure could be for that person.

The Measurement of Goods. A third essential feature of utilitarianism is its commitment to the measurement and comparison of goods. On the hedonistic view we must be able to measure pleasurable and painful states and be able to compare one person's pleasures with another's in order to decide which is greater. Bentham, for example, worked out a measurement device which he called the *hedonic calculus.* By using the calculus he could add the quantitative units of individual happiness, subtract the units of individual unhappiness, and thereby arrive at a measure of total happiness. The quantitative units of individual happiness are determined by considering the intensity, the duration, the certainty or uncertainty, the nearness or remoteness, the fecundity, the purity, and the extent of any proposed action or event. By the use of this hedonic calculus we allegedly can measure and compare individual happiness and can ultimately determine the act or practice that will provide the greatest happiness of the greatest number.

The idea that pleasurable experiences, or at least subjective preferences, can be measured and compared has had great appeal to economists and to the framers of public policy. Indeed, economic analysis was for some time expressed in utilitarian language. Many readers of this text may recall with some dismay their struggles in economics with "the law of diminishing marginal utility." This is not the place to rekindle unpleasant memories. However, a few examples will reveal how utilitarian analysis can be incorporated within economic thought. Historically, some economists have maintained that the maximum amount of goods and services can be squeezed from scarce resources through a free-market, competitive economy. These economists further believed that in maximizing the production of valued goods and services, happiness was maximized as well. Utilitarian analysis provided the bridge for that conclusion. Here is a simplified example: Suppose Sam goes to the grocery store for a six pack of beer. While there, he meets his friend Jim, who is also buying a six pack. Since both pay $1.50 for the beer, economists assume that, other things being equal, Sam and Jim receive the same satisfaction from the beer. Suppose, however, the price of beer goes up to $1.75, and Sam shifts to wine while Jim stays with the six pack. It is then assumed that Jim must obtain more satisfaction from a $1.75 six pack than Sam. By replacing Bentham's categories of certainty, nearness, fecundity, etc. with the measuring rod of *price*, economists have argued that an economy constructed along the lines of the postulates of free competition maximized utility (happiness). Economic theory was thus utilitarian at its core, and business theory borrowed and built upon that utilitarian base.

The Concept of Utility. We have discussed the notion of utility as if it could be easily understood in terms of traditional utilitarian ideas of intrinsic value. However, in recent philosophy, economics, and psychology, neither the approach of the hedonists nor that of the pluralists has prevailed. Both approaches have seemed relatively useless for purposes of objectively aggregating widely different interests in order to determine where maximal value, and therefore right action, lies. The contemporary approach is to appeal to the language of individual *preferences*. The concept of utility is understood from this perspective not in terms of experiences or states of affairs, but rather in terms of the actual preferences of an individual as determined by his behavior. In the language of business, utility is measured by what a person purchases or otherwise pursues. Accordingly, to maximize a person's utility is to provide that which he has chosen or would choose from among the available alternatives that might be produced. To maximize the utility of all persons affected by an action or policy is to maximize the utility of the aggregate group. This approach is indifferent as regards hedonistic or pluralistic construals of intrinsic value. What is intrinsically valuable is what individuals prefer to obtain, and utility is thus translated into the satisfaction of those needs and desires individuals choose to satisfy.

To many this modern approach to value seems preferable to its predecessors for two main reasons. First, disputes about hedonism and pluralism have proved interminable, sometimes ideological, and in the opinion of many irresolvable. One's choice of a range of these values seems deeply affected by personal experience, and the concept of preference seems to provide a way of avoiding such problems. Second, to make utilitarian calculations it is necessary, as we have seen, to measure values. While it is hard to know what it would mean to measure the value of pleasure or health or knowledge as a human state, it does make sense to measure preferences by devising a utility scale that measures strengths of individual and group preferences numerically. This approach has proved fruitful in recent discussions of health economics, for example, and it is bound to make a strong appeal to those in business who are both quantitatively oriented and wedded to the view that public policies and business activities should be closely related to the subjective preferences of those served by such policies and activities.

Act and Rule Utilitarianism

Utilitarian moral philosophers are conventionally divided into two types, act and rule utilitarians. An *act utilitarian* argues that in all situations one ought to perform that act which leads to the greatest good for the greatest number. Rules or practices are simply rules of thumb; they are guides to the actions that generally lead to the public good. An act utilitarian would not hesitate to violate such rules if he or she thought that in the circumstances such a violation would actually lead to the greatest good for the greatest number, for act utilitarians theoretically consider every circumstance open to any course of action, and thus no case is closed by rules.

Rule utilitarianism, on the other hand, is the theory that ethical actions and judgments should conform to firm and publicly advocated moral rules. Rules thus have a central role to play in determining correct behavior. For example, rules protect us from our own shortsightedness: when confronted with a particular situation, we are far too often tempted to believe that our case is a special case, that it is a legitimate exception to the rule. Viewing rules as merely rules of thumb only reinforces this attitude. Moreover, rule utilitarians argue that allegiance to the rules enables us to avoid acts of individual injustice. Consider a classic example: A small town has been plagued by a number of particularly vicious murders. The citizenry is near panic. Heavily armed homeowners sit behind their locked windows and doors. The local sheriff knows the identity of the killer, who has fled the country. He also knows that he will be unable to convince the local populace that the danger is over. The sheriff discovers a hobo in the freight yards. Although subsequent investigation shows that the hobo is innocent, he can be convincingly made to appear guilty. Since the hobo is without family or friends and the situation in the town is especially grave, he can be punished with a resulting increase in utility. On act utilitarian grounds, the punishment of the innocent in such circumstances seems morally required. But punishment of the innocent seems blatantly immoral. To save utilitarianism from such counter-intuitive conclusions as the punishment of innocent persons, the rule utilitarian requires that we look to rules or practices rather than to individual acts.

What can be said about a rule that permits punishment of the innocent in circumstances like those described above? Surely such a rule could not pass the test put forward by rule utilitarians. Such a rule would not, when followed generally, lead to the greatest good for the greatest number. The proper use of utilitarianism is to evaluate the rules, practices, and institutions of society to make sure they lead to the public good. However, individuals within society who are contemplating what to do should follow the rules. The test for individual action is the relevant rules or practices; and the test for rules and practices is utilitarianism itself (often called *the principle of utility*). As this applies to punishment, penal officials are duty bound to follow rules that provide for a fair trial, as well as the other relevant rules of criminal justice. These rules providing for a system of punishment are themselves justified by their utilitarian results. Many philosophers believe that rule utilitarianism is more adequate as a moral theory than act utilitarianism, because rule utilitarianism is not subject to the counterexamples (such as punishing the innocent) that plague act utilitarianism.

However, it should also be mentioned that act utilitarians have a ready reply to these criticisms advanced by rule utilitarians. Act utilitarians regard rule utilitarians as unfaithful to the fundamental demand of utilitarianism, which requires that we *maximize* happiness (or at least that we maximize intrinsic value). There are many cases in which abiding by a generally beneficial rule will not prove most beneficial to the persons involved, *even in the long run.* So the question arises whether a rule ought to be obeyed if obeying it does *not* maximize value. And, argue act utilitarians, the rule utilitarian cannot reply that it would be better that everybody should obey the rule than that nobody should. This objection fails, according to these writers, because there is a third possibility between never obeying a rule and always obeying it—viz., that it should be only sometimes obeyed. This objection perhaps reduces to the prediction that we will be better off in the moral life if we sometimes obey and sometimes disobey rules, because this kind of conduct will not fundamentally erode either moral rules or our general respect for morality. The rule utilitarian would, of course, challenge the part of this argument that claims less rather than more damage will be done to the institution of morality by adopting an act utilitarian position. Much current debate within utilitarianism focuses on this issue.

Business Morality: Egoism and Utilitarianism

Many business persons' views can be analyzed as a unique blend of egoism and utilitarianism. Business practice is egoistic in that each business is urged to pursue its own interest. Business practice is also egoistic to the extent that it is believed individuals should strive to be as successful in competition as possible. Business practice is utilitarian, however, in that it is believed that both corporate egoism and individual egoism lead to maximal utilitarian results. Although it can be argued that egoistic behavior yields utilitarian results, it is important that egoism be distinguished from utilitarianism. We can begin this task by distinguishing two varieties of egoism—psychological egoism and ethical egoism.

Psychological Egoism. Psychological egoism is the view that everyone is always motivated to act in his or her own perceived self-interest. To the obvious objection that people often claim to take the interests of others into account, the psychological egoist claims that we do so only when supporting the interests of others is in our self-interest. In loving others, for example, we strengthen their love for us. By sacrificing for our children, we take satisfaction in their achievements. By following society's moral codes, we avoid both the police and social ostracism. The egoist thus claims that the ultimate motive for any act is self-interest.

You may protest that people often act contrary to their self-interest and that some people seem to act contrary to their self-interest most of the time. The psychological egoist concedes this. People do make mistakes about what is in their self-interest, and a few people stupidly overlook their own best interest. The psychological egoist is not saying that people are motivated to act in terms of their *real* self-interest. The egoist is only committed to the view that everyone always is motivated to act in accordance with *perceived* self-interest.

As an account of the motivation of human behavior, psychological egoism has found a sympathetic response both in student quarters and in the world of business. To determine whether psychological egoism is true as a matter of psychological fact is a task too complicated for this introductory chapter. Nonetheless, two comments are in order: Since there do seem to be cases of genuinely altruistic acts that are clearly not in the interest of the individual performing them—for example, giving up one's life to save another—it is tempting for the psychological egoist to make his theory true by definition. This point can be clarified by an illustration. Suppose a biologist makes the claim that all swans are white. While traveling in Australia you discover a bird that has all the characteristics of a swan except one; it is black instead of white. Does this discovery refute the biologist? It is tempting for the biologist to claim that by definition something cannot be a swan unless it is white. If the biologist makes this move, he has given up his claim about the world and has proposed in its place a thesis about how he will use words. He will think up a new *name* for your new bird, rather than revise his scientific claim.

Psychological egoists often seem to succumb to similar temptations. When confronted with what looks like genuinely altruistic acts, they appeal to unconscious motives of self-interest or claim that every act is based on some desire of the person performing the act and that acting on that desire is what is meant by "self-interest." But this latter move is simply a verbal trick; for they have changed their definition of self-interest. At first it meant acting exclusively on behalf of one's own self-interest. Now self-interest has been redefined to mean acting on any interest one has. But of course the main question still remains. Are there two different kinds of human motives? Do we sometimes have an interest in acting for ourselves and sometimes an interest in acting on behalf of others, or do we simply act for ourselves? We often do act in terms of our own self-interest, and often our interests and the interests of others coincide, but psychology has not yet established that we never act contrary to our perceived self-interest.

The second matter about psychological egoism concerns its implications for ethical theory. An essential feature of ethics is the recognition that in some cases our self-interest comes into conflict with the interest of others. An ethical theory should specify conditions under which we *ought* to sacrifice our own interest for the interest of others. But if psychological egoism is correct, ethics is pointless. Ethics would then require that we do something which is psychologically impossible. Ethics is based on a postulate put somewhat misleadingly as "Ought implies can." This expression suggests that it is pointless to tell someone that he or she ought to do something when he or she cannot do it. If psychological egoism is true, the whole enterprise of ethics is rendered trivial: If ethics permits us to put self-interest first, the advice of ethics is redundant, and if ethics requires that we put the interests of others first, the advice of ethics is futile.

Ethical Egoism. Given the above problems (and others not here considered) some philosophers have proposed ethical egoism as an alternative to psychological egoism. Whereas psychological egoism is a psychological theory about human motivation, ethical egoism purports to be a general moral theory about what we ought to do. According to psychological egoism we always *do* act on the basis of what we believe to be our own interest. According to ethical egoism, "One *ought* always to act on the basis of one's own best interest." It is tempting to dismiss ethical egoism by saying that it is silly because it is committed to the view that we ought never to take others' interests into account. Such a characterization of ethical egoism is incorrect, however. An ethical egoist does take the interests of other persons into account when it suits his or her own interest, and usually it *is* in our interest to take the interest of others into account because it promotes our self-interest to treat them well.

Some philosophers have tried to refute ethical egoism by showing that it is a self-contradictory theory, because ultimately ethical egoism is committed to the view that it is both right and wrong to do the same act. Whether or not ethical egoism is guilty of self-contradiction is a matter of continuing philosophical controversy. More interesting for our purposes is a dispute over what the nature of society would be if ethical egoism were the prevailing moral theory. Some philosophers and political theorists would argue that anarchism and chaos would prevail. A classic statement of this position was made by the philosopher Thomas Hobbes (1588–1679): Imagine a world with limited resources, where persons are approximately equal in their ability to harm one another, and yet everyone acts exclusively in his or her own interest. Hobbes argued that in such a world everyone would be at everyone else's throat; such a "state of nature" would be plagued by anxiety, violence, and constant danger. As Hobbes put it, life would be "solitary, nasty, brutish, and short." However, Hobbes also assumed that human beings were sufficiently rational to recognize their own interests. To avoid the war of all against all he urged that they form a powerful state to protect themselves from their own individual selfishness.

An ethical egoist might well reply that both Hobbes' characterization of an egoistic world and his alleged "solution" are totally inadequate. After all, Hobbes' egoism can be challenged on grounds that he renders egoism more akin to selfishness than to self-interest and that selfish people often do not act rationally in pursuit of their self-interest. A different view, one which has been extremely influential in economics and in the personal philosophy of the business community, is that of Adam Smith. Smith believed that the public good evolves out of a suitably restrained clash of competing individual interests. As each person pursues his or her own self-interest, the interactive process is guided by an "invisible hand," so that the public interest is achieved. It is a strange irony that, according to Smith, individual egoism leads not to the war of all against all, but rather to utilitarianism, i.e., to the greatest good of the greatest number. The existence of the invisible hand is, Smith thought, a far better method of achieving the public good than the highly visible and authoritarian hand of Hobbes' all-powerful sovereign state. To protect individual freedom, government should be fairly limited. Of course, Smith recognized that concern with our own self-interest could get out of control, and hence that a minimal state is required to provide and enforce the rules of the competitive game.

Egoistic Business Practices and Utilitarian Results. Adam Smith's picture of an egoistic world has captivated many in the business community. They do not picture themselves as selfish and indifferent to the interests of others, and they recognize that a certain element of cooperation is necessary if their own interests are to flourish. At the same time, they recognize that their interests do conflict with the interests of others; and *within the established rules of the competitive game,* they should pursue their own interests. Within the rules of business practice, they see business ethics as the ethics of a restrained egoist. It is egoistic because it is an ethic based on the active pursuit of one's own interest. It is restrained because self-interest is subservient to the rules of business practice.

Many in the business community can also be considered rule utilitarians. Individual competition advances the good of the corporation. Rule-governed competition among individual firms advances the good of society as a whole. Hence, a popular view of business ethics might be captured by the phrase "individual egoism leads to utilitarianism." Or, as Adam Smith more graciously put it, as individuals pursue their individual interests, we are all led by an invisible hand to promote the public good. This kind of confident optimism has been severely challenged, however, as has the entire utilitarian philosophy. Let us now turn to some aspects of this challenge.

Criticisms of Utilitarianism

The Problem of Quantifying Goodness. One major criticism of utilitarianism centers on the commitment to the quantification and measurement of goodness. Bentham's hedonism—the view that pleasure is the sole good—has been a special object of attack. It was charged by Bentham's utilitarian successor, John Stuart Mill, that on Bentham's account it would be better to be a satisfied pig than a dissatisfied Socrates. Human experience, Mill argued, is such that some pleasures seem to be qualitatively better than others. Mill was convinced that it is better, all things considered, to be a dissatisfied Socrates than a satisfied pig; Socratic pleasures of the mind are qualitatively better than purely bodily pleasures. Mill thus had to grapple with a new problem of measuring value, since Bentham's hedonic calculus is no longer solely sufficient and since "qualitative betterness" is difficult and perhaps impossible to quantify. Mill's proposal was, in effect, that we should appeal to a panel of experts, where the chief criterion for membership on the panel was experience in the matters being compared.

If the members of the panel would prefer one experience over another, even though the first experience had quantitatively less pleasure than the other, the former experience was to be preferred. If it is asked, "But how can any human being take the perspective of the pig?" Mill's answer seemed rather Aristotelian. He argued that humans are qualitatively different from animals and that this natural difference protects them against desiring a lower grade of existence even if they would be in some sense happier. The ground of this qualitative distinction is our recognition of a sense of dignity. Although Mill thought this strategy preserves hedonism, it appears to many modern philosophers that it does not. After all, what special quality does a somewhat *less* pleasurable experience have that makes it better? It cannot be the pleasure itself. But if it is not pleasure alone, then hedonism must be given up, because it is theoretically committed to the view that pleasure is the sole good.

Utilitarians who were not hedonists also encountered serious problems with quantification. Economists, for example, either simply appropriated the word "utility" to denote that experience of satisfaction in which economists are interested, or they abandoned the word "utility" and talked about "preference orderings" instead. In the first case the economists simply said that a person buying a 27-cent loaf of bread received 27 cents worth of utility; they did not commit themselves to saying that the purchaser received pleasure from buying the bread. Using words in this way did not affect much of theoretical economics. However, economists could not construct social welfare functions unless they were willing to make inferences from market decisions to welfare. Without such inferences, saying that a consumer received 27 cents worth of utility from the purchase of a loaf of bread amounts to nothing more than saying that a consumer purchased a 27-cent loaf of bread. In other words, the inability to make inferences from behavior to welfare eliminated the possibility of making the policy decisions and ethical judgments that utilitarianism was traditionally designed to provide. Such a weakened utilitarianism was of no interest to a philosopher interested in ethics.

The other approach used by economists was to substitute "preference orderings" for "utility." As indicated earlier, an attempt was made to understand utilitarianism in terms of the choices people actually make. But many philosophers remain skeptical that defining utility this way will resolve the measurability problem. Suppose Jim prefers to spend his 27 cents on milk and Sally prefers to spend her 27 cents on bread. Suppose neither Sally nor Jim has any money and we have only 40 cents to distribute. What can utilitarianism advise when utility is limited to preference orderings? It seems that no advice is possible unless some inferences are made which enable us to go from revealed preferences to considerations of welfare and happiness. The difficulty in justifying such inferences creates questions about the adequacy of the utilitarian method.

Pluralistic utilitarians argued that many things are intrinsically good— pleasure, beauty, truth, and moral virtue, to name a few of the most commonly accepted intrinsically good things. Although the view that there are many intrinsically valuable things may have a certain plausibility in light of how people talk about the good, such a view creates problems of its own for utilitarianism. Pluralistic utilitarianism faces an even more severe measurability problem, because it is extremely difficult to discern how truth, goodness, and virtue can be measured and tradeoffs negotiated on the basis of such measurements.

One further problem in measurement focuses on what to measure. Utilitarianism stipulates that in matters of ethics only consequences count. Suppose we accept this claim for the moment. What is to count as a consequence of an act, and how far into the future must consequences be considered? There is much dispute within utilitarianism on this point, and these debates are not unrelated to problems of business ethics. For most of our country's history the so-called "externalities" of business practice were not taken into account in calculating the cost of doing business. Specific examples include air and water pollution, noise, and ugliness, to name but a few. Environmental deterioration has now reached a point where such consequences as externalities must be counted as part of the social *cost* of doing business. This changing perception of what is to be counted as part of the costs and consequences of business has had unsettling effects. The rules of the game are changing, and as a result ethical dilemmas multiply. The issues which result from redefining the consequences of doing business are discussed in several chapters of this text.

A related problem might be called the comparison problem, or the apples and oranges problem. Can individual pleasures or units of happiness be quantified and compared? How does one compare the pleasure of a swim on a hot summer day with the pleasure of listening to Beethoven? Did Lyndon Johnson or John Kennedy have the happier life? This difficulty in comparing different experiences extends to business firms as well. For example, one device suggested for measuring corporate responsibility is the corporate social audit. In addition to providing a financial picture of the company, the social audit is supposed to provide a picture of the company's ethical merits. However, problems have arisen in the measurement and comparison of a corporation's ethical assets and liabilities that have left the corporate social audit in a relatively primitive state. We will examine these issues of measurement surrounding the corporate social audit in Chapter 4.

The Problem of Unjust Consequences. In addition to all the criticisms surrounding utilitarian attempts to measure and calculate happiness, utilitarianism has also been challenged on the grounds that it can lead to injustice. We have already encountered one form of this criticism when we discussed the punishment-of-the-innocent argument advanced against act utilitarianism. While rule utilitarians argue that their particular version of utilitarianism avoids this criticism, many philosophers are not convinced. They see no reason why the objection could not be reformulated against the rule utilitarian. Consider an extreme example. Suppose a slave society produced the greatest happiness for the greatest number. Wouldn't a rule utilitarian have to say that the practice of slavery in that particular society is morally obligatory? The standard response of a rule utilitarian is to deny that as a *matter of fact* the world of human relations would ever be such that slavery would *in fact* lead to the greatest happiness for the greatest number.

Such a response has not seemed to some convincing, however. Many political philosophers and legal theorists have argued that documents such as the Bill of Rights in the United States Constitution contain a set of rules that *constrain* rather than serve as examples of utilitarian policy decisions. The Bill of Rights, they say, is inserted into the Constitution because those rights protect individuals even if they are *not* rules that lead to the greatest good for the greatest number; their justification must thus be nonutilitarian, for their purpose is to protect the individual rights of citizens from being sacrificed in the name of the public good. Utilitarians argue in response that the Bill of Rights can be justified on utilitarian grounds. But even if this claim were true, many philosophers would not be satisfied that utilitarianism is saved by it. If the Bill of Rights did not lead to the greatest good for the greatest number, rule utilitarians would be committed to giving it up, while anti-utilitarians would not give it up and indeed would cite the failure of the Bill of Rights always to lead to utilitarian consequences as one reason why it should be retained.

Just as some philosophers criticize the general theory of utilitarianism for not adequately taking individual rights into account, some social critics chastise utilitarian practices of business on the same basis. As a matter of historical fact, the doctrine of individual rights within business institutions has not traditionally been a major part of business ethics, though this situation seems now to be changing. Employees were and often still are fired for what superiors consider "disloyal" conduct, and employees traditionally have had no right to "blow the whistle" on corporate misconduct. Many alleged abuses have also been catalogued: Young executives are moved from one geographic area of the country to another, often at psychological hardship to them and to their families. Some companies try to regulate employee behavior outside the business. Some female employees have been expected to grant sexual favors as a condition of their employment. This familiar list could be indefinitely lengthened, and many of these complaints will be considered in later chapters of this book. At present, rights as protections against unjust business practices are being demanded, sometimes within companies and sometimes in court. The development of theories of employee rights, consumer rights, and stockholder rights, the clashes among rights claims, and the alleged clash between utilitarianism and nonutilitarian rights theories provide the framework for major contemporary debates within business ethics. Many of these issues are also discussed in later chapters of this book.

DEONTOLOGICAL THEORIES

One of the underlying assumptions of the criticisms of utilitarianism based on both justice and rights is the view that an adequate ethical theory must be deontological or nonconsequential. A deontological theory denies what teleological (and therefore what utilitarian) theories assert—namely, that in ethics only the consequences of actions and rules count. *Deontologism* (derived from the Greek term meaning "duty") maintains that the concept of duty is independent of the concept of good, and that right actions are thus not determined by the production of (nonmoral) good. Other features besides those of goodness determine the rightness of actions—e.g., features such as personal commitment, the fact of an act's being illegal, or an act's being required by a religious directive.

Deontologists argue that a variety of relationships between persons have significance independent of the *consequences* of these relationships. They do not believe that we should simply maximize goodness by considering persons in isolation from their peculiar relationship to us. Instead of being future oriented, as utilitarian theories are, deontological theories also hold that ethics must look as much to the past as to present and future consequences. What a person deserves is said to be as fundamental as the consequences he produces, and the evaluation of his motives is central in the evaluation of his act. For example, business persons do not treat each customer in abstraction from their previous relations. If the person is an old customer and the merchandise being sold is in scarce supply, the old customer will be given preferential treatment, for a relationship of commitment and trust has already been established. Or, to take another example, in considering how much to punish a criminal, we should look at what he *did.* The consequences of an attempted murder are usually less severe than the real thing; but in terms of motive, the attempted murderer is often as wicked, and sometimes more wicked, than an actual murderer. Other deontological examples center on the institution of the family. Being a father is said to place a person in a special relation of obligation. In the event of a burning apartment house, a father presumably ought to save his son first, even if the world would be better off if he saved someone else in the building who was more valuable to society. Further, the fact that one has made a promise often obligates one to keep the promise even if it becomes obvious that keeping the promise will not lead to the greatest good. For the deontologist, in short, there are many special, nonconsequential relations such as friendships, parent-child relations, and business affiliations that intrinsically enrich the moral life.

It is likely that deontological motives play as important a part in some aspects of business ethics as utilitarian ones (or even egoistic ones), though this fact is often overlooked. After all, one ground of the business enterprise is the sanctity of contracts. The contractual relationship is a form of promise keeping and the obligatoriness of promises, independent of consequences, is a standard deontological notion. (The role of promise keeping and the contractual nature of business will be discussed further in Chapters 3, 4, and 5.) Moreover, it is often argued that employers stand in special relationships to employees or to their customers and that, as a result, corporations have *special moral obligations* to their employees or customers, independent of the general good. Deontologically grounded duties are from this perspective an irreducible feature of business ethics.

Another and extremely important difference between utilitarians and deontologists arises from the characteristic means/end reasoning used by utilitarians. We have seen that utilitarians focus on goals and on the most efficient means to these ends—a conception of the moral life that both empirical scientists and business persons may find congenial. Deontologists, however, think it is fundamentally wrong to conceptualize the moral life—or even the moral life of the business community—in such terms. It is fundamentally wrong because we seldom can be very certain of our ultimate goals, and even less do we have the capacity to predict and control the future consequences of our actions. Deontologists insist that we rarely, if ever, set out goals to be achieved in the moral life. Rather, we abruptly encounter the claims, rights, and moral problems of others, and we are called upon by morality to observe the rights of others and to help them through difficult times. This view of the moral life will be found congenial by at least some in the business community, for they will insist that moral problems and their solutions often appear almost unnoticed. *Business activities* have definite goals but the *moral boundaries* restricting those activities do not. They will insist, for example, that business codes of ethics set forth restrictions on what may be done, but in no way are such codes attempts to maximize value through the device of established goals.

The Importance of Motives

Less extreme deontologists agree with utilitarians that consequences are morally relevant to the determination of right actions. However, most deontologists also insist that the motives of the agent are morally relevant to the assessment of actions quite apart from the consequences actually produced. (A utilitarian may agree that motives are critical but will always insist that right motives are determined by one's *intention to produce the best possible consequences.*) For example, *act deontologists* argue that there is some feature of the moral act which must be taken into account in moral evaluation; and *rule deontologists* will make a similar point about a genuine moral rule. Consider two business persons signing a contract, both of whom accept the rule, "People should honor their contracts." A rule deontologist would argue that the rule, "Honor your contracts," has special characteristics; for the making of a contract binds one in a special way from the moral point of view. This obligation holds even if the consequences of keeping the contract are disadvantageous to all parties.

To understand the deontologist's point about motives, consider the example of people making personal sacrifices for a sick aunt. Fred makes the sacrifices only because he fears the social criticism that would result if he didn't. He hates making the sacrifices and secretly resents having to be involved. Bill, however, is naturally a kindhearted soul. He does not view the "sacrifice" as a genuine sacrifice at all. His deepest satisfaction comes from helping others, especially this aunt who suffers the misfortunes of illness. Sam, by contrast, derives no personal satisfaction from taking care of his sick aunt. He would rather be doing other things, and he takes care of his sick aunt purely from a sense of duty.

Let us assume that in the cases of these three differently motivated persons, the consequences are equally good, because the sick aunt is adequately cared for. Suppose we ask, however, which person is behaving in a morally praiseworthy manner. On a utilitarian theory such a question might be hard to answer, especially if act utilitarianism were in question. Most of us would focus on the different motives for acting held by the three persons. The deontologist takes this conventional reaction as confirmation of the view that in ordinary moral evaluation, motives count substantially. But which motive is morally superior? Nearly everyone would agree that Fred's motive is not a moral motive at all. It is a motive of prudence, and perhaps springs from fear. This is not to say that Fred's action does not have morally good consequences. It does. However, Fred does not deserve any special moral credit for his act, for it is purely self-interested.

This distinction between the motive for an act and the consequences of an act may prove to be extremely important for business ethics. Those who argue for a broad notion of corporate responsibility sometimes give arguments analogous to Fred's: Corporate responsibility is in the long run self-interest of the business community (See Chapter 3). To recognize the prudential basis of the beneficial consequences does not detract from the goodness of the consequences. It may be argued that, given the purpose or function of the business enterprise, the motive of self-interest may be the most appropriate motive to ensure good consequences. The only point a deontologist would make is that a business derives no special *moral* credit for acting in its own interest, even if society is benefited by and pleased by the action.

If Fred's motive is not moral, what about Bill's and Sam's? Deontologists disagree about an appropriate answer. Some identify morally correct motivation with altruistic motivation. Bill's behavior is morally right because his action is motivated by a concern for others. This altruistic attitude is absent in Sam's case, and hence Sam's action is morally inferior. However, the eighteenth-century deontologist Immanuel Kant (1734–1804) argues on behalf of the moral superiority of Sam's motive. In fact, Kant paradoxically thinks that Bill hardly deserves any more moral credit than Fred. Bill is *naturally* motivated to do the right thing. That he is so motivated represents a fortunate fact about him; but this untutored motivation hardly merits moral praise. Kant seems to be saying that you only deserve moral credit when your act is neither done for self-interested reasons nor is the result of a natural psychological urge. But actually Kant's view is more complicated. He also insists that the moral motive be universally valid; that is, he wants it to be a motive which ought to motivate all human beings. Psychological traits, like the propensity to altruism found in Bill, are not universal traits and are not morally required of everyone. Kant's search for a special motive grounded on reason itself involves a tortuous and difficult philosophical journey, which we must briefly consider now. The first step in this journey may be taken by considering the notion of conscience.

The Concept of Conscience

Although the notion of conscience has not been given much attention by recent moral philosophers, the slogan, "Let your conscience be your guide" remains an influential one in popular ethical writings; and it frequently receives attention in articles on business ethics written by business persons or business school professors. What accounts for this disparity between professional moral philosophers and the general public (including the business community) on this matter of conscience? Three factors should be mentioned. First, in the minds of many, conscience has a theological ground. Yet, the more that moral philosophers have separated ethics from theology, the more an interest in a theological interpretation of conscience has waned. Second, the discoveries of psychology have undermined the idea that there is a rational basis of conscience. Conscience has been proclaimed little more than a way of coping, and hence its ethical ground has been undermined. Third, and most important, conscience often demonstrably is not a good guide in moral matters. Not all consciences are the consciences of a Schweitzer, Gandhi, or Martin Luther King. The political terrorist and assassin, for example, appeal to conscience as a source of justification for their actions. But many of their acts remain morally heinous nonetheless. A criterion is thus needed that enables us to distinguish a good conscience from a bad one.

We might sum up these objections to the use of conscience as a ground for morality in the following way: Appeals to conscience are important, but alone they are insufficient. After all, consciences vary radically from person to person, are often altered by circumstance or training, seem subject to impulse and whim, and are rather more acute when authorities such as policemen are present. The reliability of conscience is thus not self-certifying and is always in doubt, because support is needed from some source external to conscience itself. This conclusion is further corroborated by the fact that many claims to have performed the right action on grounds that "my conscience was my guide" seem to external observers to be rationalizations for an immoral act. Conscientious action is thus hardly a firm ground for morality and cannot stand as the single basic principle deserving allegiance by persons in the world of business.

Moral Rules and Their Universality

Kant did not speak much of conscience; rather he spoke about our sense of duty. However, Kant had an enlightened view of this "sense" and never claimed that anyone acting merely from a sense of duty was acting morally. Moreover, Kant's moral philosophy cannot be summed up as "Duty for duty's sake," as it is often described. Duty is the proper motive for genuinely moral action, but duty as a motive for moral action has a special characteristic, which Kant called "universality." This odd-sounding thesis may be explained as follows: Acts done from moral duty alone have moral worth, and there is a definite source of their worth. That source is found in a principle or rule that determines how we ought to act in a certain range of cases. Kant is here returning to the importance of motives. Praise or blame depends on what our motives or intentions are, and these are spelled out by the rule or principle on which we act. And what makes these rules that determine duty correct is their universality, i.e., the fact that they consistently apply to everyone alike. Perhaps the best known such moral rule is the Golden Rule, "Do unto others as you would have them do unto you." Kant's moral philosophy can in some ways be viewed as an extensive philosophical reworking of this fundamental moral rule.

The second step in our Kantian journey leads us to consider the distinctive character of these so-called universal moral rules. Let us begin with a simple example. Suppose two teams are discussing the rules to be used for an ad hoc baseball game. The pitcher for the Red Sox argues vehemently for keeping the traditional "three strikes and you're out" rule. However, upon coming to bat, that very same pitcher now argues for four strikes. Would the pitcher be guilty of contradicting himself? Suppose the pitcher replies that he is not contradicting himself at all. When he agreed earlier to the three strike rule, he was the pitcher. Now that he is the batter, the four strike rule seems more appropriate. Such a reply would never do, but why not? Would this person allow the opposing team's pitcher to change the rule? Presumably not. To make the point another way, would this person accept a rule in which a person could change the rules of the game as he took different positions in the game? Again, presumably not.

To apply the analogy to moral problems, suppose someone were to advocate discriminatory policies against Jews. To be consistent, that person would have to advocate discrimination even if he himself should turn out to be a Jew. Presumably he would not be willing to be treated discriminatorily, and hence as a matter of *logical consistency,* he cannot recommend discriminatory practices against Jews. Morality is not simply a matter of treating others as you would like them to treat you. It is also a matter of *not* treating others in ways you would not accept if you were they. Kant's point is that morality requires consistency of action and judgment when you are both on the receiving and the giving ends. Morality requires that you not make an exception of yourself, that you not engage in practices or follow rules which you could not recommend to everyone.

Kant has a worthy point. Some of the clearest cases of immoral behavior involve a person trying to make an exception of himself or herself. Sometimes this consistency requirement is captured by the notion of justice: One should not try to push ahead in a line while attempting to buy tickets to a popular movie. A student should not cheat on exams. A business person should not engage in the practices of giving kickbacks and bribes. These practices involve making exceptions of oneself, or exempting oneself from the rules without being willing to grant similar privileges to others.

But suppose someone is willing to sanction line cutting, cheating, kickbacks, and bribes. What would Kant then say? Kant has a ready reply.

Such practices, he argues, are contradictory. They are not consistent with the larger social practices of which they are a part. Consider promising, for example. If one were consistently to recommend that anyone should lie when it worked to his or her advantage, the very practice of truth telling would be undermined. The universalization of rules that allow lying would entitle everyone to lie to you, just as you can lie to them. But in this case one could never tell if a person were telling the truth or lying. Such a rule would thus be self-defeating. Similarly, cheating undermines the practice of examinations. Kickbacks and bribes undermine business practices. All such practices are self-defeating or inconsistent because they undermine a rule or practice that they presuppose. A dilemma may be constructed that captures Kant's full point. Suppose a student were to reflect on whether it is permissible to cheat on an exam. If the student is consistent, he must agree to allow any student to cheat. If he does not allow cheating, he is contradicting himself. On the other hand, if he is consistent and recommends cheating, then the purpose of the exam is undermined and he cannot gain the advantage of his cheating. When a large number of students cheat, the professor detects the violation and the exam is not counted.

Kant's point is implicitly recognized by the business community when corporate officials despair of the immoral practices of corporations and denounce executives engaging in shady practices as undermining the business enterprise itself. Kant captures this conviction in what he calls *the categorical imperative:* "One ought never to act except in such a way that one can also will that one's maxim should become a universal law." Cheating, kickbacks, and bribes necessarily cannot be made universal laws. Such actions are universally and necessarily immoral, according to Kant, quite independent of the desires and culture of the actor. The categorical imperative is required by reason itself, and hence in Kant's view places morality on its strongest ground.

Respect for Persons

Our examination of Kant's analysis is not yet complete, however, for the categorical imperative has other formulations in Kant's philosophy, one of which should be discussed here. On its second formulation, the categorical imperative requires that people always treat each other as ends in themselves and never as means merely. Kant, in the tradition of Aristotle, recognizes that only human beings are capable of being motivated by the moral rules laid down by the categorical imperative. It is human beings that place values on other things; these other things have conditional value because they acquire this value only as the result of human action. Human beings, on the other hand, have unconditioned value, i.e., value apart from any special circumstances that confer value. Since all human beings and only human beings have this unconditional value, it is always inappropriate to use other human beings merely as means to some end, as if they had instrumental value only. This view of Kant's is sometimes briefly summarized as the principle of respect for persons.

A Kantian philosopher takes exception to utilitarianism because it appears that utilitarianism violates this second formulation of the categorical imperative. Utilitarianism counts individual value as happiness (or unhappiness) only as a means for maximizing total value or happiness in society. In so doing, each individual is treated as if he or she primarily has instrumental value for others (though of course utilitarians treat each person also as a source of intrinsic value). A Kantian would similarly take strong exception to the view that employees are to be treated like mere equipment in the production process. Human labor should never be treated like machinery, industrial plants, and capital—solely in accordance with economic laws for profit maximization. Any economic system that fails to recognize this distinction between human beings and other nonhuman factors of production is morally deficient.

We can now summarize Kant's deontological position. What is distinctive about moral acts, rules, and practices is that they conform to the categorical imperative and that the motivation for the action is done from duty. If conscience is identified with the categorical imperative, then one can say that every moral action is motivated by conscience. However, Kant's categorical imperative provides a criterion for distinguishing between those whose appeal is to the conscience supported by morality and those whose appeal to conscience is perverted.

Applications of Deontological Theories

Although almost no moral philosopher finds Kant's system fully satisfactory, many would agree that together with its contemporary elaborations it provides some of the necessary elements of a sound moral position. Using Kantian elements as a base, some have attempted to construct a more encompassing deontological theory. For example, some philosophers are using the Kantian notion of respect for persons as a ground for providing a moral theory of rights. If people do have intrinsic unconditional worth, they reason that social and economic institutions should be arranged to protect and sustain individual human worth. Philosophers subscribing to this rights orientation argue that social and economic institutions, including business enterprises, should sustain and enrich rights rather than, as is often the case, subvert them. There is still considerable controversy, however, as to the rights people actually possess. Contemporary business practice will be much affected by these discussions, and in nearly every chapter of this text, rights claims and conflicts among rights play a major part.

Other philosophers have attempted to expand Kant's philosophy by considering the special obligations we incur as a result of special roles. (Kant himself does not deal with these specific roles.) Consider the role of being a father. The fact that one is a father creates special obligations. That is why one should rescue his son first among the children in a burning building—irrespective of the considerations of the society as a whole. In that case, one's primary obligation is to one's son as a result of the special relationship. Similarly, special roles and relationships created by being a bank president or a journalist or an auditor result in special obligations and responsibilities in the world of business. This aspect of deontological ethics is perhaps best captured by the phrase "My station and its duties." This expression means, at least in part, that one's station (e.g., profession) itself creates special duties.

The business community has long accepted this notion of "my station and its duties." Since the business firm is usually characterized by a sharp hierarchical organization, this type of organization is ideally suited for an ethics tied to the special obligations of one's role. Each designated office in the hierarchical structure has duties and obligations appropriate to that office. At the macro level, the corporation itself has specific functions within society and hence has duties and obligations appropriate to that function. Some of the controversy in business ethics results from growing disagreements between the business and the public, and among business firms themselves, on what the function both of business firms and of particular offices within business firms *should* be. Recently, for example, auditors have come under criticism for not revealing "shady" practices they discover in the course of their audit. These controversies are usually the result of a changing moral climate in which society's conception of both the "station" and its resultant duties are under revision.

Summary

Our survey of two major ethical theories has shown that there are elements of each in business ethics. Within the competitive framework, business persons tend to be ethical egoists, but they argue that their egoistic behavior is justified on utilitarian grounds. Business persons also recognize the necessity of playing by the rules of the competitive game. Such rules as the sanctity of contracts provide a deontological element to business ethics. Within the corporate hierarchy the notion of "My station and its duties" seems similarly to rest on deontological considerations.

When we consider the adequacy of these traditional ethical theories, this blend of the traditions within business ethics should come as no surprise. No one theory seems to be free of serious objections. Also, no one theory provides a complete answer to the question, "What ought I to do?" Although students are often frustrated by the failure of ethical theory to provide clear-cut answers to every moral question, there are good reasons why such a demand is impossible to satisfy. One reason will suffice as an illustration. Ethical theory is ultimately directed at the actual world; it is not designed for angels or ideal worlds, but rather for human beings at a given time within given cultural circumstances. Our ethical convictions are limited by our knowledge of the facts and by the state of our own technology. The ethics of sexual relations may justifiably be very different in a society without effective means of contraception than it is in a society with effective contraception. Until the advent of highly developed medical technology, many of the acute ethical problems in medicine and in the care of elderly citizens simply did not exist. Persons died before contemporary ethical issues could become concerns. As technology changes and as our knowledge of the world changes, our ethical views must adapt. As a special branch of ethics, business ethics must thus allow for changes. However, the corporate executive who is called upon to make *actual decisions* cannot wait for the perfect ethical theory to evolve. He or she must decide on a course of action on the basis of imperfect information. Given this imperfect information and the competing traditional ethical theories, how should a corporate executive take account of ethical theory in applying it to practical problems?

PROCEDURAL JUSTICE

It may be that no ethical theory will ever provide nontentative and correct solutions for every ethical issue. In considering how to deal with this problem, and also with that of a pluralistic society, a distinction should be made between just procedures and just results. Suppose three friends order a pizza. When the pizza arrives, how should it be divided? Barring special circumstances, the result which seems most just is that each person receives an equal share. What procedure should be used to ensure that result? An appropriate procedure is to make the person cutting the pizza take the last piece. The pizza example is an illustration of perfect procedural justice. Both the procedure and the results are just.

In some cases, just procedures are solely sufficient for yielding just results. Consider a lottery as an example. It makes perfect sense to speak of the conditions of a fair lottery. Now suppose that the winner is an extremely rich man. Can we say that the lottery is unjust? Certainly not. We condemn a horse race which is fixed, but we do not condemn a horse race where the rich are winners. In situations like these, as long as the procedures are just, the results as well are just. In other cases, we know what would constitute perfect procedural justice, but practical considerations make it impossible to achieve. A perfect system of punishment which provides just results in every single case is a practical impossibility. The problem before society is to design a *system* of punishment (a set of procedures) that provides as much justice as possible.

Note that "providing as much justice as possible" need not mean maximizing the tradeoff between letting some guilty persons go free while punishing some innocent persons. A society might quite appropriately decide that protecting the innocent is more important than punishing the guilty, and hence that society might create a system of punishment whose procedures make special provision for protecting the innocent. The American system of punishment is such a system: it does place a higher value on protecting the innocent. The American system of punishment is an example of what John Rawls would call imperfect procedural justice. Our system of penal justice is imperfect because it cannot provide just results in every case. Recognizing that imperfect procedural justice is the best one can obtain shifts the ethical issue in a fundamental way. Rather than debating whether or not each individual punishment is just, the debate moves to the best criteria for a just procedure in the arrest and conviction of a person charged with commiting a crime. Once we agree on the appropriate procedures, then so long as Jones is punished according to those procedures, the *procedure* eventuating in his punishment is just—even if Jones turns out to be innocent and the *result* therefore unjust. Naturally, in situations where imperfect procedural justice is the best we can do, we should accept the results of our procedural system with a certain amount of humility and where possible we should make allowances for the inevitable errors.

Of course, shifting the issue from results to procedures does not end the ethical controversy. The various traditional theories of ethics will provide competing theories as to what counts as just procedures. Resolution of this debate will require another set of procedures. In the English common law tradition of "natural justice," procedural rules are followed such as "No party may be condemned without a hearing"; but this and other rules are subject to different interpretations and to further specification into more definite rules and procedures (e.g., procedures for the presentation of evidence). Within the American system, representative democracy is the procedure adopted, for democracy provides a just system for voting and passing laws (even if some of the laws turn out to be unjust).

It is hoped that we can avoid the problem of an infinite regress of justification. This problem arises, for example, when one asks whether representative democracy is itself morally justified and then asks if the justification offered is itself justified, etc. If different competing theories give different answers, another procedure could be required and the controversy could continue about that and all subsequent procedures. There are two ways the controversy might be brought to an end. If all the competing ethical theories agree that one procedure is in fact best, the controversy would obviously be at an end. In political theory, for example, both deontologists and utilitarians often agree that representative democracy is procedurally the best form of government.

Another means for ending the regress is by using the method which John Rawls calls *reflective equilibrium.* Rawls agrees with many moral philosophers that there are paradigm cases of immoral behavior, such as punishing the innocent, and of morally proper behavior, such as giving up your life for a friend. No moral principle which would permit such cases of immoral behavior as punishing the innocent or which would not praise a heroic act of sacrifice can be adequate. If all moral issues had such paradigm case resolutions, there would be no need for moral principles. However, many moral issues have no clear parallel solution; for example, the problems of "deceptive" advertising and environmental responsibility discussed later in this book present numerous dilemmas. The purpose of principles is to assist persons in making difficult decisions about these dilemmas. As we actively engage in making moral judgments, there is an interplay between the principles we use and the cases to which we apply our principles. We start with paradigm cases about certain acts that are either obviously morally right or morally wrong. We then search for principles which are consistent with these paradigm cases, are consistent with each other, and assist us in resolving difficult moral problems. These principles are then tested to see if they yield results which are counterintuitive. If so, they are readjusted or are given up and new principles are developed. Moral inquiry and moral practice reflect this mutual testing of cases against principles and principles against cases.

The situation in business ethics is similar. The competitive free enterprise system is viewed by business persons as a justified procedure for organizing economic institutions, although the competitive free enterprise system can lead to unjust results and is a good example of imperfect procedural justice. When criticized, some economists and business leaders admit that free enterprise distribution can lead to unjust results, but they argue that no other scheme is procedurally more satisfactory. Like the American system of retributive justice, the American system of distributive justice is hardly perfect; but in structure it may be the best we can do. Periodically, however, the general public comes to doubt the justice of the free enterprise system and to search for modifications to it. The late 1960's was one of those times. In such times, discussions in business ethics are particularly appropriate and useful, for business practices are being severely questioned in a way that behooves both the business community and its critics to enter into a dialogue and to attempt to build a new consensus about morally acceptable business practices. This book is designed to present the student with some of the major issues that must be discussed in any such dialogue.

PURPOSE AND GOODNESS

As a business person considers some of the objectives and criticisms of traditional business practices, sooner or later he or she will undoubtedly ask, "What constitutes a good business practice?" This question has the same *formal structure* as ones we have encountered at several points in this Introduction: What constitutes a good ethical theory? What constitutes a good procedure? In asking such questions, we are asking a variation of a more general question asked by Greek moral philosophers over two thousand years ago: What does it mean to be a *good* thing, whether the thing in question is a toy, a person, a business, a parade, or whatever? The Greeks posed this question by asking what the purpose or function of something is. Suppose, for example, we want to know what a good racehorse is. On the first level, a good racehorse is a horse that wins races. By studying the horses to learn what characteristics contribute to the winning of races—speed, agility, discipline, etc.—we learn the characteristics of a good racehorse. And so it is with tools, works of art, and methods of accounting. The question, "What is a good painting, or a good accountant, or a good house?" is answered by enumerating those characteristics essential to the purpose or function of a painting, accountant, or a house. This way of looking at the world of objects, events, and practices represents a common bond between our way of thinking and the thinking of these early Greek moral philosophers.

Good Objects and Good Practices

The Greeks also analyzed good human beings and good human institutions from the perspective of function or purpose. Both Plato (427–347 B.C.) and Aristotle (384–322 B.C.) argued that the purpose or function of human beings is to develop and exercise their rational capacities. For Plato, reasoning was not simply calculation, not simply the choosing of the most efficient means to reach a given end. Rather, reason enabled human beings to recognize what is truly good. In this way, the rational human being could control his or her appetites and emotions. Reason represents the highest and best aspect of human nature. Plato gave little argument for his view that reason is superior to appetite, but Aristotle had a world view that provided more powerful argument.

To understand Aristotle's argument, we might think of him as the first museum director. Alexander the Great had been a student of Aristotle's, and as Alexander's armies traveled throughout the Mediterranean world, he sent back fossils, artifacts, animals, and even constitutions. Aristotle then had to group these objects together in appropriate categories. Aristotle looked for a common characteristic that differentiated the group in question from every other group. He thought that human beings, for example, are distinguished from everything else by their reason. Appetite, including sexual desires, is something humans share with animals, and hence appetite is not distinctively human. Because Aristotle believed that the members of a species ought to emphasize the characteristic that is unique to them, he argued that a human being should not seek the life of wine, women, and frivolity, but rather should pursue the life of reason. To do otherwise is to behave more like an animal than a human being. Here the functional analysis is clearly at work. The good human being is conceived as the human being whose life embodies the characteristic of what is distinctively human, namely the life of reason.

Using this same functional analysis, Plato and Aristotle also attempted to give an account of the good state. To reach his conclusions, Plato considered the various groups or classes within the state and asked what the appropriate function of each class is. So long as each class within the state is performing its proper function, he argued, then the state is good. However, should members of one class aspire to perform the activities of another class, the state becomes disordered and no longer a good state. Plato focused on three classes: the business and labor community (as we shall call it here), the armed forces or soldiers, and the rulers or top agents of national policy. The rulers he took to be analogous to reason in the human soul, the soldiers analogous to will, and the labor and business community analogous to appetite. Business persons and workers might be annoyed at being compared with the "lower" aspect of the human soul. However, one powerful and influential view of some business persons is distinctly Platonic. They would agree with Plato that the appropriate function of the business community is *to provide for the material needs of the citizens of the state in an efficient manner;* this is Plato's larger thesis. They would also agree with Plato that the making of policies that promote the general good of the state is the proper function of government and that when members of the business community try to decide the fate of the community without legitimate authorization, such action will only lead to a confusion of functions and to general disorder.

On such matters, Plato and the contemporary economist Milton Friedman are in agreement. On Friedman's view, the statement "The business of business is business" is not an empty definition but is a Platonic moral program for the good or well-ordered state.

Because Aristotle believed that rationality is intimately bound up with sociability, he had a different view about social institutions, including business. Social institutions, including the family, the tribe, and the state, are essential if human beings are to develop into rational creatures. Individual human beings cannot become fully developed rational beings by their own efforts alone, for human beings are dependent on social institutions. It is important to note here that Aristotle's view is very different from that taken by many business executives, especially those who espouse the ideal of the self-made person. To them, the virtues of individual effort are highly praised, and those persons who depend on government for support and sustenance are viewed with suspicion, and often with hostility. On this view, the government is at most like an umpire who polices society but has little or no active role to play in the development of human beings. Such a view is in sharp contrast to Aristotle's view that the "self-made person" is a psychologically and sociologically impossible ideal. Any human being inescapably owes a great debt to social institutions, including the state. This dispute about the relation of society to the individual emerges in several of the chapters of this text.

The Purpose of Business

How does the functionalist analysis apply to good business practice? One functionalist view is that the *purpose* of business is to serve the public interest: The medieval guild, the national corporations of Great Britain such as The East India Company, and the industrial firms of nineteenth- and twentieth-century America were all permitted to do business on grounds that the existence of such business firms promoted the public interest. Moreover, in the United States the notion that businesses should operate as competitive private firms for the purpose of providing profit for the stockholders rested on the empirical claim that the pursuit of profit by private corporations works to the benefit of the public. It is a mistake from this perspective to say that the function of the corporation is primarily to maximize the profit of the stockholder. And should it be shown that the emphasis by firms on obtaining profits for stockholders does not lead to the public good, the practices of the firm could be changed without changing the function of the firm. Indeed, reformed practices might well be more faithful to the purpose or function of the firm. Hence, from this view, the first step in the moral evaluation of business practices is to *ascertain the function or purpose of business.* Those business practices which are in accord with the function of business are *good* business practices. Those functions which are in some sense in conflict with the purpose of business are bad business practices. Fine. But what is the distinctive or at least primary function of business? The above suggestions were that businesses are chartered for the public good. But what exactly does this mean, and is this function the defining one for business activity? Such questions will recur repeatedly in the readings in this book. We believe there are some illuminating, even if not fully convincing, answers to be found in these readings.

Chapter 2

THEORIES OF ECONOMIC JUSTICE

INTRODUCTION

We have all noticed economic disparities between individuals and nations, and most of us have come to question some aspects of domestic and international systems for distributing wealth. We wonder whether tax burdens are unfairly distributed. For example, we may think that individuals are overtaxed and that wealthy corporations are undertaxed. We may wonder whether such wealthy corporations and their stockholders actually *deserve* their abundant profits, and whether their executives deserve the generous salaries that usually attend such positions. On the other hand, we may wonder whether it is fair that hard-earned corporate and individual incomes should be taxed in order to redistribute the money through social welfare. These questions are notoriously subject to different answers, but underlying any sophisticated answer is a theory of economic justice, i.e., an answer to the problem of how economic goods and services are to be distributed. This chapter deals with various problems of economic justice, with emphasis on the major distinctions, principles, and methods of moral argument employed by influential writers on the subject. Each author attempts to develop a definite framework for understanding the wider implications of a particular *theory* of economic justice.

THE CONCEPTS OF JUSTICE AND DISTRIBUTIVE JUSTICE

Many moral philosophers have argued that our basic notion of justice is more akin to the notion of fairness than to almost any other moral notion. While they are right to insist on the close conceptual connections between these terms, perhaps the single word most broadly linked to the general meaning of "justice" is "desert." One has acted justly toward a person when that person has been given what he or she is due or owed, and therefore has been given what he or she deserves or can legitimately claim. It may be that a person deserves to be awarded a prize, for example, in which case justice has been done when that person receives the prize. What persons deserve or can legitimately claim is based on certain relevant properties they possess. If a person possesses the property of being a lawbreaker or of otherwise wrongly treating others, we are justified in allocating an appropriate punishment. But it is wrong, as a matter of justice, to allocate a punishment or reward if the person does *not* possess the relevant property. Similarly, it is unjust to reward a supervisor for the work of his or her subordinates when it was not the supervisor's guidance that led to the rewardable productivity.

The expression "distributive justice" refers to the proper distribution (or intentional nondistribution, as Nozick suggests) of social benefits and burdens. Paying taxes and serving on juries are distributed burdens, while welfare checks and foundation grants are distributed benefits. Most recent literature on distributive justice dealing with issues of fair *economic* distribution has focused on unjust distributions in the form of inequalities of income among different classes of persons and unfair tax burdens on certain classes. But there are other problems of economic justice, as we shall see.

Distributive justice is a notion that applies only to the distribution of scarce benefits, where there is some competition for them. If there are plenty of fish in a river so that everyone can have as many as he or she can catch, we do not establish patterns limiting fishermen or the fishing industry. It is only when we are worried that the fish supply will be exhausted or that future fishermen will be unfairly affected by present fishing that we set limits to the number of fish they may catch. There are, of course, various patterns that could serve as models for the distribution; but that fact is irrelevant to the present point. The point is that there are no problems of distributive justice and no need of principles of distributive justice until some measure of scarcity exists. Even when burdens rather than benefits are being allocated, there is competition for the least disadvantageous distribution.

David Hume pointed out that we have developed the concept of justice in order to handle situations where claims are pressed by parties with conflicting interests. As he put it, there would be no point to having rules of justice unless society were composed of persons in competition for scarce resources. The rules of justice serve to strike a balance between conflicting interests and claims that repeatedly occur in society. This shows a close link between the lawful society and the just society, since law and morality are our explicit tools for balancing conflicting claims. Nonetheless, the law may be unjust; and there may be many rules of justice that are not connected to the law or to legal enforcement.

PRINCIPLES AND THEORIES OF DISTRIBUTIVE JUSTICE

In the philosophy of distributive justice there are a few widely discussed (so-called material) principles of distributive justice. Each principle mentions a relevant property on the basis of which burdens and benefits should be distributed. That is, each principle asserts a standard of relevance for purposes of distribution. The following is a fairly standard list of the major candidates for the position of valid principles of distributive justice (though longer lists have been proposed):

1. To each person an equal share
2. To each person according to individual need
3. To each person according to individual effort
4. To each person according to societal contribution
5. To each person according to merit

There is no obvious barrier to acceptance of more than one of these principles, and some theories of justice accept all five as valid. Most societies use several of them, applying different principles of distribution in different contexts. In the United States, for example, unemployment and welfare payments are distributed on the basis of need (and to some extent on the basis of previous length of employment); jobs and promotions are in many sectors awarded (distributed) on the basis of demonstrated achievement and merit; the higher incomes of wealthy professionals are allowed (distributed) on the grounds of superior effort or merit or social contribution (or perhaps all three); and, at least theoretically, the opportunity for elementary and secondary education is distributed equally to all citizens.

Theories of distributive justice are commonly developed by emphasizing and elaborating one or more of the above principles of distributive justice, perhaps in conjunction with other moral principles. Thus, *egalitarian* theories emphasize equal access to primary goods; *Marxist* theories emphasize need and social efforts to meet needs; *libertarian* theories emphasize contribution, merit, and the operation of a free market; *utilitarian* theories emphasize a mixed use of such criteria so that public and private utility are maximized, etc. The viability of any such theory of justice is determined by the quality of its moral argument to the conclusion that some one or more selected principles of justice ought to be given priority (or perhaps even exclusive consideration) over the others.

The first two sections of this chapter present three theories of economic justice that have had enormous impact in recent philosophy. An egalitarian theory of justice is presented in two selections excerpted from John Rawls's book *A Theory of Justice*. A libertarian theory is supported in the articles by Robert Nozick and by Jan Narveson. (Nozick's general theory of justice is applied to problems of free market justice in the selection by Narveson.) The utilitarian account of justice is defended in the articles by Rolf Sartorius and Peter Singer. Finally, Carl Cohen attempts a synthesis of these disparate views by focusing on the question, "How should we make decisions about priorities in matters of justice?" In the third section of this chapter the Marxist conception of justice is discussed in two articles by Marxist writers. These authors are especially concerned with defending a theory of economic justice that challenges what they regard as capitalist presuppositions present in the egalitarian, libertarian, and utilitarian arguments of the earlier authors in this chapter. But before we turn to the Marxist challenge, let us briefly consider the philosophical presuppositions and orientations located in the three allegedly "capitalistic" theories.

The utilitarian theory (here represented by Sartorius and Singer) follows from the explanation of utilitarianism in Chapter 1. Economic justice is viewed as merely one among a number of problems about how to maximize value in society. The ideal economic distribution, utilitarians argue, is *any* arrangement that would have this maximizing effect. According to Singer, this thesis leads directly to a position diametrically opposed to libertarianism: a heavy element of political and economic planning are said to be morally required in order that justice be done to individuals. In his defense of an *egalitarian theory,* John Rawls argues that a social contract account of justice is more acceptable than the utilitarian view. Rawls then attempts to justify two basic principles of justice by appeal to a hypothetical situation in which fully rational agents choose the principles of distribution they wish to govern everyone in society. Rawls's central contention is that we would choose to distribute economic goods and services *equally* except in those cases where an unequal distribution would actually work to everyone's advantage, especially to the benefit of the worst off in society. Both utilitarianism and egalitarianism are rejected in Robert Nozick's *libertarian theory.* He argues that a theory of justice should work to protect our rights not to be coerced and should not propound a thesis intended to "pattern" society through distributive arrangements that redistribute economic benefits and burdens. Any economic arrangements that we freely choose are thus just. Nozick develops an entitlement theory according to which we have a right, without interference, to economic benefits we produce for ourselves, as well as a right to our voluntary economic transactions. Narveson supports this same point of view but does not think it entails a rejection of utilitarianism.

THE MARXIST CHALLENGE

In our discussion of utilitarianism in the previous chapter we distinguished the justification of individual actions from the justification of social practices. A judge sentencing a convicted criminal must follow the established rules. However, a legislator voting on the adoption of sentencing rules should consider the merits and demerits of the various rules themselves. Much of the discussion of business ethics takes place within a given social and economic structure. In a discussion of advertising ethics, for example, the competitive free market is taken as given. In this way the person discussing advertising ethics is in the same position as a judge sentencing a convicted criminal. Both operate from within a given social framework that establishes their roles and thereby their duties.

Some philosophers would insist that the really important questions do not arise *within capitalism* but rather arise as the result of *external criticisms* directed at the competitive market economy itself. Rather than discussing advertising ethics from within the capitalist framework, according to this viewpoint, we should be assessing the merits and demerits of the capitalist economic system. Perhaps the strongest and best-known challenge to capitalism comes from the political and social philosophy of Marxism. In this chapter we find two selections which specifically criticize standard operating assumptions in contemporary American business.

The focus of Marx's criticisms is on the notion of the voluntary exchange of private property—a notion which is fundamental to capitalist economic organization, as Nozick's theory clearly indicates. Exchange takes place when I surrender something of mine in return for something of yours that I want more. As industrial society develops, industries utilize the principle of the division of labor. As a result, men and women have little, if any, need for what they themselves produce. They produce only for their "share" of the money that their products represent. Since what they produce is simply a means toward something else, Marxists claim that workers are "alienated" from their product. A worker's creation of a product has no intrinsic value; one works simply in order to acquire products produced by others.

Under voluntary exchange, one's relations to other workers suffer as well, according to Marxists. We view fellow workers and the fruits of their labor solely as a means for satisfying our own as yet unfulfilled wants. We are interested neither in our fellow workers nor in their products as objects of value in themselves. Rather, our interest in them is purely instrumental. (They are a means to our end.) Moreover, our *only* interest in others occurs when they produce something we value; otherwise they have no other interest to us at all. In this way voluntary exchange based on private property corrupts a worker's relation both to his own product and to his fellow workers.

This Marxist theme has been developed by later Marxists such as Herbert Marcuse. These Marxists argue that through the manipulation of language and technology, the dominant social class has successfully compromised the working class: the working class has come to desire the useless products of industry. The inevitable frustration and alienation of the working class have been successfully redirected away from the ruling class into the abuse of some of the products of the consuming society, such as racing cars, guns, and power tools. Marcuse's critique is a direct challenge to the notion of consumer sovereignty. The purchases of the affluent consumer society are not really *free* purchases at all. A genuinely free purchase is one that is supportive of essential features of human nature. Since the products of advanced capitalist society are antithetical to the true nature of mankind, no purchase of these products is genuinely free. (This Marxist challenge to the notion of consumer choice is one of the focal points in our discussion of advertising in Chapter 7.)

One might think it possible to embrace Marxists' criticisms of capitalism while also arguing that the capitalist system can be reformed. In the other selection the contemporary American socialist Michael Harrington provides three arguments why such reform is impossible. He adds a novel twist on Marx's argument that capitalism contains within itself the seeds of its own destruction. Harrington then outlines what he considers a viable socialist program of economic justice for the last quarter of the twentieth century.

INTERNATIONAL ECONOMIC JUSTICE

The Marxist challenge to capitalism is not the only challenge that can be leveled against the entire system within which business ethics takes place. In most discussions of economic justice the framework for the discussion is a national state. We ask, should taxes in the United States be made more progressive? Should Saudi Arabia put more of its oil wealth into public works projects? However, given the wide disparity in the standard of living between the developed industrial countries and the largely underdeveloped agricultural or single resource countries, perhaps an equally appropriate question of economic justice should focus on whether or not rich countries should sacrifice some of their standard of living (wealth) for the benefit of poorer countries.

In answering such a question, a number of crucial ethical variables must be discussed. The first focuses on the question of responsibility. Who is responsible for the famine and malnutrition in many under-developed countries? Some argue that the persons living in under-developed countries are responsible themselves primarily because they have failed to keep their population under control. In such cases, some have argued that not only are the persons who are living in industrial countries under no obligation to provide food, but it would be wrong to do so. The most influential publication espousing this point of view is Garrett Hardin's "The Tragedy of the Commons." He uses the analogy of a public grazing ground to illustrate his point about famine. As more and more animals are allowed to graze on the common, the food supply is depleted and everyone is reduced to a desperate state. If we encourage overpopulation by providing food for victims of famine, we are in danger of creating the tragedy of the commons on a global scale.

Hardin's thesis, as might be expected, has created great controversy. One common line of criticism is that more variables than overpopulation must be mentioned to explain malnutrition and starvation in certain underdeveloped countries. In a provocative article, Onora O'Neill argues that the international business activities of many corporations is at least partially responsible for the dire conditions in certain underdeveloped countries. She focuses particularly on the foreign investment activities and on the policies of commodity pricing. Since the economic chains linking U.S. multinationals and the foreign policy of the U.S. government extend to U.S. citizens, there is a relevant sense, she claims, in which almost all of us are responsible for the deaths of famine victims. Our duty, then, is to redirect the policies of the U.S. government and the multinational corporations.

Howard Richards adds yet another consideration to this discussion of international economic justice. Too often discussions focus simply on formulas for *distribution* without considering the productive side of economic arrangements. One obvious way to improve the situation in underdeveloped countries is to improve their productive capacities. Richards believes that production provides the most appropriate strategy of all. What good does it do, he asks, to redistribute scarce resources when there simply are not enough resources to go around? Increasing the supply so that *no one* suffers is certainly better than simply spreading misery about more equitably. This view is obviously more sympathetic to the orientation that business persons might be expected to take to problems of international economic justice. Richards goes on to provide five "considerations" he thinks would convince rational men and women that principles of distributive justice must be supplemented by principles of productive justice. Richards believes that by recognizing the importance of principles of productive justice, concerned persons might make a more effective response to problems of hunger and malnutrition.

T.L.B.

N.E.B.

AN EGALITARIAN THEORY OF JUSTICE

John Rawls

THE ROLE OF JUSTICE

Justice is the first virtue of social institutions, as truth is of systems of thought. A theory however elegant and economical must be rejected or revised if it is untrue; likewise laws and institutions no matter how efficient and well-arranged must be reformed or abolished if they are unjust. Each person possesses an inviolability founded on justice that even the welfare of society as a whole cannot override. For this reason justice denies that the loss of freedom for some is made right by a greater good shared by others. It does not allow that the sacrifices imposed on a few are outweighed by the larger sum of advantages enjoyed by many. Therefore in a just society the liberties of equal citizenship are taken as settled; the rights secured by justice are not subject to political bargaining or to the calculus of social interests. The only thing that permits us to acquiesce in an erroneous theory is the lack of a better one; analogously, an injustice is tolerable only when it is necessary to avoid an even greater injustice. Being first virtues of human activities, truth and justice are uncompromising.

These propositions seem to express our intuitive conviction of the primacy of justice. No doubt they are expressed too strongly. In any event I wish to inquire whether these contentions or others similar to them are sound, and if so how they can be accounted for. To this end it is necessary to work out a theory of justice in the light of which these assertions can be interpreted and assessed. I shall begin by considering the role of the principles of justice. Let us assume, to fix ideas, that a society is a more or less self-sufficient association of persons who in their relations to one another recognize certain rules of conduct as binding and who for the most part act in accordance with them. Suppose further that these rules specify a system of cooperation designed to advance the good of those taking part in it. Then, although a society is a cooperative venture for mutual advantage, it is typically marked by a conflict as well as by an identity of interests. There is an identity of interests since social cooperation makes possible a better life for all than any would have if each were to live solely by his own efforts. There is a conflict of interests since persons are not indifferent as to how the greater benefits produced by their collaboration are distributed, for in order to pursue their ends they each prefer a larger to a lesser share. A set of principles is required for choosing among the various social arrangements which determine this division of advantages and for underwriting an agreement on the proper distributive shares. These principles are the principles of social justice: they provide a way of assigning rights and duties in the basic institutions of society and they define the appropraite distribution of the benefits and burdens of social cooperation. . . .

THE MAIN IDEA OF THE THEORY OF JUSTICE

My aim is to present a conception of justice which generalizes and carries to a higher level of abstraction the familiar theory of the social contract as found, say, in Locke, Rousseau, and Kant. In order to do this we are not to think of the original contract as one to enter a particular society or to set up a particular form of government. Rather, the guiding idea is that the principles of justice for the basic structure of society are the object of the original agreement. They are the principles that free and rational persons concerned to further their own interests would accept in an initial position of equality as defining the fundamental terms of their association. These principles are to regulate all further agreements; they specify the kinds of social cooperation that can be entered into and the forms of government that can be established. This way of regarding the principles of justice I shall call justice as fairness.

Thus we are to imagine that those who engage in social cooperation choose together, in one joint act, the principles which are to assign basic rights and duties and to determine the division of social benefits. Men are to decide in advance how they are to regulate their claims against one another and what is to be the foundation charter of their society. Just as each person must decide by rational reflection what constitutes his good, that is, the system of ends which it is rational for him to pursue, so a group of persons must decide once and for all what is to count among them as

just and unjust. The choice which rational men would make in this hypothetical situation of equal liberty, assuming for the present that this
choice problem has a solution, determines the principles of justice.

In justice as fairness the original position of equality corresponds to
the state of nature in the traditional theory of the social contract. This
original position is not, of course, thought of as an actual historical state
of affairs, much less as a primitive condition of culture. It is understood
as a purely hypothetical situation characterized so as to lead to a certain
conception of justice. Among the essential features of this situation is that
no one knows his place in society, his class position or social status, nor
does any one know his fortune in the distribution of natural assets and
abilities, his intelligence, strength, and the like. I shall even assume that
the parties do not know their conceptions of the good or their special
psychological propensities. The principles of justice are chosen behind
a veil of ignorance. This ensures that no one is advantaged or disadvantaged in the choice of principles by the outcome of natural chance or the
contingency of social circumstances. Since all are similarly situated and
no one is able to design principles to favor his particular condition, the
principles of justice are the result of a fair agreement or bargain. For
given the circumstances of the original position, the symmetry of everyone's relations to each other, this initial situation is fair between individuals as moral persons, that is, as rational beings with their own ends and
capable, I shall assume, of a sense of justice. The original position is, one
might say, the appropriate initial status quo, and thus the fundamental
agreements reached in it are fair. This explains the propriety of the name
"justice as fairness": it conveys the idea that the principles of justice are
agreed to in an initial situation that is fair. The name does not mean that
the concepts of justice and fairness are the same, any more than the
phrase "poetry as metaphor" means that the concepts of poetry and
metaphor are the same.

Justice as fairness begins, as I have said, with one of the most general
of all choices which persons might make together, namely, with the choice
of the first principles of a conception of justice which is to regulate all
subsequent criticism and reform of institutions. Then, having chosen a
conception of justice, we can suppose that they are to choose a constitution and a legislature to enact laws, and so on, all in accordance with the
principles of justice initially agreed upon. Our social situation is just if it
is such that by this sequence of hypothetical agreements we would have
contracted into the general system of rules which defines it.

. . . It may be observed, however, that once the principles of justice are
thought of as arising from an original agreement in a situation of equality,
it is an open question whether the principle of utility would be acknowledged. Offhand it hardly seems likely that persons who view themselves
as equals, entitled to press their claims upon one another, would agree
to a principle which may require lesser life prospects for some simply for
the sake of a greater sum of advantages enjoyed by others. Since each
desires to protect his interests, his capacity to advance his conception of
the good, no one has a reason to acquiesce in an enduring loss for himself

in order to bring about a greater net balance of satisfaction. In the absence of strong and lasting benevolent impulses, a rational man would not accept a basic structure merely because it maximized the algebraic sum of advantages irrespective of its permanent effects on his own basic rights and interests. Thus it seems that the principle of utility is incompatible with the conception of social cooperation among equals for mutual advantage. It appears to be inconsistent with the idea of reciprocity implicit in the notion of a well-ordered society. Or, at any rate, so I shall argue.

I shall maintain instead that the persons in the initial situation would choose two rather different principles: the first requires equality in the assignment of basic rights and duties, while the second holds that social and economic inequalities, for example inequalities of wealth and authority, are just only if they result in compensating benefits for everyone, and in particular for the least advantaged members of society. These principles rule out justifying institutions on the grounds that the hardships of some are offset by a greater good in the aggregate. It may be expedient but it is not just that some should have less in order that others may prosper. But there is no injustice in the greater benefits earned by a few provided that the situation of persons not so fortunate is thereby improved. The intuitive idea is that since everyone's well-being depends upon a scheme of cooperation without which no one could have a satisfactory life, the division of advantages should be such as to draw forth the willing cooperation of everyone taking part in it, including those less well situated. Yet this can be expected only if reasonable terms are proposed. The two principles mentioned seem to be a fair agreement on the basis of which those better endowed, or more fortunate in their social position, neither of which we can be said to deserve, could expect the willing cooperation of others when some workable scheme is a necessary condition of the welfare of all. Once we decide to look for a conception of justice that nullifies the accidents of natural endowment and the contingencies of social circumstance as counters in quest for political and economic advantage, we are led to these principles. They express the result of leaving aside those aspects of the social world that seem arbitrary from a moral point of view. . . .

THE ORIGINAL POSITION AND JUSTIFICATION

. . . The idea here is simply to make vivid to ourselves the restrictions that it seems reasonable to impose on arguments for principles of justice, and therefore on these principles themselves. Thus it seems reasonable and generally acceptable that no one should be advantaged or disadvantaged by natural fortune or social circumstances in the choice of principles. It also seems widely agreed that it should be impossible to tailor principles to the circumstances of one's own case. We should insure further that particular inclinations and aspirations, and persons' conceptions of their good, do not affect the principles adopted. The aim is to rule out those principles that it would be rational to propose for acceptance, however little the chance of success, only if one knew certain things that are irrelevant from the standpoint of justice. For example, if a man knew that he was wealthy, he might find it rational to advance the principle that various taxes for welfare measures be counted unjust; if he knew that he was poor, he would most likely propose the contrary principle. To represent the desired restrictions one imagines a situation in which everyone is deprived of this sort of information. One excludes the knowledge of those contingencies which sets men at odds and allows them to be guided by their prejudices. In this manner the veil of ignorance is arrived at in a natural way. . . .

Two Principles of Justice

I shall now state in a provisional form the two principles of justice that I believe would be chosen in the original position. . . .

The first statement of the two principles reads as follows.

First: each person is to have an equal right to the most extensive basic liberty compatible with a similar liberty for others.

Second: social and economic inequalities are to be arranged so that they are both (a) reasonably expected to be to everyone's advantage, and (b) attached to positions and offices open to all. . . . [The Difference Principle]

By way of general comment, these principles primarily apply, as I have said, to the basic structure of society. They are to govern the assignment of rights and duties and to regulate the distribution of social and economic advantages. As their formulation suggests, these principles presuppose that the social structure can be divided into two more or less distinct parts, the first principle applying to the one, the second to the other. They distinguish between those aspects of the social system that define and secure the equal liberties of citizenship and those that specify and establish social and economic inequalities. The basic liberties of citizens are, roughly speaking, political liberty (the right to vote and to be eligible for public office) together with freedom of speech and assembly; liberty of conscience and freedom of thought; freedom of the person along with the right to hold (personal) property; and freedom from arbitrary arrest and seizure as defined by the concept of the rule of law. These liberties are all required to be equal by the first principle, since citizens of a just society are to have the same basic rights.

The second principle applies, in the first approximation, to the distribution of income and wealth and to the design of organizations that make use of differences in authority and responsibility, or chains of command. While the distribution of wealth and income need not be equal, it must be to everyone's advantage, and at the same time, positions of authority and offices of command must be accessible to all. One applies the second principle by holding positions open, and then, subject to this constraint, arranges social and economic inequalities so that everyone benefits.

These principles are to be arranged in a serial order with the first principle prior to the second. This ordering means that a departure from the institutions of equal liberty required by the first principle cannot be justified, or compensated for, by greater social and economic advantages. The distribution of wealth and income, and the hierarchies of authority, must be consistent with both the liberties of equal citizenship and equality of opportunity.

It is clear that these principles are rather specific in their content, and their acceptance rests on certain assumptions that I must eventually try to explain and justify. A theory of justice depends upon a theory of society in ways that will become evident as we proceed. For the present, it should be observed that the two principles (and this holds for all formulations) are a special case of a more general conception of justice that can be expressed as follows.

All social values—liberty and opportunity, income and wealth, and the bases of self-respect—are to be distributed equally unless an unequal distribution of any, or all, of these values is to everyone's advantage.

Injustice, then, is simply inequalities that are not to the benefit of all. Of course, this conception is extremely vague and requires interpretation.

As a first step, suppose that the basic structure of society distributes certain primary goods, that is, things that every rational man is presumed to want. These goods normally have a use whatever a person's rational plan of life. For simplicity, assume that the chief primary goods at the disposition of society are rights and liberties, powers and opportunities, income and wealth. These are the social primary goods. Other primary goods such as health and vigor, intelligence and imagination, are natural goods; although their possession is influenced by the basic structure, they are not so directly under its control. Imagine, then, a hypothetical initial arrangement in which all the social primary goods are equally distributed: everyone has similar rights and duties, and income and wealth are evenly shared. This state of affairs provides a benchmark for judging improvements. If certain inequalities of wealth and organizational powers would make everyone better off than in this hypothetical starting situation, then they accord with the general conception.

Now it is possible, at least theoretically, that by giving up some of their fundamental liberties men are sufficiently compensated by the resulting social and economic gains. The general conception of justice imposes no restrictions on what sort of inequalities are permissible; it only requires that everyone's position be improved. . . .

Now the second principle insists that each person benefit from permissible inequalities in the basic structure. This means that it must be reasonable for each relevant representative man defined by this structure, when he views it as a going concern, to prefer his prospects with the inequality to his prospects without it. One is not allowed to justify differences in income or organizational powers on the ground that the disadvantages of those in one position are outweighed by the greater advantages of those in another. Much less can infringements of liberty be counterbalanced in this way. Applied to the basic structure, the principle of utility would have us maximize the sum of expectations of representative men (weighted by the number of persons they represent, on the classical view); and this would permit us to compensate for the losses of some by the gains of others. Instead, the two principles require that everyone benefit from economic and social inequalities. . . .

THE TENDENCY TO EQUALITY

I wish to conclude this discussion of the two principles by explaining the sense in which they express an egalitarian conception of justice. Also I should like to forestall the objection to the principle of fair opportunity that it leads to a callous meritocratic society. In order to prepare the way for doing this, I note several aspects of the conception of justice that I have set out.

First we may observe that the difference principle gives some weight to the considerations singled out by the principle of redress. This is the principle that undeserved inequalities call for redress; and since inequalities of birth and natural endowment are undeserved, these inequalities are to be somehow compensated for. Thus the principle holds that in order to treat all persons equally, to provide genuine equality of opportunity, society must give more attention to those with fewer native assets and to those born into the less favorable social positions. The idea is to redress the bias of contingencies in the direction of equality. In pursuit of this principle greater resources might be spent on the education of the less rather than the more intelligent, at least over a certain time of life, say the earlier years of school.

Now the principle of redress has not to my knowledge been proposed as the sole criterion of justice, as the single aim of the social order. It is plausible as most such principles are only as a prima facie principle, one that is to be weighed in the balance with others. For example, we are to weigh it against the principle to improve the average standard of life, or to advance the common good. But whatever other principles we hold, the claims of redress are to be taken into account. It is thought to represent one of the elements in our conception of justice. Now the difference principle is not of course the principle of redress. It does not require society to try to even out handicaps as if all were expected to compete on a fair basis in the same race. But the difference principle would allocate resources in education, say, so as to improve the long-term expectation of the least favored. If this end is attained by giving more attention to the better endowed, it is permissible; otherwise not. And in making this decision, the value of education should not be assessed only in terms of economic efficiency and social welfare. Equally if not more important is the role of education in enabling a person to enjoy the culture of his society and to take part in its affairs, and in this way to provide for each individual a secure sense of his own worth.

Thus although the difference principle is not the same as that of redress, it does achieve some of the intent of the latter principle. It transforms the aims of the basic structure so that the total scheme of institutions no longer emphasizes social efficiency and technocratic values. . . .

. . . The natural distribution is neither just nor unjust; nor is it unjust that men are born into society at some particular position. These are simply natural facts. What is just and unjust is the way that institutions deal with these facts. Artistocratic and caste societies are unjust because they make these contingencies the ascriptive basis for belonging to more or less enclosed and privileged social classes. The basic structure of these societies incorporates the arbitrariness found in nature. But there is no necessity for men to resign themselves to these contingencies. The social system is not an unchangeable order beyond human control but a pattern of human action. In justice as fairness men agree to share one another's fate. In designing institutions they undertake to avail themselves of the accidents of nature and social circumstance only when doing so is for the common benefit. The two principles are a fair way of meeting the arbitrariness of fortune; and while no doubt imperfect in other ways, the institutions which satisfy these principles are just. . . .

There is a natural inclination to object that those better situated deserve their greater advantages whether or not they are to the benefit of others. At this point it is necessary to be clear about the notion of desert. It is perfectly true that given a just system of cooperation as a scheme of public rules and the expectations set up by it, those who, with the prospect of improving their condition, have done what the system announces that it will reward are entitled to their advantages. In this sense the more fortunate have a claim to their better situation; their claims are legitimate expectations established by social institutions, and the community is obligated to meet them. But this sense of desert presupposes the existence of the cooperative scheme; it is irrelevant to the question whether in the first place the scheme is to be designed in accordance with the difference principle or some other criterion.

Perhaps some will think that the person with greater natural endowments deserves those assets and the superior character that made their development possible. Because he is more worthy in this sense, he deserves the greater advantages that he could achieve with them. This view, however, is surely incorrect. It seems to be one of the fixed points of our considered judgments that no one deserves his place in the distribution of native endowments, any more than one deserves one's initial starting place in society. The assertion that a man deserves the superior character that enables him to make the effort to cultivate his abilities is equally problematic; for his character depends in large part upon fortunate family and social circumstances for which he can claim no credit. The notion of desert seems not to apply to these cases. Thus the more advantaged representative man cannot say that he deserves and therefore has a right to a scheme of cooperation in which he is permitted to acquire benefits in ways that do not contribute to the welfare of others. There is no basis for his making this claim. From the standpoint of common sense, then, the difference principle appears to be acceptable both to the more advantaged and to the less advantaged individual.

A LIBERTARIAN THEORY OF JUSTICE

Robert Nozick

The minimal state is the most extensive state that can be justified. Any state more extensive violates people's rights. Yet many persons have put forth reasons purporting to justify a more extensive state. It is impossible within the compass of this book to examine all the reasons that have been put forth. Therefore, I shall focus upon those generally acknowledged to be most weighty and influential, to see precisely wherein they fail. In this chapter we consider the claim that a more extensive state is justified, because necessary (or the best instrument) to achieve distributive justice. . . .

The term "distributive justice" is not a neutral one. Hearing the term "distribution," most people presume that some thing or mechanism uses some principle or criterion to give out a supply of things. Into this process of distributing shares some error may have crept. So it is an open question, at least, whether *re*distribution should take place; whether we should do again what has already been done once, though poorly. However, we are not in the position of children who have been given portions of pie by someone who now makes last minute adjustments to rectify careless cutting. There is no *central* distribution, no person or group entitled to control all the resources, jointly deciding how they are to be doled out. What each person gets, he gets from others who give to him in exchange for something, or as a gift. In a free society, diverse persons control different resources, and new holdings arise out of the voluntary exchanges and actions of persons. . . .

SECTION I: THE ENTITLEMENT THEORY

The subject of justice in holdings consists of three major topics. The first is the *original acquisition of holdings,* the appropriation of unheld things. This includes the issues of how unheld things may come to be held, the process, or processes, by which unheld things may come to be held, the things that may come to be held by these processes, the extent of what comes to be held by a particular process, and so on. We shall refer to the complicated truth about this topic, which we shall not formulate here, as the principle of justice in acquisition. The second topic concerns the *transfer of holdings* from one person to another. By what processes may a person transfer holdings to another? How may a person acquire a holding from another who holds it? Under this topic come general descriptions of voluntary exchange, and gift and (on the other hand) fraud, as well as reference to particular conventional details fixed upon in a given society. The complicated truth about this subject (with placeholders for conventional details) we shall call the principle of justice in transfer. (And we shall suppose it also includes principles governing how a person may divest himself of a holding, passing it into an unheld state.)

If the world were wholly just, the following inductive definition would exhaustively cover the subject of justice in holdings.

1. A person who acquires a holding in accordance with the principle of justice in acquisition is entitled to that holding.
2. A person who acquires a holding in accordance with the principle of justice in transfer, from someone else entitled to the holding, is entitled to the holding.
3. No one is entitled to a holding except by (repeated) applications of 1 and 2.

The complete principle of distributive justice would say simply that a distribution is just if everyone is entitled to the holdings they possess under the distribution.

A distribution is just if it arises from another just distribution by legitimate means. The legitimate means of moving from one distribution to another are specified by the principle of justice in transfer. The legitimate first "moves" are specified by the principle of justice in acquisition. Whatever arises from a just situation by just steps is itself just. The means of change specified by the principle of justice in transfer preserve justice. As correct rules of inference are truth-preserving, and any conclusion deduced via repeated application of such rules from only true premises is itself true, so the means of transition from one situation to another specified by the principle of justice in transfer are justice-preserving, and any situation actually arising from repeated transitions in accordance with the principle from a just situation is itself just. The parallel between justice-preserving transformations and truth-preserving transformations illuminates where it fails as well as where it holds. That a conclusion could have been deduced by truth-preserving means from premises that are true suffices to show its truth. That from a just situation a situation *could* have arisen via justice-preserving means does *not* suffice to show its justice. The fact that a thief's victims voluntarily *could* have presented him with gifts does not entitle the thief to his ill-gotten gains. Justice in holdings is historical; it depends upon what actually has happened. We shall return to this point later.

Not all actual situations are generated in accordance with the two principles of justice in holdings: the principle of justice in acquisition and the principle of justice in transfer. Some people steal from others, or defraud them, or enslave them, seizing their product and preventing them from living as they choose, or forcibly exclude others from competing in exchanges. None of these are permissible modes of transition from one situation to another. And some persons acquire holdings by means not sanctioned by the principle of justice in acquisition. The existence of past injustice (previous violations of the first two principles of justice in holdings) raises the third major topic under justice in holdings: the *rectification of injustice in holdings*. If past injustice has shaped present holdings in various ways, some identifiable and some not, what now, if anything, ought to be done to rectify these injustices? What obligations do the performers of injustice have toward those whose position is worse than it would have been had the injustice not been done? Or, than it would have been had compensation been paid promptly? How, if at all, do things change if the beneficiaries and those made worse off are not the direct parties in the act of injustice, but, for example, their descendants? Is an injustice done to someone whose holding was itself based upon an unrectified injustice? How far back must one go in wiping clean the historical slate of injustices? What may victims of injustice permissibly do in order to rectify the injustices being done to them, including the many injustices done by persons acting through their government? I do not know of a thorough or theoretically sophisticated treatment of such issues. Idealizing greatly, let us suppose theoretical investigation will produce a principle of rectification. This principle uses historical information about previous situations and injustices done in them (as defined by the first two principles of justice and rights against interference), and information about the actual course of events that flowed from these injustices, until the present, and it yields a description (or descriptions) of holdings in the society. The principle of rectification presumably will make use of its best estimate of subjunctive information about what would have occurred (or a probability distribution over what might have occurred, using the expected value) if the injustice had not taken place. If the actual description of holdings turns out not to be one of the descriptions yielded by the principle, then one of the descriptions yielded must be realized.

The general outlines of the theory of justice in holdings are that the holdings of a person are just if he is entitled to them by the principles of justice in acquisition and transfer, or by the principle of rectification of injustice (as specified by the first two principles). If each person's holdings are just, then the total set (distribution) of holdings is just. To turn these general outlines into a specific theory we would have to specify the details of each of the three principles of justice in holdings: the principle of acquisition of holdings, the principle of transfer of holdings, and the principle of rectification of violations of the first two principles. I shall not attempt that task here. (Locke's principle of justice in acquisition is discussed below.)

Historical Principles and End-result Principles

The general outlines of the entitlement theory illuminate the nature and defects of other conceptions of distributive justice. The entitlement theory of justice in distribution is *historical;* whether a distribution is just depends upon how it came about. In contrast, *current time-slice principles* of justice hold that the justice of a distribution is determined by how things are distributed (who has what) as judged by some *structural* principle(s) of just distribution. A utilitarian who judges between any two distributions by seeing which has the greater sum of utility and, if the sums tie, applies some fixed equality criterion to choose the more equal distribution, would hold a current time-slice principle of justice. As would someone who had a fixed schedule of trade-offs between the sum of happiness and equality. According to a current time-slice principle, all that needs to be looked at, in judging the justice of a distribution, is who ends up with what; in comparing any two distributions one need look only at the matrix presenting the distributions. No further information need be fed into a principle of justice. It is a consequence of such principles of justice that any two structurally identical distributions are equally just. (Two distributions are structurally identical if they present the same profile, but perhaps have different persons occupying the particular slots. My having ten and your having five, and my having five and your having ten are structurally identical distributions.) Welfare economics is the theory of current time-slice principles of justice. The subject is conceived as operating on matrices representing only current information about distribution. This, as well as some of the usual conditions (for example, the choice of distribution is invariant under relabeling of columns), guarantees that welfare economics will be a current time-slice theory, with all of its inadequacies.

Most persons do not accept current time-slice principles as constituting the whole story about distributive shares. They think it relevant in assessing the justice of a situation to consider not only the distribution it embodies, but also how that distribution came about. If some persons are in prison for murder or war crimes, we do not say that to assess the justice of the distribution in the society we must look only at what this person has, and that person has, and that person has, . . . at the current time. We think it relevant to ask whether someone did something so that he *deserved* to be punished, deserved to have a lower share. . . .

Patterning

. . . Almost every suggested principle of distributive justice is patterned: to each according to his moral merit, or needs, or marginal product, or how hard he tries, or the weighted sum of the foregoing, and so on. The principle of entitlement we have sketched is *not* patterned. There is no one natural dimension or weighted sum or combination of a small number of natural dimensions that yields the distributions generated in accordance with the principle of entitlement. The set of holdings that results when some persons receive their marginal products, others win at gambling, others receive a share of their mate's income, others receive gifts from foundations, others receive interest on loans, others receive gifts from admirers, others receive returns on investment, others make for themselves much of what they have, others find things, and so on, will not be patterned. . . .

To think that the task of a theory of distributive justice is to fill in the blank in "to each according to his _____" is to be predisposed to search for a pattern; and the separate treatment of "from each according to his _____" treats production and distribution as two separate and independent issues. On an entitlement view these are *not* two separate questions. Whoever makes something, having bought or contracted for all other held resources used in the process (transferring some of his holdings for these cooperating factors), is entitled to it. . . .

So entrenched are maxims of the usual form that perhaps we should present the entitlement conception as a competitor. Ignoring acquisition and rectification, we might say:

> From each according to what he chooses to do, to each according to what he makes for himself (perhaps with the contracted aid of others) and what others choose to do for him and choose to give him of what they've been given previously (under this maxim) and haven't yet expended or transferred.

This, the discerning reader will have noticed, has its defects as a slogan. So as a summary and great simplification (and not as a maxim with any independent meaning) we have:

> *From each as they choose, to each as they are chosen.*

How Liberty Upsets Patterns

It is not clear how those holding alternative conceptions of distributive justice can reject the entitlement conception of justice in holdings. For suppose a distribution favored by one of these non-entitlement conceptions is realized. Let us suppose it is your favorite one and let us call this distribution D_1; perhaps everyone has an equal share, perhaps shares vary in accordance with some dimension you treasure. Now suppose that Wilt Chamberlain is greatly in demand by basketball teams, being a great gate attraction. (Also suppose contracts run only for a year, with players being free agents.) He signs the following sort of contract with a team: In each home game, twenty-five cents from the price of each ticket of admission goes to him. (We ignore the question of whether he is "gouging" the owners, letting them look out for themselves.) The season starts, and people cheerfully attend his team's games; they buy their tickets, each time dropping a separate twenty-five cents of their admission price into a special box with Chamberlain's name on it. They are excited about seeing him play; it is worth the total admission price to them. Let us suppose that in one season one million persons attend his home games, and Wilt Chamberlain winds up with $250,000, a much larger sum than the average income and larger even than anyone else has. Is he entitled to this income? Is this new distribution D_2, unjust? If so, why? There is *no* question about whether each of the people was entitled to the control over the resources they held in D_1; because that was the distribution (your favorite) that (for the purposes of argument) we assumed was acceptable. Each of these persons *chose* to give twenty-five cents of their money to Chamberlain. They could have spent it on going to the movies, or on candy bars, or on copies of *Dissent* magazine, or of *Monthly Review*. But they all, at least one million of them, converged on giving it to Wilt Chamberlain in exchange for watching him play basketball. If D_1 was a just distribution, and people voluntarily moved from it to D_2, transferring parts of their shares they were given under D_1 (what was it for if not to do something with?), isn't D_2 also just? If the people were entitled to dispose of the resources to which they were entitled (under D_1), didn't this include their being entitled to give it to, or exchange it with, Wilt Chamberlain? Can anyone else complain on grounds of justice? Each other person already has his legitimate share under D_1. Under D_1, there is nothing that anyone has that anyone else has a claim of justice against. After someone transfers something to Wilt Chamberlain, third parties *still* have their legitimate shares; *their* shares are not changed. By what process could such a transfer among two persons give rise to a legitimate claim of distributive justice on a portion of what was transferred, by a third party who had no claim of justice on any holding of the others *before* the transfer? To cut off objections irrelevant here, we might imagine the exchanges occurring in a socialist society, after hours. After playing whatever basketball he does in his daily work, or doing whatever other daily work he does, Wilt Chamberlain decides to put in *overtime* to earn additional money. (First his work quota is set; he works time over that.) Or imagine it is a skilled juggler people like to see, who puts on shows after hours. . . .

The general point illustrated by the Wilt Chamberlain example is that no end-state principle or distributional patterned principle of justice can be continuously realized without continuous interference with people's lives. Any favored pattern would be transformed into one unfavored by the principle, by people choosing to act in various ways; for example, by people exchanging goods and services with other people, or giving things to other people, things the transferrers are entitled to under the favored distributional pattern. To maintain a pattern one must either continually interfere to stop people from transferring resources as they wish to, or continually (or periodically) interfere to take from some persons resources that others for some reason chose to transfer to them. . . .

Patterned principles of distributive justice necessitate *re*distributive activities. The likelihood is small that any actual freely-arrived-at set of holdings fits a given pattern; and the likelihood is nil that it will continue to fit the pattern as people exchange and give. From the point of view of an entitlement theory, redistribution is a serious matter indeed, involving, as it does, the violation of people's rights. (An exception is those takings that fall under the principle of the rectification of injustices.) From other points of view, also, it is serious.

Taxation of earnings from labor is on a par with forced labor. Some persons find this claim obviously true: taking the earnings of n hours labor is like taking n hours from the person; it is like forcing the person to work n hours for another's purpose. Others find the claim absurd. But even these, *if* they object to forced labor, would oppose forcing unemployed hippies to work for the benefit of the needy. And they would also object to forcing each person to work five extra hours each week for the benefit of the needy. But a system that takes five hours wages in taxes does not seem to them like one that forces someone to work five hours, since it offers the person forced a wider range of choice in activities than does taxation in kind with the particular labor specified. . . .

Whether it is done through taxation on wages or on wages over a certain amount, or through seizure of profits, or through there being a big *social pot* so that it's not clear what's coming from where and what's going where, patterned principles of distributive justice involve appropriating the actions of other persons. Seizing the results of someone's labor is equivalent to seizing hours from him and directing him to carry on various activities. If people force you to do certain work, or unrewarded work, for a certain period of time, they decide what you are to do and what purposes your work is to serve apart from your decisions. This process whereby they take this decision from you makes them a *part-owner* of you; it gives them a property right in you. Just as having such partial control and power of decision, by right, over an animal or inanimate object would be to have a property right in it. . . .

Locke's Theory of Acquisition

Before we turn to consider other theories of justice in detail, we must introduce an additional bit of complexity into the structure of the entitlement theory. This is best approached by considering Locke's attempt to specify a principle of justice in acquisition. Locke views property rights in an unowned object as originating through someone's mixing his labor with it. This gives rise to many questions. What are the boundaries of what labor is mixed with? If a private astronaut clears a place on Mars, has he mixed his labor with (so that he comes to own) the whole planet, the whole uninhabited universe, or just a particular plot? Which plot does an act bring under ownership? . . .

Locke's proviso that there be "enough and as good left in common for others" is meant to ensure that the situation of others is not worsened. . . .

. . . I assume that any adequate theory of justice in acquisition will contain a proviso similar to [Locke's]. A process normally giving rise to a permanent bequeathable property right in a previously unowned thing will not do so if the position of others no longer at liberty to use the thing is thereby worsened. It is important to specify *this* particular mode of worsening the situation of others, for the proviso does not encompass other modes. It does not include the worsening due to more limited opportunities to appropriate . . . and it does not include how I "worsen" a seller's position if I appropriate materials to make some of what he is selling, and then enter into competition with him. Someone whose appropriation otherwise would violate the proviso still may appropriate provided he compensates the others so that their situation is not thereby worsened; unless he does compensate these others, his appropriation will violate the proviso of the principle of justice in acquisition and will be an illegitimate one. A theory of appropriation incorporating this Lockean proviso will handle correctly the cases (objections to the theory lacking the proviso) where someone appropriates the total supply of something necessary for life.

A theory which includes this proviso in its principle of justice in acquisition must also contain a more complex principle of justice in transfer. Some reflection of the proviso about appropriation constrains later actions. If my appropriating all of a certain substance violates the Lockean proviso, then so does my appropriating some and purchasing all the rest from others who obtained it without otherwise violating the Lockean proviso. If the proviso excludes someone's appropriating all the drinkable water in the world, it also excludes his purchasing it all. (More weakly, and messily, it may exclude his charging certain prices for some of his supply.) This proviso (almost?) never will come into effect; the more someone acquires of a scarce substance which others want, the higher the price of the rest will go, and the more difficult it will become for him to acquire it all. But still, we can imagine, at least, that something like this occurs: someone makes simultaneous secret bids to the separate owners of a substance, each of whom sells assuming he can easily purchase more from the other owners; or some natural catastrophe destroys all of the supply of something except that in one person's possession. The total supply could not be permissibly appropriated by one person at the beginning. His later acquisition of it all does not show that the original appropriation violated the proviso. . . . Rather, it is the combination of the original appropriation *plus* all the later transfers and actions that violates the Lockean proviso.

Each owner's title to his holding includes the historical shadow of the Lockean proviso on appropriation. This excludes his transferring it into an agglomeration that does violate the Lockean proviso and excludes his using it in a way, in coordination with others or independently of them, so as to violate the proviso by making the situation of others worse than their baseline situation. Once it is known that someone's ownership runs afoul of the Lockean proviso, there are stringent limits on what he may do with (what it is difficult any longer unreservedly to call) "his property." Thus a person may not appropriate the only water hole in the desert and charge what he will. Nor may he charge what he will if he possesses one, and unfortunately it happens that all the water holes in the desert dry up, except for his. This unfortunate circumstance, admittedly no fault of his, brings into operation the Lockean proviso and limits his property rights. Similarly, an owner's property right in the only island in an area does not allow him to order a castaway from a shipwreck off his island as a trespasser, for this would violate the Lockean proviso.

Notice that the theory does not say that owners do not have these rights, but that the rights are overridden to avoid some catastrophe. (Overridden rights do not disappear; they leave a trace of a sort absent in the cases under discussion.) There is no such external (and *ad hoc?*) overriding. Considerations internal to the theory of property itself, to its theory of acquisition and appropriation, provide the means for handling such cases. . . .

I believe that the free operation of a market system will not actually run afoul of the Lockean proviso. . . . If this is correct, the proviso will not . . . provide a significant opportunity for future state action.

A UTILITARIAN THEORY OF JUSTICE

Rolf E. Sartorius

A stable social order in large part depends upon a common conviction that basic social institutions—economic, political, educational, etc.—are just. But one of the most persistent complaints against act-utilitarianism is that it is unable to account for our considered moral judgments concerning social justice. The fundamental principles of a just moral and political order, it is contended, demand that utilitarian considerations sometimes be subordinated to individual claims of entitlement based upon principles of just desert. Whether it is political liberty, economic benefits, or personal freedom that is involved, it is contended that act-utilitarianism would override the morally legitimate claims of the individual as a means of furthering the common good. If men are to be treated as moral ends rather than as mere means to the satisfaction of the interests of others, and are to be secure in their expectations that they will receive from their social institutions that which they are due, principles of distributive and retributive justice which are independent of, and absolute with respect to, the principle of utility must, it is claimed, prevail.

. . . I shall attempt to defend act-utilitarianism against the charge that it would permit the unwarranted sacrifice of the some to the many (or the few, for that matter) with respect to the distribution of economic burdens and benefits (distributive justice) and the application of legal sanctions (retributive justice).

1. UTILITARIAN PRINCIPLES OF JUSTICE

. . . John Rawls has recently contended that the choice and public acceptance of principles of justice by the members of a hypothetical community of rational utilitarians would be tantamount to their abandonment of utilitarianism as a moral theory. If it is believed that the direct employment of the act-utilitarian principle itself in the distribution of primary goods would have undesirable consequences, and if principles of justice which are absolute with respect to considerations of utility are instead chosen as the basis for designing and criticizing institutions created for that purpose, utilitarianism, it is claimed, has been rejected.

A major purpose of this essay [is] to demonstrate how and why just this kind of claim is radically mistaken. . . .

2. JUSTICE AS FAIRNESS

. . . I shall first comment briefly on Rawls's conception of the particular form of social contract theory within the framework of which his account is developed.

Justice as fairness is a mere fragment of a comprehensive moral theory of *rightness as fairness.* The principles of right in this view are those which would be unanimously chosen by individuals in a hypothetical original position in which none would be aware of those inequalities, arbitrary from a moral point of view, which permit natural men to take unfair advantage of one another. Mutually self-interested men with roughly similar needs and abilities, acting behind a veil of ignorance as to what their particular life plans and social position will be in the real world, must reach agreement in advance on those principles which will serve as the basis for the design and criticism of their fundamental social institutions insofar as they are concerned with the distribution of primary social goods. Although self-interested, they are free from envy, and are subject to the constraints of having a morality in the sense that each will conform to the principles originally agreed upon even if so doing works to his disadvantage in specific cases once the veil of ignorance is removed. As Rawls himself emphasizes, this conception of morality makes the theory of right in general, and thus the theory of justice in particular, part of the more general theory of rational choice. What is right is what is in accord with those principles which would be chosen by rational men in a hypothetical position of fair equality as the best means of promoting their individual ends. Moral principles are the result of a fair bargain amongst equals.

Regardless of what view he takes of the principles of justice (or any others) that would be adopted under such circumstances, this conception of moral theory is one which the utilitarian must reject. Even though Rawls admits that with slight changes in the motivation assumptions which characterize his description of the original position, it is the utilitarian principle, and not his principles of justice, which would be adopted as the fundamental charter of society,[1] all of this must be deemed irrelevant by the utilitarian. Most men as they are exhibit an inclination to act upon both benevolent and selfish motives. The act-utilitarian's conception of moral theory is that it appeals directly to the former, psychological egoism being just one of a number of empirical facts which must be taken into account in the application of the utilitarian principle. Rawls, on the other hand, treats the inclination to further narrow self-interest not only as a psychological fact but as the fundamental basis for the concept of morality itself. Although he hedges on his description of what self-interest comes to,[2] his view is essentially Hobbesian, even though he must assume that men are benevolent enough to be willing to save for the benefit of future generations and are subject to what he calls "the constraints of having a morality."[3] Indeed, both the strictly Hobbesian man and the benevolent man may reply to Rawls that they fail to see the relevance, to them, of the principles which Rawls's hypothetical men (essentially Hobbesian, but of limited benevolence in certain crucial re-spects) *would* adopt under hypothetical conditions which fail to obtain in their real lives. The consistent Hobbesian, who finds himself in a real world where some *can* take advantage of others, will see no reason to conform to the principles of justice when so doing would be contrary to the dictates of narrow self-interest, and he will not be moved by a consideration of what is in the interest of future generations. The utilitarian will not be surprised if it turns out that the principles of justice which would be adopted by essentially Hobbesian men are not the same as those which merit support on the basis of a principle of benevolence.

I conclude, therefore, that Rawls's argument for his principles of justice in terms of the notion of which principles would be adopted in the initial position of fair equality as he characterizes it carries little weight, wherever it may lead. What remains is the notion that acceptable principles of justice are those which best accord with particular considered moral judgments about matters of social justice, and are consistent with the other principles contained in a comprehensive moral theory. Of course, if it turns out that such substantive principles are the ones which would be adopted under the hypothetical situation as Rawls describes it, this would give a privileged position to arguments from his hypothetical situation to other moral principles. My own view is that the principles which Rawls defends neither are in accord with our considered moral judgments nor are they the ones which would be adopted in the initial situation, even as Rawls describes it.

3. DISTRIBUTIVE JUSTICE: RAWLS'S ACCOUNT

The act-utilitarian is concerned only with the sum total of satisfaction consequent upon the distribution of any fixed quantity of goods and services; where they lead to the same net utility level, he is indifferent to the pattern in which either the satisfactions or that which produces them is distributed. Potshots may be taken at act-utilitarianism by pointing out that unequal distributions may thus be viewed as either indifferent to or even preferable to equal ones on the grounds that a failure to satisfy the desires of some is compensated for by the satisfactions of others. To such complaints the utilitarian may reply that the plausibility of such putative counter examples typically rests upon confusing the pattern of goods and services with the pattern of distribution of the associated satisfactions. There are sound empirical grounds—considerations of envy, diminishing marginal utility, etc.—for the act-utilitarian not being indifferent to the former. But, the utilitarian may ask, what *reasons* can be given for preferring one distribution to another when the levels of satisfaction associated with both—*all* things considered—are equal? To answer such a question, one must have a comprehensive non-utilitarian *theory* of justice.

And this is what Rawls has. . . . [But] some quite general considerations will demonstrate, I believe, that Rawls has failed to provide a plausible alternative to a utilitarian account of distributive justice.

The difference principle represents the unwillingness of Rawls's hypothetically situated individuals to gamble on landing in a less advantaged position than they can assure themselves of as the price to be paid for the higher payoffs attached to other positions which they might have the good fortune to find themselves occupying once the veil of ignorance is removed. Unequal social and economic benefits are acceptable only if their existence works out to the benefit of the least, as well as the more, advantaged. Each individual, in acting as if he assumed that he would turn out to be one of the least rather than the more advantaged, is, as Rawls once put it, acting as if his own worst enemy would put him in his social and economic place.[4]

Rawls's hypothetical individual acting behind a veil of ignorance is employing what decision theorists call the *maximin rule* for choice under conditions of uncertainty.[5] The decision-maker is viewed as having to make a choice amongst a finite number of alternative acts with each of which is associated a finite number of possible outcomes,[6] which one will eventuate if the act is performed depending upon which of a number of possible states of affairs obtain in the world. Since probabilities cannot be assigned to these different states of nature, they cannot be assigned to the outcomes associated with each act-state pair. The decision-maker therefore cannot employ that decision rule, appropriate for choice under conditions of risk, which requires choosing that act which has associated with it the highest expected utility. The maximin rule requires one to play things safe and to perform that act which has associated with it the highest minimum payoff. . . .

4. Distributive Justice: A Utilitarian Account

The utilitarian, I have argued above, may criticize Rawls on the very same score on which Rawls and others have objected to utilitarianism: The principles which he adopts would lead to the unjust sacrifice of the interests of some to those of others. But assuming that interpersonal utility comparisons may be put upon a firm foundation, the act-utilitarian must admit—indeed, urge—that unequal distributions may sometimes be justified because the satisfactions of those who receive more outweigh the dissatisfactions of those who receive less. This is an undeniable consequence of act-utilitarianism which will be welcomed by benevolent men.

To the charge that the act-utilitarian is thus committed to treating (at least some) men as means rather than as moral ends, thus depriving them of the basis of self-respect, a number of replies are in order. Firstly, insofar as an individual act or social policy will result in damage to the self-esteem of some of those who are likely to be affected by it, this is an important disutility of which the act-utilitarian can and must take account. Indeed, he may even agree with Rawls's suggestion that self-respect is the most important primary good, although he will of course refuse to give it *absolute* weight. Secondly, it may be argued that in the only clear sense that can be given to this notion, the act-utilitarian does treat all men as moral ends: It is only their satisfactions and dissatisfactions which are held to be of value, and the preferences of each are given the same absolute weight on an intersubjective scale of value. All men, and their happiness and unhappiness, are treated as being of equal moral worth. Thirdly, insofar as unequal distributions of the things that men desire are justified on the grounds that the happiness of some outweighs the unhappiness of others, it is reasonable to assume that many of these inequalities will be randomly distributed over time. The one who benefits from the sacrifices of others today is likely to be called upon to subordinate different interests of his own to those of others tomorrow. In the proverbial long run, inequalities may balance out in a manner which permits each to view himself as having received roughly equal treatment with others. It is a defect of many contemporary social institutions that some receive more, and others less, of virtually everything over time. But who would seriously suggest that such institutions could be justified in terms of the utilitarian principle? Finally, benevolent men will not only take positive pleasure in knowing that the burdens which they assume enhance the well-being of others; they will view themselves as most fully realizing their potential to act as moral agents in those instances in which they voluntarily accept those disadvantages which work to the advantage of others.

As has already been suggested, though, there is, in spite of the above, good reason for limiting the scope of the direct operation of the utilitarian principle when it comes to the distribution of primary social goods.

In many instances, equal distribution (up to a certain ground-floor level, at least) is called for by obvious but all too often ignored features of a world in which the majority of people are ill-fed, ill-housed, ill-clothed, and uneducated. Roughly equal needs for (similar utility functions over) primary social goods, diminishing marginal utility of those goods past a minimum attainable by all, and the inefficiency of constructing mechanisms which would be sensitive to differences where they do exist—all are the best of reasons for designing institutions which conform to traditional liberal ideas of social justice.

Where basic needs and desires are no longer in question, though, there is nothing inherently immoral about designing institutions which will foster inequalities the justification of which lies simply in the fact that some need pay only a modest price to considerably heighten the satisfactions of others. This is not to deny, of course, that one may have more confidence that institutionally fostered inequalities are justified when, as is demanded by Rawls's principles, the inequalities appear to work out to the advantage of others than those whom they most directly and substantially benefit. A system of higher education to which there is limited competitive access, but which is supported by a tax burden shared by all, perhaps may not be justified by either of these principles taken in isolation, although it may be by their conjunction. On the one hand, it must be admitted that all are being required to make a small contribution to the support of an institution the primary and substantial beneficiaries of which are those who receive the education, and associated earning power, in question. On the other hand, failing widespread benevolence, the system would probably be politically unacceptable if it were not also believed that the better educated would in the long run make valuable contributions to the general social good which would otherwise be lost.

Rawls's admission that the principles with which his theory is concerned are to a considerable extent ones of what he calls *pure procedural justice,* consistent with any de facto distribution of primary goods which yields the required payoff schedules for his representative, average men,[7] serves to highlight the point that what just institutions do is to create and maintain certain stable sets of expectations amongst the members of a social group. It is like knowing that a game of chance is fair; if fairly played, the outcome is just, whatever it may be. But although I don't know whether I'll win, lose, or come out even, I do know a number of things which permit me to make rational decisions (in terms of betting behavior) that I could not otherwise make. So with just institutions: They support rational expectations which permit those whose lives they affect to make plans and take risks which it would otherwise be irrational for them to undertake. Viewed in this manner, they are but another instance of conventions which serve to redirect human behavior into channels which it would otherwise not take by restructuring the sets of considerations of consequences upon which those employing a consequentialist choice principle will base their decisions.

There is no doubt but that a community of rational act-utilitarians would perceive the desirability of institutional mechanisms for distributing primary goods which subordinate direct considerations of utility to simpler and much more predictable considerations. Without them, the security of expectations required for the formation of rational long range life plans would to a considerable degree be lacking. To what extent such institutions would conform to Rawls's two principles of justice is an empirical question the answer to which must depend upon the contingent features of any actual social situation. But I am confident that there are few, if any, real historical contexts in which it is plausible to claim that it would be reasonable to attempt to meet all of the demands made by Rawls's principles. Even admitting that what Rawls's principles require may be overridden, if not by considerations of utility, at least by other considerations of justice, and leaving aside the difficulties with them already mentioned, the priority rules associated with them—which cannot be abandoned without abandoning the theory—would seem to prohibit just the sort of trade-offs which are demanded by the realities of social existence. Whereas political liberty and equal opportunity are, according to Rawls's principles, to strictly dominate considerations of social and economic advantage, this is just the sort of justice the achievement of which may appear to be a hollow victory indeed for those who live under relatively liberal governments and yet exist from day to day without knowing where their next meal is coming from. Most inhabitants of undeveloped countries, I suspect, would with good reason take the view that Rawls's principles had the priorities reversed from their most plausible natural ordering.

With respect to the distribution of social and economic benefits, I thus conclude that what justice demands can only be determined by the application of the act-utilitarian principle to complex problems of institutional design under concrete social conditions, there being at best a presumption in favor of equal distribution of certain primary goods (up to a point) under conditions of abundance and equal need which are admittedly quite widespread. As far as principles of distributive justice which have to do with economic and social advantages are concerned, the act-utilitarian will thus view them, with caution, as little more than rules of thumb. Except within the most technologically and socially static societies, economic and social conditions are simply too variable and changeable to warrant such principles being raised to the status of conventional moral rules, let alone constitutional guarantees.

Notes

1. Rawls, *Theory of Justice*, Sections 27 and 28.
2. Rawls writes of his hypothetical men in the original position that "although the interests advanced . . . are not assumed to be interests in the self, they are the interests of a self that regards its conception of the good as worthy of recognition and that advances claims in its behalf as deserving satisfaction." *Theory of Justice*, 127.
3. See Rawls, *Theory of Justice*, 128 and following pages, on the just savings principle and the motivational assumptions needed to derive it. On the constraints of the concept of right, see Section 23.
4. Rawls, *Theory of Justice*, 152–153.
5. For a general discussion of a variety of criteria which have been proposed for rational choice under uncertainty, see Luce and Raiffa, *Games and Decisions*, Chapter 13.
6. For there to be a genuine choice problem, at least one act must have more than one possible outcome associated with it, and there must be at least two acts with different possible outcomes.
7. Rawls, *Theory of Justice*, Section 14.

ECONOMIC SYSTEMS

John Rawls

SOME REMARKS ABOUT ECONOMIC SYSTEMS

. . . An economic system regulates what things are produced and by what means, who receives them and in return for which contributions, and how large a fraction of social resources is devoted to saving and to the provision of public goods. Ideally all of these matters should be arranged in ways that satisfy the two principles of justice. But we have to ask whether this is possible and what in particular these principles require.

To begin with, it is helpful to distinguish between two aspects of the public sector, otherwise the difference between a private-property economy and socialism is left unclear. The first aspect has to do with the ownership of the means of production. The classical distinction is that the size of the public sector under socialism (as measured by the fraction of total output produced by state-owned firms and managed either by state officials or by workers' councils) is much larger. In a private-property economy the number of publicly owned firms is presumably small and in any event limited to special cases such as public utilities and transportation.

A second quite different feature of the public sector is the proportion of total social resources devoted to public goods. The distinction between public and private goods raises a number of intricate points, but the main idea is that a public good has two characteristic features, indivisibility and publicness.[1] That is, there are many individuals, a public so to speak, who want more or less of this good, but if they are to enjoy it at all must each enjoy the same amount. The quantity produced cannot be divided up as private goods can and purchased by individuals according to their preferences for more and less. There are various kinds of public goods depending upon their degree of indivisibility and the size of the relevant public. The polar case of a public good is full indivisibility over the whole society. A standard example is the defense of the nation against (unjustified) foreign attack. All citizens must be provided with this good in the same amount; they cannot be given varying protection depending on their wishes. The consequences of indivisibility and publicness in these cases is that the provision of public goods must be arranged for through the political process and not through the market. Both the amount to be produced and its financing need to be worked out by legislation. Since there is no problem of distribution in the sense that all citizens receive the same quantity, distribution costs are zero.

Various features of public goods derive from these two characteristics. First of all, there is the free-rider problem. Where the public is large and includes many individuals, there is a temptation for each person to try to avoid doing his share. This is because whatever one man does his action will not significantly affect the amount produced. He regards the collective action of others as already given one way or the other. If the public good is produced his enjoyment of it is not decreased by his not making a contribution. If it is not produced his action would not have changed the situation anyway. A citizen receives the same protection from foreign invasion regardless of whether he has paid his taxes. Therefore in the polar case trade and voluntary agreements cannot be expected to develop.

It follows that arranging for and financing public goods must be taken over by the state and some binding rule requiring payment must be enforced. Even if all citizens were willing to pay their share, they would presumably do so only when they are assured that others will pay theirs as well. Thus once citizens have agreed to act collectively and not as isolated individuals taking the actions of the others as given, there is still the task of tying down the agreement. . . .

Another aspect of the public goods situation is that of externality. When goods are public and indivisible, their production will cause benefits and losses to others which may not be taken into account by those who arrange for these goods or who decide to produce them. Thus in the polar case, if but a part of the citizenry pays taxes to cover the expenditure on public goods, the whole society is still affected by the items provided. Yet those who agree to these levies may not consider these effects, and so the amount of public expenditure is presumably different from what it would be if all benefits and losses had been considered. The everyday cases are those where the indivisibility is partial and the public is smaller. Someone who has himself inoculated against a contagious disease helps others as well as himself; and while it may not pay him to obtain this protection, it may be worth it to the local community when all advantages are tallied up. And, of course, there are the striking cases of public harms, as when industries sully and erode the natural environment. These costs are not normally reckoned with by the market so that the commodities produced are sold at much less than their marginal social costs. There is a divergence between private and social accounting that the market fails to register. One essential task of law and government is to institute the necessary corrections.

It is evident, then, that the indivisibility and publicness of certain essential goods, and the externalities and temptations to which they give rise, necessitate collective agreements organized and enforced by the state. That political rule is founded solely on men's propensity to self-interest and injustice is a superficial view. For even among just men, once goods are indivisible over large numbers of individuals, their actions decided upon in isolation from one another will not lead to the general good. Some collective arrangement is necessary and everyone wants assurance that it will be adhered to if he is willingly to do his part. . . .

. . . The idea that competitive prices under normal conditions are just or fair goes back at least to medieval times. While the notion that a market economy is in some sense the best scheme has been most carefully investigated by so-called bourgeois economists, this connection is a historical contingency in that, theoretically at least, a socialist regime can avail itself of the advantages of this system. One of these advantages is efficiency. Under certain conditions competitive prices select the goods to be produced and allocate resources to their production in such a manner that there is no way to improve upon either the choice of productive methods by firms, or the distribution of goods that arises from the purchase of households. There exists no rearrangement of the resulting economic configuration that makes one household better off (in view of its preferences) without making another worse off. No further mutually advantageous trades are possible; nor are there any feasible productive processes that will yield more of some desired commodity without requiring a cutback in another. For if this were not so, the situation of some individuals could be made more advantageous without a loss for anyone else. The theory of general equilibrium explains how, given the appropriate conditions, the information supplied by prices leads economic agents to act in ways that sum up to achieve this outcome. Perfect competition is a perfect procedure with respect to efficiency. Of course, the requisite conditions are highly special ones and they are seldom if ever fully satisfied in the real world. Moreover, market failures and imperfections are often serious, and compensation adjustments must be made by the allocation branch. Monopolistic restrictions, lack of information, external economies and diseconomies, and the like must be recognized and corrected. And the market fails altogether in the case of public goods. But these matters need not concern us here. These idealized arrangements are mentioned in order to clarify the related notion of pure procedural justice. The ideal conception may then be used to appraise existing arrangements and as a framework for identifying the changes that should be undertaken.

A further and more significant advantage of a market system is that, given the requisite background institutions, it is consistent with equal liberties and fair equality of opportunity. Citizens have a free choice of careers and occupations. There is no reason at all for the forced and central direction of labor. Indeed, in the absence of some differences in earnings as these arise in a competitive scheme, it is hard to see how, under ordinary circumstances anyway, certain aspects of a command society inconsistent with liberty can be avoided. Moreover, a system of markets decentralizes the exercise of economic power. Whatever the internal nature of firms, whether they are privately or state owned, or whether they are run by entrepreneurs or by managers elected by workers, they take the prices of outputs and inputs as given and draw up their plans accordingly. When markets are truly competitive, firms do not engage in price wars or other contests for market power. In conformity with political decision reached democratically, the government regulates the economic climate by adjusting certain elements under its control, such as the overall amount of investment, the rate of interest, and the quantity of money, and so on. There is no necessity for comprehensive direct planning. Individual households and firms are free to make their decisions independently, subject to the general conditions of the economy.

In noting the consistency of market arrangements with socialist institutions, it is essential to distinguish between the allocative and the distributive functions of prices. The former is connected with their use to achieve economic efficiency, the latter with their determining the income to be received by individuals in return for what they contribute. It is perfectly consistent for a socialist regime to establish an interest rate to allocate resources among investment projects and to compute rental charges for the use of capital and scarce natural assets such as land and forests. Indeed, this must be done if these means of production are to be employed in the best way. For even if these assets should fall out of the sky without human effort, they are nevertheless productive in the sense that when combined with other factors a greater output results. It does not follow, however, that there need be private persons who as owners of these assets receive the monetary equivalents of these evaluations. Rather these accounting prices are indicators for drawing up an efficient schedule of economic activities. Except in the case of work of all kinds, prices under socialism do not correspond to income paid over to private individuals. Instead, the income imputed to natural and collective assets accrues to the state, and therefore their prices have no distributive function.

It is necessary, then, to recognize that market institutions are common to both private-property and socialist regimes, and to distinguish between the allocative and the distributive function of prices. Since under socialism the means of production and natural resources are publicly owned, the distributive function is greatly restricted, whereas a private-property system uses prices in varying degrees for both purposes. Which of these systems and the many intermediate forms most fully answers to the requirements of justice cannot, I think, be determined in advance. There is presumably no general answer to this question, since it depends in large part upon the traditions, institutions, and social forces of each country, and its particular historical circumstances. The theory of justice does not include these matters. But what it can do is to set out in a schematic way the outlines of a just economic system that admits of several variations. The political judgment in any given case will then turn on which variation is most likely to work out best in practice. A conception of justice is a necessary part of any such political assessment, but it is not sufficient. . . .

Background Institutions for Distributive Justice

The main problem of distributive justice is the choice of a social system. The principles of justice apply to the basic structure and regulate how its major institutions are combined into one scheme. Now, as we have seen, the idea of justice as fairness is to use the notion of pure procedural justice to handle the contingencies of particular situations. The social system is to be designed so that the resulting distribution is just however things turn out. To achieve this end it is necessary to set the social and economic process within the surroundings of suitable political and legal institutions. Without an appropriate scheme of these background institutions the outcome of the distributive process will not be just. Background fairness is lacking. I shall give a brief description of these supporting institutions as they might exist in a properly organized democratic state that allows private ownership of capital and natural resources. . . .

In establishing these background institutions the government may be thought of as divided into four branches.[2] Each branch consists of various agencies, or activities thereof, charged with preserving certain social and economic conditions. These divisions do not overlap with the usual organization of government but are to be understood as different functions. The allocation branch, for example, is to keep the price system workably competitive and to prevent the formation of unreasonable market power. Such power does not exist as long as markets cannot be made more competitive consistent with the requirements of efficiency and the facts of geography and the preferences of households. The allocation branch is also charged with identifying and correcting, say by suitable taxes and subsidies and by changes in the definition of property rights, the more obvious departures from efficiency caused by the failure of prices to measure accurately social benefits and costs. To this end suitable taxes and subsidies may be used, or the scope and definition of property rights may be revised. The stabilization branch, on the other hand, strives to bring about reasonably full employment in the sense that those who want work can find it and the free choice of occupation and the deployment of finance are supported by strong effective demand. These two branches together are to maintain the efficiency of the market economy generally.

The social minimum is the responsibility of the transfer branch. . . . The essential idea is that the workings of this branch take needs into account and assign them an appropriate weight with respect to other claims. A competitive price system gives no consideration to needs and therefore it cannot be the sole device of distribution. There must be a division of labor between the parts of the social system in answering to the common sense precepts of justice. Different institutions meet different claims. Competitive markets properly regulated secure free choice of occupation and lead to an efficient use of resources and allocation of commodities to households. They set a weight on the conventional precepts associated with wages and earnings, whereas the transfer branch guarantees a certain level of well-being and honors the claims of need. . . .

It is clear that the justice of distributive shares depends on the background institutions and how they allocate total income, wages and other income plus transfers. There is with reason strong objection to the competitive determination of total income, since this ignores the claims of need and an appropriate standard of life. From the standpoint of the legislative stage it is rational to insure oneself and one's descendants against these contingencies of the market. Indeed, the difference principle presumably requires this. But once a suitable minimum is provided by transfers, it may be perfectly fair that the rest of total income be settled by the price system, assuming that it is moderately efficient and free from monopolistic restrictions, and unreasonable externalities have been eliminated. Moreover, this way of dealing with the claims of need would appear to be more effective than trying to regulate income by minimum wage standards, and the like. It is better to assign to each branch only such tasks as are compatible with one another. Since the market is not suited to answer the claims of need, these should be met by a separate arrangement. Whether the principles of justice are satisfied, then, turns on whether the total income of the least advantaged (wages plus transfers) is such as to maximize their long-run expectations (consistent with the constraints of equal liberty and fair equality of opportunity).

Finally, there is a distribution branch. Its task is to preserve an approximate justice in distributive shares by means of taxation and the necessary adjustments in the rights of property. Two aspects of this branch may be distinguished. First of all, it imposes a number of inheritance and gift taxes, and sets restrictions on the rights of bequest. The purpose of these levies and regulations is not to raise revenue (release resources to government) but gradually and continually to correct the distribution of wealth and to prevent concentrations of power detrimental to the fair value of political liberty and fair equality of opportunity. For example, the progressive principle might be applied at the beneficiary's end.[3] Doing this would encourage the wide dispersal of property which is a necessary condition, it seems, if the fair value of the equal liberties is to be maintained.

Notes

1. For a discussion of public goods, see J. M. Buchanan, *The Demand and Supply of Public Goods* (Chicago: Rand McNally, 1968), esp. Ch. IX. This work contains useful bibliographical appendixes to the literature.
2. For the idea of branches of government, see R. A. Musgrave, *The Theory of Public Finance* (New York: McGraw-Hill, 1959), Ch. I.
3. See Meade, *Efficiency, Equality and the Ownership of Property,* pp. 56f.

JUSTICE AND THE BUSINESS SOCIETY

Jan Narveson

"We're not in business for our health, Mister!" "Madam, at that price you're not asking for a bargain—you're asking for charity!" Remarks like these illustrate the basic facts—and raise the basic questions—about that realm of human activity known to us as "business." What is the "business world"? What are its main assumptions? The classic answers to these questions are well known and clear. Business transactions occur between free and independent persons presumed to be rationally seeking to promote their own advantage. The standard business relationship is between people who are neither friends nor enemies, neither allies in a common

Original essay written especially for this text. Reprinted by permission of the author.

cause nor hated competitors out to do each other dirt. It is almost impossible to overemphasize either of these facets. (1) On the one hand, business may be done between people who not only do not love each other but, indeed, don't even know each other. Such ties are entirely unnecessary—and might even get in the way. (One of the reasons why the supermarket has largely replaced the corner store is precisely because of its impersonal character. You don't feel compelled to discuss the weather, the latest political developments, or, worst of all, the goings-on of your new neighbors' children with the check-out person at the supermarket—who in any case is too busy for such things.) (2) On the other hand, there is no call for attributing malice even to the most avid competitors in the business world. A's loss is not identical with B's gain: A and B both want the business, but that's all they want. The satisfaction of one's own firm's getting the contract is due to getting the contract, not to the other fellow's not getting it.

Parties to any business transaction—from the lowliest purchase of an onion at the Farmer's Market to deals involving billions of dollars—may be as different as you like; yet business enables each party to benefit from the other. The free exchange of goods or services which is the essence of business is possible because each party has something which the other party values *more* than what he already has. If both possessed identical commodities, and especially if they were also in exactly the same circumstances, then mutually advantageous exchange could not readily happen. In business, our differences unite us. This is so, as economic analysis can readily demonstrate, even when our values are not only different but, in a rather important sense, incomparable. For profitable exchange, it is unnecessary for us to be able to say, "Ahah—you are getting five units of Ultimate Value out of this, whereas I'm getting only three!" It is necessary merely that we consider what our options are, know which we prefer to which, and believe that what the other fellow has to offer is the best we can do in the circumstances. Given this, we are "ready to do business."

There is a great deal to be said for business transactions as the paradigm cases of human relationships. For consider the alternatives. On the one hand, imagine trying genuinely to live in accordance with Jesus Christ's injunction, "Love ye one another!" Any decently realistic view of the human situation will quickly reveal that this injunction is neither possible nor even desirable for the typical case. It is not *possible* because, in any but the most trivialized sense of the term "love," our capacity to love is wildly outstripped by the enormous number of people toward whom it might be directed. Anyone who thinks this is possible has probably never been in love, never really loved anyone, or has forgotten for the moment what loving involves. And even if it were *possible,* would it be *desirable?* Is it not far better to know a few people well, give them the kind of devoted attention and warmth of feeling which makes love so important and so fine an element in the good life, than to divide oneself a thousand and million ways, driving oneself crazy in the attempt to honor all those commitments?

On the other hand, consider how awful it would be, how intolerable and miserable, to regard all mankind as The Enemy. Quite apart from the fear, suspicion, and hatred inspired in us by the thought of someone who regards all of his fellows as evil and diabolical, do we not, on reflection, have the greatest pity for anyone like that? What could be a worse and more desperate frame of mind than to walk the streets in constant rage against the rest of mankind? This, of course, quite apart from the evils sure to be visited upon you if you take the actions appropriate to such paranoid beliefs.

No, neither of these alternatives will do. And then, isn't it inevitable that with regard to the greater part of mankind, either we simply have nothing to do with them at all, because they are much too far away, or we engage in relationships which are neither too onerously personal and involving nor dangerous and thoroughly unpleasant? And is there any better basis for such relationships than those of mutual profit and advantage? But that structure, in principle, is the world of business. Here we are not presumed to *owe* each other anything more than to leave each other in peace, to go about, as we say, his business; and if we do relate to each other, then we do so on terms of mutual advantage. There is no expectation, no insistence that the other fellow will give me the shirt off his back. Rather, the assumption is that, apart from ordinary good manners, he will do something for me only if I reciprocally do something for him.

One of the ablest current writers[1] has coined an admirable phrase to characterize the ethics of what we might call Business Person. The phrase is "constrained maximization." The person operating on such a policy is one who is, indeed, out to get the best deal possible for himself; but he stops short in those cases where for all concerned to pursue such a policy would make each worse off. In such cases, he cooperates with the others involved, renouncing the policy of unlimited self-seeking and adhering instead to mutually satisfactory agreements.

It is possible to think that a world in which everyone adhered to the business orientation in his dealings with the world at large would be quite a good world, even, perhaps, the very best world we could humanly and reasonably expect. Yet there are plenty of people nowadays who are anything but convinced of that possibility. Why is this so?

The main reason has to do with a difference of view on the subject of Justice. Those who share the view that a Business World would be the best of all realistically possible worlds are apt to think of justice as the keeping of honestly made agreements and the avoidance of violence. On that general conception of justice, it will be noted, justice has no necessary connection with Equality. If we each make and reliably keep the best deals we can, there is no certainty, and indeed small probability, that the result, even in the long run, will be to yield approximately the same level of income, wealth, welfare, or happiness for everyone. Indeed, there is no limit to the discrepancies which could in principle arise as the result of successive just dealings, on this view of the matter.[2] But some—quite a few, evidently—want to insist that a just world is also an equal world.

Usually such people have especially in mind the avoidance of poverty as the goal of justice;[3] but sometimes they proclaim the goal of real equality in the stronger sense, not merely that none will be in desperate want but also that the difference in wealth between the poorest and the richest would be negligible, which of course is to say that there would be no "poor" or "rich."[4]

Indeed, there are those who think that equality is so obviously a goal, or even *the* goal of justice that they accuse those who espouse the business world of ignoring or even opposing justice. But this accusation is unfair. Those who think that the world in which our typical relations with our fellows are those of free transactions for mutual advantage think that that *is* a just world. And they think that a world in which such transactions are substantially "interfered with" in the interests of equality is, on the contrary, an unjust world. For they think that to intervene forcibly in an activity carried on between mature people who have freely agreed to do what they do and who are not working for the detriment of anyone else is unjust.

It may at first seem that here is a ground-floor disagreement, one which it is scarcely possible to resolve. And this may be true, but we must not be too hasty. For the plot thickens when we consider more carefully the description which I have just produced of the business advocate's view of injustice. It is not so clear, in fact, that the advocate of equality must, or will, disagree that that description, just as it stands, is one of injustice. He may well agree that *if* an agreement between two normal and rational beings has been genuinely reached *freely,* and if indeed the resulting activity really does not work to the detriment of anyone else— *then* to interfere in this activity would be wrong or unjust, at least other things being more or less equal. But they will claim that this is not typically the case in the business world. They will insist that business agreements are not struck in perfect freedom, and that even if they were, they systematically work to disadvantage others. Is there any reason to think this is so?

First, why might it be felt that these agreements are not struck freely? In some cases, we may all agree, there is fraud, deception, or dishonesty involved. And in others, there is coercion or even violence. If I sell you what I have described as a can of peanuts, and upon opening it you find instead wood chips, then something has gone wrong and injustice may well be involved. Or if I give you your choice between paying me $10,000 and winding up in cement shoes at the bottom of the Welland Canal one fine evening, then again we do not have a "free agreement." Injustice not only may well be, but certainly is, involved. But does the egalitarian think that either of these kinds of shortcomings is involved in typical business transactions?

He might. Along the former lines, he might, for instance, point to the use of advertising. He might claim that the customer in the contemporary world is typically bamboozled into buying, that the product is made to look alluring, and that in any case the "need" which the item allegedly satisfies is not a *real* need.[5] In turn, he may claim that in much of this world there are monopolies doing the supplying, so that the consumer has no real choice. Or in the case of labor contracts, he may say that the workman has no real choice either: he must either work or starve.

All these points are susceptible to cogent replies, however. The point about advertising simply doesn't establish what it needs to establish, for it is not claimed that typical ads are fraudulent. If they attempt to create an aura of attractiveness about the products being advertised, why shouldn't they? So does the New Testament, in its efforts to persuade us of the merits of the Christian religion. Does anyone think that it should be outlawed? And if advertisers insinuate that you will live a better life if you buy their products, why on earth *shouldn't* they do this? And if we are to have a centralized censor making decisions about what we should and shouldn't be told by sellers, or what we should or shouldn't buy, then how, please, is this argument going to be represented as that of a friend of "freedom"?

The other two arguments suffer from a different defect. They assume that it is the duty of the seller not only to offer the consumer the products he offers, but also to make sure that there are plenty of other sellers on the market with attractive alternatives! But if *that* is the argument, then there isn't genuinely an agreement about our original hypothesis that interference with freedom is on the face of it unjust. If I, the seller, had begun by forcibly depriving you of alternatives, in the manner of the mobster with his protection racket, then of course we would not have a situation of freedom between buyer and seller. But that is not what happens. The business person does not in general create the situation in which there is a potential market for his product. Rather, he discerns this situation, and he moves to supply it. *Not,* let us recall, out of motives of charity, but out of a desire for profit. And others are free to enter the market, too, if they've a mind to.

The business-world view of justice does, certainly, have its hard-nosed aspects. In that world, we do not *owe* each other even a minimum standard of living, let alone an equal one. I may be starving in the gutter and in rags: this still does not make it your obligation to feed and clothe me, even if you are exceedingly wealthy. Why not? Because there is no antecedent agreement, struck on terms of mutual self-interest, which requires me to do this. Had there been one, that would be another matter. But there may well not have. And if not, then what?

Well, one thing is that if I am in such desperate straits, I ought to be willing to accept any offer of employment which will get me out of them. And you, in turn, can make me a very favorable offer, from your point of view. The likelihood is that you will indeed make such an offer. After all, low labor costs are a main road to profit, are they not? Thus will industry move to depressed areas, provided that there are no minimum-wage laws standing in the way. Thus will our cotton shirts and our transistor radios come to be made in India or Hong Kong. It's good business—for *both* parties. The egalitarian, of course, will denounce this as Imperialism. Imperialism appears when you hire foreigners for 50 cents an hour—

several times what they have ever earned before, quite likely!—when instead you could be hiring your fellow citizens for $6 an hour, plus time and a half, plus union featherbedding in the bargain. Obviously Justice will call upon us to leave the Indians, the Chinese, and the Mexicans to stay undernourished in their hovels in the interests of Equality for our fellow Americans or Canadians, right? And so our other fellow North Americans will pay 50 percent more for their shirts and their radios, thus making their fair sacrifice to equality too—even if they happen to be making less than $6 an hour themselves and do not belong to unions.

Is there a duty to our fellowman, as our fellowman, to attend to his health and welfare? To provide him with a tolerable diet if he doesn't already have one? To send him off to the public schools (whether he wants to go or not, of course!)? And to pay his way through a fine public university when he gets out of that public school? Or are we confusing the question of whether these would be *desirable* things to happen to him with the question of whether it is our duty, as a matter of justice, to provide him with them if we can afford to and he cannot? If we are, that might go far to explain the mixture of feelings we may well have when we consider these matters. For after all, how can any humane and decent person deny that it is *better* that people be healthy, well fed and clothed, and well educated than that they should be sick, starving, and ignorant? The fact that it is better, however, may not show that it is a matter of justice that those of us in a position to promote these ends *must* promote them.

What is the difference between these two, if they are different—between the desirable and the just? Between, to invoke two recent political slogans, the Good Society and the Just Society? Although these are difficult questions, with a long history of philosophical dispute behind them, I believe that a considerable part of the answer is not so difficult to come by. The difference I have in mind is the difference between what, as rational beings, we *should* do and what we *must* do. When we address ourselves to the former sort of questions, the assumption is that we are free to choose: we can make better or worse choices, and if we make a worse one we may come to regret it, and others may properly deplore the choice—but it remains that the choice is ours to make. In the latter case, however, the case of justice, things are different. Justice *requires* us to do some things and to refrain from others. More especially, others may properly not only upbraid us for failing to do what justice requires, but may even properly make us do it. Our freedom may properly be restricted, if it's a matter of justice; but not if it isn't. (Some theorists will want to have it that justice involves *rights,* whereas goodness and the desirable do not. But I believe that this formulation will be found to come to the same thing as what I have just said.)[6]

The question whether we have a duty in justice to part with some of our fairly gotten gains to help the unfortunate is, then, the question whether we may properly be *forced* to do so. If we may, then taxation, for instance, is in order—taxes being payments which we have no choice but to make, payments we must make whether we like it or not, and even whether we think the objects for which the money will be spent are desirable or not, whether the money is being spent wisely or foolishly. But if we may *not* be forced to do so, then taxation is out of order, even if the result is that some will be in want.

Do we think that this sort of thing is a matter of justice and duty? If it is so thought, then there is at least one problem to face: viz., why does it matter whether those in want are next door or in other countries, however far away? And how much of our incomes may we be required to part with in order to promote this end? These two questions cannot be tidily separated. For if justice requires that we help those less fortunate than ourselves, and if we could, literally, afford to help many more than only those in our own country before we began to be in desperation ourselves, then it is not obvious why justice should extend only to the borders of one's own country. And if, on the other hand, it *should* stop there, then it cannot be due to the sheer fact that others are in want and we can help that justice requires us to help them. It makes no sense to say, "X is a human right, and therefore we should see that everybody *who is subject to the same government we are* gets X." And this shows that we do not really believe that welfare *is* a human right.

But mightn't it still be a politically based right, that is, a right derived from common membership in the same political system? There will, again, be those who think so, perhaps on the ground that we all have the equal right to vote, and hence to whatever a democratic procedure provides in the way of welfare rights or whatever other kinds of rights there might be. But do we believe this, either? Do we not, on the contrary, think that genuine rights are beyond the reach of majorities? Such rights as free speech, assembly, religion, and so on are surely not rights which we think a majority can properly abrogate. Why should property rights, then, be an exception?

Among those who still think it should be an exception are, principally, people who take the view that inert nature, unlike the various bodies and minds which are around, does not intrinsically *belong* to anyone. Attempts, such as that of Locke, to get external nature into the sphere of private ownership by acts of appropriation of labor, for instance, are difficult to carry out satisfactorily for reasons which have lately been rather exquisitely set forth by Robert Nozick.[7] But while this may be so, it remains that there is likewise no obvious reason for saying that external nature belongs to *everyone*—to all of us equally or jointly or whatever.[8] And there is a strong reason for pointing out that the lion's share of what there is to own is man-made. If we add to this the inordinate difficulties of coherently articulating socialism in this area, we shall find it very hard to improve on property rights which are likewise strong enough to resist the blandishments of majority rule. When a person has acquired property or purchasing power through fair exchange and honest effort, it is not easy to resist the conclusion that to take some or all of it from him simply on the say-so of an obscure majority is as unjust as it would be to take some of his limbs, or some of his time. Indeed, it is tantamount to taking the latter, for if you take from me some important (to me) and replaceable thing, my only option is to expend some more of my precious time in replacing it.

These last arguments look uncomfortably like appeals to Natural Right. And such appeals have a notable potential for becoming dead ends. However, the situation may not be so bad as all that. I want to conclude this quick survey of a great deal of pertinent territory with two observations.

The first observation is that while the business conception of justice does not make it a duty to contribute to those in need, it does not preclude voluntary contributions to that end either. And if it is, as I have suggested above, so obvious that such contributions are a good thing, is it unbelievable that a system in which taxation was not resorted to in order to cater to needs would be able to cope sufficiently with them? Even in the current dispensation, after all, generosity is not unusual even among people of means and among business enterprises. The typical human breast is far from devoid of sympathy, and those who think that business society exterminates such sentiments have probably never served on fund-raising committees for charitable enterprises. And shouldn't we also ask why it is that motives of charity and humanity should make us resort to a sort of organized theft—which, after all, taxation appears to be equivalent to? There is also, of course, the question whether an unlimited free market would not do far better for problems of unemployment and the like; and who can doubt that full employment would be a far more efficient cure for poverty and its related ills than any amount either of tax-induced expenditure on welfare or of charitable contribution by the better-off? All in all, the upshot may be that the Just Society, if justice is measured by the business outlook, would also in fact be the Good Society! Perhaps, then, our predilection for governmental cures to problems is a function of two of the oldest enemies of mankind: fear and ignorance—fear of liberty ("dreadful freedom"!) and ignorance of economics.

The second observation is a more general theoretical cousin of the first. Those who defend the market economy, the business view of justice, on grounds of Natural Right cannot, of course, consistently base their defense of that society on such arguments as the above. But the rest of us can. And is it really believable that a society might be both perfectly just and perfectly miserable? Not readily, I think. But there is not, as has often been thought, a great gulf fixed between a theory of justice involving strong property rights and a theory based on general utility. Those who have supposed that there must be such a gulf have, I suspect, overlooked an important point about the terms of reference of a utilitarian outlook on these matters. For they suppose that the utilitarian must simply equate the just with what has maximal utility; and so, for instance, they suppose that if from the utilitarian point of view it would be preferable for A to have less and B to have more, then straightaway we must conclude that the just thing to do, on the utilitarian view, must be to bring it about, by whatever means, that A has less and B has more. Not so, however. For what must be evaluated is not simply the end result—A's level of material wellbeing versus B's, for instance—but *also* the means by which it is brought about that A and B each has what he has. For if we can bring about this result only by taking from A what he has acquired fairly through a highly natural and intuitive system of acquisition, and by giving it to B, who has not, then we have to evaluate the consequences of that *as well as* the distributive end result. And it is no longer so obvious that the arrangement of A having less and B more by virtue of A having been forcibly deprived of what B ends up with *is* going to be better on the whole—particularly if B, after all, was welcome to pursue his living on the same terms as A, if he was all that anxious to achieve what A has.

It is a very long way from the sort of society we in fact have to the sort of society envisaged by the proponent of the noninterventionist free market—a fact of considerable importance when we encounter the kind of diatribes against the latter currently fashionable in Western intellectual circles, since much of their complaint seems to be based on the assumption that current economic society is a good enough model of the free market to do. It is not very easy to say how things would be in a free market society; and further, so far as I can see, the theory of that kind of society is by no means complete. But we owe it to ourselves to take seriously the philosophical underpinnings of that view. This brief account is designed to suggest that those foundations are neither silly nor even inhumane.

Notes

1. David Gauthier, "Reason and Maximization," *Canadian Journal of Philosophy*, March 1975. Gauthier, I should note, does not coin this phrase especially to describe business society, but rather, to describe the normative stance of rational man. It fits and leads to the Business Society, however.
2. This is brought forcibly home in the brilliant exposition of this point of view by Robert Nozick, in *Anarchy, State and Utopia* (Basic Books, 1974). Cf. especially pp. 150–164.
3. For example, Nicholas Rescher's *Distributive Justice* (Bobbs-Merrill, 1966) advocates a "Utility Floor" (cf. Ch. 2, Sect. 2), and suggests a concept of "Effective Average" which tends in the direction of equality. The more recent *A Theory of Justice*, by John Rawls (Harvard, 1971), proposes principles of justice which favor the bottom classes of society rather strongly.
4. Many Marxists appear to embrace full equality, at least as an ultimate goal.
5. This point of view is urged, in rather delightful prose, by John Kenneth Galbraith in many places, e.g. *The New Industrial State* (Houghton Mifflin, 1967), especially Ch. xiii.
6. J. S. Mill's *Utilitarianism*, Chapter V ("On the Connection between Justice and Utility") in effect proposes a way to accomplish this. It is followed up in the author's *Morality and Utility* (Johns Hopkins, 1967), Chapter VI.
7. Nozick, *op. cit.*, pp. 174–175 especially.
8. Nozick, again, p. 178. A good deal of the inspiration for this essay, I should say, comes from reading Nozick's stimulating book.

RIGHTS AND THE MARKET

Peter Singer

INTRODUCTION

How should goods and services be distributed? In theory there is a wide range of possible answers to this question: in accordance with need, utility, merit, effort, contribution to production, seniority, strict equality, competitive examinations, ancestry as determined by a free market, and so on. At some time each of these answers has been endorsed by some thinkers, and each has been put into practice as the basis of distribution of at least some goods and services in some societies. Within limited spheres, each is still used today. This use is often controversial. Should seniority be a ground for promotion, as it frequently is in areas of employment like teaching and the civil service? Should a person be able to inherit great wealth merely because he is the most direct living descendant of a miserly recluse who died without leaving a will? Should university places be allocated strictly in accordance with examination grades? Interesting as such issues are, they tend to be overshadowed by a more fundamental division of opinion: should distribution by and large be left to the workings of a free market, in which individuals trade voluntarily, or should society as a whole, through the agency of the government, seek to distribute goods and services in accordance with some criterion generally regarded as desirable? It is this issue which is at the center of the political division between right and left, and consequently is the subject of dispute between political parties, in most nations which have political parties, as well as between philosophers, who, like Robert Nozick, are clearly aligned with the free market advocates and those who, like John Rawls, support distribution in accordance with a favored criterion of justice.

This essay deals with only one aspect of this basic disagreement, though a central one. Those who favor leaving distribution to the market have used two distinct types of argument. One is utilitarian in character. It asserts that if we leave distribution to the market we shall end up with a better outcome than if we interfere with the market because the market will promote efficient methods of production and exchange, and hence will lead to more people getting what they want than any alternative means of distribution. I shall not discuss this type of argument here. It is obvious that, although difficult to test, the utilitarian argument rests on a factual claim and consequently would have to be given up if non-market modes of distribution could be shown to be compatible with as much or more efficiency in production and exchange as the market. This line of

From John Arthur and William H. Shaw, eds., *Justice and Economic Distribution.* Copyright © 1978, pp. 207–221. Reprinted by permission of Prentice-Hall, Inc., Englewood Cliffs, N.J.

argument is not, therefore, a defense of the market in principle, but rather a defense of the market as a means to an end—the end of maximum satisfaction, or something similar.[1]

Nozick's View

The second line of argument is less vulnerable to empirical criticism, for it does not defend the market as a means to an end. Nozick's position is an extreme instance of this. He rejects altogether the idea that institutions—or actions, for that matter—are ultimately to be judged by the ends they promote. That an institution maximizes happiness and minimizes pain would not, in Nozick's view, be a sufficient reason for recommending the institution. If the institution violates rights, then he would consider the institution unjustifiable, no matter how great its superiority in producing happiness or alleviating pain may be. Nor would other goals, like the maximization of freedom, or even the minimization of violations of rights, suffice to justify an institution which violates rights. Nozick's system takes absolute (or virtually absolute) "side constraints" as primary, and hence is structurally distinct from any "maximizing" view.[2]

Nozick therefore defends distribution through the market on the grounds that this method does not violate rights, whereas alternatives such as government distribution in accordance with, say, need do. For, Nozick would say, market distribution is distribution in accordance with the voluntary decisions of individuals to buy or sell goods and services, while government distribution in accordance with need will, in practice, involve the government in taking resources from some individuals, usually by taxation, to give to others, irrespective of whether those from whom the resources are taken wish to give to those in need. Nozick sees the voluntary nature of each of the many individual exchanges which together make up the market system as proof that the market does not violate rights, and the coercion by the government of those from whom resources are taken as proof that government distribution does violate rights.

Empirical investigation of how the market distributes goods and services will not refute this second type of defense of the market. Nozick acknowledges that any distribution at all can result from the market. Some may trade shrewdly and make great fortunes; others may gamble recklessly and lose everything. Even if everyone worked equally hard and traded equally wisely, fortune would favor some and ruin others. So far as justice is concerned this is all, in Nozick's view, irrelevant: any distribution, no matter how unequal, is just, if it has arisen from an originally just position through transfers which do not violate rights. This defense of the market is a philosophical argument. So far as its application to the real world is concerned it might be met by arguing—as Marxists have frequently argued—that the "free market" is a figment of the imagination of bourgeois economists, that all actual markets fall under the dominant influence of a few monopolists, and so do not allow consumers or producers to choose freely after all. Let us take Nozick's argument on a more theoretical level, however, and consider what philosophical objections can be brought against it. One strong philosophical objection is to the moral stance on which it is based. I have elsewhere suggested that the grounds Nozick offers for rejecting utilitarianism are inadequate, and that the utilitarian theory of distribution is preferable to Nozick's own view.[3] But it is also worth considering if such defenses of the market can be shown to be unsatisfactory even within the terms of a moral theory which takes the prohibition of violations of rights as prior to the maximization of utility, and on the assumption that a free market would not be distorted by monopolistic practices.

The first point to be made is that it is only if we accept a very narrow conception of the nature of rights that the market has any chance at all of being shown to be necessarily superior to other systems of distribution in avoiding violations of rights. To see this, consider, for instance, the right to life. It is commonly said that we have a right to life that comprises, not merely a right not to be killed by attackers, but also a right to food if we are starving while others have plenty, and a right to a minimal level of medical care if the society in which we live can afford to provide it. If a society allows people to die from starvation when there is more than enough food to go around, or to die from diseases because they are too poor or too ignorant to obtain a simple and inexpensive injection, we would not consider that society to be one in which the right to life is greatly respected. The right to life, in other words, is widely seen as a right of *recipience,* as well as a right against interference.[4] Another important and frequently claimed right of recipience is the right to education. Clearly, if there are such rights, the market will not necessarily protect them; if it does protect them at a particular time in a particular society, it does so only accidentally, since the market is not structured to produce any particular distribution. A planned distribution, financed by taxation, on the other hand, could aim directly at protecting such rights, and could thereby protect them more effectively.

Nozick recognizes that his position requires a narrow interpretation of rights. With reference to someone who argues, as he himself does, that the state should not interfere in distribution, he says that the position

> will be a consistent one if his conception of rights holds that your being *forced* to contribute to another's welfare violates your rights, whereas someone else's not providing you with things you need greatly, including things essential to protection of your rights, does not *itself* violate your rights.[5]

Oddly, while Nozick is aware of the importance of this conception of rights to his general position, he provides no argument for it. Instead, he appears to take it as a natural consequence of his starting point, which is Locke's state of nature. If we start, as Hobbes, and following him Locke, do, with independent individuals in a state of nature, we may be led naturally enough to a conception of rights in which so long as each leaves the other alone, no rights are violated. This line of reasoning seems to go: "If I do not make you any worse off than you would have been if I had never come into contact with you, then I do not violate your rights, for I might quite properly have maintained my independent existence if I had wished to do so." But why should we start with such an unhistorical, abstract, and ultimately inexplicable idea as an independent individual? It is now well known that our ancestors were social beings long before they were human beings, and could not have become human beings, with the abilities and capacities of human beings, had they not been social beings first.

Admittedly, Nozick does not present his picture of the state of nature as an historical account of how the state actually arose. He says: "We learn much by seeing how the state could have arisen, even if it didn't arise that way."[6] But if we know that, human nature being what it is, the state could *not* have arisen that way, maybe we don't learn so much. On the mistakenly individualistic aspect of Locke's view of society, however, enough has been said by others and there is no need for repetition here. It is surprising that Nozick should ignore this extensive literature and accept Locke's starting point without providing any reply to these damaging criticisms.[7]

If we reject the idea of independent individuals and start with people living together in a community, it is by no means obvious that rights must be restricted to rights against interference. When people live together, they may be born into, grow up with, and live in, a web of rights and obligations which include obligations to help others in need, and rights to be helped oneself when in need.[8] It is reasonable to suppose that such altruistic practices are the very foundation of our moral concepts.

It is also worth noting that Nozick's conception of rights cannot be supported by appeal to the only other ethical tradition on which Nozick draws, that of Kant. Nozick defends his ethic of "side constraints" rather than goals as a reflection of "the underlying Kantian principle that individuals are ends and not merely means; they may not be sacrificed or used for the achieving of other ends without their consent."[9]

The Kantian principle to which Nozick refers, however, cannot bear the gloss Nozick places on it. Any undergraduate who has studied Kant's famous (notorious?) four examples of the application of the categorical imperative knows that Kant thinks we have an obligation to help others in distress. Elsewhere he describes charity as "an act of duty imposed upon us by the rights of others and the debt we owe to them." Only if "none of us drew to himself a greater share of the world's wealth than his neighbour" would this debt and the consequent rights and duties not exist.[10]

It can, indeed, well be argued that rational beings have rights of recipience precisely *because* they are ends in themselves, and that to refuse a starving person the food he needs to survive is to fail to treat him with the respect due to a being that is an end in itself. Nor does it follow from the fact that people are autonomous, in the Kantian sense in which autonomy of the will is opposed to heteronomy of the will, that it is always wrong to force a person to do what he does not do voluntarily.[11]

The distinction between "civil society" conceived as Locke and Nozick conceive it, as an association of fully formed independent human beings, and the alternative conception of a community bound together by moral ties which affect the nature of the human beings who grow up in it, has been illustrated in a recent empirical study which is directly relevant to the choice between market and non-market modes of distributing goods: *The Gift Relationship* by R. M. Titmuss.[12] This work is worth examining in some detail, because it presents a rare opportunity to compare, not in theory but in the real world, the operation of market and non-market modes of distribution. Thereby it enables us to observe how rights and freedoms are affected by the two systems of distribution. We shall see that the question is a much more subtle and complex one than libertarian defenders of the market assume.

The good whose distribution Titmuss studied is blood. In Britain, human blood required for medical purposes is obtained by means far removed from the market. It is neither bought nor sold. It is given voluntarily, and without reward beyond a cup of tea and a biscuit. It is available to anyone who needs it without charge and without obligation. Donors gain no preference over non-donors; but since enough blood is available for all, they need no preference. Nor does the donor have any hope of a return favor from the recipient. Although the gift is in one way a very intimate one—the blood that now flows in the donor's veins will soon flow in those of the recipient—the donor will never know whom he or she has helped. It is a gift from one stranger to another. The system is as close to a perfect example of institutionalized generosity as can be imagined.

By contrast, in the United States, only about 7 percent of the blood obtained for medical purposes comes from similar voluntary donations. Around 40 percent is given to avoid having to pay for blood received, or to build up credit so that blood will be available without charge if needed. Approximately half of the blood and plasma obtained in America is bought and sold on a strictly commercial basis, like any other commodity.

Which of these contrasting systems of blood collection violates rights, and which does not? One obvious point is that if we accept that there is a right of recipience to a level of medical care consonant with the community's resources, then the British system provides for this right, while a pure market system would not. It is only the intervention of the state which can guarantee that everyone who needs blood will receive it. Under a market system those needing large quantities of blood have to be extremely wealthy to survive. Hemophiliacs, for example, may require treatment with large quantities of blood plasma twenty or thirty times a year. In the United States each such treatment costs around $2250. Not surprisingly, the private health insurance market considers hemophiliacs "bad risks" and will not insure them. In Britain hemophiliacs receive the blood they need free of charge.[13] If hemophiliacs have a right to life, which goes beyond the right not to be killed, the market cannot protect this right.

Titmuss's study also reveals some more subtle ways in which the market may violate rights, including rights which are not rights of recipience. It does this in two ways. First, it provides an example of how individual actions which appear harmless can contribute to the restriction of the freedom of others. Second, it shows that one cannot assume without a great deal of argument about the nature of rights, that the state acts neutrally when it allows people to trade without restriction. I shall take this second point first. Supporters of laissez faire overlook the extent to which one's conception of a "neutral" position is affected by one's view about what rights people have. If we ask: "Under which system does the individual have the right to choose whether to give or to sell his blood?" the answer must be that this right is recognized only when there is a commercial system as well as a voluntary one. This aspect of the situation is the basis of the claim made by many advocates of the market, that the market simply allows people to sell what is theirs if they so desire— providing they can find buyers—and thus grants a right to sell without in any way impairing the right of anyone else to give away his or her property if he or she prefers to do so.[14] Why, these supporters of the market ask, should we prohibit the selling of blood? Is it not a flagrant infringement of people's freedom to prevent them doing something which harms no one and is, literally, their own business?

This approach overlooks the fact that the existence of a market in goods or services changes the way in which these goods or services are perceived in the community. On the basis of statistical data, as well as the results of a questionnaire Titmuss carried out on blood donors in Britain, Titmuss has shown that the existence of a commercial system discourages voluntary donors.[15] This is not because those who would otherwise have made voluntary donations choose to sell their blood—donors and sellers come from, in the main, different sections of the population—but because the fact that blood is available as a commodity, to be bought and sold, affects the nature of the gift that is made when blood is given.

If blood is a commodity with a price, to give blood means merely to save someone money. Blood has a cash value of a certain number of dollars, and the importance of the gift will vary with the wealth of the recipient. If blood cannot be bought, however, the gift's value depends upon the need of the recipient. Often, it will be worth life itself. Under these circumstances blood becomes a very special kind of gift, and giving it means providing for strangers, without hope of reward, something they cannot buy and without which they may die. The gift relates strangers in a manner that is not possible when blood is a commodity.

This may sound like a philosopher's abstraction, far removed from the thoughts of ordinary people. On the contrary, it is an idea spontaneously expressed by British donors in response to Titmuss's questionnaire. As one woman, a machine operator, wrote in reply to the question why she first decided to become a blood donor:

> You can't get blood from supermarkets and chain stores. People themselves
> must come forward; sick people can't get out of bed to ask you for a pint
> to save their life, so I came forward in hopes to help somebody who needs
> blood.[16]

The implication of this answer, and others like it, is that even if the
formal right to give blood can coexist with commercial blood banks, the
respondent's action would have lost much of its significance to her, and
the blood would probably not have been given at all. When blood is a
commodity, and can be purchased if it is not given, altruism becomes
unnecessary, and so loosens the bonds that can otherwise exist between
strangers in a community. The existence of a market in blood does not
threaten the formal right to give blood: but it does away with the right
to give blood which cannot be bought, has no cash value, and must be
given freely if it is to be obtained at all. If there is such a right, it is
incompatible with the right to sell blood, and we cannot avoid violating
one of these rights when we grant the other.

Is there really a right to give something that is outside the sphere of
the market? Supporters of the market will no doubt deny the existence
of any such right. They might argue against it on the grounds that any
such right would be one that can be violated by two individuals trading,
and trading seems to be a private act between consenting parties. (Compare Nozick's dictum: "The socialist society would have to forbid capitalist acts between consenting adults.") Acts which make commodities of
things which were not previously commodities are not, however, purely
private acts, for they have an impact on society as a whole.

If we do not now take the commercialization of a previously non-
commercial process very seriously, it is because we have grown used to
almost everything being commercialized. We are still, perhaps, vaguely
uneasy when we see the few remaining non-commercial areas of our lives
disappearing: when sport becomes a means of earning a living, instead
of an activity entered into for its intrinsic qualities; when once-independ-
ent publishing houses, now swallowed by giant corporations, begin ruth-
lessly pruning the less profitable types of work from their lists; and when,
as is now beginning to happen, a market develops in organs for transplan-
tation.[17] But our unease is stilled by the belief that these developments
are "inevitable" and that they bring gains as well as losses. The continuing commercialization of our lives is, however, no more inevitable than
the American Supersonic Transport, and as Titmuss has convincingly
shown in the case of blood, the alleged gains of commercialization are
often illusory, and where not illusory, outweighed by the losses.[18]

Nozick's political theory itself represents the ultimate triumph of commercialization, for in his theory rights themselves become commodities
with a price. Nozick often writes as if he holds that it is always wrong to
violate someone's rights. In fact, however, he holds nothing of the kind:
he holds that it is always wrong to violate someone's rights *unless* you
compensate them for the violation. The distinction is crucial. If Nozick
never allowed violations of rights with compensation, life in a world
governed by his conception of rights would become impossible. One

could not even move around without first obtaining the permission of the owners of the land one wished to cross—and one might well not be able to obtain this permission without moving on to the land first in order to locate the owner. Nozick recognizes the necessity of allowing violations of rights with compensation (Ch. 4, especially pp. 71–84) but he does not realize that implicit in allowing these violations is the assumption that rights have some monetary or at least barter value. For what can compensation be except money or the bartering of goods and services? But what if there is no monetary or other compensation that I am willing to accept in exchange for the violation of my rights? This is not an implausible assumption. Someone who has enough to feed and clothe himself may well prize solitude, quiet, or clean air above all compensation. So to violate rights, with an intention to compensate, may be an unconditional violation of rights—for in any given instance no adequate compensation may be possible. Hence Nozick's theory does not really protect rights at all. It can only be thought to do so if one assumes that every right has its price.

What must be borne in mind about the process of commercialization is that whether an act constitutes an interference in the lives of others cannot be decided independently of the nature of the society in which the act takes place, and the significance of existing social practices in the lives of the individuals who make up that society. Advocates of the market commonly claim, as Nozick does, that "the market is neutral between persons' desires" and merely "reflects and transmits widely scattered information via prices and coordinates persons' activities."[19] In fact, however, the market is not neutral. It affects the way in which goods and services are perceived, and it affects, as Titmuss has shown, how people act. If a prohibition on the buying and selling of a particular "commodity" interferes with those who wish to buy or sell it, the making of something into a commodity is also a form of interference with those for whom the fact that the good or service was not previously a commodity is significant. Whether we should recognize a right to buy and sell anything that is one's own, or whether, instead, we should recognize the conflicting rights of people to retain certain goods and services outside the influence of the commercial sphere is therefore not a question that can be denied by adhering to strictures about avoiding interference or remaining neutral between people's desires; it can properly be decided only if we take into consideration how recognition of these rights affects people, not only directly but also indirectly, through its effect on society as a whole.

These broader issues are entirely overlooked by most defenders of the market, who pay attention to the forms of freedom and ignore its substance. They regard every law extending the range of choices formally open to people as an increase in their freedom, and every law diminishing this range of choice as a decrease in their freedom; whether the choice is a real or attractive one is irrelevant. Nor is any consideration given to the long-range consequences of a large number of individual choices, each of which may be rational from the point of view of the interests of each individual at the time of making the choice, although the cumulative effects may be disastrous for everyone. Titmuss's study suggests that the decision to sell one's blood could be in this category.

INDIVIDUAL RATIONALITY AND COLLECTIVE IRRATIONALITY

Other examples of this phenomenon of individual rationality and collective irrationality are now well known. If public transport is poor, it is in my interest to travel to work by car, for the car will get me there faster and more comfortably, and the marginal increase my additional vehicle makes to pollution, traffic jams and the depletion of oil reserves does not materially affect me. If everyone has this same choice of transportation and makes the same rationally self-interested decision, however, the result is a dangerous level of air pollution, choked roads and swift exhaustion of oil reserves, none of which anyone wants. It would therefore be in all our interests if steps were taken to improve public transport; but once a pattern of private transport has set in, public transport can only be economically viable if people are deterred from using their own vehicles. Hence restrictions on the use of cars may well be in everyone's interest.

Suppose that in the above situation a law is enacted prohibiting the use of private vehicles in a defined inner city area. In one sense the range of choice of transport open to people has been reduced; but on the other hand a new choice now opens up—the choice of using a fast and frequent public transport system at a moderate cost. Most reasonable people, given the choice between, say, an hour's crawl along congested, exhaust-filled roads and 20 minutes' comfortable ride on a bus or train, would have little hesitation in choosing the latter. Let us assume that for economic reasons the possibility of choosing the quick and comfortable ride on public transport would not have existed if private transport had not been restricted. Nevertheless, because the choice of driving oneself to work has been eliminated by a deliberate human act, the defenders of laissez faire will regard this restriction as an interference with freedom; and they will not accept that the nonexistence of the option of efficient public transport, if private transport is not restricted, is a comparable interference with freedom, the removal of which compensates for the restriction of private transport. They will argue that it is circumstances, not deliberate human acts, which preclude the coexistence of efficient public transport and the unrestricted use of private vehicles. In the view of laissez-faire theorists—and some other philosophers as well—freedom is not restricted, and rights are not infringed, by "circumstances," but only by deliberate human acts.[20] This position makes, in my view, an untenable moral distinction between an overt act and the omission of an act. If we can act to alter circumstances but decide not to do so, then we must take responsibility for our omission, just as we must take responsibility for our overt act.[21] Therefore circumstances which it is within our power to alter may limit our freedom as much as deliberate human acts.

Turning back now to the subject of a market in human blood we can see that here too profound social consequences, though of a more subtle kind, can arise from the cumulative effect of many seemingly insignificant decisions. We know that altruistic behavior by some can foster further altruistic acts in others.[22] Titmuss has suggested that a society which has and encourages institutions in which some members of society freely render important services to other members of the society, including others with whom they are not acquainted, whose identity they may never know, and from whom they can expect no reward, tends to differ in other important aspects from a society in which people are not expected or encouraged to perform services for strangers except for a direct, and usually monetary, reward. The difference is related to the different views of the state held by philosophers like Hobbes and Locke, on the one hand, and Rousseau, Hegel and Marx on the other. For Hobbes and Locke, as we have seen, the state is composed of people who join and remain in society for the advantage they get out of it. The state then becomes an association of self-interested individuals, which exists because, and as long as, all or most of its members find it useful and profitable. Rousseau and his successors, on the other hand, see the state more as a community which, in addition to merely providing opportunities for material gains, gives meaning to the individual's existence and inevitably has a formative influence on the nature of the people who grow up in it. Through this influence human beings become social beings, and see the interests of the community and of other members of it as a part of their own interests. While for Hobbes and Locke the state can do no more than paper over the ultimately irresolvable difference between the interests of its members, providing at best a superficial, temporary harmony which is always liable to break down, for Rousseau, Hegel and Marx a good society creates a genuine, deep-seated harmony because it actually resolves the differences between the interests of its members.[23]

The phenomenon of cumulative irrationality of individually rational choices, and the still more fundamental point that the nature of human beings is influenced by the institutions of the society in which they live, both point in the same direction: the need to recognize the rights of members of a society to act collectively to control their lives and to determine the nature of the society in which they live. Even if the distinction between laws which interfere with others (like laws prohibiting the sale of blood, or the driving of cars in a prescribed area) from laws which purportedly do not so interfere (like laws allowing people to sell their blood, or drive their cars to work) can be rescued from the objections I have offered, I would still argue that if a majority of the members of a society should decide that unless they interfere with the actions of others the lives of most members of society will become significantly worse—as in the examples we have been discussing—then the majority have a right to interfere. (This does not justify unlimited interference. The extent and nature of the interference that is permissible would vary with the seriousness of the harm that it is intended to avert; but this topic is too large to discuss here.[24])

It might be said that to allow the majority a right to interfere is dangerous, in that it sacrifices the individual to the collective, and leads straight to a totalitarian dictatorship of the majority. There is, however, no reason why the right I would allow the majority should lead to totalitarianism. It is quite compatible with many valid anti-totalitarian arguments, including utilitarian arguments against totalitarianism, and most of the arguments for individual liberty advanced by John Stuart Mill in *On Liberty.* These arguments are sufficient to rebut the claims of totalitarians. If, despite this, it is claimed that we need to uphold the absolute inviolability of individual rights because any other position, while not itself supporting totalitarianism, is always likely to be distorted by those seeking to establish a totalitarian state, then the appropriate reply is that it is fallacious to object to a principle because one objects to the actions of those who distort the principle for their own ends. If it is only through distortion that the principle lends support to totalitarianism, then it is to the distortion, and not to the principle itself, that objections should be made.[25]

In contrast to the dangers of granting a right to the majority to interfere with individual members of the society, which exist only if this principle is distorted or added to in objectionable ways, the dangers of the opposite position are real enough and are truly entailed by the position itself. The effect of the doctrine that our freedom is not diminished and our rights are not violated by circumstances—including the cumulative effect of individual choices, each of which would be quite harmless on its own—is to tie our hands against effective action in situations which threaten the survival of our species. Pollution, overpopulation, economic depression, the breakdown of social cohesion—all of these may be brought about by millions of separate acts, each one falling within what is normally perceived as the sphere of individual rights.

Nozick and other defenders of individual rights may assert that the moral status of rights does not depend on the consequences of not violating them; but if they leave people with no legitimate means of controlling the course their society is to take, with no legitimate means, even, of steering away from looming disaster, then they have not succeeded in providing a plausible theory of rights.

Nozick might reply that what my argument shows is that these individual actions do violate rights after all, and his theory of rights can therefore cope with them by the usual procedures for violations of rights, namely prohibition or compensation. In the case of pollution, Nozick does outline a scheme for enforcing the payment of compensation to those whose *property* is damaged by pollution, but he concedes that his discussion is incomplete in that it does not cover the pollution of unowned things like the sky or the sea.[26] Perhaps we can imagine how Nozick would extend his view to handle those cases, but I at least cannot see any way in which it could deal satisfactorily with, for instance, overpopulation. The claim that having children violates the rights of others would be difficult to reconcile with other elements of Nozick's view of rights. Yet by comparison with the problem of overpopulation, the pollution problems Nozick thinks he can cope with are only symptoms, not causes, of the real problem. Nozick might, I suppose, take a hard line and say that when it comes to the crunch, evolutionary forces will take care of the population problem, and only the fittest will survive. Any moral theory that reaches this conclusion reveals its inadequacy more convincingly than I could ever hope to do.

CONCLUSIONS

There are, then, three main conclusions which have emerged from this discussion of the effects of markets on rights. First, the view that the market necessarily respects rights, while government systems of distribution involving coercion do not, requires a peculiarly narrow conception of rights which lacks justification once its basis in an individualistic theory of the "state of nature" is rejected. Second, it is incorrect to hold that the state acts neutrally by allowing markets to operate without restriction in any commodity. A market can interfere with people, and may reasonably be said to violate their rights. To draw a line between interference and non-interference is a far more complex task than advocates of the unrestricted market generally assume. Third, and finally, on any plausible theory of rights, some social and economic planning must be permissible. Individuals cannot have an absolute right to buy and sell without interference, any more than they can have an absolute right to pollute or to populate without interference. To grant individuals these rights is to make social planning impossible, and hence to deny to the "individuals" who make up that society the right to control their own lives.[27]

Notes

1. I discuss the utilitarian argument for the market, in respect of the provision of health care, in "Freedoms and Utilities in the Distribution of Health Care" in R. Veatch and R. Branson (eds.), *Ethics and Health Policy* (Ballinger, Cambridge, Mass., 1976).
2. *Anarchy, State and Utopia,* pp. 28–33. My hesitation about the degree of absoluteness is prompted by the final paragraph of the footnote commencing on p. 29, in which Nozick refrains from stating whether his side-constraints may be violated to avoid catastrophic moral horror. If he were to say that they may be, he would need to show how this thin end of the utilitarian wedge can be accommodated while resistance to other utilitarian considerations is maintained. Since I cannot predict how Nozick would overcome this difficulty I shall henceforth ignore the possibility that his side-constraints may not be quite absolute.
3. See my review of *Anarchy, State and Utopia* in *The New York Review of Books,* March 6, 1975; and see also J. J. C. Smart's essay in this volume, pp. 103–115.
4. I take the term "right of recipience" from H. J. McCloskey, "Rights—Some Conceptual Issues," *Australasian Journal of Philosophy,* vol. 54 (1976), p. 103.
5. *Anarchy, State and Utopia,* p. 30.
6. *Ibid.,* p. 9.
7. The political philosophies of Hegel, Marx and their successors are built upon the rejection of Locke's individualist starting point. The classic, though char-

acteristically obscure, reference in Hegel is Paragraph 258 of *The Philosophy of Right.* Marx makes the general point on several occasions. The following example is from the *Economic and Philosophical Manuscripts of 1844:*

> Above all we must avoid postulating "Society" again as an abstraction *vis-à-vis* the individual. The individual *is the social being.* (trans. Martin Milligan, International Publishers, New York, 1964, pp. 137–138).

A more recent and more fully argued philosophical critique of the individualism of Hobbes and Locke is to be found in C. B. Macpherson's *The Political Theory of Possessive Individualism* (Clarendon Press, Oxford, 1962). Further discussion of the literature on individualism can be found in Steven Lukes, *Individualism* (Blackwells, Oxford, 1973). For a dramatic introduction to the factual material bearing on the social nature of our ancestors, see Robert Ardrey, *The Social Contract* (Collins, London, 1970). Ardrey himself is unreliable, but his bibliography and references are useful.

 8. It seems likely that our moral concepts have developed out of those altruistic practices. See, for instance, Edward O. Wilson *Sociobiology: The New Synthesis* (Belknap Press, Cambridge, Mass., 1975) and Richard Brandt, "The Psychology of Benevolence and Its Implications for Philosophy," *Journal of Philosophy,* LXXIII (1976), pp. 429–453.
 9. *Anarchy, State and Utopia,* pp. 30–31.
10. See the *Groundwork of the Metaphysics of Morals,* trans. H. J. Paton under the title *The Moral Law* (Hutchinson, London, 1948), p. 86; and *Lectures on Ethics,* trans. L. Infield (Harper, New York, 1963), pp. 194, 236.
11. I am indebted to H. J. McCloskey for these points about Kant, although Alan H. Goldman makes a similar point in "The Entitlement Theory of Distributive Justice," *Journal of Philosophy,* LXXIII, pp. 823–835 (Dec. 2, 1976).
12. Allen & Unwin, London, 1970. The substance of the following paragraphs is taken from the article cited in Note 1, above, and also appeared in "Altruism and Commerce: A Defense of Titmuss against Arrow," *Philosophy and Public Affairs,* 2 (1973), pp. 312–320.
13. *The Gift Relationship,* pp. 206–207. The price quoted is a 1966 figure, and has no doubt risen considerably.
14. Cf. Kenneth Arrow, "Gifts and Exchanges," *Philosophy and Public Affairs,* 1 (1972), p. 350.
15. *The Gift Relationship, passim.* For a summary of the evidence see "Altruism and Commerce: A Defense of Titmuss against Arrow," pp. 314–315.
16. *The Gift Relationship,* p. 277. Spelling and punctuation have been corrected.
17. Amitai Etzioni, *Genetic Fix* (Harper & Row, New York, 1973), p. 137; *Wall Street Journal,* Dec. 16, 1975.
18. *The Gift Relationship,* especially Chapters 8 & 9. Again, I am indebted to H. J. McCloskey for bringing the significance of Nozick's use of compensation to my attention.
19. *Anarchy, State and Utopia,* pp. 163–164.
20. For instance, F. A. Hayek: " 'Freedom' refers solely to a relation of men to other men, and the only infringement on it is coercion by men." (*The Constitution of Liberty,* Routledge & Kegan Paul, London, 1960, p. 12); and for a similar view, Isaiah Berlin, "Two Concepts of Liberty" in *Four Essays on Liberty,* p. 122. The discussion on pp. 237–238 of *Anarchy, State and Utopia* indicates that Nozick, though primarily concerned with rights rather than freedom, also holds that my rights are not infringed if the collective result of a series of legitimate individual actions by others is a drastic curtailment

of my freedom of action. On this question see the discussion by Thomas Scanlon in "Nozick on Rights, Liberty and Property," *Philosophy and Public Affairs,* vol. 5, no. 1 (Fall, 1976), especially pp. 14–15. Scanlon writes:

> It is the connection with justification that makes plausible Nozick's restriction of attention to limitations on alternatives that are brought about by human action. Even though acts of nature may limit our alternatives, they are not subject to demands for justification. But individual human acts are not the only things subject to such demands; we are also concerned with social institutions that make it possible for agents to do what they do.

Scanlon is right to point out that social institutions need to be justified, but he lets Nozick off too lightly in respect to acts of nature. When acts of nature are preventable, the omission of human acts that would have prevented them may require justification.

21. See Michael Tooley, "Abortion and Infanticide," *Philosophy and Public Affairs,* 2 (1972), especially p. 50 ff; James Rachels, "Active and Passive Euthanasia," *New England Journal of Medicine,* 292 (1975), pp. 78–80.
22. Derek Wright, *The Psychology of Moral Behaviour* (Penguin, London, 1971), pp. 133–139.
23. One does not, of course, have to accept in their entirety the views of any of these philosophers in order to accept the central point that the structure of a society influences the nature of those who are members of it, and that given this influence will occur, it is better that it be directed toward a community of interests than toward a conflict of interests.
24. I have touched upon it—though in a different context—in *Democracy and Disobedience* (Clarendon Press, Oxford, 1973), especially pp. 64–72.
25. Much of the argument against the positive concept of liberty in Berlin's "Two Concepts of Liberty" commits this fallacy.
26. *Anarchy, State and Utopia,* pp. 79–81.
27. H. J. McCloskey, J. J. C. Smart, C. L. Ten and Robert Young made useful criticisms of an earlier version of this article.

HOW SHOULD WE DECIDE WHO SHOULD DECIDE WHAT COMES BEFORE WHAT?

Carl Cohen

Most of us are democrats. We believe—whether as an outcome of careful reflection or of early indoctrination—that when a community of equals is to determine its priorities collectively it should do so by giving to each of the members an equal voice. The machinery of democracy (voting systems, and so on) has the job of somehow justly integrating all

Original essay written especially for this text. Reprinted by permission of the author.

the expressed preferences. But not all decisions should be put to a democratic vote; e.g., how many classical records should be produced in any
given year? When should a group determine its priorities collectively, and
when individually? This hard question underlies most disputes between
honestly democratic advocates of private and of public enterprise.

Both parties commonly contend that democracy itself is on their side.
Each side claims that, in addition to the benefits of efficiency (or fairness,
or economy, etc.) to be gained from its mode of enterprise, the making
of decisions its way is the more consonant with the nature of democracy.
It is well, therefore, to see what can and what cannot be derived from
democracy itself on the question of what should be publicly and what
privately decided. The role of democracy in that enterprise is what I am
to explore.

Consider the essential features of democratic process as applied to the
critical business of setting priorities. The actor in many situations is not
an individual human being but some community of human beings. "We"
then refers to our group collectively, rather than to our selves singly. The
priorities of the community are established through democratic process
when an ordering emerges as the outcome of a process in which individual members of the deciding community may participate with equal voting strength, each member counting for one. Democracy is sometimes
identified, mistakenly, with particular mechanisms for accomplishing this:
majority rule, secret ballot, balance of powers, proportional representation, etc. The merits and demerits of alternative mechanisms I bypass
here entirely. Democracy is a process of collective decision-making in a
community of equals, in which (for our purposes, by hypothesis) the
devices for weighing the judgments contributed by each member of the
community are agreed upon and reasonably just.

We will pursue the concrete implementation of the democratic process
when the decisions are to be made by the group, collectively. But when
shall decisions be made in that way? Priorities must be established, obviously. But when must the community establish its collective priorities,
and when may the ordering be left to individuals or subgroups deciding
for themselves? This issue lies at the core of much dispute among democrats, especially dispute over conflicting visions of the ideal economy.
Who (the group or the individual) should decide what comes before
what? And *how* should that choice of *who* be made?

Progress with this question will be easier with some concrete case
before us. For a first concrete setting I shall consider the range of problems facing a community and its members respecting the delivery of mail.

No one doubts the need for an effective postal system. But what shall
its character be? How shall that be decided? Each of the many members
of the community has several varying ends in view in using the mails:
keeping contact with loved ones, paying bills, receiving packages, advertising and distributing products, and so on. The priorities of each user
(respecting these functions) will greatly differ, of course. In the performance of the several functions envisaged, any given system will have

differing merits and demerits—all of concern to all, but with very different weights: safety in delivery, speed in delivery, cost of delivery, frequency of delivery, equitability of charges and services, and so on. When alternative postal systems are considered, the arguments in behalf of the candidates are vastly complicated by the variety of functions in the users' minds, and by the variety of factors entering into each evaluation of each system's performance of each function. The priority system of each user (supposing it known) may be thought of as a choice tree with a preferred path, and the community of users as creating an overlapping thicket of such trees. In this tangled thicket, what is the role of *democratic* decision-making?

The question itself can be taken to ask different things. We may be asking:

1. Given the public nature of the postal service, how shall we make a democratic determination of the priorities for that service? American practice has supposed that a postal system should pay for itself, be supported by user charges, and that the calculation of possible services to be offered must take place within the parameters of economic self-support. When the postal system goes "into the red," we raise rates or trim services to make ends meet. Other communities give much lower priority to economic self-sufficiency; some might give it virtually no weight at all. Speed of delivery will probably be weighed more heavily by business users; cheapness of service will be given different priority by different users. One question, then, is whether (and how) we are to get a democratic reading of the will of the community with respect to priorities of this kind, priorities among the features the postal service might display.

2. Priority questions of another kind arise when a public service function (the postal system, the park system, the welfare system) competes against other service systems for its share of public support. Suppose it is agreed that a postal system need not be self-supporting but, rather, is a public service function properly maintained by the community through general taxation, supplemented by some moderate level of user charges. It must then compete against welfare services, public transport, national security, each claiming great chunks of the available resources. No one of these need be wholly excluded. Yet some priorities will be essential if the community is to budget its revenues rationally. The second type of priority questions for democrats, then, is how a fair determination is to be made for the relative priority of the postal service among other services.

These two questions are largely independent in that a priority choice of the first kind (say, safety over speed) takes place at one level in the means-end chain, while a priority choice of the second kind (say, postal service over park service) takes place at a different level. Decisions on both levels will have reciprocal impact, of course. But the same ordering of priorities within the postal service itself (say, safety over speed) might be rationally chosen even when a different set of larger values (say, a much lower relative placement of the postal service) has been adopted by the community. If a democratic community provides postal services for its members, priority issues of both kinds must be faced.

3. But a third and very different kind of priority issue may also be opened. Is the delivery of mail a service the community wants (or should want) to conduct collectively? The widespread conviction that the postal service must be a public monopoly, wholly owned and operated by the community, keeps this question (in this community, for this service) from being much discussed. The common affirmative answer may be the wisest one, but it is reached largely through default. In other spheres we make the reverse assumption, almost as mechanically. The production and distribution of clothing or toys (for example) are activities in which we forbid monopoly, supposing that decisions about manufacturing and selling are better made when widely dispersed among private producers, retailers, and customers. Neither the question "Should we collectivize the clothing industry?" nor the question "Should we privatize the postal service?" is commonly put to us.

I do not argue for doing the one or the other. Even if convinced that our way of dealing with mail or clothes is much the best, we are instructed by the arguments on the other side—if only to learn how present systems can be improved. The classical arguments for private or public enterprise I shall not review. My aim is to examine the impact of our desires for democracy upon our choice between private and public enterprise.

Every making or serving goes forward with certain ends in view. Whether we choose a private or a public mode for the conduct of that activity, the choice of mode is rational insofar as it advances the achievement of our several ends in appropriate degree. Some argue for privatizing the postal service (and other services now publicly run). They contend that what we want from a postal system—fast, convenient, safe service, equitably paid for—will be more surely and more economically achieved if the entire system were decentralized and power over it more widely dispersed. Some argue for collectivizing the clothing industry (and other industries now privately run). They contend that what we want from healthy industry—good-quality products, attractively made and widely and fairly distributed—will be more surely and more economically attained when intelligent centralized planning is introduced. Whatever the wisdom of these two proposals, we (as a community) *could* adopt either or both of them. Nothing stops us from considering those options; nothing stops the democratic body politic from accepting either—save habits of mind, and the judgment that one or both would be unwise.

Does democracy tell us which of these paths to choose? It does not. Each member of the community, supposing the issue were put to a vote, would have to decide whether the private or the public way was more likely (in that sphere) to advance his scheme of priorities. Greater economy for the resulting products will be claimed by the advocates of a collectivized clothing industry; greater efficiency and speed in mail delivery will be claimed by the advocates of a privatized postal service. These and countless other claims would have to be weighed by the community, through its representatives, should the choice be put in a way obliging response. But democracy does not tell us which way to go. Democracy is a way of deciding how to do it, not a decision about what to do.

One of the things we want is to continue to make such decisions *that way,* democratically. Our having that want, democracy itself becomes an end as well as a means. We want both to make decisions about the economy through the equal participation of each member of the community, and to reach decisions that are most likely to increase the likelihood that that is the way we will decide things (in the economy and elsewhere) in the future. From this point of view, holding democracy in mind both as means and as end, what is there about democracy that can help us to decide whether it is wise to collectivize the clothing industry, or privatize the postal system? There are considerations flowing from the nature of democracy, and from the conditions of its success, that bear upon this issue, but they are not controlling, partly because these considerations cut in both directions. That is, it may be correctly argued that democracy, viewed as an end, will in some respects be advanced by the community's choice of private enterprise solutions; *and* it may be correctly argued that the choice of collectivized enterprise also advances the process of democracy in some—but of course in different—respects. Where democracy is end as well as means, the several facets of democracy itself, and the several conditions of its continued success, complicate the problems of choosing through the democratic process. These complications are double edged.

On the collective side the argument goes something like this: "Economics forms the base of community life. The production and distribution of goods and services is *the* fundamental concern of the entire citizenry. Whatever the expressed desires of the community on political questions, it cannot achieve its will unless it, the community acting as a whole, controls those economic levers. Hence the *political* democracy that is so commonly extolled presupposes *economic* democracy, that is, requires the public management of the production and distribution of goods and services. We want democracy as an end-in-view because we want it to serve as means for the attainment of a great array of other, future ends. At a more fundamental level, we want collectivized economic functions as a means not only to effect greater efficiency in production and service, but [the argument concludes] as a means to support the power of the community to work its own will in this and every other sphere."

On the private side the argument goes something like this: "Democracy is a system in which the ultimate power rests in the hands of the members of the community viewed distributively, not collectively. Talk about "the community as a whole" is misleading; *it* is no more than *they* (or *we*), taken together. Democracy is just, precisely because it is designed to protect the effective voice of each member of the body politic. Each member must have the opportunity to make independent judgments, judgments that count. Democracy is therefore strengthened by every policy decision that safeguards or enlarges those opportunities for judgment. The decentralization of power is the heart of democracy; measures supporting that decentralization feed it at its roots. Economic decision-making should be designed, therefore, to reinforce this decentralization. Private enterprise does just this [the argument concludes]. By giving each member the opportunity to act in pursuit of his own interests, to choose for himself among competing goods and services, it strengthens, in spirit and in substance, the deepest element of democratic government—the choosing, by individuals, of what serves or pleases them."

Both of these arguments have merit. The process of democracy itself, viewed as valued end, will be furthered in differing respects by differing modes of economic operation.

That democracy can be furthered by both collective control and the private market may be seen more clearly if we identify the *kinds* of priorities more effectively determined by each of the two economic modes. On one side: A collectivized clothing industry, or cosmetics industry, would give the community taken as a whole the opportunity to make some judgments about the priority of needs in these areas—for clothing or for deodorants—as competing against other needs, say those for housing or for recreation. The resources of the community, in money and human energy, are limited. What we invest in cosmetics we cannot invest in parks. By giving us the chance to register our priorities on such matters, collectivization serves democracy. Moreover, democracy thrives as a general system only where the practice of reaching compromise and consensus on important and controversial matters is well established. By obliging that process in the economic sphere, public management reinforces democracy.

On the other side: A privatized postal system, for example, would give the members of the community, taken individually, the opportunity to make effective their independent priority judgments regarding possible features of the service in question. Individual users of the mails have differing needs: convenience, safety, economy, whatever. Among these we do not need to determine *an* order; perhaps we ought not determine a single system of preferences for the community as a whole. The power to choose among competing enterprisers, some of whom are faster, some safer, some cheaper, gives each user an opportunity—not just indirectly by vote, but concretely in the expenditure of his resources—to make his priorities within the system manifest. The collectivized mail service fore-closes that opportunity; it advances the expression of one kind of priority among systems (indeed it forces that) but at the cost of precluding the expression of the specific priorities that democracy is designed to protect. Moreover, democracy thrives as a general system only where there are established habits of informed deliberation and of forthright defense of judgments reached independently. The spirit of such individualized ex-pression—the inclination of each citizen to think of himself as effective agent—is the psychological root of democracy. By keeping economic decisions out of the collective arena where individuals are only remotely influential on distant questions, and retaining the immediate effective-ness of the individual on smaller issues of direct concern to him, we safeguard that psychological root. By private management democracy is reinforced.

Of the two opposing arguments, neither clearly dominates. Some honest private enterprise democrats contend that without a decentralized, privately owned and operated economy, democracy in other spheres cannot survive, that real democracy is impossible under socialism. This is patently mistaken; it is evident that a community can decide to put industrial decisions into the public arena, for reasons it thinks good, and to continue to make decisions in that and other spheres jointly and fairly. He is blind who would deny the democracy of some communities in which a high degree of collectivization has been introduced and freely maintained by a community membership that could make a different choice. Some honest socialists, on the other hand, contend that without a publicly owned and controlled economy, democracy in other spheres cannot survive, that without "economic democracy" the shell of "political democracy" is a fraud, real democracy impossible under capitalism. This, too, is patently mistaken. It is evident that a community can leave many or most of the economic decisions—to make, to work, to buy, to invest —in the hands of private parties operating in a reasonably free or partly regulated market. He is blind who would deny the democracy of some communities in which a high degree of private economic enterprise has been introduced and freely maintained by a community membership that could make a different choice.

The conclusion to be drawn is very important, just because it has been denied with such passion by partisans of both extremes. Democracy, as a decision-making process in which the members of the community participate, does not entail any particular economic system. It does not entail any particular degree of government regulation. That is not to say that there are not good reasons for doing things one way (privately) or the other (collectively). It is to say that the advancement of democracy, here taken as end, although relevant to each member's choice, is relevant in differing and opposing ways, and therefore is not dispositive.

The advancement of democracy is not dispositive for another important reason. The kinds of ends for which most decisions about collectivization or privatization are made—efficiency or cheapness of service, and the like—may incline the rational chooser to prefer one way of doing things, while his judgment of the impact of that mode of doing them upon democracy as an end may incline him to prefer the other way. He may believe (for example) that *democracy* really is best served over the long term by community control of the ongoing decisions of industry, and for that reason want a collectively owned and operated clothing industry, while he believes at the same time that the *quality* and *variety* of clothes, and *efficiency* in serving the clothing needs of the citizens, are more effectively advanced by leaving the industry in private hands in a free or regulated market. Or (to take the opposite case) one may believe that the wide dispersion of economic decisions in the offering and choosing of essential community services is important for the health of the democracy, but believe also that certain essential but profitless services (e.g., the home delivery of rural mail) can only be provided to many who must have them if the burden of their provision is taken on by the whole community.

Tensions like these may prove embarrassing. Most democrats seldom feel them because, committed by habit or persuaded by reason, we implicitly suppose consonance. That is, we assume that, in a given sphere, the merits of private (or public) enterprise on the one side (its support for democracy itself) are always consonant with its merits on the other side (its impact on efficiency, quality, and the like).

Honesty will compel the admission, however, that at least in some spheres (utilities? basic industries? insurance? other?) the assumption of consonance between good process and good results is dubious. Deciding how we want to decide—whether collectively or privately—requires the ordering of our preferences respecting the immediate objects of the activity concerned (efficiency, etc.), and may require more complicated priority judgments when the advancement of those objects and the advancement of democracy itself are not in harmony. It may also require judgments concerning which of the kinds of arguments sketched above (regarding long-term service to democracy) is dominant. That, in turn, requires a judgment about which kind of priority—the priorities of the community in the budgeting of its resources, or the priorities of individuals in the realization of their private preferences—must take priority.

In choosing democracy, we never promised ourselves a rose garden. Understanding complications does not overcome them. Each of us confronts a great tangle of ends and means, in which democracy plays a multiple role. We are obliged to consider the many ramifications of our commitment to democratic decision-making upon decisions about who should decide what comes before what.

ALIENATED LABOR VERSUS *TRULY HUMAN PRODUCTION*

Karl Marx

The *exchange* of human activity within production itself as well as the exchange of *human products* with one another is equivalent to the *generic activity* and generic spirit whose actual, conscious, and authentic existence is *social* activity and *social* satisfaction. As *human* nature is the *true common life [Gemeinwesen]* of man, men through the activation of their

From *Writings of the Young Marx on Philosophy and Society,* trans. and ed. by L. D. Easton and K. H. Guddat (New York: Doubleday & Company, Inc., 1967). Reprinted by permission.

nature create and produce a human *common life,* a social essence which is no abstractly universal power opposed to the single individual, but is the essence or nature of every single individual, his own activity, his own life, his own spirit, his own wealth. *Authentic common life* arises not through reflection; rather it comes about from the *need* and *egoism* of individuals, that is, immediately from the activation of their very existence. It is not up to man whether this common life exists or not. However, so long as man does not recognize himself as man and does not organize the world humanly, this *common life* appears in the form of *alienation,* because its *subject,* man, is a being alienated from itself. Men as actual, living, particular individuals, not in an abstraction, *constitute* this common life. It is, therefore, *what* men are. To say that *man* alienates himself is the same as saying that the *society* of this alienated man is the caricature of his *actual common life,* of his true generic life. His activity, therefore, appears as torment, his own creation as a force alien to him, his wealth as poverty, the *essential bond* connecting him with other men as something unessential so that the separation from other men appears as his true existence. His life appears as the sacrifice of his life, the realization of his nature as the diminution of his life, his production as the production of his destruction, his power over the object as the power of the object over him; the master of his creation appears as its slave.

Political economy understands the *common life of man,* the self-activating *human* essence and mutual redintegration toward generic and truly human life, in the form of *exchange* and *commerce. Society,* says Destutt de Tracy, is a *series of multilateral exchanges.* It is constituted by this movement of multilateral integration. *Society,* says Adam Smith, is a *commercial enterprise.* Each of its members is a *merchant.* It is evident that political economy *establishes* an *alienated* form of social intercourse as the *essential, original,* and definitive human form.

Economics—like the actual process itself—proceeds from the *relationship of man to man* and from the relationship of one *property owner to another.* Let us presuppose man as *property owner,* that is, an exclusive possessor who maintains his personality and distinguishes himself from other men and relates himself to them through this exclusive possession. Private property is his personal existence, his *distinguishing* and hence essential existence. The *loss* or *relinquishing* of private property, then, is an *externalization of man* as well as of *private property.* We are concerned here only with the latter. When I yield my private property to another person, it ceases being mine. It becomes something independent of me and *outside* my sphere, something *external* to me. I *externalize* my private property. So far as I am concerned, it is *externalized* private property. I see it only as something generally *externalized;* I only transcend my *personal* relationship to it; and I return it to the *elemental* forces of nature when I externalize it only in relation to myself. It only becomes externalized *private property* as it ceases being *my* private property without ceasing to be *private property* in general, that is, when it acquires the same relationship to *another* man *outside* of me, as it had to me—in a word, when it becomes the *private property* of *another* man. Apart from the situation of *force,* what causes me to externalize *my* private property to another person? Economics answers correctly: *need* and *want.* The other person is also a property owner, but of *another* object which I lack and which I neither can nor want to be without, an object which to me seems to be something *needed* for the redintegration of my existence and the realization of my nature.

The bond relating the two property owners to each other is the *specific nature of the object.* The fact that either property owner desires and wants objects makes him aware that he has another *essential* relationship to objects outside of property and that he is not the particular being he takes himself to be but rather a *total* being whose wants have a relationship of *inner* property to the products of the labor of the other person. For the need of an object is the most evident and irrefutable proof that the object belongs to *my* nature and that the existence of the object for me and its *property* are the property appropriate to my essence. Both owners are thus impelled to relinquish their property, but in such a way that at the same time they reaffirm that property; or they are impelled to relinquish that property within the relationship of private property. Each thus externalizes a part of his property in the other person.

The *social* relationship of both owners is thus the *mutuality of externalization,* the relationship of externalization on both sides—or *externalization* as the relationship of both owners—while in simple private property *externalization* takes place only one-sidedly, in relationship to itself.

Exchange or *barter,* therefore, is the social, generic act, the common essence, the social intercourse and integration of man within *private property,* and the external, the *externalized* generic act. For that very reason it appears as *barter.* And hence it is likewise the opposite of the *social* relationship.

Through the mutual externalization or alienation of private property, *private property* itself has been determined as *externalized* private property. First of all it has ceased being the product of labor and being the exclusive, distinctive personality of its owner because the owner has externalized it; it has been removed from the owner whose product it was and has acquired a personal significance for the person who did *not* produce it. It has lost its personal significance for the owner. In the second place it has been related to and equated with another private property. A private property of a *different* nature has taken its place, just as it itself takes the position of a private property of a *different* nature. On both sides, then, private property appears as a representative of private property of a different nature, as the *equivalence* of another natural product. Both sides are so related that each represents the existence of the *other* and they mutually serve as *substitutes* for themselves and the other. The existence of private property as such has thus become a *substitute,* an *equivalent.* Instead of its immediate self-unity it exists only in relationship to *something else.* As an *equivalent* its existence is no longer something peculiarly appropriate to it. It has become *value* and immediately *exchange value.* Its existence as *value* is a determination of *itself,* different from its immediate existence, outside of its specific nature, and *externalized*—only a *relative* existence. . . .

The relationship of exchange being presupposed, *labor immediately* becomes *wage-labor.* This relationship of alienated labor reaches its apex only by the fact (1) that on the one side *wage-labor,* the product of the laborer, stands in no *immediate* relationship to his need and to his *status* but is rather determined in both directions through social combinations alien to the laborer; (2) that the *buyer* of the product is not himself productive but exchanges what has been produced by others. In the crude form of *externalized* private property, *barter,* each of the two private owners produces what his need, his inclination, and the existing raw material induces him to produce. They exchange only the surplus of their production. To be sure, labor was for each one the immediate *source of his subsistence;* at the same time, however, it was also the confirmation of his *individual existence.* Through exchange, his *labor* has partly become his *source of income.* The purpose and existence of labor have changed. The product is created as *value, exchange value,* and an *equivalent* and no longer because of its immediate personal relationship to the producer. The more varied production becomes—in other words, the more varied the needs become on the one hand and the more one-sided the producer's output becomes on the other—the more does his labor fall into the category of *wage-labor,* until it is eventually nothing but wage-labor and until it becomes entirely *incidental* and *unessential* whether the producer immediately enjoys and needs his product and whether the *activity,* the action of labor itself, is his self-satisfaction and the realization of his natural dispositions and spiritual aims.

The following elements are contained in *wage-labor:* (1) the chance relationship and alienation of labor from the laboring subject; (2) the chance relationship and alienation of labor from its object; (3) the determination of the laborer through social needs which are an alien compulsion to him, a compulsion to which he submits out of egoistic need and distress—these social needs are merely a source of providing the necessities of life for him, just as he is merely a slave for them; (4) the maintenance of his individual existence appears to the worker as the *goal* of his activity and his real action is only a means; he lives to acquire the means of *living.*

The greater and the more articulated the social power is within the relationship of private property, the more *egoistic* and asocial man becomes, the more he becomes alienated from his own nature.

Just as the mutual exchange of products of *human activity* appears as *trading* and *bargaining,* so does the mutual redintegration and exchange of the activity itself appear as the *division of labor* making man as far as possible an abstract being, an automaton, and transforming him into a spiritual and physical monster.

Precisely the unity of human labor is regarded as being its *division* because its social nature comes into being only as its opposite, in the form of alienation. The *division of labor* increases with civilization.

Within the presupposition of the division of labor, the product and material of private property gradually acquire for the individual the significance of an *equivalent.* He no longer exchanges his *surplus,* and he can become *indifferent* to the object of his production. He no longer immediately exchanges his product for the product he *needs*. The equivalent becomes an equivalent in *money* which is the immediate result of wage-labor and the *medium* of exchange.

The complete domination of the alienated object *over* man is evident in *money* and the complete disregard of the nature of the material, the specific nature of private property as well as the personality of the proprietor.

What formerly was the domination of one person over another has now become the general domination of the *thing* over the *person,* the domination of the product over the producer. Just as the determination of the *externalization* of private property lay in the *equivalent* and in value, so is *money* the sensuous, self-objectified existence of this *externalization.* . . .

It is the basic presupposition of private property that man *produces* only in order to *own.* The purpose of production is to *own.* It not only has such a *useful* purpose; it also has a *selfish* purpose. Man only produces in order to *own* something for himself. The object of his production is the objectification of his *immediate,* selfish *need.* Man—in his wild, barbaric condition—determines his production by the *extent* of his immediate need whose content is the *immediately* produced object itself.

In that condition man produces *no more* than he immediately needs. The *limit of his need* is the *limit of his production.* Demand and supply coincide. Production is *determined* by need. Either no exchange takes place or the exchange is reduced to the exchange of man's labor for the product of his labor, and this exchange is the latent form (the germ) of real exchange.

As soon as exchange occurs, there is an overproduction beyond the immediate boundary of ownership. But this overproduction does not exceed selfish need. Rather it is only an *indirect* way of satisfying a need which finds its objectification in the production of another person. Production has become a *source of income,* labor for profit. While formerly need determined the extent of production, now production, or rather the *owning of the product,* determines how far needs can be satisfied.

I have produced for myself and not for you, just as you have produced for yourself and not for me. The result of my production as such has as little direct connection with you as the result of your production has with me, that is, our production is not production of man for man as man, not *socialized* production. No one is gratified by the product of another. Our mutual production means nothing for us as human beings. Our exchange, therefore, cannot be the mediating movement in which it would be acknowledged that my product means anything for you because it is an *objectification* of your being, your need. *Human nature* is not the bond of our production for each other. Exchange can only set in *motion* and confirm the *relationship* which each of us has to his own product and to the production of the other person. Each of us sees in his product only his *own* objectified self-interest and in the product of another person, *another* self-interest which is independent, alien, and objectified.

As a human being, however, you do have a human relation to my product; you *want* my product. It is the object of your desire and your will. But your want, desire, and will for my product are impotent. In other words, your *human* nature, necessarily and intimately related to my human production, is not your *power,* not your sharing in this production, because the *power* of human nature is not acknowledged in my production. Rather it is in the *bond* which makes you dependent upon me because it makes you dependent on my product. It is far from being the *means* of giving you *power* over my production; rather it is the *means* of giving me power over you.

When I produce *more* than I can consume, I subtly *reckon* with your need. I produce only the *semblance* of a surplus of the object. In truth I produce a *different* object, the object of your production which I plan to exchange for this surplus, an exchange already accomplished in thought. My *social* relationship with you and my labor for your want is just plain *deception* and our mutual redintegration is *deception* just as well. Mutual pillaging is its base. Its background is the intent to pillage, to defraud. Since our exchange is selfish on your side as well as mine and since every self-interest attempts to surpass that of another person, we necessarily attempt to defraud each other. The power I give my object over yours, however, requires your *acknowledgment* to become real. Our mutual acknowledgment of the mutual power of our objects is a battle and the one with more insight, energy, power, and cleverness is the winner. If my physical strength suffices, I pillage you directly. If there is no physical power, we mutually dissemble and the more adroit comes out on top. It makes no difference for the *entire* relationship who the winner is, for the *ideal* and *intended* victory takes place on both sides; in his own judgment each of the two has overcome the other.

On both sides exchange necessarily requires the *object* of mutual production and mutual ownership. The ideal relationship to the mutual objects of our production is our mutual need. But the *real* and *truly effective* relationship is only the mutually *exclusive ownership* of mutual production. It is your *object,* the *equivalent* of my object, that gives your want for my object *value, dignity,* and *efficacy* for me. Our mutual product, therefore, is the *means,* the *intermediary,* the *instrument,* the *acknowledged power* of our mutual needs. Your *demand* and the *equivalent of your property* are terms which for me are *synonymous* and equally valid, and your demand is effective only when it has an effect on me. Without this effect your demand is merely an unsatisfied effort on your part and without consequence for me. You have no relationship to my object as a human being because I *myself* have no human relation to it. But the *means* is the *real power* over an object, and we mutually regard our product as the *power* each one has over the other and over himself. In other words, our own product is turned against us. It appeared to be our property, but actually we are its property. We ourselves are excluded from *true* property because our *property* excludes the other human being.

Our objects in their relation to one another constitute the only intelligible language we use with one another. We would not understand a human language, and it would remain without effect. On the one hand, it would be felt and spoken as a plea, as begging, and as *humiliation* and hence uttered with shame and with a feeling of supplication; on the other hand, it would be heard and rejected as *effrontery* or *madness*. We are so much mutually alienated from human nature that the direct language of this nature is an *injury to human dignity* for us, while the alienated language of objective values appears as justified, self-confident, and self-accepted human dignity.

To be sure, from your point of view your product is an *instrument,* a *means* for the appropriation of my product and for the satisfaction of your need. But from my point of view it is the *goal* of our exchange. I regard you as a means and instrument for the production of this object, that is, my goal, and much more so than I regard you as related to my object. But (1) each of us actually *does* what the other thinks he is doing. You actually made yourself the means, the instrument, and the producer of *your* own object in order to appropriate mine; (2) for you, your own object is only the *sensuous shell* and *concealed form* of my object; its production *means* and *expressly is* the acquisition of my object. You indeed become the *means* and *instrument* of your object; your greed is the *slave* of this object, and you performed slavish services so that the object is never again a remission of your greed. This mutual servitude to the object is actually manifested to us at the beginning of its development as the relationship of *lordship* and *slavery,* and is only the *crude* and *frank* expression of our *essential* relationship.

Our *mutual* value is the *value* of our mutual objects for us. Man himself, therefore, is mutually *valueless* for us.

Suppose we had produced things as human beings: in his production each of us would have *twice affirmed* himself and the other. (1) In my *production* I would have objectified my *individuality* and its *particularity,* and in the course of the activity I would have enjoyed an individual *life;* in viewing the object I would have experienced the individual joy of knowing my personality as an *objective, sensuously perceptible,* and *indubitable* power. (2) In your satisfaction and your use of my product I would have had the *direct* and conscious satisfaction that my work satisfied a *human* need, that it objectified *human* nature, and that it created an object appropriate to the need of another *human* being. (3) I would have been the *mediator* between you and the species and you would have experienced me as a redintegration of your own nature and a necessary part of your self; I would have been affirmed in your thought as well as your love. (4) In my individual life I would have directly created your life; in my individual activity I would have immediately *confirmed* and *realized* my true *human* and *social* nature.

Our productions would be so many mirrors reflecting our nature.

What happens so far as I am concerned would also apply to you.

Let us summarize the various factors in the supposition above:

My labor would be a *free manifestation of life* and an *enjoyment* of *life.* Under the presupposition of private property it is an *externalization of life* because I work *in order to live* and provide for myself the *means* of living. Working *is not* living.

Furthermore, in my labor the *particularity* of my individuality would be affirmed because my *individual* life is affirmed. Labor then would be *true, active property*. Under the presupposition of private property my individuality is externalized to the point where I *hate* this *activity* and where it is a *torment* for me. Rather it is then only the *semblance* of an activity, only a *forced* activity, imposed upon me only by *external* and accidental necessity and *not* by an *internal* and *determined* necessity.

My labor can appear in my object only according to its nature; it cannot appear as something *different* from itself. My labor, therefore, is manifested as the objective, sensuous, perceptible, and indubitable expression of my *self-loss* and my *powerlessness*.

BEYOND THE WELFARE STATE

Michael Harrington

The basic socialist indictment of capitalism is more true today than it was in the nineteenth century. The corporations have progressively "socialized" the economy, basing production on science and the most intricate web of human cooperation. Yet, for all the changes in capitalist attitudes, decision-making and appropriation have remained private even when they are exercised by corporate managers rather than owners. And so, as Marx and the early socialists predicted, the contradiction between unprecedented social productivity and the private institutions that direct it has become more and more intolerable, and made us progressively fearful of our own ingenuity. We purchase progress at the expense of the poor, the minorities, the old; we are even more threatened by our affluence than by our poverty.

The socialist solution remains utterly relevant: the social means of production must be socialized and made subject to democratic control. The crisis of socialism, then, does not concern what to do about the epoch, but rather what to do about tomorrow morning. . . .

I

There are three basic reasons why the reform of the welfare state will not solve our most urgent problems: the class structure of capitalist society vitiates, or subverts, almost every such effort toward social justice; private corporate power cannot tolerate the comprehensive and demo-

From *Socialism* by Michael Harrington. Copyright © 1972 by Michael Harrington. Reprinted by permission of the publisher, E. P. Dutton. (A Saturday Review Press book.)

cratic planning we desperately need; and even if these first two obstacles to providing every citizen with a decent house, income and job were overcome, the system still has an inherent tendency to make affluence self-destructive. . . .

First of all, the welfare state, for all the value of its institutions, tends to provide benefits in inverse relationship to human needs. And not—the point is crucial—because of a conspiracy by the affluent, but as a "natural" consequence of a society divided into unequal social classes. . . .

The class divisions of welfare capitalism, which are the root cause of this problem within neo-capitalism, are not, it must be stressed at the outset, simply unfair in some abstract sense. Were that the case, a sophisticated conservative argument might be persuasive: since to some extent the growth of the economy benefits everyone, even those who are worst off, there is no point in endangering these gains on behalf of some ultimate egalitarianism. What really concerns the poor, this theory continues, is not the rise or fall of their *relative* share of affluence but the steady increase in their absolute standard of living. Actually, inequality does not merely mean that there are sharply unequal proportions of goods distributed among the various social sectors of the population. It signifies a socio-economic process, at once dynamic and destructive, which determines that public and private resources shall be spent in an increasingly anti-social way and thereby threatens the well-being of the entire society.

Housing is an excellent case in point. The Government, even under liberal administrations, has been much more solicitous about the comfort of the rich than the shelter of the poor. This policy is not only morally outrageous, it has had disastrous social consequences as well. Yet it must be emphasized that in thereby investing billions in the creation of public problems, Washington did not act maliciously but only followed—unconsciously, automatically, "naturally"—the priorities that are structured into America's class divisions. Thus:

in 1962 the value of a single tax deduction to the 20 percent of Americans with the highest incomes was worth twice as much as all the monies spent on public housing for the one fifth who were poorest; and this figure does not even take into account Government support of below-market rates of interest to build suburbia;

in 1969, the *Wall Street Journal* reported, the $2.5 billion for urban freeways was a far greater subsidy to car owners who daily fled the central city than was the $175 million provided for mass transit to city dwellers; and Richard Nixon's 1970 budget continued this perverse allocation of resources by providing public transportation with only 6 percent of the funds assigned to highways;

and, as the National Commission on Civil Disorders (The "Riot Commission" of 1968) computed the figures, during roughly the same thirty-year period, the Government helped to construct over ten million housing units for home builders, i.e., for the middle class and the rich, but provided only 650,000 units of low-cost housing for the poor.

But it would be a mistake to think that Washington discriminates only against the poor. For, as a White House Conference told President Johnson in 1966, *the entire lower half of the American population is excluded from the market for new housing,* a market that could not exist without massive Federal support. This point needs special emphasis, if only because many people, with the best of intentions, concluded from the rediscovery of poverty in America in the sixties that the bulk of the nation was affluent while only a minority were poor. But the statistics, far from describing a simple division between the rich and the poverty-stricken, show that we have in this country a *majority,* composed of the poor, the near-poor, more than half the workers and the lower middle class, which does not even have a "moderate standard of living" as defined by the Government itself.

So when Washington used its powers to improve conditions for a wealthy elite, the poor suffered most because they had the most urgent claim on the funds thus squandered on the upper class, but a majority of the people, including tens of millions who were not poor, were also deprived of benefits that should have rightfully been theirs. . . .

. . . And, to turn now to the second major reason why American society on its current basis cannot deal with its crises, there must also be national economic and social planning on a scale that our present institutional arrangements will not tolerate.

There is no question but that the seventies will see planning in the United States. The really crucial questions are: What kind of planning? Planning for whom? The problems of welfare capitalist society are becoming so obvious and overwhelming that conservatives and even reactionaries have understood the need for state intervention—if only to maintain as much of the old order as possible. . . .

The first distinction between capitalist and socialist planning has to do with money. . . . In 1967 Senator Abraham Ribicoff noted that the various existing programs don't even reach people with incomes of $8,000 a year. In December, 1969, three years of inflation later, *Fortune* reported that "the shortage of acceptable shelter that has been afflicting the poor and the black is reaching to the white middle class and even to quite affluent families." And in mid-1970, George Romney, the Secretary of Housing and Urban Development, estimated that 80 percent of U.S. families could not afford the average cost of a new house. To deal with a crisis of this magnitude will clearly require a shift of massive resources from the private to the public sector, since the market is not even reaching a majority of the people. . . .

A second basic distinction between capitalist and socialist planning has to do with comprehensiveness.

When President Eisenhower proposed in May, 1968, that there be new, integrated communities with jobs, schools and parks and high-speed transportation links to the old cities, he was unwittingly committing himself to radical innovation. Assembling an integrated population and providing its members with decent work, education and transportation is not something to be accomplished by Adam Smith's "invisible hand." It requires long-range projections and a conscious coordination of Government policies. It could not be done, to take but one crucial example, if land were left to private speculation. For in order to assemble the huge areas needed for such extensive projects at a remotely reasonable cost, the public authority would have to use its power of eminent domain and establish land banks. So conservatives may be forced to recognize the magnitude of the urban crisis but they cannot solve it within their own economic calculus. What Eisenhower, Nixon and Stans really were talking about in their advocacy of new cities is a version of the old schemes to provide Federal subsidies to private interests, which are then supposed to fulfill a social purpose. But even supposing that such a tactic could provide the necessary billions in money (it cannot), the housing industry hardly has the resources, the overview or the legal right to engage in national, regional and metropolitan planning. . . .

The third major reason why capitalist society must be basically transformed is this: Let us assume that the system proves to be much more ingenious than the preceding analysis suggests. Suppose it constructs a welfare state that really does respond to the needs of the poor and that, without fundamental changes in structure, it manages to accommodate itself to democratic planning. Even then—and I admit this possibility for the purpose of argument only—even then, it would be necessary to go beyond capitalism to socialism. For if this society somehow found a way to deal with poverty, racism, inequality and unmet social needs, it would still be incapable of dealing with its own prosperity.

This problem is not a consequence of wrong-headed choices on the part of muddled executives; it is a trend within the system and cannot be corrected without sweeping changes. The economic theory of "external economies" and "external diseconomies" helps to explain why.

An external economy occurs when an act of consumption creates a collective good, e.g., when the decision of a high school student to remain in school raises his skill level and makes him a more productive worker rather than a candidate for welfare. External economies usually derive from public investments in schools, hospitals and the like. External diseconomies are a result of an opposite phenomenon: acts of consumption that create a collective evil, e.g., the air pollution visited upon society by a private automobile. These are particularly associated with giant industries and, as one moderate economist put it, "seem to be far more prevalent than external economies."

So the fundamental tendencies of late capitalist economies toward bigness and concentration will produce goods whose social costs often exceed their social benefits. This, it must be emphasized, is an inherent pattern in a society where huge investments are privately made. To offset this trend, such decisions would have to be made with major consideration of the social costs—a kind of calculus (as will be seen shortly) that is at odds with the very character of the capitalist economy. There follows an extraordinary paradox: the richer capitalism becomes, the more self-destructive it is. (This is a sort of economic analogue to Freud's psychological insight that the more sophisticated society becomes, the more repressive it is, since instinctual energy must be disciplined in order to make large-scale organization possible.)

In traditional Marxist theory economic crisis was the result of overproduction within a society of systematically limited consumption. Many contemporary economists now argue that the cyclical breakdown of capitalism, which turned relative abundance into immediate want, has been mastered. That . . . is much too optimistic an analysis, since the contradictions of capitalism bedevil Keynesians as well as anti-Keynesian conservatives. But even if we do assume for a moment that the cyclical crisis of capitalism is under control, it has been succeeded by an even more bizarre problem: that affluence itself is becoming increasingly counterproductive. . . .

So contemporary capitalism is not only heir to many of the traditional evils of the system, even if sometimes in ameliorated ways, it also cannot deal adequately, no matter how sophisticated it has become with either poverty or affluence. Left to itself, the system creates a welfare state that provides some benefits for all, yet favors the rich and discriminates against the desperate; it generates problems, like those of the urban environment, that demand comprehensive planning; and even when it functions to produce the highest standard of living the world has known, the social consequences of that achievement are so appalling as to vitiate much of it.

We socialists support every struggle for the partial and liberal reform of this inadequate structure. Yet we insist—and I believe that the previous analysis has documented the point—that the fundamental solution of these problems requires measures that go beyond the limits of the capitalist economy.

II

Neo-capitalism, for all its sophistication, cannot make desperately needed social investments, plan comprehensively and massively or cope with either poverty or affluence. Socialism can. . . .

First of all—and this is urgent practical politics within the present confines of capitalism as well as a step toward socialism—investment must be socialized.

There are, as has just been seen, huge decisive areas of economic life in which private capital will not invest because there is no prospect of sufficient profitability (or, what amounts to the same thing, where antisocial allocations are more profitable than social allocations would be). This is true of the fundamental determinants of the urban environment, like housing and transportation. Therefore the society must shift resources from the privately profitable sector of the economy to the socially necessary. This is a decision that only the Government has the power to make and which must be taken as a result of a democratic process. And it can only be accomplished on a national scale and within the framework of planning. . . .

There should be an Office of the Future in the White House. Each year the President should make a Report on the Future—with projections ranging five, ten or even twenty years ahead—which would be submitted to a Joint Congressional Committee where it would be debated, amended and then presented to the entire Congress for decision. This process should establish the broad priorities of the society and annually monitor the result of past efforts. It would be, for instance, the proper forum for establishing the broad concept of regional planning; but it would not engage in the actual planning of individual projects.

At this point, a candid admission is in order. The changes outlined in the previous paragraph could be welcomed by social engineers and technocrats determined to impose their values on the people. They could be used by sophisticated corporate leaders to make the status quo more rational and stable. And they might create an entrenched bureaucracy with a self-interest of its own. The critics of socialism who cite such dangers ignore, or conceal, the fact that they are the consequence of the complexity of *all forms* of modern technological society and that socialism is the only movement that seeks to make a structural and democratic challenge to the trend. But even more important, it must be understood that there is no institutional reform that, in and of itself, can guarantee genuine popular participation in this process. Only a vibrant movement of the people can do that. That is why socialists do not foresee an ultimate stage of human existence in which all questions are answered and all conflicts resolved. Even in the very best of societies the democratic majority must be on the alert. . . .

Profit is still another function of property that must be subjected to social control. In 1967 the Council of Economic Advisors—hardly an anti-capitalist agency—noted that Government direction of the economy had smoothed out the cycle of boom and bust and therefore removed a great deal of the risk in the market-place. Under such conditions, it argued, business should be prepared to take a lower rate of return. But in point of fact, American corporations chafed under the voluntary controls of the Kennedy and Johnson administrations, even though their profits rose by 78.7 percent between 1960 and 1970 and their cash flow (profits plus depreciation) was up by 85 percent in the same period. When Richard Nixon came into office, he abandoned all efforts to persuade industry and labor to obey guidelines in price and wage policy. Whereupon, the London *Economist* reported, the steel industry increased its prices in twelve months by 7 percent—as contrasted to a 6 percent rise in the previous ten years. And in 1971 a major price increase by Bethlehem Steel finally forced even the conservative Mr. Nixon to proclaim a contrary public interest.

So government cannot leave profit policy up to the good conscience of the corporation, but it can use an array of techniques to socialize this important area of economic life: selective price and wage controls in an inflationary period; a requirement that big companies open up their books and justify any increase in prices before an independent board; the use of vigorous tax policy (more on this shortly). But however it is done, the fundamental purpose of this reform is clear enough. The society cannot afford to leave to private decision how the prices of basic goods are to be set—or how the huge annual increments in wealth are to be distributed. . . .

There is still another avenue of socialist action. . . . The vigorous use of tax policy as a means of achieving a more egalitarian society is relevant to the immediate neo-capitalist present.

To a considerable extent, the Left has ignored the enormous potential of tax reform in forwarding the transition to a decent society. If . . . there is a tendency under capitalism for reforms, and even structural changes like nationalization, to benefit the wealthy rather than the poor, then taxes provide a most important corrective. It is not simply a question of seeing to it that the wealth generated by the intervention of the state serves the society on a democratic basis, but also of the possibility of transforming the very organization of inequality itself.

In most cases the discussion of maldistribution focuses upon income, for that is an area of abundant government statistics. But if one begins instead by examining the shares of *wealth*— "the sum total of equity in a home or business, liquid assets, investment assets, the value of automobiles owned, and miscellaneous assets, such as assets held in trust, loans to individuals, oil royalties, etc."—the disproportions are even more shocking. One quarter of the consumer units in the United States have no wealth at all (or "negative" wealth, i.e., more debt that assets); 61 percent of the consumer units own 7 percent of the wealth while a little over 2 percent of the total have 43 percent. Indeed a majority of the wealth in the United States—57 percent, to be exact—is held by just a bit over 6 percent of the consumer units. It is this permanent structure of inequality which underlies, and is reinforced by, the annual inequities in income.

Thus, there has been no significant change in the distribution of income since 1944. Moreover, the effective rate of taxation on the rich and the upper middle class (the top 15 percent of the society as measured by incomes) declined in the years between 1952 and 1967. Many of the taxes in this country—for Social Security and Unemployment Insurance, to take Federal examples, and on consumption in the case of state levies—are regressive. All of these tax rates are based on reported rather than actual income and do not take into account the command over resources in expense accounts, pensions and other perquisites which are rampant in the upper reaches of the economy. The same trends can be observed in England despite the achievements of the Attlee and Wilson governments.

So the American and other advanced capitalist tax systems are a labyrinth designed to favor the wealthy who can afford lawyers and accountants. "Income," as defined by the Internal Revenue Service in the United States, is not income at all: it excludes a good portion of capital gains, worth $7 billion a year; it does not tax the rent a middle-class family saves by owning a house, an item worth $8 billion a year; it exempts various state and local bonds; and so on. In this setting, the simple equitable act of making income equal income for purposes of tax computation would be a major contribution to social justice.

But even such a modest reform is intolerable on the basis of the capitalist ideology. In the summer of 1969 when the Congress considered —and promptly forgot—the idea of limiting some of the privileges of stock speculators by changing the favored status of capital gains somewhat, the *Wall Street Journal* responded in an angry editorial. By requiring these people to pay a little more in the direction of a fair share, the Government would "punish the nation's most productive citizens." And this disincentive to the stockholder could actually lead to a decrease in economic activity and Federal revenues: "Obviously enough the tax reformer's chief aim is not more money for Uncle Sam but more 'justice' as among individual taxpayers."

Among the many problems with this analysis is the fact that it is based on an obsolete model of capitalist society. If the stock market had as its prime function bringing together risk capitalists and industrial innovators, it is indeed possible that an increase in justice would lower the rate of return on such money and slow down economic change. But in reality, American corporations more and more accumulate their own investment funds internally or else turn to institutional investors. In 1964, for instance, after paying taxes and dividends the corporations retained $59 billion to finance their future plans. And a good many of the people in the Market, far from being the "nation's most productive citizens," are functionless parasites. As Joan Robinson put it, "The shareholders and rentiers, indeed, make a great negative contribution to industry, for much of the best talent of every generation is engaged, one way or another, in the lucrative business of swapping securities around amongst them and so is kept from constructive activities. The notion that the Stock Exchange, with all its ancillary apparatus, is the most efficacious means of supplying finance to industry, compared with other available methods, is a fig leaf which it wears to preserve its self respect."

Effective inheritance taxes would be another important source of social funds and an opportunity for working toward greater equality. In the United States they are quite low—or quite avoidable, which amounts to the same thing. In classic capitalist theory a man must be able to leave his fortune to his children if he is to have an incentive to work hard all his life. That motive could be easily protected by providing for relatively low death duties on the first transfer from father to son, which would encourage the father, and very high rates on the second transfer, from son to grandson, which would give the son a reason to strive as hard as his father. This is something like that ingenious Saint-Simonian notion of abolishing inheritance over three generations and counting on the greed of the first generation to make it indifferent to what happens to its grandchildren.

In all these reforms, in short, the point would not be to penalize hard work or actual risk-taking but to severely limit, and eventually eliminate, the tribute society pays to passive wealth or to stock gamblers. For as the process of accumulation becomes much more social with industry generating its own investment funds or getting them from institutions, it becomes absurd to pay generations of functionless coupon-clippers on the grounds that their distant ancestors made a signal contribution to the society. So it is property income that would be the target, and it is easy enough to distinguish between it and the reward for present accomplishment. One would also seek to get the enormous increase in land values which take place without any effort on the part of the owner. This was $25 billion a year in the United States between 1956 and 1966.

Moreover, of all the reforms proposed here, the use of taxes as a means of increasing justice and equality should be the most politically promising, for it attacks the wealth of a functionless minority and would provide benefits for a huge majority. If all the artful outlived rationales for favoring the rich can be shown to be what they are, masses would support their abolition.

So there are three main areas of transitional programs moving in the direction of a socialist democratization of economic power: the socialization of investment; the progressive socialization of the functions of corporate property, and then that of property itself; the employment of tax policy as an instrument for social justice. Each one of these structural reforms corresponds to a need in the society which can be documented in the official reports, and more to the political point, several of them could become quite popular with the majority of the people.

There is, then, still very much meaning to the idea of socialism as it relates to the middle distance.... If socialists no longer imagine an existing society of total perfection, they must hold fast to a vision of a new order which can animate all the approximations of it.

LIFEBOAT EARTH

Onora O'Neill

If in the fairly near future millions of people die of starvation, will those who survive be in any way to blame for those deaths? Is there anything which people ought to do now, and from now on, if they are to be able to avoid responsibility for unjustifiable deaths in famine years? I shall argue from the assumption that persons have a right not to be killed unjustifiably to the claim that we have a duty to try to prevent and postpone famine deaths. A corollary of this claim is that if we do nothing we shall bear some blame for some deaths.

From *Philosophy and Public Affairs,* 4, no. 3 (Spring 1975). Copyright © 1975 by Princeton University Press. Excerpts reprinted by permission.

I shall assume that persons have a right not to be killed and a corresponding duty not to kill. . . .

Let us imagine six survivors on a lifeboat. There are two possible levels of provisions:

1. Provisions are on all reasonable calculations sufficient to last until rescue. Either the boat is near land, or it is amply provisioned or it has gear for distilling water, catching fish, etc.
2. Provisions are on all reasonable calculations unlikely to be sufficient for all six to survive until rescue.

We can call situation (1) *the well-equipped lifeboat situation;* situation (2) *the under-equipped lifeboat situation.* . . . On an under-equipped lifeboat it is not possible for all to survive until rescue. . . . Lifeboat situations do not occur very frequently. We are not often confronted starkly with the choice between killing or being killed by the application of a decision to distribute scarce rations in a certain way. Yet this is becoming the situation of the human species on this globe. The current metaphor "spaceship Earth" suggests more drama and less danger; if we are feeling sober about the situation, "lifeboat Earth" may be more suggestive.

Some may object to the metaphor "lifeboat Earth." A lifeboat is small; all aboard have equal claims to be there and to share equally in the provisions. Whereas the earth is vast and while all may have equal rights to be there, some also have property rights which give them special rights to consume, while others do not. The starving millions are far away and have no right to what is owned by affluent individuals or nations, even if it could prevent their deaths. If they die, it will be said, this is a violation at most of their right not to be allowed to die. And this I have not established or assumed.

I think that this could reasonably have been said in times past. The poverty and consequent deaths of far-off persons was something which the affluent might perhaps have done something to prevent, but which they had (often) done nothing to bring about. Hence they had not violated the right not to be killed of those living far off. But the economic and technological interdependence of today alters this situation. Sometimes deaths are produced by some persons or groups of persons in distant, usually affluent, nations. Sometimes such persons and groups of persons violate not only some persons' alleged right not to be allowed to die but also their more fundamental right not to be killed. . . .

FIRST CLASS VERSUS STEERAGE ON LIFEBOAT EARTH

If we imagine a lifeboat in which special quarters are provided for the (recently) first-class passengers, and on which the food and water for all passengers are stowed in those quarters, then we have a fair, if crude, model of the present human situation on lifeboat Earth. For even on the assumption that there is at present sufficient for all to survive, some have control over the means of survival and so, indirectly, over others' survival. Sometimes the exercise of control can lead, even on a well-equipped lifeboat, to the starvation and death of some of those who lack control. On an ill-equipped lifeboat some must die in any case. . . . Corresponding situations can, do, and will arise on lifeboat Earth, and it is to these that we should turn our attention, covering both the presumed present situation of global sufficiency of the means of survival and the expected future situation of global insufficiency.

Sufficiency Situations

Aboard a well-equipped lifeboat any distribution of food and water which leads to a death is a killing and not just a case of permitting a death. For the acts of those who distribute the food and water are the causes of a death which would not have occurred had those agents either had no causal influence or done other acts. . . .

It is not far-fetched to think that at present the economic activity of some groups of persons leads to others' deaths. I shall choose a couple of examples of the sort of activity which can do so, but I do not think that these examples do more than begin a list of cases of killing by economic activities. Neither of these examples depends on questioning the existence of unequal property rights; they assume only that such rights do not override a right not to be killed. Neither example is one for which it is plausible to think that the killing could be justified as undertaken in self-defense.

Case one might be called the *foreign investment* situation. A group of investors may form a company which invests abroad—perhaps in a plantation or in a mine—and so manage their affairs that a high level of profits is repatriated, while the wages for the laborers are so minimal that their survival rate is lowered, that is, their expectation of life is lower than it might have been had the company not invested there. In such a case the investors and company management do not act alone, do not cause immediate deaths, and do not know in advance who will die; it is also likely that they intend no deaths. But by their involvement in the economy of an underdeveloped area they cannot claim, as can another company which has no investments there, that they are "doing nothing." On the contrary, they are setting the policies which determine the living standards which determine the survival rate. When persons die because of the lowered standard of living established by a firm or a number of firms which dominate a local economy and either limit persons to employment on their terms or lower the other prospects for employment by damaging traditional economic structures, and these firms could either pay higher wages or stay out of the area altogether, then those who establish these policies are violating some persons' rights not to be killed. Foreign investment which *raises* living standards, even to a still abysmal level, could not be held to kill, for it causes no additional deaths, unless there are special circumstances, as in the following example.

Even when a company investing in an underdeveloped country establishes high wages and benefits and raises the expectation of life for its workers, it often manages to combine these payments with high profitability only by having achieved a tax-exempt status. In such cases the company is being subsidized by the general tax revenue of the underdeveloped economy. It makes no contribution to the infrastructure—e.g., roads and harbors and airports—from which it benefits. In this way many underdeveloped economies have come to include developed enclaves whose development is achieved in part at the expense of the poorer majority. In such cases, government and company policy combine to produce a high wage sector at the expense of a low wage sector; in consequence, some of the persons in the low wage sector, who would not otherwise have died, may die; these persons, whoever they may be, are killed and not merely allowed to die. Such killings may sometimes be justifiable—perhaps, if they are outnumbered by lives saved through having a developed sector—but they are killings nonetheless, since the victims might have survived if not burdened by transfer payments to the developed sector.

But, one may say, the management of such a corporation and its investors should be distinguished more sharply. Even if the management may choose a level of wages, and consequently of survival, the investors usually know nothing of this. But the investors, even if ignorant, are responsible for company policy. They may often fail to exercise control, but by law they have control. They choose to invest in a company with certain foreign investments; they profit from it; they can, and others cannot, affect company policy in fundamental ways. To be sure the investors are not murderers—they do not intend to bring about the deaths of any persons; nor do the company managers usually intend any of the deaths company policies cause. Even so, investors and management acting together with the sorts of results just described do violate some persons' rights not to be killed and usually cannot justify such killings either as required for self-defense or as unavoidable.

Case two, where even under sufficiency conditions some persons' economic activities result in the deaths of other persons, might be called the *commodity pricing* case. Underdeveloped countries often depend heavily on the price level of a few commodities. So a sharp drop in the world price of coffee or sugar or cocoa may spell ruin and lowered survival rates for whole regions. Yet such drops in price levels are not in all cases due to factors beyond human control. Where they are the result of action by investors, brokers, or government agencies, these persons and bodies are choosing policies which will kill some people. Once again, to be sure, the killing is not single-handed, it is not instantaneous, the killers cannot foresee exactly who will die, and they may not intend anybody to die.

Because of the economic interdependence of different countries, deaths can also be caused by rises in the prices of various commodities. For example, . . . famine in the Sahelian region of Africa and in the Indian subcontinent is attributed by agronomists partly to climatic shifts and partly to the increased prices of oil and hence of fertilizer, wheat, and other grains.

> The recent doubling in international prices of essential foodstuffs will, of necessity, be reflected in higher death rates among the world's lowest income groups, who lack the income to increase their food expenditures proportionately, but live on diets near the subsistence level to begin with.[1]

Of course, not all of those who die will be killed. Those who die of drought will merely be allowed to die, and some of those who die because less has been grown with less fertilizer will also die because of forces beyond the control of any human agency. But to the extent that the raising of oil prices is an achievement of Arab diplomacy and oil company management rather than a windfall, the consequent deaths are killings. Some of them may perhaps be justifiable killings (perhaps if outnumbered by lives saved within the Arab world by industrialization), but killings nonetheless.

Even on a sufficiently equipped earth some persons are killed by others' distribution decisions. The causal chains leading to death-producing distributions are often extremely complex. Where they can be perceived with reasonable clarity we ought, if we take seriously the right not to be killed and seek not merely to avoid killing others but to prevent third parties from doing so, to support policies which reduce deaths. For example—and these are only examples—we should support certain sorts of aid policies rather than others; we should oppose certain sorts of foreign investment; we should oppose certain sorts of commodity speculation, and perhaps support certain sorts of price support agreements for some commodities (e.g., those which try to maintain high prices for products on whose sale poverty stricken economies depend).

If we take the view that we have no duty to enforce the rights of others, then we cannot draw so general a conclusion about our duty to support various economic policies which might avoid some unjustifiable killings. But we might still find that we should take action of certain sorts either because our lives are threatened by certain economic activities of others or because our own economic activities threaten others' lives. Only if we knew that we were not part of any system of activities causing unjustifiable deaths could we have no duties to support policies which seek to avoid such deaths. Modern economic causal chains are so complex that it is likely that only those who are economically isolated and self-sufficient could know that they are part of no such systems of activities. Persons who believe that they are involved in some death-producing activities will have some of the same duties as those who think they have a duty to enforce others' rights not to be killed.

Note

1. Lester R. Brown and Erik P. Eckholm, "The Empty Breadbasket," *Ceres* (F.A.O. Review on Development), March–April 1974, p. 59. See also N. Borlaug and R. Ewell, "The Shrinking Margin," in the same issue.

PRODUCTIVE JUSTICE

Howard Richards

There is too little food in the world, and what little there is is unjustly distributed. The latter proposition, that the distribution of food is unjust, need not posit equality of food distribution as the standard of justice, but requires only the premise that no defensible doctrine of distributive justice, be it based on the needs of persons, their work, their worth, their productivity, their rights, their effort, or any judicious combination of such personal characteristics, would yield an ideal distribution of food that would be coincident with or reasonably similar to that which obtains. However, this paper will not disillusion those persons, if there are any, who find that food is justly distributed, but instead address itself to the question whether it is unjust that there is too little food.

Five considerations will be discussed, and it will be concluded that in combination they are sufficient to determine a reflective mind to believe that it is not unreasonable to hold that the present food shortage is unjust, and, moreover, that principles of productive justice are needed as supplements to principles of distributive justice. If this paper is sound, and if all, or even many, reflective minds should give due thought to the considerations brought forward in it, then moral progress will be made, since it is a feature of justice that if all who duly reflect come to hold that something is unjust, then that something will be unjust. And without taking an overly optimistic view of history, one can believe that a wrong that is recognized as an injustice is more likely to be righted than it otherwise would be.

Before discussing the considerations in question, I shall list them briefly:

1. The practices responsible for keeping world food production at harmfully low levels are unjust, because they cause harm that could be averted, at a cost of only minor, morally insignificant, sacrifices.
2. Indeed, unproductive practices kill people, and they are unjust because they are analogous to homicide in the morally relevant respects.
3. The hungry of the earth have a right to a reasonably high level of agricultural production.
4. Distributive justice cannot be achieved without production, from which it follows that justice requires production.
5. It is misleading and mischievous to say that practices which sacrifice distributive justice in order to increase production are just (which we often say) without also saying that production is a requirement of justice. . . .

... The first of them is a variant of an argument made by Peter Singer, to the effect that we have a duty to aid the hungry, such a duty being an instance, or set of instances, of the more general proposition that we should prevent bad occurrences (i.e., harm) unless, to do so, we have to sacrifice something morally significant.[1] The argument as presented by Singer supports a duty of benevolence more than a principle of justice, seems to apply more to private acts than to social practices, and seems to put more emphasis on sharing what we have than on working more (and more efficiently) in order to produce more. But if Singer's position is correct, it would seem reasonable to accept also a similar argument, *mutatis mutandis,* for a principle of justice calling on us to amend our social practices, to produce more as well as to share more, when we cannot without so doing prevent famine. There may be disagreement as to the exact point where sacrifice becomes great enough that it is morally significant, i.e., the point where the harm done to some people by the adoption of practices that prevent the starvation of other people becomes great enough that it deserves consideration; but wherever this point may be located, it seems evident that we are not near it. The part of the argument that may be found objectionable is the part that asserts a duty to prevent bad occurrences, for it is traditionally and commonly held that our duties dissipate "like the ripples made by throwing a stone into a pond,"[2] in proportion as the claimants are less intimately associated with us, so that one's duty to one's starving mother is strong, but one's duty to a starving stranger is weak. An objector might say that no Briton has any duty to the peasants of Bangladesh. Furthermore, morality is more stringent with respect to actions than with respect to inertia; so that, while it would be immoral for a Briton to fly to Bangladesh, and there lock a Bengali in a cage with no food, causing, by this means, death by starvation, it is less immoral, or not immoral at all, for the same Briton to stay at home and do nothing while the same Bengali starves. Singer's position might be taken, if this objection is found to be persuasive, not as an analysis of our present moral condition—for our present rules have exceptions that have the effect of allowing more hardheartedness than Singer approves of—but rather as a direct appeal back to utilitarian premises and/or to moral sensibility, coupled with calling attention to pertinent facts about the extent and causes of suffering. One may hope that his paper will help to persuade people that the range of persons whom it is our duty to help should be extended, and the scope of permissible inertia diminished.

A second consideration which can be interpreted as a reinforcement of the first, has been advanced by Onora Nell [O'Neill], who holds that allowing people to starve to death is morally equivalent to killing them.[3] (Nell develops her case using criteria for "killing" drawn from the literature on the moral controversy over abortion, and relies on the assumption that persons have a right not to be killed.) If a case of homicide can be made out, the effect should be to extend the duty to strangers, since it is not ordinarily just (some hold it is never just) to kill anybody at all, and also to reduce the force of excuses that rely on the custom of excusing omissions more easily than commissions. The fact that many people cooperate to bring about the deaths in question does not weaken the case for homicide, since all of the accomplices to such a crime are guilty, no matter how numerous they may be. The fact that the number of victims is uncertain, there being many borderline cases where it is not clear that malnutrition is a necessary condition of death, is not decisive as long as we know that there are some deaths, that they are not excusable, and that even one such killing is morally prohibited. However, most persons whose actions and omissions support the practices that lead to death are not aware of the role that they play, nor aware of what they might do, if they would, in order to avert killing. Consequently, homicide fails to be a valid analogy, for lack of intent, with respect to those persons who do not perceive the effects of their conduct and viable alternatives. The argument for productive justice, on the ground that our failure to organize human institutions efficiently results in killing, will become stronger as the mass media and the schools increase public awareness of what needs to be done; since it will thereby become correct to ascribe malicious intent to those who continue to fail to take constructive steps to prevent famine.

Turning now to a third consideration, Gregory Vlastos has called attention to the rule that a trustee of property is obliged to manage it with a reasonably high degree of efficiency; if the trustee manages it badly, so that the income is, say, one-half of what it would be if it were well managed, then the beneficiaries can justly claim that they are being cheated of part of the income that is due them.[4] The case of the right of the beneficiaries of a trust to the proper management of it is, perhaps, a representative of the general principle that if all and only certain persons have a claim on the proceeds produced by a property, then they have a right to insist that it be well managed. Now, the persons who can lay claim to the earth's production are all and only the inhabitants of the earth, from which it should follow that everyone, including the hungry, has a right to an earth that is as productive as people can reasonably be expected to make it; from this latter proposition it follows that unproductive practices (at least large-scale ones) are unjust. But the general principle in question will not persuade persons who deny that producers have anything like a fiduciary duty to consumers; someone may hold, for example, that a man who owns farmland in fee simple has not only a legal but also a moral right to use it inefficiently or not to use it at all, and, further, he may hold that the institutions that define and protect such rights are just ones. For this reason, Vlastos' suggestion is likely to be accepted only by those who already believe that property rights should be morally evaluated in the light of their social functions, e.g., in the case of farmland, the function of agricultural production: Vlastos' suggestion should be especially welcome to those who hold, for religious reasons, that God is the Owner of the earth, and that mortal property owners are, and should conduct themselves as, His stewards.

The fourth consideration may be stated briefly: If distributive justice requires, for whatever reason, a minimum standard below which no one (or no one with some minimal level of merit) should fall, then distributive justice cannot be achieved without production. Production then becomes a requirement of justice. Consider, too, that distributive justice could too easily be evaded if production were not an obligation, for the employer who does not pay a just wage could discharge his obligation by closing the enterprise; there would then be no revenue, no employees, and no wages at all. But we would not always say in such cases that the man who had been unjust, because he paid unjust wages, had become just by ceasing to produce, nor that institutions that oblige him to take such a step, or reward him for doing so, are just institutions.

To introduce the fifth consideration, let us assume, quite realistically, that distributive justice calls for a more egalitarian distribution of incomes than that which now exists. Now consider the position of an Economics Minister (perhaps Ludwig Erhard, or Antonio Delfim Neto) who believes that even more inequality is needed in order to produce more goods, including more food. In such a case it would be natural to argue that although it is true that distributive justice calls for more equal incomes, there is another kind of justice, productive justice, which calls for less equal incomes. Such an argument appears to be implicit in the following statement made by President Geisel of Brazil on 19 March 1974. After citing statistics showing that there is a high degree of inequality of income in Brazil, he said: "A careful examination of the problem reveals that the improvement of the distribution of income, in order to make it compatible with the maintenance of high levels of economic growth, is a process that demands time and rationality. The easy distributivism that tries to reduce individual injustices by the prodigality of increases in nominal salaries, is condemned to failure because it generates inflationary tensions, limits opportunities for employment, and mutilates the potential for savings and development. Our experience prior to the revolution of 1964 and similar experiences in other countries definitely refute this emotional distributivism."[5] . . .

On Whether Productive Justice Is Different from Distributive Justice

Some persons may be inclined to understand the foregoing considerations not as reasons for seeking principles of productive justice, but rather as reasons for incorporating the requirements of production into standards of distributive justice. In other words, they may wish to hold that what is needed is not a new concept (productive justice), but merely the proper application of an old concept (distributive justice). One's reasons for agreeing or disagreeing with these hypothetical persons who hold that the concept of distributive justice provides an umbrella wide enough to take account of the obligation to produce, are likely to vary according to what meaning one assigns to the phrase "distributive jus-

tice," and accordingly I shall divide my effort to show that productive
justice is different from distributive justice into several parts, corresponding to each of several meanings that are commonly given to the latter.[6]

The Aristotelian and Thomist tradition has it that distributive justice
is a proportion, such that goods are distributed in proportion to merit.[7]
If, for example, the criterion of merit is number of hours worked, then
distributive justice requires that if A works two hours and B one hour,
then A should be paid twice as much as B.[8] An example of this type shows
that it is frequently plausible to equate productive and distributive justice, for if people are paid according to how long they work, then it seems
reasonable to say both that production will be augmented (because workmen have an incentive to work long hours) and the rewards are just
(because they are proportional to how much one works).[9] In order to
show, as I wish to do, that distributive justice and productive justice are
not the same, it would suffice to exhibit a case in which distributive justice
requires one result and productive justice another. Superficially, at least,
it appears that such cases abound, for it is common for leaders of developing countries to say that it is regrettably necessary to postpone considerations of distributive justice in order to stimulate economic growth. For
purposes of analysis, however, let us assume a single case, in which the
facts are stipulated. Much of the arable land of Nicaragua is devoted to
natural pasture for cattle, producing 10 kilos of protein per hectare per
year, protein which is consumed in the form of beef by the small portion
of the population that can afford it. There is an obvious distributive
injustice here, for it is not fair that some eat meat while others starve. But
this is not the injustice to which I draw attention. My point concerns the
need to change production goals and techniques. It turns out to be the
case, let us stipulate, that the only way to feed the population is to
produce protein-rich legumes and grains, at a rate of 100 kilos of protein
per hectare per year. And it turns out to be the case that the only feasible
way to do that is to increase the rewards of cultivators, and decrease those
of ranchers.

In such a case, the merits of cultivators and ranchers may be, for all
we know, the same, but productive justice requires that the former be
rewarded. This might be true even if *(per impossibile)* the change from 10
to 100 kilos of protein per hectare were accompanied by an egalitarian
social revolution, such that everyone's material rewards were the same,
for it might still be a necessary condition of feeding the population that
esteem or other nonmaterial rewards be accorded to possessors of culti-
vating skills, to the detriment of possessors of ranching skills. Under such
circumstances, distributive justice calls for equal treatment, while productive justice requires preferential treatment.[10] It follows that productive justice cannot be subsumed under the rubric of distributive justice,
where the latter is defined as distribution proportional to merit.

John Rawls may be taken as representative of a class of philosophers
who do not emphasize the word "distributive," but who nonetheless treat
of that concept of justice which applies "whenever there is an allotment
of something rationally regarded as advantageous or disadvanta-

geous."[11] Rawls sets out to solve Aristotle's problem (namely, that of just allotment), but he does not propose to solve it in Aristotle's way (he will not conclude that distribution should be according to merit). It might be further observed that Rawls follows in Aristotle's footsteps in the respect that he addresses himself to the question, under what circumstances can one justify departure from the standard of equal distribution of goods— Aristotle's answer to that question being that it is justified when merit is unequal, and Rawls's answer being that it is justified when inequality benefits everyone, including those worst off.[12] It is a noteworthy feature of Rawls's position that the best off need demonstrate no merit in order for it to be just that they receive a more-than-equal share. It suffices that their having more in fact leads through some sequence of causal relationship to benefit for the worst off. It follows that productive considerations which represent necessary conditions for benefiting the worst off (or, for that matter, for benefiting anybody at all) must enter into Rawls's criteria for the allotment of advantages. Rawls has a good reason, therefore, for not emphasizing the word "distributive," for his theory of justice in fact calls for a combination of distributive and productive justice.

One might, no doubt, decide to broaden the scope of the phrase "distributive justice" so that it is simply a name for whatever pattern of property distribution ought to obtain. On such a view, whatever might be the proper inputs to the decision-making process, the name of the output would be "distributive justice." I have already said enough to make it unnecessary to repeat my reasons for believing that to decide to use the phrase in this way would neither accord with ordinary usage, nor respect tradition, nor illuminate the issues at stake. Here I shall add that even if the unwise decision to use the phrase in this broad and somewhat amorphous way were taken, productive justice would still refer to something above and beyond distributive justice, if the duty to produce has implications not only for who should have what, but also for what people should do with property when they have it.

FURTHER IMPLICATIONS FOR THE WORLD HUNGER PROBLEM

It is often observed that even if the population explosion could be brought under control, and even if the rich were to share their surplus with the poor, the world hunger problem would not be solved, because surpluses are not large enough to meet world needs. Such observations (sometimes abetted by the assumption that the population explosion cannot be brought under control) are used to justify apathy and inaction on the grounds that nothing can be done. They may even be used to claim that the rich should not share their food, on the ground that a world where some are rich and some are poor is better than a world where all are poor. But those who argue in this vein overlook productive justice completely. The point is not what would happen if we should share what we have—the point is what would happen if we should share what we can produce. It is possible production and not presently existing food supplies that sets the moral standard. And we need not think in terms of producing more artichokes, coffee, and tobacco, but rather in terms of producing more of those foods that most efficiently satisfy human nutritional requirements. Looking at the matter in this way, and taking a reasonably optimistic view of the population problem, there is every reason to believe that the world hunger problem can be solved, no reason for apathy, and no reason for inaction.[13]

Our thinking should not be limited only to what the United States could do if it should employ its agricultural potential, and in any event no one wants the poor nations to be forever dependent on the United States for their food supplies. Within the poor countries themselves productive justice usually fares no better than distributive or social justice, and there is much to be done in the areas of reducing waste, inefficiency, and idleness.

These considerations suggest that the moral indignation that is expressed on food issues is frequently misplaced. It is not the starving child and the extravagant banquet that should awaken our moral sentiments, but the underutilized land, the unemployed work force, and the factories that are closed waiting for passenger car sales to pick up when they could be making tractors. We should retrain our sentiments so that we will be made indignant not by the effects, but by the causes. Our sentiments will then be more constructive, because they will be more likely to lead to actions that will solve the problem.

It is, of course, one thing to see what needs to be done on a physical level (e.g., soybeans need to be planted) and another thing to design the economic system that will organize cooperative effort so that what needs to be done will be done. As a first step, the study of economic systems should feature the evaluation of the economic performance of a society in terms of how well that society complies with the obligation to produce. To borrow a phrase from the field of operations research, an economy should be judged according to how closely slack variables (which represent unused resources) approach zero.

On a political level, the concept of productive justice throws into relief a far-reaching implication of one of the main justifications of human inequality. If inequality is justified because it augments production, then it follows that production ought to be augmented. The same argument that makes it morally plausible to say that some should have more than others, adds weight to the claim that resources ought to be mobilized in order to satisfy human needs.

Notes

1. Peter Singer, "Famine, Affluence, and Morality," *Philosophy and Public Affairs*, I, no. 3 (Spring 1972), pp. 229–243.
2. The phrase quoted is from Sidgwick, *The Methods of Ethics*, p. 271.

3. Onora Nell [O'Neill], "On Why Abortion Is the Wrong Topic for Moral Philosophy to Bog Down In," (unpublished), p. 21: "If all persons have a right not to be killed and a corollary duty not to kill others, then we are bound to insure that famine is . . . minimized."
4. Gregory Vlastos, "Justice and Equality," in Richard B. Brandt, ed., *Social Justice* (Englewood Cliffs, N.J.: Prentice-Hall, 1962), Section III. Vlastos actually holds that men are jointly entitled to benefit from the means of well-being, at the highest level at which it may be secured (p. 59). If he is correct, then my weaker version should be correct *a fortiori*.
5. Ernesto Geisel, remarks to first cabinet meeting, 19 March 1974, mimeographed (Brasilia: Ministry of Foreign Affairs, 1974).
6. Note that the question is the same whether or not one defines justice wholly or partly by reference to what persons would agree to under fair conditions. On such a (Rawlsian) view, one asks whether those principles that would be agreed to under fair conditions can properly be described as only principles of distributive justice.
7. For Aristotle see Book V of the *Nichomachean Ethics*. For St. Thomas see, for example, *Summa Theologica*, II, II, Q. 58, article 11. Merit ($\kappa \alpha \tau \alpha \ \alpha \xi \iota o \nu$) is, for Aristotle, a flexible term, and any number of personal characteristics can be taken to constitute merit. But for something to be a criterion of merit, that thing must be a characteristic of a person whose merit it is. Productive justice sometimes requires preferential treatment that is not premised on a person's characteristics, hence *a fortiori* not on his merits.
8. St. Thomas uses this example. See his *Commentary on the Nichomachean Ethics* (Chicago: Henry Regnery Co., 1964), Section 941.
9. If some workmen work harder in an hour or get more done in less time, then the criterion of merit can be adjusted to count harder or better work as more meritorious, in such a way that it will remain plausible to say that distributive and productive justice are identical.
10. To make the point more sharply, one can suppose that ten years ago the people of Nicaragua could be fed by letting cattle graze on natural pastures. Population growth and climatic variations have now changed circumstances, while the relevant characteristics of the persons concerned (ranchers and cultivators) have not changed. These suppositions make it easy to focus on the point that preference for cultivators is premised on circumstances independent of their personal characteristics.
11. Rawls, *A Theory of Justice*, p. 7.
12. Rawls's theory is, of course, much more complicated than this, but a fuller account of his views here would not affect the point being made.
13. See John McHale, and Magda Cordell McHale, *Human Requirements, Supply Levels and Outer Bounds: A Framework for Thinking about the Planetary Bargain* (New York: The Aspen Institute for Humanistic Studies, 1975).

SUGGESTED SUPPLEMENTARY READINGS

ACTON, H. B. *The Morals of Markets: An Ethical Exploration.* London: Longman Group Limited, 1971.

AIKEN, WILLIAM, and HUGH LAFOLLETTE. *World Hunger and Moral Obligation.* Englewood Cliffs, N.J.: Prentice-Hall, 1977.

ARTHUR, JOHN, and WILLIAM H. SHAW, eds. *Justice and Economic Distribution.* Englewood Cliffs, N.J.: Prentice-Hall, 1978.

BEAUCHAMP, TOM L. "Distributive Justice." In *Appendix to the Belmont Paper: Ethical Guidelines for the Protection of Human Subjects.* Washington, D.C.: National Commission for the Protection of Human Subjects of Biomedical and Behavioral Research. DHEW Publication No. (OS) 78-0013, 1978. Reprinted in *Bioethics Digest,* I, no. 7 (November 1976).

BOWIE, NORMAN. *Towards a New Theory of Distributive Justice.* Amherst, Mass.: University of Massachusetts Press, 1971.

BRANDT, R. B. "The Concept of Welfare." In *Talking About Welfare: Readings in Philosophy and Public Policy,* ed. Noel Timms and David Watson. London: Routledge and Kegan Paul, 1976.

BRANDT, R. B., ed. *Social Justice.* Englewood Cliffs, N.J.: Prentice-Hall, 1962.

CHAMBERLAIN, NEIL W. *The Place of Business in America's Future: A Study in Social Values.* New York: Basic Books, 1973.

DANIELS, NORMAN, ed. *Reading Rawls: Critical Studies of a Theory of Justice.* New York: Basic Books, 1976.

DWORKIN, GERALD, GORDON BERMANTO, and PETER G. BROWN, eds. *Markets and Morals.* Washington, D.C.: Hemisphere Publishing Corp., 1977.

EDWARDS, RICHARD C., MICHAEL REICH, and THOMAS E. WEISSKOPF, eds. *The Capitalist System* (2nd ed.). Englewood Cliffs, N.J.: Prentice-Hall, 1978.

FUCHS, VICTOR R. *Who Shall Live?: Health, Economics, and Social Choice.* New York: Basic Books, 1974.

HARDIN, GARRETT, "Living on a Lifeboat." *BioScience,* October 1974.

HARRINGTON, MICHAEL. *Socialism.* New York: Saturday Review Press, 1972.

LUCAS, GEORGE, and THOMAS W. OGLETREE, eds. *Lifeboat Ethics.* New York: Harper and Row, 1976.

MARCUSE, HERBERT. *An Essay on Liberation.* Boston: Beacon Press, 1969.

MILLER, DAVID. *Social Justice.* Oxford: Clarendon Press, 1976.

NOZICK, ROBERT. *Anarchy, State, and Utopia.* New York: Basic Books, 1974.

OLAFSON, FREDERICK A., ed. *Justice and Social Policy.* Englewood Cliffs, N.J.: Prentice-Hall, 1961.

PHELPS, E. S., ed. *Economic Justice: Selected Readings.* Baltimore: Penguin Books, 1973.

RAWLS, JOHN. *A Theory of Justice.* Cambridge, Mass.: Harvard University Press, 1971.

SINGER, PETER. "Famine, Affluence, and Morality." *Philosophy and Public Affairs,* 1, no. 3 (1972).

TUCKER, ROBERT C., ed. *The Marx-Engels Reader* (2nd ed.). New York: W. W. Norton and Co., 1978.

WOLFF, ROBERT PAUL. *Understanding Rawls: A Reconstruction and Critique of a Theory of Justice.* Princeton, N.J.: Princeton University Press, 1977.

Chapter 3

CORPORATE SOCIAL RESPONSIBILITY

case 1: The Sloane Products Case

Sloane Products is a regional manufacturer of metal dispensers for paper products used in restaurants, hotels, and passenger terminals. The products bear the Sloane brand and are advertised in trade journals. Sloane sells its products through wholesalers. There is no information on the amount of output eventually sold in minority-operated establishments. Sloane assumes the amount is relatively small. The manufacturing plant, however, is in an older metropolitan area with a large black population, though the plant itself is far from the center of the black neighborhoods and the firm has only a few black employees.

In response to pleas from the metropolitan chapter of the National Alliance of Business, Sloane's board adopted the following policy on minority purchasing:

> Sloane managers are expected to make extra efforts to find minority suppliers and even to help minority enterprises adjust to Sloane's purchasing requirements. The board's instructions also made it clear that the effort was not expected to impose any serious disruption on Sloane's operations.

Right after the procurement directive was issued, Frank Gambetta, head of purchasing, had found a local firm, Diamond Carton Company, a black owned and managed producer of corrugated boxes for shipping merchandise. For quotation purposes, Gambetta's office had given Diamond information on quantity, quality, sizes, and delivery requirements.

Adapted from a case by Lawrence G. Lavengood, Professor of Business History, Graduate School of Management, Northwestern University.

Diamond had admitted being new to the business but assured the people at Sloane that Diamond could meet the product and delivery specifications.

Diamond had sent quotations to Gambetta's office. After some negotiation, Diamond was awarded a contract by Sloane, who then reduced quantities purchased from other sources.

However, Diamond did not provide samples for pre-production approval at the time specified in the original agreement. When samples eventually appeared, they proved to be below standard. Gambetta and production chief Sam Fritzel then spent time helping the managers at Diamond work out the defects, and eventually Diamond did produce samples that could be approved.

First production deliveries were satisfactory, but since then every delivery has been either late or substandard. This has been going on for four months.

Fritzel is ready to end the agreement on the grounds that the relationship with Diamond is disrupting Sloane's operations.

case 2: The Olin Corporation Case

Saltville is a small community of 2,500 located in rural southwest Virginia. Since 1892 it had been the epitome of the one-company town. By 1954, the original Mathieson Alkali Works had been taken over by the giant Olin Corporation. Although some of the symbols of the one-company town— e.g., company houses and a company store—had become a thing of the past, the Olin Company was the foundation of Saltville's economic and psychological support.

In 1960, Olin Corporation's Saltville facilities employed about 1,500 people. By 1970, that employment figure had dwindled to about 800. In 1970, Olin Corporation announced that it would close its soda ash facilities in Saltville. The closing would occur in a phaseout over a two-and-one-half-year period. Presumably, a phaseout rather than an abrupt shutdown would give Olin's Saltville employees an opportunity to find other work.

In making its announcement, the company contended that three economic factors had led to its decision: (1) the failure of a 1968 modernization program of Olin's Saltville facilities to raise production, (2) the resulting rise in production costs as a result of the failure, and (3) stricter requirements by the Virginia Water Control Board that would require a $2 million expenditure at the Saltville facilities. Company officials placed most of the emphasis on the economic impact of the Virginia Water Control Board's decision.

Some were unconvinced that revised water pollution standards were the chief reason for the closing. In addition to the failure of the modernization program, the parent company had made a major error in the timing of its investment in aluminum production. Others focused on environmental issues. One study showed that Olin's Saltville facilities caused $2 million in damages per year to the river. Olin was in effect being asked to make total expenditures for pollution reduction equipment, which were equal to the damage it caused in one year. In any case, Olin never appealed the Board's decision, and the state granted Olin a two-and-one-half-year exemption so that the shutdown of the Saltville facilities might be orderly.

The assumption that most people would not be out of work until mid-1972 was shattered in June 1971. It was announced that the soda ash facilities would close permanently July 1, 1971. Worsening economic factors represented by an inventory buildup were given as the cause. On November 18, 1971, Olin announced it would close its Saltville caustic soda plant on March 1, 1972. Increasing production costs and needed modernization costs were given as the reasons. The final blow fell when the Navy failed to renew a contract with an Olin Saltville hydrazine plant. Instead, the contract was given to another Olin company facility in Louisiana. Again, economic factors were cited. On June 30, 1972, all Olin facilities in Saltville were closed.

Despite the economic motivation for the closedowns, Olin took several steps to mitigate the charge that Saltville had been heartlessly sacrificed on the altar of profits. A generous severance plan and early retirement plan were implemented. Olin established a relocation assistance service. Olin donated plant, property, and equipment to Saltville and contributed $600,000 to compensate for lost taxes and for planning and development. Some were unimpressed with Olin's generosity. The company "gifts" represented huge tax write-offs, and in any case did not fully compensate Saltville for the harms it suffered.

INTRODUCTION

THE CLASSICAL THEORY OF CORPORATE RESPONSIBILITY

Some of the demands for increased corporate social responsibility arose from the civil rights conflicts of the 1960's. After the bombing of a black church in Birmingham, Alabama, September 15, 1963, which resulted in the deaths of four black children attending Sunday school, business leaders in Birmingham, particularly those affiliated with U.S. Steel, were sharply criticized for not taking more initiative in improving race relations within Birmingham. Eventually, Roger Blough, Chairman of U.S. Steel, responded in a news conference at which he made the following point:

> I do not either believe that it would be a wise thing for United States Steel to be other than a good citizen in a community, or to attempt to have its ideas of what is right for the community enforced upon that community by some sort of economic means.
> ... When we as individuals are citizens in a community, we can exercise what small influence we may have as citizens, but for a corporation to attempt to exert any kind of economic compulsion to achieve a particular end in the racial area seems to me quite beyond what a corporation should do, and I will say also, quite beyond what a corporation can do.[1]

These remarks were widely quoted in the press and rekindled the flames of an old debate: What are the nature and scope of corporate social responsibility? A classical view, frequently referred to as the narrow view of corporate social responsibility,[2] limits corporate responsibility to making profits for its shareholders. Defenders of the narrow view, like Milton Friedman, indicate that business, like labor, government, and consumers, has its appropriate function, which is making a profit, and that in a free and good society, each group within society should simply work at performing its own particular function well (a perspective closely approximating the functional analysis of the Greeks). The notion that various groups within society have discrete functions supports a commitment to pluralism. The doctrine of pluralism has its roots in Federalist Paper #10, written by James Madison. According to this theory, the key feature of pluralism is the advocacy of multiple centers of power, and the chief danger to democracy and to individual freedom is the centralization of power, especially government power.

Many concerned business persons fear that calls for increased social responsibility on the part of business persons will only increase government control. An argument on behalf of this limitation of increased government control presupposes the functional analysis, for it is generally recognized that the function of government is to look after the public interest. If business were to expand its function from making profits to looking after the public interest, it would be exercising prerogatives appropriate to government and hence put itself under government control. Other business people fear that calls for increased corporate responsibility will put too much power in the hands of corporate officials. After all, corporate officials, unlike government officials, are not elected representatives charged with determining the public good. In a democratic society, corporate executives have neither the expertise nor the right to implement their own views of the public good. Both of these concerns about excess centralized power are discussed in the article by Theodore Levitt.

Finally, the classical view that a corporation's primary responsibility is to maximize the profit of stockholders is embodied in *Dodge* v. *Ford Motor Company*, which begins the selections in this chapter. Even such a relatively narrow concern as the responsibility of Ford to his workers could not take priority over the interests of the stockholders. It was not until 1953 in the case of *A. P. Smith Manufacturing Company* v. *Barlow*, et al. that corporate officials had something approaching legal permission to undertake acts designed to promote the public good.

This case, partially reprinted in this chapter, marks a watershed in the history of the development of corporate responsibility. It recognizes that the corporate good and the good of society are bound together. To twist a saying, "What is good for America is good for General Motors." Legal recognition of the interrelation of public good and corporate good permits a broader view of corporate social responsibility.

DOES BUSINESS HAVE A CONTRACT WITH SOCIETY

Another way to approach the question of the specific obligations and duties of corporations is through the notion of a contract. Contract arguments are both familiar to and well accepted by the business community. Any incorporated business is chartered. A charter is a kind of contract in which society permits the corporation to do business. It is presumed that the business practices will lead to the public good. Original charters were based on the assumption that the pursuit of profit yielded utilitarian results. In other words, the narrow view of corporate responsibility represented by Friedman and Levitt was assumed to be in the best interest of the public at large. If that assumption were successfully challenged, one would have grounds for justifying a broader conception of social responsibility. One of the reasons for the current interest in business ethics is that many members of society are challenging the traditional view and are demanding that the social contract with business be changed. The idea of changing the social contract with business is the focal point of Melvin Anshen's provocative article.

Any fundamental change in our society's understanding of the function of business or in the basis on which society charters corporations (enters into contracts with business) raises fundamental moral issues of its own. Those, like Friedman and Levitt, who take the so-called narrow view of corporate responsibility could raise a legitimate moral point in the face of society's demands that the social contract with business be changed. After all, the making of a contract is a type of promise making. Just as one party cannot simply break a promise when the keeping of the promise would be inconvenient, so society cannot change the rules under which business operates whenever it would be convenient for society to do so. To put the point another way, isn't society treating business unjustly when it demands changes in the rules? The selection by Norman

Bowie not only addresses this issue, but considers some of the moral principles which should govern any attempt to rewrite the social contract with business.

In addition to determination of moral grounds for changing contracts between society and business, some attention must be given to the content of any new contract. Unfortunately, there are a large number of competing views as to what moral obligations should be embodied in any contract. Robert Holmes provides a useful classification scheme for understanding these competing views. Often, debates on corporate responsibility focus on the "conservative" extreme that corporations ought not to assume social responsibilities and on the "liberal" extreme that corporations ought to assume extensive social responsibilities even at the expense of profit maximization. Holmes develops several intermediary positions, including one which uses the profit maximization principle as a justification for a corporation's undertaking some social responsibilities. He also shows how the extreme conservative position that corporations ought to have no social responsibilities can be defended as resting on a moral base.

Holmes then considers two arguments which maintain that business ethics is impossible. The first maintains that morality has no application to corporations since corporations are not persons and only persons can be held morally responsible. The second maintains that persons within corporations cannot have moral obligations, given the position of the individual in the corporation. With these arguments out of the way, Holmes concludes with a useful taxonomy of the kinds of social responsibility a corporation can undertake.

Certainly a requirement that business do whatever it can, regardless of the effects on profits, is much too broad. Yet, many business people argue that many critics of business espouse a principle quite close to that impossibly broad one. John Simon, Charles Powers, and Jon Gunnemann draw a distinction between negative injunctions and affirmative duties. Their distinction is based on the distinction between not causing harm and doing everything one can to promote the good. They argue that although society cannot legitimately impose affirmative duties on corporations, society certainly can legitimately impose negative injunctions on corporations, i.e., society can legitimately insist that corporate activities not cause harm. These authors recognize that many of our actions indirectly cause harm and hence that some criteria are needed for determining what harms fall under a person's or corporation's area of responsibility. By analyzing the tragic murder of Kitty Genovese, the authors suggest four criteria for determining when one is responsible for causing or helping to cause a social injury.

A much broader set of social responsibilities for business is envisioned in the selection by Keith Davis. Davis analyzes some of the sociological facts about business, society, and the relation between them. His analysis of these facts provides a rationale for some of the demands society is currently making on corporations. Davis then proposes five propositions which constitute new rules for business practice which will correct current inadequacies.

LOCATING THE MORAL AGENT

Any broad general discussion of corporate responsibility inevitably raises a number of important sub-issues. First, since a corporation is an artificial creation, how can society hold it morally responsible? Normally only individuals are held morally responsible. A corporation is not a real individual person; since it was created by society, it is at most a fictitious person. As a result, some philosophers, such as Holmes, hold that in talking about corporate responsibility we can be talking only about the moral responsibilities of corporate officers. This approach may not do, however. Although one can speak fairly easily of holding the president of General Motors responsible for some act that he did, often company decisions are not the result of the actions of any one individual or set of identifiable individuals, but rather emerge from the interactions among company officials. For example, a policy statement prepared by the Vice-President for Corporate Planning might be prepared and distributed to the board of officers in advance of a board meeting. Each board member will have his or her own idea of what the policy should be. In effect, each board member will have his or her own policy. It is perfectly plausible to think that the final policy statement issued by the board on behalf of the company is *not* identical with any of the various statements presented at the meeting. Suppose that the policy adopted is an immoral one. Who or what is responsible and how should they or it be punished? Peter French uses the notion of a corporation's internal decision structure to propose how a corporation might be held morally responsible. French makes use of the fact that corporations have established procedures for accomplishing specific tasks. These procedures can be justified in terms of larger corporate goals. After all, the procedures are created so that the corporation can achieve its end. French argues that the actions of a corporate official(s) can be described in two ways—in terms of the personal intentions of the corporate official and in terms of the procedures and objectives of the corporation. On the basis of this distinction, French tries to explain how a corporation, as distinct from corporate officials, can be held morally responsible.

THE CORPORATION: PRIVATE OR PUBLIC PROPERTY

A second topic inextricably linked with discussions of corporate responsibility is the topic of private property. Those who hold the narrow view of corporate responsibility will argue that both society's attempt to impose social responsibility on corporate management and the individual manager's own decision to engage in beneficent actions are violations of the property rights of shareholders. As Kelso and Adler put it:

> For management of a corporate enterprise to dispose of what rightfully belongs to its stockholders without their free, present, and affirmatively expressed consent is despotism and it remains despotism no matter how benevolent or wise management is in acting for what it thinks to be in the best interests of its stockholders.[3]

Those who hold a broader view of corporate responsibility have counterattacked by showing that a stockholder's relation to his property is very different from the traditional property/property-owner relationship. The unique situation of the shareholder received its classic statement in Adolf A. Berle, Jr., and Gardiner E. Means's *The Modern Corporation and Private Property.* The shareholder is envisioned as unlike the traditional property holder in that he has voluntarily surrendered control and responsibility to management. The shareholder does this to relieve himself of certain personal responsibilities with respect to his property. A shareholder's ownership is passive rather than active. The attitudes and behavior of a shareholder are thus regarded as very different from those of a homeowner, for example.

As a result of Berle and Means's work, new theories of corporate property have arisen. A common conception is to view the corporation as a special type of public property. Most socialists would argue that since the corporation was created to advance the public good and since the ramification of its activities impinges on the wider public, the corporation should be treated as public property. Society can then legitimately require that the corporation take on a wider range of social responsibilities. Despite the growing popularity of this view, James Fisher and Michael Hoffman, in a provocative article, argue that the old notion of private property is more effective in controlling certain types of socially undesirable corporate behavior.

N.E.B.

Notes

1. Quoted from Clarence C. Walton, *Corporate Social Responsibilities* (Belmont, Calif.: Wadsworth Publishing Co., 1967), pp. 169–170.
2. *Ibid.* pp. 54–82.
3. Louis Kelso and Mortimer Adler, *The Capitalist Manifesto* (New York: Random House, 1958), p. 211.

OPINION IN DODGE v. FORD MOTOR CO.

Justice J. Ostrander

... When plaintiffs made their complaint and demand for further dividends the Ford Motor Company had concluded its most prosperous year of business. The demand for its cars at the price of the preceding year continued. It could make and could market in the year beginning August 1, 1916, more than 500,000 cars. Sales of parts and repairs would necessarily increase. The cost of materials was likely to advance, and perhaps the price of labor, but it reasonably might have expected a profit for the year of upwards of $60,000,000. . . .

In justification, the defendants have offered testimony tending to prove, and which does prove, the following facts. It had been the policy of the corporation for a considerable time to annually reduce the selling price of cars, while keeping up, or improving, their quality. As early as in June, 1915, a general plan for the expansion of the productive capacity of the concern by a practical duplication of its plant had been talked over by the executive officers and directors and agreed upon, not all of the details having been settled and no formal action of directors having been taken. The erection of a smelter was considered, and engineering and other data in connection therewith secured. . . .

The plan, as affecting the profits of the business for the year beginning August 1, 1916, and thereafter, calls for a reduction in the selling price of the cars. . . . In short, the plan does not call for and is not intended to produce immediately a more profitable business but a less profitable one; not only less profitable than formerly but less profitable than it is admitted it might be made. The apparent immediate effect will be to diminish the value of shares and the returns to shareholders.

It is the contention of plaintiffs that the apparent effect of the plan is intended . . . to continue the corporation henceforth as a semi-eleemosynary institution and not as a business institution. In support of this contention they point to the attitude and to the expressions of Mr. Henry Ford. . . .

> "My ambition," said Mr. Ford, "is to employ still more men to spread the benefits of this industrial system to the greatest possible number, to help them build up their lives and their homes. To do this we are putting the greatest share of our profits back in the business."

Supreme Court of Michigan, 1919. 204 Mich. 459, 170 N.W. 668 3 A.L.R. 413.

"With regard to dividends, the company paid sixty per cent on its capitalization of two million dollars, or $1,200,000, leaving $58,000,000 to reinvest for the growth of the company. This is Mr. Ford's policy at present, and it is understood that the other stockholders cheerfully accede to this plan."

He had made up his mind in the summer of 1916 that no dividends other than the regular dividends should be paid, "for the present." . . .

The record, and especially the testimony of Mr. Ford, convinces that he has to some extent the attitude towards shareholders of one who has dispensed and distributed to them large gains and that they should be content to take what he chooses to give. His testimony creates the impression, also, that he thinks the Ford Motor Company has made too much money, has had too large profits, and that although large profits might be still earned, a sharing of them with the public, by reducing the price of the output of the company, ought to be undertaken. We have no doubt that certain sentiments, philanthropic and altruistic, creditable to Mr. Ford, had large influence in determining the policy to be pursued by the Ford Motor Company—the policy which has been herein referred to.

It is said by his counsel that—

"Although a manufacturing corporation cannot engage in humanitarian works as its principal business, the fact that it is organized for profit does not prevent the existence of implied powers to carry on with humanitarian motives such charitable works as are incidental to the main business of the corporation." . . .

In discussing this proposition, counsel have referred to decisions [citations omitted]. These cases, after all, like all others in which the subject is treated, turn finally upon the point, the question, whether it appears that the directors were not acting for the best interests of the corporation. . . . There should be no confusion (of which there is evidence) of the duties which Mr. Ford conceives that he and the stockholders owe to the general public and the duties which in law he and his codirectors owe to protesting, minority stockholders. A business corporation is organized and carried on primarily for the profit of the stockholders. The powers of the directors are to be employed for that end. The discretion of directors is to be exercised in the choice of means to attain that end and does not extend to a change in the end itself, to the reduction of profits or to the nondistribution of profits among stockholders in order to devote them to other purposes.

. . . As we have pointed out, and the proposition does not require argument to sustain it, it is not within the lawful powers of a board of directors to shape and conduct the affairs of a corporation for the merely incidental benefit of shareholders and for the primary purpose of benefiting others, and no one will contend that if the avowed purpose of the defendant directors was to sacrifice the interests of shareholders it would not be the duty of the courts to interfere.

We are not, however, persuaded that we should interfere with the proposed expansion of the business of the Ford Motor Company. In view of the fact that the selling price of products may be increased at any time, the ultimate results of the larger business cannot be certainly estimated. The judges are not business experts. . . . We are not satisfied that the alleged motives of the directors, in so far as they are reflected in the conduct of the business, menace the interests of shareholders. It is enough to say, perhaps, that the court of equity is at all times open to complaining shareholders having a just grievance. . . .

. . . The large sum appropriated for the smelter plant was payable over a considerable period of time. So that, without going further, it would appear that, accepting and approving the plan of the directors, it was their duty to distribute on or near the first of August, 1916, a very large sum of money to stockholders.

. . . It is obvious that an annual dividend of sixty per cent upon $2,-000,000 or $1,200,000, is the equivalent of a very small dividend upon $100,000,000, or more.

The decree of the court below fixing and determining the specific amount to be distributed to stockholders is affirmed. . . .

OPINION IN A. P. SMITH MANUFACTURING CO. v. BARLOW

Judge J. S. C. Stein

[1] This controversy presents questions of transcendent importance, the solution of which is not without considerable difficulty. . . . While the contest here relates to a very modest donation, $1,500, made by the directors of the plaintiff company, a large and prosperous corporation, to Princeton University for the latter's general educational purposes, the questions thereby provoked and here presented are of great public interest and very materially touch the public welfare. Stripped to its simplest

Atlantic Reporter 97A 2d 186, pp. 189–192 (edited).

form, the question calling for decision is whether a New Jersey corporation, organized in 1896 to engage in industry for purposes of profit, may lawfully in 1951 donate from its funds for the general maintenance of an educational institution like Princeton University, private in nature, in the sense that it is privately supported, it being an institution where learning is advanced by the teaching of learned languages, the liberal arts and sciences, architecture, engineering, and political science. The plaintiff company, speaking through its directors, answers this question affirmatively and seeks justification in two acts of our Legislature. . . .

[2] Now as to the particular facts upon which the court is asked to consider the legislation aforementioned. The facts are not in dispute. . . . At Princeton, as at most American universities and colleges, the tuition paid for instruction meets only fractionally the per capita cost of the education furnished. Not only that, but a large segment of the student body is assisted by scholarships and by direct financial aid from the school's treasury. So widespread has been for many years this policy of aid to the needy student that it cannot in truth be said that any deserving youth of ambition and promise cannot obtain at some American university or college that aid, in whole or in part, necessary to put him through an undergraduate career and even a post-graduate course. Unlike the system of higher education in other countries, the tremendous growth and expansion over the years of the American universities and colleges have created and furnished to the youth of the land the broadest of opportunity for instruction and development in the area of advanced learning in arts and pure and applied science and in the field of economics and government. It is from the millions of young men and women who are the products of higher American education that industry has picked, and will have need to pick, its scientists and its business executives. It is the youth of today which also furnishes tomorrow's leaders in economics and in government, thereby erecting a strong breastwork against any onslaught from hostile forces which would change our way of life either in respect of private enterprise or democratic self-government. The proofs before me are abundant that Princeton emphasizes by precept and indoctrination the principles which are very vital to the preservation of our own democratic system of business and government, particularly vital at this time when alien ideologies seek to impose themselves upon our habits and our dreams for the future. I cannot conceive of any greater benefit to corporations in this country than to build, and continue to build, respect for and adherence to a system of free enterprise and democratic government, the serious impairment of either of which may well spell the destruction of all corporate enterprise. Nothing that aids or promotes the growth and service of the American university or college in respect of the matters here discussed can possibly be anything short of direct benefit to every corporation in the land. The college-trained men and women are a ready reservoir from which industry may draw to satisfy its need for scientific or executive talent. It is no answer to say that a company is not so benefited unless such need is immediate. A long-

range view must be taken of the matter. A small company today might be under no imperative requirement to engage the services of a research chemist or other scientist, but its growth in a few years may be such that it must have available an ample pool from which it may obtain the needed service. It must also be remembered that industry cannot function efficiently or enjoy development and expansion unless it have at all times the advantage of enlightened leadership and direction. The value of that kind of service depends in great measure upon the training, ideologies and character of the personnel available. All of these considerations must lead the reflecting mind to the conclusion that nothing conducive to public welfare, other than perhaps public safety, is more important than the preservation of the privately supported institutions of learning which embrace in their enrollment about half the college-attending youth of the country. Even public safety depends heavily upon the educated mind; witness what scientific research at Princeton and elsewhere was able to accomplish in discovering and making of practical utilization what had since the beginning of time been the mystery of the atom. Princeton is preeminent in its encouragement of the searching mind both in science and in public affairs. Its preservation is indeed of first importance to the welfare of the State.

The court was furnished with proofs that Princeton, like most other privately supported institutions of higher education, is presently facing a serious threat, if not to its very existence then certainly to the extent of its public usefulness. High taxation against individual incomes and inflationary living costs have dried up the sources which heretofore nourished and sustained the school's activities. The school's budgetary deficits are mounting and are assuming threatening proportions. To turn to the State for help carries with it a certain decided disadvantage. The award of state funds is a matter of political administration. Such grants certainly present the hazard of political interference or control. The experience of the University of Louisiana, a state university, can hardly be forgotten. That school for a time became a political football, a condition hardly to be courted. I am strongly persuaded by the evidence that the only hope for the survival of the privately supported American college and university lies in the willingness of corporate wealth to furnish in moderation some support to institutions which are so essential to public welfare and therefore, of necessity, to corporate welfare. What promotes the general good inescapably advances the corporate weal. I hold that corporate contributions to Princeton and institutions rendering the like public service are, if held within reasonable limitations, a matter of direct benefit to the giving corporations, and this without regard to the extent or sweep of the donors' business. The benefits derived from such contributions are nation-wide and promote the welfare of everyone anywhere in the land. . . .

. . . The defendants, who object to the aforementioned resolution passed by the company's directors, contend that the $1,500 contribution to Princeton, granted though not yet paid, is *ultra vires* [beyond the power of], since there is no power in the charter of the company to make such contribution as the resolution calls for. They argue that the company may not use any of its corporate funds except in furtherance of its business needs, and only for the purpose of creating profit for its stockholders....

[3, 4] ... It is settled law here and in England that a corporation or association possesses not only those powers which are expressly conferred upon it by its charter, franchise or articles of association, but also all incidental powers reasonably designed or required to give fuller or greater effect to the expressed powers. An expressed power to a company to sell its wares does not require that with it there be also expressed the right to advertise its merchandise by the public press, radio, television, or any of the infinite variety of media of publicity and promotion. Such activity is a power present by necessary implication. So in respect of good-will. Anything that tends to promote with the public a company's good-will is a reasonable measure towards the corporate objective of earning profits. It is this philosophy which moved Congress to allow corporations to give up to 5% of their earnings to any established or recognized charity, educational institution (public or private), or other welfare organization. Contributions to such beneficiaries engender respect and appreciation on the part of the general public and certainly place the giving corporation on a better platform of public esteem than the one who padlocks its treasury against appeals for the public good. Therefore, in a real sense the contribution here under consideration is one that would have a tendency to enlarge upon and improve that goodwill which the plaintiff company already enjoys. Individuals who give to schools, hospitals, Red Cross, and the like enjoy far greater respect from their fellowmen than do those persons who tighten their purses against all appeals for such help. What is true as between individuals has undoubtedly the same impact between companies and between companies and individuals. There is also the broader question here involved, namely, that the contribution here in question is towards a cause which is intimately tied into the preservation of American business and the American way of life. Such giving may be called an incidental power, but when it is considered in its essential character, it may well be regarded as a major, though unwritten, corporate power. It is even more than that. In the court's view of the case it amounts to a solemn duty.

THE SOCIAL RESPONSIBILITY OF BUSINESS

Milton Friedman

The view has been gaining widespread acceptance that corporate officials and labor leaders have a "social responsibility" that goes beyond serving the interest of their stockholders or their members. This view shows a fundamental misconception of the character and nature of a free economy. In such an economy, there is one and only one social responsibility of business—to use its resources and engage in activities designed to increase its profits so long as it stays within the rules of the game, which is to say, engages in open and free competition, without deception or fraud. Similarly, the "social responsibility" of labor leaders is to serve the interests of the members of their unions. It is the responsibility of the rest of us to establish a framework of law such that an individual in pursuing his own interest is, to quote Adam Smith again, "led by an invisible hand to promote an end which was no part of his intention. Nor is it always the worse for the society that it was no part of it. By pursuing his own interest, he frequently promotes that of the society more effectually than when he really intends to promote it. I have never known much good done by those who affected to trade for the public good."[1]

Few trends could so thoroughly undermine the very foundations of our free society as the acceptance by corporate officials of a social responsibility other than to make as much money for their stockholders as possible. This is a fundamentally subversive doctrine. If businessmen do have a social responsibility other than making maximum profits for stockholders, how are they to know what it is? Can self-selected private individuals decide what the social interest is? Can they decide how great a burden they are justified in placing on themselves or their stockholders to serve that social interest? Is it tolerable that these public functions of taxation, expenditure, and control be exercised by the people who happen at the moment to be in charge of particular enterprises, chosen for those posts by strictly private groups? If businessmen are civil servants rather than the employees of their stockholders then in a democracy they will, sooner or later, be chosen by the public techniques of election and appointment.

And long before this occurs, their decision-making power will have been taken away from them. A dramatic illustration was the cancellation of a steel price increase by U.S. Steel in April 1962 through the medium of a public display of anger by President Kennedy and threats of reprisals on levels ranging from anti-trust suits to examination of the tax reports of steel executives. This was a striking episode because of the public display of the vast powers concentrated in Washington. We were all made aware of how much of the power needed for a police state was already available. It illustrates the present point as well. If the price of steel is a public decision, as the doctrine of social responsibility declares, then it cannot be permitted to be made privately.

The particular aspect of the doctrine which this example illustrates, and which has been most prominent recently, is an alleged social responsibility of business and labor to keep prices and wage rates down in order to avoid price inflation. Suppose that at a time when there was upward pressure on prices . . . every businessman and labor leader were to accept this responsibility and suppose all could succeed in keeping any price from rising, so we had voluntary price and wage control without open inflation. What would be the result? Clearly product shortages, labor shortages, gray markets, black markets. If prices are not allowed to ration goods and workers, there must be some other means to do so. Can the alternative rationing schemes be private? Perhaps for a time in a small and unimportant area. But if the goods involved are many and important, there will necessarily be pressure, and probably irresistible pressure, for governmental rationing of goods, a governmental wage policy, and governmental measures for allocating and distributing labor.

Price controls, whether legal or voluntary, if effectively enforced would eventually lead to the destruction of the free-enterprise system and its replacement by a centrally controlled system. And it would not even be effective in preventing inflation. History offers ample evidence that what determines the average level of prices and wages is the amount of money in the economy and not the greediness of businessmen or of workers. Governments ask for the self-restraint of business and labor because of their inability to manage their own affairs—which includes the control of money—and the natural human tendency to pass the buck.

One topic in the area of social responsibility that I feel duty-bound to touch on, because it affects my own personal interests, has been the claim that business should contribute to the support of charitable activities and especially to universities. Such giving by corporations is an inappropriate use of corporate funds in a free-enterprise society.

The corporation is an instrument of the stockholders who own it. If the corporation makes a contribution, it prevents the individual stockholder from himself deciding how he should dispose of his funds. With the corporation tax and the deductibility of contributions, stockholders may of course want the corporation to make a gift on their behalf, since this would enable them to make a larger gift. The best solution would be the abolition of the corporate tax. But so long as there is a corporate tax, there is no justification for permitting deductions for contributions to charitable and educational institutions. Such contributions should be made by the individuals who are the ultimate owners of property in our society.

People who urge extension of the deductibility of this kind of corporate contribution in the name of free enterprise are fundamentally working against their own interest. A major complaint made frequently against modern business is that it involves the separation of ownership and control—that the corporation has become a social institution that is a law unto itself, with irresponsible executives who do not serve the interests of their stockholders. This charge is not true. But the direction in which policy is now moving, of permitting corporations to make contributions for charitable purposes and allowing deductions for income tax, is a step in the direction of creating a true divorce between ownership and control and of undermining the basic nature and character of our society. It is a step away from an individualistic society and toward the corporate state.

Note

1. Adam Smith, *The Wealth of Nations* (1776) Bk. IV, Chapter ii, (Cannon ed., London, 1930) p. 421.

THE DANGERS OF SOCIAL RESPONSIBILITY

Theodore Levitt

The function of business is to produce sustained high-level profits. The essence of free enterprise is to go after profit in any way that is consistent with its own survival as an economic system. The catch, some-one will quickly say, is "consistent with." This is true. In addition, lack of profits is not the only thing that can destroy business. Bureaucratic ossification, hostile legislation, and revolution can do it much better. Let me examine the matter further. Capitalism as we like it can thrive only in an environment of political democracy and personal freedom. These require a pluralistic society—where there is division, not centralization, of power; variety, not unanimity, of opinion; and separation, not unification, of workaday economic, political, social, and spiritual functions.

We all fear an omnipotent state because it creates a dull and frightening conformity—a monolithic society. We do not want a society with one locus of power, one authority, one arbiter of propriety. We want and need variety, diversity, spontaneity, competition—in short, pluralism. We do not want our lives shaped by a single viewpoint or by a single way of doing

From *Harvard Business Review,* September–October 1958. Copyright © 1958 by the President and Fellows of Harvard College; all rights reserved.

things, even if the material consequences are bountiful and the intentions are honorable. . . .

Now there is nothing wrong as such with the corporation's narrow ambitions or needs. Indeed, if there is anything wrong today, it is that the corporation conceives its ambitions and needs much too broadly. The trouble is not that it is too narrowly profit-oriented, but that it is not narrowly profit-oriented *enough*. In its guilt-driven urge to transcend the narrow limits of derived standards, the modern corporation is reshaping not simply the economic but also the institutional, social, cultural, and political topography of society.

And there's the rub. For while the corporation also transforms itself in the process, at bottom its outlook will always remain narrowly materialistic. What we have, then, is the frightening spectacle of a powerful economic functional group whose future and perception are shaped in a tight materialistic context of money and things but which imposes its narrow ideas about a broad spectrum of unrelated noneconomic subjects on the mass of man and society.

Even if its outlook were the purest kind of good will, that would not recommend the corporation as an arbiter of our lives. What is bad for this or any other country is for society to be consciously and aggressively shaped by a single functional group or a single ideology, whatever it may be.

If the corporation believes its long-run profitability to be strengthened by these peripheral involvements—if it believes that they are not charity but self-interest—then that much the worse. For, if this is so, it puts much more apparent justification and impulse behind activities which are essentially bad for man, bad for society, and ultimately bad for the corporation itself. . . .

Business wants to survive. It wants security from attack and restriction; it wants to minimize what it believes is its greatest potential enemy—the state. So it takes the steam out of the state's lumbering engines by employing numerous schemes to win its employees and the general public to its side. It is felt that these are the best possible investments it can make for its own survival. And that is precisely where the reasoning has gone wrong. These investments are only superficially *easy* solutions, not the best.

Welfare and society are not the corporation's business. Its business is making money, not sweet music. The same goes for unions. Their business is "bread and butter" and job rights. In a free enterprise system, welfare is supposed to be automatic; and where it is not, it becomes government's job. This is the concept of pluralism. Government's job is not business, and business's job is not government. And unless these functions are resolutely separated in all respects, they are eventually combined in every respect. In the end the danger is not that government will run business, or that business will run government, but rather that the two of them will coalesce, as we saw, into a single power, unopposed and unopposable.

The only political function of business, labor, and agriculture is to fight each other so that none becomes or remains dominant for long. When one does reach overwhelming power and control, at the very best the state will eventually take over on the pretense of protecting everybody else. At that point the big business executives, claiming possession of the tools of large-scale management, will come in, as they do in war, to become the bureaucrats who run the state.

The final victor then is neither government, as the representative of the people, nor the people, as represented by government. The new leviathan will be the professional corporate bureaucrat operating at a more engrossing and exalted level than the architects of capitalism ever dreamed possible.

The functions of the four main groups in our economy—government, business, labor, agriculture—must be kept separate and separable. As soon as they become amalgamated and indistinguishable, they likewise become monstrous and restrictive. . . .

Business will have a much better chance of surviving if there is no nonsense about its goals—that is, if long-run profit maximization is the one dominant objective in practice as well as in theory. Business should recognize what government's functions are and let it go at that, stopping only to fight government where government directly intrudes itself into business. It should let government take care of the general welfare so that business can take care of the more material aspects of welfare.

The results of any such single-minded devotion to profit should be invigorating. With none of the corrosive distractions and costly bureaucracies that now serve the pious cause of welfare, politics, society, and putting up a pleasant front, with none of these draining its vitality, management can shoot for the economic moon. It will be able to thrust ahead in whatever way seems consistent with its money-making goals. If laws and threats stand in its way, it should test and fight them, relenting only if the courts have ruled against it, and then probing again to test the limits of the rules. And when business fights, it should fight with uncompromising relish and self-assertiveness, instead of using all the rhetorical dodges and pious embellishments that are now so often its stock in trade.

Practicing self-restraint behind the cloak of the insipid dictum that "an ounce of prevention is worth a pound of cure" has only limited justification. Certainly it often pays not to squeeze the last dollar out of a market —especially when good will is a factor in the long-term outlook. But too often self-restraint masquerades for capitulation. Businessmen complain about legislative and other attacks on aggressive profit seeking but then lamely go forth to slay the dragon with speeches that simply concede business's function to be service. The critic quickly pounces on this admission with unconcealed relish—"Then why *don't* you serve?" But the fact is, no matter how much business "serves," it will never be enough for its critics. . . .

If the all-out competitive prescription sounds austere or harsh, that is only because we persist in judging things in terms of utopian standards. Altruism, self-denial, charity, and similar values are vital in certain walks of our life—areas which, because of that fact, are more important to the long-run future than business. But for the most part those virtues are alien to competitive economics.

If it sounds callous to hold such a view, and suicidal to publicize it, that is only because business has done nothing to prepare the community to agree with it. There is only one way to do that: to perform at top ability and to speak vigorously *for* (not in defense of) what business does. . . . But it is only a beginning.

In the end business has only two responsibilities—to obey the elementary canons of everyday face-to-face civility (honesty, good faith, and so on) and to seek material gain. The fact that it is the butt of demagogical critics is no reason for management to lose its nerve—to buckle under to reformers—lest more severe restrictions emerge to throttle business completely. Few people will man the barricades against capitalism if it is a good provider, minds its own business, and supports government in the things which are properly government's. Even today, most American critics want only to curb capitalism, not to destroy it. And curbing efforts will not destroy it if there is free and open discussion about its singular function.

To the extent that there is conflict, can it not be a good thing? Every book, every piece of history, even every religion testifies to the fact that conflict is and always has been the subject, origin, and life blood of society. Struggle helps to keep us alive, to give élan to life. We should try to make the most of it, not avoid it.

Lord Acton has said of the past that people sacrificed freedom by grasping at impossible justice. The contemporary school of business morality seems intent on adding its own caveat to that unhappy consequence. The gospel of tranquility is a soporific. Instead of fighting for its survival by means of a series of strategic retreats masquerading as industrial statesmanship, business must fight as if it were at war. And, like a good war, it should be fought gallantly, daringly, and, above all, *not* morally.

CHANGING THE SOCIAL CONTRACT:
A Role for Business

Melvin Anshen

Among the problems confronting top corporate officers none is more disturbing than the demand that they modify or abandon their traditional responsibility to devote their best talent and energy to the management

From *The Columbia Journal of World Business,* V, no. 6, November–December 1970.

of resources with the goal of maximizing the return on the owners' investment.

This demand takes many forms. It may appear as pressure:

> to withhold price increases to cover rising costs;
>
> to give special financial support to black ghetto properties and businesses;
>
> to provide special training and jobs for the hard-core unemployed;
>
> to invest in equipment designed to minimize environmental contamination by controlling, scrubbing or eliminating industrial process discharges into air or water;
>
> to contribute generously to the support of charitable, educational and artistic organizations and activities;
>
> to refuse to solicit or accept defense and defense-related contracts;
>
> to avoid or dispose of investments in countries where racial or political policies and practices offend elements of the citizenry;
>
> to provide for "public" or "consumer" representation on boards of directors;
>
> to make executives available to serve without compensation on public boards or other non-business assignments.

The common element in all these pressures is their departure from, even contradiction of, the economic considerations which have been regarded as appropriate criteria for determining the allocation and use of private resources. They challenge the thesis that decisions taken with a view to maximizing private profit also maximize public benefits. They deny the working of Adam Smith's "invisible hand."

This cluster of pressures is not limited to alleged deficiencies in the traditional elements of management decision making. It also raises fundamental questions about the intellectual ability of business managers—reflecting their education, experience and norms of behavior—to respond adaptively and creatively to new goals, new criteria for administering resources, new measures of performance. . . .

One way of comprehending the whole development is to view it as an emerging demand for a new set of relationships among business, government, non-economic organizations and individuals. Some such set of relationships, of changing character and composition, has existed throughout recorded history. Without some implicit and broadly accepted design for living together, man's existence with his fellow men would be chaotic beyond endurance.

Philosophers and political theorists have observed the persistence and the necessity of this organizing concept. They have even coined a useful descriptive phrase for it: "the social contract.". . .

The ultimate determinant of the structure and performance of any society is a set of reciprocal, institutionalized duties and obligations which are broadly accepted by its citizens. The acceptance may be described as an implicit social contract. Without such a contract, not less real or powerful for being implicit, a society would lack cohesiveness, order and continuity. Individuals would be confused about their own behavior and commitments as well as about their appropriate expectations with respect to the behavior and commitments of the private and public institutions which employ them, service them and govern them. . . .

The concept of the implied social contract is an old one in Western civilization. It found early expression in the writings of the Greek philosopher Epictetus. It was central to the intellectual system developed by Thomas Hobbes in the first half of the seventeenth century. Without such an implicit contract, he observed, man faces the terror of anarchy, for the natural condition of man is "solitary, short, brutish and nasty." Hobbes used his concept to rationalize the power of the state to compel obedience to the terms of the implied contract. A few decades later, John Locke converted this view of compulsion as the lever to the view of consent as the lever—the consent of the citizens to a relationship of reciprocal duties and obligations.

In the next century, Jean Jacques Rousseau expanded the idea into an intellectual system in which each member of society entered into an implicit contract with every other member, a contract that defined the norms of human behavior and the terms of exchanges and trade-offs among individuals and organizations, private and public. His view even provided for handling disagreements about ends and means. The implied social contract, he wrote, stipulated that the minority would accept the decisions of the majority, would express its opposition through legitimate channels of dissent, and would yield before proceeding to rebellion. To Rousseau, therefore, the act of rebellion signified not what it appeared to be on the surface—a rebellion against the ends and means favored by the majority—but rather a rejection of the very terms of the contract itself.

Most recently, the fundamental thrust of such a book as John Kenneth Galbraith's *The New Industrial State* challenges the terms of the implicit social contract that defines, among other things, the function and role of private enterprise in today's society, the popular view of the responsibilities and performance of private corporations and the network of reciprocal relationships among corporations, government, and citizens. Galbraith's description of the enterprise system is distorted and incomplete, but his perception of the fundamental contract and its pervasive influence is accurate.

The terms of the historic social contract for private business, now coming under critical attack, are brilliantly clear. They existed for more than a hundred years with only minor modifications. Indeed, they acquired a popular, almost mythic, concept which purported to define a set of institutional arrangements uniquely advantageous for the national well-being, superior to all alternatives. . . .

These contractual terms were an outgrowth of interlaced economic, social and technological considerations in which the economic issues were overwhelmingly dominant. Economic growth, summed in the grand measure of gross national product, was viewed as the source of all progress. The clear assumption was that social progress (including those benefits associated with ideas about the quality of life) was a by-product of economic progress and impossible to achieve without it. Technological advance both fueled economic progress and was fueled by it in a closed, self-generating system.

The engine of economic growth was identified as the drive for profits by unfettered, competitive, private enterprise. Natural and human resources were bought in an open market and were administered in the interest of profit maximization. Constraints were applied only at the margins and were designed either to assure the continuance of the system (as in anti-trust legislation and administration) or to protect those who could not protect themselves in the open market (as in legislation prohibiting child labor, assuring labor's right to organize or restraining deliberate injury to consumers). These and similiar constraints were "the rules of the game," a suggestive term. The rules protected the game and assured its continuance as a constructive activity.

The implicit social contract stipulated that business could operate freely within the rules. Subject only to the constraints on conduct imposed by the rules, the responsibility of business was to search for and produce profits. In doing this competitively, business yielded benefits for society in the form of products and services wanted by consumers who earned the purchasing power to supply their wants by working at jobs created by business. . . .

The most dramatic element for business in the emerging new contract is a shift in the conceptual relation between economic progress and social progress. Until recently, the primacy of economic growth as the chief engine of civilization was generally not seriously questioned. Some of its unpleasant or wounding by-products were, to be sure, superficially deplored from time to time. But they were accepted by most people as fundamentally inevitable and were appraised as a reasonable price to pay for the benefits of a steadily rising gross national product. As a result, the by-products were rarely studied in depth, their economic and social costs were not measured—indeed, little was done even to develop accounting techniques for tooling such measurement.

Michael Harrington's book, *The Other America,* with its quantitative documentation of the existence of an unacknowledged poor nation within a rich nation, could strike with genuine shock on the mind and conscience of many professional and managerial leaders in public and private organizations. The facts of urban decay and the implications of trends projected into the future were not analyzed and reported in terms that would permit a realistic assessment of their present and future costs. Nor, certainly until the outbreak of mass riots in minority ghettos, was there penetrating consideration of the relation of social disturbance to continued economic progress.

While much remains to be done in scientific research and analysis of the side effects of economic progress, the accumulating formal and informal documentation has begun to influence the set of general ideas that constitute the terms of the contract for business. The clause in the contract that stipulated the primacy of economic growth, and thereby gave a charter to free enterprise within broad rules of competitive economic behavior, is now widely challenged. It is becoming clear that in the emerging new contract, social progress (the quality of life) will weigh equally in the balance with economic progress. . . .

Such equality foreshadows some drastic revisions in the rules of the game. As one example, it will no longer be acceptable for corporations to manage their affairs solely in terms of the traditional internal costs of doing business, while thrusting external costs on the public. Since the 1930s, of course, some external costs have been partially returned to business firms, as in the case of unemployment compensation. But most have not, and this situation is on the edge of revision. This means, as is even now beginning to occur, that the costs associated with environmental contamination will be transferred from the public sector to the business firms which generate the contamination. It also means that corporations whose economic activities are judged to create safety hazards (from automobiles to atomic power plants) will be compelled to internalize the costs of minimizing these hazards by conforming with stipulated levels of acceptable risk or of mandatory manufacturing and performance specifications.

To be rigorously correct, it should be noted that industry's new cost structure will be reflected in its prices. Purchasers of goods and services will be the ultimate underwriters of the increased expenses. But a moment's reflection on the supply-demand charts that sprinkle the pages of economics texts will demonstrate that a new schedule of supply prices will intersect demand curves at different points than formerly. This may lead to a changed set of customer purchase preferences among the total assortment of goods and services. What is implied is not a simple pass-through of newly internalized social costs. The ultimate results will alter relative market positions among whole industries and, within industries, among firms. Choices from available options in short-term technological adjustments to the new contamination and safety requirements and in long-term pricing strategies to reflect higher costs will, in the familiar competitive way, determine success or failure for a number of companies. Some interesting management decisions lie ahead.

The internalization of traditional social costs of private operations is the most obvious of the changes that will follow on striking a new balance between economic and social progress. More subtle, and eventually more radical, relocations of responsibility can be foreseen. The complex cluster of socio-economic problems associated with urbanization, population shifts and the needs of disadvantaged minorities are already overwhelming the administrative capacities, probably also the resources, of city, county and state governments. Evidence is accumulating that the public expects private business to contribute brains and resources to the amelioration and resolution of these massive strains. History suggests that such expectations will be transformed into demands. . . .

If the thrust of this analysis is generally on target, the principal lesson for private management is clear. It must participate actively in the redesign of the social contract. There can be no greater danger than to permit the new rules to be formulated by either the small group of critics armed only with malevolence toward the existing system or the much larger group sincerely motivated by concern for ameliorating social ills but grossly handicapped by their ignorance of the techniques and dynamism of private enterprise. . . .

A good place to begin would be the uncharted jungle of cost estimates. We need concepts and techniques for measuring and accounting for the real costs of environmental contamination. We need to build a body of reliable information about what the costs are in all their complexity, where they originate, where they impact. We also need to evaluate present and potential technologies for suppressing or removing contaminants, along both engineering and economic parameters. Using history, experimentation and game theory, we need to study the relative effectiveness of all types of cost transfer instruments, both inducements and penalties. One might speculate that the conclusion will be in favor of applying a variety of devices, each fitted to a specific set of technical and economic circumstances, rather than a single instrument. But this is a foresighted guess, not a basis for public policy determination.

A second area where business competence can make a contribution is the cluster of problems associated with poverty in the midst of plenty, unemployed or underemployed minorities, and urban decay. Less clearly defined than the contamination issue, this area possesses much greater potential for violent disruption that could mortally shred the fabric of our society. If this occurs (and there are too many recent examples of limited local disruptions to be comfortably skeptical about the possibilities ahead), many of the environmental conditions essential for the private enterprise system will disappear. There can be little doubt that what would follow would be an authoritarian, social-service, rigid society in which the conditions of production and distribution would be severely controlled. In such a setting, the dynamism, creativeness and flexibility of the economy would disappear, together with all the incentives for individual achievement in any arena other than, possibly, the political.

It is not easy to project with confidence how private business might move effectively into this area while retaining its fundamental profit orientation. One interesting possibility is to transfer the concept of the defense contractor to the non-defense sector. The brute economics of low-cost urban housing, for example, may rule out unsubsidized, business-initiated investment. Not ruled out, however, is business as contractor, remodeler and operator under negotiated or competitive-bid contracts. There has been limited experimentation in arrangements of this type, in housing, education, urban systems analysis and planning, and other fields. Freer exploration in diverse circumstances and in public-private relationships might discover an attractive potential for alleviating and removing major causes of gross social discontent while retaining a large degree of private initiative and the familiar web of revenue-cost relationships. The true social costs remaining, representing the layer of subsidies that may be found necessary to absorb the remaining expenses of an acceptable ground level of general welfare, could then be allocated through the tax system.

This is obviously not the only possibility in sight. Business has made only a few limited experiments in the application of incentives. More extensive analysis and trial might suggest at least the special circumstances in which this tool could effectively supplement or supplant the public contractor device. A third possibility is suggested by the concept embodied in Comsat—the mixed public-private corporation. Other options, including combinations of the foregoing, await imaginative creation.

The incentive for business management to enroll as a participant in the general exploration of ways and means for removing the cancerous growth in the vitals of society is classically selfish. Somehow, this cancer will be removed. The recognition is spreading rapidly that its continuance is intolerable. Some of the proposed or still-to-be-proposed lines of attack may be destructive of other elements in society, including the private enterprise system. Management is in a position to contribute rational analysis, technical competence and imaginative innovations. The interests served by continuing the enterprise system coincide here with other social interests.

These and comparable innovations imply for private managers a willingness to think about new economic roles and social relationships that many will see as dangerous cracks in the wall of custom. It is not unreasonable, however, to suggest that we are considering nothing more adventurous than the explorations and commitments that managers have long been accustomed to underwrite in administering resources. The only significant difference is that the stakes are higher. In place of the marginal calculus of profit and loss, what may be involved is the preservation of the civilization that has created such an unparalleled record of wealth and growth.

CHANGING THE RULES

Norman E. Bowie

It is not merely the introductory philosophy students who ask, "Why be moral?" An examination of much of the contemporary literature in business ethics indicates that the "Why be moral" question is very much on the mind of business persons as well.

One possibility for providing an answer to the "why be moral" question is to indicate the contractual basis on which business rests. The operation of a business, particularly when the business is a corporation, is not a matter of right. Rather the individuals enter into a contract with society. In turn for the permission to do business, the society places certain obligations and duties on the business. The corporation is created by society for a specific purpose or purposes. Robert A. Dahl has put the point this way:

> Today it is absurd to regard the corporation simply as an enterprise established for the sole purpose of allowing profit making. We the citizens give them special rights, powers, and privileges, protection, and benefits on the understanding that their activities will fulfill purposes. Corporations exist only as they continue to benefit us. . . . Every corporation should be thought of as a social enterprise whose existence and decisions can be justified only insofar as they serve public or social purposes.[1]

Actually not only does Dahl's quotation indicate that the relation between business and society is contractual, but Dahl spells out the nature of that contract. The corporation must not only benefit those who create it, it must benefit those who permit it (namely society as a whole).

In many discussions of business ethics no one defines terms like "moral" or "corporate responsibility." This inadequacy can be corrected by adopting the perspective of the contract analysis. The morality of business or corporate responsibility is determined by the terms of the contract with society. The corporation has those obligations which the society imposes on it in its charter of incorporation. In accepting its charter, the corporation accepts those moral constraints. Failure to be moral is a violation of the principle of fairness. The corporation which violates the moral rules contained in or implied by its charter is in the position of agreeing to the rules and then violating them. It is in the position of one who makes a promise and then breaks it. Such unfairness is often considered a paradigm case of injustice and immorality. The corporation which finds itself in the position of breaking the agreements it has made is in a particularly vulnerable position, since the corporate enterprise depends for its survival on the integrity of contractual relations. Understanding business as a contractual relation between the corporation and the society as a whole provides a preliminary answer to our "why be moral" question. The corporation should be moral because it has agreed to be. However, what a corporation's moral obligations are is contained in the contract itself.

Although this analysis does provide the framework for showing that certain corporate activities are immoral and provides a moral *reason* for indicating why a corporation should not engage in them, many complicated questions remain to be answered.

The first focuses on the content of the contract. Many corporate executives could accept the contract analysis as outlined thus far and argue that current demands on corporations to be more socially responsible are themselves violations of the contract. After all, corporate charters do not contain an open-ended moral requirement that the corporation promote the public interest. Rather, corporations are founded primarily to promote the financial interests of the investors (the stockholders). Society had believed that by furthering the interests of the stockholders, society as a whole benefited. Now society has changed its mind, and frustrated corporation executives rightly argue that it is the corporate responsibility zealots and not the corporate executives who are changing the terms of the contract.

In several respects the corporate response is appropriate. Society is changing the rules of the game and it is appropriate to ask why corporations should acquiesce in these unilateral changes. Before considering these issues, however, I should like to point out one respect in which the corporate officials' charge that the rules are being changed is incorrect. In addition to the obligations spelled out in the contract itself, there are certain moral requirements, moral background conditions, if you will, which are assumed. Certain moral rules are rules that are required if contracts are to be made at all. These moral requirements are as obligatory as the obligations spelled out in the contract itself. After all, when I agree to pay my bills in order to get a Master Charge card, I do not also sign a meta-agreement that I keep my agreements. The whole market exchange mechanism rests on conditions of trust which can be embodied in moral principles. What is shocking about some of the current corporate scandals—bribery, falsification of records, theft, and corporate espionage—is that these acts violate the conditions for making contracts and market exchanges, conditions which are at the very heart of the free enterprise system. Such violations cannot be excused by saying that they do not appear in the contract. Such excuses are almost as absurd as someone defending the murder of a creditor by saying: I only promised to pay him back; I didn't promise not to murder him. Hence we can conclude that a company has moral obligations in the contract it makes with society and it has obligations to those moral rules which make contracts possible. Its agreement in the former is explicit; its agreement in the latter, implicit. Violation of either is a violation of fairness—a failure to keep one's promises.

We can now return to the charge that it is society which is changing the terms of the contract. Fortunately, not all the charges of immorality and irresponsibility leveled at corporations are directed at violations of contractual morality. Corporations are charged with neglecting to solve such social problems as pollution, racism, sexism, and urban blight. They are charged with sins of omission. At this point the corporation can argue that they have no obligation to resolve all of society's problems. Such a broad-based moral obligation is not a part of their contract with society. That corporations do not have such general contractual obligations is conceded by most experts in the field.

We now face a more complicated form of the "why be moral" question. Why should the corporation agree to a rewriting of its contract with society—a rewriting which will impose greatly expanded social responsibilities on it?

One answer is prudential. It is in the interests of the corporation to do so. This idea has been expressed in the form of a law called the Iron Law of Responsibility: In the long run those who do not use power in a manner which society considers socially responsible will tend to lose it.[2] If society demands a rewriting of the contract, society has the *power* to rewrite it unilaterally. However, can we go beyond prudence to offer any moral reasons for business to revise its agreements? I believe there are several.

One might be called the principle of contribution: If one contributes to a social harm, then one has a proportional obligation to contribute to its alleviation. Since business clearly does contribute to social problems, it has at least some obligation to correct them. In saying that business has some responsibility, I do not wish to imply that it has the only responsibility. Government, labor, and all of us as consumers contribute our part to the problems and hence have some responsibility to work toward solutions. It is neither fair nor prudent to expect one segment of society to shoulder the entire burden. Hence only a *contribution* is required.

Another moral reason for business to accept a new contract might be based on the notion of power. Those constituents of society which have the most in the way of resources should contribute the most to resolving social ills. Since business is either the most powerful force or second only to the federal government, its superior resources impose special obligations upon it. There is an analogy here to arguments made on behalf of progressive taxation.

If the moral arguments are sound, there are moral reasons as well as a very strong prudential reason for corporations to revise their contractual relations with society. However, the corporation can reciprocally require certain agreements on the part of society. First, since a contract should be mutually acceptable, the contract cannot be rewritten unilaterally. Representatives from the corporate sector have a right to participate in the redrafting. Second, grounds of consistency require that other contributors to society's problems also contribute to their solution and that the requirements for the more powerful constituencies be stronger. So long as these conditions are met, corporations should agree to a revised contract and our original fairness arguments can be used to show why individual corporations should follow it.

Notes

1. Robert A. Dahl, "A Prelude to Corporate Reform." In *Corporate Social Policy,* ed. Robert L. Heilbroner and Paul London (Reading, Mass.: Addison-Wesley Publishing Company, 1975), pp. 18–19.
2. Keith Davis and Robert L. Blomstrom, *Business and Society: Environment and Responsibility,* 3rd ed. (New York: McGraw-Hill Book Company, 1975), p. 50.

THE CONCEPT OF CORPORATE
RESPONSIBILITY

Robert L. Holmes

Both sides in the debate over corporate responsibility agree that corporations have responsibilities. They disagree only over what those responsibilities are—specifically over whether they are purely economic, that is, to maximize profits,[1] or include social responsibilities as well—and if the latter, over how far corporations should go in meeting them.

But this issue is more complex than it at first appears, and it raises a number of difficult ethical and metaethical issues. Some of the debate, for example, isn't primarily over whether corporations have social responsibilities at all, but over whether they have social responsibilities which conflict with and sometimes override the responsibility to maximize profits.[2] Many who oppose the idea of corporate social responsibility do so because they see it as a threat to the successful performance of the corporation's central economic functions, and they would not object otherwise. I say many wouldn't, but some would.[3] And this distinction marks an important difference among opponents of social responsibility. Some hold only that corporations have no obligation to assume social responsibilities, but leave it open that they *may* do so provided it doesn't jeopardize profits. Others hold the stronger position that corporations not only have no social responsibilities but would be acting wrongly to assume such responsibilities.[4]

I

Let us make this clearer by formulating three principles in terms of which the Liberal and Conservative positions (as I shall respectively label those which favor and those which oppose corporate responsibility) can be stated.

1. Corporations ought not to assume social responsibilities.
2. Corporations may (but aren't obligated to) assume social responsibilities:
   a. when doing so is consistent with profit maximization; or
   b. even at the expense of profit maximization.
3. Corporations ought to assume social responsibilities:
   a. when doing so is consistent with, or in the interest of, profit maximization; or
   b. even at the expense of profit maximization.

What we may call the Pure Conservative position can then be defined as the acceptance of (1) and the Pure Liberal position as the acceptance of

Original essay especially written for this text. Reprinted by permission of the author.

3(b). Qualified Conservatism will be the acceptance of 2(a) and Qualified Liberalism the acceptance of either 2(b) or 3(a).

Now it is often assumed that the Liberal in this debate is arguing from a moral position and the Conservative from a nonmoral position. But this needn't be so. Each of the above can be held on either moral or nonmoral grounds (whether defensibly or not we shall consider in Part II). Each says only what corporations should (or may) do, not why they should do it, or what the justification is of their doing it. For the latter we need to look to more basic positions.

These can be broken down into two, each resting upon a specific claim regarding obligation. The first, which we may call the classical view,[5] in deference to the common but misleading belief that it is the unqualified view of classical economists, is as follows:

> C: *The sole obligation of corporations is to maximize profits.*

On the relatively unproblematic assumption that the maximization of profits *simpliciter* isn't a moral end, this doesn't express a moral obligation, and, in fact, in light of the word "sole," it entails that coporations have no moral obligations. It is compatible with both the Conservative principle (1) and with the Qualified Conservative principle 2(a). It would even be compatible with the Liberal principle 3(a) if the latter weren't taken (as it is here intended) to imply an obligation. Aside from that, it rules out only 2(b) and 3(b). It means—in line with the Kantian precept[6] that to will an end is to will the indispensable means to its attainment— that corporations ought to do whatever is necessary to maximize profits. The reason this is compatible with some forms of Liberal position is that it is conceivable, and in fact argued by some contemporary writers, that the most effective means to that end in the long run is through the assumption of social responsibilities, even at risk of a short-term diminution of profits.[7]

A convenient way of formulating the second basic position, which we may call the moralist's view, is as follows:

> M: *The basic obligation of corporations is always to act morally.*

This leaves it open what morality specifically requires and whether it be teleological or deontological in character. But it would sanction any of the Liberal and Conservative positions if they could be shown to be justified by the basic principle(s) of morality. It could even support C if C were amended to read: The sole derivative obligation of corporations is to maximize profits. Such a possibility is suggested by Adam Smith when he says:

> Every individual is continuously exerting himself to find the most advanta-
> geous employment for whatever capital he can command. It is his own
> advantage, indeed, and not that of the society, which he has in view. But

the study of his own advantage naturally, or rather necessarily, leads him
to prefer that employment which is most advantageous to the society. . . .
   In this, as in many other cases, he is led by an invisible hand to promote
an end which was no part of his intention.[8]

Though it is unclear whether Smith takes the interest of society to be the
end which ultimately justifies the pursuit of self-interest (and by extension to our present concern, the pursuit of profit maximization by corporations), one very well might, in which case the justification of
self-interest would be a putatively moral one. It is perfectly consistent to
hold that people should promote the greatest good, or the general happiness, or some such putative moral end, but that the most effective means
to that end is the pursuit by each person of his or her own interest. All
that is required is the assumption—though a large one—that morality and
self-interest coincide. The invisible hand, on this view, would then be a
moral hand, perhaps a utilitarian one, as suggested by the quote.
Whether the basic principles of morality be teleological or deontological,
it is conceivable that human conduct will more nearly accord with them
if people act upon some other principle(s) rather than attempting to
implement them directly.[9]

II

Both sides, I've said, assume that corporations have responsibilities.
But, strictly speaking, this assumption isn't warranted. Corporations
aren't living, rational beings and accordingly can't have obligations and
responsibilities or be proper objects of moral praise or blame.[10] Even if
they were, there would be no considerations, moral or otherwise, bearing
upon their conduct which wouldn't bear equally upon the conduct of
individuals who stand in the appropriate relationships to them (e.g., as
directors, managers, stockholders) so that any obligations corporations
had would devolve ultimately upon persons. Thus there is no advantage
to hypostatizing corporations. They have life only through the choices
and decisions of individual persons. We nevertheless do speak of corporations as acting and making decisions as though they were persons, and
there is no harm in this so long as it is understood that such talk must
be transposable into statements about the conduct of individuals—not
necessarily without remainder, but with sufficient completeness to enable
us to formulate the appropriate moral judgments about the latter.

Bearing this in mind, let us ask whether corporations, understood now
in the manner indicated, have moral responsibilities, as the moralist
affirms and the classicist denies. It might seem evident that they do, but
there are two lines of argument by which this view might be challenged.

The first is to contend that morality has no application to corporations
at all, and for that reason that the imputation to corporations of moral
responsibilities makes no sense. The second is to allow that corporations
are governed by morality but to maintain that it is a morality of a different
type than applies to individuals—a collective as opposed to a personal

morality—so that although corporations can have responsibilities of the former sort, they can't of the latter.

The first view can be handled with dispatch. The reply to it is implicit in what we said above about the relationship between corporate and individual conduct. Corporations can fail to have moral responsibilities only if corporate managers can fail to have moral responsibilities. And this the latter cannot do. No conduct is immune from moral assessment. Behavior sometimes is, as when it is deranged or psychotic. But self-directed, uncoerced action—conduct in the fullest sense of the term—is always appraisable as right or wrong. Morality isn't a compartment of human affairs which we step out of by passing through the door of an executive suite, or assuming public office, or putting on a military uniform. It constrains us in all that we do. To suppose otherwise is to indicate a misunderstanding of what it is all about.

The second, and more challenging, position is suggested by the following passage:

> The individual cannot be moral in independence. The modern business collectives force a collective morality. Just as the individual cannot resist the combination, so individual morality must give place to a more robust or social type.[11]

By "individual" here, the authors mean primarily the shareholder; their concern is with whether he can invest in a morally responsible way. But we can adapt the point to the case of corporate executives and ask whether they, qua corporate executives, are forced into a different morality than that which governs them in their capacity as ordinary persons—whether, if you like, corporations as collectivities unavoidably operate within a different moral framework than individuals.

Notice that the first sentence of the quotation may be taken in a number of ways. It may mean that individuals in independence (1) cannot act morally as opposed to immorally (i.e., cannot do what is morally right), or (2) cannot act morally as opposed to nonmorally (i.e., cannot bring their conduct even within the scope of morality), or (3) cannot be morally effective in changing things. Now (3) is often true of individuals with limited power in large institutions or in society at large. But the problem it highlights is that of how to render right action effective, not that of whether right action is possible. (1) and (2), on the other hand, bear upon our present concern, so let us take them in turn.

The first, adapted to the case of corporate managers, suggests that there is something about the circumstances in which they carry on their work which makes moral conduct impossible. It might be said, for example, that the business system itself is inherently immoral, and that for that reason individuals within it cannot act morally.[12] And if they cannot, it might be added, then corporations, whose actions theirs constitute, cannot act morally, hence cannot have moral responsibilities. But this involves a confusion. It isn't conceptually possible for a person to be in a situation in which all of the alternatives are immoral. It is possible of course to be in a situation in which all of the alternatives are bad; depending upon one's outlook on life that happens rather often. But we're here concerned with right and wrong, not good and bad. The most that follows from the fact that one is in a situation in which all of the alternatives are bad is that all of the alternatives are right or permissible.[13] If "ought" implies "can," and one cannot avoid doing what has bad consequences, then one cannot be obligated to avoid doing what has bad consequences. But if, by hypothesis, all alternatives are immoral, then it should be permissible to do some immoral act, that is, it should be right to do what is wrong—and this is unintelligible. So given that "ought" implies "can," we cannot make sense of saying that one must ever act immorally.

Let us look therefore at interpretation (2). The position it represents would be of little interest, of course, if it held that the imperatives of the two alleged moralities coincide; what it implies is that the morality to which corporations are beholden sanctions conduct that is wrong according to personal morality, and that when there is such a conflict it supersedes the latter. This is a common outlook on the conduct of nations and is equally applicable to that of corporations.

Consider a possible line of reasoning in support of this position. It runs as follows: The ordinary person isn't the architect of the socioeconomic system in which he finds himself, or of the institutions that system comprises. These are given. And unless he dedicates himself to a life of reform or revolution—which, if justified at all, is supererogatory—he can only accept them. The most he can reasonably be expected to do is to conduct himself responsibly in the working out of whatever plan of life he chooses within that framework. A part of that plan may call for a career with a corporation, either because he likes the money, or finds the work rewarding, or simply believes in the value of the institution and of the capitalist system as a whole. Be that as it may, he is no more the creator of the duties and responsibilities attaching to the role he finds himself playing within such an institution than he is of the broader system of which it is a part. He may certainly be able to modify the former to a greater extent than he can the latter, but by and large they are fixed, and he either accepts them or finds another job. If, moreover—in the course, let us say, of managing a corporation or of implementing the decisions of those who do—those duties call for some conduct which in some of his other capacities (citizen, neighbor, Christian, Jew, etc.) would be adjudged wrong, he should allow the former to override the latter. Only in that way can he avoid obstructing the relatively smooth operation of the system which provides the setting for these other roles and makes the quality of life associated with them possible. Thus he cannot but recognize two different, and at some points incongruent, moralities, and to allow the higher, the collective, to override the lower, the personal.

This is a sketch of *an* argument, I say, for the recognition of two moralities. It's oversimplified, of course, but one can see the direction in which it moves and feel some of its force. It's true that it would commit us to an extreme form of moral relativism. If what the individual is permitted or even obligated to do from the standpoint of one morality is prohibited by the other, then one and the same act would be both right and wrong. One then either does whatever he pleases, which is tantamount to disregarding morality from the start, or he allows one of these moralities to supersede the other, as the argument intends. Despite this problem, it's the only line of reasoning in support of this conclusion that I find remotely plausible. Yet it is unsatisfactory for two reasons.

The first is that it is difficult to render fully intelligible the judgment that one morality ought to override the other, much less to provide a basis for that judgment. For the "ought" it contains is either moral or nonmoral. If it is moral, and set in one of the competing moralities itself, then there is no more reason to accede to it than to its counterpart in the opposing morality. If, on the other hand, it is nonmoral, then it must represent a point of view from which one can judge the imperatives of morality—and not only judge them (which one can do in any event from such points of view as self-interest, economics, national interest, and so on) but judge them with authority. And there is no such point of view. There is no higher appeal than to morality—certainly not to the point of view of business or economics, since that already has representation in the collective morality, and it is the latter's claim to supremacy over the individual morality that is at issue. What is needed is a vantage point outside of both moralities from which to choose between them with authority. And there is no such vantage point.

It is tempting to respond at this point that the collective morality should supersede the personal because there is a greater good to be achieved by it, and that that good (principal parts of which would be social cohesion and stability) is a precondition of whatever is of value in the personal morality. People simply cannot maintain the quality of life they enjoy, or carry out the responsibilities and obligations of personal morality, apart from the broader social context made possible by the collective morality.[14]

The thought behind this argument—that the best lives are possible only within a social context—may be granted. Philosophers from Plato to the present have made that same point in various ways (differing, of course, over what kind of social context is required). But this doesn't establish the existence of two moralities, much less the supremacy of one over the other. This can be shown by turning to the second reason why the main argument is unsatisfactory.

The second and principal reason why the main argument is unsatisfactory is that its conclusion is a non sequitur. One might grant virtually all of its premises without conceding the conclusion. Whatever concrete moral judgments one holds with regard to the priorities of business and economic conduct *vis-à-vis* interpersonal conduct can be defended without the assumption of different moralities. One need only say that there are within morality conflicting prima facie obligations, and that these often confront the corporate executive. The problems they pose may be vexing. Indeed, one cannot overstate the complexity of some of the dilemmas corporate managers face when confronted with the interests of shareholders on one side, and those of employees and society (and perhaps other societies as well in the case of multinationals) on the other. But it doesn't advance our understanding of these dilemmas, or aid in their resolution, to think that they arise because of competing moralities.

The response to our first objection, which stated that collective morality should supersede personal morality, can now be dealt with by saying that if it is indeed true (and we're not now challenging the correctness of this claim, though one well might) that, when they conflict, the prima facie social imperative to preserve a certain kind of status quo in society outweighs the more immediate prima facie obligations of personal life, this means only that what morality dictates on balance is that our obligation lies ultimately on the side of society. Nothing in this requires the postulation of two moralities. Whatever we may want to say on either side of this issue can be accommodated within the framework of a single morality. This doesn't, of course, prevent one from assuming that there are two moralities nonetheless, but it shows that assumption to be otiose.

III

If what we have said is correct, then although both the Liberal and Conservative positions can be held on either moral or nonmoral grounds, only the moral can justify either position. This means that corporations do indeed have moral responsibilities. But what those responsibilities are, and specifically whether they include social responsibilities in the sense under consideration, remains open.

We can nevertheless answer this latter question, at least in part, on the basis of our findings thus far.

To do this, let us consider what social responsibilities corporations might be alleged to have. These break down,[15] first, into internal and external responsibilities: the internal being to employees, and pertaining to such matters as working conditions, benefits, job training, and the like; the external being all those which are not internal, and pertaining to such things as racial and sexual discrimination, pollution, depletion of natural resources, and urban decay. Though often neglected by both sides to the debate, there are also possible external responsibilities of the same sort as those just characterized, but extending beyond our own society. These are particularly relevant in assessing problems raised by multinational corporations, whose operations have direct consequences for persons in foreign countries.[16] Additionally, there are those responsibilities related to social costs and those which are not. Social costs have been characterized in different ways, but we may follow Kapp in taking them to cover

> all direct and indirect losses suffered by third persons or the general public as a result of private economic activities. . . . all those harmful consequences and damages which third persons or the community sustain as a result of the productive process.[17]

Social costs would include losses resulting from pollution, destruction of wildlife habitats, relocation of corporations, and so forth. Non social cost related responsibilities would include obligations to support charities, to contribute to universities, or to open facilities to the public for recreational use. Possible social responsibilities thus break down as follows:

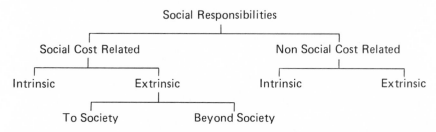

Now whether or not corporations have any obligation to do good, that is, have responsibilities in the area of non social cost related matters, it is clear that they have an obligation not to do harm. That is, they have at least a prima facie duty of nonmaleficence.[18] If there are any duties at all, we all have such a duty, corporation managers included. It is morally wrong for corporations to deceive the public into thinking that harmful drugs are beneficial, or that unsafe automobiles are safe, or knowingly to allow employees to work under conditions detrimental to health; all of these are wrong whether or not in violation of any laws. Moreover, if corporations have a duty of nonmaleficence, then it is plausible to maintain that they also have a duty of reparation when they have acted maleficently. The mere fact of having caused harm[19] creates a prima facie obligation to remedy that harm. This doesn't mean that every conceivable harm is of sufficient importance to require remedy, or that it will be possible to remedy all harms, or that all harms can even be calculated. Nor does it mean that every corporate action with social costs is wrong; if that were so, little that corporations do would be justified. Many social costs are offset by sufficient benefits as to be justified on balance.[20] What it does mean is that corporations have at least *some* social cost related responsibilities.

What specific social responsibilities a given corporation has this doesn't tell us, of course. To do that would require a case-by-case examination of alleged harms. The preceding doesn't in principle even presuppose that any corporation has in fact ever harmed anyone. All it says is that corporations have a moral obligation *not* to harm anyone, and that they owe reparations for such harm if it occurs. If that much is granted, then corporations have a social responsibility and the conservative position is refuted. The only questions remaining—and they are of the first importance, but from a practical moral standpoint, not that of the fundamental philosophical issue—concern which corporations have which responsibilities, and which responsibilities should take precedence in cases of conflict. These deserve the most thorough analysis and discussion. But the debate over whether corporations have social responsibilities should be put to rest.

Notes

1. Within the limits of the law it is usually assumed, though not always stated, that the responsibilities of a corporation are purely economic.
2. Milton Friedman virtually defines "social responsibility" in such a way that it must conflict with the interests of a corporation. See his "The Social Responsibility of Business Is to Increase Its Profits," *The New York Times Magazine,* September 13, 1970. For other statements of his views on this general topic, see also his *Capitalism and Freedom* (Chicago: University of Chicago Press, 1962), Chap. VIII; and "Milton Friedman Responds," A *Business and Society* Interview, *Business and Society,* Spring 1972, No. 1, 5–17.
3. Theodore Levitt, for example, says that business involvement in social issues yields the frightening spectacle of ". . . a powerful economic functional group whose future and perception are shaped in a tight materialistic context of money and things but which imposes its narrow ideas about a broad spectrum of unrelated noneconomic subjects on the mass of man and society"; in "The Dangers of Social Responsibility," *Harvard Business Review,* September–October 1958, p. 44. See also his "Business Should Stay Out of Politics," *Business Horizons,* 3 (1960), 45–51.
4. We have used "responsibilities" ambiguously here, as it is often used in discussions of this topic. In the first occurrence it is roughly synonymous with "obligations"; in the second, with "voluntarily undertaken commitments."
5. Following Clarence C. Walton, *Corporate Social Responsibilities* (Belmont, Calif.: Wadsworth Publishing Co., 1967), p. 54.
6. Widely accepted in one form or another as a principle of rationality in much of contemporary social science.
7. See, for example, Melvin Anshen, "The Socially Responsible Corporation: From Concept to Implementation," in *Managing the Socially Responsible Corporation* (New York: Macmillan, 1974), p. 6; and George Steiner, *Business and Society* (New York: Random House, 1971), p. 144. This outlook is explicit in an advertisement by the Eastman Kodak Company in which, after describing their various efforts at socially responsible action, they say: "In short, it's simply good business. And we're in business to make a profit. But in furthering our business interests, we also further society's interests." Reprinted in Robert Baum, ed., *Ethical Arguments for Analysis,* 2nd ed. (New York: Holt, Rinehart & Winston, 1976), p. 210.
8. *The Wealth of Nations,* Bk. V, Ch. II.
9. This view gains in credibility if one thinks, with Dewey, for example, that the end, say, of utilitarianism is just too remote to be an effective guide to practical conduct, and that more accessible ends—ends-in-view—are a better guide to the realization of social good.
10. As Friedman maintains. See "The Social Responsibility of Corporations Is to Increase Its Profits," and "Milton Friedman Responds," A *Business and Society* Interview.
11. John Dewey and James H. Tufts, *Ethics* (New York: Henry Holt & Co., 1908), p. 519.
12. This view is suggested by Robert Freedman, Jr., in "The Challenge of Business Ethics," in William T. Greenwood, ed., *Issues in Business and Society,* 1st ed. (Boston: Houghton Mifflin Co., 1964), p. 307.
13. And even this follows only if the alternatives are equally bad and if there are no other overriding moral considerations.

14. Robert L. Heilbroner acknowledges the force behind some of this reasoning even while sharply attacking corporations: "Thus when corporations rape the environment or abuse us as guinea pigs, suddenly we awaken to the realities of our individual powerlessness *and of our dependence on their smooth and presumably benign functioning.*" In Robert L. Heilbroner and others, *In the Name of Profit* (New York: Doubleday & Co., 1972), pp. 235f.

15. Following Steiner, *Business and Society,* p. 141.

16. There are at least two dimensions to this problem. On the one hand there is the question of whether corporations should operate in countries like South Africa, which institutionalize racism (or engage in equally objectionable practices). On the other hand, there is the question of whether corporations should transfer production to other countries at all, if the effect is to export employment from the United States to countries with large labor forces employable at cheaper wages (on this, see Richard J. Barnet and Ronald E. Muller, "U.S. Unemployment Is Clearly Affected by the Spread of Multinationals," *The New York Times,* December 22, 1974). The former raises the question of whether corporations have social responsibilities to the citizens of other countries; the latter whether, even if they do, responsibilities to citizens of our own country override those in case of conflict.

17. K. William Kapp, *The Social Costs of Private Enterprise* (New York: Schocken Books, 1950), pp. 13f.

18. In this and what follows I am following the analysis of W. D. Ross in *The Right and the Good* (Oxford: The Clarendon Press, 1930).

19. And by "harm" I mean that which makes one worse off on balance.

20. Whether being offset by benefits is sufficient to justify all social costs, for example, in terms of the rights of persons who may not prefer the benefit over the cost, is a matter we cannot go into at present.

THE RESPONSIBILITIES OF CORPORATIONS AND THEIR OWNERS

John G. Simon
Charles W. Powers
Jon P. Gunnemann

For better or worse, the modern American business corporation is increasingly being asked to assume more responsibility for social problems and the public welfare. How corporate responsibility is understood,

From *The Ethical Investor: Universities and Corporate Responsibility* by John G. Simon, Charles W. Powers, and Jon P. Gunnemann. Copyright © 1972 by Yale University Press, New Haven, Conn. Reprinted by permission of the publisher.

and whether it is perceived to be for better or worse, may depend in the last analysis on the beholder's emotional reaction to the corporation itself: one either extols the corporation as part of the creative process or condemns it as the work of the Devil. Thus, almost four centuries ago the English jurist Sir Edward Coke wrote of corporations that "they cannot commit treason nor be outlawed nor excommunicated for they have no souls," while more recently Justice Louis D. Brandeis characterized the corporation as the "master instrument of civilized life. . . ."[1]

Our analysis of the controversies surrounding the notion of corporate responsibility—and the suggestion that the university as an investor should be concerned with corporate responsibility—proceeds in large part from our approach to certain issues in the area of social responsibility and public morals. In particular, we (1) make a distinction between negative injunctions and affirmative duties; (2) assert that all men have the "moral minimum" obligation not to impose social injury; (3) delineate those conditions under which one is held responsible for social injury, even where it is not clear that the injury was self-caused; and (4) take a position in the argument between those who strive for moral purity and those who strive for moral effectiveness.

NEGATIVE INJUNCTIONS AND AFFIRMATIVE DUTIES

A distinction which informs much of our discussion differentiates between injunctions against activities that injure others and duties which require the affirmative pursuit of some good. The failure to make this distinction in debate on public ethics often results in false dichotomies, a point illustrated by an article which appeared just over a decade ago in the *Harvard Business Review*. In that article, which provoked considerable debate in the business community, Theodore Levitt argued against corporate social responsibility both because it was dangerous for society and because it detracted from the primary goal of business, the making of profit. We deal with the merits of these arguments later; what is important for our immediate purpose, however, is Levitt's designation of those activities and concerns which constitute social responsibility. He notes that the corporation has become "more concerned about the needs of its employees, about schools, hospitals, welfare agencies and even aesthetics," and that it is "fashionable . . . for the corporation to show that it is a great innovator; more specifically, a great public benefactor; and, very particularly, that it exists 'to serve the public.' "[2] Having so delimited the notion of corporate responsibility, Levitt presents the reader with a choice between, on the one hand, getting involved in the management of society, "creating munificence for one and all," and, on the other hand, fulfilling the profit-making function. But such a choice excludes another meaning of corporate responsibility: the making of profits in such a way as to minimize social injury. Levitt at no point considers the possibility that business activity may at times injure others and that it may be necessary to regulate the social consequences of one's business activities accordingly. . . .

Our public discourse abounds with similar failures to distinguish between positive and perhaps lofty ideals and minimal requirements of social organization. During the election campaigns of the 1950's and the civil rights movement of the early 1960's, the slogan, "You can't legislate morality," was a popular cry on many fronts. Obviously, we have not succeeded in devising laws that create within our citizens a predisposition to love and kindness; but we can devise laws which will minimize the injury that one citizen must suffer at the hands of another. Although the virtue of love may be the possession of a few, justice—in the minimal sense of not injuring others—can be required of all.

The distinction between negative injunctions and affirmative duties is old, having roots in common law and equity jurisprudence.[3] Here it is based on the premise that it is easier to specify and enjoin a civil wrong than to state what should be done. In the Ten Commandments, affirmative duties are spelled out only for one's relations with God and parents; for the more public relationships, we are given only the negative injunction: "Thou shalt not. . . ." Similarly, the Bill of Rights contains only negative injunctions.

AVOIDANCE AND CORRECTION OF SOCIAL INJURY AS A "MORAL MINIMUM"

We do not mean to distinguish between negative injunctions and affirmative duties solely in the interests of analytical precision. The negative injunction to avoid and correct social injury threads its way through all morality. We call it a "moral minimum," implying that however one may choose to limit the concept of social responsibility, one cannot exclude this negative injunction. Although reasons may exist why certain persons or institutions cannot or should not be required to pursue moral or social good in all situations, there are many fewer reasons why one should be excused from the injunction against injuring others. Any citizen, individual or institutional, may have competing obligations which could, under some circumstances, override this negative injunction. But these special circumstances do not wipe away the prima facie obligation to avoid harming others.

In emphasizing the central role of the negative injunction, we do not suggest that affirmative duties are never important. A society where citizens go well beyond the requirement to avoid damage to others will surely be a better community. But we do recognize that individuals exhibit varying degrees of commitment to promote affirmatively the public welfare, whereas we expect everyone equally to refrain from injuring others.

The view that all citizens are equally obligated to avoid or correct any social injury which is self-caused finds support in our legal as well as our moral tradition. H. L. A. Hart and A. M. Honoré have written:

> In the moral judgments of ordinary life, we have occasion to blame people because they have caused harm to others, and also, if less frequently, to insist that morally they are bound to compensate those to whom they have

caused harm. These are the moral analogues of more precise legal conceptions: for, in all legal systems liability to be punished or to make compensation frequently depends on whether actions (or omissions) have caused harm. Moral blame is not of course confined to such cases of causing harm.[4]

We know of no societies, from the literature of anthropology or comparative ethics, whose moral codes do not contain some injunction against harming others. The specific notion of *harm* or *social injury* may vary, as well as the mode of correction and restitution, but the injunctions are present.

In using the term *moral minimum* to describe this obligation, we mean to avoid any suggestion that the injunction against doing injury to others can serve as the basis for deriving the full content of morality. Moreover, we have used an expression which does not imply that the injunction is in any way dependent upon a natural law point of view. A person who subscribed to some form of natural law theory might indeed agree with our position, but so could someone who maintained that all morality is based on convention, agreement, or contract. Social contract theorists have generally maintained that the granting of rights to individuals by mutual consent involves some limitation on the actions of all individuals in the contract: to guarantee the liberty of all members, it is essential that each be enjoined against violating the rights of others.[5]

We asserted earlier that it is easier to enjoin and correct a wrong than it is to prescribe affirmatively what is good for society and what ought to be done. Notions of the public good and the values that men actively seek to implement are subjects of intense disagreement. In this realm, pluralism is almost inevitable, and some would argue that it is healthy. Yet there can also be disagreement about what constitutes social injury or harm. What some people think are affirmative duties may be seen by others as correction of social injury. For example, the notion that business corporations should make special effort to train and employ members of minority groups could be understood by some to fulfill an affirmative duty on the part of corporations to meet society's problems; but it could be interpreted by others as the correction of a social injury caused by years of institutional racism. As a more extreme example, a Marxist would in all probability contend that *all* corporate activity is socially injurious and that therefore all social pursuits by corporations are corrective responses rather than affirmative actions.[6]

Although the notion of *social injury* is imprecise and although many hard cases will be encountered in applying it, we think that it is a helpful designation and that cases can be decided on the basis of it. In the law, many notions (such as *negligence* in the law of torts or *consideration* in the law of contracts) are equally vague but have received content from repeated decision-making over time. We would hope that under our proposed Guidelines similar "case law" would develop. Moreover, our Guidelines attempt to give some content to the notion of *social injury* by referring to external norms: *social injury* is defined as "particularly including activities which violate, or frustrate the enforcement of, rules of domestic or international law intended to protect individuals against deprivation of health, safety or basic freedoms."[7]

In sum, we would affirm the prima facie obligation of all citizens, both individual and institutional, to avoid and correct self-caused social injury. Much more in the way of affirmative acts may be expected of certain kinds of citizens, but none is exempt from this "moral minimum."

In some cases it may not be true—or at least it may not be clear—that one has caused or helped to cause social injury, and yet one may bear responsibility for correcting or averting the injury. We consider next the circumstances under which this responsibility may arise.

NEED, PROXIMITY, CAPABILITY, AND LAST RESORT (THE KEW GARDENS PRINCIPLE)

Several years ago the public was shocked by the news accounts of the stabbing and agonizingly slow death of Kitty Genovese in the Kew Gardens section of New York City while thirty-eight people watched or heard and did nothing.[8] What so deeply disturbed the public's moral sensibilities was that in the face of a critical human need, people who were close to that need and had the power to do something about it failed to act.

The public's reaction suggests that, no matter how narrowly one may conceive of social responsibility, there are some situations in which a combination of circumstances thrusts upon us an obligation to respond. Life is fraught with emergency situations in which a failure to respond is a special form of violation of the negative injunction against causing social injury: a sin of omission becomes a sin of commission.

Legal responsibility for aiding someone in cases of grave distress or injury, even when caused by another, is recognized by many European civil codes and by the criminal laws of one of our states:

> (A) A person who knows that another is exposed to grave physical harm shall, to the extent that the same can be rendered without danger or peril to himself or without interference with important duties owed to others, give reasonable assistance to the exposed person unless that assistance or care is being provided by others....
> (C) A person who wilfully violates subsection (A) of this section shall be fined not more than $100.00.[9]

This Vermont statute recognizes that it is not reasonable in all cases to require a person to give assistance to someone who is endangered. If such aid imperils himself, or interferes with duties owed to others, or if there are others providing the aid, the person is excepted from the obligation. These conditions of responsibility give some shape to difficult cases and are in striking parallel with the conditions which existed at Kew Gardens. The salient features of the Kitty Genovese case are (1) critical need; (2) the proximity of the thirty-eight spectators; (3) the capability of the spectators to act helpfully (at least to telephone the police); and (4) the absence of other (including official) help; i.e., the thirty-eight were the last resort. There would, we believe, be widespread agreement that a moral obligation to aid another arises when these four features are present. What we have called the "moral minimum" (the duty to avoid and correct self-caused social injury) is an obvious and easy example of fulfillment of these criteria—so obvious that there is little need to go through step-by-step analysis of these factors. Where the injury is not clearly self-caused, the application of these criteria aids in deciding responsibility. We have called this combination of features governing difficult cases the "Kew Gardens Principle." There follows a more detailed examination of each of the features:

Need. In cases where the other three criteria are constant, increased need increases responsibility. Just as there is no precise definition of social injury (one kind of need), there is no precise definition of need or way of measuring its extent.

Proximity. The thirty-eight witnesses of the Genovese slaying were geographically close to the deed. But proximity to a situation of need is not necessarily spatial. Proximity is largely a function of notice: we hold a person blameworthy if he knows of imperilment and does not do what he reasonably can do to remedy the situation. Thus, the thirty-eight at Kew Gardens were delinquent not because they were near but because nearness enabled them to know that someone was in need. A deaf person who could not hear the cries for help would not be considered blameworthy even if he were closer than those who could hear. So also, a man in Afghanistan is uniquely responsible for the serious illness of a man in Peoria, Illinois, if he has knowledge of the man's illness, if he can telephone a doctor about it, and if he alone has that notice. When we become aware of a wrongdoing or a social injury, we take on obligations that we did not have while ignorant.

Notice does not exhaust the meaning of proximity, however. It is reasonable to maintain that the sick man's neighbors in Peoria were to some extent blameworthy if they made no effort to inquire into the man's welfare. Ignorance cannot always be helped, but we do expect certain persons and perhaps institutions to look harder for information about critical need.[10] In this sense, proximity has to do with the network of social expectations that flow from notions of civic duty, duties to one's family, and so on. Thus, we expect a man to be more alert to the plight of his next-door neighbor than to the needs of a child in East Pakistan, just as we expect a man to be more alert to the situation of his own children than to the problems of the family down the block. The failure of the man to act in conformance with this expectation does not give him actual notice of need, but it creates what the law would call *constructive notice.* Both factors—actual notice and constructive notice growing out of social expectation—enter into the determination of responsibility and blame.

Capability. Even if there is a need to which a person has proximity, that person is not usually held responsible unless there is something he can reasonably be expected to do to meet the need. To follow Immanuel Kant, *ought* assumes *can.* What one is reasonably capable of doing, of course, admits to some variety of interpretation. In the Kew Gardens incident, it might not have been reasonable to expect someone to place his body between the girl and the knife. It was surely reasonable to expect someone to call the police. So also it would not seem to be within the canons of reasonability for a university to sacrifice education for charity. . . . But if the university is able, by non-self-sacrificial means, to mitigate injury caused by a company of which it is an owner, it would not seem unreasonable to ask it to do so.

Last Resort. In the emergency situations we have been describing, one becomes more responsible the less likely it is that someone else will be able to aid. Physical proximity is a factor here, as is time. If the knife is drawn, one cannot wait for the policeman. It is important to note here that determination of last resort becomes more difficult the more complex the social situation or organization. The man on the road to Jericho, in spite of the presence of a few other travelers, probably had a fairly good notion that he was the only person who could help the man attacked by thieves. But on a street in New York City, there is always the hope that someone else will step forward to give aid. Surely this rationalization entered into the silence of each of the thirty-eight: there were, after all, thirty-seven others. Similarly, within large corporations it is difficult to know not only whether one alone has notice of a wrongdoing, but also whether there is anyone else who is able to respond. Because of this diffusion of responsibility in complex organizations and societies, the notion of last resort is less useful than the other Kew Gardens criteria in determining whether one ought to act in aid of someone in need or to avert or correct social injury. Failure to act because one hopes someone else will act—or because one is trying to find out who is the last resort —may frequently lead to a situation in which no one acts at all.[11] This fact, we think, places more weight on the first three features of the Kew Gardens Principle in determining responsibility, and it creates a presumption in favor of taking action when those three conditions are present.[12]

Notes

1. We are indebted for the juxtaposition of these two quotes to Harris Wofford, president of Bryn Mawr College. From some points of view, of course, being the "master instrument of civilized life" is to be convicted of soullessness.

   Debate about the corporation in American society and about its desirability in a democratic nation goes back at least to the writers of the American Constitution: Hamilton wanted to give the federal government the power to issue corporate charters for the purpose of promoting trade and industry; Madison felt that corporations would prevent men from participating in public action and were thus a threat to freedom. The debate was resolved in Madison's favor—although in later years some federal charters were issued.

   For a brief discussion of the early debates between the Jeffersonians and the Hamiltonians, see Harvey C. Bunke, *A Primer on American Economic History* (New York, 1969), Ch. 3, and Edwin M. Epstein, *The Corporation in American Politics* (Englewood Cliffs, N.J., 1969). For fuller discussion, see Oscar and

Mary Handlin, "Origins of the American Business Corporation," *Journal of Economic History* 5 (May 1945), and Joseph S. David, *Essays in the Earlier History of American Corporations* vol. 2 (Cambridge, Mass., 1917).

2. Theodore Levitt, "The Dangers of Social Responsibility," in Marshall, ed., *Business and Government,* pp. 22–23.

3. We are grateful to President Edward Bloustein of Rutgers University for suggesting this terminology and for inviting our attention to its historical antecedents. Further analysis of the distinction between *negative injunctions* and *affirmative duties* is given in the following sections of this chapter.

4. H. L. A. Hart and A. M. Honoré, *Causation in the Law* (Oxford, 1959), p. 59.

5. Jeremy Bentham wrote that "... [A]ll rights are made at the expense of liberty.... [There is] no right without a correspondent obligation.... All coercive law, therefore ... and in particular all laws creative of liberty, are, as far as they go, abrogative of liberty." "Anarchical Fallacies," in *Society, Law and Morality,* ed. F. A. Olafsson (Englewood Cliffs, N.J., 1961), p. 350. Clearly, Bentham understood that any creation of rights or liberties under the law entailed recognition of an injunction against violating the rights of others.

6. The notion of social injury may also change over time. External norms in the form of government regulations now provide that failure to actively recruit minority group members constitutes discrimination, i.e., is a matter of social injury. See the "affirmative action" requirements, including recruiting measures, imposed on all federal contractors by the federal "contract compliance" regulations. 41 *Code of Federal Regulations,* Section 60–62. At one time, such recruitment was not subject to a negative injunction.

7. We do not suggest that social injury is identical to violation of the legal norms to which we are referring. (In other words, we recognize that some laws themselves cause social injury in the eyes of many persons, and also that not all social injury is prohibited by law.) We are only saying that reference to legal norms will help individuals and institutions to make their own judgments about social injury.

8. See A. M. Rosenthal, *Thirty-Eight Witnesses* (New York, 1964).

9. "Duty to Aid the Endangered Act," *Vt. Stat. Ann.,* Ch. 12, § 519 (Supp. 1968). See G. Hughes, "Criminal Omissions," 67 *Yale L. J.* 590 (1958).

10. See, for example, Albert Speer's reflection on his role during the Hitler regime: "For being in a position to know and nevertheless shunning knowledge creates direct responsibility for the consequences—from the very beginning." *Inside the Third Reich* (New York, 1970), p. 19.

11. Failure to respond to need in social situations may also have another effect, equally detrimental to public morality: it suggests to others who might have stepped forward that the situation is really not serious. Thus, two psychologists, John M. Darley and Bibb Latané, after conducting experiments on social reaction to simulated emergencies, concluded that "it is possible for a state of 'pluralistic ignorance' to develop, in which each bystander is led by the apparent lack of concern of the others to interpret the situation as being less serious than he would if alone. To the extent that he does not feel the situation is an emergency, he will be unlikely to take any helpful action." Darley and Latané, *The Unresponsive Bystander: Why Doesn't He Help?* (New York, 1970), cited by Israel Shenker, *New York Times,* 10 April 1971, p. 25. The latter article was based on a separate experiment conducted by Prof. Darley and Dr. C. Daniel Batson at Princeton Theological Seminary designed to determine why people do not help. A group of students were given biblical

texts to record, then given individual directions to the recording studio that required them to pass a writhing, gasping student lying in a doorway. It was found that the only significant differentiating factor in determining whether a student stopped to aid was the amount of time he thought he had; those who were told that they were late for the recording session stopped to help much less often (10 per cent) than those who were told that they had sufficient time (63 per cent). It made no statistical difference that half of the seminary students had been given the Parable of the Good Samaritan to record.

12. We do not invoke the Kew Gardens Principle to establish corporate responsibility for clearly self-caused social harm, but rather to demonstrate how shareholders—who may not appear to be directly involved in corporate-caused injury—are obligated to attempt to avert or avoid such injury.

FIVE PROPOSITIONS FOR SOCIAL RESPONSIBILITY

Keith Davis

Business's need for social response and social responsibility has been discussed loudly and at length. What does it all mean? One way to understand the issues is to examine the basic propositions offered in the social responsibility debate.

Modern society presents business with immensely complicated problems. Technology has advanced to a level that tests intellectual capacities, markets have become more complex and international in scope, and difficult new problems of social issues and social responsibility have arisen. In earlier periods, the mission of business was clear. It was strictly an economic one—to produce the best quality of goods and services at the lowest possible price and to distribute them effectively. The accomplishment of this mission was remarkably effective, so effective that large numbers of the population found their minimum economic needs reasonably satisfied and began to turn their thoughts toward other needs.

Beginning in the 1950s, the public's mood shifted sharply toward social concerns, and this mood was reflected in extensive social demands made on institutions. Since business interacts extensively with all of society, perhaps more of these demands were made on business than any other institution. By sticking strictly to its economic role in the past,

From *Business Horizons*, Vol. XVIII, no. 3, June 1975. Copyright © 1975 by the Foundation for the School of Business at Indiana University. Reprinted by permission.

business had left the social side of its activities largely untended and was unprepared to deal effectively with social issues. However, the public also was unprepared for its new role as social protagonist, and, as a result, churning and ferment have marked discussion of social priorities, how they are to be accomplished, and what role business should play in this accomplishment.

After more than twenty years of controversy, the debate over business and social issues has now reached some maturity. Out of this maturity, a degree of uniform support is developing for certain social propositions to guide the conduct of business as well as of other institutions. These guidelines apply to a greater or lesser degree according to individual circumstances, but the important point is that they do apply. Intelligent businessmen will take heed of these guidelines if they wish to avoid unnecessary confrontations with society. This article examines five of these guidelines which are supported by a degree of consensus. These guidelines collectively will be called the social responsibility mode.

SOCIAL RESPONSIBILITY AND POWER

One basic proposition is that *social responsibility arises from social power.* Modern business has immense social power in such areas as minority employment and environmental pollution. If business has the power, then a just relationship demands that business also bear responsibility for its actions in these areas. Social responsibility arises from concern about the consequences of business's acts as they affect the interests of others. Business decisions do have social consequences. Businessmen cannot make decisions that are solely economic decisions, because they are inter-related with the whole social system. This situation requires that busi-nessmen's thinking be broadened beyond the company gate to the whole social system. Systems thinking is required.

Social responsibility implies that a business decision maker in the process of serving his own business interests is obliged to take actions that also protect and enhance society's interests. The net effect is to improve the quality of life in the broadest possible way, however quality of life is defined by society. In this manner, harmony is achieved between business's actions and the larger social system. The businessman becomes concerned with social as well as economic outputs and with the total effect of his institutional actions on society.

Business institutions that ignore responsibility for their social power are threatened by what Keith Davis and Robert L. Blomstrom call the Iron Law of Responsibility: "In the long run, those who do not use power in a manner which society considers responsible will tend to lose it."[1] The record of history has supported operation of this law as one institution after another has found its power either eroded or overthrown when it fails to use power responsibly. The implication for business is that, if it wishes to retain its viability and significance as a major social institution, then it must give responsible attention to social issues.

The fundamental assumption of this model is that society has entrusted to business large amounts of society's resources to accomplish its mission, and business is expected to manage these resources as a wise trustee for society. In addition to the traditional role of economic entrepreneurship, business now has a new social role of trusteeship. As trustee for society's resources, it serves the interests of all claimants on the organization, rather than only those of owners, or consumers, or labor. . . .

AN OPEN SYSTEM INTERFACE

A second basic proposition is that *business shall operate as a two-way open system with open receipt of inputs from society and open disclosure of its operations to the public.* An open interface in both directions is essential. Business has been charged with consistently turning a deaf ear toward many of the inputs directed toward it. The executive suite has been geared to send messages but not to receive them. Under the best of conditions, business has offered an untrained ear to social inputs so that it misunderstood the message or heard only selected parts.

The social responsibility model expects business to turn both a sensitive and a trained ear to social needs and wants. If these inputs do not flow freely from society, perhaps because of society's past frustrations with communication efforts, business will seek them just as avidly as it seeks market information for traditional economic purposes. Business must know what is going on in society if business is to respond to social needs.

With regard to business communication outputs, the charge is that most outward communication has been a public relations facade, usually revealing the good but rarely the bad about business products or operations. The social responsibility model, however, postulates a policy of full disclosure in which both product and social data about a firm are available in the same way that economic data are now available. To accomplish the objective of full disclosure the social audit is proposed.[2] Such an audit would serve the same purpose in social areas that an accounting audit serves in economic areas. It is a necessary instrument to determine whether a business has been using its social assets responsibly. It shows where progress has been made and where deficiencies remain. It is a useful guide to management for improving its performance, a check and balance on mismanagement of resources, and an open disclosure to those with a bona fide interest in social performance.

The model of the social audit is, of course, an ideal. At the present, it is hardly operational and decades may pass before it reaches the proficiency of today's accounting audits, but it is a justifiable model in support of an open business system. Though the ideal of open communication probably can never be reached fully because of inherent difficulties in the communication process, the social responsibility model postulates that considerable improvement is both possible and necessary.

Some aspects of consumerism are examples of the beginning of open disclosure. For example, the public has insisted that installment debt charges be fully disclosed, that grocery prices allow comparative price shopping, that containers not be misleading, and that labels disclose the dangers of products.

CALCULATION OF SOCIAL COSTS

A third basic proposition is that *social costs as well as benefits of an activity, product, or service shall be thoroughly calculated and considered in order to decide whether to proceed with it.* In the past, business has been required to consider only two factors in deciding whether to proceed with an activity. These factors were technical feasibility and economic profitability. If they were favorable, the activity was launched. Now business has a third factor to consider—the social effect of an activity. Only if all factors are favorable is it safe to proceed.

In making these kinds of decisions, both short- and long-run costs must be considered. For example, a firm that builds row upon row of look-alike houses may be saving $500 on each house and passing along $400 of the saving to each buyer, thus serving consumer interests. In the long run, however, this kind of construction may encourage the rapid development of a city slum. In this instance, the lack of a long-range outlook may result in serious social costs.

Long-run cost data need to be diligently sought; business cannot assume that if nothing negative is evident, there is no problem. The automobile industry, for example, is faulted for the myopic vision that prevented it from perceiving the serious environmental problems that developed from automobile emissions. Even though it was a transportation expert on which the public depended, the industry was unable to foresee and prevent the environmental degradation that resulted from its products. Similarly, the chemical industry did not foresee the health-damaging effects of vinyl chloride gas even though it was known as a powerful chemical.

If better forecasting cannot be developed, then is it worthwhile to initiate potentially damaging activities even when they bring short-run benefits? In the future, for example, extreme caution may be required for introduction of new products from dangerous chemical families.

In sum, the expectation of the social responsibility model is that a detailed cost/benefit analysis will be made prior to determining whether to proceed with an activity and that social costs will be given significant weight in the decision-making process. Almost any business action will entail some social costs. The basic question is whether the benefits outweigh the costs so that there is a net social benefit. Many questions of judgment arise, and there are no precise mathematical measures in the social field, but rational and wise judgments can be made if the issues are first thoroughly explored.

For major business projects, such as the doubling of a plant's capacity and employment in a suburban area, the social responsibility model implies that society may eventually require social impact statements comparable with today's environmental impact statements. Then affected parties could become involved in considering a project before decisions have been made. In other instances, such as the introduction of new drugs, the public wants the government to act in the public's interest through regulatory agencies.

What is being threatened is the business decision-making process itself. Business is expected to make responsible decisions based on thorough examination of costs and benefits and, if necessary, only after those groups affected have been involved, such as a community. If business cannot establish a track record of responsible decisions, then the Iron Law of Responsibility will force business to share its decision-making powers with government and representatives of affected interest groups. Business will have a less free hand in making decisions with a social impact.

THE USER PAYS

A fourth basic proposition is that the *social costs of each activity, product, or service shall be priced into it so that the consumer (user) pays for the effects of his consumption on society.* This philosophy holds that a fair consumer price for a product or service is one that includes all costs of production, including social costs. Historically, society or someone else has had to bear these social costs while the consumer benefited from reduced product prices.

Consider the case of the environment. For the most part, the environment has been an economic free good that a business could use, passing much of the saving on to the consumer. It was a public common available to all without substantial charge. The strip miner could mine coal without the cost of restoring the topsoil, thus providing cheaper electricity for consumers. The steelmaker could use oxygen from the air for his blast furnace without paying society a penny for it, and he also could use the air as a dumping ground for his wastes. Similarly, he could draw water from the river and discharge his wastes into it without paying for this service.

Society placed no economic value on these public commons. They were free goods. Therefore, both the businessman and his customers avoided paying for degradation of the common, and these costs were transferred to society as social costs. This was not a serious problem as long as the load on the common was light, but when it became heavy, society found itself burdened with costs that it did not wish to bear. The social responsibility model assumes that generally society should not bear these costs. The consumer should pay for his consumption, including social costs of preventing pollution. That is a fair price; any other would be unfair to the public or to innocent third parties.

The philosophy that the user pays is a general guide, not a hard and fast rule. There will be many exceptions including instances when the costs are unknown at the time the user makes his purchase or when the costs are so minimal that they will be ignored. In other cases, a remedy may not be technologically feasible and so no costs are established, for example, the removal of sulfate chemicals from the stacks of coal-burning electrical generating stations. Technology is not available for the complete removal of these pollutants, so some are allowed and no additional charge is transmitted to the consumer. Thus he buys his electricity more cheaply than he could if total removal were technologically feasible and the removal equipment required. In other instances, the government may underwrite part of the costs in the name of the public interest, passing costs on to taxpayers rather than to users of that particular product or service.

Nevertheless, the general philosophy that the user pays still applies. The reasoning is that since his consumption incurs the social cost, he should bear as much of it as possible. If the added costs discourage his consumption, the result is still beneficial because certain social costs are avoided.

SOCIAL RESPONSIBILITIES AS CITIZENS

A fifth basic proposition is that *beyond social costs business institutions as citizens have responsibilities for social involvement in areas of their competence where major social needs exist.* The four preceding propositions concern social costs directly caused by business. In the fifth proposition, business actions are only indirectly related to certain social problems, but nevertheless business is obliged to help solve them.

The fifth proposition is based essentially on the reasoning that business is a major social institution that should bear the same kinds of citizenship costs for society that an individual citizen bears. Business will benefit from a better society just as any citizen will benefit; therefore, business has a responsibility to recognize social problems and actively contribute its talents to help solve them.

Such involvement is expected of any citizen, and business should fulfill a citizenship role. Business will not have primary responsibility for solving problems, but it should provide significant assistance. For example, business did not directly cause educational problems, but it does stand to gain some benefit from their solution; therefore, it has some responsibility to help develop and apply solutions.

A MATTER OF HARMONY

The thrust of the foregoing propositions is that business, like any individual, needs to act responsibly regarding the consequences of its actions. The socially responsible organization behaves in such a way that it protects and improves the social quality of life along with its own quality of life. In essence, quality of life refers to the degree to which people live in harmony with their inner spirit, their fellow man, and nature's physical environment. Business has a significant effect on each of these, particularly the last two. It can support harmony among people as well as in the environment if it will take the larger system's view.

Although quality of life embraces harmony, it is not a static concept that seeks to preserve a utopian status quo. Rather, it is a dynamic concept in which people live harmoniously with the changes occurring in nature and in themselves. It is, however, a utopian concept in the sense that most people use it as an ultimate goal that they realize probably will never be obtained absolutely. It is essentially a set of criteria by which judgments may be made about social progress. The social responsibility model seeks to improve the' quality of life through its five propositions.

Certain observations can be made concerning the implementation of the social responsibility model.

First, it applies to all organizations. Although this discussion has been presented in the context of business, the social responsibility model does not single out business for special treatment. All organizations have equal responsibilities for the consequences of their actions.

Similarly, social responsibility applies to all persons in all of their life roles, whether employee, camper, renter, or automobile driver. An individual who tosses his rubbish along a roadside is just as irresponsible as a business that pours pollutants into a river. The individual may argue that his offense is less in magnitude, but when his rubbish is added to all the rest, it becomes a massive offense against the public interest.

As a matter of fact, quality of life will be improved less than people expect if only business is socially responsible. Substantial improvement will be achieved only when most organizations and persons act in socially responsible ways.

Second, the movement toward greater social responsibility is not a fad but a fundamental change in social directions. Business executives will do their organizations grievous damage if they assume social responsibility is merely something to be assigned to a third assistant with action to be taken only when absolutely necessary and when the organization is backed into a corner.

Social responsibility is here to stay despite its intangibles and imponderables. As stated earlier, business probably has been a significant cause of the rise of social responsibility ideas because it did its economic job so well that it released people from economic want, freeing them to pursue new social goals.

Third, social response by business will increase business's economic costs. Social responsibility is not a free ride or a matter of simple goodwill. Actions such as the reduction of pollution take large amounts of economic resources. The costs are there. It is true that some of these costs are transferred from other segments of society, so society as a whole may not bear higher costs for some actions; however, these costs are brought into the business system and, in most instances, will flow through in the form of higher prices.

This situation is likely to put further strain on business-consumer relations. It may even lead to consumer demands for less social involvement in the short run, but the long-run secular trend toward more social involvement is likely to remain.

Notes

1. Keith Davis and Robert L. Blomstrom, *Business and Society: Environment and Responsibility*, 3rd ed. (New York: McGraw-Hill Book Company, 1975), p. 50. Italics in original. A number of analysts believe that the desirable course of events is for business to lose a substantial part of its power. That is a separate issue not treated in this article, but for details the reader is referred to the review of Richard Barnet and Ronald Muller's *Global Reach: The Power of the Multinational Corporation,* in William G. Ryan, "The Runaway Global Corporation," *Business Horizons* (February 1975), pp. 91–95.
2. Further discussion of the social audit is found in Raymond A. Bauer and Dan H. Fenn, Jr., *The Corporate Social Audit* (New York: The Russell Sage Foundation, 1972); and John J. Corson and George A. Steiner, *Measuring Business's Social Performance: The Corporate Social Audit* (New York: Committee for Economic Development, 1975). The social audit for business originally was proposed by Howard R. Bowen, *Social Responsibilities of the Businessman* (New York: Harper & Brothers, 1953), pp. 155–156.

CORPORATE MORAL AGENCY*

Peter A. French

1. In one of his *New York Times* columns of not too long ago Tom Wicker's ire was aroused by a Gulf Oil Corporation advertisement that "pointed the finger of blame" for the energy crisis at all elements of our society (and supposedly away from the oil company). Wicker attacked Gulf Oil as the major, if not the sole, perpetrator of that crisis and virtually every other social ill, with the possible exception of venereal disease. I do not know if Wicker was serious or sarcastic in making all of his charges; I have a sinking suspicion that he was in deadly earnest, but I have doubts as to whether Wicker understands or if many people understand what sense such ascriptions of moral responsibility make when their subjects are corporations. My interest is to argue for a theory that accepts

From "The Corporation as a Moral Person" by Peter A. French. Paper presented at the Ethics and Economics Conference, University of Delaware, November 11, 1977. Copyright © 1977 by Peter A. French. Reprinted by permission of the author.

*I am grateful to Professors Donald Davidson, J. L. Mackie, Howard Wettstein, and T. E. Uehling for their helpful comments on earlier versions of this paper. I wish also to acknowledge the support of the University of Minnesota Graduate School.

corporations as members of the moral community, of equal standing with the traditionally acknowledged residents—biological human beings—and hence treats Wicker-type responsibility ascriptions as unexceptionable instances of a perfectly proper sort without having to paraphrase them. In short, I shall argue that corporations should be treated as full-fledged moral persons and hence that they can have whatever privileges, rights, and duties as are, in the normal course of affairs, accorded to moral persons.

2. There are at least two significantly different types of responsibility ascriptions that I want to distinguish in ordinary usage (not counting the laudatory recommendation, "He is a responsible lad.") The first type pins responsibility on someone or something, the who-dun-it or what-dun-it sense. Austin has pointed out that it is usually used when an event or action is thought by the speaker to be untoward. (Perhaps we are more interested in the failures rather than the successes that punctuate our lives.)

The second type of responsibility ascription, parasitic upon the first, involves the notion of accountability.[1] "Having a responsibility" is interwoven with the notion "Having a liability to answer," and having such a liability or obligation seems to imply (as Anscombe has noted[2]) the existence of some sort of authority relationship either between people, or between people and a deity, or in some weaker versions between people and social norms. The kernel of insight that I find intuitively compelling is that for someone to legitimately hold someone else responsible for some event, there must exist or have existed a responsibility relationship between them such that in regard to the event in question the latter was answerable to the former. In other words, a responsibility ascription of the second type is properly uttered by someone Z if he or she can hold X accountable for what he or she has done. Responsibility relationships are created in a multitude of ways, e.g., through promises, contracts, compacts, hirings, assignments, appointments, by agreeing to enter a Rawlsian original position, etc. The "right" to hold responsible is often delegatable to third parties; but importantly, in the case of moral responsibility, no delegation occurs because no person is excluded from the relationship: moral responsibility relationships hold reciprocally and without prior agreements among all moral persons. No special arrangement needs to be established between parties for anyone to hold someone morally responsible for his or her acts or, what amounts to the same thing, every person is a party to a responsibility relationship with all other persons as regards the doing or refraining from doing of certain acts: those that take descriptions that use moral notions.

Because our interest is in the criteria of moral personhood and not the content of morality, we need not pursue this idea further. What I have maintained is that moral responsibility, although it is neither contractual nor optional, is not a class apart but an extension of ordinary, garden-variety responsibility. What is needed in regard to the present subject, then, is an account of the requirements into *any* responsibility relationship.[3]

3. A responsibility ascription of the second type amounts to the assertion that the person held responsible is the cause of an event (usually an untoward one) and that the action in question was intended by the subject or that the event was the direct result of an intentional act of the subject. In addition to what it asserts, it implies that the subject is liable to account to the speaker (who the speaker is or what the speaker is, a member of the "moral community," a surrogate for that aggregate). The primary focus of responsibility ascriptions of the second type is on the subject's intentions rather than, though not to the exclusion of, occasions.[4]

4. For a corporation to be treated as a responsible agent it must be the case that some things that happen, some events, are describable in a way that makes certain sentences true, sentences that say that some of the things a corporation does were intended by the corporation itself. That is not accomplished if attributing intentions to a corporation is only a shorthand way of attributing intentions to the biological persons who comprise, for example, its board of directors. If that were to turn out to be the case, then on metaphysical if not logical grounds there would be no way to distinguish between corporations and mobs. I shall argue, however, that a corporation's CID Structure (the *C*orporate *I*nternal *D*ecision Structure) is the requisite redescription device that licenses the predication of corporate intentionality.

It is obvious that a corporation's doing something involves or includes human beings' doing things and that the human beings who occupy various positions in a corporation usually can be described as having reasons for *their* behavior. In virtue of those descriptions they may be properly held responsible for their behavior, *ceteris paribus*. What needs to be shown is that there is sense in saying that corporations, and not just the people who work in them, have reasons for doing what they do. Typically, we will be told that it is the directors, or the managers, etc. that really have the corporate reasons and desires, etc. and that although corporate actions may not be reducible without remainder, corporate intentions are always reducible to human intentions.

5. Every corporation must have an internal decision structure. The CID Structure has two elements of interest to us here: (1) an organizational or responsibility flow chart that delineates stations and levels within the corporate power structure and (2) corporate decision recognition rule(s) (usually embedded in something called "corporate policy"). The CID Structure is the personnel organization for the exercise of the corporation's power with respect to its ventures, and as such its primary function is to draw experience from various levels of the corporation into a decision-making and ratification process. When operative and properly activated, the CID Structure accomplishes a subordination and synthesis of the intentions and acts of various biological persons into a corporate decision. When viewed in another way the CID Structure licenses the descriptive transformation of events seen under another aspect as the acts of biological persons (those who occupy various stations on the organizational chart) as corporate acts by exposing the corporate character of those events. A functioning CID Structure *incorporates* acts of bio-

logical persons. For illustrative purposes, suppose we imagine that an event E has at least two aspects, that is, can be described in two nonidentical ways. One of those aspects is "Executive X's doing y" and one is "Corporation C's doing z." The corporate act and the individual act may have different properties; indeed they have different causal ancestors though they are causally inseparable.[5]

Although I doubt he is aware of the metaphysical reading that can be given to this process, J. K. Galbraith rather neatly captures what I have in mind when he writes in his recent popular book on the history of economics:

> From [the] interpersonal exercise of power, the interaction . . . of the participants, comes the *personality* of the corporation.[6]

I take Galbraith here to be quite literally correct, but it is important to spell out how a CID Structure works this "miracle."

In philosophy in recent years we have grown accustomed to the use of games as models for understanding institutional behavior. We all have some understanding of how rules of games make certain descriptions of events possible that would not be so if those rules were nonexistent. The CID Structure of a corporation is a kind of constitutive rule (or rules) analogous to the game rules with which we are familiar. The organization chart of, for example, the Burlington Northern Corporation (See Appendix I) distinguishes "players" and clarifies their rank and the interwoven lines of responsibility within the corporation. The Burlington chart lists only titles, not unlike King, Queen, Rook, etc. in chess. What it tells us is that anyone holding the title "Executive Vice President for Finance and Administration" stands in a certain relationship to anyone holding the title "Director of Internal Audit" and to anyone holding the title "Treasurer," etc. Also it expresses, or maps, the interdependent and dependent relationships that are involved in determinations of corporate decisions and actions. In effect, it tells us what anyone who occupies any of the positions is *vis-à-vis* the decision structure of the whole. The organizational chart provides what might be called the grammar of corporate decision-making. What I shall call internal recognition rules provide its logic.[7]

Recognition rules are of two sorts. Partially embedded in the organizational chart are the procedural recognitors: we see that decisions are to be reached collectively at certain levels and that they are to be ratified at higher levels (or at inner circles, if one prefers the Galbraithean model). A corporate decision is recognized internally not only by the procedure of its making, but by the policy it instantiates. Hence every corporation creates an image (not to be confused with its public image) or a general policy, what G. C. Buzby of the Chilton Company has called the "basic belief of the corporation,"[8] that must inform its decisions for them to be properly described as being those of that corporation. "The moment policy is side-stepped or violated, it is no longer the policy of that company."[9]

Peter Drucker has seen the importance of the basic policy recognitors in the CID Structure (though he treats matters rather differently from the way I am recommending). Drucker writes:

> Because the corporation is an institution it must have a basic policy. For it must subordinate individual ambitions and decisions to the *needs* of the corporation's welfare and survival. That means that it must have a set of principles and a rule of conduct which limit and direct individual actions and behavior. [10]

6. Suppose, for illustrative purposes, we activate a CID Structure in a corporation, Wicker's favorite, the Gulf Oil Corporation. Imagine then that three executives X, Y, and Z have the task of deciding whether or not Gulf Oil will join a world uranium cartel (I trust this may catch Mr. Wicker's attention and hopefully also that of Jerry McAfee, current Gulf Oil Corporation president). X, Y, and Z have before them an Everest of papers that have been prepared by lower echelon executives. Some of the reports will be purely factual in nature, some will be contingency plans, some will be in the form of position papers developed by various departments, some will outline financial considerations, some will be legal opinions, and so on. Insofar as these will all have been processed through Gulf's CID Structure system, the personal reasons, if any, individual executives may have had when writing their reports and recommendations in a specific way will have been diluted by the subordination of individual inputs to peer group input even before X, Y, and Z review the matter. X, Y, and Z take a vote. Their taking of a vote is authorized procedure in the Gulf CID Structure, which is to say that under these circumstances the vote of X, Y, and Z can be redescribed as the corporation's making a decision: that is, the event "X Y Z voting" may be redescribed to expose an aspect otherwise unrevealed, that is quite different from its other aspects, e.g., from X's voting in the affirmative.

But the CID Structure, as already suggested, also provides the grounds in its nonprocedural recognitor for such an attribution of corporate intentionality. Simply, when the corporate act is consistent with the implementation of established corporate policy, then it is proper to describe it as having been done for corporate reasons, as having been caused by a corporate desire coupled with a corporate belief and so, in other words, as corporate intentional.

An event may, under one of its aspects, be described as the conjunctive act "X did a (or as X intentionally did a) and Y did a (or as Y intentionally did a) and Z did a (or as Z intentionally did a)" (where a = voted in the affirmative on the question of Gulf Oil joining the cartel). Given the Gulf CID Structure—formulated in this instance as the conjunction of rules: when the occupants of positions A, B, and C on the organizational chart unanimously vote to do something and if doing that something is consistent with an implementation of general corporate policy, other things being equal, then the corporation has decided to do it for corporate reasons—the event is redescribable as "the Gulf Oil Corporation did j for corporate reasons f" (where j is "decided to join the cartel" and f is any

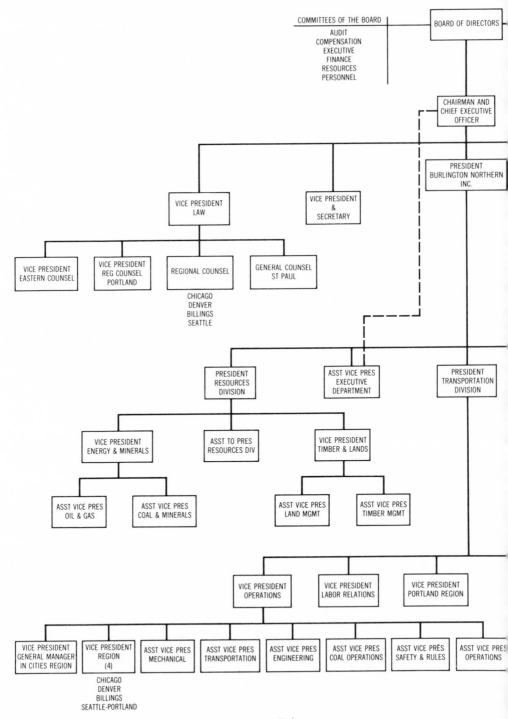

Appendix I

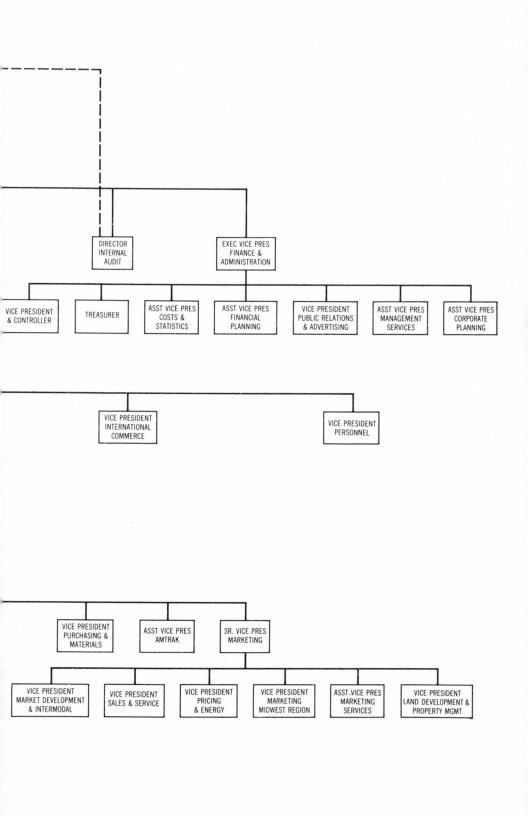

reason [desire + belief] consistent with basic policy of Gulf Oil, e.g., increasing profits) or simply as "Gulf Oil Corporation intentionally did *j.*" This is a rather technical way of saying that in these circumstances the executives voting are, given its CID Structure, also the corporation deciding to do something, and that regardless of the personal reasons the executives have for voting as they do, and even if their reasons are inconsistent with established corporate policy or even if one of them has no reason at all for voting as he does, the corporation still has reasons for joining the cartel; that is, joining is consistent with the inviolate corporate general policies as encrusted in the precedent of previous corporate actions and its statements of purpose as recorded in its certificate of incorporation, annual reports, etc. The corporation's only method of achieving its desires or goals is the activation of the personnel who occupy its various positions. However, if X voted affirmatively purely for reasons of personal monetary gain (suppose he had been bribed to do so), that does not alter the fact that the corporate reason for joining the cartel was to minimize competition and hence pay higher dividends to its shareholders. Corporations have reasons because they have interests in doing those things that are likely to result in realization of their established corporate goals regardless of the transient self-interest of directors, managers, etc. If there is a difference between corporate goals and desires and those of human beings, it is probably that the corporate ones are relatively stable and not very wide ranging, but that is only because corporations can do relatively fewer things than human beings, being confined in action predominately to a limited socioeconomic sphere. It is, of course, in a corporation's interest that its component membership view the corporate purposes as instrumental in the achievement of their own goals. (Financial reward is the most common way this is achieved.)

It will be objected that a corporation's policies reflect only the current goals of its directors. But that is certainly not logically necessary nor is it in practice totally true for most large corporations. Usually, of course, the original incorporators will have organized to further their individual interests and/or to meet goals which they shared. But even in infancy the melding of disparate interests and purposes gives rise to a corporate long-range point of view that is distinct from the intents and purposes of the collection of incorporators viewed individually. Also corporate basic purposes and policies, as already mentioned, tend to be relatively stable when compared to those of individuals (for example, see Appendix II-1-3, statements of the John Deere, 3M, and Campbell Soup Companies) and not couched in the kind of language that would be appropriate to individual purposes. Furthermore, as histories of corporations will show, when policies are amended or altered it is usually only peripheral issues and matters of style that are involved. Radical policy alteration constitutes a new corporation. This point is captured in the incorporation laws of such states as Delaware. ("Any power which is not enumerated in the charter or which cannot be inferred from it is *ultra vires**   of the corporation.") Obviously underlying the objection is an

---

*Beyond the legal competence.

DEERE & COMPANY

John Deere Road, Moline, Illinois 61265

1 December 1975   Bulletin No. 2

JOHN DEERE'S BUSINESS AND CORPORATE OBJECTIVES

Although it is seldom necessary to refer specifically to the distinguishing characteristics and fundamental objectives of our business, a basic understanding of their nature can contribute greatly to the sense of purpose needed for coordinated progress toward our goals without wasteful diversion of efforts and resources.

The John Deere organization has a special purpose which underlies its principal business:

> to provide those who work the land, build upon it, and there spend their leisure—on farms, in forests, in parks and open places and in towns and cities throughout the world—reliable mechanical power and equipment of superior quality to increase their productivity and satisfaction in mutually beneficial ways.

Our overriding objective is to serve the requirements of our customers in such a fashion that the Company's long-term economic performance will ensure investor confidence and will enable it to make its full contribution to the welfare of its customers, employees, stockholders and the general public.

To achieve a high level of economic performance, the Company's product policy and strategy will be aimed at world markets, and its resources will be managed on a worldwide basis.

To make appropriate contributions to the general welfare, the Company will strive actively to enhance the conditions that make achievement of its economic goals possible and sustainable: namely, a nondiscriminatory, opportunity oriented and equitably rewarding working environment for employees; and progressive improvements of the physical, economic social and cultural environments in which the Company operates.

WILLIAM A. HEWITT

Chairman

Appendix II-1

3M COMPANY
BOARD OF DIRECTORS

"The objective of 3M Company is to produce quality goods and services that are useful and needed by the public, acceptable to the public, and in the best interests of the global economy—and thereby to earn a profit, which is essential to perpetuation of the useful role of the Company. 3M profit is not an abstraction. It is the wherewithal to support individuals, government and social institutions through salaries, taxes, dividends, purchases of goods and services, contributions, and to provide growth and additional job opportunities."

Appendix II-2

Campbell Soup Company

PRINCIPLES OF OPERATION

Our Company has been in existence for a great many years. It has been consistently successful and characterized by exceptional growth. This record stems in large part from our intense desire that the Company be successful and that it grow. In the pursuit of that goal, we have followed aggressive, forward-looking policies which are administered conservatively. These policies are as follows:

Prepare and market products that represent superior values to consumers and constantly improve these values. Our products are sound values because they are made from superior quality ingredients, blended skillfully and always made uniformly. They are made and marketed efficiently and delivered to consumers at low prices in relation to their value.

Make our business grow in a sound manner. Our history is one of growth and our ambition is to continue that growth. We are geared for growth and to that end we vigorously pursue research for better ingredients, better operating methods, better equipment, improved products, new product developments, new markets and improved marketing efforts.

Provide fair treatment. To have a successful, growing business there must be good relationships with employees, stockholders, customers, suppliers and the public. These relationships are good because they are based on fair and uniform treatment, opportunities for betterment and mutual respect.

All of our plans and our decisions are made in the light of these objectives. When we fail to match our efforts and achievements with these policies, we hold back our Company's progress. Conversely, when we follow them, we contribute to our Company's and our own advancement.

Appendix II-3

uneasiness about the fact that corporate intent is dependent upon policy and purpose that is but an artifact of the sociopsychology of a group of biological persons. Corporate intent seems somehow to be a tarnished, illegitimate, offspring of human intent. But this objection is a form of the anthropocentric bias that pervades traditional moral theory. By concentrating on possible descriptions of events and by acknowledging only that the possibility of describing something as an agent depends upon whether or not it can be properly described as having done something for a reason, we avoid the temptation of trying to reduce all agents to human referents.

The CID Structure licenses redescriptions of events as corporate and attributions of corporate intentionality while it does not obscure the private acts of executives, directors, etc. Although X voted to support the joining of the cartel because he was bribed to do so, X did not join the cartel: Gulf Oil Corporation joined the cartel. Consequently, we may say that X did something for which he should be held morally responsible, yet whether or not Gulf Oil Corporation should be held morally responsible for joining the cartel is a question that turns on issues that may be unrelated to X's having accepted a bribe.

Of course Gulf Oil Corporation cannot join the cartel unless X or somebody who occupies position A on the organizational chart votes in the affirmative. What that shows, however, is that corporations are collectivities. That should not, however, rule out the possibility of their having metaphysical status and being thereby full-fledged moral persons.

This much seems to me clear: We can describe many events in terms of certain physical movements of human beings and we also can sometimes describe those events as done for reasons by those human beings, but further we also can sometimes describe those events as corporate and still further as done for corporate reasons that are qualitatively different from whatever personal reasons, if any, component members may have for doing what they do.

Corporate agency resides in the possibility of CID Structure licensed redescription of events as corporate intentional. That may still appear to be downright mysterious, although I do not think it is, for human agency, as I have suggested, resides in the possibility of description as well. On the basis of the foregoing analysis, however, I think that grounds have been provided for holding corporations *per se* to account for what they do, for treating them as metaphysical persons *qua* moral persons.

A. A. Berle has written:

> The medieval feudal power system set the "lords spiritual" over and against the "lords temporal." These were the men of learning and of the church who in theory were able to say to the greatest power in the world: "You have committed a sin; therefore either you are excommunicated or you must mend your ways." The lords temporal could reply: "I can kill you." But the lords spiritual could retort: "Yes that you can, but you cannot change the philosophical fact." In a sense this is the great lacuna in the economic power system today.[11]

I have tried to fill that gap by providing reasons for thinking that the moral world is not necessarily composed of homogeneous entities. It is sobering to keep in mind that the Gulf Oil Corporation certainly knows what "You are held responsible for payment in full of the amount recorded on your statement" means. I hope I have provided the beginnings of a basis for an understanding of what "The Gulf Oil Corporation should be held responsible for destroying the ecological balance of the bay" means.

Notes

1. For which there are good lexical grounds. See *Oxford English Dictionary,* especially entry, Accountability.
2. G. E. M. Anscombe, "Modern Moral Philosophy," *Philosophy* 33, 1958, pp. 1–19.
3. For a more detailed discussion, see my *Foundations of Corporate Responsibility,* forthcoming. In that book I show that the notion of the juristic person does not provide a sufficient account. For example, the deceased in a probate case cannot be *held* responsible in the relevant way by anyone, even though the deceased is a juristic person, a subject of rights.
4. J. L. Austin, "Three Ways of Spilling Ink," in *Philosophical Papers* (Oxford: Clarendon Press, 1970), p. 273. "In considering responsibility, few things are considered more important than to establish whether a man *intended* to do A, or whether he did A intentionally." Moreover, to be the subject of a responsibility ascription of the second type, to be a party in responsibility relationships, hence to be a moral person, the subject must be, at minimum, what I shall call a Davidsonian agent. If corporations are moral persons, they will be noneliminatable Davidsonian agents. See, for example, Donald Davidson, "Agency," in *Agent, Action, and Reason,* ed. Binkley, Bronaugh and Marros (Toronto: University of Toronto Press, 1971).
5. The causal inseparability of these acts I hope to show is a product of the CID Structure, X's doing y is not the cause of C's doing z nor is C's doing z the cause of X's doing y, although if X's doing y causes Event E then C's doing z causes E and vice versa.
6. John Kenneth Galbraith, *The Age of Uncertainty* (Boston: Houghton Mifflin, 1977), p. 261.
7. By "recognition rule(s)" I mean what Hart, in another context, calls "conclusive affirmative indication" that a decision on an act has been made or performed for corporate reasons. H. L. A. Hart, *The Concept of Law* (Oxford: Clarendon Press, 1961), Chap. VI.
8. G. C. Buzby, "Policies—A Guide to What a Company Stands For," *Management Record* (March 1962), p. 5.
9. *Ibid.*
10. Peter Drucker, *Concept of the Corporation* (New York: John Day Co., 1946/1972), pp. 36–37.
11. A. A. Berle, "Economic Power and the Free Society," *The Corporate Take-Over,* ed. Andrew Hacker (Garden City, N.Y.: Doubleday, 1964), p. 99.

CORPORATE RESPONSIBILITY:
Property and Liability

W. Michael Hoffman
James V. Fisher

I

Daniel Bell suggested in the early seventies that the question of social responsibility would be the crux of a debate that would serve as a turning point for the corporation in modern society.[1] This thought has been echoed recently by George Lodge in his book *The New American Ideology.* Bell and Lodge are the most recent in a line of social theorists who portray our society—and particularly the world of business—as in the midst of one of the great transformations of Western civilization. Old ideas that once legitimized our institutions are eroding in the face of changing operational realities. And one of the most important of these ideas being challenged is that of private property.[2] For example Lodge says:

> A curious thing has happened to private property—it has stopped being very important. After all, *what difference* does it really make today *whether a person owns or just enjoys property?* . . . The value of property as a legitimizing idea and basis of authority has eroded as well. It is obvious that our large public corporations are not private property at all. . . . It was to (the) notion of *community need,* for example, that ITT appealed in 1971 when it sought to prevent the Justice Department from divesting it of Hartford Fire Insurance. . . . Note that here, *as so often happens, it was the company that argued the ideologically radical case.*[3] [Emphasis added]

At the heart of the entire debate is the question of the nature of the corporation. Is the corporation primarily an instrument of owners or is it an autonomous enterprise which can freely decide where its economic and moral responsibilities lie? This question arose with the advent of the megacorporation and its *de facto* separation of ownership and control. Stockholding owners today have little or no direct control over what they "own," control being for all practical purposes totally in the specially trained hands of management. With this operational shift of power to management, corporate objectives have enlarged to include at least a recognition of social obligations other than providing the greatest possible financial gain or advantage for their stockholders. But herein lie questions not only as to what these corporate social obligations are and how they are to be acted upon, but more importantly, as to what conceptually justifies and legitimizes the corporation itself now that private

Paper presented at the Ethics and Economics Conference, University of Delaware, Nov. 12, 1977. Copyright © 1977 by W. Michael Hoffman and James V. Fisher. Reprinted by permission of the authors.

property theory is said to have eroded. Answers to the former clearly are dependent on answers to the latter.

Through a variety of rather slippery normative moves, corporate revisionists like Galbraith seem to argue that the great corporation must now simply be regarded as no longer a private but really a public institution. This would, presumably, provide a basis for corporate social responsibility that goes significantly beyond Friedman's "one and only one" social responsibility of business—to increase its profits.[4] Such a "corporate revolution" would appear to mean that the corporation is moving away (whether consciously or unconsciously) from legitimizing itself as *private property* to legitimizing itself as more like *common property*. In fact, perhaps the modern corporation should be seen as an exemplification of the philosophical unsoundness of private property, a strange development, to be sure, since the theory of private property has ostensibly been the essential pillar of capitalism itself.

It is important to note that the analysis which we have just sketched has focused almost exclusively on the issue of *control*. Traditionally, three elements have characterized property: the right to control, to benefit from, and to alienate (to sell or dispose of) something. An analysis of property which focuses exclusively on *control*, however, is seriously deficient, and a somewhat different picture of the question of corporate social responsibility begins to emerge when one focuses on the property rights of benefit and alienation. Clearly there are dangers to a society in the midst of radical change if it proceeds to discard basic legitimizing ideas of such social import as that of private property before it carefully considers the logic of that move.

It is an interesting fact to ponder that no fully adequate explication of a theory of justification of property acquisition has yet been achieved in modern Western social philosophy. By fully adequate is meant (a) a theory which goes beyond the "justification" that possession *is* ownership, i.e., that having an enforceable claim to something is to be understood as having the power to enforce that claim, and (b) a theory which is reasonably congruent with social realities.[5] The lack of a fully adequate theory of property, however, does not preclude examination of the notion of property itself.

In this paper our primary interest is with the internal logic of the notion of property. The logic of *private property*, it will be argued, indicates a class of things which cannot become (or at least remain) private property, and thus the concept of private property suggests an inevitable transition from (some kinds of) private property to common property. Moreover, the theory of the "managerial revolution" will be seen to result in a gerrymandered definition of private property rather than in an innocent discarding of the idea. The social analysts who have focused on corporate control have made an important empirical observation, but, in reference to the issue of the relation of the corporation, private property, and social responsibility, they have generated serious conceptual confusion. Nor have the philosophers helped very much.

II

The property rights of control, benefit, and alienation always imply the right to exclude. Since we intend to focus on the right to benefit, the following is proposed as a working definition of *private property* in order to clarify and highlight the logic of the notion of property.[6]

(1a) *Something* (x) *is the private property of someone (S) if and only if S has the right to exclude all others from the use or benefit of* x.

The right to alienate will be considered directly, though no attempt will be made in this paper to develop a satisfactory definition integrating the errant element of control.

Common property, on the other hand, must be defined in such a way as to include the individual rights of those who share ownership as well as the collective right of the owners to exclude all others.

(2a) *Something* (x) *is the common property of two or more people (S_1, S_2, etc.) if and only if S_1, S_2, etc. together have the right to exclude all others from the use or benefit of* x, *and S_1, S_2, etc. each has the right* not to be excluded *from the use or benefit of* x.

These definitions which emphasize the right to exclude or the right not to be excluded are, it will be argued, incomplete. There is, in fact, a *double-edged* exclusion which will become obvious when we consider the right to alienate or dispose of something.

To elaborate further the concept of common property, let us consider what it means for something to be common property. Suppose an apple tree is the common property of S_1, S_2, etc., and suppose further that it is autumn and the apple tree in question is now full of ripe apples. If S_1 were to pick one of those ripe apples and eat it, and assuming no prior agreement to refrain from eating any apples (say, for example, to save them all for pressing cider), then it would make little sense for S_2 to say to S_1: "You had no right to eat that apple since it was common property and you have now excluded the rest of us from the use or benefit of it." Here being common property would appear to mean (again in the absence of some specific agreement) that while S_1 had indeed excluded S_2 from the use or benefit of that apple, nevertheless S_2 had not been excluded from the use or benefit of the apple tree—at least as long as there is another ripe apple for S_2. The problem becomes somewhat more complicated if that autumn the apple tree in question were to have borne only one edible apple (each gets one bite?), but clearly any individual commoner's right not to be excluded cannot be taken to mean an *absolute* preclusion of any other individual commoner's actual use of the common property. What this suggests is that any notion of common property is incomplete without some (implicit or explicit) procedure for "fair-taking/using."

III

It was Hegel who pointed out, though no one seems to have followed up on the point, that *owning* something is an action. To put the same point somewhat differently, a necessary condition for S's owning x is S's intention to own x. As Hegel put it, ". . . a person puts his (or her) will into a thing—this is just the concept of property . . ."[7] Clearly I may possess, use, or benefit from something *without* intending or claiming to own it. I cannot *own* something accidentally (though possible modifications of this will be noted in a moment). Without S's intention to own x, S's possession of x is no more ownership than S's arm moving would be S's action without S's intending that S's arm move. It follows, then, that S's property is S's in precisely the same way and for the same reason that S's action is S's. Since this is true for any theory of property, the (perhaps surprising) consequences apply for any and all theories of property.

In modern Western society it has commonly been assumed that the term "property" automatically (or even necessarily) meant *private* property. It should be clear, however, that if we can talk about common or joint action, we can also talk about common property. We need no such notion as that of some (fictitious) corporate intention (the intention of the whole as if there were such a thing as a group mind). In other words, there is a clear parallel between "S_1 and S_2 together do something (joint action)" and "S_1 and S_2 together own something (common property)." What should be said is *not* that property necessarily takes the form of private property, but that property is a right which necessarily takes the form of an *individual right*. And this is true whether it is a *right to exclude*, on the one hand, or on the other, a *right not to be excluded*, i.e., whether it is a private property or a common property right.

We can talk about at least three modes in which an individual makes a claim (at least a *de facto* claim) to *own* something: (1) taking possession; (2) use; and (3) alienating or *disowning* it. We will elaborate (1) briefly and then move to (3), since it is of greatest interest for the argument being developed in this paper.

Under the first category, taking possession, at least three elements can be distinguished: directly grasping something physically—what is referred to in legal contracts as "taking possession;" shaping, forming, or developing something; and taking possession by simply marking something as one's own. Note the function of the concept of intention in all three of these activities. Not only is it a necessary element in ownership, its scope extends beyond the immediate relation to the thing itself. Thus the claim to ownership extends to not only such things as unknown parts (mineral deposits, etc.) and organic results (eggs, the offspring, etc.), but also connections made by chance subsequent to the original acquisition (alluvial deposits, jetsam, etc.). This is even more explicit when I take possession by shaping or forming something. By shaping or forming it, I take more than just the immediate constituents into my possession. This applies to the organic (breeding of cattle, etc.) as well as to the reshaping of raw materials and the "forces of nature." The point that needs to be emphasized is that marking something as my own is an action that extends my intention to ownership beyond the immediate thing itself, a principle that has been long accepted in legal theory and in social practice (and in fact is at the basis of our patent laws, etc.).

It is with the third category, however, that we come to the most interesting move. In a sense when I *disown* something (e.g., by selling it) I intend the thing in its entirety (I intend, so to speak, to be rid of it) and so presuppose the claim that it is/was most completely my own.

It is at this point that we can see clearly the missing half of our definitions of property. Note that it is generally held that there are two ways of *disowning* something:

(i)   I may yield it to the intention (will) of another, i.e., to another's claim to ownership (usually in exchange for something I deem valuable, though it may be an outright gift as long as the recipient accepts it as his or her own); or

(ii) I may abandon it (as *res nullius,* the property of no one? or as now the common property of all?).

The first option is clear enough and if we pursued that discussion the questions would center around the issue of what constitutes a fair exchange. But what about the second option? Where does the logic of disowning lead us? Consider the following case:

Suppose S, being perceptive and industrious, notes that there is a good market for tiger skins (well tanned, handsome to the eye, and luxurious to the touch). Furthermore, there are wild tigers in S's vicinity and the tigers may rightfully be appropriated by anyone and thus become the private property of the one who appropriates them (there being plenty of tigers in the vicinity relative to the number of people, etc.). By virtue of S's physical strength, cunning, and dexterity (as well as industriousness), S is able to capture several of these tigers intending to breed them in captivity for their very fine skins. Suppose further that S is successful initially in breeding the tigers, but it soon develops that they do not live long enough in captivity to grow to a size to produce sufficiently luxurious skins. But S is undaunted and eventually, by ingenuity and much hard labor, is successful in breeding stock that is long-lived, very handsome and adequately large.

Let's suppose further that as a result of this ingenious breeding process S produces a tiger, we can call it T_n, which has two very special and advantageous characteristics: (a) T_n regularly sheds its skin, leaving each time a very fine tiger skin ready to be tanned and sold; and (b) T_n appears to be immune to the aging process and even impervious to anything which might harm or even kill it. T_n appears to be indestructible, a source, it seems, of an infinite number of fine tiger skins.

Can it be doubted that T_n is the private property of S, that S has the right to exclude all others from the use or benefit of T_n? If anything could ever satisfy the traditional property accounts like those of Kant, Locke, and Hegel, surely S's ownership of T_n could.

Now let's imagine that one day T_n begins to show signs of a developing nasty temperament, and finally it becomes painfully clear to S that T_n is a serious danger to S (far outweighing the amazing advantages which T_n

manifests), and as well a danger to those in S's immediate living unit, S's neighbors, and even S's whole community. But T_n is indestructible (or at least no one has yet found a way to do away with T_n). What is S to do? The danger is critical.

Aha! S, using what precautions are possible, takes T_n one day to the village green and in the presence of the (not too happy) villagers makes the following announcement: "I, S, who have rightfully acquired this tiger, T_n, as my private property, do here and now publicly renounce, relinquish, and abandon my property in T_n." We are assuming, of course, that S has attempted to transfer property in T_n to someone else, to yield S's property in T_n to the will of another and so into that person's possession, but understandably has found no takers.

Imagine then that the next day S's neighbor appears at S's door, cut and scratched and bearing the remains of a flock of sheep which had been destroyed during the night. "Look what your tiger has done," says the neighbor to S. "My tiger?" responds S. "I renounced and abandoned my property in that tiger yesterday. That's not *my* tiger." No doubt we would be more than a little sympathetic with the neighbor's reply: "The hell it's not *your* tiger!"

It is interesting to observe that Kant, Locke, and Hegel (to name only a few) all treat property *only* as if it were a good, i.e., as if the right to exclude all others was something always desirable (note our use of the term "goods"). Why is it that these pillars of modern Western social and political philosophy have apparently ignored what we might call the "garbage factor"? (Which is not to say that those involved with the practice of law and politics have likewise ignored this factor.) Is it because we no longer live in an age when people commonly throw their garbage out the window? Or because there are now so many of us? Or because of such things as radioactive nuclear wastes and breeder reactors? No matter. It is in any case clear that the initial definition of private property must now be revised along the following lines:

(1a) x *is S's private porperty if and only if S has the right to exclude all others from the use or benefit of* x AND

(1b) *each of these others has the right to be excluded from liability for the maleficence of* x.

The term "liability" ("responsibility" does equally as well) is chosen for etymological reasons—the root of "liability" being *ligare,* to bind. It is not intended in any technical legal sense. This is what we may call the *double-edged exclusionary definition* of private property.

What will become obvious on reflection is that *if S's property is S's in precisely the same sense and for the same reason that S's action is S's, then the discussion of morality is also a discussion of property.*

Consider for a moment the question of the relation of intention to responsibility. In one sense I cannot be held responsible for an act that was not, in some significant sense, intentional. But I doubt that we want to take this in the strictest sense, i.e., that I have a right to recognize as my action—and to accept responsibility for—only those aspects of the deed of which I was conscious in my aim and which were contained in my original purpose. Surely, even though one may intend only to bring about a single, immediate state of affairs, there are consequences which are implicit within that state of affairs or connected with it empirically of which I ought to be aware and for which I am therefore morally responsible.

There is a clear parallel between how we deal with the question of someone's liability and how we deal with the beneficial additions to someone's property (by nature, chance, etc.) which, though subsequent to the time and intention of the acquisition of that property, are judged to be *part* of that property. It is directly analogous to the distinction between having an action imputed to me and being responsible for the consequences of an action. I may be responsible for a criminal act, though it does not follow that the thing done may be directly imputed to me. To apply this to our case of T_n, we might say that on the one hand we do not want to confuse S with T_n, though on the other hand we may want to hold S responsible for the consequences that follow.

Hegel observes: "To act is to expose oneself to bad luck. Thus bad luck has a right over me and is an embodiment of my own will (intention)."[8]

It is fair, we think, to paraphrase Hegel: "To acquire property is to expose oneself to bad luck."

The case of T_n, we argue, demonstrates that we are inclined to hold T_n's owner liable for the consequences, an inclination that finds expression in positive legislation in contemporary society. If we hold S liable for T_n, it is clear that what we are saying is that not only does S have rights in reference to T_n, but all others do as well. All the story of T_n does is to make explicit that the *double-edged exclusionary definition* represents what has always been, and indeed must be, implicit in the notion of private property.

The abandonment mode of disowning makes sense, then, *only if* property is *only* considered a good. Or rather we might say, it is morally justified only if what is abandoned *is* good. If it is acknowledged that property also entails liability for maleficence, then it follows (especially where the negative consequences of something are serious) that such a mode of disowning is really tantamount to ascribing to the thing in question the *de facto* status of common property of all—and that without the express (or implied) consent of those to whom the liability is transferred. Or perhaps we should say that the thing in question *ought* to be the common property of all, since in fact the negative consequences may fall more heavily on some than on others. Note that the definition of common property must also be revised to pick up the double-edged aspect.

(2a) x *is the common property of* S_1, S_2, *etc., if and only if* S_1, S_2, *etc. together have the right to exclude all others from the use or benefit of* x, *and* S_1, S_2. *etc. each has the right not to be excluded from the use or benefit of* x

(2b) *BUT not the right to be excluded from liability for the maleficence of* x.

IV

Given this interpretation of the logic of the notion of property, now reconsider a view which is current these days among some social theorists and popularized in Lodge's eclectic *The New American Ideology:* the view that the notion of (private) property is passé in our "post-industrial" era. Here Lodge suggests, as we have indicated above, that "(t)he value of property as a legitimizing idea and basis of authority has eroded . . . (and that it) is obvious that our large public corporations are not private property at all."

This "ideological" change, reflecting the operational changes in management practice in large "public" corporations, has been characterized as a *managerial revolution.* If we are to use a metaphor like "revolution" here, then it might be said that the managerial revolution is a revolution, to be sure, a revolution in the concept of property. That is, what seems to be implicit in the theory of the managerial revolution is not a move away from the notion of private property to some new basis of legitimation for the modern corporation, but rather a radical change in the concept of property itself. The implicit change (or revolution) is a *gerrymandering* of the concept of property out of parts of the concepts of private and common property. It would then appear to be something like the following:

(1a) *S has the right to exclude all others from the use or benefit of* x *BUT*
(2b) *these others do not have the right to be excluded from liability for the maleficence of* x.

This is, of course, a bit oversimplified, but recent cases like that of the Lockheed Corporation suggest that it is not far off the mark in characterizing our contemporary situation. We should entertain such (implicit) proposals for a gerrymandered definition of private property, we suggest, with considerable hesitation and even skepticism. Too easily giving up the notion of private property runs the danger of giving up the right to hold accountable for *x* those people who have the sole right to the use or benefit of *x*. What would be more rational (and not merely conceptually conservative, we are arguing) is to say that *when all others are to be held liable for S's* x, *then each of those others should also have the right not to be excluded from the use or benefit of* x—in other words, that *x* become common property. Or, one might say, logically some kind of social revolution is what is called for, not a conceptual revolution.

One of the many questions which now arise concerns the problem of symmetry (or fairness). Why should it be considered right to put a limit on liability (or to recognize a *de facto* limit, e.g., bankruptcy laws, etc.), but not to have some sort of similar limit on the use or benefits? (But would that not turn private property rights into common property rights, i.e., some procedure for fair taking/using?) The question becomes especially critical in situations where the negative consequences of something are actual while the benefits only potential. Thus, for example, S may declare the intention to assume liability for x commensurate with the potential benefits from x (or even commensurate with the total assets of S), but how does this help when the negative consequences are actual and the benefits only potential (or when the potential negative effects far outweigh the potential benefits)?

Lest one think that this is a purely hypothetical situation, consider the case of the 1957 Price-Anderson Act.

> In 1954, when the government decided to encourage electric utilities to venture into nuclear power, the companies at first were enthusiastic; but after studying the consequences of a possible major nuclear accident, they and such equipment manufacturers as General Electric and Westinghouse backed off. They feared damage claims that could bankrupt them. Insurers refused then and refuse now to provide full coverage. And so the utilities told Congress they would build nuclear plants only if they first were to be immunized from full liability. Congress responded with the Price-Anderson Act of 1957. Because of this law—a law that legalized financial unaccountability—nuclear power technology exists and is growing today. . . . In 1965, when it recommended that the Price-Anderson Act be renewed, the Congressional Joint Committee on Atomic Energy "reported that one of the Act's objectives had been achieved—the deterrent to industrial participation in the atomic energy program had been removed by eliminating the threat of large liability claims." . . . In December 1975 . . . Congress voted to extend the law for ten more years.[9]

In the face of such policies we have attempted to demonstrate that the logic of property leads one from the notion of private property (the right to exclude) with a kind of inevitability to the notion of common property (the right not to be excluded)—unless one proposes gerrymandering the concept of private property. At least this is true with respect to certain kinds of things which have traditionally been seen to fall within the range of what can rightfully become (and remain) private property. A more elaborate specification of what kinds of things these might be is a topic that goes much beyond the scope of this paper. And, of course, there remains the task of filling out our incomplete notion of common property, i.e., formulating the principles for procedures for fair-taking and fair-using.

Notes

1. Daniel Bell, *The Coming of Post-Industrial Society: A Venture in Social Forecasting* (New York: Basic Books, 1973), p. 291.
2. The classic analysis which generated much of the contemporary discussion is A. A. Berle, Jr., and G. G. Means, *The Modern Corporation and Private Property* (New York: The Macmillan Company, 1932). See also A. A. Berle, Jr., *Power Without Property* (London: Sidgwick and Jackson, 1959).
3. George C. Lodge, *The New American Ideology* (New York: Alfred A. Knopf, Inc., 1975), pp. 17–19. Also see his article "Business Ethics and Ideology" delivered

at Bentley College's "First National Conference on Business Ethics," published in the Conference *Proceedings,* edited by W. Michael Hoffman, Center for Business Ethics, 1977.

4. Milton Friedman, *Capitalism and Freedom* (Chicago: University of Chicago Press, 1962), p. 133.

5. A more detailed discussion of this issue is contained in J. V. Fisher, "Hegel and Private Property (or, the Case of T_n the Tiger)" (unpublished manuscript), from which portions of this paper were adapted. See also Lawrence Becker, *Property Rights: Philosophic Foundations* (London: Routledge and Kegan Paul, 1978).

6. These definitions are adapted from C. B. Macpherson, "A Political Theory of Property," in *Democratic Theory: Essays in Retrieval* (Oxford: Clarendon Press, 1973), p. 128.

7. Hegel, *Philosophy of Right,* trans. T. M. Knox (Oxford University Press, 1952), §51A.

8. Hegel, §119A.

9. Morton Mintz and Jerry S. Cohen, *Power, Inc.* (New York: The Viking Press, 1976), pp. 513f. Other such liability exclusionary examples could be cited.

SUGGESTED SUPPLEMENTARY READINGS

ANSHEN, MELVIN, ed. *Managing the Socially Responsible Corporation.* New York: Macmillan Publishing Co., 1974.

BLUMBERG, PHILLIP I. "Selected Materials on Corporate Social Responsibility." *Business Lawyer,* July 1972.

CHAMBERLAIN, NEIL W. *The Limits of Corporate Responsibility.* New York: Basic Books, 1973.

Committee for Economic Development (CED). *Social Responsibilities of Business Corporations.* New York: CED, 1971.

DAHL, ROBERT. "A Prelude to Corporate Reform." *Business and Society Review,* 1 (Spring 1972).

DAVIS, KEITH, and ROBERT L. BLOMSTROM. *Business and Society: Environment and Responsibility* (3rd ed.). New York: McGraw Hill Book Company, 1975.

DEGEORGE, RICHARD T., and JOSEPH A. PICHLER, eds. *Ethics, Free Enterprise, and Public Policy: Original Essays on Moral Issues in Business.* New York: Oxford University Press, 1978.

EILBIRT, HENRY, and I. R. PARKET. "The Corporate Responsibility Officer: A New Position on the Organizational Chart." *Business Horizons,* February 1973.

GILLESPIE, NORMAN C. "The Business of Ethics." *Business Review,* XXVII (November 1975).

HODGES, LUTHER H., and MILTON FRIEDMAN. "Does Business Have a Social Responsibility?" *Magazine of Bank Administration,* 47 (April 1971).

HOFFMAN, W. MICHAEL. *Proceedings of the First National Conference on Business Ethics.* Business Values and Social Justice: Compatibility or Contradiction? Waltham, Mass.: Center for Business Ethics at Bentley College, 1977.

JACOBY, NEIL H. *Corporate Power and Social Responsibility.* New York: Macmillan Publishing Co., 1973.

KAPP, K. WILLIAM. *The Social Costs of Private Enterprise.* New York: Schocken Books, 1971.

Reprints from Harvard Business Review. *Ethics for Executives Series.* Cambridge, Mass.: Harvard University Press, contents copyrighted 1955–61, 1966–68.

SETHI, PRAKASH, S. *Up Against the Corporate Wall: Modern Corporations and Social Issues of the Seventies* (3rd ed.). Englewood Cliffs, N.J.: Prentice-Hall, 1977.

SILK, LEONARD, and DAVID VOGEL. *Ethics and Profits: The Crisis of Confidence in American Business.* New York: Simon and Schuster, 1976.

STEINER, GEORGE A. *Business and Society* (2nd ed.). New York: Random House, 1975.

STONE, CHRISTOPHER D. *Where the Law Ends: The Social Control of Corporate Behavior.* New York: Harper and Row, 1975.

WALTON, CLARENCE C. *Corporate Social Responsibilities.* Belmont, Calif.: Wadsworth Publishing Company, 1967.

Chapter 4

SELF-REGULATION AND GOVERNMENT REGULATION

---

case 1 The Advertising Code Case

The Advertising Code of American Business reads as follows:

1. TRUTH. Advertising shall tell the truth, and shall reveal significant facts, the concealment of which would mislead the public.
2. RESPONSIBILITY. Advertising agencies and advertisers shall be willing to provide substantiation of claims made.
3. TASTE AND DECENCY. Advertising shall be free of statement, illustrations or implications which are offensive to good taste or public decency.
4. BAIT ADVERTISING. Advertising shall offer only merchandise or services which are readily available for purchase at the advertised price.
5. GUARANTEES AND WARRANTIES. Advertising of guarantees and warranties shall be explicit. Advertising of any guarantee or warranty shall clearly and conspicuously disclose its nature and extent, the manner in which the guarantor or warrantor will perform, and the identity of the guarantor or warrantor.
6. PRICE CLAIMS. Advertising shall avoid price or savings claims which are false or misleading, or which do not offer provable bargains or savings.
7. UNPROVABLE CLAIMS. Advertising shall avoid the use of exaggerated or unprovable claims.
8. TESTIMONIALS. Advertising containing testimonials shall be limited to those of competent witnesses who are reflecting a real and honest choice.

The Advertising Code of American Business was part of a program of industry self-regulation announced September 28, 1971. Participating in the announcement were the American Advertising Federation (AAF), the American Association of Advertising Agencies (AAA), the Association of National Advertisers (ANA), and the Council of Better Business Bureaus,

Inc. (CBBB). This program arose in response to mounting public criticism of the advertising industry, to more aggressive action by federal regulatory agencies, and to fears of even greater government control in the future. The public had become aroused over cigarette advertising, the advertising of over-the-counter medicine such as sleeping pills, and TV advertising, particularly by cereal companies, aimed especially at children. The Federal Trade Commission (FTC) had already required cigarette ads to carry the warning: "Caution: Cigarette smoking may be hazardous to your health." It had also banned cigarette advertising on television. Discussion was under way on several programs for greater regulatory control including the use of counter-advertising.

In announcing the new program of self-regulation, enforcement was emphasized. Complaints are received or initiated by the National Advertising Division (NAD) of the Council of Better Business Bureaus. During the first year, 337 complaints were placed on the table. Of these 337, investigations were completed on 184. Seventy-two of those complaints were upheld. In every case, the advertiser either agreed to withdraw the objectionable ad or to modify it. Six of the cases which were dismissed were appealed to a higher body, the National Advertising Review Board. Of the six cases, the NARB accepted the decision of the NAD in four cases, but agreed with two complaints. In these two cases, the challenged ads were withdrawn. All complaints were settled within several months. Supporters of the NAD applaud their time record for handling complaints as compared with frequent delays of several years in federal suits.*

It should be noted that the review boards dealt with matters of truth and accuracy, but not with matters of taste.

case 2:   The OSHA-Benzene Case

In May of 1977 the Occupational Safety and Health Administration (OSHA) of the United States government issued an emergency temporary standard (ETS) ordering that worker exposure to the chemical benzene—which is widely present in industrial manufacturing—be reduced from the existing regulated level of 10 parts per million (ppm) to 1 ppm [time weighted average (TWA)], with a 15-minute ceiling for any one day of 5

*These figures may be found in Howard H. Bell's "Self-Regulation by the Advertising Industry," in *The Unstable Ground: Corporate Social Policy in a Dynamic Society,* ed S. Prakash Sethi (Los Angeles: Melville Publishing Company, 1974).

ppm exposure. In addition, OSHA proposed to make this a permanent standard for benzene exposure in all industries (except gasoline distribution and sales), pending a hearing (as required by section 6 of the Occupational Safety and Health Act).

OSHA's action was precipitated by a report to the National Institutes of Health in 1977 of excessive leukemia deaths related to benzene. These deaths occurred in two rubber pliofilm plants in Ohio. On this basis, and in the absence either of animal studies relating benzene to leukemia or of studies showing a relation of benzene to leukemia in humans at levels of exposure below 50–100 ppm, OSHA determined benzene to be a leukemogen (leukemia-causing agent) and ruled that worker safety demanded reduction of exposure to the lowest technologically feasible levels.

OSHA and industry determined, subsequent to publication of the standard, that compliance costs would be in the hundreds of millions of dollars, with no indication of the number of workers likely to be protected from cancer. OSHA's general assumption was that lowered exposure to a potential carcinogen is desirable; but little medical evidence existed of a relation between benzene and cancer at already *established* levels. Nor were cost/benefit studies undertaken to show that a reduction in the level of the chemical is indefinitely worth the cost merely because each reduction is technically achievable. Because there is some scientific evidence to indicate that there are no-effect exposure levels, the oil industry questioned the wisdom of OSHA's expending large public and private resources in the regulation of a chemical which most agree is a weak leukemogen.

On the other hand, benzene seems definitely to be a carcinogen and workers can be affected by it. The public thus cannot simply allow the manufacture of benzene at any level, and it would seem that OSHA has a legitimate interest in the regulation of industrial manufacture. Still under study is the *level* at which the chemical will be allowed in the environment —a conclusion that probably will be based largely on data gathered by animal testing.

INTRODUCTION

The last chapter focused on problems in determining the moral requirements of a socially responsible corporation. In this chapter we discuss how to motivate a corporation to carry out its responsibilities.

A corporation or group of corporations can be viewed as analogous to an individual who has committed himself or herself to the moral point of view and who now wishes to put that perspective into practice. Individuals face a distinctive problem in practicing their morality that is commonly referred to as "weakness of will." Simply put, individuals sometimes yield to the temptation to do what they know is morally wrong. They therefore face the question, "How should weakness of the will be compensated for or overcome?" There are two fundamental strategies for overcoming weakness of the will. One relies on internal mechanisms of self-control and the other on external constraints on behavior. These same two strategies have been adopted in the corporate setting to overcome weakness of will in business. Internal mechanisms for self-control include business codes of ethics and the corporate social audit. The chief external constraint is government regulation. In this chapter, the strengths and weaknesses of these mechanisms for self-regulation and of government regulation are discussed.

PROBLEMS IN FIXING RESPONSIBILITY

While it now seems obvious to many businesses that they do have certain responsibilities to control their own activities, it seems unclear both how much is to be left to the private sector and at what point the public legitimately obtains a right to interfere. This issue is the major one addressed throughout the body of this chapter, but a prior question deserves first consideration: can we clearly establish the *boundaries* between the responsibilities of *companies* to act in resolution of social problems and the responsibilities of *government*?

On the question of fixing the boundaries of responsibility, it is important to notice that business persons have themselves found this issue troublesome, and even dilemmatic. Businesses have generally wanted the government to restrain the kind of cutthroat competition that would drive their own businesses out of existence. On the other hand, they have wanted the government to leave them alone to pursue their own avenues of competition. The same conflicting interests are also present regarding business' social responsibility. Business wants the government to force irresponsible agents into responsible conduct when the irresponsible action is damaging the reputation and activity of business; yet business always prefers the ideal of self-regulation to that of federal regulation. The issue is actually far more complicated than this simple juxtaposition of conflicting objectives makes it appear. As the first nonlegal reading in this chapter makes evident, broad societal goals directly affect the action of both business and government; and neither institution is solely committed to economic benefit above all other goals. Problems arise because of unclarity about whose responsibility it is to ensure that goals other than those of maximizing profits are achieved, both by rational planning and by ensuing courses of action.

Specifically, Thomas Schelling argues in this chapter that business persons are often powerless to respond to matters of conscience and that it is unclear even within the corporate structure which individuals ought to be held responsible and subject to federal actions. He also notes that government is presently a more pervasive force in controlling business by *assisting* it than is generally supposed—especially where the assistance involves the provision of certain policing activities. And finally, he maintains that most issues of responsibility are not ones of "Should we do the right things?" but rather of "What is the right thing to do?" His point is that the most insistent ethical problems about public policy are ones of determining which course of action is in the public interest, rather than ones of determining whether it is the province of business or of government to take the proper course of action. In his view, this uncertainty is the inevitable result of a situation in which most issues of business responsibility are new, indeterminate, and very complex. He concludes that we generally cannot make out a case for the *irresponsibility* of business, even if we can locate a *failure of initiative.* He seems also to imply that much the same judgment must be reached about federal regulatory action.

SELF-REGULATION

It is axiomatic for most business executives that self-regulation is superior to government regulation. In public utterances business persons argue that government regulation is cumbersome, uncertain, frequently unfair, and ultimately damaging to economic efficiency. However, in contemporary practice the business community finds some government regulation desirable. Why are these views held, and are they consistent?

Some argue that government regulation reduces competition and risk, and hence advantages already established firms. Such an argument provides no *moral* reason on behalf of government regulation, even if it is correct. There is a different argument that might provide a moral case for limited state control: Sometimes an essential function or purpose of business makes it impossible for the corporation to do the morally appropriate act. Suppose, for example, that textile company A is polluting the river and that expensive technology is now available to enable company A to greatly reduce pollution. On the basis of the harm analysis provided by Simon, Powers, and Gunnemann (Chapter 3), it seems that company A ought to install the pollution control device. However, suppose that company A can show that all other textile companies are similarly polluting rivers. If company A installs the pollution control devices and the other textile companies do not, company A's products will rise in price and hence will run the risk of becoming noncompetitive. Eventually company A may be forced out of business. The competitive situation thus makes it unfair and perhaps impossible for company A to do the morally appropriate thing. Only a rule that requires *all* textile companies to install pollution control devices will be fair and effective. It is often maintained that in situations paralleling this textile pollution case, government regulation is the only viable and appropriate answer.

Kenneth Arrow argues, however, that the textile pollution case can be resolved by an alternative to government regulation—industry-wide codes of ethics. At least some evidence exists that industry-wide codes can work. In general, not all moral problems of personal conflict in society are resolved in courts by law or by regulatory agencies. Some are suitably handled by society's moral codes. Indeed, if moral codes were not widely efficacious, the legal and regulatory systems would be overwhelmed. For this reason Arrow argues that business codes of ethics should be taken seriously as a means of regulation.

On the other hand, business codes of ethics have been treated with considerable skepticism by the public and by many business executives as well. Although these criticisms have been taken seriously, they need not be decisive. Mario Salvadori describes why and how the code of ethics for the American Society of Civil Engineers was rewritten as a response to traditional criticisms. In his discussion he presents several basic criteria for evaluating codes and argues for the necessity of enforcement.

In the third article, Norman Bowie considers the charge that the wording of codes of ethics is so broad and amorphous that such codes are of little practical value. Bowie argues that these problems in the wording of codes are characteristic of language in general and present no special problems for codes of ethics. Despite these problems inherent in language, Bowie argues that codes of ethics have advantages over other alternatives for promoting ethical behavior and that the problems of wording are manageable. Nonetheless, Bowie admits that codes of ethics alone are not sufficient for the successful self-regulation of business.

If self-regulation is to be judged effective, it would be useful if there were some way of measuring results—parallel perhaps to standard audit and accounting procedures for annual financial reports to stockholders. It has been suggested that the notion of an audit should be extended beyond the state of a corporation's financial health to the state of its moral health. The figures on the next two pages from the First National Bank of Minneapolis Social-Environmental Audit, provide an example of a corporate social audit. When first discussed, the notion of a corporate social audit was received with some enthusiasm by the business community. Indeed, the Committee for Economic Development commissioned a study of the corporate social audit. That study, a portion of which is included in this chapter, explained the function of a corporate social audit and gave the concept some respectability in the business community. However, difficulties in implementation have muted the initial enthusiasm for the corporate social audit, and some observers predict its imminent demise.

The chief problem with the implementation of corporate social audits comes in knowing what to measure and how to make acceptable measurements. The notion of the corporate social audit has utilitarian roots, and problems of measurability that plague utilitarianism similarly constitute one of the chief stumbling blocks to the successful implementation of the corporate social audit. The specific problems of measurement affecting such a social audit are discussed in the selection by Blake, Frederick, and Myers. Further discussion of the measurability problems common to both self-regulation and government regulation is also found in the concluding section of this chapter on regulating through cost/benefit analysis.

1974 Internal Social-Environmental Audit
FIRST NATIONAL BANK OF MINNEAPOLIS

		1974 Performance Level	Net Percentage Performance Differential '73-'74 [2]	1974 Objectives [3]	1974 Social Performance Index [4]	1975 Objectives [5]
Housing 1 [1]	1. Number of residential mortgage loans originated in 1974 to families living in	a.) 360	35%	+	↑	a.) 360
	a.) Minneapolis b.) Suburbs & St. Paul	b.) 967	30	+	↓	b.) 967
	2. Dollar amount of residential mortgage loans originated in 1974 to families in	a.) $ 8,861,000	25	+	↑	a.) $ 8,861,000
	a.) Minneapolis b.) Suburbs & St. Paul	b.) $29,324,000	20	+	↑	b.) $29,324,000
	3. Number of outstanding home improvement loans made to families living in	a.) 357	15			a.) 655
	a.) Minneapolis b.) Suburbs & St. Paul	b.) 744	10			b.) 676
	4. Ratio originated residential mortgage loans to bank's total resources	1:50	5			1:50
	5. Foundation contribution	$10,000	0	$10,920	.92	$10,000
Education 2	1. Number of classes taken by employees paid by bank	363	5%	+	↓	
	a.) internal	164	4	+	↑	
	b.) external	199		+	↓	
	2. Number of employees in bank college gift matching program	48	3	+	↑	55
			2			
	3. Employee community involvement man-hours per month	1,129	1	+	↑	1,241
	4. Foundation contribution to educational institutions	$51,750	0	$50,006	1.03	$55,000
Public Safety 3	1. Accidents on bank premises involving employees — 1974 (Does not include sports)	26	80% 80 40			26
	2. Accidents involving non-employees	14	20 0			14
Income 4	1. Clerical employees — monthly income related to area-wide averages	1:1.01				1:1
	2. Clerical employees — composite productivity relation to base 1973	1:1.06				1:1.10
Job Opportunities 5	1. Percent officers, managers and professionals (EEO defined)	a.) 19.8	80% 60	+	↑	a.) 23.8
	a.) women b.) racial minority	b.) 3.5	40 0	+	↑	b.) 4.2
	2. Percent of job categories posted	77	20 0	75	1.03	77
Health 6	1. Estimated commitment to treatment of alcoholism	a.) $5,460	50%	+ 50%	.61	
	a.) money b.) man-hours	b.) 222		+ 100%	1.39	
	2. Number of days missed due to health problems per capita	a.) 3.43	40	a.) 5.0	a.) 1.7	a.) 3.43
	a.) women b.) men	b.) 1.65	30	b.) 2.3	b.) 4.3	b.) 1.65
	3. Prepaid health services (HMO) as employee health option		20			
	a.) services offered	a.) 0	10			a.) 0
	b.) dollar	b.) $1,000		+	↓	b.) $1,500
	c.) man-hours	c.) 141	0	+	↑	c.) 150
Transportation 7	1. Percent employees taking bus to work	61	50% 40	50	1.22	65
	2. Percent employees who come to work in car pools	17	30 20	30	.56	20
	3. Percent employees who drive to work alone	19	10 0	15	.79	15
Participation 8	1. Man-hours per month spent by employees in community activity	4,632	50%			5,095
	a.) on bank time	585	40	380	1.54	643
	b.) non-bank time	4,047	30	+	↑	4,451
	2. Percent employees donating to United Way	83	20	+	↑	85
	3. Percent employees voting Nov. '74	75	10 0			

GOVERNMENT REGULATION IN "THE PUBLIC INTEREST"

As social and economic systems have grown more complex in European and North American nations, there has been a correlative increase in the scope of government regulation of business (and of all economic activity). Sometimes the government intervenes for the purpose of shoring up the economic system itself, while at other times intervention is

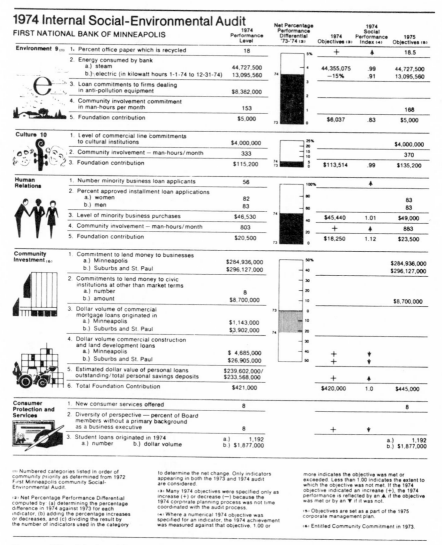

1974 Internal Social-Environmental Audit

FIRST NATIONAL BANK OF MINNEAPOLIS

		1974 Performance Level	Net Percentage Performance Differential '73-'74 [2]	1974 Objectives [3]	1974 Social Performance Index [4]	1975 Objectives [5]
Environment 9 [1]	1. Percent office paper which is recycled	18		+	▲	18.5
	2. Energy consumed by bank a.) steam	44,727,500		44,355,075	.99	44,727,500
	b.) electric (in kilowatt hours 1-1-74 to 12-31-74)	13,095,560		−15%	.91	13,095,560
	3. Loan commitments to firms dealing in anti-pollution equipment	$8,382,000				
	4. Community involvement commitment in man-hours per month	153				168
	5. Foundation contribution	$5,000		$6,037	.83	$5,000
Culture 10	1. Level of commercial line commitments to cultural institutions	$4,000,000				$4,000,000
	2. Community involvement — man-hours/month	333				370
	3. Foundation contribution	$115,200		$113,514	.99	$135,200
Human Relations	1. Number minority business loan applicants	56		▲		
	2. Percent approved installment loan applications a.) women	82				83
	b.) men	83				83
	3. Level of minority business purchases	$46,530		$45,440	1.01	$49,000
	4. Community involvement — man-hours/month	803		+	▲	883
	5. Foundation contribution	$20,500		$18,250	1.12	$23,500
Community Investment [6]	1. Commitment to lend money to businesses a.) Minneapolis	$284,936,000				$284,936,000
	b.) Suburbs and St. Paul	$296,127,000				$296,127,000
	2. Commitments to lend money to civic institutions at other than market terms a.) number	8				
	b.) amount	$8,700,000				$8,700,000
	3. Dollar volume of commercial mortgage loans originated in a.) Minneapolis	$1,143,000				
	b.) Suburbs and St. Paul	$3,902,000				
	4. Dollar volume commercial construction and land development loans a.) Minneapolis	$ 4,685,000		+	▼	
	b.) Suburbs and St. Paul	$26,905,000		+	▼	
	5. Estimated dollar value of personal loans outstanding/total personal savings deposits	$239,602,000/ $233,568,000		+	▲	
	6. Total Foundation Contribution	$421,000		$420,000	1.0	$445,000
Consumer Protection and Services	1. New consumer services offered	8				8
	2. Diversity of perspective — percent of Board members without a primary background as a business executive	8		+	▼	
	3. Student loans originated in 1974 a.) number b.) dollar volume	a.) 1,192 b.) $1,877,000				a.) 1,192 b.) $1,877,000

[1] Numbered categories listed in order of community priority as determined from 1972 First Minneapolis community Social-Environmental Audit.

[2] Net Percentage Performance Differential computed by (a) determining the percentage difference in 1974 against 1973 for each indicator, (b) adding the percentage increases or decreases, and (c) dividing the result by the number of indicators used in the category

to determine the net change. Only indicators appearing in both the 1973 and 1974 audit are considered.

[3] Many 1974 objectives were specified only as increase (+) or decrease (−) because the 1974 corporate planning process was not time coordinated with the audit process.

[4] Where a numerical 1974 objective was specified for an indicator, the 1974 achievement was measured against that objective. 1.00 or

more indicates the objective was met or exceeded. Less than 1.00 indicates the extent to which the objective was not met. If the 1974 objective indicated an increase (+), the 1974 performance is reflected by an ▲ if the objective was met or by an ▼ if it was not.

[5] Objectives are set as a part of the 1975 corporate management plan.

[6] Entitled Community Commitment in 1973.

Source: *First National Bank of Minneapolis. 1974 Annual Report.* Used by permission.

undertaken to support certain socially approved goals. Whatever the exact purpose, government regulation of business is now an enormous undertaking. Because this phenomenon has emerged so rapidly and amid such a constant swirl of controversy, an historical survey of the setting and reasons for modern regulation of business in the United States will be helpful.

In the nineteenth and early twentieth centuries, an individualist philosophy prevailed in both government and business, according to which the success of business is due largely to individual effort, which the government restricts only at society's economic peril. The proper role of government relative to industry is thus that of encouraging the growth of unregulated business. Action in light of this philosophy led to a situation in which the corporation was privileged: tariffs intended to prevent foreign competition were erected, corporate taxes were kept at low levels, and the corporation enjoyed an advantaged status under law. Giant corporations quickly began to control the economy of the country. Before the turn of the twentieth century, the 200 largest corporations produced more of the GNP than the next 100,000 largest corporations combined. These monopolies stifled competition and inflated prices. While their corporate profits rapidly increased, wages were decreasing and the cost of living was soaring. At the same time, these corporations engaged in a number of ethically unacceptable practices, such as lowering product quality without warning, watering down the value of stock, etc.

In 1887 the Interstate Commerce Act was passed to protect farmers and small business persons from monopolistic practices, especially by the railroads. A federal regulatory agency, the Interstate Commerce Commission, was created to monitor the railroads, though it was given no real power to do so, and the act thus had little immediate effect. Only three years later, in 1890, the Sherman Anti-trust Act was passed to protect small businesses from a wide variety of monopolistic practices. However, for many years thereafter the courts continued to favor monopolistic interests, and not until Theodore Roosevelt's administration was a stricter interpretation placed on the Sherman Act. Finally, in 1914 both the Clayton Act and the Federal Trade Commission Act were enacted to control anti-competitive practices. The basic idea was to free the free enterprise system from monopoly and deceptive maneuvers. Shortly thereafter, a World War I boom restored confidence in business, and not until the Depression was there renewed pressure for further regulation. However, from 1930 until the present a broad range of federal legislation has been enacted to control those business activities believed to involve unfairnesses or inefficiencies analogous to those that earlier had resulted from unregulated industry. Thus, unfair advertising, deceptive trade, sluggish competition, powerful anti-competitive mergers, questionable investment practices, waste discharges, discrimination in hiring, etc. all gradually came under federal regulation. Many state and local government controls were also enacted. As a result, federal regulation now affects virtually every business in the country. And as the regulation has increased, so has the critical response.

Presumably everyone would like to see the federal regulatory process achieve vital social ends without obstructing the productive capacity of the marketplace. We sometimes use shorthand to express this view by saying that we want business regulated "in the public interest." Yet what is the public interest, and do regulatory agencies now function so that this interest is best served? Virtually no one is satisfied with the current state of regulatory practices in the United States. Critics across a wide spectrum of political opinion accuse federal agencies of either too much, too little, or inefficient regulation. The claim that these agencies serve to regulate in the public interest is severely criticized in the article by Louis Kohlmeier in this chapter. As Kohlmeier sees the situation, the public interest is not served, largely because the agencies both *regulate* industry and *protect* it from competitive influences. He thus argues against the thesis of those public interest groups (such as Ralph Nader's) that aim at forcing the regulative branches of government to act in the public interest. No manner of reform or pushing will lead such agencies, in Kohlmeier's view, to desirable outcomes. Indeed, Kohlmeier's conclusion is severely critical, for he claims that present regulatory agencies serve neither the interests of the public, nor those of industry, nor those of the government itself.

In a more optimistic assessment, Dan H. Fenn reexamines certain "myths about federal agencies." For example, he argues against a view known as the "capture theory," according to which the regulatory agencies have been captured by representatives of industry. He contends that federal agencies are themselves a diverse lot and that each has a heterogeneous cast capable of a variety of responses to problems. We will never understand the problems of regulation, he argues, unless we examine the functioning of each agency independently. He does, however, list a number of internal agency problems intended to show that the agencies are shackled by organizational difficulties and dilemmas. Finally, in a constructive attempt, he offers some recommendations intended to improve federal regulatory agencies so that they will better serve the public interest.

MORAL REASONING AND COST/BENEFIT ANALYSIS

In recent years, especially in the regulative agencies of government, a particular method has been widely touted as a means of applying legal standards to the regulation of industry. This method is generally referred to as cost/benefit analysis, one segment of which is risk/benefit analysis. This method has also been employed by individual firms. For example, some corporate social audits are based on cost/benefit principles. The purpose is to provide a systematic method to facilitate tasks of decision making—whether decisions apply to the regulation of business or to the corporate management of a business. Since both management and the government have definite goals that fit the limits within which they operate (e.g., the firm strives to maximize profits), they are naturally interested in the most efficient means to those ends. It is here that cost/benefit reasoning plays a role, for this method is intended to show how one can bring about the desired result with the least possible expenditure.

The simple idea behind cost/benefit procedures is that one can *measure* costs and benefits by some acceptable device, at the same time identifying uncertainties and possible tradeoffs, in order to present policy makers or business persons with specific, relevant information on the basis of which a decision can be reached. Although such analysis usually proceeds by measuring different quantitative units—e.g., the number of worker accidents, statistical deaths, dollars expended, and number of workers fired —cost/benefit analysis (in the ideal) attempts in the end to convert and express these seemingly incommensurable units of measurement into a common one, usually a monetary unit. It is this ultimate reduction that gives the method its power in the minds of many, because judgments about tradeoffs can be made on the basis of perfectly comparable quantities. For example, it has been argued that among its other uses it can be employed to make financially explicit such tradeoffs (reached in government policy decisions) as those between environmental quality and factory productivity and between the quality of gasoline and the quality of the health of those who produce it.

Cost/benefit analysis has been widely criticized as a technique, especially when suggested for public policy purposes. First, the method has proved difficult to implement. Economists have been concerned largely with spelling out how such analyses can be carried out in *theory* rather than with providing practical and already quantified examples. The fact that many important variables are difficult to ascertain and reliably quantify—so difficult that we may never be very confident about the ending net sum—is a major reason why cost/benefit analysis has not been more widely used and has seemed to many a nonviable technique. This conclusion has been particularly drawn in the case of evaluating projects which would improve the quality of life, as opposed to considerations merely about the purchase of capital goods. A second and common objection to cost/benefit analysis is that we may not want it for *moral* reasons, and especially for reasons of (distributive) justice. It may be that some cost/benefit analyses will tell us that a particular device would be highly beneficial as compared to its costs, and yet provision of this benefit might function in an economy to deny more basic services to those who desperately need them. Perhaps instead, as a matter of justice, such needy persons ought to be subsidized, either in terms of services or financial awards, no matter what cost/benefit analyses reveal. When this problem is coupled with the generally acknowledged fact that the language of "costs" and "benefits" itself harbors implicit value judgments about positive and negative consequences, it appears that some fundamental moral thinking must be done, not only about whether to accept a *particular* cost/benefit model as decisive, but also about the acceptability of the *notions* of costs and benefits.

A critical estimate of cost/benefit analysis is offered in this chapter by Alasdair MacIntyre, who provides five reasons why this method as well as the utilitarian reasoning underlying it may be questioned. MacIntyre finds them both wanting because of certain problems that arise in attempts to measure different cost/benefit units for purposes of comparison, in attempts to predict and limit the scope of the consequences of an action, and in attempts to specify whose values, preferences, and assessments are to be relied upon in cases of a conflict. However, a defense of utilitarian and cost/benefit reasoning has been offered by some philosophers. In this chapter, Tom Beauchamp attempts to refute each of MacIntyre's criticisms. Beauchamp warmly endorses the use of cost/benefit analysis for purposes of deciding public policy dilemmas. He argues explicitly against those, such as MacIntyre, who advance *moral* reservations about such reasoning. According to Beauchamp, cost/benefit analysis not only is a morally acceptable method but actually produces the fairest outcomes of any method now available and holds out the greatest promise of a workable and rational methodology for public policy analysis. This defense of utilitarianism is buttressed in further respects in the concluding essay by R. B. Brandt, who deals specifically with the measurement problem. He argues that we can make sufficiently accurate quantitative comparisons that public policies may be based on them.

T.L.B.
N.E.B.

LICENSEE RESPONSIBILITY TO REVIEW RECORDS BEFORE THEIR BROADCAST

Federal Communications Commission

A number of complaints received by the Commission concerning the lyrics of records played on broadcasting stations relate to a subject of current and pressing concern: the use of language tending to promote or glorify the use of illegal drugs as marijuana, LSD, "speed," etc. This Notice points up the licensee's long-established responsibilities in this area.

Whether a particular record depicts the dangers of drug abuse, or, to the contrary, promotes such illegal drug usage is a question for the judgment of the licensee. The thrust of this Notice is simply that the licensee must make that judgment and cannot properly follow a policy of playing such records without someone in a responsible position (i.e., a management level executive at the station) knowing the content of the lyrics. Such a pattern of operation is clearly a violation of the basic principle of the licensee's responsibility for, and duty to exercise adequate control over, the broadcast material presented over his station. It raises serious questions as to whether continued operation of the station is in the public interest, just as in the case of a failure to exercise adequate control over foreign-language programs.

Public Notice of March 5, 1971, 28 F.C.C. 2d 409.

In short, we expect broadcast licensees to ascertain, before broadcast, the words or lyrics of recorded musical or spoken selections played on their stations. Just as in the case of the foreign-language broadcasts, this may also entail reasonable efforts to ascertain the meaning of words or phrases used in the lyrics. While this duty may be delegated by licensees to responsible employees, the licensee remains fully responsible for its fulfillment.

Thus, here as in so many other areas, it is a question of responsible, good faith action by the public trustee to whom the frequency has been licensed. No more, but certainly no less, is called for.

Action by the Commission February 24, 1971. Commissioners Burch (Chairman), Wells and Robert E. Lee with Commissioner Lee issuing a statement, Commissioners H. Rex Lee and Houser concurring and issuing statements, Commissioner Johnson dissenting and issuing a statement, and Commissioner Bartley abstaining from voting.

STATEMENT OF COMMISSIONER ROBERT E. LEE

I sincerely hope that the action of the Commission today in releasing a "Public Notice" with respect to *Licensee Responsibility to Review Records Before Their Broadcast* will discourage, if not eliminate the playing of records which tend to promote and/or glorify the use of illegal drugs.

We are all aware of the deep concern in our local communities with respect to the use of illegal drugs particularly among the younger segment of our population. Public officials, at all levels of government, as well as all interested citizens are attempting to cope with this problem.

It is in this context that I expect the Broadcast Industry to meet its responsibilities of reviewing records before they are played. Obviously, if such records promote the use of illegal drugs, the licensee will exercise appropriate judgment in determining whether the broadcasting of such records is in the public interest.

CONCURRING STATEMENT OF COMMISSIONER H. REX LEE

While the title of the notice seemingly applies to the licensee's responsibility to review all records before they are broadcast, the notice itself is directed solely at records which allegedly use "language tending to promote or glorify the use of illegal drugs. . . ."

Although I am concurring, I would have preferred it if the Commission had not decided to restrict today's notice to so-called "drug lyrics." The Commission may appear to many young people as not being so concerned with other pressing broadcasting problem areas. And to many of these young people (and not just to that segment who use illegal drugs) the Commission may appear as "an ominous government agency" merely out to clamp down on *their* music.

A preferable approach would have been to repeat, with an additional reference to drug abuse of all kinds, our *1960 Program Policy Statement* wherein we stated:

> Broadcasting licensees must assume responsibility for all material which is broadcast through their facilities. *This includes all programs and advertising material which they present to the public.* . . . This duty is personal to the licensee and may not be delegated. He is obligated to bring his positive responsibility affirmatively to bear upon all who have a hand in providing broadcast material for transmission through his facilities so as to assure the discharge of his duty to provide acceptable program schedule consonant with operating in the public interest in his community.[1] [Emphasis added.]

Because of the Commission's expressed concern with the drug problem, I would hope that we could initiate action with other appropriate Federal agencies to require a reassessment by pharmaceutical manufacturers, advertisers, and the media, looking toward the reform of advertising practices in the non-prescription drug industry. *Advertising Age* expressed its concern with the increased use of drugs—both the legal and illegal types—when it stated in an editorial:

> With an estimated $289,000,000 being spent annually on TV advertising of medicines, this serious question is being raised: Is the flood of advertising for such medicines so pervasive that it is convincing viewers that there is a medical panacea for any and all of their problems, medical and otherwise? Are we being so consistently bombarded with pills for this and pills for that and pills for the other thing that we have developed a sort of Pavlovian reaction which makes us reach for a pill everytime we are faced with an anxious moment, be it of physical or psychic origin?[2]

Drug abuse *is* a serious problem in the United States. It is found in every sector of the population, not merely among the young who listen to hard rock music.

I believe the broadcasting industry has made a good start in helping to discourage illegal drug abuse. Many local radio and television stations and the four networks have broadcast documentaries and specials, carried spot announcements, helped to raise funds for local drug abuse clinics and information centers, and have helped to establish "tie-lines" and "switchboards" where all people can call for free medical and psychological help and guidance. These activities represent "communicating" in the best sense of the word.

My concurrence in this notice, therefore, should not be regarded as a reflection on the good start that I think most broadcasters have made in dealing with this problem. They must continue with even more determination and support from everyone.

Notes

1. *Report and Statement of Policy re: Commission En Banc Programming Inquiry,* FCC 60–970, 20 R.R. 1901, 1912–1913 (July 27, 1960).
2. *Advertising Age* (May 11, 1970), p. 24.

MAJORITY OPINION IN ENVIRONMENTAL DEFENSE FUND v. WILLIAM D. RUCKELSHAUS AND THE ENVIRONMENTAL PROTECTION AGENCY

Judge David Bazelon

This is a petition for review of an order of the Secretary of Agriculture, refusing to suspend the federal registration of the pesticide DDT or to commence the formal administrative procedures that could terminate that registration. We conclude that the order was based on an incorrect interpretation of the controlling statute, and accordingly remand the case for further proceedings.

At the outset, we reject respondents' contention that this court lacks jurisdiction to entertain the petition. The Federal Insecticide, Fungicide, and Rodenticide Act (FIFRA) provides that for certain purposes pesticides must be registered with the Secretary of Agriculture, and that in order to be registered a pesticide must conform to the statutory standards for product safety. When it appears that a registered pesticide fails to conform to these standards, its registration is subject to cancellation in accordance with procedures prescribed by statute. In the ordinary case, the administrative process begins when the Secretary issues a notice of cancellation to the registrant. The matter may then be referred, at the request of the registrant, to a scientific advisory committee, and to a public hearing, before the Secretary issues the order that effectively cancels or continues the registration. Instead of issuing a notice of cancellation, the Secretary may alternatively initiate the process by summarily suspending a registration, when "necessary to prevent imminent hazard to the public.". . .

Petitioners here are organizations engaged in activities relating to environmental protection. On October 31, 1969, they submitted a petition to the Secretary requesting him to issue notices of cancellation with respect to all registrations of pesticides containing DDT, and further, to suspend those registrations pending the conclusion of the administrative proceedings. They submitted extensive scientific documentation in support of their petition. The Secretary initially issued notices of cancellation with respect to some uses of DDT, and published in the Federal Register a notice announcing his intention to issue cancellation notices with respect to all other DDT uses that are not essential for the protection of human health; he invited comments on that proposal. No action was taken on the request for summary suspension.

On May 28, 1970, this court concluded that the Secretary's silence on

439 f. 2d58.

the request for suspension was equivalent to a denial of that request, and that the denial was reviewable as a final order, because of its immediate impact on the parties. The court remanded the case to the Secretary for a fresh determination on the question of suspension and for a statement of the reasons for his decision. . . .

The relevant question . . . is whether the FIFRA requires the Secretary to issue cancellation notices in the circumstances of this case. The statute provides that "[t]he Secretary, in accordance with the procedures specified herein, may suspend or cancel the registration of an economic poison whenever it does not appear that the article or its labeling or other material required to be submitted complies with the provisions of sections 135-135k of this title." That language vests discretion in the Secretary to determine whether an article is in compliance with the act, and to decide what action should be taken with respect to a nonconforming article. Nevertheless, his decisions are reviewable for abuse of discretion. For guidance in defining the limits of his discretion, we must turn to the legislative history and to the statutory scheme as a whole.

Prior to 1964, the FIFRA required the Secretary to register "under protest" any pesticide or other item that failed to meet the statutory requirements. The product remained on the market, and the Secretary reported the violation to the United States Attorney for possible prosecution. In 1964 the statute was amended to eliminate the system of protest registration, and substitute the present administrative mechanism for cancelling registrations. The stated purpose of the amendment was to protect the public by removing from the market any product whose safety or effectiveness was doubted by the Secretary. The legislative history supports the conclusion that Congress intended any substantial question of safety to trigger the issuance of cancellation notices, shifting to the manufacturer the burden of proving the safety of his product.

Not only the legislative history, but also the statutory scheme itself points to the conclusion that the FIFRA requires the Secretary to issue notices and thereby initiate the administrative process whenever there is a substantial question about the safety of a registered pesticide. For when Congress creates a procedure that gives the public a role in deciding important questions of public policy, that procedure may not lightly be sidestepped by administrators. The cancellation decision does not turn on a scientific assessment of hazard alone. The statute leaves room to balance the benefits of a pesticide against its risks. The process is a delicate one, in which greater weight should be accorded the value of a pesticide for the control of disease, and less weight should be accorded its value for protection of a commercial crop. The statutory scheme contemplates that these questions will be explored in the full light of a public hearing and not resolved behind the closed doors of the Secretary. There may well be countervailing factors that would justify an administrative decision, after committee consideration and a public hearing, to continue a registration despite a substantial degree of risk, but those factors cannot justify a refusal to issue the notices that trigger the administrative process.

In this case the Secretary has made a number of findings with respect to DDT. On the basis of the available scientific evidence he has concluded that (1) DDT in large doses has produced cancer in test animals and various injuries in man, but in small doses its effect on man is unknown; (2) DDT is toxic to certain birds, bees, and fish, but there is no evidence of harm to the vast majority of species of nontarget organisms; (3) DDT has important beneficial uses in connection with disease control and protection of various crops. These and other findings led the Secretary to conclude "[t]hat the use of DDT should continue to be reduced in an orderly, practicable manner which will not deprive mankind of uses which are essential to the public health and welfare. To this end there should be continuation of the comprehensive study of essentiality of particular uses and evaluations of potential substitutes."

There is no reason, however, for that study to be conducted outside the procedures provided by statute. The Secretary may, of course, conduct a reasonable preliminary investigation before taking action under the statute. Indeed, the statute expressly authorizes him to consult a scientific advisory committee, apart from the committee that may be appointed after the issuance of a cancellation notice. But when, as in this case, he reaches the conclusion that there is a substantial question about the safety of a registered item, he is obliged to initiate the statutory procedure that results in referring the matter first to a scientific advisory committee and then to a public hearing. We recognize, of course, that one important function of that procedure is to afford the registrant an opportunity to challenge the initial decision of the Secretary. But the hearing, in particular, serves other functions as well. Public hearings bring the public into the decision-making process, and create a record that facilitates judicial review. If hearings are held only after the Secretary is convinced beyond a doubt that cancellation is necessary, then they will be held too seldom and too late in the process to serve either of those functions effectively.

The Secretary's statement in this case makes it plain that he found a substantial question concerning the safety of DDT, which in his view warranted further study. Since we have concluded that that is the standard for the issuance of cancellation notices under the FIFRA, the case must be remanded to the Secretary with instructions to issue notices with respect to the remaining uses of DDT, and thereby commence the administrative process.

While the Secretary recognized a substantial question concerning the safety of DDT, he concluded that the evidence did not warrant summary suspension of its registration for any purpose. That conclusion reflects both a factual determination and the application of a legal standard. Suspension is designed to protect the public from an "imminent hazard" during the course of further administrative proceedings. In order to decide whether it is warranted in a particular case, the Secretary must first determine what harm, if any, is likely to flow from the use of the product in question during the course of administrative proceedings. He must consider both the magnitude of the anticipated harm, and the likelihood that it will occur. Then, on the basis of that factual determination, he must decide whether the anticipated harm amounts to an "imminent hazard to the public."

Petitioners do not challenge the Secretary's determination of the kinds of harm that may be associated with DDT. They argue that his estimate of the probability that harm will occur is too low, in light of the available reports of scientific studies. They also argue that he has set the standard of proof too high, in light of the clear legislative purpose. On the first point, we think it appropriate in the circumstances of this case to defer to the administrative judgment. We have neither an evidentiary record, nor the scientific expertise, that would permit us to review the Secretary's findings with respect to the probability of harm. We have found no error of law that infects the Secretary's inferences from the scientific data. And we have recognized that it is particularly appropriate to defer to administrative findings of fact in reviewing a decision on a question of interim relief.

The second part of the petitioners' challenge, however, is entirely appropriate for judicial consideration at this time. The formulation of standards for suspension is entrusted to the Secretary in the first instance, but the court has an obligation to ensure that the administrative standards conform to the legislative purpose, and that they are uniformly applied in individual cases.

The statute provides for suspension in order "to prevent an imminent hazard to the public." Congress clearly intended to protect the public from some risks by summary administrative action pending further proceedings. The administrator's problem is to determine which risks fall in that class. The Secretary has made no attempt to deal with that problem, either by issuing regulations relating to suspension, or by explaining his decision on this case. If regulations of general applicability were formulated, it would of course be possible to explain individual decisions by reference to the appropriate regulation. It may well be, however, that standards for suspension can best be developed piecemeal, as the Secretary evaluates the hazards presented by particular products. Even so, he has an obligation to articulate the criteria that he develops in making each individual decision. We cannot assume, in the absence of adequate explanation, that proper standards are implicit in every exercise of administrative discretion.

Since the Secretary has not yet provided an adequate explanation for his decision to deny interim relief in this case, it will be necessary to remand the case once more, for a fresh determination on that issue. On remand, the Secretary should consider whether the information presently available to him calls for suspension of any registrations of products containing DDT, identifying the factors relevant to that determination, and relating the evidence to those factors in a statement of the reasons for his decision.

In the course of this and subsequent litigation, the Secretary has identified some of the factors he deems relevant to the question of suspension, and resolved some questions of statutory interpretation. He has concluded that the most important element of an "imminent hazard to the public" is a serious threat to public health, that a hazard may be "imminent" even if its impact will not be apparent for many years, and that the "public" protected by the suspension provision includes fish and wildlife. These interpretations all seem consistent with the statutory language and purpose. An important beginning has been made, and the task of formulating standards must not be abandoned now.

We stand on the threshold of a new era in the history of the long and fruitful collaboration of administrative agencies and reviewing courts. For many years, courts have treated administrative policy decisions with great deference, confining judicial attention primarily to matters of procedure. On matters of substance, the courts regularly upheld agency action, with a nod in the direction of the "substantial evidence" test, and a bow to the mysteries of administrative expertise. Courts occasionally asserted, but less often exercised, the power to set aside agency action on the ground that an impermissible factor had entered into the decision, or a crucial factor had not been considered. Gradually, however, that power has come into more frequent use, and with it, the requirement that administrators articulate the factors on which they base their decisions. . . .

Courts should require administrative officers to articulate the standards and principles that govern their discretionary decisions in as much detail as possible. Rules and regulations should be freely formulated by administrators, and revised when necessary. Discretionary decisions should more often be supported with findings of fact and reasoned opinions. When administrators provide a framework for principled decision-making, the result will be to diminish the importance of judicial review by enhancing the integrity of the administrative process, and to improve the quality of judicial review in those cases where judicial review is sought.

> Remanded for further proceedings
> consistent with this opinion.

DISSENTING OPINION IN ENVIRONMENTAL DEFENSE FUND v. WILLIAM D. RUCKELSHAUS AND THE ENVIRONMENTAL PROTECTION AGENCY

Judge C. J. Ross

In my view the majority opinion substitutes the judgment of this court for the judgment of the Secretary in a matter committed to his discretion by law. This action is taken without the benefit of any administrative hearing in which the validity of the petitioner's forebodings and the soundness of the Secretary's discretionary action might be tested. In effect, the court is undertaking to manage the Department of Agriculture. Finding nothing in the statutes that gives us such authority, I respectfully dissent.

COMMAND AND CONTROL

Thomas C. Schelling

Part of the problem of the "social responsibility of business" is that captains of industry are hell-bent for profits or too beset by competition to indulge their social consciences. But another part is that, say, the president of a telephone company may be no more able to institute equal rights for women than the president of a university or the director of a nonprofit hospital. He usually can't even fire people for disobeying his directives. And if he could, he might still be unable to devise a system that would monitor the way minority applicants were treated in a personnel office. . . .

For setting public policy with respect to business, two important implications emerge from these initial insights. First, business, as a "black box" to be dealt with through government action, will not be instantly

439 F. 2d 58.

From *Social Responsibility and the Business Predicament*, ed. James W. McKie. Copyright © 1974 by the Brookings Institution, Washington, D.C. Reprinted by permission.

and effectively responsive either to the consciences of managers or to the market incentives—taxes and subsidies, property rights and liabilities—that may be designed as "proxies" for conscience. Second, in thinking about social responsibility, it may often be a mistake to think of "the company" as the unit of action. Business is not a population of unitary entities—"firms" in the private sector. On the contrary, it is a number of small societies comprising many people with different interests, opportunities, information, motivations, and group interests.

Taking the Lid off the Black Box

For some purposes it will be necessary to "disaggregate" the firm and to deal with the social responsibility of subdivisions and individuals, applying the incentives and sanctions directly on the people or on the transactions that constitute the business and its activity, rather than to conceptualize the firm or the industry as the target of attention.

A clear-cut example would be to impose criminal liability on individuals for, say, activity contrary to the antitrust laws. One can apply sanctions on the firm; or one can make people individually liable for their actions as managers, supervisors, even salesmen. . . .

I am drawing a distinction, not a conclusion. The question of *where* it is most efficacious to locate responsibility within the business is a complicated one. It is an enormous convenience to government if "policy" can be directed toward the firm and not toward the people who work for it. But sometimes it won't work. Sometimes the firm is impotent. Sometimes the firm is a clumsy instrument to work with. Sometimes the firm has little control over the activities that the authorities wish to regulate. (Sometimes the firm can take refuge in its own impotence!) And even when the firm is the appropriate target for policy, it is difficult to identify the level of corporate decentralization or the mixture of stock holdings that determine just which entity is "the business." . . .

Discipline and the Supportive Role of Government

. . . It is interesting to note to what extent government may substitute for the firm's own management, or augment the firm's capability, or supplement the firm's efforts to enforce policy directives within the firm, and particularly policy directives that represent a social responsibility.

To indicate what I have in mind, let me begin with a few clear cases. Certain forms of personal violence and material sabotage are criminal offenses, and a company is also presumably helped by the police in enforcing the rules against prostitution, drug peddling, and gambling on company time. Similarly with theft and embezzlement. Certain regulations that reduce the hazards of fire and disease are more easily enforced within the firm if there are local ordinances that can be adverted to or if certain careless actions are violations of law as well as of company policy.

For a case that is a small step closer to the government's monitoring the activities of a firm's employees, consider a taxi company. The company may want a reputation for courtesy and safety—it may even want actual courtesy and safety. But it may be unable to enforce its own regulations about seat belts, double parking, illegal U-turns, or drinking on the job. The police, the Registry of Motor Vehicles, or other public authorities may have to do the monitoring. . . .

It is worth noticing that the licensing both of airline pilots and of cab drivers is done by government. Though one may expect the airlines to demand higher standards of pilot competence than are prescribed by the regulations, there is no thought that the profit motive alone should be counted on to guarantee the competence of those airline employees to whom are entrusted the airborne mixed cargoes of people and kerosene.

Now, how does this bear on our subject? Business firms may indeed want government to help them police their employees or their customers, to help protect the firm itself—its profits, its reputation, its legal security. May it also need some direct intervention of government in the command-and-control process to meet some social responsibilities? What are the specific areas of social responsibility in which a business firm might lack the discipline, the information, the incentives, or the moral authority to command performance or restraint on the part of everyone whose cooperation is required?

One possibility is that employees are personally irresponsible and out of laziness or for personal gain fail in their performance. Trash collectors leave debris in the gutters; fishing boats dump garbage in the harbor; sanitary regulations are neglected in a fruit-processing plant; nurses sleep and airline ground crews drink on duty; truck drivers make up for an extra-long lunch hour by driving through an off-limits tunnel with a dangerous cargo. . . .

Whether we have in mind criminal charges or damage suits, it will turn out in many cases that the government does best to make it an obligation of *people* in a firm, not of the firm as a profit-making entity, to behave properly. Just as the police can keep a delivery truck from double parking even though the home office of the delivery truck may not be able to, the holding of individuals personally responsible for hazardous behavior in the plant, for violation of civil rights, misrepresentation of a product, or the destruction of beauty or quiet can sometimes be more effectively managed by government directly than by government attempting to manipulate rewards and penalties on stockholder dividends.

The issue is one of comparative advantage. Technology may make it easier for the trucking firm than for the Registry of Motor Vehicles to monitor the emission of gaseous pollutants. Or it may not. . . .

MORAL CHOICE OR POLICY CHOICE

In discussing "social responsibility" there is a tendency to take for granted that more of it is a good thing. (Those who don't think so probably don't spend much time discussing it.) There may be limits to how much one would demand, but, if one thinks of a unidimensional scale

—"responsibility" at one end and "irresponsibility" at the other—responsibility seems to be something we can always wish for more of.

At least, it does until somebody feels morally compelled to persuade us to his faith in some god or some food, or to protect us from books or card games, to make us salute the flag or refuse to salute the flag, to prohibit smoking in the cafeteria or to make us stop using the masculine pronoun in referring to everybody.

There are of course situations in which responsibility means considerateness, less selfishness, helping or supporting someone and offending no one. Flammable children's pajamas without warning labels, the clandestine dumping of garbage, and reset odometers on second-hand cars are not likely to cause any moral dilemmas. But at a time when, urged by the brother of two assassination victims, the Senate can barely muster a majority in moral support of suppression of the cheap and easily obtainable handguns known as "Saturday night specials"; when the town dogcatcher is still among the least-loved public servants; when abortions are construed by some as an inalienable freedom and by others as a sin to be publicly suppressed; when Academy Awards are won by pictures that couldn't have been shown ten years ago; when many black people are genuinely apprehensive about the dilution of their culture and the co-opting of their leaders by "integrationist" campaigns reflecting the best of intentions—at such a time responsibility is often not a quantity (something a person can have more or less of) but a *policy choice,* a choice among the alternative values that one can be responsible to.

There are dangers in urging business to let its responsibilities be defined by some subset of its customers, by the special interests of its employees, by whatever ethnic group in the community is most articulate or most threatening, by people who love dogs or by people who are allergic to dog hair. There is no need to be alarmist, but it is worthwhile to recall that, even in matters of business responsibility, especially social responsibility, there are always conflicts of interest to be found; and they often correspond to conflicts of responsibility. Protective tariffs, safety inspection of marginal coal mines, pets in apartment buildings, and of course the gun laws are reminders of this principle. Some of the issues may be strictly distributional: higher-cost low-sulphur fuels clean the air for the people who live downwind from the smokestacks; and use of these same fuels may add to the cost of electric power and other commodities, with an incidence that falls disproportionately on the poor. Pity the "responsible" refuse company that has to decide in which community to locate its dumping ground.

My purpose at this point is not to be destructive of the idea of responsibility or to suggest that all efforts at responsibility are doomed to violate somebody's principles. It is rather to point out that being responsible for a business firm is a little like being responsible as a senator or as a university president. Often the question is not, "Do I want to do the right thing?" It arises in the form, "What is the right thing to want to do?" The choice is not always between some selfish temptation and some obvious responsible course. The choice is often a policy decision.

What should a business do about drug addiction among its employees? What should it do about admitting men to jobs that have been tradition-ally women's—secretaries, receptionists, or file clerks? Or smoking on the job? Or eliminating some hazard in the product by producing it more expensively and selling it at a higher price? Or letting a black organization dictate policy toward blacks, letting a women's organization negotiate on behalf of women? Consider the business that is under pressure to discon-tinue operations in South Africa, throwing people out of work there. What is the right thing to do? To whom should the company defer in deciding the right thing to do? Is there a "right thing" in this case or just a choice between equally unsatisfactory options?

Many of today's issues in business responsibility are new. There is no easy answer to the question of whether the Sierra Club or a farm group speaks for the responsible position, and they may take opposite sides. One thing seems sure: on the issues that exercise people today, especially the issues of the social responsibility of business, there is often no source of reliable guidance, no acknowledged source of policy, no easy choice between the responsible and the selfish.

Not all problems of responsibility involve dilemmas of conscience. Ambiguity about what is right is no excuse for doing wrong. But we should usually be careful not to adopt the idea that it is easy to know what is right and responsible and that the choice is only between responsibility and irresponsibility. People in business who have the decisiveness to do the responsible thing will often be the people who, because they did something decisive, are accused of irresponsibility. Even the prejudiced employer may have trouble deciding whether or not his responsibility is to his community and its traditional values; it is the unprejudiced em-ployer who may have the hardest time deciding how much of a handicap it is appropriate to give some disadvantaged minority.

IRRESPONSIBLE OR UNRESPONSIVE

The vexed and ambiguous character of many modern problems of business responsibility has been exemplified, if in an exaggerated way, by the tantalizing problem of aircraft hijacking. In addition to the dramatic crisis of responsibility that is bound to occur when an actual hijacking is attempted or in process and perilous decisions of an unforeseen and often unique kind have to be reached in a hurry, a multitude of nearly routine decisions with a bearing on hijacking remained on the agenda for a good many years without being settled.

There is, for example, the straightforward matter of baggage handling, about which nothing has been done. Maybe nothing should be done. Baggage in the cabin is evidently important, as evidenced by the search procedures that were initiated in early 1973. Until a dozen years ago we checked our bags; then, with the large-diameter fuselage that goes with jet airplanes, it became feasible to elevate the seats off the floor to accom-modate overnight bags. Most baggage is apparently carried aboard for quick retrieval, not because anyone wants to shave or wear his bathrobe in flight. Maybe passengers could be induced to surrender their baggage or eventually to invest in specially designed aircraft luggage that yielded more readily to search.

Instead we have search procedures. Whatever their efficacy, one thing is certain: if it made sense to institute them in 1973, it would have made sense to institute them several years earlier. There were halfhearted efforts by some airlines. Eventually federal regulation made the procedures mandatory.

There were some procedures for screening passengers, by reference to "behavior profiles" of real and potential hijackers. It was apparently left to busy passenger agents, on their own responsibility and with no very clear system of penalties for either kind of mistake—overzealous and heavy-handed screening or laxity or laziness—to enforce or even to legitimize the procedure. Little or nothing was done about airport security or the design of aircraft or of loading facilities. Nothing noticeable was done about aircraft operating procedures, personnel selection, or restrictions on passenger seating and behavior in relation to hijacking.

The point in rehearsing this unimpressive history of efforts to cope with the danger of hijacking is not to disparage what the airlines did, to give them low marks for responsibility, or to complain that solvable problems went unsolved. The point is rather to observe how difficult it may be to identify social responsibility.

In the first place, it was not clear just where primary responsibility rested. The matter involved criminal behavior and airline safety. While the federal government fumbled its own policies and failed to specify clearly where responsibility lay, an airline executive could only have been bewildered about even what responsibility would be allowed him if he were to assume it. It was by no means evident how jurisdiction was divided among agencies of the federal government or between levels of government.

Second, many of the measures that airlines might have considered depended largely on collective action, perhaps uniform arrangements common to all airlines. It may not have been clear how far the CAB (Civil Aeronautics Board) or the Antitrust Division of the Department of Justice would have let them go. And many changes in operating procedures would have required the active cooperation of air-terminal facilities, which for the most part the airlines neither own nor control.

In the third place, it is not altogether clear toward whom the airlines ought to feel responsible or whose interest the airlines should responsibly try to serve. Airline managers can feel responsible for the safety of their firm's own passengers, or for all passengers on all airlines, or more generally for helping to prevent an epidemic of violence. They could have a sense of obligation not to use ethnic data in the screening and selective search or interrogation of passengers. They could feel responsible for protecting passengers from illegal or improper search and seizure. Responsibility for the safety of employees is still another consideration, as well as a responsibility not to waste the stockholders' resources.

If a senior executive of an airline had resolved, as many of them may have done for all I know, to be guided by his sense of social responsibility on all matters relating to hijacking, it is not clear what he would have done. A responsible objective could have been to avoid unduly alarming passengers, to avoid making a dramatic and enticing game out of efforts to thwart hijackers, to avoid burdening passengers or crew with any sense of obligation to risk their lives in heroics, and of course to avoid any behavior that would so exaggerate the hazards of flying as to impair airline travel seriously, at high cost to passengers and stockholders alike. . . .

One cannot easily make a case of *irresponsibility* against the airlines. What we have instead is simply a *lack* of any commanding sense of *responsibility*, of any initiative toward assumption of responsibility, of any leadership or collective action inspired by social responsibility. The lack seemed even more conspicuous on the part of federal agencies than on the part of private airlines. One of the differences between irresponsibility and lack of responsibility may be that conscience or legal liability can help to safeguard against the former, but some real initiative is required to overcome the latter. The diagnosis involves the organizational basis for behavior, not merely the private consciences of people. The discouragement of wrongdoing is different from the stimulation of something right. . . .

THE TWO FACES OF REGULATION

. . . Consider some alarming byproducts of ordinary commercial activity. There is the dumping of noxious substances into rivers and lakes; there is strip mining; there is the production of electric power by combustion of cheap fuels that fill the air with sulphuric acid. It appears to be typical of producers that they resist being identified with the harms that they promulgate and being saddled with compulsory efforts to clean up or to change their technology. In some cases there is a transparent motive behind their resistance: fear that they will be put out of business by an aroused populace. In some cases there may be fear that the image of their product will be contaminated by association with noxious by-products. People may come to associate potato chips with dead fish or associate the harmful effects of insecticides with the foods protected by them, even though there is no physical connection between the harms and the foods. . . .

I am not now raising a question of responsibility. I am trying only, in an area related to "responsibility," to get at the question of what business motivation ought to be expected to be. One of the phrases that has been popularized in the last decade is "built-in obsolescence." It is alleged that automobile companies and companies that produce television sets or electric freezers like to see this year's product become unacceptable to consumers next year or the year after. What could more reliably promise "built-in obsolescence" than a federal law prohibiting internal combustion engines in automobiles after the year 1980? . . .

Of course there is a strong sentiment against antibusiness regulation.

There may be great apprehension, not always unjustified, that, when government intrudes into a field of production, it bodes ill for the companies intruded on. This attitude may not have much to do with profits: people don't like, or pretend not to like, being told what to do. One is provoked to wonder, nevertheless, whether government regulation is quite as menacing as it is seen to be.

There is growing recognition that firms may acquiesce in standards that penalize them no more than their competitors. A "responsible" firm can wish to comply with some social standards but refuse to adopt them unilaterally while its competitors ignore them. My suggestion here is that the standards, once adopted by all, may not even turn out to be onerous. Often measures that perforce increase business costs (or internalize costs) turn out to be neutral or even beneficial in relation to business profits.

The False Dichotomy of Voluntarism and Coercion

The question is sometimes posed where the line should be drawn between reliance on the voluntary assumption of responsibility by business and the coercion of "responsible" performance by government sanctions. So many techniques, instruments, and philosophies exist beyond or in addition to these two rather pure forms that that may be a poor way of posing a choice.

Posing the question in terms of drawing a line suggests gratuitously that what is needed is something business firms "ought" to have done voluntarily but did not, so that coercion is both corrective and punitive. It may also suggest, inadvertently and often wrongly, that business firms prefer (or naturally should prefer) public reliance on their voluntary assumption of responsibility and that coercion is what they always and naturally wish to avoid.

Taking off from that last point, an interesting alternative approach is that of permitting businesses *to coerce themselves.* "Mutual coercion, mutually agreed on," a term recently publicized by Garrett Hardin in connection with population policy, could appeal to firms that are prepared to incur costs but only on condition that competitors do also. The coercion could take the form of the government's responding to a plea to enforce a mandatory regulation. Alternatively, the government might allow, in the public interest, a voluntary contractual arrangement that would otherwise run afoul of the antitrust laws. As still another arrangement for the same purpose, there could be legislation that would make mandatory the application to all firms in an industry of an agreement that had been ratified by some substantial number; retail price maintenance in some states may be a near example.

Sometimes what business may need is an ability to *concert on a uniform practice* or simply the information by which they could coordinate their activities. Heterogeneous phonograph speeds may not have been a sufficient nuisance to consumers to arouse a demand for regulatory action, but bumper heights are a different matter. The sheer power of suggestion could become almost "coercive" on domestic automobile manufacturers if a simple, identifiable, easily remembered standard could be impressed on consumers and insurance companies. The primary enforcement of daylight saving is merely the publicized announcement of the date for setting clocks forward or backward and everybody's expectation that, if they don't participate, they'll only confuse themselves and their friends.

Another alternative to the voluntarism-coercion dichotomy (one much discussed recently in the professional economics literature) is the *relocation of legal obligations.* Property rights and liabilities for damage are important ways of dealing with externalities. No-fault insurance is a current, dramatic example.

Still another approach is *leadership in the public sector.* In addition to setting an example, government purchasing power can often overcome the overhead costs of, say, redesign of a product; and government contracting has long been used as a way of enforcing, with at least some success, certain hiring practices. The government may reach an industry indirectly through its powers of regulation over suppliers to that industry. Both these techniques have affected automobile design: seat belts, direction signals, and bumper standards can be influenced by requiring police cars and other government vehicles, and taxis, to meet the new standards. (Now that legislation protecting pension plans has been enacted, the federal government can help reform retirement practices in private business by remodeling its own practices to set the example.)

Changing the rules of the game has been another important way that government has redefined and restructured the responsibility of business. The National Labor Relations Act is an example. Both legislatively and through the courts a similar shift of bargaining advantage may occur, or may now be occurring, with respect to multiple-tenant landlords.

Schemes that operate in the market can have an element both of the voluntary and of the coercive. A tax that is discretionary rather than prohibitive is a flexible kind of coercion. Subsidies are much the same, though harsh words like "coercion" are typically not used when the firm is, on balance, a beneficiary and not a victim. Tax relief and cost-sharing arrangements are somewhat less "coercive" than straightforward regulation.

Similarly, government-financed research and development and government provision of goods and services (not necessarily "public goods" in the economist's jargon) offer a way of bypassing the coercion-voluntarism issue.

Thus the coercive and the voluntary are not exhaustive alternatives. They are not even opposite ends of a scale, since many techniques have little to do with either category.

BUSINESS CODES AND
ECONOMIC EFFICIENCY

Kenneth J. Arrow

This paper makes some observations on the widespread notion that the individual has some responsibility to others in the conduct of his economic affairs. It is held that there are a number of circumstances under which the economic agent should forgo profit or other benefits to himself in order to achieve some social goal, especially to avoid a disservice to other individuals. For the purpose of keeping the discussion within bounds, I shall confine my attention to the obligations that might be imposed on business firms. . . . Is it reasonable to expect that ethical codes will arise or be created? . . . This may seem to be a strange possiblity for an economist to raise. But when there is a wide difference in knowledge between the two sides of the market, recognized ethical codes can be, as has already been suggested, a great contribution to economic efficiency. Actually we do have examples of this in our everyday lives, but in very limited areas. The case of medical ethics is the most striking. By its very nature there is a very large difference in knowledge between the buyer and the seller. One is, in fact, buying precisely the service of someone with much more knowledge than you have. To make this relationship a viable one, ethical codes have grown up over the centuries, both to avoid the possibility of exploitation by the physician and to assure the buyer of medical services that he is not being exploited. I am not suggesting that these are universally obeyed, but there is a strong presumption that the doctor is going to perform to a large extent with your welfare in mind. Unnecessary medical expenses or other abuses are perceived as violations of ethics. There is a powerful ethical background against which we make this judgment. Behavior that we would regard as highly reprehensible in a physician is judged less harshly when found among businessmen. The medical profession is typical of professions in general. All professions involve a situation in which knowledge is unequal on two sides of the market by the very definition of the profession, and therefore there have grown up ethical principles that afford some protection to the client. Notice there is a mutual benefit in this. The fact is that if you had suffcient distrust of a doctor's services, you wouldn't buy them. Therefore the physician wants an ethical code to act as assurance to the buyer, and he certainly wants his competitors to obey this same code,

From "Social Responsibility and Economic Efficiency" by Kenneth J. Arrow, in *Public Policy*, vol. XXI, no. 3, Summer 1973. Copyright © 1973 by the President and Fellows of Harvard College. Reprinted by permission of John Wiley & Sons, Inc.

partly because any violation may put him at a disadvantage but more especially because the violation will reflect on him, since the buyer of the medical services may not be able to distinguish one doctor from another. A close look reveals that a great deal of economic life depends for its viability on a certain limited degree of ethical commitment. Purely selfish behavior of individuals is really incompatible with any kind of settled economic life. There is almost invariably some element of trust and confidence. Much business is done on the basis of verbal assurance. It would be too elaborate to try to get written commitments on every possible point. Every contract depends for its observance on a mass of unspecified conditions which suggest that the performance will be carried out in good faith without insistence on sticking literally to its wording. To put the matter in its simplest form, in almost every economic transaction, in any exchange of goods for money, somebody gives up his valuable asset before he gets the other's; either the goods are given before the money or the money is given before the goods. Moreover there is a general confidence that there won't be any violation of the implicit agreement. Another example in daily life of this kind of ethics is the observance of queue discipline. People line up; there are people who try to break in ahead of you, but there is an ethic which holds that this is bad. It is clearly an ethic which is in everybody's interest to preserve; one waits at the end of the line this time, and one is protected against somebody's coming in ahead of him.

In the context of product safety, efficiency would be greatly enhanced by accepted ethical rules. Sometimes it may be enough to have an ethical compulsion to reveal all the information available and let the buyer choose. This is not necessarily always the best. It can be argued that under some circumstances setting minimum safety standards and simply not putting out products that do not meet them would be desirable and should be felt by the businessman to be an obligation.

Now I've said that ethical codes are desirable. It doesn't follow from that that they will come about. An ethical code is useful only if it is widely accepted. Its implications for specific behavior must be moderately clear, and above all it must be clearly perceived that the acceptance of these ethical obligations by everybody does involve mutual gain. Ethical codes that lack the latter property are unlikely to be viable. How do such codes develop? They may develop as a consensus out of lengthy public discussion of obligations, discussion which will take place in legislatures, lecture halls, business journals, and other public forums. The codes are communicated by the very process of coming to an agreement. A more formal alternative would be to have some highly prestigious group discuss ethical codes for safety standards. In either case to become and to remain a part of the economic environment, the codes have to be accepted by the significant operating institutions and transmitted from one generation of executives to the next through standard operating procedures, through education in business schools, and through indoctrination of one kind or another. If we seriously expect such codes to develop and to be maintained, we might ask how the agreements develop and above all, how the codes remain stable. After all, an ethical code, however much it may be in the interest of all, is, as we remarked earlier, not in the interest of any one firm. The code may be of value to the running of the system as a whole, it may be of value to all firms if all firms maintain it, and yet it will be to the advantage of any one firm to cheat—in fact the more so, the more other firms are sticking to it. But there are some reasons for thinking that ethical codes can develop and be stable. These codes will not develop completely without institutional support. That is to say, there will be need for focal organizations, such as government agencies, trade associations, and consumer defense groups, or all combined to make the codes explicit, to iterate their doctrine and to make their presence felt. Given that help, I think the emergence of ethical codes on matters such as safety, at least, is possible. One positive factor here is something that is a negative factor in other contexts, namely that our economic organization is to such a large extent composed of large firms. The corporation is no longer a single individual; it is a social organization with internal social ties and internal pressures for acceptability and esteem. The individual members of the corporation are not only parts of the corporation but also members of a larger society whose esteem is desired. Power in a large corporation is necessarily diffused; not many individuals in such organizations feel so thoroughly identified with the corporation that other kinds of social pressures become irrelevant. Furthermore, in a large, complex firm where many people have to participate in any decision, there are likely to be some who are motivated to call attention to violations of the code. This kind of check has been conspicuous in government in recent years. The Pentagon Papers are an outstanding illustration of the fact that within the organization there are those who recognize moral guilt and take occasion to blow the whistle. I expect the same sort of behavior to occur in any large organization when there are well-defined ethical rules whose violation can be observed.

One can still ask if the codes are likely to be stable. Since it may well be possible and profitable for a minority to cheat, will it not be true that the whole system may break down? In fact, however, some of the pressures work in the other direction. It is clearly in the interest of those who are obeying the codes to enforce them, to call attention to violations, to use the ethical and social pressures of the society at large against their less scrupulous rivals. At the same time the value of maintaining the system may well be apparent to all, and no doubt ways will be found to use the assurance of quality generated by the system as a positive asset in attracting consumers and workers.

One must not expect miraculous transformations in human behavior. Ethical codes, if they are to be viable, should be limited in their scope. They are not a universal substitute for the weapons mentioned earlier, the institutions, taxes, regulations, and legal remedies. Further, we should expect the codes to apply only in situations where the firm has superior knowledge of the situation. I would not want the firm to act in

accordance with some ethical principles in regard to matters of which it
has little knowledge. For example, with quality standards which consumers can observe, it may not be desirable that the firm decide for itself, at
least on ethical grounds, because it is depriving the consumer of the
freedom of choice between high-quality, high-cost and low-quality, low-
cost products. It is in areas where someone is typically misinformed or
imperfectly informed that ethical codes can contribute to economic efficiency.

THE CODE OF ETHICS OF THE AMERICAN
SOCIETY OF CIVIL ENGINEERS

Mario G. Salvadori

INTRODUCTION

Each human society is governed by a set of laws, but each responsible
group in a society is governed, in addition, by a written or unwritten code
of ethics. The code of ethics represents an ideal and is morally binding
to the members of the group. Every professional group with activities
having an important bearing on the working of the society has a code of
ethics. The officers of an army, and the members of the medical, legal,
and teaching professions subscribe to such codes.

The codes are enforced by the group, which uses reprimand or ostracism to this purpose. The strictness of the enforcement of the code
should be in accordance with the degree of influence the group has on
society.

It is in this light that the codes of ethics of the engineering societies
must be considered. At a time of great moral upheaval, when the political,
business, educational, and professional leaderships are challenged all the
way to the top, it is imperative that the engineering societies make their
code of ethics significant, binding, enforceable, and enforced.

From *Engineering Issues*, vol. 101, no. E12, April 1975. Reprinted by permission of
Professional Publications, ASCE, New York.

Recently, other engineering societies have reassessed their goals and proposed basic changes in their code of ethics. ASCE encompasses the activity of a group whose influence on society has grown substantially in the last decade and whose image looms large in the eyes of the public. Because of this increased importance, it is essential that the code of ethics of ASCE be revised, after a thorough airing of its articles on the part of ASCE members. The following considerations are addressed to initiating this process.

Present Code of Ethics

The present Code of Ethics of the Society (as amended on October 1971, with a note added in July 1972, and a note on foreign engineering work adopted by ASCE Board of Direction in October 1963) is a short document consisting of nine separate articles followed by a "guide to professional practice under the code of ethics," in which the articles of the code are illustrated by means of specific examples.

The Code of Ethics consists of nine "don'ts." On the other hand, the Society has also endorsed the "fundamental principles of professional engineering ethics of the Canons of Ethics as adopted by the Engineers Council for Professional Development on September 1963, by Board action of May 1964." The Canons consist of three "dos."

It is obvious from a reading of the Code that its nine articles represent a concern about: (1) The relationship of the engineer to his employer or client; and (2) the relationship between engineers and the public image of the civil engineering profession. *But it is concerned about nothing else.* The Code is written mostly from the viewpoint of the engineer as a consultant or an employer of engineers and not as an employee, while today the large majority of civil engineers are employees.

The Canon of Ethics of Engineers, again, is concerned with the duties of the engineer as an employee, with the relationship between an engineer and his clients, and with the competence and prestige of the engineering profession. But, in contrast with the Code, it is concerned with the goal of the engineer as a potential benefactor to humanity.

It is useful to analyze briefly the nine articles of the Code and to group them under specific headings. Article 1 requires that the engineer be a faithful agent or trustee for his client and for his employer. No mention is made of requirements of the engineer as employer. Articles 2 and 8 refer to bribes and undue influence. Articles 3, 4, 5, and 7 regulate the relationships among engineers and, obviously, refer to engineers as consultants. Article 9 is a catchall concerned with "the honor, integrity, or dignity of the engineering profession." This analysis of the nine articles, incomplete as it is, shows the limited scope of the Code. A careful reading of the examples in the "Guide" reinforces such conclusion.

Basic Criteria for Evaluation of Present Code

To evaluate the present Code and to suggest possible improvements, one should consider the responsibilities of the engineer and establish a set of priorities for these responsibilities. As suggested by H. B. Koning, a member of the American Society of Mechanical Engineers, "the engineer interacts in his professional work with four groups of people: (1) the public, (2) his employer, (3) the customers of his employer (or in the case of self-employed engineers, his own customers), and (4) his engineering colleagues."

It would seem undebatable that the engineer's responsibility to the public should have first priority, responsibility to his employer or customer second priority, and responsibility to his engineering colleagues third priority. (This list of priorities, except for the first, actually may be interchangeable, depending on the issue.) The present Code of Ethics does not concern itself *at all* with priority No. 1 (responsibility to the public), gives very high priority to the responsibility of the engineer as an employee, and has a lot to say about the relationships among engineers. Thus, the entire emphasis of the Code is opposite to what is today an acceptable set of priorities in the eyes of both the engineering profession and the public.

The Canons of Ethics, while giving high priority to the conduct of the engineer as an employee, recognize clearly in the third article the responsibility of the engineer to the public "for the advancement of human welfare." It must be noted, though, that while this article makes it mandatory for the engineer to use his knowledge and skill for this purpose, it only *implies* that the engineer must *not* use his knowledge and skill in actions contrary to this purpose.

Thus, the combined articles of the Code and the Canons do not present the engineer, whatever his position, with a positive, encompassing, and clearly stated guide to his actions on the basis of ethics.

Guidelines to Professional Employment for Engineers and Scientists

Most of the engineering and other professional societies have adopted (in January 1973) guidelines to professional employment that ethically supplement the Codes and the Canons in a minor way. The guidelines are said to be "a guide to mutually satisfying relationships between professional employees and their employers" and to "represent desirable general goals rather than a set of specific minimum standards." As such, the guidelines are concerned with the responsibilities of the engineer as employer and employee.

In addition, Article 2 of the Terms of Employment, which concerns the professional employee, states in part: "Where the technical adequacy of a process or product is involved, he (the employee) should protect the

231

public and his employer by withholding approval of plans that do not meet accepted professional standards and by presenting clearly the consequences to be expected if his professional judgment is not followed." Thus, some consideration is given to the responsibility of the engineer to the public and to the influence of this responsibility on his relationship to his employer.

NOTES TO CODE OF ETHICS

The Code of Ethics was implemented in October 1963, by a note indicating in clear terms that the United States engineer is *not* bound by the ASCE Code of Ethics in foreign engineering work, except when only United States engineering firms are being considered for the work.

It is unsavory, to say the least, that such a note, obviously disparaging to all engineers except United States engineers, should still be in our Code at a time when international work is carried out by engineers of all nations, on a foot of equality, in competition with United States engineers.

Another note, added in July 1972, reflects the decision of the United States Courts that the prohibition of submitting fee quotations for engineering work is a restraint of trade. ASCE is said to be "constrained from prohibiting or limiting this practice." Although the reluctant acceptance of the Courts' decision on the part of ASCE is somewhat understandable, this note puts an end to a practice that over the years had become only theoretically unacceptable. It should not be considered necessary to keep it in the Code.

On the basis of the principles and considerations of the preceding paragraphs, the following draft of a new Code of Ethics is suggested for discussion by the members of ASCE. No footnotes are attached to it, nor is mention of the Canons of Ethics required by this suggested Code.

PROPOSED CODE OF ETHICS

Every member of the American Society of Civil Engineers:

1. Will use his knowledge and skill for the advancement of human welfare and refuse any assignment contrary to this goal.
2. Will act for his client or employer as a faithful agent or trustee, provided the consequences of his work are consonant with the goals of this Code.
3. Will encourage his employees to increase their knowledge and their skills and will not require of them actions contrary to the letter and spirit of this Code.
4. Will deal honestly and fairly with his colleagues as an employer, an employee, a consultant, and a client. Therefore:
    (a) He will not attempt to supplant another engineer in a particular engagement after definite steps have been taken towards his employment.
    (b) He will not attempt to injure, falsely or maliciously, the professional reputation, business, or employment position of another engineer.

    (c) He will not review the work of another engineer for the same client, except with the knowledge of such engineer, unless such engineer's engagement on the work that is subject to review has been terminated.

    (d) He will not use the advantages of a salaried position to compete unfairly with other engineers.

    (e) He will not exert undue influence or offer, solicit, or accept compensation for the purpose of affecting negotiations for an engineering engagement.

    (f) He will not accept remunerations for engineering services rendered other than from his client or his employer without their prior knowledge.

5. Will act in a manner compatible with the honor, integrity, and dignity of the engineering profession so as to increase its competence and prestige. (The proposed code has been approved in principle by the Environmental and Social Concerns Committee of the Construction Division.)

CODE ENFORCEMENT

At the present time, the mechanism for the enforcement of the Code of Ethics is cumbersome, slow, and not particularly attractive. Any complaints concerning the unethical behavior of members of the Society are to be presented to a Committee on Professional Practice that reviews them and reports to the Board of the Society. The Board then issues a statement, which cannot be appealed. The extremely limited number of complaints that have been dealt with by the Board over the years indicates that this mechanism is not ideal for the enforcement of the Code. In contrast to this, similar complaints are presented in large numbers to the ethics committees of the lawyers' and doctors' associations, are made public, and are dealt with in strict adherence to the spirit and the letter of the codes.

Following the adoption of the Rules of Employment for Engineers and Scientists by ASCE and assuming that some version of the suggested Code be adopted by the Society, it becomes clear that complaints concerning the relationships between engineering employees and engineering or nonengineering employers may well become numerous and that a new mechanism will be needed to make the new Code enforceable and enforced.

There are various levels at which the Society may intervene in matters of ethics in employee-employer relations. The minimum involvement would require the acceptance of complaints from employees, employers, and third interested parties, and the discussion of such complaints on the part of a *Committee on Ethics* to be created for this purpose. The activities of this Committee should be made public and the availability of a mechanism for redressing wrongs stemming from ethical considerations should be advertised widely in the literature of the Society. It would seem neither practical nor wise to have every decision of the Committee on Ethics referred to the Board, but it would be legally correct to delegate to the Board the role of Board of Appeals from the decisions of the Committee on Ethics. The deliberations of this Committee should be of a quasilegal nature, with plaintiff and defendant represented by counsel, if so desired. Obviously, the legal counsel of ASCE must advise on how the powers of the Committee should be defined and on how the process of complaints and deliberations should be carried out. The Committee, with the advice of the Society's counsel, should publish a pamphlet of its procedures and should list the types of judgments they would be entitled to consider, from simple reprimands to expulsion from the Society. Also, it should be possible for the Society to participate either as *amicus curiae* or as witness for the plaintiff or the defendant in actual legal proceedings, or in extralegal proceedings, e.g., personnel actions by corporations not governed by the ASCE Code of Ethics. Here again the advice of the Society's legal counsel should be requested, case by case.

It is clear that the enforcement of the Code under the articles considered in its new suggested version would entail expenses to the Society as well as serious involvement on the part of the members of the Committee on Ethics and the Board. On the other hand, this is what other professional societies have been doing for years and, unless ASCE takes upon itself this kind of burden, obviously, its new potential members, who expect much more from the Society than what it has given so far, will not consider it a professional society and will refuse to join it. Without debating here whether the Society should become an engineering "union," it seems clear that the Society cannot expect the support of its young membership unless it adopts in the near future the kind of attitude sketched in this article.

It may be well to remember that in jurisprudence a law that is unenforceable is considered invalid. By analogy, a Code of Ethics that is not enforced or enforceable should not be on the books of the Society.

BUSINESS CODES OF ETHICS:
Window Dressing or Legitimate Alternative to Government Regulation?

Norman E. Bowie

The problem is to find some mechanism for ensuring that *all* corporations adhere to the minimum conditions of business ethics. Most corporations believe that it is clearly in the enlightened self-interest of the free enterprise system to ensure adherence to ethical standards through self-regulation. Unethical conditions should not be allowed to develop to the point where government regulation takes over. Government regulation of corporate ethics is viewed on a scale from distrust to horror. There are several reasons why government regulation is opposed. These include:

1. A recognition that government regulation would diminish the power and the prestige of corporate officials.
2. A fear that government officials would interfere with incentives and efficiency and hence reduce profit.
3. A judgment that government officials do not understand business and hence that its regulations would be unrealistic and hence unworkable.
4. A judgment that government officials are in no position to comment on the ethics of others.
5. A judgment that the federal government is already too powerful in a pluralistic society so that it is inappropriate to increase the power of government in this way.
6. A judgment that government regulation violates the legitimate freedom and moral rights of corporations.

When compared to the spectre of government regulations, codes of ethics at least deserve a second look. Codes of good business practice do serve a useful function and are not new. After all, one of the purposes of the Better Business Bureau is to protect both the consumer and the legitimate business operator from the "fly-by-night operator." The lesson we learn from the Better Business Bureau is that business ethics is not simply in the interest of the consumer, it is in the vital interest of the business community as well. Business activity depends on a high level of trust and confidence. If a firm or industry loses the confidence of the public, it will have a difficult time in selling its products. Kenneth Arrow has made this point in an earlier selection. An important result follows from the argument that business codes are in the general interest of business. To be effective, codes of business ethics must be adopted industry-wide. Otherwise, it is not to the competitive advantage of the individual firm to follow them. For example, it would not make sense for Bethlehem Steel to initiate the installation of anti-pollution devices for their own plants. In the absence of similar initiatives on the part of other steel companies, Bethlehem's steel would become more expensive and hence Bethlehem would suffer at the hands of its competitors.

An industry-wide code based on rational self-interest would help rebut a frequent criticism of the codes of individual firms. Often the cynical reaction of the public to any individual code is that it is a mere exercise in public relations. For arguments already given, there is good reason for that public reaction. An individual code by a particular firm on matters of industry-wide significance runs the danger of being nothing but window dressing if the firm is not to be at a competitive disadvantage. However an industry-wide code designed to protect legitimate businesses from the unethical acts of their competitors is not mere public relations; it is designed to preserve the trust and confidence of the public which is necessary for the survival of the industry itself. For the purpose of protecting the consumer and hence ultimately for the protection of industry itself, industry-wide codes of ethics are in theory a viable alternative to government regulation.

If industry-wide codes of ethics make sense on grounds of self-interest, why don't we have more successful examples? Two factors explain the basic situation. The first has to do with the scope of the regulations, and the second has to do with enforcement.

First, it is hard to make regulations flexible enough to meet a wide variety of situations, especially new situations, and yet simple enough to guide people's behavior in ways that will hold them accountable. Many criticize professional codes of ethics because they are too broad and amorphous. For example, consider four of the first six standards of the Public Relations Society of America.

1. A member has a general duty of fair dealing towards his clients or employees, past and present, his fellow members and the general public.
2. A member shall conduct his professional life in accord with the public welfare.
3. A member has the affirmative duty of adhering to generally accepted standards of accuracy, truth, and good taste.
6. A member shall not engage in any practice which tends to corrupt the integrity of channels of public communication.

By using such terms as "fair dealing," "public welfare," "generally accepted standards," and "corrupt the integrity," the code of standards of the PRSA could be charged with being too general and vague.

Before giving up on codes on this account, a few comments about the nature of language are in order. Except in the use of proper names, language is always general and is always in need of interpretation. Consider a municipal law: "No vehicles are allowed in the park." What counts as a vehicle? A bicycle? A skateboard? A baby carriage? Moreover, whenever we have a definition, there are certain borderline cases. When is a person bald or middle-aged? I used to think 35 was middle-aged. Now I am not so sure. The point of these comments is to show that some of the criticisms of business codes are really not criticisms of the codes but of language itself.

One should note, however, that none of these remarks refutes the criticism that business codes of ethics are too general and amorphous. Indeed these codes must be supplemented by other forms of self-regulation. First, the codes must provide procedures for interpreting what the code means and what it requires. Just as the Constitution needs the Supreme Court, a code of business ethics needs something similar. A serious code of business ethics can have its vagueness and generality corrected in ways not dissimilar from the mechanisms used by the law to correct vagueness problems in statutes and precedents. Perhaps a professional association could serve as the necessary analogue. Business codes of ethics do not have unique problems here.

Now we come to the second basic factor underlying the lack of successful existing codes of ethics: the difficulty of adequate enforcement procedures. There is a validity to the saying that a law which is unenforceable is really not a law at all. Any code of ethics worth having is worth enforcing and enforcing effectively.

First, the codes must be taken seriously in the sense that failure to follow them will carry the same penalties that failure to meet other company objectives carries. The trouble with many corporate codes of ethics is that employees see the codes as peripheral to their main concerns. After all, what is important is the bottom line. Experience demonstrates that when the crunch comes, ethics takes a back seat.

If they were philosophers, the employees could put their point in the form of a syllogism. (1) If management is serious about a policy, management will enforce it; (2) management doesn't enforce its codes of ethics; (3) therefore management isn't really serious about its codes of ethics.

If codes of ethics are to work they must be enforced, and the first step in getting them enforced is to get them taken seriously by the management. How is that to be done? Phillip T. Drotning of Standard Oil of Indiana puts it this way:

> Several generations of corporate history have demonstrated that any significant corporate activity must be locked into the mainstream of corporate operations or it doesn't get done. Social policies will remain placebos for the tortured executive conscience until they are implemented with the same iron fisted management tools that are routinely employed in other areas of activity to measure performance, secure accountability, and distribute penalties and rewards.[1]

In a home where discipline is taken seriously a certain atmosphere pervades. I submit that in a company where ethics is taken seriously, a certain atmosphere will also pervade. Since I do not work in a business corporation, I cannot identify all the signs which indicate that the right atmosphere exists, but I can mention some possibilities discussed in the literature. These include:

1. Recognition that ethical behavior transcends the requirements of the law. The attitude that if it's not illegal it's okay is wrong. It's wrong first because at most the law prescribes minimum standards of ethical behavior. The public desires higher standards and the desire of the public is legitimate although I will not argue for this point here. Moreover, the attitude "if it's not illegal, it's okay" is wrong because it is ultimately self-defeating. By depending upon the law, one is encouraging the government regulations most business persons strongly object to. The American Institute for Certified Public Accountants recognizes this point when it describes its code of professional ethics as a voluntary assumption of self-discipline above and beyond the requirements of law.

2. A high level officer, presumably a vice-president, with suitable staff support, being empowered to interpret and enforce the code. This vice-president should have the same status as the vice-presidents for marketing, production, personnel, etc. The vice-president should also be responsible for measuring performance.

3. Utilization of the device of the corporate social audit as part of the measurement of performance. The corporate social audit has come to have a number of different meanings. What I have in mind, however, is a revision of the corporation's profit and loss statement and balance sheet. Following the ideas of David Linowes, on the credit side all voluntary expenditures not required by law aimed at improving the employees and the public would be entered. On the debit side would be known expenditures which a reasonably prudent socially aware management would make, but didn't make. Such debit entries represent lost opportunities which the company should not have lost.

I recognize that many of these suggestions are highly controversial and I do not want the discussion to shift away from our main topic. This discussion does reiterate, however, an important point made before. Codes of ethics by themselves are not sufficient devices to provide the climate for a desirable record on business ethics. Codes of ethics must be buttressed by internal mechanisms within the corporation if they are to be effective. They must be adequately interpreted and effectively enforced.

Given these criticisms, we should remind ourselves why written codes, both legal and moral, are viewed as desirable despite their inadequacies. Laws or codes of conduct provide more stable permanent guides to right or wrong than do human personalities. As you recall, God recognized that the charismatic leadership of Moses needed to be replaced by the Ten Commandments. Codes of ethics or rules of law provide guidance especially in ethically ambiguous situations. When one is tempted to commit a wrong act, laws also provide the basis for appeal in interpersonal situations. Professor Henry P. Sims, Jr., Professor of Organizational Behavior at Penn State, has done some research with graduate students confronted with decision-making opportunities. His results show that a clear company policy forbidding kickbacks lowers the tendency of the graduate students to permit kickbacks. A business code of ethics can provide an independent ground of appeal when one is urged by a friend or associate to commit an unethical act. "I'm sorry, but company policy strictly forbids it," is a gracious way of ending a conversation about a "shady" deal.

Codes of ethics have another advantage. They not only guide the behavior of average citizens or employees, they control the power of the leaders and employers. For Plato, questions of political morality were to be decided by philosopher kings. Plato had adopted this approach after observing the bad decisions of the Athenian participatory democracy. Aristotle, however, saw the danger that Plato's elitism could easily lead to tyranny. The actions of human beings needed to be held in check by law. The English and American tradition is similar. One means for controlling the king or other governing officials is through a constitution. The Bill of Rights of our own Constitution protects the individual from the tyranny of the majority. A strict company code of ethics would help provide a needed defense for an employee ordered by a superior to do something immoral. "I'm sorry but company regulations forbid that" does have some bite to it.

Finally, during the time when conflicting standards of ethics are being pushed on the business community, a code of ethics would help clarify the ethical responsibilities of business. One of the most frustrating aspects of the current debate about business ethics is that no one knows what the rules are. Most business leaders recognize that the social responsibilities of business must expand and that businessmen and women will be held to higher ethical standards than in the past. However there are some obvious limits. A blanket ethical demand that business solve all social problems is arbitrary and unrealistic. Business codes of ethics acceptable both to the business community and to the general public would help bring some order out of the chaos.

Let me conclude by providing some suggestions for writing an effective code of ethics. I am taking these suggestions directly from an article by Neil H. Offen, Senior Vice-President and Legal Counsel of the Direct Selling Association.

1. Be clear on your objectives, and make sure of your constituent's support. It is important to get the commitment from the president of each company.
2. Set up a realistic timetable for developing and implementing your code.
3. Know the costs of running a code program, and be sure you have long-term as well as short-term funding.
4. Make sure to provide for changing the code to meet new situations and challenges. It should be a living document.
5. Gear your code to the problems faced by your industry or profession.
6. Be aware of the latest developments and trends in the area of self-regulation. Pay particular attention to FTC, Justice Department, and Congressional activities.
7. Make sure legal counsel is consulted and the code is legally defensible.
8. Get expert advice on how to promote the code and how to go about educating the public.
9. Watch your rhetoric. Don't promise more than you can deliver.
10. Write it as simply as possible. Avoid jargon and gobbledygook.
11. Be totally committed to being responsive and objective.
12. Select an independent administrator of unquestionable competence and integrity.
13. Be patient, maintain your perspective, and don't lose your sense of humor.[2]

Notes

1. Phillip T. Drotning, "Organizing the Company for Social Action," in S. Prakash Sethi, *The Unstable Ground: Corporate Social Policy in a Dynamic Society* (Los Angeles: Melville Publishing Co., 1974), p. 259.
2. Neil H. Offen, "Commentary on Code of Ethics of Direct Selling Association," in *The Ethical Basis of Economic Freedom* (Chapel Hill, N.C.: American Viewpoint, Inc. 1976), pp. 274–75.

THE LOGIC, SCOPE, AND FEASIBILITY OF THE CORPORATE SOCIAL AUDIT

John J. Corson
George A. Steiner
in collaboration with Robert C. Meehan

The corporation, like the government, the hospital, the university, and the church, is being held accountable to its constituencies and to the general public in an unprecedented fashion today.

This demand is an inevitable consequence of the emergence of the compact society in which many more units—business firms, governments, hospitals, colleges, universities, and others—compete with one another in markedly limited living space to serve a people that expect a better quality of life than has previously been available to them. Each unit is being held accountable for contributing to making life safer, more secure, more healthful, more equitable, and more rewarding of honest effort, and to offering greater opportunity for every individual. These two trends (the increasing demand for accountability by the individual unit and the rising expectations as to the acceptable quality of life) underlie the development of the social audit. . . .

Historically, the primary *social* responsibility of the corporation has been to discover and develop goods and services that satisfy the needs of people. The accomplishment of that end—the production of an increasing abundance of steadily improving goods and services—has long been regarded as of such great value to the society as to warrant the earning of profits.[1]

As the basic wants for food, clothing, shelter, and health care of most members of American society have been satisfied, society's expectations have grown to include not only new and better goods and services but other things as well. For example: (1) services of clear social utility that were once provided by government and are now provided by corporations at a *profit;* such services include postsecondary education (e.g., the schools and educational services marketed by Bell and Howell Company) and providing food services for school programs and for aged and invalid persons in their homes; (2) a widening range of amenities, services, and information for employees, consumers, shareholders, and the community, without prospect of profit and at the cost of the corporation.

If the social audit is to catalogue all such activities, verify the costs entailed, and evaluate the benefits produced, it becomes an evaluation of everything a corporation is doing. When the scope is thus defined, it becomes impractical to accomplish a social audit and, indeed, the information it would present would likely be too massive to be useful.

If, on the other hand, the scope of the audit—that is, the activities to be catalogued, verified, and evaluated—is limited, it will not demonstrate to the constituencies the extent to which the corporation's social performance measures up to what the constituents expect. For example, the social audit will not perform this principal function if it is limited to (1) those activities for which a corporation's executives are particularly concerned about accomplishments and/or costs incurred; (2) those activities about which information is publicized to better the corporation's public image.

Therefore, the scope of the social audit (like the scope of the financial audit) is determined by the informational needs of those it is designed to serve—employees, consumers, concerned shareholders, the general public, and those who influence the shaping of public opinion. In the course of time those needs will undoubtedly change, but in the main they will include the need for information about: (1) statutorily required activities (e.g., the provision of equal employment opportunities for minority group members); (2) voluntary activities (e.g., the making of contributions to health, educational, and cultural agencies and the "adoption" of a local high school); and (3) socially useful activities undertaken for the making of profits (e.g., contracting to provide teaching services in the schools).

The key task for the corporation is to specify what activities are of concern to its constituencies at a particular time.[2] It is a difficult task, and new ways and means must be developed to accomplish it. . . .

Few social audits made today embrace the categories of activities that fall logically within its scope as suggested here. The scope of few if any of these audits is determined by the standard of social expectations that has been proposed. The failure to attain this ideal is to be expected at this early stage in the evolution of this form of appraisal. A methodology for identifying social expectations and appraising corporate social performance is still being developed. To indicate the point that has been reached, we will describe ways of determining what society expects of the corporation and examine existing yardsticks for measuring the corporation's performance of various social activities.

Society communicates its expectations in several ways. This is done through the crusading of reformers. It is also done by businessmen with social foresight who by taking advanced steps communicate the needs of society by example. Such examples have been set by Henry Ford when he established the $5 per-day wage in the automobile industry, by George Eastman and Marion B. Folsom when in the 1930s Eastman Kodak Company established its wage-dividend and pension policies, and by International Business Machines Corporation and Xerox Corporation more recently in granting leaves at full pay to employees who choose to engage in community activities.

Group pressures are another means by which society communicates its expectations. The National Consumers League in the 1930s and the United Farm Workers in 1972 communicated what they contended were the expectations of the society by mobilizing consumers to force employers to better conditions for their workers. Strikes, boycotts, sit-ins, and demonstrations have been used to convey other expectations to corporate leadership.

In theory, society communicates its expectations to corporate leadership through the voices of the corporation's stockholders. Many recent stockholders' meetings illustrate both the theoretical process as well as its ineffectiveness. A score of issues ranging from the corporation's efforts to curb pollution and employ women to changing its operations in South Africa have been presented by small, articulate minorities in the form of resolutions for stockholder approval which have been regularly voted down. The presentation of such resolutions by a few stockholders, despite their usual rejection, nevertheless forces corporate management to consider whether society expects it to perform the actions proposed.

Society conveys its expectations most clearly when they are finally enacted into law. Prior to 1935, a few employers provided pensions for employees who had spent much of their adult life in their employ. Unemployment and suffering among the aged during the depression of the 1930s attracted public concern and resulted in the enactment of the Social Security Act. By means of this law, society converted a growing public desire and the example of a few employers into an obligation for all employers. Other examples of such actions are apparent in the labeling requirements and product quality standards set by the Food and Drug Administration and the Federal Trade Commission, in the water quality standards established by the state governments, and in the financial reporting practices stipulated by the Securities and Exchange Commission.

Such channels of information provided the corporation executive with indications of society's expectations.[3] However, much of what is transmitted through these channels (other than actual legislation) is distorted by the opposing views of others in the society, is blurred by emotions, or is simply inaccurate. The executive is thus left with the task of weighing these messages and deciding what expectations have gained general acceptance among consumers, employers, stockholders, and citizens so strongly as to suggest, if not require, that the corporation take action. His problem is one of determining what social responsibilities are of such critical and continuing importance to the constituencies his firm serves as to warrant its acceptance of the associated costs and obligations.[4]

The methodology to make this determination has not been perfected but is now being developed. Staff members of the larger corporation usually have an understanding of the demands as well as threats made on the company at the present time and those that will be made in the future. What the corporation more often lacks is the capacity for objectively weighing its obligation to meet such demands. Yet some larger companies, General Electric Company, for instance, have made such assessments.[5] They have demonstrated that decisions can be made by staff, when guided by clear policy, about the relationship that the corporation strives to maintain to the society.[6] To ensure objectivity the corporation's staff and managers can be aided by market surveys and polls of constituent opinion that provide reliable indications of social expectations. From the results managers then can select those activities they think they should pursue to meet the most urgent needs of society. . . .

Presuming that the scope of a social audit can be determined, what yardsticks are available to measure the costs and accomplishments of activities included in the social audit? Without credible measures of business's social performance the social audit will make little progress. Many business executives hold views similar to that expressed by one respondent to [a] survey, who stated: "Most of the elements involved cannot be quantified in any meaningful way and . . . a balance sheet would result only in an oversimplified representation which might lend itself to puffery." Measures of accomplishment for many activities, as this respondent has accurately pointed out, do not yet exist, and the identification of costs is sometimes difficult. The problems involved in developing measures of accomplishment and in identifying relevant costs are substantial, yet the development of useful measures is progressing.

The financial auditor has numerous acceptable yardsticks for evaluating the financial operations of a business enterprise. They include unit production costs, the ratio of each category of costs to the sales dollar, the current ratio, inventory turnover, the aging of receivables, cash flow analyses, the ratio of net earnings to interest on debt, and others. The social auditor is at an early stage in forging similar yardsticks and faces formidable obstacles in perfecting measures for a number of social activities. . . .

The development of the social audit today is hobbled, as our survey indicates, by confusion as to purpose as well as by difficulties confronted in striving to measure costs and accomplishments. If the social audit is to inform insiders alone, one set of measures focusing on costs and efficiency of performance is needed. If the social audit is designed to meet the demands of outsiders for an assessment of social performance, a different set of measures is required.

If we assume that both needs must be served, the problem of measurement still remains. By definition an audit is a "methodical examination and review," but many businessmen view an audit as necessarily involving quantification, and, as we have stated, the quantification of costs and accomplishments is difficult, the latter more so than the former.

The costs involved in many social activities, although not all, are difficult to isolate. The benefits received by the company itself or those contributed to society are difficult to appraise. For example, what cost/benefit is involved in the maintenance by corporations of deposits in minority-owned and -operated banks? In increasing the proportion of blacks in the corporate work force? If the cost of building a plant in the inner city rather than moving it to the suburbs can be identified, how can the auditor measure the benefits produced for the company? For the community? What is the value to society of contributions to the support of black colleges and universities? Of the service of corporate employees on leave to teach in universities? Of the stimulation of interest in liturgical music?

The quantification that is involved in the financial audit (which conditions thinking as to the nature of a social audit) evolved over many years. Gradually accountants have found ways of quantifying concepts that at an earlier time were dealt with only or primarily as subjective judgments (e.g., cash flow). But even today some important concepts of costs and value are difficult to quantify and are treated in descriptive footnotes to corporate financial statements.

Methods for quantifying accomplishments of social activities are being developed. For those activities that are now required by government, some yardsticks that quantify what is expected have been established; for example, state and federal governments have established air quality and water quality standards. Yardsticks are evolving for some activities that are generally accepted by corporations as responsibilities they should bear, for example, the proportion of net income the corporation contributes to charitable, educational, religious, and welfare institutions. For many activities that corporations have undertaken, no yardsticks of accomplishment are yet available. To illustrate, there are no yardsticks to measure the performance of a company in helping society to improve its transportation systems or to preserve animal life or to recycle materials. . . . Gradually ways must and, hopefully, will be found to evaluate the worth as well as the cost of many activities that are now unmeasurable. . . .

One-half of the companies responding to our survey stated that they made the results of their audit of social activities available only to the company's executives and directors. Less than half the respondent companies made the results available to stockholders and to the public. Do these practices constitute the kind of accountability being called for?

When one assesses the demands from constituents and the breadth of the social audits being made by the pioneering companies, the answer must be "No." Yet, an increasing number of corporations are now including statements in their annual and quarterly reports to stockholders describing what they have done in particular fields of social activity.[7] A few corporations use newspaper advertising to tell the general public about social activities they are engaged in,* and some others have prepared special reports describing rather comprehensively their activities and have made them generally available.

Examples of such special reports are those made in 1972, 1973, and 1974 by the General Motors Corporation entitled *Report on Progress in Areas of Public Concern*. These reports explain what General Motors did in these years to meet the problems of automobile pollution and automobile safety. They refine and make more generally known the corporation's policy relative to investments in South Africa, its policy and accomplishments in hiring members of minority groups, its efforts to assist minority

---

*For example, the Chase Manhattan Bank advertised in a number of newspapers and journals that "We helped the Black magazine *(Black Enterprise)* that's helping Black businessmen."

group members to conduct their own businesses, and its efforts to seek the views of the consumers of its products and act upon their complaints.[8]

Notes

1. Criticisms of the "large corporation as a malevolent conscious force" ignore the central fact that "the large bureaucratized industrial enterprise is the principal tool that we have available for providing those resources which are needed to improve the quality of life." Joseph L. Bower, "On the Amoral Organization," in Marris, *The Corporate Society*, p. 178.
2. For a list of fourteen major constituencies likely to exert pressure that the corporation must consider in its strategic planning processes, see Ian H. Wilson, "Reforming the Strategic Planning Process: Integration of Social Responsibility and Business Needs," in Sethi, *The Unstable Ground*, pp. 245–255.
3. For views that have aided us in developing this analysis, see Dow Votaw, "Corporate Social Reform: An Educator's Viewpoint"; and George P. Hinckley and James E. Post, "The Performance Context of Corporate Responsibility," in Sethi, *The Unstable Ground*, pp. 14–23; 293–302.
4. For an ingenious method for making such determinations, see Allan D. Shocker and S. Prakash Sethi, "An Approach to Incorporating Social Preferences in Developing Corporate Action Strategies," in Sethi, *The Unstable Ground*, pp. 67–80.
5. For a discussion and evaluation of some ninety-seven demands made in this company, see Robert M. Estes, "Today's Demands on Business," in *The Changing Business Role in Modern Society*, ed. George A. Steiner (Los Angeles: University of California at Los Angeles, Graduate School of Management, 1974), pp. 160–178.
6. For an excellent example of such policy, see "What Should a Corporation Do?" *Roper Report*, no. 2 (October 1971), pp. 2–3. This contains an excerpt of the philosophy and goals of the Standard Oil Company (N.J.), now the Exxon Corporation.
7. Fry Consultants, *Social Responsibilities II* (Washington, D.C., 1971), p. 2.
8. Other companies that distribute similar reports for public consumption include the Bank of America, CNA Financial Corporation, Dayton Hudson Corporation, Eastern Gas and Fuel Associates, and Ford Motor Company.

MEASUREMENT PROBLEMS IN THE SOCIAL AUDIT

David H. Blake
William C. Frederick
Mildred S. Myers

When those interested in social auditing gather together, questions about social measurement invariably arise. Those that get the most attention are (1) Is it possible to measure social factors with an acceptable degree of precision?; and (2) What standards will be used to judge the social performance of corporations? Both matters are complex, and discussions of them tend to bristle with such exotic phrases as "utiles," "pareto optima," "consensual norms," "cost-benefit analysis," and "independent attest function."

One result of these discussions is the creation of the erroneous impression that measurement problems are purely technical matters better left to experts who speak the language of mathematics, economics, and accounting. However, a closer look reveals a different story.

Measurement problems tend to be related to questions of definition and identification, two factors that can—and usually do—permit wide-ranging individual interpretation. Consider, for example, the definition of the goals of a social program. A social auditor looking at a program within a company may well find that the chief executive officer has one set of goals and sees the program fulfilling one particular purpose, while the manager and employees of the department administering the program view it differently. The government may see yet another purpose for the program, and the people (inside or outside the company) who are affected by the program will obviously have still different goals for it. Whose goals, then, should the social auditor consider in the attempt to, first, identify the *program's* goals and, second, evaluate whether or how the goals are being achieved? The answer is probably that the goals of everyone concerned should be examined, but if this is the case, how should the goals be weighted when the time comes to evaluate the program's effectiveness? Should the president's goals be considered more important than those of the recipients of the program's benefits? Goals have a personal and subjective dimension as well as a social and organizational meaning, and they are vitally important in any attempt to measure a program's effectiveness. Efforts to appy traditional measurement and weighting systems inevitably involve the consideration of individualized and nonobjective factors.

Definitional problems, too, affect attempts to quantify, standardize, and measure. Terminology that has one unquestioned meaning in traditional financial or economic contexts may be misunderstood, misconstrued, misleading, or simply inappropriate when it is applied to situations other than those for which it was formulated. There has been enough discussion about whether or not "social auditing" is a legitimate term to make this point clear. If "auditing" is to mean strictly what it means in accounting terminology, then we may be a long way from "social auditing"; indeed, in those terms, it may be impossible to do. If, however, the term takes on a different meaning in a different context, "social auditing" is being done. These terminology problems become attitudinal difficulties when they lead to dissension about whether "social auditing" is or is not—or should be—"auditing." If it is auditing, should accountants be the only people who do it? If it is not auditing in the traditional sense—or should not be—what is it, whose ground rules should be used, what standards should be applied? These two examples indicate clearly that while there are genuine methodological problems and dilemmas, measurement is inextricably intertwined with political, social, and attitudinal issues.

Whose Standards Should Be Used?

Consider the question of the criteria to be used in judging a corporation's social performance. Whose standards should prevail respecting air pollution? Those of an aroused citizen group? Of the Environment Protection Agency? Of scientists testifying for the polluting industry or of those who testify against it? Of employees who may lose their jobs if the plant is forced to shut down? Or should profit-oriented stockholder values prevail?

Not only will this conflict be resolved through the process of bargaining and negotiation (a political process), but the outcome will represent some compromise of the positions and viewpoints of various parties. The technical measurement experts ask the question "Whose values will constitute the criteria for corporate performance?" with an air of despair, as if there is no answer. True, there is no pristine answer, free from the pulling and hauling of everyday problems, and the outcome might not be as neatly packaged as one would like. Criteria may be arbitrary, shifting, and difficult to quantify precisely. But from the negotiating process, some standards do emerge. Ambient air standards now exist, representing a compromise of the views of many interested groups. The same can be said for minority employment standards, for product safety standards, for drug effectiveness standards, and for standards in other areas of social concern.

What Should Be Measured and How?

Deciding what and how to measure are also questions of value choices. Since none of us exists in a social or political vacuum, those choices about what is worth measuring are inevitably affected by sociopolitical factors.

What do you identify as racial or sexual discrimination? You can compute the numbers of jobs held by minority persons and compare those figures with jobs held by the dominant majority, and such measures are important to make. But what about the more subtle factors such as racial and sexual attitudes, feelings, deep-seated prejudices? Many social factors simply cannot be stated or measured in quantitative terms, or the figures that can be developed do not really capture the essence of the problem. One way out of this dilemma is to design meaningful nonquantitative measures that will allow comparisons to be made. Another possibility is to find ways to state qualitative factors in quantitative terms. Some encouraging developments are under way now to design "social indicators" that will help measure a community's social well-being, just as various "economic indicators" are used to help calculate economic well-being. . . .

Assuming that adequate social measuring sticks can be developed, one encounters the further problem of deciding which criteria to use in assessing a company's social performance. What is the standard of social "good" or "bad"? For example, how many blacks must be hired before a company or a union is nondiscriminatory? Should the number be equal to their proportion in the general population? Or to the population in the particular community in which the social audit is being made? Or should employment opportunities be made even greater than either of these percentage figures, as a way of compensating today's blacks for the long history of discrimination? Similar difficulties arise in the case of women. Because women constitute more than half of the population, is any company guilty of sexual discrimination if the majority of its employees are male? If a percentage figure is used, for blacks or women, should it be a percentage of the total employee force, in all ranks and all jobs? Or should the figure be divided by job classification and rank, for both blacks and women?

In these examples as well as in others that could be cited, social auditors need generally accepted social standards against which to measure, but these standards frequently do not exist, or data that do exist may not be usable to reach any kind of consensus on social criteria. Here, too, help may come as current research on the development and application of social indicators goes forward.

Clearly, even deciding *how* to measure social elements—a decision that would seem, at first glance, to be just as technical as it can be—is a process that reflects philosophic attitudes and points of view. When Abt Associates set out to convert social costs and benefits into dollars, there was a storm of protest from those who said it couldn't—and/or shouldn't—be done. There are values in life that are not reducible to such crass calculations, claimed some of the critics. Others maintained that Abt's dollar figures give an incomplete and misleading rundown on a company's social posture. Closely allied to this view is the one that maintains that social auditing has the same dim future enjoyed by all attempts to attach numbers to the values that are important to individuals and to society. Welfare economists who have attempted for years to quantify the fugitive elements of "preference," "utility," and "indifference" have taken their share of criticism for even making the attempts. On the other side of the controversy are those who urge that progress lies in the direction of quantifying everything. Their attitude tends to be that if measures don't exist now, we should get on with the job of designing them.

What these conflicting positions tell us is that measurement, even in its most technical manifestations, is very much a political, philosophical, and "human" undertaking. Virtually all corporate actions have economic and social results and involve large numbers of people from different groups. Each group may feel more strongly about one issue than another, leading to immense difficulties in comparing different areas of social action and concern. It is difficult, if not impossible, to find a standard of comparison applicable to, for example, industrial pollution and employment discrimination. The net result is that moral, ethical, and political problems emerge as equally important to technical problems, and the latter may become the former. The prevailing sociopolitical structure and process exert great influence upon the measurement enterprise by helping to decide whose values will be used as criteria, what social elements will be measured, and how the measurement will be done.

METHODOLOGICAL PROBLEMS

All of the foregoing is not to imply that there are not genuine methodological problems associated with social auditing. The literature abounds with descriptions of attempts to develop measurement and reporting methods that will be useful and accurate . . . And for every article outlining a proposed measurement system, there is a response indicating the reasons why that system will not work. A number of examples will illustrate these methodological dilemmas.

What indicators should be used in attempts to measure the effects of pollution? Tons of pollutants? Number of days the plant had to shut down because the air pollution level in the area was too high? Dollar cost to others of either the pollution or the shut-downs? The Environmental Protection Agency has set standards, but perusal of the daily newspapers in any large city shows clearly that not everyone agrees with or abides by these criteria. The standards that are set may not be accurate indicators. A plant may have no shut-down days at all and still be a high polluter; if it is the only plant in the area, the total level of air pollution in that area may never reach the stage where shut-down is required. But this is no measure of what the plant is doing that causes pollution or what it is doing to prevent pollution.

Suppose a corporation wants to evaluate the ways in which it attempts to improve the quality of life for its employees. The company's goal might be identified as a desire to provide a positive work environment and to enhance the quality of life in the corporation's entities. One step in this direction, it might be decided, is to improve the lighting in the plants. Does this plan, when it is effected, help meet the goal? There are various elements to be evaluated, some of which are measurable and some not.

In this example, it may be possible to measure directly some effects but not others. How much the lighting in a plant has been improved is measurable quantitatively, but what this improvement means to the workers may not be. One can measure the input—what changes in lighting occurred—and, perhaps, an output—increased worker productivity, for example, if there is such an increase. The output may be an effect of the input and may well be measurable, at least in part. But, if an attempt is being made to measure ways in which the corporation is thereby improving the quality of working life, there are other effects that should be measured. These could be called perceived effects (for example, the workers' reactions to and feelings about the improved lighting) that are not easily measurable, if at all.

Even factors that seem relatively simple to measure may turn out to have hidden difficulties. Consider the area of plant safety and reduction of accidents. This seems to be an easy area to measure because accidents are identifiable; they must be reported and tabulated, and the Occupational Safety and Health Administration has definite requirements for these reports. But, to what extent are all accidents really reported? Are there some incidents that are not entered in the statistics? Are the official definition of an accident and the workers' perceptions one and the same? What was actually reported? Was the accident reported the one that really occurred?

Another quantification technique that has generated a flurry of interest is human resource accounting, in which a firm attempts to measure the cost and value of people to the organization. Items normally considered to be expenses, such as employee training and benefits, are treated as investments that contribute to building up resources. In terms of social benefits, the idea of seeing human resources as assets may bolster employees' morale. In speeches, in internal publications, and even in annual reports, executives frequently say something to the effect that "our employees are our most valuable resources and assets." But until the recent attempts at human resource accounting, these valuable resources and assets never appeared in a financial statement. So there may well be some social value (at the least, in a public relations sense; at best, in the company's truly perceiving and treating employees as assets) in human resource accounting.

The technical problem with trying to put human resources into the balance sheet as an asset is that these resources have no separate existence of their own, as do a patent or trademark or a piece of equipment or property. The Coca Cola formula and trademark, for example, would have value to another organization and could be sold for a set dollar amount. The labor force does not necessarily perform functions that would be conveyable or salable by the company. In addition, human assets could take a sudden decline in value that could not be forecasted or systematically depreciated.

Various attempts have been made, by David Linowes and others, to construct accounting systems to measure social data. But these systems may leave out some important information. Truthful and informative marketing and advertising practices are very positive socially, but it could be extremely difficult to put an identifiable cost figure on them when compared with misleading or false advertising. Another problem with some proposed systems of social measurement is the danger of misunderstanding, misinterpretation, and negativism.

> . . . a company with superb engineering might design its pollution-control procedures to increase the efficiency of its production technology to the point that better pollution control costs little or nothing. A company with poorer technical ability would be perceived as making a contribution because its pollution-control apparatus yielded a net loss. Or an entire industry might, by virtue of its technology, appear to be more (or less) socially responsible depending on how efficiently its technology permitted it to handle pollution.[1]

The point is that social reporting must guard against measuring only deficiencies. When this happens, the report becomes a negative document saying, in effect, "Why haven't you solved the whole problem?" rather than indicating progress that has been made. This approach runs the risk of making the whole concept of social auditing seem negative, critical, and carping. The objections raised may be similar to those sometimes voiced about the "management by exception" technique in which a manager's performance is evaluated, and only those items or ratios that are unfavorable receive attention.

ACCENTING THE POSITIVE

It is clear that those who bemoan the difficulties of social measurement are not merely attempting to bury the social audit or to avoid the other problems associated with it. There are real and serious methodological and technical difficulties. But selective information about selected areas is available or able to be generated, as in the areas of pollution control, occupational safety and health, and employment discrimination, and work on social indicators is proceeding rapidly. As time goes on, existing information and criteria may be altered, strengthened, or more clearly delineated and defined. Government, corporate, and public consensus may be reached about measurements in some areas considered to be of national importance. Companies have already begun to try social audits of program areas that are of particular importance or interest to the company, its workers, or its community, or about which management needs and wants some systematic information, whether it be quantitative or qualitative, objective or subjective, or some combination.

The difficulties are real and must be recognized, but they should not be used as excuses for not proceeding. The more social auditing is tried, using a variety of methods, the more likely social auditors are to find their way through the maze of measurement problems, to recognize the attitudinal, organizational, and political implications of such problems, and to realize that if we cannot make our way through the morass, perhaps we ought to be looking for a way around it—for alternatives to traditional measurement as tools for social auditing.

Note

1. Raymond A. Bauer, "Commentary on 'Let's Get on With the Social Audit'," from *Business and Society Review*, Winter 1972–73, p. 44. Copyright © 1972, Warren, Gorham, and Lamont, Inc., 210 South St., Boston, Mass. All Rights Reserved.

EFFECTIVE REGULATION IN THE PUBLIC INTEREST

Louis M. Kohlmeier, Jr.

FEDERAL REGULATORY AGENCIES

The Populists, who created the mold when the ICC was born in 1887, thought they had invented the perfect instrument of public administration in the structurally independent, politically bipartisan, multimember regulatory commission. The agencies were to be above partisan politics and beyond the reach of both politicians and vested interests. In splendid isolation, they were to be free to address themselves to complex economic and social problems, guided only by the wisdom of expert knowledge and experience in their respective fields of endeavor. The Supreme Court described the intended function of the agencies very well when it said they were created by Congress "with the avowed purpose of lodging functions in a body specifically competent to deal with them by reason of information, experience and careful study of the business and economic conditions of the industry affected."[1]

The great body of criticism of the agencies has been built by traditionalists—by latter-day Populists, up to and including Ralph Nader and his still-growing tribe of Nader's Raiders—who still believe that the independent regulatory commissions are capable of performing in the public interest. They insist that there is nothing wrong with regulation that cannot be cured by men of good will. The specific cures that have been and still are recommended depend to some degree on the predilections of the specific reformers. By and large, the legal community has sought to make the procedures of the agencies more like those of courts and thus presumably to make them more fair. Various economists have criticized the agencies for their failure to make bolder use of their rule-making powers and thus their failure to engage enthusiastically in economic planning. Some politicians have criticized the agencies for listening to

From S. Prakash Sethi, ed., *The Unstable Ground: Corporate Social Policy in a Dynamic Society.* Copyright © 1974 by Melville Publishing Co., Los Angeles. Reprinted by permission of John Wiley & Sons, Inc.

other politicians. And some other reformers have been critical simply because many of the regulators appointed by various presidents have not had full faith and trust in the regulatory statutes, and probably lacked the ability to regulate well even if they possessed the faith.

The point is that all of the traditional criticism of the agencies and the efforts to reform them have shared a belief in the system of independent, bipartisan, multimember commissions. The reformers insist that the regulators would perform in the public interest if only better men and women manned the agencies, if the agencies were more fair and more efficient (conflicting objectives in themselves), or if some other tinkering could be accomplished.

In my opinion, the Naders of the world are wrong, the flaws in the regulatory process are fatal, and the time has come to admit that the independent regulatory agencies never have been and never will be permanent, trustworthy repositories of the public interest as that term was defined by the Populists and is defined now by liberal reformers. . . .

REFORMS IN REGULATORY AGENCIES

I do not contend that all regulation at all times in all agencies has failed to serve the public interest. For example, there was a time in history, many years ago, when the ICC kept railroads' rates low, as Congress intended. To take another and more recent example, it seems to me that the National Labor Relations Board (NLRB) has been reasonably true to its mandate, through Republican as well as Democratic administrations, which is to ensure employees of the right to organize and bargain collectively with their employers. Unions do not and should not always get their way at the NLRB, but the ever-flowing river of employer appeals from NLRB decisions would seem to be evidence enough that the board by and large has remained true to its mandate.

After a dozen years in Washington, I also do not believe that regulators are venal men and women who can be bought by regulated industries. A few regulators have accepted vicuna coats and assorted other gifts, either from industry lobbyists or from the lobbyists' political allies in Congress or the White House. But I do not find convincing evidence that the public interest has been compromised simply because a few regulators have accepted gifts or even because many more regulators have been wined and dined by industry executives and lobbyists. It seems to me that bureaucrats are no less and no more honest, trustworthy, and efficient than similarly situated men and women at other very large institutions, such as General Motors or a large university.

Nor do I agree with the liberals who wrap all their criticisms of the regulators together and swing hard with the allegation that regulation has failed to serve the public interest because the regulators have been captured by the regulated. This charge seems to be enjoying a new popularity these days. . . . I think history supports the generalization that the affected industry almost invariably has fought against the initial enactment by Congress of new regulatory programs, and I am certain that after a regulatory agency has been in existence for some years its industry constituency is its strongest supporter. But to draw from this the conclusion simply that the regulators have been captured by the regulated is of no real help. The allegation tends to ignore industry dynamics, political realities, and the strange place in which the weary regulators find themselves today.

Finally, I must include in this list of demurrers a willing acknowledgment that the traditionalist reformers have scored some points over the years. Regulation undoubtedly is more uniformly fair among the agencies because of the Administrative Procedure Act of 1946, which was peculiarly the legal profession's contribution to reform. Maybe there is hope even that some public good will flow from the Freedom of Information Act, an amendment to the 1946 law that President Johnson signed into law on July 4, 1966. Some have hope even for the institutionalized tinkering, which became possible in 1964 with the creation of the Administrative Conference of the United States as a permanent body. Admittedly, there have been other reforms, or at least changes. Most would agree, I think, that President Nixon named better men to the FTC because of the criticisms of it that were voiced late in the Johnson administration by Ralph Nader and early in the Nixon administration by an American Bar Association committee. The FTC nowadays unquestionably is enforcing laws against false advertising with vastly greater effectiveness than prior to these criticisms. . . .

The reform forces in recent years have made two additional advances that, although tentative, offer additional hope for the future of regulation in the public interest. First, the antitrust division of the Department of Justice has been taking a more active role as a party to specific cases and as a court intervenor in issues before a number of agencies, including the ICC, the Civil Aeronautics Board (CAB), and the Securities and Exchange Commission (SEC). The antitrust division, for instance, has opposed some railroad and airline merger proposals on the ground that they are not in the public interest because they are unnecessarily anticompetitive. The antitrusters also have argued before the SEC that the New York Stock Exchange should be required to open its "private club" trading facilities to pension funds and other institutional investors.

The second of these tentative advances consists of various court decisions requiring some of the regulatory agencies to allow certain public-interest groups some sort of participation in particular pending cases. The best evidence of this new crack in the regulators' doors probably is the flood of challenges that have been filed at the FCC to applications of radio and television stations for renewal of their licenses.

In sum, I respect the reformers for their accomplishments, but I fear they are too little and too late. Court orders requiring the regulatory agencies to listen to public-interest groups, such as those representing a television station's audience, do not by any means require the regulators to adopt the views of the public-interest groups. Indeed, there is no substantial reason for believing that the challenged station owners really are in danger of losing their licenses. Similarly, the antitrust division's arguments and interventions are no guarantee whatsoever that the anti-trusters' view of the public interest will be adopted by the regulators. To the contrary, the Supreme Court has declined, wisely it would seem, to enter this t[h]icket; the Court generally has upheld the regulators and thrown out the antitrusters, not explicitly because the antitrusters are wrong but because Congress entrusted such matters to the expertise of the regulatory agencies.

THE POWER AND CAPABILITY OF REGULATORY AGENCIES

... The problems of regulation may reach the heart of the democratic process itself. I would suggest further that perhaps these public agencies are inherently incapable of regulating in the public interest, as they are now constituted within our form of government.

It has been said often enough that the agencies combine the three functions—legislative, executive, and judicial—that are divided among the three constitutional branches of the federal government. The agencies make rules that have the force of law; they are prosecutors as well as planners; and they sit in judgment on the cases they bring. This concentration of all three kinds of powers has bothered some constitutional purists, but the powers would not seem to pose a public danger because they are distributed through many agencies and each is small when compared with an executive branch department, such as Health, Education and Welfare, or Justice. This is not to say that the agencies are not powerful; they are uniquely powerful in our form of government. But the power of each is confined to a particular sphere, and Congress divided spheres such as transportation among three regulatory agencies. (The three are the ICC, the CAB, and the Federal Maritime Commission, although the total number of federal offices that have transportation functions, including those in the executive branch with some regulatory powers, is more than a dozen.)

The independent exercise of all three kinds of power poses a certain dilemma, however. The U.S. Constitution provides certain checks and balances that are intended to assure the independence of the executive, the legislative, and the judicial branches, one from another. In constitutional theory, the regulatory agencies are extensions of Congress' assigned power to regulate commerce and are arms of Congress. Congress could have accomplished many regulatory purposes through legislation but chose not to do so, mostly perhaps because political considerations mitigated against such drastic legislation.[2] Instead, in most instances, Congress created an agency and, frequently in vague and even contradictory terms, directed the agency to solve a pressing economic or social issue of the day.

Thus, the regulators were launched on stormy, uncharted seas with very little in the way of foul-weather gear. Congress provided them with no sure means of protecting their independence and is unlikely to do so. It gave them specified terms of office, usually five or seven years, but has never seriously considered giving regulators the lifetime tenure that the Founding Fathers deemed a necessary protection for federal judges. The only readily apparent alternative would be to allow regulators to run for office and thereby acquire the protection that is afforded by an elective constituency, but Congress also has not seriously entertained this alternative.

Thus, the regulators are functionally independent and powerful, yet they are almost defenseless when their independence is challenged. It seems to me that history bears out the conclusions that the regulatory agencies have set their courses independently, without direct or indirect communication with publicly constituted authority. The public interest that the regulators are supposed to act for is too diverse and unorganized a force to make itself heard. Congress by and large ignores the agencies and presidents take the attitude that, since the regulators owe them nothing, they will utilize the agencies for political patronage appointments and little more.

The regulators thus are left with the only constituency available to them, and indeed the only protection that may be available: the regulated. Even at that, it probably is true that the regulators do not get untoward amounts of help or hindrance from the regulated on board policy matters. Rather, the storms inevitably hit hardest when the regulators decide specific cases to which real price tags are attached. For example, when the FCC threatens to deny renewal of a television station license worth $20 million or more to its holder, the regulated typically do not run straight to the regulators. They run to Congress and, if possible, to the White House; the poor and weary regulators are left to muse over the public interest. Worse, Congress may enact legislation to prevent the regulators from doing what they intended or to undo what the regulators have done: such legislation was threatened to prevent the FCC from engaging in any wholesale denial of radio- and television-station licenses, and legislation was enacted to foreclose the FTC from requiring cigarette manufacturers to advertise a stern warning that smoking can cause cancer. Worse still, regulators who persist in defying presidents and Congress know from history that they will not be reappointed.

Congresses and presidents have inflicted other, perhaps more serious, indignities on the regulators. With and without the help of industry lobbyists, regulatory laws have been enacted that require the regulators to promote as well as to regulate an industry. Thus, many of the laws are ambiguous as well as vague. The Atomic Energy Commission and the CAB, for example, were directed to promote as well as regulate, and they were created before there was a real atomic energy industry or a commercial aviation industry. On the other hand, Congress clearly had the welfare of the railroad industry in mind when it told the ICC to promote railroads in 1940.

To make matters worse, congresses and presidents have created new programs and agencies that conflict with the existing mandates of regulatory agencies. The prime example, of course, is the Highway Trust Fund, under which the urban and rural portions of the interstate highway system have been financed. The motor vehicle traffic that the new system spawned has made it difficult or impossible for the ICC to fulfill its mandate to promote and regulate the nation's railroads. And, to complicate matters further, Congress for many years subsidized the airlines and the regulated merchant shipping industry, and the lawmakers to this day are a long way from providing equal treatment to railroads and urban mass transit.

Still another complication is worthy of note. Occasionally, when Congress has failed to act, the Supreme Court abandoned caution and marched into the thicket, with consequences no less disastrous. The Court in 1954 ordered the Federal Power Commission to regulate natural gas producers' prices, which until then had been regulated by the forces of competition. It seems to me that coincidence alone does not explain the fact that after 1954 exploratory discoveries of new natural gas sources in this country declined, and today the nation faces the possibility of severe gas shortages, even though there is ample gas in the ground.

One additional dilemma of regulation by a multiplicity of independent agencies is worthy of note. Reformers often charge the agencies with being slow to react or with failing entirely to react to technological and social change. The charge has some validity, but I wonder whether these agencies, as they are presently constituted, are institutionally capable of reacting in the public interest. For example, the NLRB was created in 1935 to secure labor's right to organize and bargain and, in my opinion, it has remained reasonably true to its mandate. But in the years since 1935, organized labor has grown very powerful, and when Senator McGovern during the recent election campaign merely suggested that labor's power now bears a certain likeness to industry power, George Meany reacted with a wrath worthy of any big industrialist. The point is that times have changed and in theory the NLRB should address itself to the new balance of power and the possibility that labor also is capable of abusing the public interest. But the NLRB has not and very probably never will.

The conclusion suggested is that independent regulatory agencies tend to be static and inflexible. They were created, some of them many years ago, to respond to quite specific economic or social crises of the day, and it is important to recognize also that they were created to bring about some change or development that Congress in its wisdom believed would not or could not be brought about by the forces of free competition. It should not be surprising then that the regulators' bag of tools is loaded with protectionist, anticompetitive devices. Protectionism is indigenous to their trade. When the FCC drew up the master plan for television in this country, it chose a plan that restricted the number of commercial stations more than technological considerations required, and the nation presumably will be burdened forevermore with that essentially protectionist master plan. The SEC, effective as it has been in ridding the stock market of manipulators, always has been and still is quite protective of the dominant "private club" position of the New York Stock Exchange. The CAB has never allowed a new trunkline to enter the commercial aviation business since the board was created in 1938. The CAB's answers to the airline industry's financial ills never seem to go beyond more mergers and higher fares, no matter how many empty seats there are on ever bigger aircraft. And the ICC is almost as protective in approving railroad mergers, ruling against the entry of new competitors into the trucking business, and approving rate increases for both railroads and trucks. The ICC, of course, forced the bankrupt New York, New Haven & Hartford Railroad on the old Pennsylvania and New York Central Railroads before it would approve the merger of the Pennsy with the Central, and then the entire structure collapsed. The ICC is not responsible for highway competition, and maybe the Penn Central would have collapsed anyway. But the dreary experience seems not to have dimmed the ICC's enthusiasm for mergers, quite possibly because it knows no alternatives.

Conclusions

I have painted a dreadfully pessimistic picture, but I hope I have suggested the reasons why, in my opinion, the problems of the independent regulatory agencies are substantially more serious than acknowledged by . . . [a] long line of traditionalist reformers. . . . Whatever the chances of reform might have been in the past, there is reason to believe that the problems of the agencies today are too large and too burdensome. In brief, there is reason to conclude that the agencies are not serving the public interests of consumers, the private interests of regulated industries, or the interests of government itself. And, meanwhile, public aspirations for economic stability and security have been rising.

Notes

1. Federal Trade Commission v. R. F. Keppel and Bros. Inc., 291 U.S. 304, 314 (1934).
2. See Henry J. Friendly, *The Federal Administrative Agencies: The Need for Better Definition of Standards* (Cambridge: Harvard University Press, 1962), pp. 141–175.

DILEMMAS FOR THE REGULATOR

Dan H. Fenn, Jr.

How can regulatory agencies be the repository of the public interest? By and large, the public assumes that they are not today, an assumption often made intuitively without criteria, measurement, or testing. Some people believe that these agencies have failed because they have been captured by big business. Some businessmen, on the other hand, assert that they have been captured by the politicians, the consumerists, or the bird-and-bunny people. Some observe that the laws are poorly drafted or that many agencies are mandated to promote the industry without statutory provision for the consumer. Some say it is because the commissioners are so often lawyers, not economists, or perhaps that they are bad or poor economists. So the explanations may vary, but the judgment is the same.

If regulatory agencies are indeed failing to protect the public interest and if we want to improve them, we need to start by understanding why they perform as they do. It would also help if we could reach some kind of agreement either on what the "public interest" is or, at least, on the most appropriate and credible mechanism by which that determination could be made at a given time. I am constantly intrigued, incidentally, by the tenacity with which we cling to a kind of Platonic vision of the public interest despite the way the public policy-making process works. . . .

REEXAMINING MYTHS ABOUT REGULATORY AGENCIES

I want to try to make a contribution to this effort by looking at the agency from one particular perspective: that of the regulator himself. In so doing, I am encouraged by the blockbuster impact caused by Raymond Bauer and his colleagues, Ithiel Poole and Lewis Dexter, when they took a similar (though far more rigorously formulated) approach to legislative bodies.[1] . . .

Bauer et al. found that one man's "heavy pressure" went unnoticed by his neighbor who was receiving the same phone calls and letters; that one woman's "key issue" was a routine matter to her colleague; that the legislator himself plays a much more dynamic role in the system than the "birch-tree" model would indicate; and, above all, that there are real people in the operation whose personalities, aspirations, and views of their jobs vary enormously, so that the process turns out to be far more complex, intriguing, and messy than we had been taught in high school. That, of course, any skilled lobbyist or articulate legislator could have

From S. Prakash Sethi, ed., *The Unstable Ground: Corporate Social Policy in a Dynamic Society.* Copyright © 1974 by Melville Publishing Co., Los Angeles. Reprinted by permission of John Wiley & Sons Inc.

told us long ago if we had asked him and then listened with open minds and ears.

I welcome what I see as a developing trend to apply the same kind of scrutiny to our traditional views of regulatory agencies and how they operate. Thus, my larger purpose, beyond simply describing the dilemmas of a regulator as I see them, is to contribute to and stimulate a reexamination of the shibboleths about regulation that we were taught in our youth and that we glibly perpetuate—notably the "capture theory," which holds that regulators are subservient to the industries for which they are responsible.

An extremely important point needs to be made at this point—so important, in fact, that it deserves an article of its own. We are extremely casual in our definition of "regulation," forcing together under that umbrella term a host of different agencies and different functions. We are *never* going to unscramble the question of why regulation operates as it does until we stop looking at agencies and start looking, separately, at the *functions* that such agencies perform. They set rates, grant licenses, suggest legislation, settle disputes, find facts and make reports, draw up industry rules, promote an industry, bring complaints, interpret vague laws, and provide expert advice to the President and Congress. In this article I am consciously generalizing across agencies, because the perspective I am taking here permits it, but no comprehensive analysis can be made of the regulatory process until we look at it by activity instead of as a whole.

SELECTION OF REGULATORS

The place to start in a look at the regulator is: How did he get there? We all know, of course, that he is nominated (and appointed) by the President by and with the consent of the Senate. But how does the President happen to nominate him in the first place?

There are two determinants of the type of person who ends up as a regulator: the method of selection and the criteria for selection.

Broadly speaking, presidents have gone in one of two directions in their methods of selection. The first, which has been irreverently called "BOGSAT" (Bunch of Guys Sitting Around a Table), is not commonly characterized by an active recruiting effort, at least at the White House level. Rather, it draws on a reservoir of names that may or may not be related to a particular job, which come in from Congress, the national committees, industry, consumer groups, other office holders, White House staff members, friends of the administration outside the government, or the potential office holder himself. The staff's function here is to winnow, to select from the pile those who, for one reason or another, they deem the most appropriate to suggest to the President. . . .

What about the criteria for nomination? Although they tend to be imprecise and undefined, seldom going beyond a phrase like "our kind of guy," they have real content nonetheless. At the beginning of his administration, Dwight Eisenhower appointed several men to head agencies in whose programs they did not believe, such as T. Coleman Andrews at the Internal Revenue Service and Congressman Albert Cole at the Housing and Home Finance Administration. Sounds strange, but given his initial commitment to minimal government, it makes sense: Who would be more likely to cut an agency down to the barest essentials than someone who did not believe in its program?

President Kennedy's version of "our kind of guy" for the regulatory agencies was a person who was bright, young, aggressive, innovative, and activist, consumer-oriented, willing to make mistakes, knowledgeable about how to make things happen, and skilled in dealing in a political environment. President Johnson, on the other hand, was more inclined toward the judicial, the umpire, the low-key regulator.

Presumably, then, with a more systematic approach to the recruitment and selection of regulatory commissioners and a penchant for activist, consumer-oriented appointees, the Kennedy regulators should all have looked and sounded like Newton Minow, conforming to the President's concept of what was in the public interest. But, of course, they did not. I can recall at least five who were considerably less than bright; at least three, including a chairman, who were primarily interested in keeping everything as calm and quiet as possible both inside and outside the agency; perhaps five whose devotion to the consumer was so slight as to be undiscernable; maybe eight who showed no evidence of having had a new idea in the past quarter century. (Obviously some people are showing up in several of these unhappy categories.)

Why did it turn out this way? Recently I went through about 25 regulatory appointments where I felt I knew pretty well what had happened. I separated them into different piles: those where the quality of the man was the major reason for his appointment; congressional "musts" (and we had only about 30 of those in the course of a year, many of whom did not end up in presidentially appointed posts); appointments made to solve a personnel problem in another agency; those where there were some personal ties of friendship or association with White House staff (in some cases, friendships that developed during a campaign); and those who fell into a minority group. Granting some overlaps, including one man who clearly fell in two groupings, I found that 11 were in the "quality" file, five in the "congressional must" group, seven in the "personal friendship" box, two "personnel problems" elsewhere, and two minority appointees.

Incidentally, I have not mentioned "pressure from industry." That omission is not inadvertent; most direct suggestions from business came to the White House during the Kennedy years via Congress, and it was simply one factor in the complex equation that went into each nomination, sometimes a positive and sometimes a negative. Interestingly enough, the most direct, persistent, orchestrated, obviously organized, and manipulated intervention we ever had on an appointment was from the educational fraternity on the selection of a commissioner of education.

What conclusion can we draw from all this? An important one, to my

mind. Given the fact that the road to appointment as a regulatory commissioner is such an uncertain one, that men and women were selected
for very different reasons and by different criteria, even within the framework of one administration never mind over the course of several, it is
hazardous indeed to generalize about these people. I know one commissioner who wanted to be a judge, one to be a senator, one to reshape his
agency, one to stay on until he retired, one to become a public figure, one
to help the consumer, one to have a nice, quiet, prestigious job. They had
different aspirations, different reasons for being there, different views of
the job, different friends and associations, different career goals and
paths. Consequently, they faced different dilemmas and, like Bauer's
legislators, felt different pressures, and grave doubt is thrown on the
simplistic "capture theory" unless it is broadened to embrace a variety
of constituencies.

So much for the process of appointment: What does a regulator find
when he sits down in his new office?

THE REGULATOR'S DILEMMAS

In the first place, the regulator cannot help but be struck by the enormous advantages of his position. He is an independent operator in an
independent agency. He has a term appointment; he cannot be removed
unless he is caught with his arm in the cookie jar up to the elbow. His vote
is his own; no one can tell him how to cast it. People can talk to him, urge
him, argue with him, but no one can order him to say aye or nay. This
is, indeed, an extraordinary privilege for a public officer in the executive
branch, and a vital distinction for the observer to bear in mind. If a person
"succumbs to pressure," to use the common idiom, it is his choice; it is
because he sees that as the appropriate thing for him to do under the
circumstances. But it is his choice and no one else's. The Secretary of
Commerce can be ordered by the President to make decisions against the
exportation of walnut logs even contrary to his better judgment, but the
President has no way of enforcing an order to the FCC commissioner to
vote for X applicant for a TV channel in preference to Y.

Concomitantly, his voice is his own. If he wants to make a speech for
or against a policy or write a decision, no one can tell him not to do so.
He can make his choices on whatever basis he wishes, and can explain that
statement however he wants to and he is protected. He is blessed with
the governmental version of academic freedom. The fact that commissioners often do not exercise that freedom does not mean they do not
have it.

All this does not mean that the commission is free of an entangling
series of dilemmas. The first and most important of these is the question:
What kind of a commissioner do I want to be?

Let me now list some of the subquestions under that key one:

1. Do I want to play an essentially judicial role here, judging cases even-
   handedly as they come before me, or do I want to be an advocate for the
   consumer, for the businessman, for the political interests of the administration, or for the prevailing congressional opinion?

2. Do I want to operate on a case-by-case basis, like a judge, or do I want to hew closer to the original conception of the regulatory agency as a policy-making body somewhere between the Congress and the President?
3. Do I want to be an "inside commissioner," trying to persuade my colleagues and win some votes for what I think is right by negotiating with them and accreting support? Or do I want to follow the lead of men like Commissioner Nicholas Johnson who says that he decided within his first three weeks on the FCC that this course was hopeless (and perhaps temperamentally unattractive), so he went "outside" and made his pitch to public opinion?
4. Do I want to accept a managerial responsibility in the large sense of that term, working to shape this agency along lines that I think are appropriate, or do I want simply to let it run by itself and concern myself exclusively with cases as they come up?
5. Do I want to be an activist, an innovator, or do I want to maintain the status quo?

Different men and women will answer such questions differently, depending on their personal aspirations, their concept of their job, their future plans, and the administration that they serve.

The issues posed here break into two parts: the commissioner as a substantive decision maker and the commissioner as a top executive of a federal agency.

To start with the first category, a certain number of cases will virtually decide themselves. I remember a dumping decision we had on the Tariff Commission. A petitioner came in and declared that he was being injured by peat moss coming into the United States from Canada at unfairly cheap prices. So the Treasury Department went to work and found that the prices were, in fact, unfair. They then sent the matter to the commission, which conducted an expensive extensive investigation and discovered that none of the Canadian peat moss was coming anywhere near the area where the complainant was selling his goods. So there was no way he could have been injured.

But a number of other cases and questions with which a commissioner is faced will be tough to decide, and the sheer facts will not provide him with the answer. How, for example, do you determine which of five competing applicants should be given a permit to operate a TV station, assuming they are all decent, out of jail, and financially competent?

At this point, the dilemmas rise up around the office. For example: What does the law say? What should the law say? What does the law mean? What did Congress intend? What is fair? What makes sense? What can I conscientiously defend? What will my colleagues, the press, the courts, my staff, the industry, and Ralph Nader think and say? What will the people who practice before us—who I see all the time at this party or that reception—what will they think of me? What will officials in other agencies say? What will the professors writing in law reviews or business journals say? What will the National Association of Concerned Business Students think?

Different commissioners will be troubled by a different mix of these questions. My erstwhile colleague on the Tariff Commission, Dr. James

W. Culliton, former Dean of the Notre Dame Business School, might tend to be interested in the professors and deans and aggressively disinterested in the people in the industry or the Tariff Commission bar. Commissioner Nicholas Johnson might be interested in what the industry says and what his colleagues think in a reverse kind of way: if they did not roast him, he'd feel he had failed! One chairman I can recall, who was once a staff man on the Hill, would not care very much about the NACBS, but he would surely be interested in congressional reaction. Another former colleague of mine was highly concerned with how the other commissioners, particularly the chairman, felt about the matter and especially sensitive to the interests of a certain industry in the district he had once represented in Congress.

So, like Bauer's legislators, different commissioners feel and respond to different dilemmas and pressures.

I suggested that a commissioner has, potentially, two kinds of responsibilities: deciding specific cases, and managing the agency with which he is associated. By "managing," I am not talking about counting paper clips and drawing organization charts; I am talking about determining what function he thinks his agency should play, what direction it should take, and what resources it needs to get there. It means assembling those resources and either persuading the existing staff of his objective or bringing people on board to support him. . . .

There is, of course, room in all this for industry intervention. . . . I can easily see a business group—or a consumer group for that matter—getting wind of some changes being worked in a regulatory agency, say in terms of staff appointments and responsibilities, and going to key congressmen to try and stop it. Whether or not they succeed would depend, of course, on the degree of interest of the congressman and the kind of people on the commission at the time. I should suppose if they were—or a majority of them were—industry-oriented, calls from Congressman Don Riegel and Senator William Proxmire would cut relatively little ice. But the point is that there are many forces other than industry holding these agencies in place and there is nothing inherent in them that automatically gives industry an open hand.

Let me make mention here of another source of potential intervention and that is the President or the presidency. One aspect of the capture theory holds that industry impinges on the President who, in turn, impacts on the commissioner through his power of reappointment. I hope that my earlier remarks have indicated that this might or might not be effective depending on the commissioner being approached. Some would be deeply affronted and be led to look eagerly for chances to vote against such a president's wishes; others would brush it aside because they planned to retire shortly anyway; still others would accede; and a fourth group who either did not want or did not need another term would ignore the suggestions being made.

But whatever the theoretical possibilities are, how to respond to White House intervention is not a dilemma that commissioners now have to face. It is true, of course, that a president telegraphs his general line of thought by the appointments he makes, by the questions his budget examiners ask, by structural changes he may seek, or new legislation he sends to the Hill. At the Kennedy Library[2] there is a transcript of a panel discussion between Newton Minow, Joseph Swidler, William Tucker, Alan Boyd, and William Cary about the regulatory agencies during the Kennedy administration. It is not so startling that these men were never called on individual cases; the fire that was lit under Sherman Adams during the Eisenhower years truly singed the pants of presidential aides even unto the present day. But it is interesting to note that most of these men had virtually no contact with the White House, never mind the President, on any kind of question, even including whether or not they were doing a good job. But they felt those judgments all the same through a kind of osmosis: offhand remarks at press conferences, comments on the role of the regulatory agency in a speech, suggested changes in legislation like Clay Whitehead's recent proposals on news commentary, overheard or reported comments of White House staffers. And, in a larger sense, if they were doing some moving and shaking they felt they were in step because moving and shaking was going on all over the town. . . .

CONCLUSIONS

. . . If my comments have served to muddy the image of how regulatory agencies function, of how the process works, my mission will have been accomplished. The recognition of messiness may be the beginning of understanding, albeit complicating the task of the academic model-builders who reject such considerations because they invalidate their artistic designs.

Way back at the start of this paper, I mentioned the topic of this section: How can the regulatory agency be the repository of the public interest? I have not, in fact, forgotten that question.

In our society, elections are the principal mechanism we have for determining what the public interest, in a large sense, is at any given time. If we feel we want to promote the interests of industry, we elect a president and an administration that seem to tend in that direction. If we think it is time to give the consumer a break, we choose a Teddy Roosevelt or a Woodrow Wilson.

The difficulty, as I see it, is that the regulatory agency does not very rapidly or very satisfactorily follow that lead. The reason lies partly in the term system and partly in the extraordinary carelessness with which commissioners are selected. In my view, then, it follows that shorter terms for commissioners and more presidential attention to the kind of people he names offer a real opportunity to attune these agencies to the public interest as it is, rather crudely, defined by the society at that moment.

I do not mean by this statement that procedural and structural reforms are irrelevant and unnecessary. I do mean to say that there is nothing in the regulatory agency as such that makes it inevitably and automatically passive or active, consumer-oriented or business-oriented, broad-gauged or tunnel-visioned, though there are various forces that tend to nudge it into a business-oriented, passive stance unless someone consciously pushes it into another posture. In sum, therefore, we can neither understand the behavior of a regulatory agency nor shape it more to our concept of the public interest unless we understand the people at the head of it and involve ourselves vigorously in their selection.

Notes

1. Raymond A. Bauer, Ithiel Poole, and Lewis Dexter, *American Business and Public Policy* (New York: Atherton Press, 1963).
2. John F. Kennedy Library, Waltham, Mass.

UTILITARIANISM AND COST/BENEFIT ANALYSIS:
An Essay on the Relevance of Moral Philosophy to Bureaucratic Theory

Alasdair MacIntyre

INTRODUCTION

Consider . . . the way in which the business executive or the civil servant characteristically defines and conceptualizes the activities of himself, his colleagues and his clients. He or she does so in a way which appears to exclude both moral and philosophical considerations from arising within his everyday decision-making tasks. Certainly some large moral considerations may have been involved in the executive's choice of a corporation; some might not be prepared to work for an armaments firm or in the making of pornographic movies. And certainly there may

From *Values in the Electric Power Industry*, ed. Kenneth Sayre. Copyright © 1977 by the Philosophic Institute of the University of Notre Dame, Notre Dame, Ind. Reprinted by permission of the Philosophic Institute of the University of Notre Dame. Some of the materials incorporated in this work were developed with the financial support of the National Science Foundation Grant ERP73-07794. However, any opinions, findings, conclusions, or recommendations expressed herein are those of the author and do not necessarily reflect the views of the Foundation.

have been moral grounds for some of the legal constraints imposed by government—the imposition of safety regulations, for example. But once the executive is at work the aims of the public or private corporation must be taken as given. Within the boundaries imposed by corporate goals and legal constraints the executive's own tasks characteristically appear to him as merely technical. He has to calculate the most efficient, the most economical way of mobilizing the existing resources to produce the benefits of power at the lowest costs. The weighing of costs against benefits is not just his business, it is business.

The business executive does not differ in this view of his task from other bureaucrats. Bureaucracies have been conceived, since Weber, as impersonal instruments for the realization of ends which characteristically they themselves do not determine. A bureaucracy is set the task of achieving within the limits set by certain legal and physical constraints the most efficient solution of the problems of realizing such ends with the means available. . . .

The presupposed agreement on ends allows all disagreement within the organization to take place on questions of means, that is on the merits of rival policies for achieving the agreed ends. If these arguments are to be settlable, then there must also be preestablished methods both for isolating all the relevant elements in each situation and for estimating the costs and the benefits of proceeding by this route rather than that. In other words, the norms of rationality, which on a Weberian or a neo-Weberian view of bureaucracies must govern public discourse within bureaucracies and between bureaucracies and their masters, clients, customers, or other external agents, are such that the cost/benefit analysis provides the essential normative form of argument.

The effect of this is that questions of alternative policies appear to become settlable in the same way that relatively simple questions of fact are. For the question of whether these particular means will or will not bring about that particular end with less expenditure of this or that resource than some other means is of course a question of fact.

The moral philosopher will at once recognize that the discourse of bureaucracy thus conceived reproduces the argumentative forms of utilitarianism. Not perhaps those of utilitarianism largely conceived as a morality capable of dealing with every area of life, but those reflecting acceptance of J. S. Mill's judgment upon "what a philosophy like Bentham's can do. It can teach the means of organizing and regulating the merely *business* part of the social arrangements." (Leavis, 1950, p. 73.) Poetry, music, friendship, and family life, as Mill sees it may not be captured by the Benthamite calculus; but there is a part of life which may be so captured, and which therefore may be rendered calculable.

If it is correct that corporate activity embodies the argumentative forms of utilitarianism, then we ought to be able to identify the key features of utilitarianism, including its central errors and distortions, within corporate activity. The guide that I shall use to identify the argumentative forms of corporate activity will be the text-book versions of cost/benefit analysis (e.g., Mishan, 1971), which not only form the mind of the corporate executive but provide paradigmatic examples from practice. The question is whether we discover in the texts the same lacunae and incoherences as in classical utilitarianism. First we must characterize these deficiencies.

UTILITARIANISM AND ITS DEFICIENCIES

The doctrines of classical utilitarianism appear to first sight simple and elegant. Every proposed course of action is to be subjected to the test: will it produce a greater balance of pleasure over pain, of happiness over unhappiness, of benefits over harms, than any alternative course of action? . . .

Two main versions of utilitarianism have been advanced: that which holds that the utilitarian test is a test of actions and that which holds that it is a test of rules. . . .

About any version of utilitarian doctrine five major questions arise. [1]*The first concerns the range of alternative courses of action which are to be subjected to the utilitarian test. For clearly at any moment an indefinitely large range of alternative courses of action are open to most agents. In practice I may consider a very limited set of alternatives: shall I use this money to paint my house or to educate my child? But perhaps I ought to weigh every proposed expenditure of energy, time or money against the benefit that might accrue from devoting it to the solution of world population problems or the invention of labor-saving devices or the discovery of new methods to teaching music to young children. If I try to construct a list of this kind of indefinite length, all decision-making will in fact be paralyzed. I must therefore find some principle of restriction in the construction of my list of alternatives. But this principle cannot itself be utilitarian; for if it were to be justified by the test of beneficial and harmful consequences as against alternative proposed principles of restriction, we should have to find some principle of restriction in order to avoid paralysis by the construction of an indefinitely long list of principles of restriction. And so on.

Utilitarian tests therefore always presuppose the application of some prior non-utilitarian principle which sets limits upon the range of alternatives to be considered. . . .

[2] Consider [secondly] only genuine pleasures. It is clear that the-pleasure-of-climbing-a-mountain, the-pleasure-of-listening-to-Bartok and the-pleasure-of-drinking-Guinness-stout are three very disputable things. There is not some one state to the production of which the climbing, the listening and the drinking are merely alternative means. Nor is there any scale on which they can be weighed against each other. But if this is true of pleasures, how much more complex must matters become when we seek to weigh against each other such goods as those of restoring health to the sick, of scientific enquiry or of friendship. A politician has to decide whether to propose spending a given sum of money on a new clinic for aged patients or on a new infant school; a

*Numbers in brackets have been introduced in this essay by the editors.

student has to decide between embarking on a career as a musician or becoming an engineer. Both wish to promote the greatest happiness of the greatest number, but they are being called upon to decide between incommensurables—unless they can provide some prior scheme of values by means of which goods and evils, pleasures and pains, benefits and harms are to be ranked in some particular way. Such a method of rank-ordering will however have to be non-utilitarian. For like the principle which specified the range of alternatives to be considered it has to be adopted before any utilitarian test can be applied.

[3] Thirdly there is the question of whose assessment of harms and benefits is to be considered by the agent making his assessment. For it is clear not only that there are alternative methods of rank-ordering, but also that different types of people will adopt and argue for different methods. The old do not weigh harms and benefits in the same way as the young; the poor have a different perspective from the rich; the healthy and the sick often weigh pain and suffering differently. "Everybody is to count for one and nobody for more than one," declared Bentham; but others—Sir Karl Popper (Popper, 1966, chapter 5, n. 6), for one—have suggested that the relief of pain or suffering always should take precedence over the promotion of pleasure or happiness. So we have at least two contingently incompatible proposals immediately, for the outcome of Bentham's rule clearly will often conflict with the results of applying Popper's maxim.

[4] Fourthly there is the question of what is to count as a consequence of a given action. We might be tempted to suppose this a very straightforward question, but it is not. For the apparently straightforward answer "All the predictable effects of my action are to be counted as consequences of my action" at once raises the question, "What are reasonable standards of prediction?" How much care and effort am I required to exert before I make my decision? Once again certain maxims must be adopted prior to the utilitarian test. But this is not the only difficulty which arises over the notion of a consequence. In the Anglo-Saxon legal tradition chains of cause-and-effect arising from an action are often thought to be modified when they pass through another responsible agent in such a way that the later effects are no longer held to be consequences of my action. I am a teacher grading a student's examination. I give him a well-deserved C–. The student, who has hoped for an A, goes home and in his anger beats his wife. Suppose that I could somehow or other have reasonably predicted this outcome; ought I to have counted the wife-beating as a consequence of my action in grading the paper? Ought I to have weighed this consequence against others before deciding on what grade to give the paper? Classical utilitarianism appears to be committed to the answer "Yes," the Anglo-Saxon legal tradition by and large to the answer "No." About what are they disagreeing? Obviously it is about the range of effects of an action for which the agent can be held responsible. Thus it turns out that some particular theory of responsibility must be adopted before we can have a criterion for deciding what effects are to count as consequences.

[5] Fifthly, a decision must be made about the time-scale which is to be used in assessing consequences. Clearly if we adopt a longer time-scale we have to reckon with a much less predictable future than if we adopt a shorter one. Our assessment of long-term risks and of long-term probabilities is generally more liable to error than our assessment of short-term risks and probabilities. Moreover, it is not clear how we ought to weigh short-term harms and benefits against long-term contingencies; are our responsibilities the same to future generations as they are to the present one or to our own children? How far ought the present to be sacrificed to the future? Here again we have a range of questions to which non-utilitarian answers have to be given or at least presupposed before any utilitarian test can be applied.

Utilitarianism thus requires a background of beliefs and of evaluative commitments, a fact that has usually gone unnoticed by utilitarians themselves. They are able to apply the test of utility only because they have already implicitly decided that the world ought to be viewed in one way rather than another, that experience ought to be structured and evaluated in one way rather than another. The world which they inhabit is one of discrete variables, of a reasonably high degree of predictability; it is one in which questions of value have become questions of fact and in which the aim and the vindication of theory is its success in increasing our manipulative powers. The utilitarian vision of the world and the bureaucratic vision of the world match each other closely.

Yet this is not just a matter of resemblance; the bureaucratic world contains a number of devices for ensuring that thought, perception and action are organized in a utilitarian way. The most important of such devices in contemporary bureaucracy is probably the cost/benefit analysis.

Cost/Benefit Analysis and Bureaucratic Decision-Making

The cost/benefit analysis is an instrument of practical reason, and it is one of the central features of practical reason that it operates under time constraints in a way that theoretical reason does not. Nothing counts as a solution of a practical problem which does not meet a required deadline; it is no good achieving a perfect solution for defeating Wellington at Waterloo on June 19, if the battle had to be fought on June 18. Hence problems cannot be left unsolved to await future solutions. But problems of a cost/benefit kind—of a utilitarian kind in general—can only be solved when all the elements of the problems are treated as belonging to the realm of the calculable and the predictable. Hence the executive is always under pressure to treat the social world as predictable and calculable and to ignore any arbitrariness involved in so doing. This pressure may operate in either of two opposite ways. It may appear in a tendency to restrict our operations to what is genuinely predictable and calculable; one manifestation of this will be a tendency to prefer short-term to long-term planning, since clearly the near future is generally more predictable than the more distant future. But the same pressure may equally appear in an opposite tendency to try to present all that we encounter as calculable and predictable, a tendency to overcome apparent difficulties in calculation by adopting *ad hoc* devices of various kinds. These conflicting pressures may appear in the way in which decisions are taken or evaluative commitments are made in any of the five areas which define the background of utilitarianism and which in a precisely parallel way define the background of cost/benefit analyses.

[1] There is first of all the restriction of alternatives so that the benefits and the costs of doing this rather than that are weighed against one another, but neither alternative is assessed against an indeterminately large range of other alternatives. Yet ever so often in corporate or governmental or private life the range of alternatives for which cost/benefit analyses are sought changes; and this change always signals a change in underlying evaluative commitments. Up to a certain point in the history of a marriage, divorce remains an unthinkable alternative; up to a certain point in the history of a foreign policy, embarking on an aggressive war remains an unthinkable alternative; up to a certain point in the history of a war, truce or withdrawal remains unthinkable. Corporate parallels are not difficult to think of. The history of publishing or of automobile manufacture abound with them. The one-volume novel or the cheap intellectually substantial paperback were once unthinkable; so was the car which could be advertised primarily for safety factors.

Corporate executives may respond to this by saying that what restricts the range of alternatives which they consider is simply profitability. They can attend only to those alternatives which in the shorter or longer run will yield their stockholders a competitive return in the market. What this reply fails to notice is that what is profitable is partly determined by the range of evaluative commitments shared in the community. Sir Allen had to make the intellectual paperback profitable for the very first time and for that a firm conviction about intellectual values was required. What attitude both automobile manufacturers and the public take to death on the roads changes what is profitable. Consumer markets are made, not just given. Underlying the restricted range of alternatives considered by corporate executives we may therefore find both covert evaluative commitments and also unspelled-out assumptions about human wants and needs. . . .

[2] Secondly, the use of cost/benefit analyses clearly presupposes a prior decision as to what is a cost and what a benefit; but more than that it presupposes some method of ordering costs and benefits so that what otherwise would be incommensurable becomes commensurable. How are we to weigh the benefits of slightly cheaper power against the loss forever of just one beautiful landscape? How are we to weigh the benefits of increased employment and lessened poverty in Detroit against a marginal increase in deaths from automobile accidents? Once somebody has to consider both factors within a cost/benefit analysis framework these questions have to be answered. Considerable ingenuity has in fact been exercised in answering them.

Consider for example how we may carry through a calculation where one of the costs we may have to take into account is the shortening of human life. One recent example occurred in the argument over whether the Anglo-French supersonic aircraft *Concorde* should be allowed to land at United States airports. It is reasonably clear that the greater the use of *Concorde* the greater—as a result of the effects on those layers of the atmosphere which filter the sun's rays—the number of cases of skin cancer. How are we to include such deaths in our calculations?

Writers on cost/benefit analysis techniques have devised four alternative methods for computing the cost of a person's life. One is that of discounting to the present the person's expected future earnings; a second is that of computing the losses to others from the person's death so as to calculate their present discounted value; a third is that of examining the value placed on an individual life by presently established social policies and practices, e.g., the benefits in increased motor traffic which society at the present moment is prepared to exchange for a higher fatal accident rate; and a fourth is to ask what value a person placed on his or her own life, by looking at the risks which that person is or was prepared to take and the insurance premiums which he or she was prepared to pay. Clearly, those four criteria will yield very different answers on occasion; the range of possible different answers to one and the same question that you can extract from the same techniques of cost/benefit analysis makes it clear that all the mathematical sophistication and rigor that may go into the modes of computation may be undermined by the arbitrariness (relative to the mathematics) of the choice to adopt one principle for quantifying rather than another. Thus there once more appears behind the ordered world of discrete, calculable, variable elements in which the cost/benefit analysis is at home, a range of relatively arbitrary decisions presupposed—and sometimes actually made—by the analyst himself.

[3] Thirdly, once more as with utilitarianism in general, the application of cost/benefit analysis presupposes a decision as to *whose* values and preferences are to be taken into account in assessing costs and benefits. Indeed the choice of a method for weighing costs against benefits, the adoption of the type of principle discussed immediately above, will often involve equally a decision as to which voices are to be heard. Consider once again the different methods employed to estimate the cost of a human death. One of these considers the individual's own earnings, one the losses to others, one certain socially established norms, and one the individual's own risk-taking. The last is an attempt to give the individual the value which he sets on himself; the second gives him the value he has to others; the third the value he has in the eyes of "society"; the fourth perhaps the value that he has in the eyes of the taxation system. To adopt one of these methods rather than another is precisely to decide *who* is to decide what counts as a cost and what counts as a benefit.

Consider the range of possible decision-makers with whom a corporate executive might be concerned: his superiors, the consumers of his product, the stockholders, the labor force, the other members of his profession (if he is, say, a lawyer or an actuary), the community in which the corporation is sited, the government, and the public at large. What makes the question "Who decides?" so crucial is another feature of cost/benefit analyses. Very often, perhaps characteristically, neither future costs nor future benefits can be restricted to identifiable individuals. After the event we can say who died in the road deaths accompanying an increase in automobile traffic, or which children were deformed by the side-effects of a new drug, or who in fact got skin cancer after an increase in use of higher flying jet aeroplanes. But beforehand all that is predictable at best is what proportion of a given population will be harmed (or will benefit). It is a chance of harm or benefit which is assigned now to each member of the population. Therefore the question is: who shall decide how the chances are distributed over a population?

There are some alien cultures where a family's ancestors are given an important voice in decision-making; so it is in traditional Vietnamese culture, for example. There are cultures where the old have a very special voice. In our own culture our explicit beliefs label the former as a superstition and our dominant practices show that we implicitly label the latter a superstition too. This is directly relevant to, for example, the policies of public utility companies. Light and heat are peculiarly important to old people; ought therefore the old to receive special consideration from public utility corporation executives in determining what is to count as a cost and what as a benefit? Implicitly or explicitly a decision will have been taken on this point whenever a cost/benefit analysis is offered in a relevant context.

[4] Fourthly, the parallel with utilitarianism is maintained in the way in which the questions of what is to count as a consequence of some particular action or course of action arises for cost/benefit analyses. Any answer to this question, as I suggested earlier, presupposes a prior answer to the question: for what range of effects of his actions is an agent to be considered liable or responsible? . . .

. . . Once a businessman is assured of the goodness of what he supplies he has a sanction for what he does that leaves him free not to think about this aspect of his activity any more. In his dealings with consumers, in his investment policies, and in his dealings with his labor force he can press ahead exactly as he would do with any other product (except for technological considerations). The wants of the consumer for the good supplied are to be taken as given; whatever is asked for in the form of market demand will, so far as possible, be supplied. It is only as creators of demand that consumers appear in this picture.

It follows that the consequences of any course of action terminate for such an executive when the consumer has been successfully supplied. The further consequences of supplying demand—the trivialization of the culture by the major television networks, for example—are beyond the scope of any consideration by those who supply the electric power for such enterprises. Once again the cost/benefit analysis is not an evaluatively neutral instrument of choice.

[5] The fifth and last parallel with utilitarianism concerns the time-scale on which costs and benefits are to be assessed. When we make a

decision—implicitly or explicitly, recognizing it or failing to recognize it —about the time-span within which we are going to reckon up costs and benefits, . . . different kinds of consideration will affect our decision. The first of these concerns the fact that both types and rates of change for different cost and benefit factors may vary so that by choosing one time-length rather than another the relation of costs to benefits will appear quite differently. If I am deciding how to transport commodities from one place to another (by building a road, building a railway, maintaining a canal or whatever) changes in the price of land, the prices of raw materials, the size of the labor force, the demand for utilization of surplus carrying capacity, the technologies involved, the alternative uses to which each type of resource might be put, will all change in such a way that, even if I am a perfect predictor, the choice of dates within which costs and benefits are to be assessed may give strikingly different results. Of course in a private profit-seeking corporation the current rates of return expected on investment will place constraints on such a choice of dates; and in public corporations the need to vindicate policies within terms ultimately specified by electoral laws will set not dissimilar constraints. Nonetheless even within such limits a certain arbitrariness is likely to appear.

Secondly it is not just that the different factors in a situation will be subject to different types and different rates of change; they will also differ in the degree to which they are predictable. [Several] types of unpredictability are likely to be generated in the relevant types of situation. One springs from the sheer complexity of so many of the relevant types of situation and their vulnerability to contingencies of an in-practice unpredictable kind: earthquakes, viruses, panics. A second springs from the systematic unpredictability of all innovation that involves radical conceptual invention. . . .

It may be said that the author of a cost/benefit analysis simply cannot be expected to deal with unpredictability at all. If this were indeed so it would be equivalent to saying that he must exclude from his view a central feature of social reality—as in fact seems to happen with many studies of organization and management as well as with many conventional texts on the methodology of the social sciences. But of course this consciously or unconsciously willed blindness is not necessary. Reasoning of a cost/benefit analysis kind may include—often does include—some provision for unforeseen contingencies. But once again how much and what types of unpredictability are allowed for will rest upon judgments independent of and prior to the cost/benefit analysis itself. Among these judgments will once again be those as to the length of time within which costs and benefits are to be reckoned; and once again there is, relative to the cost/benefit analysis, an element that seems purely arbitrary. . . .

Any cost/benefit analysis therefore has to be understood against *some* background of assumptions about identity and time; and because it is impossible to speak of the identity of organizations except in terms of some evaluative commitment, these assumptions will be in part evaluative. . . .

. . . The moral structure underlying the corporate executive's thinking is one of which he remains almost entirely unaware. He does not recognize himself as a classical utilitarian; and he cannot therefore recognize that the presuppositions of classical utilitarianism which he shares—which the utilitarians themselves did not recognize—must go doubly unrecognized by himself and his colleagues. His vision of himself remains that of a man engaged in the exercise of a purely technical competence to whom moral concerns are at best marginal, engaging him rather *qua* citizen or *qua* consumer than *qua* executive. Does this false consciousness of the executive, whether in the private corporation or in government, itself have a function? It is plausible to suppose that it does. To consider what that function is, imagine what would occur if all these considerations became manifest rather than latent.

The executive would then be presented with a set of moral problems, or moral conflicts, on which he would have to make overt decisions, over which he would have to take sides in the course of his work. What sort of issues are these? The claims of the environment *versus* the claims of cheaper power, the claims of need (for example, of the old) against those of the urgent present, the claims of rival institutions—government, church, school—in certain respects, the claims of rival judgments of intelligence, integrity and courage. Now it is a crucial feature of our moral culture that we have no established way of deciding between radically different moral views. Moral arguments are in our culture generally unsettlable. This is not just a matter of one party to a dispute generally being unable to find any natural method to convince other contending parties. It is also the case that we seem unable to settle these matters within ourselves without a certain arbitrary taking of sides.

It follows that to allow moral issues to become overt and explicit is to create at least the risk of and more probably the fact of open and rationally unmanageable conflict both between executives and within each executive. The avoidance of such conflict necessitates two kinds of device. Where the recognition of moral considerations is avoidable they must be apportioned out between the different areas of the self and its social life, so that what is done and thought in one area will not impinge upon, let alone conflict with, what is done and thought in another. Boundaries must be drawn between areas of social action whose effectiveness will depend upon them not being recognized for what they are.

Where however it is unavoidable that moral issues arise *within* one and the same area, then they must be disguised from the agent so that he can deal with them, so far as is humanly possible, as merely technical issues. Their moral and evaluative character must be relegated to a realm of latent presuppositions. But it is obvious at once that both these devices are central to the structures of life of the corporate executive, as I described them earlier. The morality of 'contract with the autonomous consumer and the morality of governmental regulation operate in carefully defined areas so that questions of their coherence or conflict with each other or with other moral considerations are prevented from arising. The moral considerations underlying cost/benefit analysis are simply suppressed.

REFERENCES

LEAVIS, F. R., ed. *Mill on Bentham and Coleridge.* Chatto and Windus, London, 1950.

MISHAN, E. J. *Cost-Benefit Analysis.* Praeger, New York, 1971.

POPPER, SIR KARL. *The Open Society and Its Enemies,* Vol. 1, 5th ed. Routledge & Kegan Paul, London, 1966.

UTILITARIANISM AND COST/BENEFIT ANALYSIS:
A Reply to MacIntyre

Tom L. Beauchamp

I

A formidable series of philosophical objections to the use of utilitarian and cost/benefit reasoning in business and government has recently been offered by Alasdair MacIntyre in his essay "Utilitarianism and Cost Benefit Analysis."[1] MacIntyre supposes that the business executive and the government bureaucrat commonly think in cost/benefit terms. He offers five criticisms of this mode of reasoning, effectively concluding that cost/benefit analysis cannot serve executives and social planners in any socially useful and morally significant way. I shall argue that MacIntyre is quite mistaken in this claim—both about cost/benefit analysis and about utilitarianism.

In brief, MacIntyre's criticisms are the following: First, he argues that bureaucrats and executives are always faced with a large range of alternative courses of action, a range so vast that all the possible options could never be seriously considered. Some "principles of restriction" are thus needed that limit the options to those that can actually be considered. Such principles of restriction cannot themselves be utilitarian, according to MacIntyre; and it will not do, he says, to argue that the alternatives are restricted by goals operative in a context—for example, by arguing that *profitability* limits goals and options in a business context. The ends are themselves selected by some (nonutilitarian) evaluative choice, argues MacIntyre. Moreover, markets and the goals of government are created by wants and needs, and thus some evaluative choices must be made that are not purely cost/benefit in character.

MacIntyre's second objection springs from the notorious problem of measuring, comparing, and weighing alternative courses of action. He argues that there is no scale on which alternatives can be weighed: "If this is true of pleasures, how much more complex must matters become when we seek to weigh against each other such goods as those of restoring health to the sick, of scientific enquiry or of friendship." He is particularly concerned about the problem of calculating costs, where the costs include ones of shortening human life. To use MacIntyre's example, by allowing the Concorde to land in the United States, the likelihood of skin cancer is increased. Weighing the former convenience against the likelihood of the latter untoward event is not one that can be done in cost/benefit terms, in his judgment, because it will be arbitrary how a principle of choice is to be determined; i.e., it is arbitrary "to adopt one principle for quantifying rather than another."

MacIntyre's third objection ponders whose values are to count in the weighing and assessment of harms and benefits. The old and the young weigh priorities differently, and some but not all persons place the absence of suffering over the promotion of happiness—to take only two examples. MacIntyre argues that this fact of plurality forces a choice concerning whose voice is to be heard. Moreover, he claims that labeling something a cost (say, environmental damage) or a benefit (say, electric power) itself depends upon an already formed evaluative viewpoint. And, as is typical of MacIntyre's conclusions, he thinks nonutilitarian evaluation *precedes* and itself critically influences cost/benefit outcomes.

His fourth objection turns on the nature of a predicted *consequence* of an action. Remote consequences such as the television industry's trivializing of a culture are said to be beyond the ethical scope of both business and government agencies because of the rules under which the culture operates, though utilitarianism is unable to tell us that this consequence is irrelevant to a moral judgment. Hence, the electric power industry apparently ought not to take into account such consequences in setting its policies, in MacIntyre's view, even though they *are* consequences of the policies.

Finally, MacIntyre adds a reservation about unpredictability and the consequence-regarding character of utilitarianism. "Time frame" problems are alleged to emerge—e.g., how much should be sacrificed in the present in order to benefit the future, by, say, benefiting our children or future generations? MacIntyre contends that this question cannot be answered in cost/benefit terms, because predictability over time—given changes, inherent unpredictability, inflation, conceptual changes, and unknowable historical developments—can rarely be accurately achieved.

As I interpret MacIntyre, his five objections reduce to three general problems for utilitarianism and cost/benefit analysis: problems in the measurement and comparison of different cost/benefit units, problems both in limiting the scope of and in predicting the consequences of actions, and problems in the specification of whose values, preferences, and assessments are to be counted in cases of conflict. While these problems are indeed practical difficulties inhibiting the actual use of utilitarian and cost/benefit reasoning in government and business, I do not believe they present insurmountable *theoretical* problems.

II

MacIntyre's arguments seem problematic in at least three respects.

(1) He asks perfect predictability of utilitarians (in objections 1, 4 and 5), something that no scientific or moral theory could possibly provide. Utilitarianism certainly is a *consequentialist* theory, but one need not be able to foresee all future consequences over a time frame that includes the historical shifts to which he alludes. It is possible to adopt a criterion of *reasonable* predictability that is serviceable for cost/benefit analysis and other utilitarian purposes, without demanding perfect predictability. To take an elementary example, in that famous controversy over whether the chemical TRIS should be used in manufacturing children's pajamas, cost/benefit determinations were made regarding the benefits of TRIS as a flame retardant and the risks of TRIS as a cancer-causing chemical. (TRIS had been ascertained to be a carcinogen.) On the basis of available evidence, the risk of cancer seemed to far outweigh the risk of being burned. Such projections were then used as aids in reaching a determination about the acceptability of manufacturing TRIS for any purpose.

MacIntyre seems to overlook the promise of cost/benefit analysis as a method for making explicit tradeoffs of this sort that everywhere must be made by business executives and government officials. For example, tradeoffs must be made between lives that will be lost under certain working conditions (e.g., in coal mines) and money expended to reduce the statistical level of lost lives, or between the quality of a product such as gasoline and the health of those who produce it (see the benzene case that introduces this chapter).

The simple idea behind the cost/benefit approach is that costs and benefits should be measured or at least systematically arrayed, while uncertainties and tradeoffs are similarly outlined, in order to present decision makers with specific, relevant information that can serve to provide an impartial conclusion where a decision must be reached. Although it is desirable to use such quantitative units as the number of accidents and dollars expended, cost/benefit judgments must often be made when quantitative data are unavailable. Although MacIntyre fails to appreciate this nonquantitative use of the term "cost/benefit analysis," this meaning is now common, especially in bureaucratic and business circles, as we see in the following definition offered by the Committee on Public Engineering Policy of the National Academy of Engineering:

> *Benefit-cost* . . . refers to an evaluation of *all* the benefits and the costs of proposed action. It is a much broader concept than that of the traditional cost-benefit analysis involving only economic factors.[2]

This way of understanding cost/benefit analysis does not reduce it to the triviality that in decision making we should weigh the advantages against the disadvantages of an action. Rather, the intent is to supply objective data that restrain decision makers from reaching conclusions on any alternative basis. Consider MacIntyre's own example of the Concorde: Secretary Coleman's decision to allow limited Concorde landings was based on the method of political compromise. If he had been required to accept a cost/benefit analysis, such a compromise route would not have been permitted. Cost/benefit analysis, in other words, is not simply a method of stockpiling information on the basis of which a decision can be reached; it is actually a *method of deciding,* for its conclusion should also serve as the conclusion of the deliberation (unless, as we shall later see, there are built-in utilitarian *constraints* against a straightforward acceptance of individual cost/benefit conclusions).

This use of the term "cost/benefit analysis" does not, however, require that all costs and benefits be fully quantified and reduced to commensurable units. Rather, the method requires that principles and standards for calculating costs and benefits that are operative in cost/benefit decisions be stated in detail so that as much unclarity in the judgmental process is reduced as possible. It is this reduction of intuitive weighing and the avoidance of purely political calculations in making decisions that in my judgment are of greatest significance in the cost/benefit approach, for this form of arbitrary decision-making is at present the most flawed dimension of the decisions of regulatory agencies of government.

Moreover, MacIntyre seems to me to overestimate the demands of the utilitarian moral theory. While we should attempt to make accurate measurements of the preferences of others, this seldom can be accomplished in detail because of limited knowledge and time. Often in everyday affairs we must act on severely limited knowledge of the consequences of our action. The utilitarian does not condemn any sincere *attempt* to maximize value merely because the *actual consequences* turn out to be less than maximal (because of incomplete information, e.g.). What is important, morally speaking, is that one conscientiously projects the most acceptable action based on the best available data, and then with equal deliberateness attempts to perform it. Since common sense and ordinary deliberation about desires and consequences will generally suffice for these calculations, utilitarians cannot fairly be accused of presenting overly demanding moral requirements. MacIntyre's problems about restricting the range of alternatives, as well as his difficulties over specifying relevant consequences of actions (see objections 1, 4, and 5), seem to me far less troublesome than he would admit. While he is correct in insisting that some "arbitrariness" in selecting variables and principles is bound to creep into human calculations, this problem is no greater for utilitarianism than for other moral theories.

(2) Second, MacIntyre specifies no alternative approach that leaves us with a workable methodology for public policy purposes. The most powerful reason favoring the adoption of cost/benefit analysis is its instrumental value for deciding which alternative to pursue in *dilemmatic* cases. That it provides the most reliable method and perhaps the only method for reaching this goal is a powerful justification in itself, even if the

method does occasionally eventuate in minor injustices or other than perfectly just outcomes.

It is worth noting at this point that any applied ethical system, utilitarian or nonutilitarian, needs *some* principle as a means of balancing possible benefits against harms, benefits against alternative benefits, and harms against alternative harms. The moral life is not so uncomplicated that ethical theory can merely exhort us to produce benefits and avoid harms. Balancing beneficent and nonmaleficent objectives is essential, and to the extent that an ethical theory fails to provide a balancing principle, to that extent it is deficient.

(3) Finally, MacIntyre fails to take account of at least two important theses that are basic to recent utilitarian thinking. These theses center on the concept of utility itself and on the difference between act and rule utilitarianism. I want now to recall these two guiding utilitarian notions and to show how they provide responses to MacIntyre.

(A) *The Nature of Utility.* Several of MacIntyre's arguments are intended to show that a value scheme is presupposed by utilitarians and that it is difficult to specify whose values and assessments are to count (see objections 1, 2, and 3). MacIntyre is especially tough on the now outmoded views of classical utilitarians, who adopt a hedonistic position. In my view, these theoretical problems can be significantly diminished by the adoption of a proper account of the nature of utility, one that includes a specification of whose utility is to count. In recent philosophy, individual *preferences* have been used to explicate the concept of utility: To maximize a single person's utility is to provide what he has chosen or would choose from among the available alternatives that might be produced. To maximize the utility of all persons affected by an action or policy is to maximize the utility of the aggregate group. Utility is translated into the satisfaction of those needs and desires that individuals choose to satisfy. MacIntyre is thus right when he says that an evaluation scheme is presupposed, but this is hardly an argument *against* utilitarianism. Utilitarians do not attempt by cost/benefit techniques to ascertain what people *ought* to prefer. They attempt, rather, to determine what ought to be done based on what people *do* prefer. Evaluation does indeed *precede* cost/benefit calculations; there could be no cost/benefit determinations without prior evaluation, and no utilitarian would deny it.

Utilitarian calculations based on individual preferences (perhaps determined by social scientists) thus can form a basis for deciding the course of action that maximizes value (or minimizes disvalue) for all affected by an action. Moreover, and contrary to MacIntyre's objections (2 and 3), standard decision procedures in business and government include techniques for determining whose values and preferences are to be considered, how these preferences are to be ordered, and how we are to ascertain initially that something is a cost or a benefit. I would admit that such information is often difficult to obtain and to interpret. It also may not always be the only or even the most relevant information for business and public policy purposes (think, for example, of the range of costs and benefits that must be considered in MacIntyre's Concorde example). But such information is on all occasions *a* relevant even if not the *overriding* consideration. And this often is all that we can ask or need ask of cost/benefit calculations, even though we might hope for more decisive conclusions.

(B) *The Distinction Between Act and Rule Utilitarianism.* This distinction is also ignored by MacIntyre. Consider his objections resting on the argument that we cannot determine "what is to count as a consequence of a given action" and that such consequences as "the trivialization of a culture by the major television networks," though ethically significant, generally must go ignored or be discounted because only the wants of consumers are to be considered (see objections 4 and 5). The act–rule distinction is of vital importance for judging the cost/benefit assessments here in question. Utilitarian rules function to provide what in the cost/benefit literature are often called "constraints" on the use of *single* cost/benefit studies on single occasions (i.e., single act rather than rule contexts). For example, in this literature it is said that there are physical, legal, social, institutional, and environmental constraints on the use of cost/benefit analyses. A rule utilitarian rightly would say that there are *moral* constraints as well, as determined by utility-based moral rules. MacIntyre ignores this built-in utilitarian constraint on cost/benefit analysis in arguing that utilitarians cannot decide which effects count as consequences and that utilitarian decisions are "not evaluatively neutral." If a *particular* cost/benefit study would lead to actions that seriously violate a moral rule, rule utilitarians would not accept the study as determinative. Thus, cost/benefit analyses are not to be isolated from the restraining control of moral rules. MacIntyre's arguments thus fail as objections against the most influential form of utilitarianism. But let us consider this problem further.

Opponents of cost/benefit analysis, including MacIntyre I should think, would reply to this argument as follows: At least some cost/benefit analyses will reveal that a particular measure will prove highly beneficial as compared to its costs, and yet provision of this benefit might function prejudicially in a free-market economy by denying basic goods and services to seriously disadvantaged members of society. But, as a matter of justice, the disadvantaged ought to be subsidized, either in terms of health and welfare services or financial awards, no matter what cost/benefit analyses reveal. As applied to business, economics, and public policy, Daniel Bell has explicitly accused utilitarians of committing what he calls the "utilitarian fallacy" of equating a social decision in the public interest with the sum total of individual preferences in society. Bell believes this procedure leads to injustices and proposes that we guide allocative schemes by some explicit nonutilitarian vision of social justice, rather than by an economic and utilitarian conception.[3]

There is some point to this form of objection, but in the end it fails. For the reasons just advanced, it would not always be permissible to follow the dictates of *single, short-range* cost/benefit calculations. For example, suppose that the employment of pregnant women in battery factories has, as has been alleged, a serious and irreversibly damaging effect on human fetuses, as well as some effect on the health of the mother. Yet suppose that allowing such employment significantly increases the profits of a business over the profits that would be realized by using new employees and paying to relocate pregnant women in other jobs. Suppose further (and quite hypothetically) that 6 of every 100 fetuses exposed to the battery factory environment are stillborn as a direct result. It would be immoral not to require some way for these women to escape employment in this environment, even if statistical calculations demonstrated that a highly favorable cost/benefit equation would result by a continuation of prevailing employment practices. There is a lower limit on the risk of harm that can be permitted by the utilization of immediate cost/benefit calculations, and we cannot pass below this limit without abusing justice.

But no utilitarian would deny any of this. The battery factory example —which represents a common variety of counterexamples thrown up against utilitarians—is not compelling, for several reasons. First, *all* of the entailed costs and benefits must be considered. These would include difficulties in hiring new workers, losses through insurance schemes and strikes, impairment to social ideals, effects on the family, the costs associated with defective fetuses, etc. When all these costs are included, it is highly unlikely that cost/benefit analysis would suggest employment in an environment that kills fetuses. Second, as previously argued, sophisticated utilitarian analyses never suggest that single cost/benefit determinations be accepted, because they propose that general rules of justice ought to constrain particular actions or uses of cost/benefit analysis in all cases. Moreover, choices between justice-regarding reasons and utilitarian cost/benefit reasons should seldom, if ever, occur. Utility in the form of cost/benefit analysis itself provides an *appropriate principle of distributive justice,* even though utilitarian moral rules (of justice) constrain single, cost/benefit outcomes. Therefore, utilitarian considerations of justice (i.e., rules of justice grounded in utility) will suffice should individual or single cost/benefit conclusions be shown morally unacceptable.

Notes

1. Reprinted in this volume, pp. 266–276.
2. Committee on Public Engineering Policy, National Academy of Engineering, *Perspectives on Benefit-Risk Decision Making,* 3–4 (1972).
3. Daniel Bell, "The Corporation and Society in the 1970's," *The Public Interest,* 24 (1971), pp. 17f.

THE INTERPERSONAL COMPARISON
OF UTILITY

Richard B. Brandt

In order to get clear how we can support the claim to know, sometimes, that one person wants *x* more than another person wants *y*, let us take a very simple case where *x* and *y* are the same thing, say, a desire for a cold Coke. Let us assume that Mr. A is a tennis player who has just come in from three sets on a hot day, whereas Mr. B is a person who has been working in an air-conditioned office, actually had a Coke a half hour ago, says the idea of a Coke has only a slight appeal, that he doesn't think a Coke is worth a dime at the moment, although he will go along for one for the sake of the company. In these circumstances we would all *think* that Mr. A wants a cold Coke more than Mr. B does. But how might we support this knowledge claim?

In the first place, there is very good reason to think that dehydration increases the desire for liquid very substantially, and hence there is prima facie reason for thinking that the severely dehydrated Mr. A wants some liquid more than does Mr. B. It is true that wants are not a function merely of physiological deprivation; there is a long personal history which also affects one's wants—including past consummatory experiences with the goal object. In the absence of special evidence that B's experiences with Cokes have been in some way especially favorable, however, we would hesitate to think that his craving for a drink when he is not dehydrated could well equal Mr. A's. In the second place, Mr. A. clearly sets more store by a Coke than he does by keeping his dime, whereas Mr. B does not. If we are to say that Mr. B really wants a Coke as much as Mr. A, we have to accept the consequence that Mr. B values a dime more than does Mr. A. This is possible, but, if their salaries and other obligations are roughly equal, we hardly shall expect varying valuations of small sums of money without some special evidence, such as Mr. B's having been deprived when a child. Third, there are possible frustration phenomena. If the machine fails to yield a coke, Mr. A will show frustration behavior, such as swearing, beating the machine, showing an altered heart rate and g.s.r.; where Mr. B merely shrugs his shoulders, and his heart rate and g.s.r. remain steady. If we want to say that Mr. B really wanted the Coke as much as Mr. A, we might say that he has a high tolerance for frustration, a hypothesis which might not be supported by other evidence, or else we might say that when he feels frustrated, the

Revised version of a paper presented to the American Society for Value Inquiry, May 6, 1971, at the Palmer House, Chicago, in conjunction with the Meeting of the American Philosophical Association. Reprinted by permission of the author.

usual symptoms do not appear: the swearing, the heart rate change, the change in g.s.r. This proposal is not impossible, although more data are wanted about the possibility of a steady g.s.r. in face of real frustration; but at the least we should want a further story explaining the difference, either a general trait of placidness in Mr. B, a history of training in concealment of emotions, and so on.

It must be conceded that, in the face of all these facts, it is still not *inconsistent* to affirm that Mr. B's desire for a Coke is at least as strong as Mr. A's. It may be that wanting is not connected with the behavioral indices in nearly as simple a way as the principles psychologists now tend to accept and that, if we knew the real laws, we would see that wanting is strongly related to other variables which we have not even thought of; and it may be that if we knew all this we would believe that Mr. B's wanting is at least as strong as Mr. A's. Moreover, there could well be facts of the past histories of the individuals which we do not know which, if we did know them, would convince us that the state of wanting must be at least as great in Mr. A, even given the lawlike principles we currently accept. Thus *certainty* about the relative strength of the desire-states of the two men must be absent; but it would be arbitrary and highly unreasonable for anyone to claim that the wanting-states of Mr. B are at least as intense as those of Mr. A, when all the facts we do know, taken with the lawlike principles we do accept on account of their predictive and explanatory value, support the view that Mr. A's wanting-states are more intense than those of Mr. B.

In view of these considerations, I think we must reaffirm the judgment that the man who comes in from three sets of tennis on a hot day wants a cold Coke more than the one who has been working in an air-conditioned office and has recently consumed a Coke. So *some* interpersonal comparisons of wanting are justified. Furthermore, I would think, they are justified well enough to support policy decisions. Professor Ward Edwards, a student of decision theory, once wrote that "it seems utopian to hope that an experimental procedure will ever give information about individual utilities that could be of any practical use in guiding large-scale economic policy." We might grant him this contention, but nevertheless say that there are sometimes good and sufficient reasons for making comparisons of wants of different persons—reasons strong enough to justify decisions. In our present case, there is surely sufficient reason, in case someone has one and only one cold Coke to give out, to present it to the tennis player.

I do not intend to suggest, of course, that we are always in a position to make a reasonable decision, between *any* pair of individuals and for *any* pair of events, as to which person's want for the one over the other is greater. All I wish to say is that sometimes we are in a position to claim, with good and sufficient reason, that, of two given individuals, one wants one specified event over another specified event more than the other wants some specified event over another one. For some decisions, that is all we need—provided, of course, there are no reasons for thinking that the wanting of one or both needs correction in some way.

I should like to point out that this reasoning can easily be extended to cover a different but important type of case: a *gain* of something for one person over a *loss* of something else for another person. We obviously *do* think that Mr. A's desire for a good French meal, with duck à l'orange, pastry, and fine wine, is sometimes stronger than Mr. B's *aversion*, say, to a prick in the ear (made in order to get a drop of blood). How can we justify this belief? First, we can know that Mr. B would gladly take a prick in the ear in order to get something, say a martini. For Mr. B prefers the prick plus a martini to the status quo. So we are justified in saying that his want for the martini is stronger than his aversion to the prick. Now, we can use the reasoning just sketched to show that Mr. A's desire for the French dinner is greater than Mr. B's desire for a martini, at least hopefully. And, given B's greater desire for the martini as compared with his aversion to the prick in the ear, we can infer that Mr. A's want for a French dinner is stronger than Mr. B's aversion to a prick in the ear. So, assuming there are no irrationalities of desire that we need worry about, we can conclude that the gain in utility for Mr. A in having a French dinner is greater than the loss to Mr. B in suffering a prick in the ear. Again, I wish to insist that this result does not commit us to saying that it is possible to make such comparative judgments of gains against losses in all cases.

We are now ready for a further question: whether and how we can sometimes know that a social act—say an alteration in income tax rates —will bring about an enhancement of utility, taking the effects on everyone into account. This is the kind of question a utilitarian moral philosopher must be concerned with when he asks which act will maximize utility, taking everyone affected into account. If we transform this question into the simpler type of question we have been discussing so far, what it becomes is the question whether and how we can sometimes know that a social act will maximize *the satisfaction of desires*, taking the effects on everyone into account.

Let me now specify some conditions which are sufficient, but not necessary, for saying that an act has increased the total desire satisfaction. The first condition is obvious: the case in which the event produces an increase in desire-satisfaction for each and every person. Obviously, if each and every person wants his situation as it will be after the social act more than he wants the status quo, we want to say that the social act has increased the *total* desire-satisfaction. A second condition is equally obvious: one in which a social act increases the desire-satisfaction for at least one person, while leaving the situation of others either unchanged or at least equally preferable from the point of view of each, so that no one is made worse off. Again in this case we want to say that the total desire-satisfaction has been increased. It should be noticed that we can know that these two situations obtain without any *inter*personal *comparisons* at all; what we need know is simply, for the case of *other* persons, whether each prefers the new state of affairs to the old one. I come now to a third sufficient condition for saying that the want-satisfaction of a group has been increased, and we should note that in order to know that this third condition is met, we *do* have to be able to make *inter*personal comparisons of an ordinal kind. Let me spell out this third condition by means of an example, with the understanding that the third condition is just a generalization of the example. Suppose there are ten persons in a group, and as a result of an action or adoption of a policy, the want-satisfaction of three is decreased, that of five increased, and that of two unchanged. Now when might we say that the total want-satisfaction has gone up? A sufficient condition seems to be this: that among the five persons whose want-satisfaction has gone up, we can pick out three, and match them with those whose want-satisfaction has gone down, and know in each case that the want-satisfaction of the one of a pair has gone up more than, or at least as much as, the want-satisfaction has declined for the person matched with him. We accomplish this result, of course, by the kind of reasoning by which we showed that you get more want-satisfaction by awarding a French dinner to Mr. A than you lose by requiring Mr. B to undergo a pinprick in the ear. Now if we can do this, we can say that the increase of want-satisfaction for the three matched individuals at least compensates for the decrease in want-satisfaction for the three others matched with them. And, since we hypothesized that there are two individuals remaining whose want-satisfaction has been increased, we can say that the total want-satisfaction has been raised.

Of course it is not suggested that we can always be sure whether such a matching and comparison can be carried through, and obviously the comparisons must be rough. I am also not asserting that an action with such an effect on want-satisfactions is *just,* or that it is right or obligatory; all I am saying is that *when* such a comparison and matching can be carried through, and there are no reasons for saying that the wants of the individuals in question are uncriticized and need correction, then we can properly say that the *utility* of all has been increased by the action.

In view of these three simple criteria for an increase in social utility, we shall be able to say that certain actions, or changes in the moral or legal code, will increase utility. For instance, consider the moral rule that one should render a service to another in distress when this can be done at trivial cost to one's self. It seems quite clear—at least assuming that the burden of having this rule in one's conscience is so slight as to be negligible—that the utility of a group with such a rule is bound to be higher, over a period of time, then the utility of the same group with no such rule.

But can we ever say that some event or new state of affairs increases the utility of a group when one of the above conditions is *not* met? For instance, could a great many modest gains from such a change outweigh a few large losses, when the losses are so large that they cannot be matched with larger gains in the way suggested above? For instance, can we say that there has been a net gain from the introduction of air travel as compared with rail travel, if we have to base our claim on the widespread convenience and speed of air travel, albeit a diminution in safety, so that more people are killed in air accidents than would have been killed in travel by rail? Or, can our system of criminal law claim to be a contribution to general utility if it confines a thief to prison for ten years with the thought that danger to the property of many people is reduced by the deterrent effect of his confinement? Utilitarians have often assumed that we can justifiably make such claims of a net gain in utility when none of the described three conditions is satisfied. And many people have supposed that such judgments *must* be possible if the morality of certain actions or institutions is to be appraised by utilitarian standards.

I shall conclude by commenting briefly on the question whether this problem is one of much magnitude. My tentative conclusion is that probably it is a very small problem. For, I suggest, if we use our ingenuity we shall find that the number of cases for which we have to make such comparisons, that is, comparisons which cannot be made by our three criteria, is very small. I suggest that it usually turns out, when it seems that we are forced to make such a comparison, that a closer look at the facts reveals that the comparison we are really required to make is one for which one of our three criteria is appropriate. For instance, when we ask ourselves whether there is a gain in confining a man to jail for five years after conviction of grand larceny in order to provide greater security to all against loss of property, I suggest that a large factor in our thinking is that, at least normally, when robbery and break-in occur, there is also a serious threat of violence in case the attempted robbery is interrupted. And if what we are really wanting to deter is personal violence, then our problem of comparison is considerably simplified. Another point that I suggest is often overlooked is the implications of the principle of declining marginal utility, both of goods and money, for distributions. When this point is fully taken into account in the large context of an appraisal of a whole economic system, I believe we can see how questions about social utility can be answered without resorting to quantitative notions. I do not know any place where it has been shown that there are numerous questions about social utility which cannot be answered unless we can determine net social utility in some way other than by the three criteria mentioned. However, I am not prepared to say that there are *no* such questions. If there are, we may have to be prepared to say that to some questions of social utility there is no rationally defensible answer.

SUGGESTED SUPPLEMENTARY READINGS

ASHFORD, N. A., "Worker Health and Safety: An Area of Conflicts." *Monthly Labor Review,* 98 (September 1975).

BAUER, RAYMOND A., and DAN H. FENN, JR. *The Corporate Social Audit.* New York: Russell Sage Foundation, 1972.

————. "What Is a Corporate Social Audit?" *Harvard Business Review,* 51 (January 1973).

BELL, HOWARD H. "Self-Regulation by the Advertising Industry." *California Management Review,* 16 (Spring 1974).

COHEN, MANUEL F., and GEORGE J. STIGLER. "Can Regulatory Agencies Protect Consumers?" Washington: American Enterprise Institute. Rational Debate Seminar Series 5, no. 4, 1971.

DAVIS, KEITH, and ROBERT BLOMSTROM. *Business and Society* (3rd ed.), Chapter 10. New York: McGraw-Hill Book Company, 1975.

ESTES, RALPH. *Corporate Social Accounting.* New York: John Wiley and Sons, 1976.

FLATHMAN, RICHARD E. *The Public Interest.* New York: John Wiley and Sons, 1966.

GIBBONS, EDWARD F. "Making a Corporate Code of Ethics Work." In *Proceedings of the First National Conference on Business Ethics,* ed. W. Michael Hoffman. Waltham, Mass.: Center for Business Ethics at Bentley College, 1977.

HELD, VIRGINIA. *The Public Interest and Individual Interests.* New York: Basic Books, 1970.

HILL, IVAN. *The Ethical Basis of Economic Freedom.* Chapel Hill, N.C.: American Viewpoint, Inc., 1976.

JACOBY, NEIL. *The Business-Government Relationship: A Reassessment.* Pacific Palisades, Calif.: Goodyear, 1975.

LINOWES, DAVID F. *The Corporate Conscience.* New York: Hawthorn Books, Inc., 1974.

NOVICK, DAVID. "Cost/Benefit Analysis and Social Responsibility." *Business Horizons,* 16 (October 1973).

————. "Cost-Benefit Analysis in the Socially Responsible Corporation." In *Managing the Socially Responsible Corporation,* ed. Melvin Anshen. New York: Macmillan Publishing Co., 1974.

POSNER, RICHARD A. *Regulation of Advertising by the FTC.* Washington, D.C.: American Enterprise Institute for Public Policy Research, 1973.

SCHUCK, PETER H. "Why Regulation Fails." *Harper's,* 251 (September 1975).

SETHI, S. PRAKASH. "Getting a Handle on the Social Audit." *Business and Society Review,* Winter 1972–73.

SETHI, S. PRAKASH, ed. *The Unstable Ground: Corporate Social Policy in a Dynamic Society.* Los Angeles: Melville Publishing Co., 1974.

STEINER, GEORGE A. "Should Business Accept the Social Audit?" *Conference Board Record,* 9 (May 1972).

TYLER, GUS. "The Limits of Corporate Responsibility." *Montclair Journal of Social Sciences and Humanities,* 2 (Summer 1973).

WERTHER, WILLIAM B., JR. "Government Control vs. Corporate Ingenuity." *Labor Law Journal,* June 1975.

WIEDENBAUM, MURRAY L. "The High Cost of Government Regulation." *Business Horizons,* 18 (August 1975).

WILLIAMS, HARRISON A., JR. "Legislation and Responsibility: The Occupational Safety and Health Act." *Journal of Current Social Issues,* 12 (Spring 1975).

WILSON, JAMES J. "The Dead Hand of Regulation." *The Public Interest,* 25 (Fall 1971).

Chapter 5

CONFLICT OF INTEREST

AND CONFLICT

OF OBLIGATION

case 1: The Lincoln Stores Case

In 1937 a man named Grant was a director of Lincoln Stores. Two of his associates in the management structure of the company were Martin and Haley. In April of 1937 these executives learned that a small and some-what competitive store near the Lincoln Stores' Norwich, Connecticut, outlet was for sale. These three men then purchased this small-time competitor. Haley resigned to handle the management of the new store. Grant and Martin concealed their interests in the new store and continued in the employ of Lincoln Stores, though they had agreed to help Haley clandestinely in the management of the new store. They also "assisted" Haley by using inventory records and private capital information from Lincoln Stores' files, in order to plan a competitive, department-by-depart-ment strategy. In addition, they charged traveling expenses to Lincoln Stores for trips that were in fact used to plan the new company.

While reversing an earlier legal finding, the Supreme Court of Massa-chusetts rejected the idea that these three men had illegally acted by seizing a "corporate opportunity." The Court argued that Lincoln Stores itself had no need of the new store and did not intend to purchase it, and therefore there was no violation (of a duty to purchase the new store) by its employees in purchasing the new store for themselves. The Court thus did not find that these employees' interests in purchasing the store con-flicted with the interests of the company, for the company had no interest in making the purchase. However, the Court did hold that there was *some* conflict of interest and breach of the duty of loyalty by these three executives because they schemed against Lincoln Stores by obtaining information and money purely in order to compete; and the court concluded that in this respect they did damage the company. The Court thus held that it was *not* disloyal or illegal to *purchase* a competitor's business even though information about the availability for sales of the competitive business came to the executives in their employment for Lincoln Stores and potentially was competitively damaging. Compensation for damages was limited to the use of private information and travel money. In brief, the Court held that: "the wrong arose, not out of the *acquisition* of the store, but in the *operation* of the business."[1]

Note

1. *Lincoln Stores* v. *Grant.* 309 Mass. 417, 34 N.E. 2d 704. This case is briefly discussed in the article in this chapter by Jacobs. (Italics added.)

case 2:   The Bert Lance Case

Bert Lance was President Jimmy Carter's first nominee for a cabinet position—as director of the Office of Management and Budget (OMB). The Georgia banker and close personal friend of the President was quickly and routinely confirmed. However, because of past and present business activities centering on his interests in his own bank and on his personal business ventures, Lance became a center of political dispute after confirmation. In particular, he had regularly and heavily overdrawn, without the usual penalty, his account with his Georgia bank. This set of events resulted in an "enforcement agreement" between Lance's Georgia bank and the U.S. Comptroller of the Currency, who described the bank's practice as "unsafe and unsound." A bank examiner had criticized the overdrafts as "unauthorized loans." Apparently, the enforcement agreement was lifted through Lance's political influence. It also turned out that Lance, President Carter, and numerous individuals later to figure prominently in the Carter administration had used the bank's private airplane for political trips—generally without reimbursement or with very late and partial reimbursement. A third key matter also came to light: Lance had received large personal loans from other banks because of Georgia bank funds he deposited in "correspondent accounts" at those banks. These funds ostensibly helped his bank receive additional banking services, but the loans also served as inducements for the other banks to make the personal loans to Lance.

Lance argued that these practices were all "normal" in business, especially in the case of Southern banks where customers were "retained" by such practices. He maintained that no showing of unfitness for public office had been demonstrated, that while he was in charge of his Georgia bank its assets had increased from $11.9 million to $54.1 million, that his overdrafts did not result in bank "losses," and that all the charges against him were either false or were merely based on innuendo (such as that the "correspondent bank" deposits *helped* him receive personal funds). Lance eventually repaid everything he owed, but he generally did not at any given time have funds available to cover his indebtedness.

Because of what he had done with private power and political influence, gradually a political consensus emerged that Lance was unfit for public office. His resignation was forced, despite the fact that he had not been found legally liable or tried in court on any of the charges mentioned above. The prevailing journalistic opinion seemed to be that the U.S. citizens and politicians had made a judgment about propriety and about "political morality," without reaching any conclusion about legal action. However, there was widespread agreement that the case raised unresolved moral problems of conflict of interest and of the ethics of acceptable banking practices.

INTRODUCTION

Perplexing issues arise in business ethics because of conflicts of interest and conflicts among competing obligations. Several problems of conflict emerge because of differing duties and responsibilities of management and employees in the corporate setting. Just as an air of change presently prevails about the responsibilities of corporations to achieve social goals, so certain changes have been proposed regarding the responsibilities of corporations toward their employees and of employees toward corporations. There is now much discussion of the duties of corporations to employees, about the correlative rights of employees, and about related topics concerning employees' duties of loyalty and obedience. Among the many problems and cases to achieve national notoriety are the Bert Lance case, recounted above, and Ralph Nader's proposals that employees ought to "blow the whistle" on corporate wrongdoing by revealing confidential information to the Securities and Exchange Commission, the Department of Justice, a Board of Directors, or some other official and appropriate body.

Traditionally, the corporate structure has been fairly tightly controlled in these matters by legal restraints and to some extent by codes of professional responsibility. Of special importance has been a body of law governing corporations known as the "law of agency." This law, fashioned largely from legal precedents, deals with the duties of loyalty and obedience of an employee to an employer. This law has generally functioned to protect corporations more than to protect their employees. For example, in cases of a conflict of obligations it has been held that corporate executives and lawyers owe their allegiance and legal duty to the corporation and *not* to stockholders, the public, other employees, etc. In some still influential cases it has been held that disloyalty by an employee to the corporation or to its interests is in effect "private treason." Recently the trend in ethical literature has run in the other direction. Employees have increasingly been regarded as having rights to pursue free speech and courses of action potentially adverse to the interests of the employer, much as citizens have been conceived as having limited rights to pursue a course of action opposed to governmental plans and control. The ancient theory that management's primary loyalty and responsibility are owed to the corporate entity rather than to employees or the public has been somewhat eroded by these changes. The older body of law and the new trends have thus combined to form a new set of moral and legal controversies over what ought to be done in the corporate setting when conflicts of interest, conflicts of duty, and conflicts of role-responsibility arise. In this chapter we study three related problems that have emerged and remain largely unresolved: areas of conflicting obligations, areas of conflicting loyalties, and areas where a conflict of interest occurs.

CONFLICT OF OBLIGATION AND DUTIES OF MANAGEMENT

Conflicts of obligation are common in the moral life. They occur whenever our principles or commitments demand that we fulfill two or more obligations though only one can actually be fulfilled. For example, suppose that a member of a labor union has promised to deliver certain goods on a contractually-agreed-upon date and that when the date arrives he finds himself having to cross picket lines, which he has also promised not to do. His two promises cannot both be fulfilled, yet he has separate obligations to fulfill both. Such situations are often referred to as *moral* dilemmas, but conflicts between obligations can also arise from *nonmoral* sources. For example, in discussions of proper business behavior, we sometimes encounter conflicts that arise from *role*-obligations. Such professionals as physicians, professors, lawyers, and business persons commonly incur an obligation by virtue of their job or profession that may conflict with either another role obligation or a moral obligation.

Many conflicts emerge in business through what is referred to in law as the "duties of management." These duties specify the respects in which directors, officers, and other policy makers such as controlling shareholders have specific duties to the corporation and its interests. Legal duties such as those of loyalty and obedience specify how management must act within lines of authority, must be persistent in the exercise of due care, and must act to fulfill so-called "fiduciary duties." (The roles occupied by employees are said to set them in a *fiduciary relationship* with the corporation.) If management has fulfilled such duties it is usually regarded as not *legally liable* for consequences of its related actions (e.g., under the so-called "business judgment" rule). Moral problems usually occur when the role responsibilities created by these established fiduciary relationships come into conflict with a manager's moral responsibilities. This conflict occurs, for example, when a manager is tempted to "blow the whistle" for moral reasons, and yet feels constrained from doing so by the obligation of loyalty to the corporation's interests.

Duties of corporate management have generally been established through case law (where the decisions of judges form precedents) rather than by formal statute or by the writings of moral philosophers. This legal history provides one reason for the heavy emphasis on law and legal responsibility in the present chapter. These duties are usually highly general statements in law, and moral arguments are commonly employed by judges in writing their decisions. In the opening two readings in this chapter, two judges debate the merits of a corporate management case involving certain conflicts of interest. In this case the directors of one corporation (Empire Power Corporation) also owned or controlled the common stock of another corporation (Long Island Lighting Company). The directors supported the latter corporation by loans from funds provided by the former corporation. The issues in the case are whether the loans purely promoted the interests of the individuals who made them, and, if so, whether such action is unacceptable when damage is not done to the loaning corporation. The judges in this case (a split decision) seem to disagree both on critical points of law and on business morality.

The initial readings in this chapter discuss conflicting obligations that arise from the role responsibilities of management and the duties of related professionals, especially lawyers. Philip I. Blumberg discusses and evaluates recent developments in law, including a consideration of the principles of the law of agency. Blumberg points out that business ethics and other professional ethics play a major part in determining the roles and duties of employees. He argues that we are in a changing period in which traditional understandings of loyalty are being balanced against employees' and society's rights, particularly where a conflict exists between an employee's duty of loyalty and society's need for a public disclosure. In a second article, Ronald D. Rotunda discusses situations of conflict of interest for the corporate manager and lawyer. Rotunda concentrates on the issue of whether the corporate entity's interest ought always to be kept paramount by lawyers, as has been proposed by a Code of Professional Responsibility of the American Bar Association. Finally, Richard Wasserstrom argues that the *ends* sought by a client—e.g., a corporation—on many occasions ought not to determine what a lawyer should do. Wasserstrom is concerned that the lawyer might become merely an "amoral technician" by virtue of his relation of loyalty to clients such as powerful corporations. This danger for lawyers is of course equally present for business executives, who represent the corporation's interests much in the way a lawyer does. Wasserstrom does not, however, invoke the easy solution that one ought to act on one's own sincerely held private views. This recourse, he argues, could undermine valid lines of loyalty, could lead to the neglect of clients, and could even lead to a general social situation in which lawyers have far too much power and control. While Wasserstrom focuses exclusively on the profession of law and its structure of role-differentiated behavior, many of the arguments he uses apply with equal force to business professionals—as he himself points out.

The so-called "duty of loyalty" receives special attention in the next section of this chapter. In law the duty of loyalty is based on a fiduciary principle popularly expressed in scripture as "a person cannot serve two masters." This principle takes on critical significance in the world of business, because those who manage a corporation have so much more power and knowledge than those who invest in or are employed by the corporation that the latter's interest can easily be disregarded by management in favor of its own interest (as in the case of voting huge bonuses for management alone). Some special aspects of the duty of loyalty are discussed in this chapter by Blumberg, by Rotunda, and by Jacobs.

A philosophical analysis is provided by Alex Michalos of the claim that corporate executives ought to exhibit their loyalty by acting in the best interests of the corporation. Michalos argues against what he calls the Loyal Agent's Argument. This argument holds that because an agent should serve a principal's (corporation's) interest, and because interests are best served by egoistic behavior, a corporate executive ought to serve the corporation by acting egoistically in its behalf. Michalos attacks the argument by focusing on certain celebrated cases of corporate loyalty, such as that of the Board of Directors of Gulf Oil, where a similar ethical argument to that attacked by Michalos seems to be operative. Next, Norman Gillespie seeks a solution to the problem of how corporations can act internally to encourage *moral* behavior, as distinct from egoistic or blindly loyal behavior. Gillespie reverses precedent by arguing that corporations are morally obliged to structure the work environment to encourage ethical conduct, even when such conduct would be contrary to certain corporate interests. Indeed, Gillespie concludes that despite prevailing practices in industry, employees have a moral right to be protected from employers who fail to grant them the right to act against corporate interests.

CONFLICT OF INTEREST

A conflict of interest occurs in the world of business when a person has two or more interests such that if both are pursued there might result an unjustified effect on another individual or individuals. Generally such a conflict emerges where one's personal interest could be pursued to the detriment of the business one represents or with which one is engaged.

The most celebrated cases have occurred in sales, banking, and purchasing transactions; but they can occur in any context where interests can conflict—monetary or nonmonetary, management or nonmanagement. For example, if a personnel director in charge of promotions is in a position to evaluate and promote his son, he has a conflict of interest. It does not follow that he is unqualified to evaluate his son or even that he will inevitably do something against the interests of the business. It only follows that he has been placed in a position such that his interest in the promotion is so substantial that it might affect his independent judgment in his business role. Many such areas where conflict of interest may occur are studied in the article in this chapter by Leslie W. Jacobs. He studies trade secrets, corporate opportunities, interference with business relations, and unfair competition as important areas where conflicts of interest may occur. He concludes, strikingly, that what *morality* says ought to be of concern to an executive's conscience (in self-regarding matters) will generally constitute *legal* grounds in a court against an executive's nonconscientious actions.

In a companion piece, Joseph Margolis studies both the concept of a conflict of interest and its practical applications as a way of condemning certain acts as immoral. He begins by distinguishing a conflict of interest from conflicting interests. He propounds the thesis that both involve dilemmas, but of different sorts. In the case of conflict of interest, at least one of the interests "may not be legitimate," whereas in the case of merely conflicting interests all of the interests are independently legitimate. It is for this reason that we tend to think of conflict of interest as always morally condemnable, whereas we think of conflicting interests as unfortunate or even tragic but not as condemnable. When conflicting interests arise, we cannot do all the (right) things we would like to do, but in the case of a conflict of interest we can, for we can simply not serve the interest that smacks of wrongdoing. Margolis claims that this difference accounts for our feeling that conflicts of interest are avoidable and to be avoided, whereas conflicting interests are not entirely avoidable and cannot be avoided once the conflict arises. Margolis further argues that a conflict of interest situation may have either "bad motives" or bad consequences, but may nonetheless be *unfair.* Margolis concludes that what counts as a conflict of interest is only specifiable within a particular professional code or moral tradition and that such traditions inevitably reflect the doctrinal convictions of a particular society or community.

T.L.B.

MAJORITY OPINION IN EVERETT v. PHILLIPS

Judge Herbert Lehman

The plaintiff is the owner of 100 shares of the "participating stock" of Empire Power Corporation. The issued and outstanding capital stock of the corporation consists of 77,000 shares of six per cent cumulative preferred stock with a stated value of $7,133,000; 400,000 shares of "participating" stock with a stated value of $3,150,000, and 400,000 shares of common stock with a stated value of $1,000,000. The directors of the corporation and members of their families owned all the common stock and large amounts of the preferred stock and the "participating" stock. At the same time they also owned or controlled, directly or indirectly, 1,500,000 shares, constituting a majority of the common stock of Long Island Lighting Company. In 1931 and 1932 the Empire Power Corporation loaned to Long Island Lighting Company large sums of money. Payment of these loans was from time to time extended and the loans are still unpaid. Claiming that these loans and the extension of time of payment were *ultra vires* [beyond the power of] and were "not made to promote any business purpose of Empire Power Corporation, but were made for the sole purpose of promoting the interests of the individual defendants and that of Long Island Lighting Company," the plaintiff has brought an action in behalf of himself and other minority stockholders in which he has asked that directors of Empire Power Corporation named as individual defendants be compelled to demand payment of the indebtedness by Long Island Lighting Company and that "in the event that the said indebtedness cannot be collected from Long Island Lighting Company, then that the individual defendants shall be directed to pay the same." . . .

To establish his cause of action the plaintiff must show that the individual defendants in causing the Empire Power Corporation to loan the moneys to the Long Island Lighting Company and in failing to demand payment of such loans as they became due, have acted in disregard of the duties they owe Empire Power Corporation and that Empire Power Corporation has suffered, or at least may suffer, some detriment or loss. In a long line of decisions this court has held directors who control corporate action responsible for dereliction of duty where they have used the property of the corporation or managed its affairs to promote their own interests, disregarding the interests of the corporation. Power of control

Court of Appeals of New York, 1942. 288 N.Y. 227, 43 N.E. 2d 18.

carries with it a trust or duty to exercise that power faithfully to promote the corporate interests, and the courts of the State will insist upon scrupulous performance of that duty. Yet, however high may be the standard of fidelity to duty which the court may exact, *errors of judgment by directors do not alone suffice to demonstrate lack of fidelity. That is true even though the errors may be so gross that they may demonstrate the unfitness of the directors to manage the corporate affairs.* [The "business judgment" rule—ED.]

The plaintiff here is asserting a cause of action for wrong done to the corporation of which he is a minority stockholder. In such an action it is immaterial whether the minority stockholder who asserts it has a large or a small interest; but in determining whether those who have power to control the corporation have committed a wrong either to the corporation or to its stockholders, the corporate capital structure, the certificate of incorporation, and the corporate constitution or by-laws may be factors of great weight; for within limits prescribed by law these define to whom the power of control is entrusted, its scope and the manner in which it must be exercised. Directors are elected by the holders of stock which have voting rights. Here the certificate of incorporation of Empire Power Corporation provides that only the holders of common stock shall have voting rights. According to the testimony of the defendant Phillips, who has been president of the corporation from its formation in 1924 and who with George W. Olmsted, its vice-president until he died in 1940, owned or controlled, either directly or indirectly, all of its common stock, the corporation was "formed for the purpose of financing and taking care of the various companies in which we were then interested and later became interested further." They invited the public to subscribe to the capital of the corporation which would be managed by directors in whose election no other stockholders would have any part, and those who might furnish the capital which these directors would manage were not left under any illusion that the directors when acting for the corporation would be free from other interests which might prevent an unprejudiced exercise of judgment. The certificate of incorporation contained a provision that: "No contract or other transaction between the Corporation and any other corporation shall be affected or invalidated by the fact that any one or more of the directors of this Corporation is or are interested in, or is a director or officer, or are directors or officers of such other corporation, . . . and no contract, act or transaction of this Corporation with any person or persons, firm or corporation, shall be affected or invalidated by the fact that any director or directors of this Corporation is a party, or are parties to or interested in such contract, act or transaction, or in any way connected with such person or persons, firm or association, and each and every person who may become a director of this Corporation is hereby relieved from any liability that might otherwise exist from contracting with the Corporation for the benefit of himself or any firm, association or corporation in which he may be in anywise interested." It is against this background that the court must consider the claim of the appellant that he has established by the overwhelming weight of testimony that the directors were faithless to their trust.

The complaint of the plaintiff concerns, as we have said, loans made to Long Island Lighting Company. The defendants controlled that corporation. Their stock interest in it was large. According to the balance sheets of the corporation introduced in evidence by the plaintiff, the corporation in 1931 and also at the time of the trial had a very large surplus and was earning large profits, but needed money for the development of its business. Corporate balance sheets unfortunately do not always present a correct picture of the corporate finances. . . . The evidence establishes that unless it had succeeded in borrowing money it would have been obliged to discontinue payment of dividends, at least temporarily, and, to use all its earnings for needed improvements, and that perhaps the earnings might have provided insufficient moneys for its needs. The evidence establishes too that the defendants expected to derive benefit not only as stockholders but also in other ways from the moneys which, as directors, they caused Long Island Lighting Company to borrow. The question remains whether in seeking benefit for themselves and for the Long Island Lighting Company, which they controlled through stock ownership, they caused Empire Power Corporation, which the defendants also controlled through stock ownership, to make a loan, which might work harm to the Empire Power Corporation.

The Long Island Lighting Company at the end of 1930 owed banks approximately $10,500,000 on short term, unsecured notes. Though, according to the balance sheet of the Long Island Lighting Company, it had assets greatly in excess of its indebtedness, and had a net income of more than $3,000,000 a year, its financial position was not entirely safe or sound. The banks might press for payment of short term obligations at a time when Long Island Lighting Company might find it difficult to borrow elsewhere the money to pay such obligations. Moreover, the needs of the territory served by Long Island Lighting Company required constant extension of its plant. We may assume that prudent and conservative directors would, in such circumstances, have sought to obtain by an issue of bonds the money the corporation might require to refund its short term obligations and for new capital. . . .

. . . The Long Island Lighting Company did in 1932 apply to the Public Service Commission for permission to issue approximately $15,000,000 of refunding bonds. The directors of the Long Island Lighting Company preferred, however, to borrow the moneys under a plan which would not be subject to the restrictions which the Public Service Commission might impose as conditions to its approval. An inference that the directors were influenced by that consideration when they sought to borrow the moneys for Long Island Lighting Company upon notes payable within one year from that date might reasonably be drawn from the evidence in this case. The transaction would not be unlawful for that reason. The Legislature has in the public interest provided that bonds or notes evidencing loans for a longer period than one year may be issued only with the approval of the Commission. The Legislature has not decreed that the public interest requires similar safeguards for issues where the loans became due within the year. The Legislature has drawn the line, and "the very meaning of a line in the law is that you intentionally may go as close to it as you can if you do not pass it." . . .

The defendants can be charged with no wrong to the Empire Power Corporation on account of repeated renewals of the loans nor on account of the way in which they were handled, without proof that in these acts the defendants willfully failed to protect the interests of Empire Power Corporation in order to serve better their personal interests and the interests of the Long Island Lighting Company. There may be difference of opinion as to whether these defendants as directors of Empire Power Corporation acted wisely in the handling of the loans. There are many matters disclosed by the record which cast doubt upon the prudence, the wisdom, and the concern for the public interest shown by these directors. We are constrained, however, to agree with the Appellate Division that there is little, if any, evidence to sustain a finding that they have violated their trust or have failed to protect the interests of the Empire Power Corporation according to the dictates of their judgment, be that judgment good or bad. . . .

The provision of the certificate of incorporation of Empire Power Corporation expressly authorizing the directors to act even in matters where they have dual interest, has the effect of exonerating the directors, at least in part, "from adverse inferences which might otherwise be drawn against them." [*Spiegel* v. *Beacon Participations,* 297 Mass. 398, 417, 8 N.E.2d 895, 907.] We may point out here also that if by reason of these loans Empire Power Corporation should sustain a loss, the loss would fall primarily upon these defendants as owners of the entire capital stock. The proportion of stock of all classes owned by these defendants in Empire Power Corporation whose moneys they are claimed to have diverted wrongfully, is, indeed, much greater than the proportion of the stock owned by them in Long Island Lighting Company which received these moneys. The loans were not excessive in relation to the capital assets and the income of the borrower as shown in the borrower's balance sheet. The evidence demonstrates that the defendants acting as the directors of the Long Island Lighting Company borrowed moneys from Empire Power Corporation because in their opinion the loans promoted the interests of the borrower and the stockholders of the borrower; the evidence does not demonstrate that the defendants acting as directors of the Empire Power Corporation in loaning its moneys to Long Island Lighting Company did not decide upon sufficient ground that the loans would also promote the interests of the lender and its stockholders.

The judgment should be affirmed, without costs.

DISSENTING OPINION IN EVERETT v. PHILLIPS

Judge Charles S. Desmond

At all the times of which we write, the individual defendants controlled both Long Island Lighting Company and Empire Power Corporation. In dealings between those corporations these individual defendants sat on both sides of the table. They caused Empire Power Corporation, from November, 1930, to February, 1933, to loan Long Island Lighting Company $5,330,000 on the latter's unsecured notes. These notes and various renewals thereof were all made for periods of less than a year. See Public Service Law, § 69. Interest has been paid regularly but, up to the beginning of this action, nothing was ever paid on principal. The lighting company needed these moneys—and used them—to pay off from time to time, notes held by banks which were asking for payment. In 1930, when Empire made its first loan to the lighting company, the latter owed the banks more than $10,000,000 and found it increasingly difficult to persuade the banks to accept renewals of their unsecured notes. The banks had suggested to the individual defendants that the lighting company discontinue paying cash dividends, so that it might accumulate in its treasury funds with which to pay off the bank loans. This the individual defendants, who owned or controlled half of the lighting company's common stock, were unwilling to do. An application to the Public Service Commission for authority to issue mortgage bonds to raise money to pay off the banks was pending but undetermined. There was only one other convenient source of funds. A lender had to be found who would supply, without security and without question, the cash needed from time to time to satisfy the banks. Such a lender was ready at hand in Empire Power Corporation, completely controlled by these individual defendants themselves.

During 1930 and 1932 these defendants arranged loans aggregating $4,500,000 from the power corporation to the lighting company, most, if not all, of the proceeds going to pay off the bank loans. In March, 1932, when the lighting company owed the power corporation about $4,500,000 and the banks about $8,750,000, an agreement was made between the lighting company and the banks whereby the latter accepted renewals of their notes for six months, and agreed to accept renewals for another six months if necessary, on condition that the lighting company make certain payments which were intended to come from, and did come from, Empire Power Corporation. It was part of this arrangement that the whole of the lighting company's debt to Empire Power Corporation should be post-dated to that of the banks, post-dated rather than subordinated because it was felt that subordination "would be openly subject to

Court of Appeals of New York (1942), 288 N.Y. 227, 43 N.E. 2d 18.

attack on account of the unity of interest between Empire Power and Long Island Lighting."

A little later Empire's directors passed a resolution agreeing on behalf of Empire "to extend and keep extended the time of payment" of the lighting company's notes to Empire Power Corporation until the banks should be paid in full. An agreement to the same effect was made by defendant Phillips on behalf of Empire, in 1933, and approved by Empire's board of directors. Later that same year the Public Service Commission granted permission to the lighting company to sell the issue of bonds above referred to, but sale at the stipulated price was found to be impossible. Again the bank notes had to be renewed, and again Empire Power Corporation was caused to agree to subordinate its claims to those of the bank. Finally, in 1934, the authorized bond issue was sold by the lighting company under a contract which provided that the indebtedness to Empire Power Corporation would not be paid, discharged or secured by the issuance of any bonds of the lighting company secured by a lien prior to or on a parity with the lien of the bond issue. All of the proceeds of this bond issue went to the banks, none to Empire Power Corporation. In 1936 the lighting company paid off all its unsecured indebtedness, except that owing to Empire Power Corporation. Among the creditors so paid off were the common directors of the two corporations and their relatives and corporations controlled by them. Thus Empire Power Corporation, starting out with short term loans to the lighting company, ended up with what amounted to a "permanent investment" of $5,000,000 in the lighting company, in the form of unsecured notes, payment of which, if this suit fails, must await the pleasure of the defendants. . . .

A court will not attempt to pass upon questions of expediency or to control the corporate managers in the faithful exercise of their discretion. [*City Bank Farmers' Trust Co.* v. *Hewitt Realty Co.,* 257 N.Y. 62, 177 N.E. 309, 76 A.L.R. 881; *United Copper Securities Co.* v. *Amalgamated Copper Co.,* supra; *Burden* v. *Burden,* supra.] To make a case for the invalidation of such a contract there must be shown circumstances tending to prove that the contract was made in bad faith, fraud or other breach of trust, including a biased exercise of judgment. [*Globe Woolen Co.* v. *Utica Gas & Electric Co., Sage* v. *Culver, United Copper Securities Co.* v. *Amalgamated Copper Co., Koral* v. *Savory, Inc.,* supra.] Given such a showing, the burden is then upon those who would maintain the contract to establish its fairness [*Sage* v. *Culver,* supra], particularly when they themselves are shown to have exercised the dominating influence in effecting the contract. [*Geddes* v. *Anaconda Copper Mining Co.,* supra.] Whether the particular contract between these two corporations having the same directors was or was not made under circumstances amounting to a breach of the directors' fiduciary duty, is a question of fact.

Here the individual defendants who arranged the loans by Empire Power Corporation to Long Island Lighting Company, were completely aware of the latter's financial difficulties at the times the loans and renewals were made. They and their families owned the majority of the lighting company's stock; they directed its policies and managed its affairs; some of them were unsecured creditors of the lighting company in substantial amounts. It was to their interest individually, that the lighting company's urgent need of funds to pay its unsecured and demanding bank creditors be met. They met it by loaning Empire's money to Long Island on such terms that Empire's capital funds were used to pay off Long Island's bank loans in part, then these loans were made subordinate to the balances owing to the banks and finally remained wholly unpaid when all Long Island's other creditors of the same class were taken care of by the proceeds of a bond issue. The inference is unescapable that in the making of these loans, and renewals, the welfare of Empire Power Corporation was ignored and that the purpose of defendants was to benefit Long Island Lighting Company, and themselves. It is no answer to all this that Empire's financial structure may have resilience enough to absorb the risk or the damage of the loans, or that the individual defendant's stake in Empire is large and the plaintiff's small. Plain disclosure of the inequity of the situation and of the unfairness of the risk to the Empire Corporation, makes a strong appeal to the conscience of the court. It is not answered by defendants' protestations that Empire has a good investment in these loans, that they would surely be paid on a liquidation of the lighting company, that the lighting company's credit is good, etc., or by the provision in Empire Power Corporation's charter concerning contracts between that corporation and other corporations with the same officers or directors.

A court of equity in such a case as this does not stand aside and await the outcome of defendants' conduct. It acts promptly and effectively. It sets the whole transaction aside without waiting, or compelling minority stockholders to wait, to see whether those who unlawfully put a corporation's property at risk, may possibly at some undetermined time, have the skill, or luck, to get it back intact for the corporation.

The judgment of the Appellate Division should be reversed and that of the Special Term reinstated, with costs.

CORPORATE RESPONSIBILITY AND THE EMPLOYEE'S DUTY OF LOYALTY AND OBEDIENCE

Phillip I. Blumberg

THREE RECENT DEVELOPMENTS

This article constitutes a preliminary inquiry into aspects of a problem that the author believes will become an area of dynamic change in the corporate organization and in time will produce significant change in established legal concepts. It is concerned with the impact of the new view of the corporation upon traditional concepts of the duties of loyalty and obedience of the employee to his employer, firmly recognized in the law of agency. This impact has been illustrated by a number of recent developments, which have a common core: the right of the employee of the large public corporation to take action adverse to the interests of his employer in response to the employee's view as to the proper social responsibility of his corporate employer.

A. The "Public Interest Disclosure" Proposal

The outstanding example, which will serve as the major topic of this article, is the recent appeal of Mr. Ralph Nader that "professional" employees of corporations, as well as of government, disclose to private agencies information about their "employers' policies or practices that they consider harmful to public or consumer interests."[1] Mr. Nader simultaneously announced the establishment of a "Clearing House for Professional Responsibility" to solicit and receive such reports and to encourage what Mr. Nader termed "responsible whistle-blowing" by scientists, engineers, and other professional employees, and to protect employees acting as informants or tipsters from retaliation by employers. Mr. Nader originally stated his program in terms of professionalism: professional ethics should take precedence over loyalty to employers when the public interest is at stake. Although this initial statement rested on an appeal to a professional responsibility, Mr. Nader's broad reference to harm to "public or consumer interests" was apparently restricted to cases where the employer's behavior was "illegal, hazardous, or unconscionable."[2]

Subsequently, Mr. Nader substantially broadened the scope of his appeal for disclosure of confidential information by employees. He included all employees, not merely professional employees, and extended

From "Corporate Responsibility and the Employee's Duty of Loyalty and Obedience: A Preliminary Inquiry," Phillip I. Blumberg, in *Oklahoma Law Review*, vol. 24, no. 3, August 1971. Reprinted by permission of *Oklahoma Law Review*.

the area of disclosure to a wide range of information, going far beyond the original restrictions of unprofessional conduct or "illegal, hazardous, or unconscionable" behavior. The *New York Times* reported:

> One way Nader sees to alleviate the problem of individual responsibility in the bureaucracies of both the Government and corporations is to turn what he calls "whistle blowing" into an honorable action. "A whistle blower," says Nader, "is anyone in any organization who draws a line on his own account where responsibility to society transcends responsibility to his organization."[3]

Thus, the test has become a personal decision by each employee "where responsibility to society transcends responsibility to his organization." It is clear that Mr. Nader wishes to encourage the "corporate leak" to facilitate efforts of so-called "public interest" organizations in publicizing actions by the major power centers in the society—whether governmental or corporate—not deemed to be in the public interest.

In brief, any person in any organization who disagrees with a decision of his superiors in the social or environmental area is encouraged to continue the campaign (which he lost, or in which he did not have an opportunity to participate within his own organization) in the public arena via disclosure to a "public interest" organization.

Mr. James M. Roche, Chairman of General Motors Corporation, promptly attacked the proposal, stating:

> Some of the enemies of business now encourage an employee to be disloyal to the enterprise. They want to create suspicion and disharmony and pry into the proprietary interests of the business. However this is labelled— industrial espionage, whistle blowing or professional responsibility—it is another tactic for spreading disunity and creating conflict.[4]

Thus, the question arises: What is the duty of the employee to his employer? To what extent, if any, has a heightened sense of a responsibility to society—on the employee level as well as on the corporate level— changed the nature of the employee's obligations to his employer?

B. Eastern Airlines

Another example involves Eastern Airlines. The airline's procedure required pilots shortly after takeoff to jettison in the atmosphere about three gallons of excess fuel in holding tanks remaining from the previous run. A senior pilot of thirty years' experience had repeatedly requested the draining of the tanks on the ground by mechanics because of his concern of the impact of the practice on air pollution. Eastern management had refused. The pilot thereupon violated the regulation and had the kerosene drained while on the ground. Eastern maintained that "each of its 3,700 pilots cannot make his own rules" and discharged the pilot. After considerable publicity (and pressure from the Airline Pilots Association), Eastern reinstated the pilot. It subsequently went further and announced that it was endeavoring to have manufacturers develop engines to eliminate the problem by allowing excess fuel to return to the regular fuel tanks.[5]

C. *Polaroid Corporation*

A third example relates to the efforts of what appears to be a small number of black employees of Polaroid Corporation, calling themselves the Polaroid Revolutionary Workers Movement, to force Polaroid to cease doing business in South Africa by "confrontation" techniques including a boycott of Polaroid products and by picketing, disruptions and demonstrations. Polaroid responded on a number of levels, including the use of an advisory committee of employees, including black employees, who visited South Africa. The aspect of the episode with which we are concerned is the action of Polaroid management in eventually suspending one of the leaders of the Movement without pay for her "persistent activities in fomenting public disapproval" of the firm and for being "involved in a deliberate campaign calculated to damage the well being" of the company.[6]

Still another reflection of changing views as to the traditional duties of loyalty and obedience of employees is the following glimpse of the corporate future depicted in Mr. Anthony Athos' article in the *Harvard Business Review* entitled "Is the Corporation Next to Die?"

> "Within five years a president of a major corporation will be locked out of his office by his junior executives," remarked George Koch, president of the Grocery Manufacturers Association, not long ago. The very idea would have seemed outrageous and impossible only a few years ago . . . the situation is rapidly becoming ripe for the kind of action Koch predicts.[7]

The foregoing illustrations of the present and possible future world of the corporate employee require a reexamination of the traditional fundamental concepts of the employer-employee relationship: the employee's duties of loyalty and obedience to the employer, and the employer's freedom to discharge an employee. They reflect a new view of responsibility—a view that the employee's duty as a citizen transcends his duties as employee. This is a companion view to the basic tenet of the "public interest proxy campaign," such as Campaign GM, that the shareholder's interest as a citizen transcends his interest as a shareholder, and that he should act primarily for the good of the country—i.e., the public interest —rather than for the good of the company. These examples may also involve a different concept, the view that employees should play a part in the corporate decision-making process, at least in issues of public concern involving questions of corporate social responsibility.

These views—so profoundly changed from traditional values—reflect the politicalization of the corporation, which the author has discussed elsewhere.[8]

THE RESTATEMENT OF AGENCY

A review of the relevant provisions of the *Restatement of Agency* provides an obvious starting point for consideration of the new view of the role and duties of the employee.[9]

A. The Duty of Obedience

Section 383 and *Section 385* state the agent's duty to obey the principal. Section 385(1) imposes upon the agent "a duty to obey all reasonable directions" of the principal.[10] Comment *a* points out:

> In determining whether or not the orders of the principal to the agent are reasonable ... *business or professional ethics* ... are considered. [Emphasis added.]

Comment *a* continues:

> In no event would it be implied that an agent has a duty to perform acts which ... are *illegal or unethical*.... [Emphasis added.]

Thus, Comment *a* expressly excludes matters contrary to "business or professional ethics" or "illegal or unethical" acts from those which an agent would be required to perform. This frees the agent from participation in such behavior and authorizes him to withdraw from the agency relation if the principal persists. It in no way authorizes him to disclose such directions of the principal, or not to comply with an instruction of the principal not to disclose any information about the principal's affairs, even in those cases where he is privileged not to perform in accordance with the principal's instructions. The duty exists not only so long as the agent remains an agent but continues after the agency has been terminated as well.

Section 385 (2) provides:

> (2) Unless he is privileged to protect his own or another's interests, an agent is subject to a duty not to act in matters entrusted to him on account of the principal contrary to the directions of the principal....

The Comments make it clear that "an interest" which the agent is privileged to protect refers only to an economic interest, such as a lien or his business reputation. There is no suggestion that an interest which "he is privileged to protect" includes the public interest.

B. The Duty of Loyalty

Section 387 expresses the general principle that:

> an agent is subject to a duty to his principal to act solely for the benefit of the principal in all matters connected with his agency.

Comment *b* emphasizes the high degree of the duties of loyalty of the agent by stating that they "are the same as those of a trustee to his beneficiaries." It provides, however, that:

> The agent is also under a duty not to act or speak disloyally ... except in the protection of his own interests or those of others. He is not, however, necessarily prevented from acting in good faith outside his employment in a manner which injuriously affects his principal's business.

and provides the following illustration:

3. A, employed by P, a life insurance company, in good faith advocates legislation which would require a change in the policies issued by the company. A has violated no duty to P.

Thus, the agent is free to act "in good faith outside his employment," even in a manner which injures his principal's business, but is subject to a duty identical with that of a trustee with respect to "all matters connected with his agency." Under the comment and illustration, the General Motors employee may campaign in good faith for legislation imposing costly antipollution or product safety controls on automobile manufacturers, but he occupies a position equivalent to a trustee with respect to information about General Motors operations which he has acquired in the course, or on account, of his employment.

Section 394 prohibits the agent from acting:

> for persons whose interests conflict with those of the principal in matters in which the agent is employed.

The numerous examples in the comments relate to competitors or adverse parties in commercial transactions or parties with adverse claims and make it plain that the reference to conflicting "interests" means economic interests.

C. The Duty of Confidentiality

Section 395 imposes a duty upon the agent:

> not to use or to communicate information confidentially given him by the principal or acquired by him during the course of or on account of his agency . . . to the injury of the principal, on his own account or on behalf of another . . . unless the information is a matter of general knowledge.

Comment *a* emphasizes that the agency relation "permits and requires great freedom of communication between the principal and the agent." It expands the agent's duty by stating that the agent:

> also has a duty not to use information acquired by him as agent . . . for any purpose likely to cause his principal harm or to interfere with his business, although it is information not connected with the subject matter of his agency.

Comment *b* extends the duty beyond "confidential" communications to "information which the agent should know his principal would not care to have revealed to others." Both Comments *a* and *b* refer to protection of the principal against competition, but it is clear that this is merely one of the interests of the principal protected by the section.

Comment *f* creates a privilege, significantly enough for a public, not an economic, interest:

> An agent is privileged to reveal information confidentially acquired . . . in the protection of a superior interest of himself or of a third person. Thus, if the confidential information is to the effect that the principal is committing or is about to commit a crime, the agent is under no duty not to reveal it.

This is the only illustration in the *Restatement* that the term "interest" may embrace something of a noneconomic nature. The public interest in law enforcement is deemed a "superior interest" giving rise to a privilege to reveal otherwise confidential information.

If construed to include disclosure to any person, and not solely to law enforcement agencies, Comment *f* would support the "public interest disclosure" proposal to the extent it relates to "illegal" matters, without regard to the nature or seriousness of the offense. *Section 395,* Comment *f,* however, refers only to commission of a "crime." This contrasts with *Section 385(1)* relating to the duty of obedience which refers not only to "illegal" but also to "unethical" acts and to "business or professional ethics." The inclusion of these latter elements in *Section 385(1)* and their omission in *Section 395* would indicate that the release of confidential information privileged under *Section 395* does not extend beyond criminal acts.

Although *Section 395* refers only to the agent's use or communication of information "on his own account or on behalf of another" and does not literally prohibit use or communication of such information for the benefit of the public, Comment *a* prohibits such use "for any purpose likely to cause his principal harm or to interfere with his business." Comment *a* thus would appear to expand the duty of the agent beyond acts "on his own account or on behalf of another" to include disclosures made to advance the "public interest," which were not related to commission of a "crime" privileged under Comment *f....*

In summary, except in the single area of "crime," the *Restatement* provides no support for the view that the employee may disclose nonpublic information about his employer acquired as a result of the employment relationship in order to promote the superior interest of society. While prohibiting affirmative acts of the employee such as disclosure, the *Restatement* relieves the employee of any duty to obey or act for the employer not only in the case of "crime" or "illegality" but also in case of "unethical acts" or acts "contrary to public policy" or constituting a tort.

The duties of obedience, loyalty, and confidentiality enunciated by the *Restatement* and the carefully circumscribed privileged exceptions clearly proscribe the "public interest disclosure" proposal suggested by Mr. Nader. We must recognize, however, that the *Restatement* drawn from the common-law cases is drafted in terms of economic activity, economic motivation, and economic advantage and formulates duties of loyalty and obedience for the agent to prevent the agent's own economic interest from impairing his judgment, zeal, or single-minded devotion to the furtherance of his principal's economic interests. The reference in *Section 395,* Comment *f* permitting the agent to disclose confidential information concerning a criminal act committed or planned by the principal is the sole exception to a system of analysis that is otherwise exclusively concerned with matters relating to the economic position of the parties. Thus, the question may fairly be asked to what extent the *Restatement* and the common-law decisions are useful in the analysis of a proposal that rests on the concept of an agent's primary obligation as a citizen to the society, transcending his economic duty to the principal.

Are doctrines resting on a policy of protecting the economic position of the principal against impairment by reason of an agent's effort to achieve economic gain properly applicable to the employee who releases nonpublic information about his employer without intent to obtain economic advantage for himself—and motivated by a desire to promote the public good rather than to injure the principal (although such injury may in fact result)?

The duties of loyalty and obedience on the part of the agent are unquestionably central to the agency relationship, irrespective of economic considerations. But these duties, as the *Restatement* itself recognizes, have limitations. To paraphrase Mr. Justice Frankfurter's well-known admonition:[11] To say that an agent has duties of loyalty and obedience only begins analysis; it gives direction to further inquiry. It is thus not enough to say that the agent has duties of loyalty and obedience which will be impaired. One must inquire more deeply and ascertain the outer perimeter of the agent's obligations by balancing the conflicting considerations. On this critical question of how far the duties of loyalty and obedience extend, the *Restatement* enunciating the traditional rules in their economic setting provides limited guidance. . . .

THE VIEW OF THE CORPORATION AS A POLITICAL INSTITUTION

Presumably, the basis for the proposal for unauthorized disclosure of corporate conduct that is regarded as socially irresponsible rests on a judgment as to the crucial social importance of controlling the important centers of power in the nation. The disclosure proposal would appear to be another variation on Mr. Nader's theme that the large public corporation is a political institution in which forces not represented in the traditional decision-making process of the corporation, such as the public generally, should participate in the decision-making process. This theme was clearly articulated in Campaign GM where its counsel acknowledged that a major objective of the Campaign was to involve the public—not merely shareholders—in the corporate decision.

When the references to "professionalism" or "illegal, hazardous or unconscionable" activity are removed, this is the real basis of the proposal that corporate employees become informers, ready to act whenever they believe their responsibility to society requires disclosure of aspects of their employer's activities which they do not deem to be in the public interest. Emphasizing the view that the public corporation is a political institution, Mr. Nader has also called for "the popularization" of the corporation and the election of five directors out of twenty by the public —not shareholders—in a national election. The adaptation of the tolerated, if not accepted, practice of the government "leak" to corporate affairs is a simple corollary of this view.

Even without accepting the implications that Mr. Nader draws from the conclusion, it is clear that his view of the large public corporation as a political institution is in many respects sound. . . .

THE CHANGING ROLE OF THE CORPORATE EMPLOYEE

. . . In the balance of the conflicting rights of the government employee as citizen and the objective of government for efficient administration, the courts have placed a lesser value on the traditional duties of loyalty and obedience and have subordinated these duties to the employee's right of free speech in order to enable the employee to play a role as a citizen in matters of public controversy. Similarly, one may inquire whether, in time, erosion of the traditional employer-employee relation and the traditional concepts of loyalty and obedience will not also occur within the major American corporation.

A. The Developing Law

The basic problem goes to the employer's right of discharge of an employee who is publicly acting contrary to the interests of the employer: the Polaroid worker picketing in protest of Polaroid's alleged involvement with apartheid; the Eastern Airlines pilot disobeying standard operating procedures for dumping excess kerosene in the atmosphere instead of draining it on the ground; the automobile worker who protests the shipment of allegedly unsafe cars from his employer's factory; or the employee who "leaks" nonpublic information in accordance with the "public interest disclosure" proposal.

At common law, the employer's freedom to discharge was absolute. Over the years, this right of discharge has been increasingly restricted by statute and by collective bargaining agreements, but the basic principle of the employer's legal right to discharge, although challenged on the theoretical level, is still unimpaired.

In *NLRB* v. *Local Union No. 1229,* [12] the Supreme Court held that the discharge of striking employees of a television station because of their attack on the station for poor programming and service did not constitute an "unfair labor practice" under the National Labor Relations Act. The employees' effort to discredit the employer's business, as distinct from his labor practices, was held "such detrimental disloyalty" as to constitute "just cause" for discharge.

Accepting without discussion the employer's absolute right of discharge, except as limited by statute, the Court emphasized "the importance of enforcing individual plant discipline and of maintaining loyalty." Insofar as the limited purposes of the National Labor Relations Act were concerned, the Court stated: "There is no more elemental cause for discharge of an employee than disloyalty to his employer," and upheld the employer's right to discharge for "insubordination, disobedience, or disloyalty."[13]

Discharge of employees for causes not related to unionization has been upheld under the National Labor Relations Act, including such "offenses" as being a member or sympathizer of the Communist Party, or invoking the protection of the fifth amendment at a Congressional hearing or refusing to complete a defense agency security questionnaire. Discharge for testifying under subpoena against the employer in a criminal proceeding has also been upheld. On the other hand, a review of arbitration awards in this area has concluded that these activities were not normally regarded as constituting "just cause" under collective agreements, and that some "resulting adverse effect upon the employment relationship which makes the retention of the employee a detriment to the company" was required.

In an illuminating article, [14] Dean Blades has reexamined the traditional concept of employment at will and the employer's traditional power to discharge the employee at any time for any reason (or indeed for no reason) and has suggested that in time the doctrine—already hedged in by statute and collective bargaining agreements—will be modified, possibly by the legislatures, perhaps by the courts, to protect the employee against discharge for exercise of those personal rights which have no legitimate connection with the employment relationship. . . .

B. The Dynamics of the Public Climate

As one moves from the theoretical level to the practical level, one may inquire whether the employer's right of discharge has not already been impaired at least in those cases where public sympathy is squarely behind the employee, as in the case of the Eastern Airlines pilot who placed his concern with air pollution above obedience to company regulations. The rules of law may condemn such activity as a clear breach of the duty of loyalty and obedience. The corporation may be tempted to exercise its right of discharge, but its freedom of action (without regard to obligations under any union contract) will be severely restricted by the climate of public opinion which may well have been significantly influenced by the publicity attending the affair.

In the arena of public opinion, the issue will involve the merits of the conduct of the employee, not whether the conduct was contrary to instructions. In the Eastern Airlines case, the intentional violation of regulations and the impracticability of allowing each of the 3,700 Eastern Airlines pilots to "make his own rules" were not the issues before the public. The subject of the public debate was the impact of the Eastern Airlines practice on air pollution. Unless the corporation can prevail in the battle for public opinion on the merits of the conduct in issue, it must yield to public clamor or face the consequences of unfavorable public reaction. Moreover, if the employer is unionized, it is unlikely that the union efforts on behalf of the employee will be limited to the legal question of whether the conduct constitutes "just cause" for discharge under the collective agreement.

At this stage, whatever the traditional legal doctrines, the corporation's right of discharge may be illusory. The major corporation must recognize that it has become a public institution and must respond to the public climate of opinion. Thus, whether or not the major corporation in the law of the future comes to be regarded as a quasi-governmental body for some purpose, it operates today as a political as well as economic institution, subject to political behavior by those affected by it and to public debate over those of its actions which attain public visibility.

The pervasive public concern with corporate social responsibility will unquestionably lead to employee response to an appeal for disclosures of confidential information tending to show corporate participation in the creation of social or environmental problems. It is only realistic, therefore, to anticipate the appearance of the government-type "leak" in the major corporation. Whether or not it violates traditional agency concepts, a "public interest clearing house" may be expected to transact considerable business. Aggrieved employers are hardly going to feel free to resort to theoretically available legal or equitable remedies for redress so long as the unauthorized disclosures relate to "antisocial" conduct and do not reflect economic motivation. The corporation that is guilty of environmental abuse reported to the "clearing house" will not be well-advised to compound its conduct by instituting action against the "clearing house" or the employee (if it can identify him) and thereby assure even greater adverse publicity with respect to its objectionable environmental activities.

The "corporate leak" will join the "government leak" and serve the same political purposes. Whatever the incidental cost, business will survive, as has government, and indeed wrongful though it may be, the possibility of such a "leak" may serve a useful therapeutic or preventative function. Nevertheless, it may be well to review some of the inevitable aspects of the "public-interest disclosure" proposal. An official of the Federal Highway Safety Bureau commented in the *New York Times:* "Many a night I've spent late at the office trying to 'Naderproof' a regulation. The pipelines this guy has into this agency are unbelievable."[15]

Fortune similarly reports:

> Both reporters and professional politicians find him [Mr. Nader] extremely useful. "Nader has become the fifth branch of government if you count the press as fourth," says a Senate aide who has worked with Nader often in drafting legislation. "He knows all the newspaper deadlines and how to get in touch with anybody anytime. By his own hard work he has developed a network of sources in every arm of government. And believe me, no Senator turns down those calls from Ralph. He will say he's got some stuff and it's good, and the Senator can take the credit."[16]

Once the duty of loyalty yields to the primacy of what the individual in question regards as the "public interest," the door is open to widespread abuse.

In a society accustomed to governmental "leaks"—deliberately instigated by an administration as trial balloons as well as by bureaucrats dissatisfied with administrative decision—extension of the conduct described above to the corporate area will be merely more of the same, part of a tolerated pattern in a political world, embracing the major corporation as well as government. At the same time, it sharply poses the question of the desirability of encouraging the spread of such patterns of violation of the concepts of loyalty and obedience from government to major business. The proposal for disclosure to private groups—however disinterested their objective or public-spirited their purpose—seems an excessive and dangerous response to the problem of subordinating to social controls the tremendous economic and social power of the major public corporations.

The problem of unauthorized disclosure inevitably has political overtones. The significance of the erosion of the employee's traditional duties of loyalty, obedience, and confidentiality may be better appreciated if the problem is viewed in a setting that does not involve issues of social and environmental responsibility that are currently matters of such deep national concern. Such a setting may be found in the case of the university communities which are increasingly troubled by reports that the Federal Bureau of Information, the military, or the local police has been maintaining surveillance over campus activities. In some cases, university staff personnel, such as security officers and switchboard operators, apparently on an individual basis, have been supplying information about faculty, students, and campus activities. These university employees have made apparently unauthorized disclosure of nonpublic information in response to the appeals of government officials for information to enable them to discharge their concept of their public law enforcement responsibilities. No doubt, these employees were responding to their personal views of their social responsibility to cooperate with the "authorities." This problem has created deep concern at many institutions. Thus, at Swarthmore College, President Robert D. Cross responded by warning faculty, students, and staff that "those who divulged confidential information not demanded by law or college policy risked dismissal."[17]

In brief, unauthorized disclosure of confidential information presents serious problems for any organization; the matter can hardly be allowed to rest on each individual employee's decision as to the nature of his responsibilities to society and to his employer.

C. Alternatives to Unauthorized Disclosure

Other alternatives to reach the same objective without the same corrosive effect on personnel and the same potential for private abuse are available. These involve the use of governmental machinery with governmental safeguards with respect to the use of information received.

1. Traditional doctrines of agency law recognize the privilege of employees to report violations of law to proper governmental authorities. Private vigilante efforts should not be essential to achieve effective administration. "Public interest" groups would seem better advised to continue to concentrate their attention on improving the efficiency and effectiveness of the regulatory processes.

2. Another alternative is to extend further the growing statutory and administrative requirements of disclosure of conduct in areas of social

responsibility. Examples include the Employer Information Report EEO-1 on minority employment practices filed with the federal Equal Employment Opportunity Commission, the Affirmative Action Compliance Program filed with the Office of Federal Contract Compliance, the water pollution data filed under the Federal Water Pollution Control Act, and the reports on work-related deaths, injuries and illnesses under the Federal Occupational Safety and Health Act. Enforcement of such matters by public agencies under public standards and with public personnel and safeguards would serve the basic object without the serious disadvantages involved in the "public-interest disclosure" proposal.

3. Still another alternative is the development of the so-called social audit or a systematic quantitative (and possibly qualitative) review of a corporation's activities in the area of social responsibility. This proposal, suggested almost twenty years ago, has been gathering increasing attention and strength with a number of institutions and corporations endeavoring to develop a satisfactory methodolgy. Such disclosure and evaluation seem an inevitable product of the forces making for greater corporate participation in the solution of social and environmental problems. Development will obviously take some time. In the meanwhile, "public interest" groups and others have proposed resolutions calling for wider disclosure in this area for consideration at the annual meetings of such corporations as General Motors Corporation, Honeywell, Inc., American Metal Climax, Inc., Kennecott Copper Corporation, Phelps Dodge Corporation, and Gulf Oil Corporation.

D. Protection Against Discharge

Another aspect of the proposal for a "public interest clearing house" has considerable merit. This is the objective to provide protection through exposure to public opinion for corporate employees discharged for refusal to participate in illegal, immoral, or unprofessional acts. Involving no breach of confidentiality, this is a laudable effort to translate into reality the theoretical legal rights of the employee recognized at common law and in the *Restatement of Agency* in the face of the grave economic inequality between the individual employee and the giant corporate employer. Such an effort should receive the support of all interested in raising the standards of industrial morality. . . .

Statutory relief is another possible method to achieve appropriate protection for the rights of employees covering unionized and nonunionized employees alike. Antidiscrimination employment statutes already prohibit discrimination on the basis of "race, color, religion, sex, or national origin," age, or union membership. They might well be extended to make unlawful discrimination for political, social or economic views even when publicly expressed in opposition to an employer's policy. Similarly, statutory prohibition of discharge for refusal to participate in acts that are illegal or contrary to established canons of professional ethics, or for cooperation with governmental law-enforcement, legislative or executive agencies, deserves serious consideration.

Conclusion

The duties of loyalty and obedience are essential in the conduct of any enterprise—public or private. Yet, they do not serve as a basis to deprive government employees of their rights as citizens to participate in public debate and criticism of their governmental employer and should not be utilized to deprive corporate employees of similar rights.

As employee attitudes and actions reflect the increased public concern with social and environmental problems and the proper role of the corporation in participating in their solution, traditional doctrines of the employee's duties of loyalty and obedience and the employer's right of discharge will undergo increasing change. The pressure of "public interest" stockholder groups for increased corporate social responsibility will also be reflected by employees. At some point in the process, disagreement with management policies is inevitable. When the employees persist in their disagreement and the disagreement becomes public, an erosion of the traditional view of the duties of loyalty and obedience will have occurred. Yet, this hardly seems a fundamental problem for the corporation or undesirable from the point of view of the larger society. The real question is to establish civilized perimeters of permissible conduct that will not silence employees from expressing themselves on the public implications of their employers' activities in the social and environmental arena and at the same time will not introduce elements of breach of confidentiality and impairment of loyalty that will materially impair the functioning of the corporation itself. A balancing of interests, not a blind reiteration of traditional doctrines, is required. It is hoped that this preliminary review will suggest some possible solutions to the problem.

Notes

1. *New York Times,* Jan. 27, 1971, p. 32, col. 3.
2. *New York Times,* Jan. 15, 1971, p. 43, col. 2.
3. *New York Times,* March 21, 1971, § 6, p. 16, col. 5.
4. *New York Times,* March 26, 1971, p. 53, col. 5.
5. *Time,* Nov. 2, 1970, p. 40; *Boston Globe,* Nov. 8, 1970, p. 2, col. 3.
6. *Boston Globe,* Oct. 18, 1970, p. 64, col. 2; Nov. 1, 1970, p. B-31, col. 3; Nov. 25, 1970, p. 7; Feb. 11, 1971, p. 3, col. 1; *New York Times,* Jan. 13, 1971, p. 9, col. 1, p. 23; Feb. 21, 1971, p. 17, col. 1; *Business Week,* Nov. 14, 1970, p. 32; *Newsweek,* Jan. 25, 1971.
7. Athos, "Is the Corporation Next to Die?" *Harvard Business Review,* March–April 1970, pp. 49–50.
8. Blumberg, "The Politicalization of the Corporation," *Business Lawyer,* 26 (1971): 1551
9. For the purposes of this paper, "agent" should be regarded as interchangeable with "employee."
10. *Restatement (Second) of Agency* (1958), § 385(1) (hereinafter cited as *Restatement*).
11. See Mr. Justice Frankfurter in SEC v. Chenery Corp., 318 U.S. 80, 85–86, 63 S.Ct. 454, 458, 87 L.Ed. 626, 632 (1943).

12. 346 U.S. 464, 74 S.Ct. 172, 98 L.Ed. 195 (1953).
13. 346 U.S. p. 472, 74 S.Ct. p. 176, 98 L.Ed. p. 202. See NLRB v. Jones and Laughlin Steel Corp., 301 U.S. 1, 45–46, 57 S.Ct. 615, 628, 81 L.Ed. 893, 915–917 (1936).
14. See Blades, "Employment at Will v. Individual Freedom: Or Limiting the Abusive Exercise of Employer Power," 67, *Columbia Law Review,* 1404 (1967).
15. Duscha, "Stop! In the Public Interest," *New York Times,* March 21, 1971, § 6, p. 4, col. 5.
16. Armstrong, "The Passion that Rules Ralph Nader," *Fortune,* May 1971, pp. 144, 145.
17. *Chronicle of Higher Education,* May 31, 1971, p. 1, col. 1.

LAW, LAWYERS, AND MANAGERS

Ronald D. Rotunda

. . . Since ethical issues always arise in a context, abstract discussion of them without reference to that context is unproductive. I would therefore like to identify several complex areas of corporate legal ethics (focusing in particular on some conflicts-of-interest issues within the corporate entity) in order to determine how corporate managers and lawyers may help one another to fulfill their ethical and professional obligations. . . .

First I will consider some examples of corporate lawyers and managers trying to represent the diverse interests within a corporation. Then I shall turn to some of the lawyer's and manager's duties to interests outside the corporate entity, duties of loyalty to the public, and how these duties place limits on one's loyalty to the corporation.

CONFLICTS OF INTERESTS WITHIN THE CORPORATE ENTITY

We all know that the corporation is considered a legal "entity" and that, much like our own souls, it has no body. While it cannot be seen, it exists legally apart from its constituencies of officers, board, stockholders, creditors, and so on. Such a multifaceted client creates special problems of conflicts of interest for the corporate manager and lawyer.

To deal with such problems for lawyers the American Bar Association has promulgated a Code of Professional Responsibility, which most states

"Law, Lawyers, and Managers," Ronald D. Rotunda, in *The Ethics of Corporate Conduct,* ed. Clarence Walton. Copyright © 1977, The American Assembly, Columbia University, pp. 128–134, 137–141. Reprinted by permission of Prentice-Hall, Inc., Englewood Cliffs, N.J.

have adopted as law with varying modifications. This code is divided into Canons (axiomatic norms and disciplinary rules which are mandatory in character) and Ethical Considerations which suggest the aspirations that properly motivate the ethical lawyer. Canon 5 of this code deals primarily with the lawyer who confronts conflicts-of-interest situations. Recognizing the special problem of the *corporate entity* in its Ethical Consideration 5–18, the code announces that a corporation lawyer "owes his allegiance to the entity and not to a stockholder, director, officer, employee, representative, or other persons connected with the entity."

It is the entity's interests which the code insists must be kept "paramount." While the code applies only to lawyers, its entity theory is not a novel one. Corporate managers as well owe their legal duty to the corporation and not to themselves or to certain factions.

Sometimes (perhaps too rarely) the law offers mechanical tests to solve legal problems. There are, of course, a few problematic issues where the entity theory is useful in solving corporate ethical problems, but such problems are not the difficult ones. For example, if a competitor sues a corporate client alleging an antitrust violation, it is easy to conclude that the corporate lawyer does not represent a shareholder or defendant who is also a shareholder of plaintiff; rather, the lawyer represents the corporation as an entity. Similarly the corporate manager owes no duty of loyalty to another corporation simply because one of its shareholders is also a shareholder of the manager's corporation.

Derivative Suits

Aside from such rather simple problems, the entity theory proves less helpful. A good example occurs with the problem of so-called "derivative" suits. When a shareholder sues his corporation, the action may be classified as either an individual or a derivative action. If the complaint is that the corporation has individually injured him as a stockholder—by unlawfully refusing to pay mandatory dividends or by not allowing him his right to inspect corporate books—the action is called an individual action. Its characteristics are those of an ordinary lawsuit, and we expect corporate counsel to defend the corporation in the action. If the corporation loses, it must pay money or give some right to the plaintiff-shareholder.

The situation is more complex in a derivative action. In such cases the shareholder is suing because he claims that the corporation is injured. The shareholder may believe the directors have breached their duty to the corporation by mismanagement or by theft of corporate assets. If a third party stole from the corporation we could expect it to sue to recover the proceeds. But if insiders stole, the corporation may be reluctant to sue since these insiders are in control. The law thus allows the shareholders to sue on behalf of the corporation. If a money recovery is sought and recovered, the insider-defendants must normally pay that judgment to the corporation, not to the plaintiff-shareholder. To motivate shareholders to become, in effect, private attorneys-general, the courts will grant attorney fees to the plaintiff's lawyer if the suit is successful. And, as we might surmise, the expectation of attorney fees encourages frivolous lawsuits.

Role of Counsel

If the corporate directors are sued derivatively, what is the proper role of the law firm which is counsel to the corporation? Which issues may the corporation raise in defense of the derivative suit and which issues may it not? Is the lawyer in an impossible conflict-of-interest situation if he represents both the corporate insiders as well as the entity? If he represents only the corporate entity, what is his proper role?

Some court decisions and bar association ethical opinions have tried to decide these issues, supposedly by using the test of the entity theory of a corporation. But the proper resolution of most questions is still very much open. The corporation counsel's role in cases where insiders are sued derivatively—insiders who have been advised in their actions by the same counsel representing the corporation—is a particularly awkward one. In the case law we can find examples of the corporation in some instances aiding the plaintiffs suing derivatively; in other instances, the corporation has resisted the action and aided the real defendants by raising procedural defenses, such as a lack of proper service or misjoinder of causes of action, or moving to require security for costs. If these procedural hurdles have been passed, and settlement is being discussed, how does the corporate attorney advise the entity to bargain in a settlement conference of a derivative suit when some, or all, of the defendants are also insiders of the corporation? After all, if the derivative plaintiff bargains successfully, the reluctant corporation, aligned as a defendant, may find more money added to its coffers.

In all aspects of the derivative litigation the corporate lawyer's ethical response is complicated by the fact that he may represent, or appear to be controlled by, the alleged inside wrongdoers. This appearance is fortified by the lawyer's natural incentive to favor the corporate officers and directors with whom he has dealt and advised. A lawyer who ignores this fact by trying to represent only the incorporeal entity may find himself dismissed by the flesh-and-blood insiders who actually hired him.

The Lewis Case

In one leading federal case, *Lewis* v. *Shaffer Stores Co.* (1963), where the regular corporate counsel was also defending the officers and directors, the district judge ordered the entity "to retain independent counsel, who have no previous connection with the corporation, to advise it as to the position which it should take" in the derivative suit. But these new lawyers, selected pursuant to court order, are not in an enviable position. The same insiders who are being sued may be influential in selecting new counsel. This same court voiced no concern that "the selection of such independent counsel will necessarily be made by officers and directors who are defendants." And if the newly selected counsel for the corporation becomes too independent-minded, he may then be dismissed by the interested insiders. Such insiders need not be corrupt or evil men. From their perspective—a self-interested perspective to be sure—they may view the particular derivative suit against them as a frivolous one.

In those cases where the corporation is aligned as a defendant with its insiders, a rule could require the corporation to raise no defenses or otherwise participate. It would be passive though, in theory, a defendant. In such cases, the law might instead, allow the real defendants having their own counsel to assert the corporate and individual defenses. But this rule would completely deprive the shareholders of their corporation's participation in important litigation that could significantly affect it.

To expect the court to allow the insider-defendants initially to choose counsel (with the court subsequently engaging in constant monitoring of the representation process) is not realistic. It may cause excessive entanglement between one of the litigants and the impartial judge. The directors who are not being sued derivatively could choose counsel, but all directors might be sued. Or the court might find that they are influenced by the other directors who actually are defendants. The judge could choose independent counsel for the corporation only in those cases where he thinks the suit is not frivolous, but the question of frivolity really goes to the merits of the case and ought not be decided by the court in a preliminary hearing.

A Possible Approach

All of these alternatives have unsatisfactory consequences. But the problems of the court itself choosing independent counsel to represent the corporation in the derivative suit (in those cases where there are an insufficient number of independent directors who have not been sued by the plaintiffs) may be less serious than other alternatives. Court imposition of its own choice of counsel on the corporation reduces the later need for monitoring. Arguably, it does deprive the corporation of its normal right to choose its own legal representative. But in such circumstances, this normal right should not apply since there are no impartial insiders who can choose counsel on behalf of the corporation. We should not expect the defendant managers to act without regard to their self-interest.

The court should then choose independent outside counsel to represent the corporation, to examine the suit, and to determine the positions the corporate entity should take. The role of the corporation and its appointed counsel in such derivative litigation need not be entirely passive, but it should not be completely active either. That is, corporate counsel's main concern should be to protect those rights peculiar to the corporation which neither the derivative plaintiff nor the other defendants have any real incentive to protect. For example, corporate counsel should assure that discovery of corporate papers does not violate trade secrets, but the appointed lawyers should not seek to use the special court-appointed position merely to aid one or the other side in the lawsuit.

To insure that the corporate lawyers' independence is not shortlived, the appointed counsel should be prohibited from later being retained by the corporation. Otherwise, the new lawyers may seek to please the allegedly wrongdoing directors in order to secure more permanent employment later on. The court will probably also have to approve counsel's fees to verify that the new lawyers have not overbilled their involuntary client.

CORPORATE TAKEOVERS

The entity theory is perhaps even less helpful in a takeover situation. Assume that a larger corporation plans a takeover attempt of a carefully selected target. Corporate counsel for the target must represent it as an entity. Therefore the attorney does not represent the significant number of minority shareholders of the target which now controls the corporate offeror or "raider" and approves of the takeover. Nor does the lawyer represent the board or officers of the target who are expected to fight the takeover.

What is the lawyer's role in such a case? What if the lawyer thinks that a takeover would probably be better for the corporation's stockholders? Perhaps he is persuaded that the raider can run the target better than the mismanagement revealed by the present board. Recall that the lawyer for the corporation is to keep that entity's interest "paramount." The board of the target, by way of defense, may suggest a charter amendment which would make it very difficult for any takeover attempt to succeed. How does the lawyer's loyalty to the "entity" resolve his possible conflicts between the interests of the present management and the present or future stockholders? Is it ethical for management to propose and urge adoption of such a charter amendment? Does duty or loyalty to the corporation require them to resist a takeover attempt? Or is their judgment to fight obviously clouded by their own self-interest? . . .

BLOWING THE WHISTLE

In the good old days, when it was thought that the sole purpose of a corporation was to make money lawfully, the entity theory was probably a useful tool to analyze the ethical aspects of corporations. But that era ended with the emergence of a belief in corporate responsibility which created a different role for corporations. This problem may be illustrated particularly well by the issues of whistle-blowing on the entity or on constituencies of the entity: board members, officers, and others. How must the corporate lawyer or manager blow the whistle? To the Board of Directors; to the Securities and Exchange Commission; to the Antitrust Division of the Department of Justice; to the Food and Drug Administration; to a state blue-sky commissioner; or to others?

The problem has been considered in detail by many commentators and no Rosetta Stone exists to offer a creative solution. From the way the law is developing, I think that lawyers should withdraw from employment rather than aid, in any way, in the preparation of a materially misleading registration statement filed with the Securities and Exchange Commission or, for that matter, in any other similar situation. Once having withdrawn, the attorney's duty of confidentiality would probably prohibit whistle-blowing to the government in all except the most unusual cases. If the corporate lawyer is willing to withdraw, the prudent manager should quickly desist from pursuing the challenged action. . . .

LAWYERS AS DIRECTORS

Related to this issue of true independence of outside counsel is the problem of lawyers who also serve as board members of their corporate clients. While I believe that corporate lawyers should be guaranteed an audience with the directors, it does not follow that the corporation's attorney should also be a member of the board. Lawyers who are directors of their clients justify this role by insisting that they are more carefully listened to in this capacity than in the capacity of an outside counsel invited to speak to the board or who insists on speaking to the board. They often feel that not only are they less likely to lose the client to another firm, but that, as lawyers, they bring an added dimension of expertise and a broader perspective to board decisions.

But there is a deficit side to this ledger. From the perspective of his own self-interest, the lawyer had better be right because he will be judged as a director with legal expertise. More importantly, from an ethical standpoint there are other difficulties. The lawyer may be motivated to serve as a director because the position allows him to attract new clients more readily and to hold old ones. Such an individual has subordinated his duty to the corporate entity to a greater loyalty to his own firm.

Tightening the Rules

The attorney's independence may also be compromised by becoming a member of the client. One distinguished New York attorney, Paul Cravath, believes that "in most cases the client is best advised by a lawyer who maintains an objective point of view and such objectivity may be impeded by a financial interest in the client's business or any participation in its management." His partner, Robert T. Swaine, wrote in the *American Bar Association Journal* of 1949, "most of us would be greatly relieved if a canon of ethics were adopted forbidding a lawyer in substance to become his own client through acting as a director or officer of a client." But he resignedly lamented that "the practice is too widespread to permit any such expectation."

In spite of Cravath's personal beliefs he himself served as chairman of Westinghouse and, at the insistence of clients, other "Cravath" partners wound up on important corporate boards. Perhaps the ultimate solution will be these prophylactic rules: *Lawyers should not be on the boards of their clients. Nor should corporate clients employ, as their outside counsel, a law firm that has one of its partners on the Corporate Board.* Corporate managers should consider the advantages of implementing such a rule. Attorneys could continue to serve on boards so long as they are not also counsel to the client.

Some corporate law firms, by specializing in an extremely narrow range of legal problems, develop a national reputation which enables them to attract corporate clients from around the country. Some corporate clients, in an unusual behavioral twist are now using as a weapon against these firms the professional rules relating to conflicts of interest. One example suffices. Let us imagine a firm which specialized in representing target companies or raiders in takeover attempts. A prospective raider-client—through one of its corporate officers—*deliberately* telephones this law firm and talks to a partner about possible representation on a takeover fight. He discusses possible theories of action, discloses some facts, and so on. But the prospective client never follows through by retaining the firm. Now the raider telephones other law firms similarly situated, proceeds in the same fashion, and does not hire any of them either. By this technique the ruthless raider can keep its regular firm as counsel. Yet, it has also been able to disqualify other firms from representing the target company since disqualification of one partner or associate is imputed to the entire firm. The Code of Professional Responsibility creates the "conflicts" rules but does not reckon with their use as a weapon. There is not merely economic harm to law firms in lost business; more importantly, a sophisticated and ingenious lay person can use such rules to limit his opponent's choice of attorneys.

It would not be sufficient for the code to explicitly prohibit the practice because the code applies only to lawyers. Certainly the ethical manager would not seek to abuse the attorneys' professional code in such a manner. But if the opponent is not ethical and does not use them, how can the ethical manager fight back? Should the Code of Professional Responsibility create a defense to such activity? If so, how would that defense work? The client will not be happy with a rule of law which requires a lawyer to spend a half year or more making preliminary motions just to establish his defense to a conflicts-of-interest charge. After all, the legal time meter keeps running throughout the entire period.

The legal conflicts problem could be significantly reduced if we allowed the presently "disqualified" law firm to take the case on the proviso that it would insulate its disqualified member. Under such a role we would not impute to the entire firm the conflict of one of its partners or associates. But this "walling-off" technique would not be satisfactory to the opponents who may always suspect leaks from a poorly insulated wall.

The Corporate Lawyer and the Public

Corporate Lawyers in Public Capacities

The expertise of corporate lawyers often leads to their involvement in special bar association projects or other public service activities. A city or state bar association may wish to invite a particular corporate lawyer to sit on one of its major committees in order to bring to it a special knowledge. In such situations, lawyers often confuse their roles by acting as advocates rather than as advisers.

The Code of Professional Responsibility does not forbid lawyers to shed their client's interests in such "nonrepresentational" situations. Its Ethical Consideration (8–1) specifically encourages lawyers to propose and support legislative programs "to improve the system, without regard to the general interests or desires of clients or former clients." The code further states:

> The obligation of loyalty to his client applies only to a lawyer in the discharge of his professional duties and implies no obligation to adopt a personal viewpoint favorable to the interests or desires of his clients. While a lawyer must act always with circumspection in order that his conduct will not adversely affect the rights of a client in a matter he is then handling, he may take positions on public issues and *espouse legal reforms he favors without regard to the individual views of any client.* (Ethical Consideration 7–17; emphasis added.)

Later the code states:

> When a lawyer purports to act on behalf of the public he should espouse those changes which he conscientiously believes to be in the public interests. (Ethical Consideration 8–4)

But lawyers, in fact, do often try to "sell" their clients' positions in such situations. Sometimes this selling flows naturally from their coming to identify with client needs, but realism requires recognition of the fact that, at other times, it may be due to fear of losing clients with whom they actually disagree.

In language relating to a lawyer who "purports to act on the basis of the public . . ." the code suggests that disclosure of the lawyer's interest may be all that is required. But disclosure is not an adequate remedy in all such situations for two reasons: (1) a lawyer is not appointed to a bar committee or to any other professional group in order to represent his clients but is expected to share his professional experiences and to bring his technical knowledge to help solve various legal problems. To exploit his position, to promote client interests at the expense of his own convictions is to breach faith with those who brought him to the committee in the first place. (2) Committee members themselves are not privileged to allow use of public-service membership as a forum to lobby for a particular client or group. When committee members assent to partisan advocacy, they too are behaving unethically. They are also suggesting that in future assignments of a similar nature they too should be allowed to act as advocates of their clients.

The lawyer should divorce personal and professional beliefs from clients' interests. Yet some do treat such appointments to professional or public service committees as another advocacy opportunity. And, *a fortiori,* the attorney ought not to bill the private clients for professional time; nor should a lawyer use client resources to support public-service functions. Separation of these public and private capacities is a basic ethical necessity. Mere disclosure is not enough. Ethical corporate managers should, in turn, expect such separation of roles and never pressure an attorney in these situations.

LAWYERS AS PROFESSIONALS:
Some Moral Issues

Richard Wasserstrom

In this paper I examine two moral criticisms of lawyers which, if well-founded, are fundamental. Neither is new but each appears to apply with particular force today. Both tend to be made by those not in the mainstream of the legal profession and to be rejected by those who are in it. Both in some sense concern the lawyer-client relationship.

The first criticism centers around the lawyer's stance toward the world at large. The accusation is that the lawyer-client relationship renders the lawyer at best systematically amoral and at worst more than occasionally immoral in his or her dealings with the rest of mankind.

The second criticism focuses upon the relationship between the lawyer and the client. Here the charge is that it is the lawyer-client relationship which is morally objectionable because it is a relationship in which the lawyer dominates and in which the lawyer typically, and perhaps inevitably, treats the client in both an impersonal and a paternalistic fashion.

To a considerable degree these two criticisms of lawyers derive, I believe, from the fact that the lawyer is a professional. And to the extent to which this is the case, the more generic problems I will be exploring are those of professionalism generally. But in some respects, the lawyer's situation is different from that of other professionals. The lawyer is vulnerable to some moral criticism that does not as readily or as easily attach to any other professional. And this, too, is an issue that I shall be examining. . . .

I

One central feature of the professions in general and of law in particular is that there is a special, complicated relationship between the professional, and the client or patient. For each of the parties in this relationship, but especially for the professional, the behavior that is involved is to a very significant degree, what I call, role-differentiated behavior. And this is significant because it is the nature of role-differentiated behavior that it often makes it both appropriate and desirable for the person in a particular role to put to one side considerations of various sorts—and especially various moral considerations—that would otherwise be relevant if not decisive. Some illustrations will help to make clear what I mean both by role-differentiated behavior and by the way role-differentiated behavior often alters, if not eliminates, the significance of those moral considerations that would obtain, were it not for the presence of the role.

Reprinted by permission from *Human Rights* (Fall 1975). Copyright © 1975 American Bar Association.

Being a parent is, in probably every human culture, to be involved in role-differentiated behavior. In our own culture, and once again in most, if not all, human cultures, as a parent one is entitled, if not obligated, to prefer the interests of one's own children over those of children generally. That is to say, it is regarded as appropriate for a parent to allocate excessive goods to his or her own children, even though other children may have substantially more pressing and genuine needs for these same items. If one were trying to decide what the right way was to distribute assets among a group of children all of whom were strangers to oneself, the relevant moral considerations would be very different from those that would be thought to obtain once one's own children were in the picture. In the role of a parent, the claims of other children vis-à-vis one's own are, if not rendered morally irrelevant, certainly rendered less morally significant. In short, the role-differentiated character of the situation alters the relevant moral point of view enormously.

A similar situation is presented by the case of the scientist. For a number of years there has been debate and controversy within the scientific community over the question of whether scientists should participate in the development and elaboration of atomic theory, especially as those theoretical advances could then be translated into development of atomic weapons that would become a part of the arsenal of existing nation states. The dominant view, although it was not the unanimous one, in the scientific community was that the role of the scientist was to expand the limits of human knowledge. Atomic power was a force which had previously not been utilizable by human beings. The job of the scientist was, among other things, to develop ways and means by which that could now be done. And it was simply no part of one's role as a scientist to forego inquiry, or divert one's scientific explorations because of the fact that the fruits of the investigation could be or would be put to improper, immoral, or even catastrophic uses. The moral issues concerning whether and when to develop and use nuclear weapons were to be decided by others; by citizens and statesmen; they were not the concern of the scientist *qua* scientist.

In both of these cases it is, of course, conceivable that plausible and even thoroughly convincing arguments exist for the desirability of the role-differentiated behavior and its attendant neglect of what would otherwise be morally relevant considerations. Nonetheless, it is, I believe, also the case that the burden of proof, so to speak, is always upon the proponent of the desirability of this kind of role-differentiated behavior. For in the absence of special reasons why parents ought to prefer the interests of their children over those of children in general, the moral point of view surely requires that the claims and needs of all children receive equal consideration. But we take the rightness of parental preference so for granted, that we often neglect, I think, the fact that it is anything but self-evidently morally appropriate. My own view, for example, is that careful reflection shows that the *degree* of parental preference systematically encouraged in our own culture is far too extensive to be morally justified.

All of this is significant just because to be a professional is to be enmeshed in role-differentiated behavior of precisely this sort. One's role as a doctor, psychiatrist, or lawyer, alters one's moral universe in a fashion analogous to that described above. Of special significance here is the fact that the professional *qua* professional has a client or patient whose interests must be represented, attended to, or looked after by the professional. And that means that the role of the professional (like that of the parent) is to prefer in a variety of ways the interests of the client or patient over those of individuals generally.

Consider, more specifically, the role-differentiated behavior of the lawyer. Conventional wisdom has it that where the attorney-client relationship exists, the point of view of the attorney is properly different— and appreciably so—from that which would be appropriate in the absence of the attorney-client relationship. For where the attorney-client relationship exists, it is often appropriate and many times even obligatory for the attorney to do things that, all other things being equal, an ordinary person need not, and should not do. What is characteristic of this role of a lawyer is the lawyer's required indifference to a wide variety of ends and consequences that in other contexts would be of undeniable moral significance. Once a lawyer represents a client, the lawyer has a duty to make his or her expertise fully available in the realization of the end sought by the client, irrespective, for the most, of the moral worth to which the end will be put or the character of the client who seeks to utilize it. Provided that the end sought is not illegal, the lawyer is, in essence, an amoral technician whose peculiar skills and knowledge in respect to the law are available to those with whom the relationship of client is established. The question, as I have indicated, is whether this particular and pervasive feature of professionalism is itself justifiable. At a minimum, I do not think any of the typical, simple answers will suffice.

One such answer focuses upon and generalizes from the criminal defense lawyer. For what is probably the most familiar aspect of this role-differentiated character of the lawyer's activity is that of the defense of a client charged with a crime. The received view within the profession (and to a lesser degree within the society at large) is that having once agreed to represent the client, the lawyer is under an obligation to do his or her best to defend that person at trial, irrespective, for instance, even of the lawyer's belief in the client's innocence. There are limits, of course, to what constitutes a defense: a lawyer cannot bribe or intimidate witnesses to increase the likelihood of securing an acquittal. And there are legitimate questions, in close cases, about how those limits are to be delineated. But, however these matters get resolved, it is at least clear that it is thought both appropriate and obligatory for the attorney to put on as vigorous and persuasive a defense of a client believed to be guilty as would have been mounted by the lawyer thoroughly convinced of the client's innocence. I suspect that many persons find this an attractive and admirable feature of the life of a legal professional. I know that often I do. The justifications are varied and, as I shall argue below, probably convincing.

But part of the difficulty is that the irrelevance of the guilt or innocence of an accused client by no means exhausts the altered perspective of the

lawyer's conscience, even in criminal cases. For in the course of defending an accused, an attorney may have, as a part of his or her duty of
representation, the obligation to invoke procedures and practices which
are themselves morally objectionable and of which the lawyer in other
contexts might thoroughly disapprove. And these situations, I think, are
somewhat less comfortable to confront. For example, in California, the
case law permits a defendant in a rape case to secure in some circumstances an order from the court requiring the complaining witness, that
is the rape victim, to submit to a psychiatric examination before trial.[1] For
no other crime is such a pretrial remedy available. In no other case can
the victim of a crime be required to undergo psychiatric examination at
the request of the defendant on the ground that the results of the examination may help the defendant prove that the offense did not take place.
I think such a rule is wrong and is reflective of the sexist bias of the law
in respect to rape. I certainly do not think it right that rape victims should
be singled out by the law for this kind of special pretrial treatment, and
I am skeptical about the morality of any involuntary psychiatric examination of witnesses. Nonetheless, it appears to be part of the role-differentiated obligation of a lawyer for a defendant charged with rape to seek
to take advantage of this particular rule of law—irrespective of the independent moral view he or she may have of the rightness or wrongness of
such a rule.

　　Nor, it is important to point out, is this peculiar, strikingly amoral
behavior limited to the lawyer involved with the workings of the criminal
law. Most clients come to lawyers to get the lawyers to help them do
things that they could not easily do without the assistance provided by the
lawyer's special competence. They wish, for instance, to dispose of their
property in a certain way at death. They wish to contract for the purchase
or sale of a house or a business. They wish to set up a corporation which
will manufacture and market a new product. They wish to minimize their
income taxes. And so on. In each case, they need the assistance of the
professional, the lawyer, for he or she alone has the special skill which
will make it possible for the client to achieve the desired result.

　　And in each case, the role-differentiated character of the lawyer's way
of being tends to render irrelevant what would otherwise be morally
relevant considerations. Suppose that a client desires to make a will
disinheriting her children because they opposed the war in Vietnam.
Should the lawyer refuse to draft the will because the lawyer thinks this
a bad reason to disinherit one's children? Suppose a client can avoid the
payment of taxes through a loophole only available to a few wealthy
taxpayers. Should the lawyer refuse to tell the client of a loophole because the lawyer thinks it an unfair advantage for the rich? Suppose a
client wants to start a corporation that will manufacture, distribute and
promote a harmful but not illegal substance, e.g., cigarettes. Should the
lawyer refuse to prepare the articles of incorporation for the corporation?
In each case, the accepted view within the profession is that these matters
are just of no concern to the lawyer *qua* lawyer. The lawyer need not of
course agree to represent the client (and that is equally true for the

unpopular client accused of a heinous crime), but there is nothing wrong with representing a client whose aims and purposes are quite immoral. And having agreed to do so, the lawyer is required to provide the best possible assistance, without regard to his or her disapproval of the objective that is sought.

The lesson, on this view, is clear. The job of the lawyer, so the argument typically concludes, is not to approve or disapprove of the character of his or her client, the cause for which the client seeks the lawyer's assistance, or the avenues provided by the law to achieve that which the client wants to accomplish. The lawyer's task is, instead, to provide that competence which the client lacks and the lawyer, as professional, possesses. In this way, the lawyer as professional comes to inhabit a simplified universe which is strikingly amoral—which regards as morally irrelevant any number of factors which nonprofessional citizens might take to be important, if not decisive, in their everyday lives. And the difficulty I have with all of this is that the arguments for such a way of life seem to be not quite so convincing to me as they do to many lawyers. I am, that is, at best uncertain that it is a good thing for lawyers to be so professional—for them to embrace so completely this role-differentiated way of approaching matters.

More specifically, if it is correct that this is the perspective of lawyers in particular and professionals in general, is it right that this should be their perspective? Is it right that the lawyer should be able so easily to put to one side otherwise difficult problems with the answer: but these are not and cannot be my concern as a lawyer? What do we gain and what do we lose from having a social universe in which there are professionals such as lawyers, who, as such, inhabit a universe of the sort I have been trying to describe?

One difficulty in even thinking about all of this is that lawyers may not be very objective or detached in their attempts to work the problem through. For one feature of this simplified, intellectual world is that it is often a very comfortable one to inhabit.

To be sure, on occasion, a lawyer may find it uncomfortable to represent an extremely unpopular client. On occasion, too, a lawyer may feel ill at ease invoking a rule of law or practice which he or she thinks to be an unfair or undesirable one. Nonetheless, for most lawyers, most of the time, pursuing the interests of one's clients is an attractive and satisfying way to live in part just because the moral world of the lawyer is a simpler, less complicated, and less ambiguous world than the moral world of ordinary life. There is, I think, something quite seductive about being able to turn aside so many ostensibly difficult moral dilemmas and decisions with the reply: but that is not my concern; my job as a lawyer is not to judge the rights and wrong of the client or the cause; it is to defend as best I can my client's interests. For the ethical problems that can arise within this constricted point of view are, to say the least, typically neither momentous nor terribly vexing. Role-differentiated behavior is enticing and reassuring precisely because it does constrain and delimit an otherwise often intractable and confusing moral world.

But there is, of course, also an argument which seeks to demonstrate that it is good and not merely comfortable for lawyers to behave this way.

It is good, so the argument goes, that the lawyer's behavior and concomitant point of view are role-differentiated because the lawyer *qua* lawyer participates in a complex institution which functions well only if the individuals adhere to their institutional roles.

For example, when there is a conflict between individuals, or between the state and an individual, there is a well-established institutional mechanism by which to get that dispute resolved. That mechanism is the trial in which each side is represented by a lawyer whose job it is both to present his or her client's case in the most attractive, forceful light and to seek to expose the weaknesses and defects in the case of the opponent. . . .

. . . When the lawyer functions in his most usual role, he or she functions as a counselor, as a professional whose task it is to help people realize those objectives and ends that the law permits them to obtain and which cannot be obtained without the attorney's special competence in the law. The attorney may think it wrong to disinherit one's children because of their views about the Vietnam war, but here the attorney's complaint is really with the laws of inheritance and not with his or her client. The attorney may think the tax provision an unfair, unjustifiable loophole, but once more the complaint is really with the Internal Revenue Code and not with the client who seeks to take advantage of it. And these matters, too, lie beyond the ambit of the lawyer's moral point of view as institutional counselor and facilitator. If lawyers were to substitute their own private views of what ought to be legally permissible and impermissible for those of the legislature, this would constitute a surreptitious and undesirable shift from a democracy to an oligarchy of lawyers. For given the fact that lawyers are needed to effectuate the wishes of clients, the lawyer ought to make his or her skills available to those who seek them without regard for the particular objectives of the client. . . .

. . . I do believe that the amoral behavior of the *criminal* defense lawyer is justifiable. But I think that jurisdiction depends at least as much upon the special needs of an accused as upon any more general defense of a lawyer's role-differentiated behavior. As a matter of fact I think it likely that many persons such as myself have been misled by the special features of the criminal case. Because a deprivation of liberty is so serious, because the prosecutorial resources of the state are so vast, and because, perhaps, of a serious skepticism about the rightness of punishment even where wrongdoing has occurred, it is easy to accept the view that it makes sense to charge the defense counsel with the job of making the best possible case for the accused—without regard, so to speak, for the merits. This coupled with the fact that it is an adversarial proceeding succeeds, I think, in justifying the amorality of the criminal defense counsel. But this does not, however, justify a comparable perspective on the part of lawyers generally. Once we leave the peculiar situation of the criminal defense lawyer, I think it quite likely that the role-differentiated amorality of the lawyer is almost certainly excessive and at times inappropriate. That is to say, this special case to one side, I am inclined to think that we might all be better served if lawyers were to see themselves less as subject to role-differentiated behavior and more as subject to the demands of the moral point of view. In this sense it may be that we need a good deal less rather than more professionalism in our society generally and among lawyers in particular.

Moreover, even if I am wrong about all this, four things do seem to me to be true and important.

First, all of the arguments that support the role-differentiated amorality of the lawyer on institutional grounds can succeed only if the enormous degree of trust and confidence in the institutions themselves is itself justified. If the institutions work well and fairly, there may be good sense to deferring important moral concerns and criticisms to another time and place, to the level of institutional criticism and assessment. But the less certain we are entitled to be of either the rightness or the self-corrective nature of the larger institutions of which the professional is a part, the less apparent it is that we should encourage the professional to avoid direct engagement with the moral issues as they arise. And we are, today, I believe, certainly entitled to be quite skeptical both of the fairness and of the capacity for self-correction of our larger institutional mechanisms, including the legal system. To the degree to which the institutional rules and practices are unjust, unwise or undesirable, to that same degree is the case for the role-differentiated behavior of the lawyer weakened if not destroyed.

Second, it is clear that there are definite character traits that the professional such as the lawyer must take on if the system is to work. What is less clear is that they are admirable ones. Even if the role-differentiated amorality of the professional lawyer is justified by the virtues of the adversary system, this also means that the lawyer *qua* lawyer will be encouraged to be competitive rather than cooperative; aggressive rather than accommodating; ruthless rather than compassionate; and pragmatic rather than principled. This is, I think, part of the logic of the role-differentiated behavior of lawyers in particular, and to a lesser degree of professionals in general. It is surely neither accidental nor unimportant that these are the same character traits that are emphasized and valued by the capitalist ethic—and on precisely analogous grounds. Because the ideals of professionalism and capitalism are the dominant ones within our culture, it is harder than most of us suspect even to take seriously the suggestion that radically different styles of living, kinds of occupational outlooks, and types of social institutions might be possible, let alone preferable.

Third, there is a special feature of the role-differentiated behavior of the lawyer that distinguishes it from the comparable behavior of other professionals. What I have in mind can be brought out through the following question: Why is it that it seems far less plausible to talk critically about the amorality of the doctor, for instance, who treats all patients irrespective of their moral character than it does to talk critically about the comparable amorality of the lawyer? Why is it that it seems so obviously sensible, simple and right for the doctor's behavior to be narrowly and rigidly role-differentiated, i.e., just to try to cure those who are ill? And why is it that at the very least it seems so complicated, uncertain, and troublesome to decide whether it is right for the lawyer's behavior to be similarly role-differentiated?

The answer, I think, is twofold. To begin with (and this I think is the less interesting point) it is, so to speak, intrinsically good to try to cure disease, but in no comparable way is it intrinsically good to try to win every lawsuit or help every client realize his or her objective. In addition (and this I take to be the truly interesting point), the lawyer's behavior is different in kind from the doctor's. The lawyer—and especially the lawyer as advocate—directly says and affirms things. The lawyer makes the case for the client. He or she tries to explain, persuade and convince others that the client's cause should prevail. The lawyer lives with and within a dilemma that is not shared by other professionals. If the lawyer actually believes everything that he or she asserts on behalf of the client, then it appears to be proper to regard the lawyer as in fact embracing and endorsing the points of view that he or she articulates. If the lawyer does not in fact believe what is urged by way of argument, if the lawyer is only playing a role, then it appears to be proper to tax the lawyer with hypocrisy and insincerity. To be sure, actors in a play take on roles and say things that the characters, not the actors, believe. But we know it is a play and that they are actors. The law courts are not, however, theaters, and the lawyers both talk about justice and they genuinely seek to persuade. The fact that the lawyer's words, thoughts, and convictions are, apparently, for sale and at the service of the client helps us, I think, to understand the peculiar hostility which is more than occasionally uniquely directed by lay persons toward lawyers. The verbal, role-differentiated behavior of the lawyer *qua* advocate puts the lawyer's integrity into question in a way that distinguishes the lawyer from the other professionals.[2]

Fourth, and related closely to the three points just discussed, even if on balance the role-differentiated character of the lawyer's way of thinking and acting is ultimately deemed to be justifiable within the system on systemic instrumental grounds, it still remains the case that we do pay a social price for that way of thought and action. For to become and to be a professional, such as a lawyer, is to incorporate within oneself ways of behaving and ways of thinking that shape the whole person. It is especially hard, if not impossible, because of the nature of the professions, for one's professional way of thinking not to dominate one's entire adult life. Thus, even if the lawyers who were involved in Watergate were not, strictly speaking, then and there functioning as lawyers, their behavior was, I believe, the likely if not inevitable consequence of their legal acculturation. Having been taught to embrace and practice the lawyer's institutional role, it was natural, if not unavoidable, that they would continue to play that role even when they were somewhat removed from the specific institutional milieu in which that way of thinking and acting is arguably fitting and appropriate. The nature of the professions—the lengthy educational preparation, the prestige and economic rewards, and the concomitant enhanced sense of self—makes the role of professional a difficult one to shed even in those obvious situations in which that role is neither required nor appropriate. In important respects, one's professional role becomes and is one's dominant role, so that for many persons at least they become their professional being. This is at a minimum a heavy price to pay for the professions as we know them in our culture, and especially so for lawyers. Whether it is an inevitable price is, I think, an open question, largely because the problem has not begun to be fully perceived as such by the professionals in general, the legal profession in particular, or by the educational institutions that train professionals.

II

The role-differentiated behavior of the professional also lies at the heart of the second of the two moral issues I want to discuss, namely, the character of the interpersonal relationship that exists between the lawyer and the client. As I indicated at the outset, the charge that I want to examine here is that the relationship between the lawyer and the client is typically, if not inevitably, a morally defective one in which the client is not treated with the respect and dignity that he or she deserves.

There is the suggestion of paradox here. The discussion so far has concentrated upon defects that flow from what might be regarded as the lawyer's excessive preoccupation with and concern for the client. How then can it also be the case that the lawyer *qua* professional can at the same time be taxed with promoting and maintaining a relationship of dominance and indifference vis-à-vis his or her client? The paradox is apparent, not real. Not only are the two accusations compatible; the problem of the interpersonal relationship between the lawyer and the client is itself another feature or manifestation of the underlying issue just examined—the role-differentiated life of the professional. For the lawyer can both be overly concerned with the interest of the client and at the same time fail to view the client as a whole person, entitled to be treated in certain ways.

One way to begin to explore the problem is to see that one pervasive, and I think necessary, feature of the relationship between any professional and the client or patient is that it is in some sense a relationship of inequality. This relationship of inequality is intrinsic to the existence of professionalism. For the professional is, in some respects at least, always in a position of dominance vis-à-vis the client, and the client in a position of dependence vis-à-vis the professional. To be sure, the client can often decide whether or not to enter into a relationship with a professional. And often, too, the client has the power to decide whether to terminate the relationship. But the significant thing I want to focus upon is that while the relationship exists, there are important respects in which the relationship cannot be a relationship between equals and must be one in which it is the professional who is in control. As I have said, I believe this is a necessary and not merely a familiar characteristic of the relationship between professionals and those they serve. Its existence is brought about by the following features.

To begin with, there is the fact that one characteristic of professions is that the professional is the possessor of expert knowledge of a sort not readily or easily attainable by members of the community at large. Hence, in the most straightforward of all senses the client, typically, is dependent upon the professional's skill or knowledge because the client does not possess the same knowledge.

Moreover, virtually every profession has its own technical language, a private terminology which can only be fully understood by the members of the profession. The presence of such a language plays the dual role of creating and affirming the membership of the professionals within the profession and of preventing the client from fully discussing or understanding his or her concerns in the language of the profession.

These circumstances, together with others, produce the added consequence that the client is in a poor position effectively to evaluate how well or badly the professional performs. In the professions, the professional does not look primarily to the client to evaluate the professional's work. The assessment of ongoing professional competence is something that is largely a matter of self-assessment conducted by the practicing professional. Where external assessment does occur, it is carried out not by clients or patients but by other members of the profession, themselves. It is significant, and surely surprising to the outsider, to discover to what degree the professions are self-regulating. They control who shall be admitted to the professions and they determine (typically only if there has been a serious complaint) whether the members of the profession are performing in a minimally satisfactory way. This leads professionals to have a powerful motive to be far more concerned with the way they are viewed by their colleagues than with the way they are viewed by their clients. This means, too, that clients will necessarily lack the power to make effective evaluations and criticisms of the way the professional is responding to the client's needs.

In addition, because the matters for which professional assistance is sought usually involve things of great personal concern to the client, it is the received wisdom within the professions that the client lacks the perspective necessary to pursue in a satisfactory way his or her own best interests, and that the client requires a detached, disinterested representative to look after his or her interests. That is to say, even if the client had the same knowledge or competence that the professional had, the client would be thought to lack the objectivity required to utilize that competency effectively on his or her own behalf.

Finally, as I have indicated, to be a professional is to have been acculturated in a certain way. It is to have satisfactorily passed through a lengthy and allegedly difficult period of study and training. It is to have done something hard. Something that not everyone can do. Almost all professions encourage this way of viewing oneself; as having joined an elect group by virtue of hard work and mastery of the mysteries of the profession. In addition, the society at large treats members of a profession as members of an elite by paying them more than most people for the work they do with their heads rather than their hands, and by according them a substantial amount of social prestige and power by virtue of their membership in a profession. It is hard, I think, if not impossible, for a person to emerge from professional training and participate in a profession without the belief that he or she is a special kind of person, both different from and somewhat better than those nonprofessional members of the social order. It is equally hard for the other members of society not to hold an analogous view of the professionals. And these beliefs surely contribute, too, to the dominant role played by a professional in any professional-client relationship. . . .

. . . The lawyer *qua* professional is, of necessity, only centrally interested in that part of the client that lies within his or her special competency. And this leads any professional including the lawyer to respond to the client as an object—as a thing to be altered, corrected, or otherwise assisted by the professional rather than as a person. At best the client is viewed from the perspective of the professional not as a whole person but as a segment or aspect of a person—an interesting kidney problem, a routine marijuana possession case, or another adolescent with an identity crisis.[3]

Then, too, the fact already noted that the professions tend to have and to develop their own special languages has a lot to do with the depersonalization of the client. And this certainly holds for the lawyers. For the lawyer can and does talk to other lawyers but not to the client in the language of the profession. What is more, the lawyer goes out of his or her way to do so. It is satisfying. It is the exercise of power. Because the ability to communicate is one of the things that distinguishes persons from objects, the inability of the client to communicate with the lawyer in the lawyer's own tongue surely helps to make the client less than a person in the lawyer's eyes—and perhaps even in the eyes of the client.

The forces that operate to make the relationship a paternalistic one seem to me to be at least as powerful. If one is a member of a collection of individuals who have in common the fact that their intellects are highly trained, it is very easy to believe that one knows more than most people. If one is a member of a collection of individuals who are accorded high prestige by the society at large, it is equally easy to believe that one is better and knows better than most people. If there is, in fact, an area in which one does know things that the client doesn't know, it is extremely easy to believe that one knows generally what is best for the client. All this, too, surely holds for lawyers.

In addition there is the fact, also already noted, that the client often establishes a relationship with the lawyer because the client has a serious problem or concern which has rendered the client weak and vulnerable. This, too, surely increases the disposition to respond toward the client in a patronizing, paternalistic fashion. The client of necessity confers substantial power over his or her wellbeing upon the lawyer. Invested with all of this power both by the individual and the society, the lawyer *qua* professional responds to the client as though the client were an individual who needed to be looked after and controlled, and to have decisions made for him or her by the lawyer, with as little interference from the client as possible.

Now one can, I think, respond to the foregoing in a variety of ways. One could, to begin with, insist that the paternalistic and impersonal ways of behaving are the aberrant rather than the usual characteristics of the lawyer-client relationship. One could, therefore, argue that a minor adjustment in better legal education aimed at sensitizing prospective lawyers to the possibility of these abuses is all that is required to prevent them. Or, one could, to take the same tack described earlier, regard these features of the lawyer-client relationship as endemic but not as especially serious. One might have a view that, at least in moderation, relationships having these features are a very reasonable price to pay (if it is a price at all) for the very appreciable benefits of professionalism. The impersonality of a surgeon, for example, may make it easier rather than harder for him or for her to do a good job of operating successfully on a patient. The impersonality of a lawyer may make it easier rather than harder for him or for her to do a good job of representing a client. The paternalism of lawyers may be justified by the fact that they do in fact know better— at least within many areas of common concern to the parties involved— what is best for the client. And, it might even be claimed, clients want to be treated in this way.

But if these answers do not satisfy, if one believes that these are typical, if not systemic, features of the professional character of the lawyer-client relationship, and if one believes, as well, that these are morally objectionable features of that or any other relationship among persons, it does look as though one way to proceed is to "deprofessionalize" the law—to weaken, if not excise, those features of legal professionalism that tend to produce these kinds of interpersonal relationships.

The issue seems to me difficult just because I do think that there are important and distinctive competencies that are at the heart of the legal profession. If there were not, the solution would be simple. If there were no such competencies—if, that is, lawyers didn't really help people any more than (so it is sometimes claimed) therapists do—then no significant social goods would be furthered by the maintenance of the legal profession. But, as I have said, my own view is that there are special competencies and that they are valuable. This makes it harder to determine what to preserve and what to shed. The question, as I see it, is how to weaken the bad consequences of the role-differentiated lawyer-client relationship without destroying the good that lawyers do.

Without developing the claim at all adequately in terms of scope or detail, I want finally to suggest the direction this might take. Desirable change could be brought about in part by a sustained effort to simplify legal language and to make the legal processes less mysterious and more directly available to lay persons. The way the law works now, it is very hard for lay persons either to understand it or to evaluate or solve legal problems more on their own. But it is not at all clear that substantial revisions could not occur along these lines. Divorce, probate, and personal injury are only three fairly obvious areas where the lawyers' economic self-interest says a good deal more about resistance to change and simplification than does a consideration on the merits.

The more fundamental changes, though, would, I think, have to await an explicit effort to alter the ways in which lawyers are educated and acculturated to view themselves, their clients, and the relationships that ought to exist between them. It is, I believe, indicative of the state of legal education and of the profession that there has been to date extremely little self-conscious concern even with the possibility that these dimensions of the attorney-client relationship are worth examining—to say nothing of being capable of alteration. That awareness is, surely, the prerequisite to any serious assessment of the moral character of the attorney-client relationship as a relationship among adult human beings.

I do not know whether the typical lawyer-client relationship is as I have described it; nor do I know to what degree role-differentiation is the cause; nor do I even know very precisely what "deprofessionalization" would be like or whether it would on the whole be good or bad. I am convinced, however, that this, too, is a topic worth taking seriously and worth attending to more systematically than has been the case to date.

Notes

1. Ballard v. Superior Court, 64 Cal. 2d 159, 410 P.2d 838, 49 Cal. Rptr. 302 (1966).
2. I owe this insight, which I think is an important and seldom appreciated one, to my colleague, Leon Letwin.
3. This and other features are delineated from a somewhat different perspective in an essay by Erving Goffman. See "The Medical Model and Mental Hospitalization: Some Notes on the Vicissitudes of the Tinkering Trades" in E. Goffman, *Asylums* (1961), especially Parts V and VI of the essay.

THE LOYAL AGENT'S ARGUMENT

Alex C. Michalos

INTRODUCTION

According to the Report of the Special Review Committee of the
Board of Directors of Gulf Oil Corporation:

> It is not too much to say that the activity of those Gulf officials involved in
> making domestic political contributions with corporate funds during the
> period of approximately fourteen years under review [1960–1974] was shot
> through with illegality. The activity was generally clandestine and in disre-
> gard of federal, as well as a number of state, statutes.[1]

Nevertheless, and more importantly for our purposes, the Committee
apparently endorsed the following judgment, which was submitted by
their lawyers to the U.S. Securities and Exchange Commission.

> No evidence has been uncovered or disclosed which establishes that any
> officer, director or employee of Gulf personally profited or benefited by or
> through any use of corporate funds for contributions, gifts, entertainment
> or other expenses related to political activity. Further, Gulf has no reason
> to believe or suspect that *the motive of the employee or officer* involved in such
> use of corporate funds was anything other than *a desire to act solely in what
> he considered to be the best interests of Gulf and its shareholders.*[2] [Emphasis added.]

If we accept the views of the Committee and their lawyers, then we
have before us an interesting case of individuals performing illegal actions with altruistic motives. What they did was admittedly illegal, but
they meant well. They had good intentions, namely, to further "the best
interests of Gulf and its shareholders." Furthermore, there is no suggestion in these passages or in the rest of the report that the officials were
ordered to commit such acts. They were not ordered. On the contrary,
the acts seem to have emerged as practically natural by-products of some
employees' zeal in looking after their employer's interests. They are, we
might say, the result of overzealous attempts of agents to fulfill their
fiducial obligations.

In the following paragraphs I am going to pursue this apparently
plausible account of overzealous behavior to its bitter end. That is, I'm
going to assume for the sake of argument that there really are reasonable
people who would and do perform immoral and illegal actions with
altruistic motives, i.e., there are people who would and do perform such
actions with reasons that they regard as good in some fairly general sense.
It's not to be assumed that they are shrewd enough to see that their own
interests lie in the advancement of their employer's or client's interests.

This paper was written for the Conference on Ethics and Economics at the University
of Delaware, Newark, Delaware, November 10–12, 1977. Copyright © 1978 by Alex C.
Michalos. Reprinted by permission of the author.

They are not, I'm assuming, cleverly egoistic. If anything, they are stupidly altruistic by hypothesis. But that's beside the point now. What I want to do is construct a generalized form of an argument that I imagine would be attractive to such agents, whether or not any of them has or will ever formulate it exactly so. Then I want to try to demolish it once and for all.

THE ARGUMENT

What I will call the Loyal Agent's Argument (LAA) runs as follows:

1. *As a loyal agent of some principal, I ought to serve his interests as he would serve them himself if he had my expertise.*
2. *He would serve his own interests in a thoroughly egoistic way.*

   Therefore, as a loyal agent of this principal, I ought to operate in a thoroughly egoistic way in his behalf.

Some clarification is in order. First, in order to make full use of the fairly substantial body of legal literature related to the *law of agency*, I have adopted some of the standard legal jargon. In particular, following Powell, I'm assuming that *"an agent is a person who is authorised to act for a principal and has agreed so to act, and who has power to affect the legal relations of his principal with a third party."*[3] The standard model is an insurance agent who acts in behalf of an insurance company, his principal, to negotiate insurance contracts with third parties. More generally, lawyers, real estate agents, engineers, doctors, dentists, stockbrokers, and the Gulf Oil zealots may all be regarded as agents of some principal. Although for some purposes one might want to distinguish agents from employees, such a distinction will not be necessary here. The definition given above is broad enough to allow us to think of coal miners, Avon Ladies, zoo attendants, and Ministers of Parliament as agents.

Second, as our definition suggests, there are typically three important relationships involved in agency transactions, namely, those between agent and principal, agent and third party, and principal and third party. The law of agency has plenty to say about each of these relationships, while LAA is primarily concerned with only the first, the fiducial relation between agent and principal. It would be a mistake to regard this as mere oversight. Few of us are immune to the buck-passing syndrome. Most of us are inclined to try to narrow the range of activities for which we are prepared to accept responsibility and, at the same time, widen the range of activities for which we are prepared to accept authority. Notwithstanding the psychological theory of cognitive dissonance, most human beings seem to have sufficient mental magnanimity to accommodate this particular pair of incompatible inclinations. Like the insects, we are very adaptable creatures.

Third, I imagine that someone using an argument like LAA would, in the first place, be interested in trying to establish the fact that agents have a moral obligation to operate in a thoroughly egoistic way in their principals' behalf. If most LAA users in fact are primarily concerned with establishing their legal obligations, then perhaps what I have to say will be less interesting than I imagine to most people. Nevertheless, I'm assuming that the force of "ought" in the first premise and conclusion is moral rather than legal. For our purposes it doesn't matter what sort of an ontological analysis one gives to such obligations or what sort of a moral theory one might want to use to justify one's moral principles. It only has to be appreciated that LAA is designed to provide a moral justification for the behavior prescribed in its conclusion.

Fourth, an agent may be regarded as operating in a thoroughly egoistic way if all his actions are designed to optimize his own interests and he has no inclination at all to identify the interests of anyone else with his own. (Throughout the essay I usually let the masculine "he" abbreviate "he or she.") He may very well be a self-confident, self-starting, self-sustaining, and self-controlled individual. These are all commendable personal characteristics. But he must be selfish, self-centered, and/or self-serving. In conflict situations when there are not enough benefits to satisfy everyone, he will try to see that his own needs are satisfied, whatever happens to the needs of others. He is more interested in being first than in being nice, and he assumes that everyone else is too. He may harbor the suspicion that if everyone behaved as he does, the world's resources would be used in a maximally efficient way and everyone would be materially better off. But these are secondary considerations at best. His first consideration, which he regards as only prudent or smart, is to look out for *Número Uno,* himself.

Fifth, to say that an agent is supposed to operate in a thoroughly egoistic way in behalf of his principal is just to say that the agent is supposed to act as he believes his principal would act if his principal were an egoist. The agent is supposed to conduct the affairs of his principal with the single-minded purpose of optimizing the latter's interests and not yielding them to anyone else's interests.

The Second Premise

Now we should be talking the same language. The question is: Is the Loyal Agent's Argument sound? Can its conclusion be established or even well-supported by its premises? I think there are good reasons for giving a negative answer to these questions. Moreover, since the argument has been deliberately formulated in a logically valid form, we may proceed immediately to a closer investigation of the content of its premises.

Let's consider the second premise first. This premise can only be regarded as true of real people *a priori* if one of the assumptions we have made for the sake of argument about human motivation is false. Following the quotations from the Special Review Committee, it was pointed out that the case involved agents who apparently performed illegal actions with altruistic motives. What they did wrong, they did in behalf of Gulf Oil Corporation. Fair enough. However, if it's possible to perform illegal but altruistically motivated acts, it must be possible to perform legal but altruistically motivated acts as well. The very assumption required to give the argument initial plausibility also ensures that its second premise cannot be assumed to be generally true *a priori*. Since some people can perform nonegoistically motivated actions, the second premise of LAA requires some defense. Moreover, broadly speaking there are two directions such a defense might take, and I will consider each in turn.

Granted that users of LAA cannot consistently regard every individual as a thoroughly egoistic operator and hence guarantee the truth of the second premise *a priori*, it is still possible to try to defend this premise as a well-confirmed empirical hypothesis. That is, admitting that there are exceptions, one might still claim that if one acted as if the second premise were true, much more often than not one would be right. This is the sort of line economists have traditionally taken toward their idealized rational economic man. They realize that people are capable of altruistic action, but they figure that the capability is seldom exercised and they design their hypotheses, laws, and theories accordingly.

So far as business is concerned, the egoistic line seems to be translated into profit maximization. According to Goodman, for example:

> The Wall Street rule for persons legally charged with the management of other people's money runs as follows: Invest funds in a company with the aim of gaining the best financial return with the least financial risk for the trust beneficiaries. If you later come to disagree with the company's management, sell the stock.[4]

Similarly, in a cautious version of LAA, Friedman has claimed that:

> In a free-enterprise, private-property system, a corporate executive is an employee of the owners of the business. He has a direct responsibility to his employers. That responsibility is to conduct the business in accordance with their desires, which generally will be to make as much money as possible while conforming to the basic rules of the society, both those embodied in law and those embodied in ethical custom.[5]

Instead of challenging the accuracy of these assessments of the motives of people generally or of businessmen in the marketplace in particular now, I want to grant it straightaway for the sake of the argument. The question is: How does that affect LAA?

As you may have guessed, users of LAA are not much better off than they were. If it's a good bet that the second premise is true, then it's an equally good bet that anyone inclined to defend his actions with LAA is not an altruistic operator. No one can have it both ways. Evidence for the empirical hypothesis that people generally act as egoists is evidence for the truth of the second premise and the falsehood of the alleged altruistic motives of anyone using LAA. In short, the premise is still self-defeating.

CORPORATE PRINCIPALS

Instead of regarding the second premise as an empirical claim about real people and attempting to support it inductively, one might treat it as a logical claim justifiable by an appeal to the definitions of some of its key terms. This looks like a very promising strategy when one considers the fact that many contemporary principals, like Gulf Oil Corporation, for example, are abstract entities. Corporate persons are, after all, nothing but fictional persons invented by people with fairly specific aims. In particular, corporations have been invented to assist in the accumulation of material assets. While they typically accomplish many different tasks, the accumulation of assets is generally regarded as their basic aim. Thus, if one's principal happens to be a corporation, one might reasonably argue that it is by definition thoroughly egoistic. The business of such entities is certainly business, because that is their very reason for being, the very point of inventing them in the first place. So, the second premise of LAA could be substantiated by definitional fiat.

The strength of this approach should not be underestimated. The people who design corporate law are not dummies. "A major goal of corporate law, through many decades," Chirelstein wrote,

> has been the development of equitable restrictions and rules of restraint aimed specifically at defending the financial interests of minority shareholders. In essence, the law contemplates that corporate investment decisions shall be wholly independent of the personal tastes of the company's shareholders—whether majority or minority—and shall be based solely on a presumed universal preference for higher market values per share.[6]

In other words, he claims:

> the chief function of corporate law is to "enable," that is, to furnish a suitable formula within the existing system of fiduciary obligation by which *corporate generosity can be approved as properly self-serving.*[7] [Emphasis added.]

Apparently, then, morally conscientious corporate agents may find themselves facing lawsuits if they assume their principals are not self-serving profit maximizers and act accordingly. Legal niceties aside, there is a thought-provoking moral argument in favor of agents acting as if their principals were just as the designers of corporate law imagine them. That is, if any particular stockholder wants to give his money away or to pursue any aims other than profit maximization, he is free to do so. Investors should be and almost certainly are aware that corporations are designed to make money. If they have other aims, they shouldn't be investing in corporations. If they don't have other aims and they go into corporations with their eyes wide open, then they should appreciate and respect the interests of others who have gone in with them.

In principle the defense of the second premise of LAA on the grounds of the defining characteristic of corporations may be challenged as before. Insofar as corporations are defined as egoistic corporate persons (a rough abbreviated definition, to be sure), a serious question arises concerning the morality of becoming an agent for them—not to mention inventing them in the first place. The evils of unbridled egoism are well known and they aren't mitigated by the fact that the egoist in question is a corporate person. If anything, they are magnified because of the difficulties involved in assigning responsibility and holding corporations liable for their activities. It is demonstrably certain that if everyone only attends to what he perceives as his own interests, a socially self-destructive result may occur. That is the clear message of prisoner's dilemma studies. It's also the message of two kids in a playpen who finally tear the toys apart rather than share them.

As before, it will not help to argue that in developed countries most people work for corporations or they don't work at all. Again, self-preservation is not altruism. To serve an evil master in the interests of survival is not to serve in the interests of altruism, and users of LAA are supposed to be motivated by altruism. On the other hand, insofar as corporations are not defined as egoistic corporate persons and are granted more or less benevolent if not downright altruistic aims, the truth of the second premise of LAA is again open to question. In either case, then, an agent trying to salvage LAA with this sort of definitional defense is bound to find the task self-defeating.

THE FIRST PREMISE

Let's turn now to the first premise of LAA. In a way it's as innocuous as motherhood and apple pie. Every discussion I've read of the duties of agents according to agency law in North America and the United Kingdom has included some form of this premise. For example, Powell says, "An agent has a general duty to act solely for the benefit of his principal in all matters connected with the execution of his authority."[8] *The American Restatement of the Law of Agency* says that "an agent is subject to a duty to his principal to act solely for the benefit of the principal in all matters connected with his agency."[9] According to a standard Canadian textbook on business law, "Good faith requires that the agent place the interest of his principal above all else except the law."[10]

The only trouble with the premise is that its limitations are not clearly built into it. In this respect it is like most moral principles and rules of law. Short of turning every principle and rule into a self-contained treatise, it's impossible to indicate every possible exception. For example, no one should kill anyone, except *maybe* in self-defense, war, capital punishment, euthanasia, abortion, or suicide. Similarly, an agent ought to pursue the interests of his principal with certain exceptions. However, the *American Restatement of the Law of Agency* makes it quite clear that "In no event would it be implied that an agent has a duty to perform acts which . . . are illegal or unethical."[11] Moreover, "In determining whether or not the orders of the principal to the agent are reasonable . . . business or professional ethics . . . are considered."[12] Powell also remarks that agents have no duty "to carry out an illegal act."[13] And in the famous Nuremberg trials the Charter of the International Military Tribunal recognized

> that one who has committed criminal acts may not take refuge in superior orders nor in the doctrine that his crimes were acts of states. These twin principles working together have heretofore resulted in immunity for practically everyone concerned in the really great crimes against peace and mankind. Those in lower ranks are protected against liability by the orders

of their superiors. The superiors were protected because their orders were called acts of the state. Under the Charter, no defence based on either of these doctrines can be entertained.[14]

Thus, there is no doubt at all that the first premise of LAA cannot be regarded as a licence to break the law. No respectable court would permit it. In fact, although the courts have no special jurisdiction over moral law, they have shown no reluctance to condemn immoral acts allegedly performed in the interests of fulfilling fiduciary obligations.

Illegality and immorality aside, the first premise still gives up much more than any sane person should be willing to give up. It virtually gives a principal a licence to use an agent in any way the principal pleases, so long as the agent's activity serves the principal's interest. For example, suppose a life insurance agent agrees to sell State Farm Insurance on commission. It would be ludicrous to assume that the agent has also committed himself to painting houses, washing dogs, or doing anything else that happened to give his principal pleasure. It would also be misleading to describe such an open-ended commitment as an agreement to sell insurance. It would more accurately be described as selling oneself into bondage. Clearly, then, one must assume that the first premise of LAA presupposes some important restrictions that may have nothing to do with any sort of law.

Since they are apparently drawn from and applicable to ordinary affairs and usage, perhaps it would be instructive to mention some of the principles developed in the law of agency to address this problem. You may recall that the definition of an agent that we borrowed from Powell explicitly referred to a person being "authorised to act for a principal." An agent's duties are typically limited to a set of activities over which he is granted authority by his principal. The authority may be expressed verbally or in writing, implied by something expressed or perhaps just assumed as usual in a certain sort of transaction.[15] The last principle (i.e., of "usual authority") would be sufficient to prevent the exploitation of the hypothetical insurance agent in the preceding paragraph.

Besides a carefully developed set of principles related to the granting of authority, the law of agency recognizes some other general duties of agents like the previously considered duty of good faith. For example, an agent is expected to "exercise due care and skill in executing his authority."[16] This obviously serves the interests of all concerned, and there are plenty of principles and precedents available to explain "due care and skill." An agent is generally not authorized to delegate his responsibilities to someone else, although such delegation may be built into a particular contract.[17] He is expected to "keep proper accounts," i.e., accounts that clearly distinguish his principal's assets from his own.[18] Without some prior agreement with his principal, an agent is usually not permitted to occupy the role of the third party in a transaction in which he is also the agent.[19] It is assumed that in the absence of some agreement, an agent would seek some advantage for himself in the contract between his principal and himself as a third party. This assumption of egoistic motives is illustrated very well in a case from 1874 reported by Smyth and Soberman.

In *Robinson* v. *Mollett* a client gave a broker an order to buy tallow for him. The broker already held some tallow on his own account, and he simply sent this tallow to his client. The court held that the client did not have to accept or pay for it. There was no evidence that the broker had obtained either the best tallow or the best price for his principal. Indeed, *there is a presumption in these circumstances that the broker would obtain as much personal profit as he could.*[20] [Emphasis added.]

Keeping the preceding guidelines in mind, perhaps some form of LAA can be salvaged by tightening up the first premise. Let's suppose I'm in the advertising business and I want to use LAA by suitably restricting the scope of the first premise thus:

> 1a. *As a loyal advertising agent of some company, I ought to advertise its products as they would advertise them if they had my expertise.*

That would require a consistent modification of the second premise and conclusion, but we need not worry about that. The question is: Does this reformulated premise 1a escape the kinds of criticism leveled against premise 1?

Certainly not. If the company happens to be run by a bunch of thoroughly unscrupulous thugs, it could be immoral and illegal to advertise their products as they would if they had the agent's expertise. Even if the company is run by fools who really don't know what they make, it could be immoral and illegal to advertise their products as they would if they had the agent's expertise. For example, if the company's directors are smart enough to know that they can make more money selling drugs than they can make selling candy, but dumb enough to think that the candy they make is an effective drug, an agent could hardly be under any obligation to advertise their product as a marvelous new drug, i.e., assuming that the agent was smart enough to know that his employers were only capable of producing candy.

If you think the agent could have such an obligation, what would be its source? Clearly it is not enough to say that the agent is employed by the company. That would be tantamount to appealing to LAA in order to establish a version of its own first premise, i.e., it would be a circular salvaging effort. Something else is required to support premise 1a.

QUESTION-BEGGING AND ACT UTILITARIANISM

At this point a critic may be wondering about the justification of my claim that a knowledgeable agent could hardly be obliged to advertise the product as a marvelous new drug. Why, one might ask, isn't that just begging the question in the opposite direction? Clearly it's not enough to say that the agent has an obligation to tell the truth. After all, he also has an obligation to honor his contracts. By asserting that a loyal agent is not obliged to perform silly, illegal, or immoral acts, I am apparently assuming what must be proved, namely, that the obligation incurred by becoming an agent of another party is not superior to other obligations. This objection has some merit. Sometimes, as in the case of our hypothetical advertiser, it's impossible to satisfy both of two moral principles. Over a hundred years ago Hegel observed that such situations constitute the essential core of human tragedies. Act utilitarian theorists often regard such anomalies as decisive considerations in support of their position. According to this view, which I accept, moral principles should be regarded as rules of thumb subject to the overriding moral obligation to try to act so as to produce the greatest amount of happiness for the largest number of people. Thus, for example, an act utilitarian would argue that our hypothetical advertiser really has only one moral obligation in the candy case, namely, to refrain from advertising candy as a therapeutic drug. That is his only moral obligation in this case because, of the two options he has (to honor his commitment to serve the interests of his employer or to refrain from spreading false or misleading information), the latter will probably produce the greatest amount of happiness for the largest number of people. From this point of view, then, it is not question-begging to assert that the obligation incurred by becoming an agent of another party is not necessarily superior to other obligations.

Although the act utilitarian procedure for deciding which of two moral principles should be given precedence in conflict situations seems eminently reasonable, it has at least three disadvantages which merit some attention. First, the procedure may encounter insuperable operational problems. Someone must assume the responsibility for determining who is how happy, when, where, and why. More often than not, I think, such assessments can and are made with sufficient accuracy to maintain the viability of the act utilitarian position. For example, there is general agreement that Thalidomide should be banned because its use would produce more harm than happiness. Generally speaking, democracy is based on act utilitarian intuitions. Granted that the practice of democracy never quite lives up to the principle or the promise, it's still preferable to its alternatives.

Second, the procedure may lead to apparently perverse judgments since, for example, the greatest happiness for the greatest number of people might be produced by horrible crimes being committed against an innocent person. I believe this sort of anomaly is logically possible but not very likely. But there are two good reasons for not regarding the objection as fatal for act utilitarianism. In the first place, when one tries to justify one's judgment that another judgment is perverse, one will find that one is roughly back where we started. That is, one will be putting some moral principle against the act utilitarian judgment. But then what does one do when one's principles conflict? Clearly there must be some weighing and balancing of benefits and costs to accommodate particular circumstances. In the second place, though I can't demonstrate it here, I think every moral theory is subject to a perverse-judgment type of criticism. I haven't seen one theory that is not liable to lead to anomalies in some circumstances. That, among other things, is what over 2,000 years of moral philosophy has accomplished.

Finally, one may find the retreat to act utilitarianism disappointing because it seems to create a morally chaotic state of affairs. It seems to substitute spur-of-the-moment for principled action. This is a mistake. As indicated above, act utilitarians use moral principles as first-line principles of action. They are committed to keeping promises, honoring contracts, refraining from cheating, and so on. They believe that more often than not, by following these well-known and respected principles, more good than harm will be produced. They realize, however, that such principles are liable to lead to conflicts and other anomalies that require a finer assessment instrument. They also realize that that instrument, the act utilitarian principle, has its own problems; but they are prepared to tolerate them until something better comes along.

CONCLUSION

The announced aim of this essay was to destroy LAA once and for all. I think that has been done. It is perhaps worthwhile to emphasize that if people use LAA when, as we saw earlier, the real reason for their actions is fear (or job preservation) then they will be circulating a distorted view of the world and decreasing the chances of reform. Thus, in the interests of a clear perception and resolution of social problems related to responsible human agency, LAA deserves the sort of treatment it has received here.

Notes

1. J. J. McCloy, N. W. Pearson, and B. Matthews, *The Great Oil Spill* (New York: Chelsea House, 1976), p. 31.
2. *Ibid.*, p. 13.
3. R. Powell, *The Law of Agency* (London: Sir Isaac Pitman and Sons, Ltd., 1965), p. 7.
4. W. Goodman, "Stocks Without Sin," *Minneapolis Star and Tribune Co., Inc.* Reprinted in *Ethical Arguments for Analysis,* ed. R. Baum (New York: Holt, Rinehart & Winston, 1975), p. 206.
5. M. Friedman, "The Social Responsibility of Business Is to Increase Its Profits," *The New York Times Magazine,* September 13, 1970. Reprinted in *Ethical Arguments for Analysis,* ed. R. Baum (New York: Holt, Rinehart & Winston, 1975), p. 205.
6. M. A. Chirelstein, "Corporate Law Reform," *Social Responsibility and the Business Predicament,* ed. J. W. McKie, (Washington, D.C.: The Brookings Institution, 1974), pp. 73–74.
7. *Ibid.,* p. 73.
8. Powell, *The Law of Agency,* p. 312.
9. Section 387 as quoted in P. I. Blumberg, "Corporate Responsibility and the Employee's Duty of Loyalty and Obedience: A Preliminary Inquiry," *The Corporate Dilemma,* ed. D. Votaw and S. P. Sethi (Englewood Cliffs, N.J.: Prentice-Hall, Inc., 1973), p. 87.
10. J. E. Smyth and D. A. Soberman, *The Law and Business Administration in Canada* (Toronto: Prentice-Hall of Canada, Ltd., 1968), p. 360.
11. Section 385 as quoted in Blumberg, "Corporate Responsibility," p. 86.

12. *Ibid.*
13. Powell, *The Law of Agency,* p. 302.
14. R. Jackson, *The Nuremberg Case* as quoted in *Philosophy for a New Generation,* ed. A. K. Bierman and J. A. Gould (New York: The Macmillan Company, 1970), p. 217.
15. Powell, *The Law of Agency,* pp. 35–119.
16. *Ibid.,* p. 303.
17. *Ibid.,* p. 305.
18. *Ibid.,* p. 321.
19. *Ibid.,* p. 320.
20. Smyth and Soberman, *The Law and Business Administration in Canada,* pp. 361–362.

CORPORATE STRUCTURES AND INDIVIDUAL FREEDOM

Norman C. Gillespie

Under the heading of corporate responsibility, it is common these days to find discussions of social responsibilities—especially *pro bono* efforts to (a) alter traditional patterns of employment *via* affirmative action and training programs, (b) reduce environmental problems, and (c) in general spend money in ways that benefit society while benefiting the corporation minimally if at all. One way to characterize all these efforts is to note that they involve the internalization of "externalities," i.e., that the corporation bear the cost of alleviating *general* social and environmental problems. Advocates of such efforts have tried to discover ways in which such expenditures benefit the corporation. So, for example, when Levi Strauss "contributes 3 percent of its net after taxes to carefully chosen social programs,"[1] it is not enough that what they are doing is morally good; the *real* benefit, according to some analysts, is the excellent public relations the company achieves for its efforts in San Francisco.[2]

Critics of such efforts argue that the benefits for the company seldom match the expenditures involved; that such spending reduces profits; that it uses stockholders' money for projects that are not integral to the corporation's basic objective, which is to provide a return on investment. Indeed, some people believe that such expenditures are fundamentally subversive of the free enterprise system and the private corporation's *raison d'être.*[3] Critics also contend that corporate executives are not well-

This paper was written for the Conference on Ethics and Economics at the University of Delaware, Newark, Delaware, November 10–12, 1977. Copyright © 1978 by Norman C. Gillespie. Reprinted by permission of the author.

qualified to make such decisions, and they insist that, in any case, the corporation is not obligated to undertake such efforts.

My aim, here, is not to dispute these contentions but to see how well they apply to the idea that corporations should internally encourage rather than discourage ethical, moral, and legal behavior. To fully assess this issue it is necessary to know somewhat more about how a corporation sets out to encourage such behavior, since the methods chosen will be part of the comparison with undertaking *pro bono* social responsibilities.

The internal structure of a corporation exists in any case, and it is designed to promote certain kinds of behavior. Adding ethical conduct on the part of its employees to the list of corporate objectives simply recognizes that corporations are obligated to behave ethically, morally, and legally. The fundamental problem in this respect, is not acknowledging such obligations, but getting individuals to comply with them. The climate of subordination in an organization is crucial in this regard, and restructuring the corporate environment will shape up many managers and supervisors immediately and relieve their subordinates of the burden of "putting up with it," keeping silent, or resigning. Two ways in which this restructuring might be implemented (and I will explain the rationale for them later) are: setting up an Ethics Appeals Board within a corporation; and instituting a phone line which individuals can use to register complaints, make suggestions, ask questions, and offer criticisms. Of course, the more ethical and moral a company is, the fewer complaints there will be. So I can imagine, in some companies, an eventual withering away of the Ethics Appeals Board except as a check upon corporate irresponsibility. The less such a board has to do the better, as long as it continues to provide a form of employee relief.

Permitting individuals to question what they take to be unethical orders and inefficient practices will encourage individual responsibility and initiative. Efficiency as well as ethical conduct might be improved, and the respect for the individual manifested by this arrangement will be evident to all. According to Kant, respect for persons is morally fundamental,[4] and this proposal emphasizes that workers are persons as well as functionaries in a corporate scheme.

If corporations were completely successful in eliminating internal unethical behavior, the results would not involve the loss of any income to which the corporation is entitled. It might well mean that certain questionable practices or unfair methods of competition would be brought to light by individuals who know and disapprove of them; and it might entail that such practices would not be engaged in at all because the likelihood of their being discovered would be so much greater. But either way, the money lost would not be income to which the corporation is entitled. Instead, it would be income that the corporation should not receive in the first place.

Any costs involved would, in many instances, be more than offset by the check on individual dishonesty within the corporation. Conscientious employees could report without fear of reprisal such serious violations as theft, overcharging, etc., as well as unnecessary expenditures and inefficient practices that are costing the corporation money. The reduction of unethical and immoral demands made upon employees could be achieved along with the reduction and partial elimination of dubious or questionable practices that are contrary to company objectives.

Nor is my argument subversive of free enterprise, since it encourages both freedom and enterprise on the part of all employees, not simply those who are at the top, or are higher in the corporate ladder. It may be subversive of standard operating procedures in some corporations, but if so, these are the very practices that should change. The problems with which I am concerned are created by corporate structures which give some individuals considerable power over others, and this is a special sort of climate in which unethical behavior can flourish if not checked. Since these results, when they occur, are internal to the corporation, there is no reason why anyone else should be responsible for correcting them.

Many individuals, it may be objected, seem to lack a sense of right and wrong; some executives and managers may not *know* when they are *exceeding* the limits of what is ethical. But instead of requiring an employee to "sit at the conscience of his supervisor," as at present, one can alleviate that lack of knowledge and the problems it causes by permitting individuals who think that they are being asked to do something wrong (or wasteful or grossly inefficient) to question such a request or practice. This will solve the lack-of-knowledge problem in that the individuals who serve on a corporate appellate board will become more expert with experience, and this accumulated experience and knowledge can be diffused throughout the corporation as well as centralized for everyone's benefit. So this objection turns out to be a reason *for* my position, instead of an argument *against* it.

None of the standard objections, then, to corporations' taking on social responsibilities seem to count against the thesis that corporations have a responsibility to structure the work environment to encourage ethical and moral behavior. The one objection that does apply is that corporate executives and managers may not be well versed in ethics. But, as I have indicated, I aim to *remedy* that fact, not simply cite it as a *reason* for not changing. So, on all these counts, my position avoids those objections.

The focus in most recent discussions of corporate responsibility has been on the role of the corporation in society, treating the corporation as an individual entity with duties and responsibilities to society. But a corporation is also a collective entity with persons as members, and the focus in this paper is *internal.* Hence the mode of thinking suggested here is not the set of principles that govern the relations between individuals, but those principles that govern the relations between a collective (such as the state) and its members (e.g., citizens). Realizing that corporations are similar in this regard to states might lead one to stress *individual rights* as a limit on corporate activity, just as constitutional rights limit legitimate government interference in the lives of citizens. And that is exactly what David Ewing has done in *Freedom Inside the Organization* (1977), which is subtitled "Bringing Civil Liberties to the Workplace." In seeking to remedy the sorts of injustices suffered by employees that are illustrated by my earlier examples, Ewing advocates a "9-to-5 Bill of Rights." Ewing eschews letting "semantic difficulties deter us" (p. ix) in trying to determine what to call the position he is advocating, but it is nonetheless important to note that there are some significant disanalogies between citizens and employees. Foremost among them is that while the government is, in theory at least, the agent of its citizens, the corporation is almost never the agent of its employees. If anything, the employees are the agents of the corporation, so that the direction, so to speak, in a corporation is from top to bottom, rather than from the individual members to the agents of the collective. Furthermore, citizens exhaust the state (there are no extra members) in a way that employees do not exhaust a corporation; and the additional members of a corporation (the stockholders) play a role to which there is no comparable analogue in the state. There is also a much larger element of choice in determining whether someone is (or becomes) part of a specific corporation than there is in determining one's citizenship. Certain people are citizens (by birth) and the state must treat them as such; no corporate employees are in the same position. For these reasons, and others, I do not think that individual employees are protected by the constitution from their employers. I have argued, not that employees have a constitutional *right* to be treated ethically and fairly, but simply that they *should* be so treated.

Two familiar principles of management are part of the basis of my argument. The first is that top executives in a corporation establish the expected code of behavior in the corporation, and aspiring executives imitate the behavior they perceive as successful. Second, the way an individual treats others, including customers and competitors, is affected by the way he or she is treated within the organization. One of the crucial features in the operation of this second principle is the conception one forms of how to treat people: of *what is* and *what is not done*. (Britains often say, "It simply isn't done," to explain why no one there acts in certain ways.) So, is everyone looking out for number one? Is it rational to do otherwise—to be ethical or moral? These are the issues at stake in a corporate environment; let me explain precisely how and why this occurs.

The fundamental problem is not the quest for profits or even self-interest, although the latter is part of the problem. The real issue is power. "Power [involves] how much you can do for (or to) others. . . . [It] rests on the assumption by other people that you have the unilateral final word in matters which concern them. . . . For this reason the first step in acquiring power is to achieve autonomous control over some group of people, however small. . . ."[5] The first and sometimes the only question that comes to many people's minds in making a work-related decision is: How will this affect me (or *my standing* with my boss, or with the corporation)? If we want individuals to ask as well: Is it right? Is it ethical? we need to make it a reasonable expectation that these questions will occur to them.

Phillips Petroleum, for example, constantly makes an individual think in terms of the corporation's power over him. "When an employee [at Phillips] deviated from the unwritten company rules about dress, manners, gasoline station patronage, or other behavior, he was penalized quickly and harshly. . . . 'If you want [to work here, a lower-echelon employee explained], you simply have to cooperate with them and conform with their rules and conform to their policies.' "[6] Such a company policy completely reinforces the preoccupation with self-interest. In being other-directed, one is always concerned with how *x* affects *one's standing* with someone else. So "looking out for number one" becomes a way of life, and those individuals who fail to do this are perceived as irrational. This kind of corporate environment, therefore, can breed an excessive and almost exclusive concern with self-interest. In such an environment, morality, ethics, and fairness take a back seat, if they are considered at all.

Hence, in restructuring power relations between managers and subordinates with a view to emphasizing doing what is ethical, one can significantly alter the pattern of thought and action that is prevalent in a corporation. It makes being concerned with being ethical rational in that the cost to you is not excessive. So if the direction comes from the top, this concern for ethics and for the individual can be made evident, and everyone in a corporation can begin to think in those terms. Once that happens, if the second principle cited above is correct, then employees will begin to think in those terms in dealing with all people—including customers and competitors. So the way to improve the quality of ethics in business is to begin with an *internal* solution. The advice is ancient: Physician, heal thyself—but it is as apt in business today as ever. Focusing on the internal structure of a corporation and the way employees are regarded and treated there seems to me to be the key to altering patterns of thought and behavior that are inimical to ethics in business.

Notes

1. Gilbert Burck, "The Hazards of Corporate Responsibility," *Fortune,* vol. 87, no. 6, pp. 217–218.
2. *Ibid.*
3. Milton Friedman, *Capitalism and Freedom,* (Chicago: University of Chicago Press, 1962).
4. Immanuel Kant, *Groundwork of the Metaphysic of Morals,* trans. H. J. Paton (New York: Harper & Row, 1964), Chap. 2.
5. Michael Korda, *Power! How to Get It, How to Use It* (New York: Ballantine Books, 1977).
6. David Ewing, *Freedom Inside the Organization* (New York: E. P. Dutton Co., 1977), p. 95.

LAW, BUSINESS ETHICS, AND CONFLICT OF INTEREST:
The Obligations of a Corporate Executive

Leslie W. Jacobs

A perusal of case histories reveals that there have always been lapses in corporate responsibility, but recurring experiences of most business lawyers suggest the wisdom of a periodic examination of the extent to which legal requirements approximate ethical standards in the management of a business.... [My] concern here is with conflicts of interest which corporate fiduciaries [those having the duty to act for a corporation's benefit—Ed.] should avoid.

It is important at the outset to recognize that provisions by statute or by law for indemnity will not protect the corporate manager from liability for proven violations of his fiduciary duties. Also there are very few situations where director and officer insurance policies provide greater coverage in this situation than the indemnity statutes. The Delaware statute and the Model Business Corporation Act, which are similar on this question, and the New York Business Corporation Law all require that the corporate executive to be indemnified must have acted in good faith and in a manner reasonably believed to be in the best interests of the corporation....

The proper application of legal obligations should relate to a person's function rather than title. A corporate fiduciary is one upon whom responsibility has been placed and in whom trust is reposed for the conduct of the corporation's business. A higher standard of conduct is generally imposed on a person who is more active in the operation of the business. Thus a president, general manager or chief executive officer in most cases will be presumed to bear the most stringent burden of rejecting self-interest, regardless of his formal title, but facts involving a specific management assignment for another executive could result in a self-dealing disability of that executive which is equal to or greater than that of the president. This view of legal relations resembles basic agency principles, but other legal theories are also applicable to the analysis. Whether the corporate fiduciary's obligations are viewed from the perspective of his duties of loyalty or of his powers, it is difficult to escape the conclusion that the law directs him to act for the corporation, and to refrain from acting for himself, in a pattern of conscientious ethical behavior....

From "Business Ethics and the Law: Obligations of a Corporate Executive," Leslie W. Jacobs, in *The Business Lawyer,* July 1973. Reprinted by permission of the American Bar Association and its Section of Corporation, Banking, and Business Law.

353

Conceptualization of liability theories may turn on general legal categories such as agency, contract, property and tort principles, or it may emphasize areas of business practices such as appropriation of trade secrets or confidential information, seizure of corporate opportunities, interference with business relations, unfair competition or other conflicts of interest. . . . It is submitted that most cases which appear to involve impropriety but result in exoneration of the executive are examples of bogging down in a single course of reasoning and losing sight of the ethical standards to which the law, sometimes circuitously, leads.

Trade Secrets and Confidential Information

The acquisition of a corporation's trade secrets and confidential information by a competitor may be either legal or illegal. Quite often so-called trade secret cases do not concentrate on the method of acquisition but instead on the information's qualification as a trade secret. It is common in this situation for the issues of technology to overwhelm the court's recognition of fundamental questions of fair play. This emphasis is occasioned by a healthy concern for active competition and a sometimes obvious judicial bias against confidential matters as inherent restraints on trade. Balanced against this hesitation historically has been the need to protect what have been considered legitimate property rights.

Trade secret status has been reduced by the *Restatement*[1] to six factors:

> (1) the extent to which the information is known outside . . . [the] business; (2) the extent to which it is known by employees and others involved in . . . [the] business; (3) the extent of measures taken . . . to guard the secrecy of the information; (4) the value of the information to . . . [its owner] and to his competitors; (5) the amount of effort or money expended . . . in developing the information; (6) the ease or difficulty with which the information could be properly acquired or duplicated by others.

An additional factor which recurs in actions against individual defendants is judicial sympathy for flexibility in employment, including utilization of acquired skills and general knowledge. Weighed against this element is the question of whether disclosure or use of an alleged trade secret "constitutes a breach of confidence imposed in him."

These competing considerations in trade secret cases are not subject to precise rules. For our purposes it is significant that "breach of confidence" is crucial to the inquiry of a modern court. "One factor which is often outcome determinative in a borderline situation where the court, it seems, may go either way as to the existence of a protectable trade secret is the degree to which the employee has violated business ethics and morals."[2] . . . This phenomenon may explain the result in *E. I. DuPont de Nemours & Co.* v. *Christopher*,[3] where a competitor obtained aerial photographs of an incomplete DuPont plant before it was under roof. It is questionable whether a trade secret in the conventional sense actually existed, but the court was clearly incensed: "our devotion to free wheeling industrial competition must not force us into accepting the law of the jungle as the standard of morality expected in our commercial relations."[4]

Two points are pertinent in the application of this attitude to employee cases. First, any employee who flagrantly misuses any confidential information will run a serious risk of losing a trade secret case. But more importantly, as the employee's status approaches the executive level, a standard of simple unethical activity or lack of good faith imperceptibly replaces a court's reliance on more extreme misconduct. As an example, the court's concern with the defendant's executive capacity was repeatedly stated in *Fairchild Engine & Airplane Corp.* v. *Cox,*[5] where Cox was a former vice-president and director of plaintiff Fairchild as well as general manager of the relevant division and plants:

> Whereas the defendant contests the chief issue in controversy—the secrecy of the process—some of the salient facts emerge from the welter of evidence free from entanglement. Indisputably, while Cox was in plaintiff's employ as an officer and director, supervising the development and licensing of the process, he acquired knowledge thereof which he now threatens to disclose to General Bronze. Though Cox has a good general, liberal education—he is a graduate of Yale—he is not an engineer or a technician.
>
> Cox possesses ability. He deserves more than a modicum of credit for Whitfield and Sheshunoff's successful development of the process. Indubitably his executive contribution to that consummation was valuable. But he was well paid for his labors. And the work he performed was not for his benefit alone. He was treated handsomely. It is unfortunate that he could not or did not remain with the plaintiffs to reap larger rewards. To determine the paramount issue confronting us, it is not essential to believe that Cox designedly set out to cheat or deceive the plaintiffs or deliberately filch what belonged to them. I do not doubt that he was animated by a desire to earn a livelihood. Certainly in connection with such a legitimate and praiseworthy and necessary endeavor he cannot be deprived of his general skill and knowledge. His general experience has become a valuable part of his equipment; he cannot divorce himself from it; it cannot be dissolved. An edict to divest the defendant of his general experience would be as harsh and cruel as it would be impossible of execution. [citing cases] Yet, good faith alone is not a sufficient protection, an impenetrable armor. Fine intentions explain, they do not justify.
>
> Cox was no ordinary employee. He was entrusted with supervision of the development of the process. He became affiliated with the plaintiffs' plans at their inception. His position was executive, one of trust and confidence. His loyalty was to his employer. He was a fiduciary owing to the plaintiffs "the duty of constant and unqualified fidelity. . . ." [citing cases][6]

Similar concern is obvious in *B. F. Goodrich Co.* v. *Wohlgemuth,*[7] a well-known Ohio case where the Court of Appeals reversed the trial Court's refusal to enter an injunction. There the defendant was employed by Goodrich following graduation from college and assigned to the pressure-space suit department; he progressively was promoted to positions as materials engineer, product engineer, sales engineer, technical manager, and finally manager of the department. He was then in charge of virtually all research and development on space suits: "There is no doubt that Wohlgemuth was one of a few top executives and developers in this field of operation with the Goodrich Company. . . ."[8] There was no evidence that trade secrets had been disclosed by Wohlgemuth to his new employer, International Latex Corporation, which has recently obtained a government subcontract for space suit development. Yet the court ordered the issuance of an injunction because

> the circumstances surrounding his employment by Latex, and his own attitude as revealed by statements to fellow Goodrich employees, are sufficient to satisfy this court that a substantial threat of disclosure exists.[9]

The court has already noted Wohlgemuth's executive capacity, and apparently it did not feel his view of fiduciary duty was commensurate with his position:

> It was then said to Wohlgemuth that in leaving Goodrich "he was taking with him a body of information which did not belong to him or to any individual, but did belong to the company, and that there was a matter of company loyalty and ethics involved." Wohlgemuth replied that "loyalty and ethics had their price; insofar as he was concerned, International Latex was paying the price."[10]

The emphasis on breach of confidence in trade secret cases naturally leads to the result that judgment is easier to obtain against an executive than against a lesser employee. That result is well-founded, both as a question of responsibility and as a matter of trade secret law. The employment relationship is the foundation of the confidence to be protected from abuse, and a person with officer or other executive responsibilities almost always has necessarily broad access to confidential information of a wide variety. Other employees have much more limited duties and authority, and routine disclosure to them of information unrelated or not essential to their jobs would probably destroy its trade secret status rather than subject them to greater employee burdens.

Not every court will pass over the trade secret finding lightly before reaching the ethical question, even in the case of an executive employee. In this instance it is important, as previously noted, that the court should not become so immersed in trade secret defenses that it forgets to deal with the real merits. . . .

Corporate Opportunities

Unlike appropriation of trade secrets, the seizure of corporate opportunities inherently involves persons in a fiduciary relationship to the corporation by reason of which they are prohibited from personal preference over the corporation on an available business venture. As with the trade secret cases, it is often misleading to view a dispute between the parties only in terms of the corporate opportunity doctrine, even where it is the clearest legal category in which an executive's alleged misconduct may be classified. The law of corporate opportunity is nothing more than a convenient, but by no means exclusive, capsulization of basic legal principles prohibiting conflicts of interest. . . .

. . . The more well-reasoned decisions can be distilled into three tests that should be applied by any court in a corporate opportunity analysis:

First, did the opportunity come to the executive because of his position, or, regardless of how the executive became aware of the opportunity, would a disinterested executive after full disclosure have viewed it as potentially favorable to the corporation and consistent with its long-range business intentions?

Second, has the defendant fiduciary satisfied a burden of proving that the corporation, after full disclosure and without the influence of any personally interested executive, was unable or unwilling to pursue an opportunity which met the first test?

Third, if the opportunity was not barred to the fiduciary by the first and second tests, would his participation in it otherwise maintain a conflict with the corporation's interests. . . .

The first two rules are descriptive of the considerations in every corporate opportunity case, and they differ somewhat from the third since they may (in the unusual case) establish the corporation's right to preclude an executive's participation in a business venture which could be of value to the corporation but not necessarily a direct conflict with its interests if undertaken by a third party.

The effect of the third rule is best demonstrated by the decisions in *Durfee* v. *Durfee & Canning, Inc.*[11] and *Lincoln Stores, Inc.* v. *Grant.*[12] Defendant Canning, an officer of Durfee & Canning, organized and served as an officer of another corporation named Pacific in which he maintained a controlling beneficial interest. Canning then arranged a source of supply for Pacific, which resold much of its product to Durfee & Canning. Canning admitted "that he made no attempt at any time, then or thereafter, to get [the supplier] to sell . . . directly to Durfee & Canning. He testified in explanation and justification that he knew it was futile."[13] The court even gave this futility explanation the benefit of the doubt and conceded that "[h]ad Canning at any time so requested, it is highly conjectural whether [the supplier] would have been willing to deal directly with Durfee & Canning,"[14] but then concluded that

> In any event the argument that a fiduciary is not subject to the general rule here involved where the venture is one that the corporation itself is unable to take advantage of is not persuasive.[15]
>
> We do not concur in the argument of counsel for the defendant to the effect that the test is whether the corporation has an existing interest or an expectancy thereof in the property involved, being of the opinion that the true basis of the governing doctrine rests fundamentally on the unfairness in the particular circumstances of a director, whose relation to the corporation is fiduciary, "taking advantage of an opportunity [for his personal profit] when the interests of the corporation justly call for protection. This calls for the application of ethical standards of what is fair and equitable . . . [in] particular sets of facts."[16]

The *Lincoln Stores* case was brought against a former corporate director and manager of a retail department store operated by the corporation, a second former director and general manager of all the company's stores in the state, and a former buyer. The three were informed by a real estate broker of the availability of a neighboring department store and, according to the opinion, decided to acquire it for themselves and have the buyer resign and "take charge," while the other two would continue in the plaintiff's employ and conceal their interests. The three furthered their purpose with the all too common practices of using the plaintiff's information (in this case inventory records) to plan a competitive operation and charging some of their expenses to the plaintiff. A trade secret question as such was not raised. The court rejected the corporate opportunity doctrine, holding that the plaintiff had no need for the additional store and therefore no expectancy, despite the clear potential for more vigorous competion if it was sold by its "old-time" management. But that was not the end of the matter, for the defendants had used bad faith to exercise their right to acquire the store, scheming against the plaintiff's interest to compete with it. That alone justified an award of damages. . . .

Interference with Business Relations

The law recognizes a right of action by an injured party, not just against one who has induced a breach of a contract with the plaintiff, but also against one who has interfered with business relations creating reasonable economic expectancies in the plaintiff short of an existing contract. In both situations the earlier decisions emphasized the maliciousness or wrongful qualities of the defendant's acts. . . .

Understandably, many executives intend that their contemplated personal ventures will parallel the business of the corporation with which they are familiar. Unfortunately, all too often they do not simply model the new company upon the old, but they actually transfer some of the operations and goodwill. The forbidden interference will usually be with customer, supplier or employee relations of the corporation. In each case the gist of the action is activity incompatible with fiduciary duties while occupying an executive position. An executive may lawfully terminate his employment or resign as an officer or director and thereafter acquire the rights of an independent competitor, and consequently he must also be permitted to plan in advance, but he may not undertake anything other than the most tentative preparations while he remains responsible for the corporation's well-being.

The courts look carefully at the point of separation from the corporation in relation to the spectrum from fiduciary duties on one end to active competition on the other. In *United Board and Carton Corp.* v. *Britting*[17] the court allowed recovery for the corporate employer where several employees operated a rival company for a year before resigning. In *Standard Brands, Inc.* v. *U.S. Partition & Packaging Corp.*[18] the defendants made plans to organize a competing business and performed other disloyal acts while former employees, but they did not form their new company until after termination of their employment. In *Freemont Oil Co.* v. *Marathon Oil*

Co.[19] the period of time between agreement among a group of employees and actual termination was two months. An injunction was granted in both *Standard Brands* and *Fremont.*[20] Some cases even hold that solicitation or interference may be enjoined after resignation,[21] but absent use of confidential information that restriction has not been based solely on a former fiduciary relationship.[22]

Other Conflicts and Unfair Competition

A number of cases refer to actionable conflicts of interest involving other types of activity. Thus in *Standard Brands* the utilization of the employer's assets and withholding improvements to machinery were part of the finding of disloyalty. In *Lincoln Stores, Inc.* v. *Grant* the executives also used the corporation's assets for their own advantage. Such actions may constitute theft, embezzlement or at least conversion. But other decisions cannot point to such obvious breaches of duty, and instead they fall back on general principles illustrated by the well-known case of *Guth* v. *Loft, Inc.*[23]

> Corporate officers and directors are not permitted to use their position of trust and confidence to further their private interests. While technically not trustees, they stand in a fiduciary relation to the corporation and its stockholders. A public policy existing through the years, and derived from a profound knowledge of human characteristics and motives, has established a rule that demands of a corporate officer or director, peremptorily and inexorably, the most scrupulous observance of his duty, not only affirmatively to protect the interests of the corporation committed to his charge, but also to refrain from doing anything that would work injury to the corporation, or to deprive it of profit or advantage which his skill and ability might properly bring to it, or to enable it to make in the reasonable and lawful exercise of its powers. The rule that requires an undivided and unselfish loyalty to the corporation demands that there shall be no conflict between duty and self-interest.

The same philosophy was declared four years earlier in a more obscure Ohio decision[24] condemning self-dealing by one Bohannon, president of the foundering Peerless Corporation:

> One fact, however, is clearly established: When an official does not deal with the corporation but for the corporation, that is then a fiduciary relationship, and the official so serving is to be regarded in the nature of a trustee, who is required as a consequence to exercise absolute good faith towards his principal and *cestui*, to whom he is bound to render faithful services. Nor may he enter into competition with his corporation and have an interest which in any way conflicts with the interests of the corporation.
>
> If one deviates from this course in the slightest degree, and a profit results out of the same, whatever he has achieved inures to the benefit of his principal.[25]
>
> While we may have doubts as to some points, of one point we are definitely certain. When it came to a question of Bohannon or the corporation, Bohannon came first every time. It was clear that Bohannon who was in a position of trust was untrue to that trust. He unlawfully enriched himself at the expense of the Peerless Corporation.[26]

Bohannon throughout the trial kept talking of the success of the corporation. He is a good deal like the doctor who kept on telling his patient he was improving, until the patient died of improvement. . . . He owed loyalty and faithfulness to his corporation. It was his duty to disclose all material facts fully to his corporation directly or indirectly. He could not derive personal profit or advantage from his position to himself.[27] . . .

CONCLUSION

The corporate executive is in a fiduciary relationship with his company which imposes a personal disability on conflicts of interest. Although morality and law are not coextensive, in this context it is a fair generalization that what should concern an executive's conscience will concern a court. Hard and fast rules are difficult to formulate, but in questionable areas it should be remembered that the corporation has been entrusted to its executives' care. Consequently, the ethical presumption should be against self-dealing. Having applied that standard and reached a finding of a violation of the duty of loyalty, a wide variety of remedies is applicable to compensate the corporation for an executive's abuse and, hopefully, to deter similar transgressions by corporate fiduciaries.

Notes

1. *Restatement of Torts,* § 757, comment b.
2. Note, "Protection of Trade Secrets in the Employer-Employee Relationship," 39, *Notre Dame Law,* 200, 202 (1964).
3. 431 F.2d 1012 (5th Cir. 1970), *cert. denied,* 400 U.S. 1024 (1971), *rehearing denied,* 401 U.S. 967 (1971).
4. 431 F.2d at 1016.
5. 50 N.Y.S.2d 643 (Supt. Ct. 1944).
6. *Id.* at 649–51 and 655.
7. 117 Ohio App. 493, 192 N.E.2d 99 (1963).
8. *Id.* at 496, 192 N.E.2d at 102.
9. *Id.* at 499, 192 N.E.2d at 104–5.
10. *Id.* at 498, 192 N.E.2d at 104.
11. 323 Mass. 187, 80 N.E.2d 522 (1948).
12. 309 Mass. 417, 34 N.E.2d 704 (1941).
13. 323 Mass. at 192, 80 N.E.2d at 525.
14. *Id.*
15. *Id.* at 202, 80 N.E.2d at 530.
16. *Id.* at 199, 80 N.E.2d at 529 (inserts and deletions from original).
17. 63 N.J. Super. 517, 164 A.2d 824 (Ch. 1959).
18. 199 F. Supp. 161 (E.D. Wis. 1961).
19. 92 Ohio L. Abs. 76 (C.P. 1963).
20. *See,* Craig v. Graphic Arts Studio, Inc. 39 Del. Ch. 447, 166 A.2d 444 (1960), where the conflicting agreement was only six weeks before termination.
21. Wear-Ever Aluminum, Inc. v. Towncraft Industries, Inc., 75 N.J. Super. 135, 182 A.2d 387 (Ch. 1962).

22. Eastern Air Devices v. Gaites, 281 App. Div. 761, 118 N.Y.S.2d 258 (1953).
23. 23 Del. Ch. 255, 270, 5 A.2d 503, 510 (Sup. Ct. 1939).
24. Taylor v. Bohannon, 3 Ohio Op. 178 (C.P. 1935).
25. *Id.* at 182.
26. *Id.* at 183.
27. *Id.* at 184.

CONFLICT OF INTEREST AND CONFLICTING INTERESTS

Joseph Margolis

The notion of a conflict of interest is singularly ignored in most attempts to examine the nature of moral and legal constraints. In attempting to supply an analysis, therefore, we will be breaking relatively fresh ground. Perhaps, in so doing, we will also come to understand the sense in which a concept is first taken to have a distinctly moral application.

A conflict of interest is not to be confused with conflicting interests or, indeed, with conflicting obligations. The Greek tragedies illustrate the latter but not the former, for instance. When Antigone, in Sophocles' *Antigone,* is torn between the king's command that her brother's body remain disgraced and her perceived duty to family and gods to ensure the body an honorable burial, she is confronted with conflicting interests. How she should act is not clearly indicated: each interest is legitimate in its own right but, in the circumstances given, plainly incompatible with the other; to accede to the king's law is to violate a high tradition, and to fulfill what Antigone regards as a sacred loyalty and duty is to violate the king's legitimate authority. She must respect both interests and she cannot respect both adequately in any act she might perform. The German philosopher Hegel theorized that Greek tragedy perceived in such conflicts a disharmony in the cosmic order of things that must be restored at whatever cost to the human agents affected: more often than not, they were destroyed in the resolution. Each interest, Hegel thought, represented in its partial way the same supreme justice of the gods. Neither could be repudiated, but the contingencies of the local lives of humans had somehow managed to bring these elements into conflict. The needed resolution required restoration of the original order, not satisfaction at the human level.

Obviously, we are all caught from time to time in dilemmas of this sort —doubtless, of more modest proportions. But our sense of such situations is that each interest, separately, not only is legitimate but imposes a fair claim on our agency: we feel we ought to act in accord with each, viewed separately. Whether there is a viable or proper way to reconcile the two is either uncertain or unlikely. A community in Maine, for example, wishes to preserve the natural beauty of the land and sea unpolluted by the threatened virgin influx of heavy industrial machinery; on the other hand, the prospect of relieving its own economic depression and chronic unemployment appears to lie solely with seizing the opportunity to establish a new oil refining industry that otherwise will go elsewhere. In the Middle East, the conflicting demands of peace and security seem too elusive to reconcile; yet neither may be rightly denied. Where we speak of conflicting interests, we provisionally concede the legitimacy of each, and regard the conflict as an unfortunate contingency that ought if possible to be resolved—without discarding either interest. Compromise is normally recommended.

Where, however, we have a conflict of interest, one or the other interest may not be independently legitimate. For instance, a Congressman, functioning as a lawyer, agrees (without public disclosure) to represent a client in a case involving the federal government. The law forbids this on the grounds of a conflict of interest. He may represent his client in cases involving state governments; but, regardless of his motives, it is illegal to do so where the federal government is involved. In a conflict of interest, it is, then, precisely, the *relationship of the putative interests* that is essential; in conflicting interests, the conflict is a mere contingency (an unfortunate contingency) arising to relate *independently legitimate interests.* In the first, our moral or legal concern centers on the agent's attempt to avoid the charge of having acted in a way that betrays a conflict of interest. In the second, we tend to be interested rather in the skill or ingenuity or tact with which an agent handles an unfortunate, possibly avoidable obstacle.

It need not, of course, actually be the case that one or the other interest, in a conflict of interest, be illegitimate or illegal; the claim of a conflict is, rather, that it is morally wrong or illegal or illegitimate *to serve both interests.* There need not even be conflicting interests in a conflict of interest. Our Congressman, for instance, knows full well that, under the law, what he is doing is illegal; his joint interests are not, as in the classical case, provisionally legitimate. Psychologically, of course, he may experience a sense of conflict, since he wishes to serve in office and to pocket his fees. But that merely confirms that a genuine conflict of interest obtains; his psychological anguish is quite irrelevant to there being either a conflict of interest or conflicting interests.

However, we can easily provide for an enlargement of the notion. Imagine that our Congressman is a member of a law partnership that stands to make only a modest sum representing Indian communities holding land claims against the federal government: he himself is part Indian and, out of a deep loyalty to his heritage and his people, fearful that no one else will champion their cause, he agrees to prepare their brief. Here, we have a conflict of interest involving conflicting interests; the illegality of his action remotely recalls Antigone's dilemma, while at the same time it marks an inadmissible conjunction of interests. We sense the complexity of the matter if we ask ourselves whether the conflict would be avoided if his partners, but not he, handled the brief—or, if no financial gain were involved; or, if the firm acted in an entirely informal way.

There is, it should be said, nothing inherently wrong or inappropriate in pursuing a course that leads to a conflict of interest; what is required is that an agent avoid activating the conflict, that is, avoid *serving* both interests in the very context in which it is supposed they constitute a conflict of interest. Our Congressman may resign his post or refuse the Indians' brief or perhaps provide his legal counsel gratis and informally. Where conflicting interests obtain, an unfortunate agent is somehow bound to attempt to act properly in accord with both; where a conflict of interest obtains, he must not undertake the relevant ventures conjointly, he must divest himself of one at least. A conflict of interest obtains simply because of the plural roles individual persons occupy; conflicting interests obtain because of the various implications of any act we may perform. The first imposes an obligation to avoid acting within an avoidable relationship; the second, an obligation to act conformably with a contingently unavoidable relationship.

We have, therefore, made considerable progress in the preliminaries of our analysis of the concept of a conflict of interest. We have, for instance, noted the following:

   (i) *A conflict of interest imposes an obligation of avoidance on an agent, an obligation to avoid certain acts while in certain relationships.*

  (ii) *Pursuing a course that leads to a conflict of interest is not itself a mark of any wrongdoing on an agent's part.*

 (iii) *Relative to a conflict of interest, wrongdoing concerns only an agent's failure, when acting relevantly, to divest himself of a relationship of roles that constitutes the conflict.*

  (iv) *In a conflict of interest, the wrongness or illegality or illegitimacy of an act lies solely in its having been performed while its agent occupied roles bearing a certain relationship to one another.*

The critical consideration is that, where a conflict of interest obtains, neither the general kind of act nor the particular relationship need be wrong or inappropriate: only the particular act performed within that particular relationship—and then, only in that respect. For example, our Congressman may be otherwise quite exemplary in managing the government's interests and those of his own clients. But even if what he does benefits both, resolves an impasse threatening the well-being of an entire community, harms no one else, is originally or eventually disclosed, involves no significant advantage of any sort to himself, he has nevertheless acted wrongly. He has acted wrongly because and only because he has acted within a relationship that relevantly counts as a conflict of interest. He has, that is, acted in pursuit of joint interests so related that he should not have pursued them jointly.

Quite recently, the organization known as Common Cause has determined that special interests—medicine, labor, industry, and the like—have, in 1976, contributed more than two million dollars toward the expenses and personal funds of the members of Congress. Did this constitute a conflict of interest? These groups obviously knew (and were guided by the knowledge) that certain favored members of Congress would be responsible for legislation and inquiries affecting their own interests. They would not otherwise have contributed such sums. Was it a conflict of interest on the part of the members of Congress to accept monies thus? They might otherwise not have been able to fund their own relevant and necessary research. Perhaps it is quite reasonable that the American Medical Association, which provided about half those contributions, should to some extent support just those senators and Congressmen professionally concerned with medical insurance, medical service and practice, pharmaceutical practices, and the like; and perhaps it is equally reasonable that such public officials should count on such support from just those quarters. Perhaps it is also reasonable that Tongsun Park and the Korean government should befriend and benefit those in American government circles who might influence decisions about military aid to Korea and the continued presence of American troops. But the prospect of abuse is obvious.

Bribery is of course *par excellence* the crime of a conflict of interest. But perhaps some at least of the contributions American officials have accepted could be assimilated to the model of the American Medical Association's assistance. Certainly, acting out a conflict of interest is not always bribery or even unearned personal gain. But risks of these sorts are always pertinent—and particularly difficult to detect. So the best argument for laws disallowing conflicts of interest probably lies with the threat of a general disorder that would arise *only* if "everybody did it," that is, only if it were a general practice to act without scruples regarding a conflict of interest. Since no such general practice obtains when a particular act is so judged, the judgment may reasonably be construed solely in terms of fair play; that is, no wrong need result, not even an intention to wrong—only the violation of our sense of "the rules of [fair] play." The intended sense seems to be this: that one should avoid acting within a relationship *prone* to such abuses as bribery or unearned personal gain or favoritism or the like, abuses which are also particularly difficult to detect. One should avoid the abuses, but one should also avoid acting under avoidable circumstances in which such abuses *may* obtain. In this sense, avoiding a conflict of interest is rather like conforming to the rules of etiquette; one should avoid situations that *may* give offense, even if particular acts do not otherwise actually offend. To grasp the tenuousness of the category is to grasp as well the extent to which explicit rules

of conduct governing a conflict of interest arise from the efforts of powerful groups acting to protect their own interests.

These reflections permit us to add to our summary:

> (v) *An act that is wrong because it manifests a conflict of interest may not be wrong
>   in any other respect, for instance motivationally or consequentially.*
>
> (vi) *An act that manifests a conflict of interest is found wrong solely in virtue of being
>   unfair, inappropriate, or inadmissible—relative to more substantive policies re-
>   garding potential harm.*

A conflict of interest normally arises in legal contexts. This is not to
deny that there is a perfectly familiar moral analogue. But the emphasis
in the law (though not in morality) is always on distinctions that can be
effectively enforced with respect to a certain anticipated set of cases.
Hence, the law tends not to take cognizance of would-be conflict-of-
interest cases that are very nearly impossible to monitor. For example,
the "old boy" system in the hiring of university faculty and in university
publishing, which obviously raises the issue, is very often ignored. It is
often ignored in the moral domain as well. Is it a conflict of interest for
a former student and beneficiary of a senior professor, mentioned with
thanks in the preface of that professor's newly published book, to review
the book in a formal way in a professional journal? Is it a conflict of
interest for a journal editor refereeing a submitted manuscript to suggest
improving the paper by the addition of a brief discussion of two or three
relevant authors including himself? Going a little farther afield, is it a
conflict of interest for a theatre critic to party regularly with actors,
playwrights, directors, the public reception of whose current work he will
affect decisively? Is it a conflict of interest to referee a grant application
when the applicant has already innocently suggested that he (the referee,
not yet known as such) may be chosen to play an important part in the
program proposed? Questions of these sorts demonstrate the ubiquity of
our issue. There is no difference in principle between minor and major
cases or between cases that can and cannot be monitored. The issue is
one of fair play and, as such, is more a matter of conscience and intention
than of consequences.

Similar cases, of course, abound in the business world. Is it a conflict
of interest to recommend to one's own company a contract with another
firm in which one holds substantial stock? Is it a conflict of interest to
favor the promotion of one's own son? Is it a conflict of interest to be a
party to a rebate where bidding for a contract is open and competitive?
Is it a conflict of interest to accept gifts from a firm whose contracts one
must periodically renegotiate?

Obviously, there are no easy answers. But the reasons are not entirely
clear. It is not merely a question of enforcement, for the issue arises in
moral as well as in legal terms. We may not be able to determine, say,
whether a Congressman has voted to support a new naval hospital in his

constituency solely in order to improve the prospects of his reelection; but the possibility rankles. On the other hand, who is to say where the line should be drawn between a genuine conflict of interest and the legitimate interests of persons in particular roles? Is it or is it not the proper interest of our Congressman to improve the economic strength of his own area? Perhaps he may be guilty of a fault in judgment: there may actually be no need for the promised hospital. But is he guilty of exploiting a conflict of interest? Is it (or is it not) a conflict of interest to favor hiring persons trained and oriented in a way similar to that of one's own schooling, or is it an honest mark of conviction and assurance about effective work? What we see here is the inherent ambiguity of so much of what may be viewed as a conflict of interest. If it is to be resolved in terms of the agent's personal intentions, then considerations like those of honest (even if simple or misguided or mistaken) conviction or of self-deception are bound to muddy the public handling of the matter in the most unmanageable way.

But to say this much suggests some further qualifications. A conflict of interest *is*, fundamentally, a matter of intention. Intentions, however, are ascribed in a number of different ways; also, to the extent that conflict-of-interest cases are to be monitored in a more-or-less public way—not merely legally but, say, in terms of the traditions and self-imposed codes of particular professions—only certain ways of ascribing intentions are sufficiently realistic. It *is*, after all, very much like a conflict of interest to participate in a vote presupposing relatively objective appraisals and a measure of disinterestedness and (secretly) to cast one's vote on the basis of personal pique. (It may, of course, be more than a conflict of interest.) Suppose, for example, one colleague votes against the tenure of another on the secret grounds that, without tenure, the other will have to leave town and the first will be free to court the woman they are both interested in. Surely, that could be construed as a conflict of interest (as well as a deception or injustice of another sort). But it is hard to see how it can be monitored in a secret vote.

Here, a useful distinction suggests itself. In the vote case, there simply is no conflict of interest that can be anticipated in terms of the actual public roles of the voting colleague. If we hold that his conduct constitutes a conflict of interest—granting how difficult it may be to detect, to monitor, or to correct the wrong—we so judge on the basis of what we take to be his personal intentions. His *role* as a voting colleague requires (so we assume, in accord with the practice of his profession) that he judge the tenure of another solely in terms of whatever is pertinent to that other's professional performance. To decide the matter for the sake of some intended personal advantage may do substantive harm to a person dropped thus from his post; but it also is unfair, at least because it intrudes an interest that *creates* a conflict of interest. On the other hand, in the case of our Congressman, it is *antecedently* recognized that his representing a client in a case against the federal government constitutes a conflict of interest regardless of his personal motives or intentions. We *assign* antecedently a certain "normal" intention on the basis of his occupying the roles of lawyer and Congressman; and his acting *as he does,* within the relationship of those roles, *entails an intention to exploit a conflict of interest.* This permits us to refine our tally a little further:

> (vii) *An agent, functioning in a certain assigned or public role, may create a conflict of interest by intentionally acting in accord with personal interests incompatible with what his role requires.*

> (viii) *Where an agent occupies distinct roles having a publicly, professionally, or traditionally assigned set of interests, what constitutes a conflict of interest is relatively explicit, so that conduct construed as involving a conflict is normally taken to involve as well the agent's intention to exploit that conflict.*

We see, therefore, that, although acting in a way that embodies a conflict of interest is a matter of an agent's intention, it is sometimes and sometimes not a matter of precisely what intentions one personally harbors or could, in all candor, detect in oneself. The first of our two situations (vii) captures the general venality of man. Everyone creates, at least in secret, a conflict of interest on occasion, by favoring—against the putative interests of one's role as citizen, public official, professional, tradesman, worker, officer, parent, and the like—some interest or other of a personally compelling sort. Often, these lapses are seen as negligible. The policeman who permits a friend to park illegally without being ticketed but who tickets a stranger in the same space may be said to have created a conflict of interest—one quite easily detected, in fact, despite its form. But is it really negligible?

It is often the case, where a conflict of interest is actually embodied in a particular act, that some other liability obtains. When circumstances are serious enough, the charge of a mere conflict of interest tends to be displaced. For example, embezzling from one's firm entails a conflict of interest—not a negligible conflict, to be sure, but one in which the gravity of the consequence tends to take precedence over the purely formal matter of having acted unfairly. Still, not all conflict-of-interest cases entail harm or adverse consequences, as we have noted (v). Also, sometimes the agent is at liberty to act on his own discretion regarding a possible conflict of interest, is at liberty in effect to exploit a conflict of interest—but sometimes he is not. For instance, Bert Lance was obliged, when he joined the Carter administration, to divest himself of his banking stock. The seriousness and difficulty of detection of the *possible,* anticipated adverse *consequences* of relevant possible acts were sufficient to require eliminating the original state of conflict: Lance could not reasonably be permitted to manage the budget and related fiscal matters for the federal government while he maintained a formal interest in a private bank. On the other hand, there is no way to require in advance that a bank teller divest himself of his interest to promote his own personal fortune (by legal or illegal means). What we are inclined to say is not that the teller *is* (antecedently) in a conflict-of-interest state—as Lance would have been as private banker and Director of the Office of Management and Budget—but that, merely by pursuing his private interests at the expense of those of his assigned role, he actually creates a conflict of interest (vii). Sometimes, in fact, it is quite impossible to divest oneself of a particular role that, in a given situation, would create a conflict of interest; but then, the other role in the relationship must be avoidable. For example, it would (normally) be (perceived as) a conflict of interest for an Israeli national to serve as the Egyptian Foreign Minister: he could not divest himself of his national origin but, then, he need not serve as Foreign Minister. *If,* under other circumstances, one cannot divest himself of a pair of interests or roles, it is likelier that we are confronted, wherever relevant, with conflicting interests rather than a conflict of interest. The very idea of a conflict of interest entails its avoidability (i). Antigone, as we have seen, could not rightly divest herself of either role —sister of a dead man whose body required suitable burial and subject of a king whose legitimate command she was obliged to obey; but then, as we also saw, she was bound, not to avoid embodying the conflict in her conduct, but, precisely, to do justice to the actual pair of conflicting interests.

The case of the bank teller is additionally instructive. For, we might have said that *every* situation in which one occupies a certain *role*—like the teller's—constitutes a conflict of interest. It does so merely (one might claim) because everyone is capable of promoting, and somewhat disposed to promote, a personal interest at the expense of whatever interests are rightly assigned to the role in question. In this sense, every situation is at risk; every situation constitutes a "standing" conflict of interest, on the assumption that each of us is inclined to favor certain interests overridingly—for instance, the preservation of one's life, the reduction of one's pain, increase in one's security or personal power or effectiveness, gratification of desire and perceived needs. These may all be called prudential interests. They are ubiquitous but not always necessary for a rational life; for example, sacrificing one's life need not be irrational though it is obviously not compatible with a continued interest in preserving one's life. Nevertheless, it is quite reasonable to assume that one's prudential interests normally prevail *and* are normally served by adhering to whatever interests and duties belong to the set of roles one occupies; also, that where these fail to converge, one's prudential interests—perceived from a deeper and personal point of view—threaten to override. This explains both the bank teller case and the case of Bert Lance. The same set of prudential interests informed the dual roles that Lance would have occupied; the specific range of anticipated decisions appropriate to each would inevitably have collided. Good sense, therefore, signifies that the relationship should not have been allowed to obtain. On the other hand, the potential conflict of a *person's* perceived prudential interests and the interests of his assigned *role* is, in principle, everywhere the same: we realize this in placing people in positions of trust. But we are obliged to risk our trust; we could never eliminate all the particular forms that our risk would take—and still continue to function at all. So, in the case of an explicit conflict of interest, we remove temptation and opportunity by eliminating the relationship of the roles at risk. In the case of the universal but only potential conflict of interest (that obtains between the interests a person has in adopting any particular role and the interests that that particular role serves), we cannot stop particular agents from acting in whatever way they will. Only retrospectively, when a particular act has actually been performed, can we determine that an agent has, in acting, created a conflict of interest.

Characteristically, where such cases are actionable (morally as well as legally), there is likely to be a wrongful consequence. Otherwise, we are inclined to view the conflict as negligible, though the division may well reflect the variable convictions of different portions of a society. That is, where we cannot antecedently determine a conflict of interest or of roles, its mere creation *by* acting in a certain way (the bank teller case) tends either to be displaced by attention to its consequence (embezzlement) or to be dismissed as negligible: imagine for example that our teller uses his position to elicit tactfully medical and legal advice from his clients or to recommend a political candidate that he favors or to attempt to find job opportunities for his son. The latter sort of practice will be judged not to be a conflict of interest at all or, if it is, entirely negligible—certainly incapable of being monitored, too widespread and "natural" to be specifically guarded against, and in any case not obviously destructive in intent. We may, then, add the following:

(ix) *Where a community recognizes a substantial conflict of interest arising within a relationship of explicit roles (viii), it is reasonable to forbid the relationship to be occupied.*

(x) *Where a conflict of interest is created by exploiting the interests assigned to a certain role in favor of one's perceived prudential interests, individuals and communities are forced to attend only to the wrongful consequences of the act in question or to the untrustworthiness of the agent involved.*

There are, it may be noted, certain classic moral puzzles that one may be tempted to construe in terms of a conflict of interest. A man who breaks a promise that he has made is judged to have acted wrongly either or both because (contingently) what he does results in some wrong or harm befalling another or because (essentially) he has failed to subordinate his own contingent interests to those he acquired by promising; he may have done no substantive harm, but he has acted unfairly. The puzzle usually raised concerns the reasoning behind the judgment that conduct may be wrong not because of its consequences or even because of an intention to harm but because of a failure to have acted fairly (where so acting is reducible neither to the one nor the other charge). It is similarly suggestive to construe breach of contract, deceit, lying, even failure (within one's power) to aid another in obvious dire need, and similar cases, as species of a conflict of interest. Here, the distinctive consideration concerns the relationship between managing one's own prudential interests and the prudential interests of another person—complicated by contract, promise, putatively implicit relationships like those of sincerity or mutual human concern, or the like.

The trouble is that the notion of a conflict of interest seems insuffi-ciently explicit (and unnecessary) where the breach of a relationship is actually linked to contracts and promises, or too elastic or debatable where it is extended to such substantive matters as truth-telling and aiding others. But it is instructive to consider the extent to which standard problems regarding moral obligations can (or cannot) be plausibly con-strued in terms of our notion. For we cannot fail to see that the morally relevant distinctions already tabulated ([i]–[x]) are quite neutral to what-ever doctrinally divergent views we may hold regarding the morality of conduct. However, as we try to extend the application of our concept to relations between persons as persons (not between persons in relatively formal or traditionally well-formed roles), we see that we cannot avoid substantive quarrels about right and wrong conduct. For instance, to hold that lying to another constitutes a conflict of interest—because, say, per-sons ought to recognize that their relationship as persons entails their occupying the role of truth-tellers vis-à-vis one another (hence, that lying exploits the relationship in favor of one's perceived prudential interests) —to interpret lying thus is simply a very elaborate (and quite artificial) way of claiming that it is wrong to lie. Here, then, it is convenient (and relatively neutral) to characterize such behavior as betraying not a conflict of interest but conflicting interests—about which, of course, relevant moral questions are bound to arise. Whether one *is* justified in lying to another (for instance, to save a life or to promote an important transac-tion) is clearly debatable, but then, there is no antecedently convincing reason why the issue should be resolved at a stroke by merely appealing to some allegedly standard, regularly recognized conflict of interest (or indeed, by appeal to any similarly fixed notion). We see, therefore, that

(xi) *There are no conflicts of interest between persons solely as persons; a conflict of interest is entirely infrapersonal, confined to the relationship between the roles that any particular person occupies; plural persons may exhibit only conflicting inter-ests.*

(xii) *Persons have conflicting interests, taken singly or relationally, when it is either impossible or difficult to avoid acting in ways that cannot jointly satisfy the (putatively legitimate) interests in question.*

The force of this distinction, (xi)–(xii), cannot be stressed enough. A conflict of interest, we have argued, is itself a morally neutral condition. It may be of such a serious sort, however, that a community will act (justifiably, in terms of its own substantive convictions) to forbid in ad-vance anyone's occupying roles the relationship between which consti-tutes such a conflict (ix). This confirms, as already observed, that exploiting a conflict of interest (not the mere existence of the state) is acting wrongfully (iv), (viii). But it also confirms that *what* is wrong about so acting cannot but reflect the ulterior interests of the parties concerned: after all, no other harm or intent to harm need arise (v)–(vi). Conflicting interests, on the other hand, are taken to be provisionally legitimate: in Antigone's case, each imposed high obligations—which suggests the key

to tragedy; otherwise, such interests may be no more than the presumptive (but "natural") prudential concerns of different agents, bound to
collide contingently within the confines of real life. But then, precisely,
the appraisal of what is right or wrong regarding conflicting interests
depends on independently introduced views of what is morally required.
Hence,

>   (xiii) *To specify a conflict of interest is, in effect, to specify explicit conditions for
>   identifying wrongful conduct.*

>   (xiv)   *To specify conflicting interests is, in effect, merely to specify contexts regarding
>   which moral questions pertinently arise.*

Now, *if* conflicting interests could be reinterpreted as entailing a bona
fide conflict of interest, then, by (xiii) (and [i]–[iv]), we could derive
substantive—quite particular—moral judgments (or, by parity of reasoning, legal judgments) regarding the conduct of particular agents. For
example, if, say, certain established banking firms, the principal banks of
New York, found that their interests collided with those of such fledgling
rural banks as Bert Lance's, it might well serve their purpose to try to
construe Lance's unorthodox methods of securing loans (for himself and
his clients) as constituting a conflict of interest. Hence, it might not even
be necessary to expose their conflicting interests in order to gain their
own ends—by apparently legal or moral means. Thus construed, moral
and legal distinctions *of* what it is *to be* a conflict of interest constitute an
instrument for promoting one's own interests in a context of conflicting
interests. It may be that Lance's conduct did constitute a standard conflict-of-interest case; for example, was it a conflict of interest for Lance
to have collected large personal loans from a bank with which his own
bank (the Calhoun First National Bank) had established a correspondent
relationship? Perhaps it was—though nothing actually illegal has been
confirmed. The fact remains that Lance's practice constitutes one strategy by which poorly capitalized but enterprising banks and bankers may
attempt to break into the banking establishment; alternatively, it provides
a new arena for conflicting interests, by inviting the partisan reinterpreta-
tion again and again of the law and the code of correct banking practices.
What must be borne in mind is that, as we have seen, what is wrong in
a conflict of interest is merely to have acted in a way that manifests the
conflict (v)–(vi). There is no way in which to fix the relevant range of cases
except in accord with the convictions and practices of *interested* parties.
   In this sense, the maneuver to construe conflicting interests in terms
of a conflict of interests serves as a paradigm for the general way in which
moral and legal distinctions are defended. They cannot but reflect the
variable doctrines, ideologies, convictions of opposing groups of power
within a society. All of our tabulated findings, (i)–(xiv), are morally neutral precisely because they are entirely formal or entirely concerned with
conceptual distinctions. Only against the backdrop of the detailed life of
a community can particular conflicts of interest (or other morally relevant
constraints) be plausibly specified. But against that very background,

competing and conflicting interests first take form. Hence, however reasonable it may be to claim a conflict of interest, in accord with either (ix) or (x), there remains an ineliminable ideological element reflecting the relative power of conflicting interests within the community. Hence, finally,

> (xv) *To specify, within the law or within a professional code of conduct or within a moral tradition, what is to count as a conflict of interest must reflect in some measure the ideological or doctrinal convictions or conflicting interests within the community affected.*

SUGGESTED SUPPLEMENTARY READINGS

BARTELS, ROBERT, ed. *Ethics in Business.* Bureau of Business Research Monograph No. 111. Columbus: Ohio State University Press, 1963.

BLADES, LAWRENCE E. "Employment at Will vs. Individual Freedom: On Limiting the Abusive Exercise of Employer Power." *Columbia Law Review,* 67 (December 1967).

BLUMBERG, PHILLIP I. "The Politicization of the Corporation." *Business Lawyer,* 26 (1971).

DAVIS, KEITH. "A Law of Diminishing Returns in Organizational Behavior." *Personnel Journal,* 54 (December 1975).

EWING, DAVID W. *Freedom Inside the Organization: Bringing Civil Liberties to the Workplace.* New York: E. P. Dutton, 1977.

"Fiduciary Duty of Officers and Directors Not to Compete with the Corporation." *Harvard Law Review,* 54 (1941).

FRIEDMAN, MILTON. *Capitalism and Freedom.* Chicago: University of Chicago Press, 1962.

GLUCK, SAMUEL E. "Philosophies of Management in Philosophical Perspective." *Annals of the American Academy of Political and Social Science,* September 1962.

HENN, HARRY G. *Corporations* (2nd ed.), "Duties of Management" Section. St. Paul, Minn.: West Publishing Co., 1970.

LEYS, WAYNE A. R. "Ethics and the Rule of Law." *Annals of the American Academy of Political and Social Science,* 343 (1962).

MYERS, CHARLES A. "Management and the Employee." In *Social Responsibility and the Business Predicament,* ed. James McKie. Washington, D.C.: The Brookings Institution, 1974.

NADER, RALPH, PETER J. PETKAS, and KATE BLACKWELL, eds. *Whistle Blowing: The Report of the Conference on Professional Responsibility.* New York: Grossman, 1972.

PETERS, CHARLES, and TAYLOR BRANCH. *Blowing the Whistle: Dissent in the Public Interest.* New York: Praeger, 1972.

POWELL, R. *The Law of Agency.* London: Sir Isaac Pitman and Sons, Ltd., 1965.

Restatement (Second) of Agency, esp. Sections 383 and 385.

WALTERS, KENNETH D. "Your Employee's Right to Blow the Whistle." *Harvard Business Review,* July–August 1975.

WALTON, CLARENCE C., ed. *The Ethics of Corporate Conduct.* Englewood Cliffs, N.J.: Prentice-Hall, 1977.

Chapter **6**

INVESTMENT
AND PRODUCTION

case 1: Eastman Kodak Company, the Church and
FIGHT

On July 23–26, 1964, the prosperous city of Rochester, New York, suffered a serious race riot. Since it was widely believed that such an event could not occur in Rochester, the first reaction of the city was one of shock. Both city officials and corporate executives enumerated the programs and policies which made Rochester such an attractive city—especially for blacks. Officials from the black community and from some of the local churches pointed out the areas—particularly in public housing and in black representation—where they believed Rochester fell seriously short of being an ideal community.

The Board of Urban Ministry of the Rochester Area Council of Churches, in cooperation with the Rochester Ministers' Conference, entered into an agreement with the radical community organizer Saul Alinsky to found an organization which would unify blacks and enable the black community to achieve some of its goals. In April 1965 a group of 134 black organizations combined to form FIGHT (Freedom, Integration, God, Honor, Today).

After a 1966 convention, FIGHT concentrated its activity on the city's largest employer, Eastman Kodak. FIGHT sought to enter into an agreement with Kodak to serve as an exclusive agent for screening unemployed blacks as candidates for jobs at Kodak. Although committed to the training and hiring of unemployed blacks, Kodak refused to enter into a special agreement with FIGHT. Discussions between the two parties, often acrimonious, continued until an Assistant Vice-President, John Mulder, signed an agreement with FIGHT concerning the hiring of unemployed blacks. The December 20, 1966, agreement was repudiated by the Executive Committee on December 21, and by the Board of Directors on December 22. The fact that the "agreement" violated Kodak policy and the fact that Mr. Mulder was not authorized to bind the company were given as reasons.

The repudiation inflamed an already volatile situation, and most observers agreed that Kodak had handled the situation badly. One of FIGHT's tactics was to bring the issue of the broken agreement before the annual meeting of Kodak stockholders. To ensure its own attendance, members of FIGHT bought 10 shares of Eastman Kodak stock. More importantly, FIGHT initiated a national campaign urging Kodak stockholders to withhold the proxies the management traditionally uses in annual meetings as votes for management positions. Although the percentage of proxies withheld was very small in quantitative terms—proxies were withheld on 40,000 shares of stock out of 80.7 million shares outstanding— most of the proxies withheld were in the hands of church groups. Indeed, of the eight organizations withholding proxies, seven were religious organizations.

As justification for its actions, the church groups contended that the very nature of the church requires that it consider the justice of the operating practices of the business firms with which it does business. The church has an obligation not to support those firms whose practices are unjust.

As one would have expected, the dissidents lost badly in the actual voting. Management policies achieved 84 percent of the vote. All Kodak officers were reelected. Eventually, however, in June 1967, Kodak and FIGHT reached an agreement on the hiring of unemployed blacks.

The church's actions were highly controversial. Some disagreed with the general policy position of the National Council of Churches. Others disagreed with the choice of Kodak—admittedly one of the most socially responsible corporations in the country—as a target. Still others questioned the wisdom of supporting FIGHT, whose tactics seemed to escalate conflict and division rather than cooperation and rapprochement.

case 2:   The Artificial Sweeteners Case

The potential for cyclamates as artificial sweeteners was discovered in the 1940's, and by the 1950's they were sold commercially to diabetics and obese persons who needed to limit their intake of sugar. Since cyclamates did not leave a bitter aftertaste as saccharin did, cyclamates became the preferred sweetener. During the 1960's producers of cyclamates promoted their use to a calorie-conscious public and soon cyclamates were used in many kinds of foods. Moreover, since cyclamates were far less expensive than sugar, there was an economic incentive to substitute cyclamates for sugar. Nearly all Americans ate food with cyclamates.

Gradually the safety of cyclamates came under question. The first doubts were raised as early as 1955. By 1962 the National Academy of Sciences-National Research Council (NAS-NRC) recommended that the use of cyclamates be restricted to special dietary foods, and by November 1968 the NAS-NRC indicated that the totally unrestricted use of cyclamates was not warranted. By 1969 there was evidence that feeding cyclamates to rats caused them to develop bladder cancer. Under the terms of the Delaney Clause of the Food Additives Amendment to the Federal Food, Drug, and Cosmetic Act, cyclamates were then banned from general use. The Delaney Clause stipulates "that no additive shall be deemed to be safe if it is found to induce cancer when ingested by man or animal, or if it is found, after tests which are appropriate for the evaluation of the safety of food additives, to induce cancer in man or animal." At first the ban was only partial, but legal proceedings forced a complete ban on August 14, 1970.

After the banning of cyclamates, the only available artificial sweetener was saccharin. However, as the 1970's progressed, similar doubts were raised about its safety. A Canadian study tipped the scales and in the summer of 1977 the FDA announced plans for the banning of saccharin. If the FDA program had gone into effect, almost all dietetic products would have been removed from the market. A public outcry ensued. Some challenged the adequacy of the tests on which the FDA had relied. Others, including many physicians, argued that the risks to health associated with obesity are greater than the risks from contracting cancer. If that were correct, it would be better on cost/benefit grounds to permit products containing artificial sweeteners on the market. As a result of the public outcry, products containing saccharin remain on the market.

INTRODUCTION

This chapter on investment and production marks a kind of division in the text. The first five chapters provided the theoretical framework for discussions of business ethics. The student who has mastered the material in the previous five chapters is conversant with the major traditions in ethical theory and is also familiar with the various theories of corporate responsibility. The arguments for and against the two means for ensuring corporate responsibility—self-regulation and government regulation—

have been set forth. Finally, the theoretical issues underlying one of the most common moral problems in business ethics—situations involving conflicts of interest—have been discussed. Some of these theoretical analyses will now be applied to specific problems within business.

We have selected certain areas of business activity for further discussion. We realize of course that our choice of topics is not exhaustive and that ethical issues arise in many other areas of business activity—in accounting, for example. However, as the student works his or her way through the next four chapters, it will be obvious that the major themes developed in the first five chapters apply to a wide variety of special moral issues that arise in business activities.

ETHICAL ISSUES IN INVESTMENT

One major way corporations raise money for growth is through the issuance of stock. Many Americans personally own shares of stock in American corporations. Many more Americans indirectly own such stock as a result of their participation in pension and insurance plans. American churchgoers and students participate in institutions which have made large investments in the stocks and bonds of American corporations. Usually the underlying philosophy of the investment decisions of both institutions and individuals is to maximize return on the investment dollar. This investment policy is consistent with the traditional view of corporate responsibility outlined in Chapter 3: the social responsibility of the corporation is to maximize the profit of the stockholders (investors). However, just as this view of corporate responsibility has been challenged on moral grounds, so has the view that the investor's only concern in purchasing stock is the likely rate of return. Beginning with the Civil Rights movement of the early Sixties, both individual and institutional investors faced demands that they consider the moral character of the companies in which they invest. Some argued that it is immoral to profit from the successes of companies that engaged in morally suspect behavior. As debate about the moral criteria for investment decisions grew, a series of moral demands on investors was proposed.

The prevailing investment practice was for the individual and institutional investors, who after all *own* the company, to leave the management of the company to professional managers. So long as dividends were good, the investors were not really interested in the company. This separation between the ownership of property and the management of property has already been discussed in Chapter 3, where it was noted that many find a significant difference between the attitude a stockholder takes in the financially successful firm and the attitude a homeowner takes in a home. The difference might best be captured by the moral notion of responsibility. The typical homeowner assumes a responsibility that the typical stockholder does not take in the corporation. It is precisely this disparity between the attitude of the typical homeowner and the typical stock owner, which the reformers are trying to overcome.

It would be a mistake to think that the moral criticism of investment decisions which was so prominent in the late 1960's and early 1970's was directed solely at the choice of companies to invest in. Rather that specific criticism was part of a more general moral criticism aimed at the irresponsible attitudes of investors in general. The stockholders of the Eastman Kodak Company were among the first to be challenged by the reformers. In the Eastman Kodak case, the supporters of FIGHT convinced the churches to take an active interest in the policies of Kodak. Many church groups did not return their proxies (an action that would have implied acquiescence in management policy). Kodak was forced to justify not only its financial management but also the moral character of its policies. That the management succeeded in convincing most stockholders is not nearly as important as the fact that Kodak was obliged to explain and defend its policies to a significant minority of its shareholders.

Stockholder review of management decision is not always readily granted either by management itself or even by the government agency charged with protecting stockholders' interests. In the legal case *Medical Committee for Human Rights* v. *Securities and Exchange Commission,* it was necessary for a group of stockholders to go to court in order to force the Securities and Exchange Commission to reconsider its decision not to intervene in Dow Chemical Company's refusal to place the anti-napalm resolution before the stockholders. The excerpt included in this chapter does not consider one major issue: Does the court have a right to review the SEC on matters of this type? Instead, the excerpt centers on the court's comments about the merits of the Medical Committee for Human Rights proposal. In this case, many moral issues concerning stockholders' rights and duties are raised: e.g., What are the specific rights of stockholders, and thus the obligations of management? What are the criteria for determining the questions a stockholder can bring before a meeting?

Recognition of these new moral demands on investment policy is the focus of the article by Burton Malkiel and Richard Quandt. The authors are concerned with investment policy from the perspective of the portfolio manager. Malkiel and Quandt candidly acknowledge the difficulties that face anyone attempting to base investment decisions on other than strictly economic grounds. Despite the difficulties listed, three criteria are advanced by these authors to aid the portfolio manager in making the moral decisions.

The search for criteria in making investment decisions is taken up by Charles Powers. In discussing investment criteria, Powers considers many of the theoretical issues raised in the first five chapters of this book. In discussing the value of criteria over personal decisions in these matters, Powers pursues many issues previously addressed in our consideration of codes of business ethics. Powers concludes that the benefits on behalf of investment criteria outweigh the costs. He then enumerates different kinds of criteria that deserve analysis. Powers shares with certain philosophers and social theorists the view that just procedures are the essential matter. Since it is extremely difficult to know what counts as a correct moral decision in matters of investment policy, Powers concentrates on developing appropriate procedures for making a decision: With respect to the substance of investment issues, Powers uses the distinction between preventing harm and promoting good which served as the basis for his article in Chapter 3. The obligation of a stockholder to deter a harm-causing corporation is stronger than the obligation to encourage a company to actively promote the general welfare—although latter obligations do exist. Although the bulk of the article is directed toward criteria for shareholder responsibility, Powers concludes with a catalogue of other possible stockholder activities that could be used to effect corporate responsibility.

ETHICAL ISSUES IN PRODUCTION

Revolutions in moral thinking occur when individuals successfully challenge established ways of looking at things. Plato and Aristotle accepted slavery as natural. Until recently stereotyped sex roles concerning homemaking and child care were so established that this allegedly reflected the natural course of events. But now thoughtful men and women agree that slavery is a moral evil and that older ideas of sex roles need not be adopted at all.

In an article at the same level of revolutionary thinking, Peter Singer questions the moral appropriateness of the production and consumption of meat products. Singer's proposal is based on what he takes to be a fundamental ethical principle: Everyone is entitled to the equal consideration of his or her interests. Now certainly one objection to a system of production based on slavery is that the interests of the slaves are ignored. Singer argues that in the production of most meat products the interests of animals are ignored. The crux of Singer's analysis is his contention that there is no criterion which would allow us to take account of the suffering of humans while at the same time ignoring the suffering of animals. With respect to the capacity to suffer, humans and animals are equal in relevant respects.

In the course of his argument, Singer implicitly raises the question, "Are there some goods and services that should not be produced at all?" This question is not new, and it seems to require an affirmative answer for some products and services. For example, it is illegal to produce heroin, and in 49 states it is illegal to provide the services of a prostitute. The fact that there is great consumer demand for these services is morally irrelevant.

Yet, sometimes demand does make a difference. The grand experiment with Prohibition was a disastrous failure. Recently, many states have given in to the great propensity of Americans to gamble and have created state lotteries. Of course, yielding to public clamoring is not always right. Rights theorists continually press this point against (act) utilitarians. Basically, modern society is committed to consumer sovereignty—but not always. Singer's article invites us to consider whether the public demand for meat should be treated more like the demand for heroin or for alcoholic beverages (or neither).

We frequently take contradictory positions on the question of whether certain goods and services should be produced at all. When the product is heroin, we take one position. When the product is an R-rated movie, most of us take another position. In a brief selection from *Capitalism and Freedom,* Milton Friedman provides an argument for allowing the broadest range of tastes to be satisfied. Although many readers will not go as far as Friedman on this point, he or she will need to consider what criteria might be invoked in deciding what products and services should not be offered at all.

Suppose one resolves or ignores the question concerning which goods ought to be produced. One would still face another ethical issue: What are the responsibilities of business persons to ensure the safety and overall quality of what they produce? Manufacturers have an obligation to make their products safe, but how safe? At first one might argue for something approaching an absolute standard of safety. An example of such an absolute standard is represented by the selection from the 1958 "Food Additives Amendment" to the Federal Food, Drug, and Cosmetic Act. This selection contains the so-called Delaney Clause, which prohibits the manufacture of any substance that has a disposition to cause cancer in laboratory animals. But as our case on the artificial sweeteners shows, such a standard might be too strict. There are tradeoffs between the harms to those who might contract cancer and the harms to diabetics and obese persons which would result from a total ban on artificial sweeteners. Strict adherence to the Delaney Clause would ignore the claims of the overweight.

The contention that no product can be absolutely safe is accepted by William Lowrance. He argues that a product is safe if its risks are judged acceptable. Such judgments are in part judgments of value. In making these judgments, one must consider a number of factors. One of the most complicated factors is the probability questions in measuring risk. Making probability judgments raises complicated questions in logic and epistemology (the theory of knowledge). Consider the artificial sweeteners case. Were the doses for the rats too large? Were there sufficient tests? How are inconsistencies among the tests to be resolved? Can we generalize from rats to persons? Lowrance introduces a test of reasonableness that plays such an important role in some philosophical and legal discussions. But what is "reasonableness"? Can we measure it, even if we can define it? Should everyone be held to the same standard of reasonableness?

In any decision concerning product safety, someone must be held responsible. But who? Lowrance asks, "Should technically trained people be expected to bear any social responsibilities different from those borne by others?" Lowrance identifies five kinds of risks which ought, as he says, be taken upon the conscience of the technical community. In the legal case *Henningsen* v. *Bloomfield Motors, Inc.* a central issue focuses on what should be the responsibility of the original manufacturer for quality control as opposed to the responsibility of intermediaries. Moreover, are these responsibilities for the original manufacturer or the intermediary or both independent of warranty provisions and disclaimers? The decision in this case goes far in extending the responsibilities of the manufacturer and of limiting the liabilities to the consumer. It is interesting to note that a major portion of the rationale for this decision rests on an analysis of the function of business activity and of the various roles that manufacturers and consumers play within it.

N.E.B.

OPINION IN MEDICAL COMMITTEE FOR HUMAN RIGHTS v. SECURITIES AND EXCHANGE COMMISSION

Judge Edward A. Tamm

PROCEDURAL HISTORY OF THE CASE

On March 11, 1968, Dr. Quentin D. Young, National Chairman of the Medical Committee for Human Rights, wrote to the Secretary of the Dow Chemical Company, stating that the Medical Committee had obtained by gift several shares of Dow stock and expressing concern regarding the company's manufacture of the chemical substance napalm. In part, Dr. Young's letter said:

> After consultation with the executive body of the Medical Committee, I have been instructed to request an amendment to the charter of our company, Dow Chemical. We have learned that we are technically late in asking for an amendment at this date, but we wish to observe that it is a matter of such great urgency that we think it is imperative not to delay until the shareholders' meeting next year....
>
> We respectfully propose the following wording to be sent to the shareholders:
>
> "RESOLVED, that the shareholders of the Dow Chemical Company request the Board of Directors, in accordance with the laws of the State of Delaware, and the Composite Certificate of Incorporation of the Dow Chemical Company, to adopt a resolution setting forth an amendment to the Composite Certificate of Incorporation of the Dow Chemical Company that napalm shall not be sold to any buyer unless that buyer gives reasonable assurance that the substance will not be used on or against human beings."

Federal Reporter 432 F. 2nd 259 (1970), pp. 659–663, 676–682.

The letter concluded with the following statement:

> Finally, we wish to note that our objections to the sale of this product [are] primarily based on the concerns for human life inherent in our organization's credo. However, we are further informed by our investment advisers that this product is also bad for our company's business as it is being used in the Vietnamese War. It is now clear from company statements and press reports that it is increasingly hard to recruit the highly intelligent, well-motivated, young college men so important for company growth. There is, as well, an adverse impact on our global business, which, our advisers indicate, suffers as a result of the public reaction to this product.

Copies of this letter were forwarded to the President and the General Counsel of Dow Chemical Company, and to the Securities and Exchange Commission.

By letter dated March 21, 1968, the General Counsel of Dow Chemical replied to the Medical Committee's letter, stating that the proposal had arrived too late for inclusion in the 1968 proxy statement, but promising that the company would "study the matter and . . . communicate with you later this year" regarding inclusion of the resolution in proxy materials circulated by management in 1969. Copies of this letter, and of all subsequent correspondence, were duly filed with the Commission.

The next significant item of record is a letter dated January 6, 1969, noting that the Medical Committee was "distressed that 1968 has passed without our having received a single word from you on this important matter," and again requesting that the resolution be included in management's 1969 proxy materials. The Secretary of Dow Chemical replied to this letter on January 17, informing the Medical Committee that Dow intended to omit the resolution from its proxy statement and enclosing an opinion memorandum from Dow's General Counsel, the contents of which will be discussed in detail in part III, *infra.* On February 3 the Medical Committee responded to Dow's General Counsel, asserting that he had misconstrued the nature of their proposal in his opinion memorandum, and averring that the Medical Committee would not "presume to serve as draftsmen for an amendment to the corporate charter." The letter continued:

> We are willing to bend . . . to your belief that the management should be allowed to decide to whom and under what circumstances it will sell its products. Nevertheless, we are certain that you would agree that the company's owners have not only the legal power but also the historic and economic obligation to determine what products their company will manufacture. Therefore, [we submit] . . . our revised proposal . . . requesting the Directors to consider the advisability of adopting an amendment to the corporate charter, forbidding the company to make napalm (any such amendment would, of course, be subject to the requirements of the "Defense Production Act of 1950," as are the corporate charters and management decisions of all United States Corporations), [and] we request that the following resolution be included in this year's proxy statement:
>
> > "RESOLVED, that the shareholders of the Dow Chemical Company request that the Board of Directors, in accordance with the laws [*sic*] of the Dow Chemical Company, consider the advisability of adopting a

resolution setting forth an amendment to the composite certificate of incorporation of the Dow Chemical Company that the company shall not make napalm."

On the same date, a letter was sent to the Securities and Exchange Commission, requesting a staff review of Dow's decision if it still intended to omit the proposal, and requesting oral argument before the Commission if the staff agreed with Dow.

On February 7, 1969, Dow transmitted to the Medical Committee and to the Commission a letter and memorandum opinion of counsel, which in essence reiterated the previous arguments against inclusion of the proposal and stated the company's intention to omit it from the proxy statement. Shortly thereafter, on February 18, 1969, the Commission's Chief Counsel of the Division of Corporation Finance sent a letter to Dow, with copies to the Medical Committee, concluding that "[f]or reasons stated in your letter and the accompanying opinion of counsel, both dated January 17, 1969, this Division will not recommend any action . . . if this proposal is omitted from the management's proxy material. . . ." In a letter dated February 28—which contains the first indications of record that petitioners had retained counsel—the Medical Committee again renewed its request for a Commission review of the Division's decision. On the same day, the Medical Committee filed with the Commission a memorandum of legal arguments in support of its resolution, urging numerous errors of law in the Division's decision. Several other documents were filed by both the company and the Medical Committee; finally, on April 2, 1969, both parties were informed that "[t]he Commission has approved the recommendation of the Division of Corporation Finance that no objection be raised if the Company omits the proposals from its proxy statements for the forthcoming meeting of shareholders." The petitioners thereupon instituted the present action, and on July 10, 1969, the Commission moved to dismiss the petition for lack of jurisdiction. On October 13 we denied the motion "without prejudice to renewal thereof in the briefs and at the argument on the merits."

In its briefs and oral argument, the Commission has consistently and vigorously urged, to the exclusion of all other contentions, that this court is without jurisdiction to review its action. We find this argument unpersuasive. . . .

THE MERITS OF PETITIONER'S PROPOSAL

The Medical Committee's sole substantive contention in this petition is that its proposed resolution could not, consistently with the Congressional intent underlying section 14(a), be properly deemed a proposal which is either motivated by *general* political and moral concerns, or related to the conduct of Dow's ordinary business operations. These criteria are two of the established exceptions to the general rule that management must include all properly submitted shareholder proposals in its proxy materials. They are contained in Rule 14a–8(c), 17 C.F.R. § 240.14a–8(c) (1970), which provides in relevant part:

... [M]anagement may omit a proposal ... from its proxy statement and form of proxy under any of the following circumstances: ...

(2) If it clearly appears that the proposal is submitted by the security holder ... primarily for the purpose of promoting general economic, political, racial, religious, social or similar causes; or ...

(5) If the proposal consists of a recommendation or request that the management take action with respect to a matter relating to the conduct of the ordinary business operations of the issuer.

Despite the fact that our October 13 order in this case deferred resolution of the jurisdictional issue pending full argument on the merits (*see* part I, *supra*), the Commission has not deigned to address itself to any possible grounds for allowing management to exclude this proposal from its proxy statement. We confess to a similar puzzlement as to how the Commission reached the result which it did, and thus we are forced to remand the controversy for a more illuminating consideration and decision. Cf. *Environmental Defense Fund, Inc.* v. *Hardin, supra.* In aid of this consideration on remand, we feel constrained to explain our difficulties with the position taken by the company and endorsed by the Commission. ...

In contending that the Medical Committee's proposal was properly excludable under Rule 14a–8(c)(5), Dow's counsel asserted:

It is my opinion that *the determination of the products which the company shall manufacture,* the customers to which it shall sell the products, and the conditions under which it shall make such sales are related to the conduct of the ordinary business operations of the Company and that any attempt to amend the Certificate of Incorporation to define the circumstances under which the management of the Company shall make such determinations is contrary to the concept of corporate management, which is inherent in the Delaware General Corporation Act under which the Company is organized.

In the first place, it seems extremely dubious that this superficial analysis complies with the Commission's longstanding requirements that management must sustain the burden of proof when asserting that a shareholder proposal may properly be omitted from the proxy statement, and that "[w]here management contends that a proposal may be omitted because it is not proper under State law, it will be incumbent upon management to refer to the applicable statute or case law." 19 Fed.Reg. 246 (1954). As noted above, the Commission has formally represented to Congress that Rule 14a–8(c) (5) is intended to make state law the governing authority in determining what matters are ordinary business operations immune from shareholder control; yet, the Delaware General Corporation law provides that a company's Certificate of Incorporation may be amended to "change, substitute, enlarge or diminish the nature of [the company's] business." If there are valid reasons why the Medical Committee's proposal does not fit within the language and spirit of this provision, they certainly do not appear in the record.

The possibility that the Medical Committee's proposal could properly be omitted under Rule 14a–8(c) (2) appears somewhat more substantial in the circumstances of the instant case, although once again it may fairly be asked how Dow Chemical's arguments on this point could be deemed a rational basis for such a result: the paragraph in the company's memorandum of counsel purporting to deal with this issue[1] . . . consists entirely of a fundamentally irrelevant recitation of some of the political protests which had been directed at the company because of its manufacture of napalm, followed by the abrupt conclusion that management is therefore entitled to exclude the Medical Committee's proposal from its proxy statement. Our own examination of the issue raises substantial questions as to whether an interpretation of Rule 14a–8(c) (2) which permitted omission of this proposal as one motivated primarily by *general* political or social concerns would conflict with the congressional intent underlying section 14(a) of the Act.

As our earlier discussion indicates, the clear import of the language, legislative history, and record of administration of section 14(a) is that its overriding purpose is to assure to corporate shareholders the ability to exercise their right—some would say their duty[2]—to control the important decisions which affect them in their capacity as stockholders and owners of the corporation. Thus, the Third Circuit has cogently summarized the philosophy of section 14(a) in the statement that "[a] corporation is run for the benefit of its stockholders and not for that of its managers." *SEC* v. *Transamerica Corp.,* 163 F.2d 511, 517 (3d Cir. 1947), cert. denied, 332 U.S. 847, 68 S.Ct. 351, 92 L.Ed. 418 (1948). Here, in contrast to the situations detailed above which led to the promulgation of Rule 14a–8(c) (2), the proposal relates solely to a matter that is completely within the accepted sphere of corporate activity and control. No reason has been advanced in the present proceedings which leads to the conclusion that management may properly place obstacles in the path of shareholders who wish to present to their co-owners, in accord with applicable state law, the question of whether they wish to have their assets used in a manner which they believe to be more socially responsible but possibly less profitable than that which is dictated by present company policy. Thus, even accepting Dow's characterization of the purpose and intent of the Medical Committee's proposal, there is a strong argument that permitting the company to exclude it would contravene the purpose of section 14(a).

However, the record in this case contains indications that we are confronted with quite a different situation. The management of Dow Chemical Company is repeatedly quoted in sources which include the company's own publications as proclaiming that the decision to continue manufacturing and marketing napalm was made not *because* of business considerations, but *in spite of* them; that management in essence decided to pursue a course of activity which generated little profit for the shareholders and actively impaired the company's public relations and recruitment activities because management considered this action morally and politically desirable. (App. 40a–43a; *see also id.* at 33.) The proper political and social role of modern corporations is, of course, a matter of philosophical argument extending far beyond the scope of our present concern; the substantive wisdom or propriety of particular corporate political decisions is also completely irrelevant to the resolution of the present controversy. What *is* of immediate concern, however, is the question of whether the corporate proxy rules can be employed as a shield to isolate such managerial decisions from shareholder control. After all, it must be remembered that "[t]he control of great corporations by a very few persons was the abuse at which Congress struck in enacting Section 14(a)." *SEC* v. *Transamerica Corp., supra,* 163 F.2d at 518. We think that there is a clear and compelling distinction between management's legitimate need for freedom to apply its expertise in matters of day-to-day business judgment, and management's patently illegitimate claim of power to treat modern corporations with their vast resources as personal satrapies implementing personal, political or moral predilections. It could scarcely be argued that management is more qualified or more entitled to make these kinds of decisions than the shareholders who are the true beneficial owners of the corporation; and it seems equally implausible that an application of the proxy rules which permitted such a result could be harmonized with the philosophy of corporate democracy which Congress embodied in section 14(a) of the Securities Exchange Act of 1934.

In light of these considerations, therefore, the cause must be remanded to the Commission so that it may reconsider petitioner's claim within the proper limits of its discretionary authority as set forth above, and so that "the basis for [its] decision [may] appear clearly on the record, not in conclusory terms but in sufficient detail to permit prompt and effective review."

Remanded for further proceedings consistent with this opinion.

Notes

1. App. 10a: It is a well-known fact that the Company has been the target of protests and demonstrations for the past few years at its office and plant locations, and on the occasion of recruiting on college and university campuses, as well as at its annual meeting of stockholders held May 8, 1968. The various protests and demonstrations are a reflection of opposition on the part of certain segments of the population against the policy of the United States Government in waging the war in Viet Nam. Although The Dow Chemical Company was not among the 100 largest prime contractors with the Department of Defense during the 1967–68 Government fiscal year and was only 75th on the list in the 1966–67 fiscal year, it appears to have been singled out symbolically by the protesters. Under all of these circumstances it is my opinion that it clearly appears that the proposal is primarily for the purpose of promoting a general political, social or similar cause.

2. *See* Bayne, The Basic Rationale of Proper Subject, 34 U.Det.L.J. 575, 579 (1957):
   In so far as the shareholder has contributed an asset of value to the corporate venture, in so far as he has handed over his goods and property and money for use and increase, he has not only the clear right, but more to the point,

perhaps, he has the stringent duty to exercise control over that asset for which he must keep care, guard, guide, and in general be held seriously responsible. . . .

As much as one may surrender the immediate disposition of [his] goods, he can never shirk a supervisory and secondary duty (not just a right) to make sure these goods are used justly, morally and beneficially.

OPINION IN HENNINGSEN v. BLOOMFIELD MOTORS, INC.

Justice John J. Francis

Plaintiff Claus H. Henningsen purchased a Plymouth automobile, manufactured by defendant Chrysler Corporation, from defendant Bloomfield Motors, Inc. His wife, plaintiff Helen Henningsen, was injured while driving it and instituted suit against both defendants to recover damages on account of her injuries. Her husband joined in the action seeking compensation for his consequential losses. The complaint was predicated upon breach of express and implied warranties and upon negligence. At the trial the negligence counts were dismissed by the court and the cause was submitted to the jury for determination solely on the issues of implied warranty of merchantability. Verdicts were returned against both defendants and in favor of the plaintiffs. Defendants appealed and plaintiffs cross-appealed from the dismissal of their negligence claim. The matter was certified by this court prior to consideration in the Appellate Division. . . .

The new Plymouth was turned over to the Henningsens on May 9, 1955. No proof was adduced by the dealer to show precisely what was done in the way of mechanical or road testing beyond testimony that the manufacturer's instructions were probably followed. Mr. Henningsen drove it from the dealer's place of business in Bloomfield to their home in Keansburg. On the trip nothing unusual appeared in the way in which it operated. Thereafter, it was used for short trips on paved streets about the town. It had no servicing and no mishaps of any kind before the event of May 19. That day, Mrs. Henningsen drove to Asbury Park. On the way down and in returning the car performed in normal fashion until the accident occurred. She was proceeding north on Route 36 in Highlands, New Jersey, at 20–22 miles per hour. The highway was paved and smooth,

Atlantic Reporter 161 A2d 69, pp. 73, 75, 80–81, 83–87, 96.

and contained two lanes for northbound travel. She was riding in the right-hand lane. Suddenly she heard a loud noise "from the bottom, by the hood." It "felt as if something cracked." The steering wheel spun in her hands; the car veered sharply to the right and crashed into a highway sign and a brick wall. No other vehicle was in any way involved. A bus operator driving in the left-hand lane testified that he observed plaintiffs' car approaching in normal fashion in the opposite direction; "all of a sudden [it] veered at 90 degrees . . . and right into this wall." As a result of the impact, the front of the car was so badly damaged that it was impossible to determine if any of the parts of the steering wheel mechanism or workmanship or assembly were defective or improper prior to the accident. The condition was such that the collision insurance carrier, after inspection, declared the vehicle a total loss. It had 468 miles on the speedometer at the time. . . .

Chrysler points out that an implied warranty of merchantability is an incident of a contract of sale. It concedes, of course, the making of the original sale to Bloomfield Motors, Inc., but maintains that this transaction marked the terminal point of its contractual connection with the car. Then Chrysler urges that since it was not a party to the sale by the dealer to Henningsen, there is no privity of contract between it and the plaintiffs, and the absence of this privity eliminates any such implied warranty.

There is no doubt that under early common-law concepts of contractual liability only those persons who were parties to the bargain could sue for a breach of it. In more recent times a noticeable disposition has appeared in a number of jurisdictions to break through the narrow barrier of privity when dealing with sales of goods in order to give realistic recognition to a universally accepted fact. The fact is that the dealer and the ordinary buyer do not, and are not expected to, buy goods, whether they be foodstuffs or automobiles, exclusively for their own consumption or use. Makers and manufacturers know this and advertise and market their products on that assumption; witness, the "family" car, the baby foods, etc. The limitations of privity in contracts for the sale of goods developed their place in the law when marketing conditions were simple, when maker and buyer frequently met face to face on an equal bargaining plane and when many of the products were relatively uncomplicated and conducive to inspection by a buyer competent to evaluate their quality. See, Freezer, "Manufacturer's Liability for Injuries Caused by His Products," 37 *Mich.L.Rev.* 1 (1938). With the advent of mass marketing, the manufacturer became remote from the purchaser, sales were accomplished through intermediaries, and the demand for the product was created by advertising media. In such an economy it became obvious that the consumer was the person being cultivated. Manifestly, the connotation of "consumer" was broader than that of "buyer." He signified such a person who, in the reasonable contemplation of the parties to the sale, might be expected to use the product. Thus, where the commodities sold are such that if defectively manufactured they will be dangerous to life or limb, then society's interests can only be protected by eliminating the requirement of privity between the maker and his dealers and the reasonably expected ultimate consumer. In that way the burden of losses consequent upon use of defective articles is borne by those who are in a position to either control the danger or make an equitable distribution of the losses when they do occur. . . .

Under modern conditions the ordinary layman, on responding to the importuning of colorful advertising, has neither the opportunity nor the capacity to inspect or to determine the fitness of an automobile for use; he must rely on the manufacturer who has control of its construction, and to some degree on the dealer who, to the limited extent called for by the manufacturer's instructions, inspects and services it before delivery. In such a marketing milieu his remedies and those of persons who properly claim through him should not depend "upon the intricacies of the law of sales. The obligation of the manufacturer should not be based alone on privity of contract. It should rest, as was once said, upon 'the demands of social justice.' " *Mazetti* v. *Armour & Co.,* 75 Wash. 622, 135 P. 633, 635, 48 L.R.A.,N.S., 213 (Sup.Ct.1913). "If privity of contract is required," then, under the circumstances of modern merchandising, "privity of contract exists in the consciousness and understanding of all right-thinking persons." *Madouros* v. *Kansas City Coca-Cola Bottling Co., supra,* 90 S.W.2d at page 450.

Accordingly, we hold that under modern marketing conditions, when a manufacturer puts a new automobile in the stream of trade and promotes its purchase by the public, an implied warranty that it is reasonably suitable for use as such accompanies it into the hands of the ultimate purchaser. Absence of agency between the manufacturer and the dealer who makes the ultimate sale is immaterial. . . .

What influence should these circumstances have on the restrictive effect of Chrysler's express warranty in the framework of the purchase contract? As we have said, warranties originated in the law to safeguard the buyer and not to limit the liability of the seller or manufacturer. It seems obvious in this instance that the motive was to avoid the warranty obligations which are normally incidental to such sales. The language gave little and withdrew much. In return for the delusive remedy of replacement of defective parts at the factory, the buyer is said to have accepted the exclusion of the maker's liability for personal injuries arising from the breach of the warranty, and to have agreed to the elimination of any other express or implied warranty. An instinctively felt sense of justice cries out against such a sharp bargain. But does the doctrine that a person is bound by his signed agreement, in the absence of fraud, stand in the way of any relief? . . .

The traditional contract is the result of free bargaining of parties who are brought together by the play of the market, and who meet each other on a footing of approximate economic equality. In such a society there is no danger that freedom of contract will be a threat to the social order as a whole. But in present-day commercial life the standardized mass contract has appeared. It is used primarily by enterprises with strong bargaining power and position. "The weaker party, in need of the goods or services, is frequently not in a position to shop around for better terms, either because the author of the standard contract has a monopoly (natural or artificial) or because all competitors use the same clauses. His contractual intention is but a subjection more or less voluntary to terms dictated by the stronger party, terms whose consequences are often understood in a vague way, if at all." Kessler, "Contracts of Adhesion— Some Thoughts About Freedom of Contract," 43 *Colum.L.Rev.* 629, 632 (1943); Ehrenzweig, "Adhesion Contracts in the Conflict of Laws," 53 *Colum.L.Rev.* 1072, 1075, 1089 (1953). Such standardized contracts have been described as those in which one predominant party will dictate its law to an undetermined multiple rather than to an individual. They are said to resemble a law rather than a meeting of the minds. *Siegelman* v. *Cunard White Star,* 221 F.2d 189, 206 (2 Cir. 1955).

Vold, in the recent revision of his Law of Sales (2d ed. 1959) at page 447, wrote of this type of contract and its effect upon the ordinary buyer:

> In recent times the marketing process has been getting more highly organized than ever before. Business units have been expanding on a scale never before known. The standardized contract with its broad disclaimer clauses is drawn by legal advisers of sellers widely organized in trade associations. It is encountered on every hand. Extreme inequality of bargaining between buyer and seller in this respect is now often conspicuous. Many buyers no longer have any real choice in the matter. They must often accept what they can get though accompanied by broad disclaimers. The terms of these disclaimers deprive them of all substantial protection with regard to the quality of the goods. In effect, this is by force of contract between very unequal parties. It throws the risk of defective articles on the most dependent party. He has the least individual power to avoid the presence of defects. He also has the least individual ability to bear their disastrous consequences.

The warranty before us is a standardized form designed for mass use. It is imposed upon the automobile consumer. He takes it or leaves it, and he must take it to buy an automobile. No bargaining is engaged in with respect to it. In fact, the dealer through whom it comes to the buyer is without authority to alter it; his function is ministerial—simply to deliver it. The form warranty is not only standard with Chrysler but, as mentioned above, it is the uniform warranty of the Automobile Manufacturers Association. Members of the Association are: General Motors, Inc., Ford, Chrysler, Studebaker-Packard, American Motors, (Rambler), Willys Motors, Checker Motors Corp., and International Harvester Company. Automobile Facts and Figures (1958 Ed., Automobile Manufacturers Association) 69. Of these companies, the "Big Three" (General Motors, Ford, and Chrysler) represented 93.5% of the passenger-car production for 1958 and the independents 6.5%. Standard & Poor (Industrial Surveys, Autos, Basic Analysis, June 25, 1959) 4109. And for the same year the "Big Three" had 86.72% of the total passenger vehicle registrations. *Automotive News,* 1959 Almanac (Slocum Publishing Co., Inc.) p. 25.

The gross inequality of bargaining position occupied by the consumer in the automobile industry is thus apparent. There is no competition among the car makers in the area of the express warranty. Where can the buyer go to negotiate for better protection? Such control and limitation of his remedies are inimical to the public welfare and, at the very least, call for great care by the courts to avoid injustice through application of strict common-law principles of freedom of contract. Because there is no competition among the motor vehicle manufacturers with respect to the scope of protection guaranteed to the buyer, there is no incentive on their part to stimulate good will in that field of public relations. Thus, there is lacking a factor existing in more competitive fields, one which tends to guarantee the safe construction of the article sold. Since all competitors operate in the same way, the urge to be careful is not so pressing. See "Warranties of Kind and Quality," 57 *Yale.L.J.* 1389, 1400 (1948). . . .

The Dealer's Implied Warranty

The principles that have been expounded as to the obligation of the manufacturer apply with equal force to the separate express warranty of the dealer. This is so, irrespective of the absence of the relationship of principal and agent between these defendants, because the manufacturer and the Association establish the warranty policy for the industry. The bargaining position of the dealer is inextricably bound by practice to that of the maker and the purchaser must take or leave the automobile, accompanied and encumbered as it is by the uniform warranty.

MORAL ISSUES IN INVESTMENT POLICY

Burton G. Malkiel
Richard E. Quandt

In recent years, the portfolio managers for pension funds, for a wide variety of financial institutions, and for universities, churches, and various charitable organizations have been faced with a serious challenge to their traditional goals. Formerly, the objective of most portfolio managers was a relatively simple one: the maximization of investment returns subject to a constraint derived from the necessity to assume no more risk than was appropriate for the circumstances.

While thorny questions arose about the degree of risk appropriate to particular circumstances, at least the basic framework for the investment decision was clear. Portfolio managers would attempt to select the securi-

Burton G. Malkiel and Richard E. Quandt, "Moral Issues in Investment Policy," *Harvard Business Review,* March–April 1971. Copyright © 1971 by the President and Fellows of Harvard College; all rights reserved.

ties best suited to their needs. If the managers of companies held in the portfolio subsequently adopted policies considered undesirable by the investment manager, the security would be sold. The thought of attempting to influence a company through proxy fights or otherwise indicating one's disagreements with management was not even contemplated.

More recently, basic changes occurring both in the political climate of the country and in the investment business itself have forced many portfolio managers to retreat from such a "business as usual" attitude. The illiquidity of the market does not permit institutions (especially very large ones) to dispose of large blocks of stock easily. Such difficulties have suggested to some portfolio managers that they are in effect forced to play a larger role in corporate management decisions. Moreover, in recent years portfolio managers (especially those of nonprofit private institutions) have been asked to deploy their funds with specific reference to social, political, and moral objectives.

These requests have been made by various concerned individuals and groups, and they cover several aspects of the management of a portfolio. They include such questions as these:

• Are there companies whose securities should not be held in the portfolio for social, political, or moral reasons?
• Should the portfolio manager be guided by such considerations in voting his institution's stock?
• Should an investing institution employ any of its resources in a positive manner for the sake of social, political, or moral objectives?

If it is true, as is likely, that questions such as these will continue to be posed in concrete contexts, it is highly desirable that portfolio managers develop general principles governing the use (if any) of social, political, and moral criteria for making investment decisions and for voting their shares.

In this article, we shall first outline briefly the history of the pressures that have been brought to bear on portfolio managers with respect to the fulfillment of their social responsibility. Then we shall examine in detail the arguments for and against the use of noneconomic criteria in investment policy. Finally, we shall attempt to set down some general principles, as well as some operational details, of how the portfolio manager may respond to requests that his institution pursue social, political, or moral goals through its investments.

We should state at the outset that, although there exist some powerful reasons for arguing against institutional investors assuming responsibility for the welfare of society, forces have been gathering which may well necessitate such concerns, whether or not the portfolio manager feels these matters should affect his behavior. . . .

"CAMPAIGN GM"

The issue that has attracted the most attention thus far has been the campaign waged by a group of young lawyers (with the blessing and support of Ralph Nader) against General Motors. The "Campaign GM" group won the right to submit these two proposals for consideration by the General Motors shareholders:

1. To establish a General Motors Shareholders Committee for Corporate Responsibility; the membership to be selected by a three-man body with one representing GM, another the United Auto Workers, and the third the Campaign GM group. (The committee would be charged with preparing a report and making recommendations to the shareholders with respect to the role of the corporation in modern society with particular reference to vehicle safety, pollution, the corporation's contributions to sound national transportation policy, and so forth.)

2. To increase the number of directors by three; the additional board members to be representatives of the public.

In an attempt to enlist support, Campaign GM mailed its position papers to approximately 2,000 financial institutions and other fund managers, and called on a number of these institutions in person. General Motors responded as if its very existence had been threatened. GM prepared a 21-page pamphlet, indicating the company's efforts in combating auto pollution, which the company mailed to its 1.5 million shareholders. Moreover, GM lobbied diligently in urging the major institutional holders of its stock to uphold management.

The denouement came at the 1970 annual meeting in Detroit. GM prided itself on the fact that the proposals were soundly defeated. Neither of the Campaign GM proposals received as much as 3% of the votes cast. But the victory was a Pyrrhic one for General Motors. Several substantial institutional investors voted with the Campaign GM group, including the influential Oppenheimer Investment Fund. Moreover, many institutions which supported management on the proxy issue were sharply critical of the company's efforts in the antipollution field and offered pointed criticisms in letters accompanying their votes.

For example, the Rockefeller Foundation, while admitting that Campaign GM's proposals were "unwieldy and impractical" from a management point of view, went on to criticize GM for not embracing the goals of the proposals, which "are clearly pointed in the direction General Motors and every American corporation must move if they are to function effectively and responsibly in the difficult years ahead."[1]

It is already clear that General Motors' top management thinking has been considerably changed by these developments. Indeed, GM has already formed a "public policy committee" made up of five of its directors to "inquire into all phases of General Motors' operations that relate to matters of public policy and recommend actions to the full board."[2]

Other Developments

In addition to such campaigns to influence the policies of corporations through the proxy route, there have been several attempts to redirect institutional investments away from companies that pursue what are believed to be morally opprobrious policies and into the securities of companies which may be considered to be fostering moral and social goals.

Several universities and church groups have been petitioned to sell the shares that they own of armaments producers.

For example, Cornell and Princeton universities were asked to sell the shares they held in those corporations that "participate in the South African, Rhodesian, Angolan and Mozambique economies" because such companies were considered to be supporting racist and repressive governments.[3]

Other proposals have concerned the positive use of investment funds. The National Council of Churches has been at work on preparing a plan for the redirection of investments into more socially beneficial areas.[4] Yale University has also been studying plans for the modification of its investment policies to include social and moral considerations in channeling investment funds.

There are also numerous instances where financial institutions have made loans at below market rates of interest in certain projects considered to be socially desirable. Princeton University recently awarded a construction contract to a firm that was not the lowest bidder for the project, at least in part because of that firm's assurance that it would provide significant employment to minority group workers. In a survey of the practices of nearly 100 institutions, Peter Landau finds that "there are inescapable signs that [social and moral] concerns may sooner or later become inevitable [in investment policy]."[5] . . .

Responsibility Implications

Corporations and universities function within society, require its sanction for their continued existence, and generally benefit from the "social contract." They therefore owe society something in return, which implies that corporations and universities must become involved in the affairs of the society and be willing to undertake actions by which these organizations' responsibility to society can be discharged. Such a position has different implications for different types of organizations. Consider:

• For General Motors, the prescription of responsibility has been considered to include increasing auto safety, reducing automobile-caused pollution, providing equal opportunities for minority groups among franchised new dealers, reducing the consumer's expected cost of repairs, and so forth.[6]
• For a pension fund or a university, the prescription of responsibility has usually consisted of a plea for using the institution's portfolio in a socially constructive manner.

Thus, it is argued, if a corporation behaves in an antisocial manner, institutions holding the stock of that company have the obligation to bring pressure to bear on it by either voting proxies against management or making direct representations to management, or by actually selling the stock.

Most of the objections to the active use of an institution's portfolio for social, moral, or political purposes are discussed in the next section of this article. Nevertheless, there is one objection that has been answered by the proponents of institutional responsibility so frequently that the answers have seemingly become part of the original justification for active social involvement by companies and their portfolio managers. This objection to social involvement consists of the view that (a) corporations are innocent of all wrongdoing, (b) they have no responsibility to anyone except their owners, (c) anyone who questions these tenets is an enemy of the free market, of capitalism, and of private property itself.[7]

Defenders of this view may argue that those concerned with the pollution caused by automobiles are perpetrating a hoax on the public (i.e., it is nobody's business whether a corporation produces napalm, other materials and engines of war, and so on). However, this is clearly an indefensible evasion. Anybody has the right to be concerned with the direct effect of a company's products if they are thought to be harmful.

Equally, we are entitled to be concerned with the external effects of a company's product, such as the by-product pollution caused by cars. Both the profession of economists and the tradition of public regulation have long been familiar with the problems of such external effects; there is no reason why institutions and the public at large should not be concerned with these matters that affect the welfare of all.

Finally, a reasonable judgment of corporate activities in the United States would have to admit that companies have contributed significantly to what ails our environment in the broadest sense. However, there are serious conceptual and practical difficulties associated with directing investment policy toward moral ends.

MAJOR DIFFICULTIES

There are severe impediments to the use of noneconomic criteria in shaping investment policy. Since many of the difficulties are not always clearly understood, it will be useful to discuss *three* major ones briefly.

1. *How can one decide which companies should be favored for investment and which companies should be avoided?*

It is difficult to exaggerate the severe problems encountered when an investment manager tries to decide how he can in fact channel investment funds so as to foster social and moral objectives. An example will illustrate the kind of difficulties involved:

• In a recent article, a Harvard student was asked to discuss university sentiment about investment policies concerning a group of proposals that had been presented to the Harvard Administration.[8] Included was his recommendation "that Harvard invest in companies that *have* clearly progressive managements, and socially useful products or services. Examples would be Xerox. . . . "[9]

• Conversely, Princeton University was requested to sell its shares in companies doing business in South Africa and thus allegedly supporting apartheid and racism. Included in the list of designated companies was

Xerox, which does business in southern Africa as well as in most other parts of the world.

Thus a company that has been a leader in providing job training to disadvantaged workers and financial and other aid to ghetto businesses can be considered by some to be a prime example of a socially responsible corporation while others can consider it to represent an "immoral investment."

Even if one decides that support of the South African regime is the most heinous sin that a corporation can commit, it is still not clear which companies should be removed from the portfolio. In the requests made at Princeton, companies with subsidiaries or affiliates operating in southern Africa were proscribed from investment. It was argued that these were the companies most directly involved in strengthening the economies of southern Africa and also most visible to the oppressed black population. Consequently, these companies were symbols of support of these economies by U.S. corporations.

The difficulty with such a position is that any company that even trades with countries in southern Africa may be supporting their economies as much as corporations with affiliates or sales subsidiaries there. Indeed, it is not even clear that any portfolio could be found that is not contaminated in some way by relationships with southern Africa.

For example, even many U.S. electric utilities, which would appear to be in no way supporting the governments of southern Africa, may buy significant quantities of processed minerals that had been mined in one of the countries of southern Africa. Purely domestic banks and life insurance companies may be even more culpable, since they often hold bonds of the International Bank for Reconstruction and Development, which lends money directly to South Africa and thereby actually supports a racist government rather than simply profiting from it.

Moreover, one could not even hold a portfolio consisting entirely of cash to escape this contamination. Cash represents the noninterest-bearing debt of the U.S. government, which has given indirect but substantial support to the South African government by buying gold at $35 an ounce. Thus, even if a relatively simple criterion of immorality is chosen, it may be impossible to cleanse the portfolio of all investments that either directly or indirectly may contribute to that immorality.

Another example is provided by companies responsible for environmental pollution. Even if the portfolio manager's constituency did agree unanimously that environmental pollution was sufficiently evil from the social point of view to justify purging from the portfolio the shares of companies responsible for it, it would be extremely difficult to decide what *degree* of pollution would make corrective action necessary.

The broader issue, however, is how the portfolio manager can in fact follow a general policy of discriminating among investments on social, moral, and perhaps even political grounds. Such a policy would commit investment managers to a continuing series of decisions on possible moral-political-social effects of all investments.

Since most investments involve businesses with a wide variety of associations (some serving socially useful ends), the investment managers would be obligated to investigate and make judgments about the moral-political-social effects of all these associations. Would it be possible for the investment manager always to obtain the necessary information? Could arrangements be made for polling the relevant constituency about their desires? Might not such responsibility severely hinder investment management?

The problem is that once the precedent had been established, a case could be made for avoiding investment in virtually any company. One could easily disapprove of investment in munitions makers, companies with "unfair" labor practices, companies dealing with discriminatory unions, companies responsible for environmental pollution, companies with investments in Portugal, Israel, Syria, and so forth. It is also likely that there would be pressures to avoid investment in companies that do business with communist countries.

The dangers involved seem very clear. It is hard to imagine a company completely free of connections that might be considered objectionable on moral, political, or social grounds by some member of the portfolio manager's constituency.

2. *Is discrimination against certain forms of investments likely to be an effective means for bringing about desirable social goals?*

It may well be doubted whether the simple sale of securities in a company following morally offensive policies would have any effect in changing these policies. Any single institutional investor is likely to hold an insignificant fraction of the total number of outstanding shares of that company.

Thus the sales of these holdings would be most unlikely to have any *permanent* influence on the market prices of the shares; the shares would simply be transferred to other buyers. True, if any institutions followed suit, the market prices of these shares might fall. But such a snowball effect is unlikely, given the practices of most institutional investors.

Moreover, our securities markets are sufficiently broad—and buyers are attracted from all over the world—that new buyers could undoubtedly be attracted into the securities with relative ease. It is thus difficult to recommend security sales as an effective instrument to bring about changes in corporate practices and policies.

It would seem that if institutional investors wish to have an influence on corporate policy, a far more effective weapon is through the proxy vote and through direct contacts with corporate management. Indeed, pressing one's views through all available channels, consistently and repeatedly, may be a more realistic and ultimately perhaps even a more effective solution in the long run. Although the Campaign GM experience suggests that the effectiveness of such action is likely to be limited at best, it is already clear that General Motors has been influenced considerably by the pressure that was brought to bear.

3. *Would the application of noneconomic criteria to the selection of investments lower the returns from the portfolio and violate the investment manager's trusteeship?*

Few studies have been undertaken to determine the cost in terms of return on investment that would be suffered if noneconomic criteria were used in shaping investment policy. Some very rough estimates were prepared by Princeton University, however, in its study of the South African investment issue.[10] Based on an analysis of returns over an 18-year period, it turned out that the securities in the portfolio representing companies with some operations in southern Africa had almost a 3% higher average rate of return than the remaining securities in Princeton's portfolio. Moreover, the rates of return for the group with southern African operations tended to be more stable.

But these differences in returns cannot be explained as resulting from extra profits that accrue to American companies that exploit black workers. The companies that had provided the largest average annual returns (and thus drove up the average) were International Business Machines, Xerox, Polaroid, and others which were relatively little involved in the southern African economies. Their involvement in South Africa was minimal, since they did not manufacture their products there.

However, it is only natural that one should find many of the most aggressive U.S. corporations operating in southern Africa, because it has been the pattern for such corporations to expand their operations, if they are successful, into every major foreign market. Of course, past returns cannot be used as a reliable guide to future returns. Nevertheless, innovative and growth-minded companies will generally want to market their products worldwide.

Thus there may well be a systematic relationship between the expected profitability of an investment and the likelihood that the company will operate in all parts of the world, including southern Africa. To the extent that these corporate characteristics can be expected to affect future returns, altering the composition of the portfolio might well have significant long-term deleterious effects on the yields therefrom. In addition, the brokerage and other costs of the transactions involved in altering substantially the composition of the portfolio would be very large. This is especially true for an institution that owns large blocks of securities in relationship to the daily trading volume of the shares.

In Princeton's case, for example, it was estimated that the costs of the transactions (including brokerage charges and an estimate of the discount necessary to move the large blocks of shares in question) involved in switching all its holdings with affiliates in southern Africa would amount to approximately $5 million.

Similarly, a policy of investing in companies that follow socially desirable policies but which provide below-market rates of return could lower overall rates of return significantly.

The issue arises whether pension-fund managers, university trustees, and other investment officers can follow such policies without violating their trusteeships. The pension-fund manager's first responsibility is to provide adequate returns for the beneficiaries of the fund. He cannot deliberately penalize these beneficiaries and force them to accept lower than market returns without violating the trust placed in him.

As Arnold N. Levin put it, ". . . workers forgo current salary for future benefits. They could feel quite strongly that 'charity begins at home.' They may argue, with vehemence, that they did not authorize others to give their money away. . . ."[11]

Similarly, a university endowment-fund manager cannot deliberately accept lower investment returns when the university's regular resources are already gravely inadequate to meet its primary educational mission. The use of the university's resources for other social ends (a) will divert them from the purposes for which they have been entrusted to the university, (b) will prevent the university from taking full advantage of its unique strengths as an educational institution, and (c) may violate the prudent-man rule of managing its resources. . . .

IMPORTANT SAFEGUARDS

The preceding sections have presented in broad terms the basic arguments for and against using social, political, or moral criteria in investment policy. Whether or not a portfolio manager (or the trustees of a pension fund) considers the arguments pro weightier than those contra, he may well find himself in a situation in which considerable public pressure may seem to make the use of social or moral criteria unavoidable.

Clearly, an institution cannot guarantee to respond positively to every haphazard demand that it take into account some moral consideration, without incurring the risk of making a shambles out of the portfolio. In this section of the article, we shall therefore propose some rules of thumb which might govern an institution's response to the demand that it use its portfolio in some particular noneconomic manner.

Majority Approval

The pressures on institutions are manifold, and the groups exerting them have differing objectives. It clearly makes no sense for an institution to adopt a certain investment policy simply because one group with a legitimate interest in the policy demands its adoption. Indeed, it seems unreasonable for an institution to take any action unless that action is backed by a majority of the institution's membership.

The reason why we suggest that a majority of the portfolio manager's "constituency" approve proposed actions should be obvious; and in most matters a simple majority is deemed sufficient to decide the actions of a body. The case of a pension fund is an example where it is *not* difficult to decide what the appropriate constituency is: *the relevant constituency must consist of the individuals for whose financial benefit the fund is being operated.*

"Proscribed" Stocks

Not only do we propose that the desirability of action in investment policy be established by a majority of the institution's constituency, but we also deem it necessary to limit action to cases in which the moral or social purpose to be accomplished is a distinctive one—that is, investment in a "proscribed" stock versus a "permitted" stock. It seems neither practical from an institution's point of view, nor effective for changing social conditions, to proscribe broad categories of investments. It thus seems not very useful to instruct a portfolio manager not to invest in companies (a) responsible for pollution (probably all major corporations cause *some* pollution), (b) involved in dealing with Arab states (nearly the entire U.S. oil industry), and/or (c) maintaining sales offices in South Africa or dealing with the southern African economies in any other way.

If moral criteria are to be used at all in investment policy, they should concern themselves with a distinctive wrong rather than a general class of activities. We cannot, in this article, provide a general definition of what constitutes a distinctive wrong. It is possible, however, to offer illustrations of actions following what might be considered distinctive offenses in this category. For example, Princeton University took a specific public position against banks lending *directly* to governments maintaining a policy of apartheid. Also, the Student Christian Movement in England decided to terminate its account with Barclay's Bank.

Moreover—and this may be a corollary of the previous argument—the company against which action is proposed should be *directly* involved in the offense. Most companies and even industries buy from one another; and if sufficient levels of indirection are allowed, every industry is related to every other. Only complete paralysis can result if one were to insist that indirect participation in the activities of a company or industry (as might be traced out by using an input-output table) is sufficient reason for striking it from the portfolio.

Cost Evaluation

Different types of actions may involve very different types of costs. Divesting oneself of large blocks of common stock will undoubtedly cause the institution to incur sizable costs of transactions. It is also possible that expected rates of return on various stocks are such as to lower the overall return on the portfolio if the institution responds to demands that it switch out of proscribed stocks into permitted stocks.

The portfolio manager is entitled to evaluate different types of costs in the light of the institution's need for income. Thus a conflict may arise between satisfying one social objective (such as not investing in the stocks of certain companies, which would reduce the funds available to the institution) and another (such as providing high-quality education, which would have to be curtailed if funds were not available).

As we mentioned in the previous sections, what is perhaps even more serious is that in the case of many trust funds, such as joint labor-management trust funds, it would be contrary to law to employ the fund for general social purposes if this resulted in a deterioration of the portfolio from the strict investment point of view. In general, courts will not allow trust monies to be used in a way that does not agree with the stated goals of the trust.

There are, of course, ways in which the portfolio might be employed without incurring any costs. Voting proxies is one obvious example. In cases such as the recent attempt by Campaign GM to create a Shareholders' Committee of Corporate Responsibility, it would be difficult to argue that a university or pension fund would injure itself by voting in favor of the proposals.

Of course, one might argue that the resulting change in the corporate structure of GM would, over the long run, reduce its net earnings. But one can just as realistically argue that the ability of GM to remain a profitable enterprise depends on its success in ameliorating the pollution caused by automobiles.

Overall Assessment

If, other things being equal, an institution were favorably inclined toward the recommendation of its members that it use the portfolio for some social or moral purpose, it is nevertheless legitimate for the portfolio manager to undertake an overall assessment of the company in question. We have described earlier how the actions of a single company may create moral conflict. A company may be an enlightened leader in hiring minority group workers but implicitly support the South African economy. Another may be a leader in combating environmental pollution but have a poor record in hiring minority groups.

Since it is simply not possible to define absolutely how such conflicts should be handled, it seems therefore unavoidable that the institution or its portfolio manager undertake an overall assessment. In order to reduce, again, the haphazardness that might result from the application of overly simple principles, he might well want to undertake an examination of how extensive (as distinguished from how distinctive) a company's offensive actions are; also, whether they are mitigated by some particularly important positive contribution to social objectives that the company is making; and also, whether its offenses are inadvertent (pollution) or deliberate and intentional (manufacture of cigarettes).

The employment of criteria such as the ones discussed in this section may not make it particularly easy for a portfolio manager to respond to demands that the portfolio be used for moral or social purposes. But they seem to be minimal safeguards for a rational investment policy that is capable of responsiveness to the urgent moral issues of the day. . . .

Effective Action

Those who wish to use portfolios for the purpose of directing investment activity toward socially meaningful ends believe in the efficacy of economic pressure. Although there is a tendency to exaggerate the effectiveness of this type of pressure, there is evidence that corporations cannot fail to heed the admonitions of even small minorities of stockholders.

We have previously noted that General Motors did respond to pressure by establishing a public policy committee composed of a group of its directors. Other examples of actions by corporations apparently yielding to pressure are the discontinuance of the manufacture of napalm by

Dow Chemical and the termination of a loan agreement between a consortium of ten U.S. banks and the government of South Africa. It seems clear that corporations are hurt by unfavorable publicity and do respond to pressure.

However, it is important to note that effective pressure in these instances consisted not of the economic pressure implied by the sale of the corporation's securities but, rather, of the moral suasion exerted by the corporation's shareholders and the public at large. This suggests that the effective course of action for shareholders is not to sell their shares but to make their views known through direct contacts with the corporate management and through the exercise of their proxies.

There are at least two major problems, however, with disjoint groups of stockholders pressuring diverse corporations toward vaguely similar ends:

First, most of the reprehensible activities of companies that one may wish to eliminate and most of the constructive actions that one may wish to encourage have far-reaching external effects. It seems quite unlikely that the actions of decentralized pressure groups toward vaguely similar objectives will ever produce widespread and coherent corporate policies at an acceptable social cost.

Second, corporations may well resist pressures brought to bear on them but not on their competitors, because yielding to such pressures could put them at a serious competitive disadvantage.

Only strict legislation seems to promise (but not guarantee) to solve these two problems by bringing about coherent plans for social improvement while ensuring that all corporations in the same line of business will be treated equally. Whether it be in pollution control, hiring of minority workers, automobile safety, or other matters, what we need is a coherent plan on a national level, supported by strict legislation. If such laws existed, we would not place the burden of "judging" companies on the portfolio manager, but could leave such decisions to the courts where they intrinsically belong. Furthermore, the burden of response would not be left to isolated corporations.

The best use that can be made of pressure, then, seems to be to persuade corporations to become champions of new legislation rather than, as has often been the case, reactionary lobbyists against change. In this process of persuasion, institutional shareholders might well play a more effective role than through the often acrimonious appraisal of a corporation's guilt.

Notes

1. See Peter Landau, "Do Institutional Investors Have a Social Responsibility?" *Institutional Investor,* July 1970, p. 84.
2. *The Wall Street Journal,* September 1, 1970, p. 9.

3. See, for example, the *Report of the Ad Hoc Committee on Princeton's Investments in Companies Operating in Southern Africa* (Unpublished Princeton University Document, January 5, 1969).

4. Landau, *op. cit.,* p. 83.

5. *Ibid.,* p. 25.

6. "Campaign to Make General Motors Responsible," Proxy Statement by Campaign GM, Washington, D.C., March 25, 1970.

7. An example of this type of thinking is an article by Henry G. Manne, "Good for General Motors?" *Barron's,* May 18, 1970, p. 1.

8. David Ignatius, "Some Notes on the Harvard Experiences," *The Institutional Investor,* July 1970, p. 64.

9. *Ibid.,* p. 65.

10. *Report of the Ad Hoc Committee on Princeton's Investments, op. cit.*

11. "The Future of Employee Benefit Trusts," Part 2, *Pension and Welfare News,* February 1970, p. 57.

THE PURSUIT OF ETHICAL CRITERIA FOR SOCIAL INVESTMENT ACTIVITY

Charles W. Powers

IN PURSUIT OF CRITERIA

Proponents of the notion that institutional investors should exercise their prerogatives to encourage corporate responsibility in the corporations whose stock they own have spent most of their time defending the concept of social investment and have, therefore, given relatively little attention to the questions this paper will address, namely: How do you make an actual investment decision which involves moral or social considerations? According to what criteria should such a decision be made? . . .

Axioms of This Study

1. It is assumed that "material" definitions of important ethical terms (e.g., justice, liberty, happiness) do differ among persons in this society and that the importance attached to each of these terms differs as well. Hence, there is extant no single ethical view from which ethical criteria for social investment activity can be derived. It is also assumed that there

From *People/Profits: The Ethics of Investment,* Charles W. Powers, ed. Copyright © 1972 by the Council on Religion and International Affairs.

is no single "rational" process of ethical justification which permits the specification of "objective" definition or weighting of ethical terms. But this assumption does not require the conclusion that ethical issues are sheerly relative matters. In respect to corporate activity it is possible to specify formal categories which permit one to "sort out" levels of corporate responsibility, albeit that material specification of obligations and goals on those levels will differ.

2. The distinction between the private and public sectors has been blurred in the United States in such a way that it is appropriate—indeed requisite—for institutions in the private sector to regulate their own behavior so as to insure that it does not result in the deprivation of health, safety and basic freedoms. It is also appropriate that where they possess the capability, institutions in the private sector should seek to *enhance* health, safety and freedom.

3. Especially where institutions in the private sector possess governmentally established or sanctioned mechanisms for influencing other institutions to establish the patterns of behavior designated in Axiom 1, it is appropriate that they do so. The prerogatives of the stockholder in publicly owned corporations constitute such mechanisms.

4. Disinvestment from corporations is the least effective means of implementing Axiom 2 when the mechanism for influencing the practices of corporations involves institutional investments and, therefore, should be employed only if other "means" are impossible or would defeat the socially important purposes for which the investing organization was founded.

5. Only in unusual cases (e.g., where efforts to obtain alterations in corporate practice are both deemed likely to succeed and would be foreseen to result in the corporation's inability to provide a reasonable return on investments) could exercise of shareholder prerogatives constitute a violation of trust and/or corporate law relating to investment of institutional assets.

WHY CRITERIA?

I first appreciated the force of this question when it was put to me by a veteran church investor as we worked on a task force mandated to develop a social investment policy for one of the large Protestant denominations. This investor did not oppose the concept of social investment (although his understanding of it is not congruent with mine); what he did oppose was the development of criteria of any sort which would commit church investors to any specific approach—and especially promulgation of a policy which would specify definite guidelines to be used by church investors for the resolution of investment questions on specific moral and social issues. He often reiterated his belief that because the considerations which an investor for a religious institution must bring to bear on any given investment decision are so numerous, variegated and complex, the rest of the church would largely have to depend on the "intuitive integrity" of its investment committee.

The issue which he raised is not an instance of the philosophical and political debate concerning whether decisions in complex societies should be made by "philosopher-kings" or through the mechanisms of participatory democracy. These are ideal-types, extremes on a spectrum of possibilities. This investor did not oppose the notion that the central body of the church—in this case, a representative one—should call attention to and provide some very general direction for this neglected aspect of the church's mission. And those who differed with him on the task force were not proposing that every proxy issue faced by every church board in the denomination be submitted to the entire church membership for a vote. But the issue which he did raise was the question of *how much* discretion should be given to managers, administrators, representatives and trustees. I suggest that this will be—if it is not already—the central question for contemporary societal organizations—particularly for American organizations and institutions, public and private, where the "consensus" upon which all delegation in any organization is dependent is in real danger of collapsing.

Where the matters on which authority is delegated are *conceived* to be purely administrative or to require only technical expertise, those affected tend not to question the decisions of those with "authority." But in complex societies, social, moral and political questions *are* and are increasingly *conceived to be* inextricably involved in most decisions. It is because they recognize this that many of those in authority have tried to convince both those at whose behest they serve and those whom their actions affect that they are men of "intuitive integrity." As I understand it, this is not normally a claim to superior competence on moral and social questions (a *better* conscience); it is a claim that these persons have integrated the *common* conscience with superior technical or administrative expertise relevant to the matter they are empowered to handle. As a result, they may be trusted to responsibly use the powers delegated to them even though exercise of those powers involves moral and social judgment.

This claim is increasingly rejected. Many persons either involved in the delegation of institutional power or affected by its use have begun to question seriously whether conscience *is* common after all. The result is a crisis of legitimacy, which has resulted in pressure for constituency representation in all decisions to ensure that diverse points of view *are* heard. Despite the fact that there are many types of institutional "costs" incurred by constituency representation, this is surely one appropriate mechanism in many institutional settings. . . .

Costs: The costs lie primarily in the inhibition of creativity and flexibility in decision-making. The point which has been made by the situationalists or contextualists against the advocates of "principled" normative ethics is analogous to the one being made here. Criteria, like principles, *tend* to be conservative—in part because they are normally developed with an eye to preventing abuses or deleterious consequences which arise only in relation to some (perhaps a few) of the situations to which the criteria are applicable. The ability to act in situations in which imaginative and innovative possibilities emerge is often excluded where criteria have been developed. . . .

Benefits: One benefit is found on the other side of the coin we have just been discussing. Carefully formulated criteria can generate, indeed mandate, activities which would otherwise not be undertaken. Indeed, it can make some activities possible which would be excluded without them. An example will help. The criteria formulated in the report on university investments arise from a painfully careful assessment of the contentions which might initially seem to exclude *any* social investment activity by universities. Some of these contentions were misguided; some required carefully constructed procedures or restrictions in response. But none required exclusion of social and moral consideration from university investment policy and, therefore, our criteria will, we argue, make some social investment activity possible. An additional point: One factor which consistently inhibits institutions considering new arenas or types of activity is the fear that those activities are themselves open-ended or that they will establish precedents for other activities whose consequences are either incalculable or obviously deleterious for the institution or for others. Carefully developed criteria will minimize this risk.

There is a benefit related to the one just discussed. If an institution develops criteria for activity appropriate for it, it simultaneously limits the discretion granted to those decision-makers for the institution who, because of ignorance, malice or unconscious biases, might allow their decisions to be determined not by concern for the institution or the larger society but by interests or concerns they have in and for other groups or purposes. This point cuts both ways in respect to social investment criteria. Those who do not duly consider (or are not duly constrained by concern about) the role and purpose of the institution for which they are making decisions may tend to lead the institution into an inappropriately expansive social investment policy; or they may unnecessarily restrict social investment activity. An example of the former is a decision-maker who carelessly lays several planks of his own political platform on the investment policy of a university; an example of the latter is a businessman who enters precepts of his business ethic into the investment program of a church whose membership has approved a different social ethic. This is not to say that institutional purposes, goals and activities should not change from what they traditionally have been. It is to say that well-formulated criteria linked to those changing goals and purposes are needed if those changes are not to be abortive or quietly stifled. . . .

CRITERIA

1. Procedural Criteria

Any decision—especially one on a controverted issue—is importantly shaped by an actor's conception of the context in which he is acting. Almost inevitably presumptions for one of the contending parties in a dispute are operative, as are certain expectations about the process into which a decision will be entered and the types of options which are available to the actor.

It is, then, of extraordinary importance to determine the nature of the context in which one acts when he responds to a proposal submitted to a corporation in which he is a stockholder. The question of where the presumption lies in a situation where management and a stockholder are at odds is of crucial importance. Traditionally, the presumption has always lain with management and for quite compelling reasons. One of the primary determinants of investor choice of stock is confidence in the ability of existing management to achieve the result for which the investor enters the market, e.g., high and/or safe investment return. Only a shareholder proposal which *cogently* and *precisely* makes a case that a corporation's profitability could be enhanced by its adoption is likely to receive any attention from stockholders. One of the underlying (but normally unaddressed) questions to be raised by the growth of corporate responsibility and social investment concepts is whether that presumption in favor of management is in any way altered when the issues raised are not the traditional ones. Does it make a difference to the character of the decision-making context when profitability is no longer the sole investor concern or when the definition of profitability is undergoing redefinition in the light of changed conceptions of the corporation's role? I would suggest that . . . the fact that moral and social considerations become part of investor thinking should result in some reassessment of the presumptions that the investor brings to a shareholder proposal decision. What kind of reassessment? Perhaps the best way to answer this question is to find a decision-making context with characteristics analogous to the situation faced by a stockholder confronted with a corporate responsibility proposal. The best that I can think of (although it's far from perfect) is a citizen's decision on a school bond issue.

Let us say that the citizen generally believes the school board knows the schools' needs, that he generally favors school improvement and is willing to pay for the costs which that improvement involves. But the particular bond issue is one about which he has several doubts: *Substantively* he questions whether the city really needs another outdoor municipal pool in the middle school playground—a project the bond issue will underwrite at the same time as it underwrites improvements he favors (a higher teacher pay scale, small elementary school class size and new language labs); *procedurally,* he questions whether he should have to decide about the pool at the same time he decides about teacher salaries, since the pool is not intended to serve a specifically educational function. Since the school board is not required to and has not held open hearings to discuss the provisions of its proposed bond issue, the citizen's first notice of it is when it is published prior to the election day on which voters will pass or defeat it. Hence, when he stands in the poll booth, he has three choices: he can vote "yes," "no," or abstain. None of these choices (including abstention) is neutral, if neutral is taken to mean exercising no influence on a decision. If he votes yes, and the issue passes, he gets salary increases, pool, and a board likely to include "extra-educational" items when it makes its next proposal. If he votes no, and the issue is defeated, salaries don't go up, the playground remains a playground, and the board *may* or *may not* discern one of the reasons why the proposal has been defeated. If he abstains, he participates in throwing the decision one way or the other, although his degree of influence is only half what it would otherwise be.

In fact, however, the citizen's decision could be made far more complex than we have indicated. Let us suppose that our citizen determines on the basis of past elections and present community sentiment that the issue will almost without question pass overwhelmingly no matter how he votes. He may then decide that a "no" vote may serve to help inform the school board that, for one reason or another, there is citizen dissatisfaction with its policies. Alternatively, suppose that he is satisfied, on grounds similar to those above, that the bond issue will surely fail. Then a "yes" vote may serve to help inform the board that some of the citizenry is in favor of quality schools (although it may also help reinforce the view that it favors more pools and sponsorship of them by the school board).

In considering the options available to our citizen, we have presupposed that his only arena of influence is the polling booth. What else could he do? I will list some of the options:

Vote for the issue and:
a. inform the board of his reservations;
b. inform the board and indicate that similar "defects" on bond issues will cause him to vote against the school board in future elections;
c. inform the board that his "yes" vote was made only to show support for education generally in a situation where he was certain that the issue would be defeated.

Vote against the issue and:
a. inform the board of reasons for his "no" vote;
b. inform the board that he will support a bond issue without the specific defects in the next election;
c. inform the board that he voted "no" to register dissatisfaction with specific aspects of the issue in a situation where he was certain the bill would pass;
d. initiate a school bond issue which does not have the defects.

Abstain on the issue and:
a. inform the board of his reasons for doing so;
b. inform the board that he will support a revised version of the defeated bill in the next election;
c. initiate a school bond issue without the defects.

The role of a school board is not the same as that of a corporate board; the role of the shareholder who votes on or initiates a proxy contest is not the same as that of a citizen who steps into a polling booth or who seeks petition signatures for his own bond issue. Many of these differences can be traced to the fact that schools operate in the public sector and corporations in the private one. But there are other differences when the shareholder proposal favors a social responsibility concept. At the present time no shareholder who proposes or votes for such a proposal can reasonably do so with the expectation that the majority of shareholders will support him if the proposal is *opposed* by the management. We have relatively little history to rely on here, and as the number of institutions and individuals which include social investment considerations in their decisions grows, the figures may change. For now and for the immediate future, however, the context in which one votes for a socially motivated proposal is likely to be one in which management will be exposed to different and perhaps creative ways of thinking about the rights, responsibilities and nature of the corporation but will not be legally bound to alter its practices or procedures. Hence, corporate responsibility proposals are—and, if management is not insensitive or stubborn, may remain—persuasive rather than coercive in character.

Despite these differences, the *types* of options available to the citizen considering a school bond issue are all available to a shareholder faced with a proxy proposal. Additionally, just as all of those options may, in the proper context, be employed legitimately by a citizen, so, I think, may all of them be employed by the shareholder in the appropriate situation. The criteria listed below attempt to help specify such appropriate contexts.

I. Criteria for institutions whose institutional policy is to vote on most corporate responsibility proposals, but to take no other action (by analogy, the institution which limits itself to the polling booth). Generally, it would seem appropriate for such an institution to:

A. vote *for* a proposal involving social considerations when:

1. the proposal specifies precisely what the investing institution believes to be the proper policy or practice of the corporation;

2. the *substance* of the proposal specifies the proper policy or practice even though the mechanism for accomplishing the proposal's purpose is deemed to be only generally acceptable;

3. the substance and the procedures proposed are at least suggestive of the proper policy or practice *and* are stated in such a way as to permit management sufficient discretion in administering the proposed practice or policy;

4. the basic purposes of the substantive proposal or its procedures for implementation are proper (despite the fact that specific provisions and procedures are improper or inefficient) *and* (a) the investor is convinced that the proposal will so soundly be defeated that a similar proposal without the defects will not be resubmitted to shareholders the following year (either because management would not be required to include it or because the submitting shareholder would not again attempt to put it before the shareholder) or, (b) that management would likely interpret it not to be the will of the stockholders to adopt policies or practices generally congruent with those suggested in the proposal.

B. *abstain* on a proposal involving social considerations when:

1. the proposal is fraught with defects, even though the purposes of the proposal are proper and the situation described in A. 4. (above) does not obtain;

2. the institution cannot make a determination concerning the propriety of the proposal.

     C. generally, vote *against* a shareholder proposal in all other cases.

  II. Criteria for institutions which in addition to considering corporate responsibility proposals are willing to undertake other activities related to it (by analogy, to act outside the polling booth). Generally it would seem appropriate for such an institution to:

     A. vote *for* a proposal involving social considerations:

       1. in any of the situations listed under I.A.1–3;

       2. on proposals such as are described in I.A.4. if in addition to voting:

         a. it undertook to communicate its views to management (either by private communication or expression of its views at the annual meeting or in public announcements;

         b. and/or it undertook to explain its objections to the initiators of the proposal;

         c. and/or it determined to submit a similar proposal, without the defects, to the other stockholders at the next annual meeting.

     B. *abstain* in cases where a proposal is fraught with defects and the institution is unwilling to undertake one or more of the alternatives described in II.A.1–3. (above), or when the institution either does not have or could not have a position.

     C. vote *against* all other proposals and to explain to the management and/or the stockholders who submitted the proposal the reasons why it did so.

2. Issue Criteria

The phrase "proper policy or practice" has been used repeatedly in the foregoing section. Here an attempt is made to give some content to that phrase. There are, I think, three different types of *issues* to be raised in shareholder proposals intended to further corporate responsibility concepts. They are: (1) proposals intended to curb corporate practices which the proposing shareholder believes to be socially injurious; (2) proposals relating to affirmative action a corporation has taken or could take to improve social conditions; (3) proposals intended to alter corporate structure. We will treat these three types of issues separately since I shall argue that the criteria for evaluating them will differ.

a. Proposals to curb practices which cause social injury. Much of the confusion and debate about "corporate responsibility" has resulted from a failure to distinguish between two different types of responsibility: (1) the responsibility of a corporation to regulate the impact on others of its ordinary business activity; (2) the responsibility of a corporation to seek to ameliorate conditions which it has not itself caused[1] . . . I submit that there is a difference between (1) an attempt to halt discriminatory hiring, a misleading advertisement, or pollution of waterways, on the one hand, and (2) corporate contributions in support of universities and black community groups, or released-time arrangements to give pay to executives for helping a minority development corporation, on the other.

This descriptive difference has normative implications as well. Any man has the minimal obligation not to harm others and, where he can, to prevent others from causing harm. Hence every stockholder has an obligation, especially when given notice in the form of a shareholder proposal of a specific case, to attempt to deter the corporation of which he is a part-owner from causing social injury. . . .

b. Proposals relating to affirmative action taken to ameliorate conditions not caused by the corporation. Whereas I think that all men can agree that corporations should not cause social injury (and hence the problems arise only in determining what social injury is), it is not nearly so clear that corporations should attempt to ameliorate conditions outside their normal sphere of operation. One of the most persistently heard charges in contemporary America is that business has already had an inordinate influence on American culture; consistent proponents of this view will be dubious that shareholders should encourage any affirmative corporate action. Indeed, some have argued that a stockholder really concerned with corporate responsibility should attempt to halt corporate giving and keep executives at their desks and out of the ghettos.

One reason that affirmative corporate activity engenders controversy is that, when an institution moves out of a traditional or an easily circumscribed sphere of activity, it becomes appropriate to ask about the "system-consequences" of this activity. "System-consequences" questions are ones which policy-makers have been able to avoid, as David Braybrooke and Charles E. Lindblom argue, both because their choices have been "margin-dependent" ones and because the underlying assumption in some pluralist theory is that the deleterious consequences of decisions will be neutralized by other interest groups. Braybrooke and Lindblom argue that, in complex societies such as ours, the foreseeability of the consequences of one's actions is so limited that there is no other viable strategy of decision except the "disjointed incrementalist" one which focuses only on marginal choices. In arguing that corporations should regulate their own socially injurious impacts and in arguing that stockholders should attempt to encourage such regulations, I have already departed from at least one interpretation of the Braybrooke and Lindblom analysis: I have not made the assumption that there will always be "neutralizing" forces at work. My position then is that when one's actions are already necessarily having an effect on the lives and liberties of people, moral paralysis due to complexity is normally not excusable. Since there will be an impact of some kind anyway, it is preferable that moral and social considerations be brought to bear on the analysis of the impact.

Some of what we have said earlier applies also to some shareholder proposals relating to the *affirmative action* of the corporation. If a corporation already has entered into an *affirmative action* arena and the proposal put to stockholders relates to the *character* of that activity (as distinct from the question of whether the activity should be undertaken at all), then the issue for the stockholder is *how* not *whether* that activity should continue. When, however, the question is whether a corporation should be engaged in a particular kind of affirmative activity, categories additional to the ones I have developed are necessary.

A stockholder attempting to determine the responsibility of a corporation to engage in activity to ameliorate social conditions it has not caused will be aided in his decision if he separates out four questions about an activity which a shareholder proposal advocates:

1. Is there a need for it?
2. Does the corporation have adequate notice of that need (does it really know with some precision what is needed)?
3. Does the corporation have the capability to meet that need?
4. Is the corporation a last resort (i.e., if the corporation does not meet the need, will it simply not be met)?

When all of these factors are present, some level of responsibility is present; and when all four factors are present, growth in the intensity of any one of them results in raising the level of responsibility. Precisely because the corporation must examine and weigh more factors in determining what it should do in affirmative action programs, it is less likely that as a general rule the shareholder will be able to claim competence in making specific proposals in this area. This issue of lack of competence is most likely to arise in relation to the "capability" factor, although it may also arise in relation to the last resort category. Nevertheless, proposals which allow management some discretion in administering the activity would, as a general rule, be more acceptable than very specific ones. . . .

c. Proposals to alter corporate governance or structure. For a variety of reasons, it is generally easier for a stockholder to put a proposal relating to an alteration in corporate structure before other stockholders than to bring up one relating to specific corporate practices. Hence many shareholders concerned about corporate responsibility issues may be expected to submit proposals of this type. And yet, corporate structure proposals are ones which shareholders will generally feel less competent to judge. Management, not the stockholder, knows how the various levels of decision-making within the corporation interact; therefore the argument that management, not the shareholder, should initiate structural changes is, abstractly, a strong one. On the other hand, management can be said to have a vested interest in maintaining the structure that it has established. Is there a way of distinguishing among types of "corporate structure" proposals and determining stockholder criteria in relation to each of these types? That is a difficult assignment.

First, it should be pointed out that some "structure proposals" are closely related to "social injury" proposals. One may find in some "statements of support" appended to shareholder proposals an indication of how a shareholder hopes to deter what he considers to be socially injurious practice through an alteration in corporate structure. In such cases, an institutional stockholder could limit his evaluation of the proposal to two considerations:

1. Is the practice which the proposal seeks to remedy one which he considers to be socially injurious or to foster affirmative action of which he approves?
2. Can the structural change proposed reasonably be expected to achieve that specific result? Such an approach would excuse the stockholder from having to consider the systems-consequences of his decision; put differently, it would exhibit many of the characteristics of the "disjointed incrementalist" strategy of decision discussed earlier. But, if an institution has determined that it will vote only on corporate responsibility proposals which relate to social injury, the only consistent approach to corporate structure proposals would be the one just described. . . .

OTHER FORMS OF SOCIAL INVESTMENT ACTIVITY

We have limited our discussion of criteria to shareholder response to "corporate responsibility proposals" submitted by others. There are many other ways in which a stockholder may seek to advance social and moral views in a corporation. The following is a partial list:

1. voting to unseat management in favor of opposition slates proposed by other stockholders;
2. undertaking to propose the shareholder resolutions or alternative slates on the shareholder's *own initiative;*
3. soliciting proxies from other shareholders in order to carry out item (2);
4. joining other shareholders who are bringing litigation (derivative or individual) to enjoin certain corporate conduct;
5. bringing the litigation referred to in item (4) on the shareholder's *own initiative;*
6. taking any of the actions listed above pursuant to an agreement for concerted action with other shareholders;
7. making public announcements in connection with any of the actions listed above.

What differentiates the shareholder activities just listed from the shareholder activities discussed in the rest of the paper is that they require initiation. In every one of the examples we have discussed earlier, a moral or social issue was placed before investors by some other stockholder. Inclusion of the proposals in the corporation's proxy material meant that every shareholder in that corporation in some way affected corporate social behavior. To that extent, the agenda of each of the hypothetical institutions whose responses we have discussed had been set by others; even those organizations which informed management that they would initiate a similar proposal if management did not alter its practice were acting responsively.

But what are the criteria by which one determines that it is appropriate and needful to move from reactive to initiating activity? Are there criteria which can be employed to help make such a decision? Are there criteria by which to decide which of the available means should be used? These are questions which deserve an early and thoughtful reply. But they are questions to which only the most cryptic answers can be given in this paper.

Shareholder initiatives are in many ways similar to affirmative corporate action. One is responsible to undertake them where there is need, notice of need, capability to meet need, and no other actor capable or likely to take remedial action. Again, as in affirmative corporate action, where all of these features are present, a growth or intensification of any one of them results in an intensification of responsibility generally. For example, as the situation in East Pakistan worsened, any one of us who was aware of this situation could do something about it and was relatively certain that no one else could or was going to take the ameliorating initiative we could take, became more responsible for taking that action. In the case of shareholder initiatives, two features deserve special consideration: capability and last resort.

Capability: There are at least four questions which an institution should consider in trying to determine whether it has the capability to initiate shareholder action:

> Competence: Does the institution have, or can it command the skills required to use a shareholder's prerogative wisely and effectively?

> Financial resources: Does the institution have the funds required to initiate and/or carry out the type of activity in question?

> Proper priorities: Since every resource allocation is made in the face of competing claims upon the same resources, an institution must ask "is the benefit to be achieved by allocating the same resources to other socially important purposes?"

> Institutional constraints: Will undertaking one of these social investment activities render the organization incapable of performing its primary task; will those activities cause it to fail to fulfill legal and other obligations to which it is committed or bound?[2]

Last Resort: Three questions may be asked to help an agent (individual or institutional) to decide whether he should consider himself to be the "last resort." (1) Are there other agents more capable of taking the remedial action required? (E.g., should government be doing this?) (2) Are there other agents likely to take that action? (3) Are there other agents who can more effectively meet the need? (E.g., can government do so more equitably and with greater speed? Are there other stockholders who can better shoulder this task?)

Where the answer to these questions is "yes," responsibility is reduced but it is not yet eliminated. In complex societies, as we have repeatedly said, the response of other actors is exceedingly difficult to predetermine. Many of the residents of Kew Gardens could have answered "yes" to all of the above questions listed on the night that Kitty Genovese died. Hence, the three questions listed above are threshold questions, preparatory to the most central ones: Will someone else (whether on his own initiative or our urging) take the steps necessary to initiate ameliorative action? If the answer to this question is "no," then it is, I submit, appropriate for an institution to consider *itself* to be the "last resort."

CONCLUSION

We have given too little thought in this country to the patterns of interaction among our private institutions. There are many reasons for this: initially it was faith in an unseen hand which would magically orchestrate the interests pursued by each into a pattern which benefits us all; then it was belief that government would and could become the visible hand to perform the functions which the invisible one had failed to perform. The emergence of the concepts of social investment and corporate responsibility is but one indication that we are discovering that in many ways we must each bring moral and social concerns into areas of our common life from which they have traditionally been excluded. Exploration of what it means to have made that initial discovery is just beginning. This paper has attempted to provide some guideposts for those who are beginning to try to maneuver in one small area in which those explorations are taking place. If those guideposts have been misplaced, we must move them; if they have been mislabeled, we must find other categories and concepts. But we must be about the task of mapping or remapping the rights and responsibilities of our societal institutions; if we do not, we will career wildly between unthinking euphoria and enervating pessimism about the future of this society until the last resort is no resort at all.

Notes

1. This distinction is crucial to the development of the position set forth by John G. Simon, Jon P. Gunnemann and myself in *The Ethical Investor.* [A selection from this work is reprinted in this book, pages 160–168.]
2. It is easy for institutions to rationalize in thinking through these issues, that is, to treat these questions as potential excuses rather than criteria to be met. The tendency to rationalize is more pronounced in collectivities than individuals. And the tendency to rationalize is even greater where the action contemplated is new, controversial, or unprecedented. Institutional initiation of stockholder activities manifests all three characteristics.

ALL ANIMALS ARE EQUAL

Peter Singer

In recent years a number of oppressed groups have campaigned vigorously for equality. The classic instance is the Black Liberation movement, which demands an end to the prejudice and discrimination that has made blacks second-class citizens. The immediate appeal of the Black Liberation movement and its initial, if limited, success made it a model for other oppressed groups to follow. We became familiar with liberation movements for Spanish-Americans, gay people, and a variety of other minorities. When a majority group—women—began their campaign, some thought we had come to the end of the road. Discrimination on the basis of sex, it has been said, is the last universally accepted form of discrimination, practiced without secrecy or pretense even in those liberal circles that have long prided themselves on their freedom from prejudice against racial minorities.

One should always be wary of talking of "the last remaining form of discrimination." If we have learned anything from the liberation movements, we should have learned how difficult it is to be aware of latent prejudice in our attitudes to particular groups until this prejudice is forcefully pointed out. . . .

It is an implication of this principle of equality that our concern for others ought not to depend on what they are like, or what abilities they possess—although precisely what this concern requires us to do may vary according to the characteristics of those affected by what we do. It is on this basis that the case against racism and the case against sexism must both ultimately rest; and it is in accordance with this principle that speciesism is also to be condemned. If possessing a higher degree of intelligence does not entitle one human to use another for his own ends, how can it entitle humans to exploit nonhumans?

Many philosophers have proposed the principle of equal consideration of interests, in some form or other, as a basic moral principle; but, as we shall see in more detail shortly, not many of them have recognized that this principle applies to members of other species as well as to our own. Bentham was one of the few who did realize this. In a forward-looking passage, written at a time when black slaves in the British dominions were still being treated much as we now treat nonhuman animals, Bentham wrote:

> The day *may* come when the rest of the animal creation may acquire those rights which never could have been withholden from them but by the hand of tyranny. The French have already discovered that the blackness of the skin is no reason why a human being should be abandoned without redress to the caprice of a tormentor. It may one day come to be recognised that

From *Philosophic Exchange*, vol. 1, no. 5, Summer 1974. Reprinted by permission of the Center for Philosophic Exchange, Brockport, N.Y., and of Peter Singer.

the number of the legs, the villosity of the skin, or the termination of the *os sacrum,* are reasons equally insufficient for abandoning a sensitive being to the same fate. What else is it that should trace the insuperable line? Is it the faculty of reason, or perhaps the faculty of discourse? But a full-grown horse or dog is beyond comparison a more rational, as well as a more conversable animal, than an infant of a day, or a week, or even a month, old. But suppose they were otherwise, what would it avail? The question is not, Can they reason? nor Can they *talk?* but, *Can they suffer?*[1]

In this passage Bentham points to the capacity for suffering as the vital characteristic that gives a being the right to equal consideration. The capacity for suffering—or more strictly, for suffering and/or enjoyment or happiness—is not just another characteristic like the capacity for language, or for higher mathematics. Bentham is not saying that those who try to mark "the insuperable line" that determines whether the interests of a being should be considered happen to have selected the wrong characteristic. The capacity for suffering and enjoying things is a prerequisite for having interests at all, a condition that must be satisfied before we can speak of interests in any meaningful way. It would be nonsense to say that it was not in the interests of a stone to be kicked along the road by a schoolboy. A stone does not have interests because it cannot suffer. Nothing that we can do to it could possibly make any difference to its welfare. A mouse, on the other hand, does have an interest in not being tormented, because it will suffer if it is.

If a being suffers, there can be no moral justification for refusing to take that suffering into consideration. No matter what the nature of the being, the principle of equality requires that its suffering be counted equally with the like suffering—in so far as rough comparisons can be made—of any other being. If a being is not capable of suffering, or of experiencing enjoyment or happiness, there is nothing to be taken into account. This is why the limit of sentience (using the term as a convenient, if not strictly accurate, shorthand for the capacity to suffer or experience enjoyment or happiness) is the only defensible boundary of concern for the interests of others. To mark this boundary by some characteristic like intelligence or rationality would be to mark it in an arbitrary way. Why not choose some other characteristic, like skin color?

The racist violates the principle of equality by giving greater weight to the interests of members of his own race, when there is a clash between their interests and the interests of those of another race. Similarly the speciesist allows the interests of his own species to override the greater interests of members of other species. The pattern is the same in each case. Most human beings are speciesists. I shall now very briefly describe some of the practices that show this.

For the great majority of human beings, especially in urban, industrialized societies, the most direct form of contact with members of other species is at mealtimes: We eat them. In doing so we treat them purely as means to our ends. We regard their life and well-being as subordinate to our taste for a particular kind of dish. I say "taste" deliberately—this is purely a matter of pleasing our palate. There can be no defense of eating flesh in terms of satisfying nutritional needs, since it has been established beyond doubt that we could satisfy our need for protein and other essential nutrients far more efficiently with a diet that replaced animal flesh by soy beans, or products derived from soy beans, and other high protein vegetable products.[2]

It is not merely the act of killing that indicates what we are ready to do to other species in order to gratify our tastes. The suffering we inflict on the animals while they are alive is perhaps an even clearer indication of our speciesism than the fact that we are prepared to kill them.[3] In order to have meat on the table at a price that people can afford, our society tolerates methods of meat production that confine sentient animals in cramped, unsuitable conditions for the entire durations of their lives. Animals are treated like machines that convert fodder into flesh, and any innovation that results in a higher "conversion ratio" is liable to be adopted. As one authority on the subject has said, "cruelty is acknowledged only when profitability ceases."[4] So hens are crowded four or five to a cage with a floor area of twenty inches by eighteen inches, or around the size of a single page of the *New York Times.* The cages have wire floors, since this reduces cleaning costs, though wire is unsuitable for the hens' feet; the floors slope, since this makes the eggs roll down for easy collection, although this makes it difficult for the hens to rest comfortably. In these conditions all the birds' natural instincts are thwarted: They cannot stretch their wings fully, walk freely, dust-bathe, scratch the ground, or build a nest. Although they have never known other conditions, observers have noticed that the birds vainly try to perform these actions. Frustrated at their inability to do so, they often develop what farmers call "vices," and peck each other to death. To prevent this, the beaks of young birds are often cut off.

This kind of treatment is not limited to poultry. Pigs are now also being reared in cages inside sheds. These animals are comparable to dogs in intelligence, and need a varied, stimulating environment if they are not to suffer from stress and boredom. Anyone who kept a dog in the way in which pigs are frequently kept would be liable to prosecution, in England at least, but because our interest in exploiting pigs is greater than our interest in exploiting dogs, we object to cruelty to dogs while consuming the produce of cruelty to pigs. Of the other animals, the condition of veal calves is perhaps worst of all, since these animals are so closely confined that they cannot even turn around or get up and lie down freely. In this way they do not develop unpalatable muscle. They are also made anaemic and kept short of roughage, to keep their flesh pale, since white veal fetches a higher price; as a result they develop a craving for iron and roughage, and have been observed to gnaw wood off the sides of their stalls, and lick greedily at any rusty hinge that is within reach.

Since, as I have said, none of these practices cater to anything more than our pleasures of taste, our practice of rearing and killing other animals in order to eat them is a clear instance of the sacrifice of the most important interests of other beings in order to satisfy trivial interests of our own. To avoid speciesism we must stop this practice, and each of us has a moral obligation to cease supporting the practice. Our custom is all the support that the meat industry needs. The decision to cease giving it that support may be difficult, but it is no more difficult than it would have been for a white Southerner to go against the traditions of his society and free his slaves; if we do not change our dietary habits, how can we censure those slaveholders who would not change their own way of living?

Notes

1. *Introduction to the Principles of Morals and Legislation,* Ch.XVII.
2. In order to produce 1 lb. of protein in the form of beef or veal, we must feed 21 lbs. of protein to the animal. Other forms of livestock are slightly less inefficient, but the average ratio in the U.S. is still 1:8. It has been estimated that the amount of protein lost to humans in this way is equivalent to 90% of the annual world protein deficit. For a brief account, see Frances Moore Lappe, *Diet for a Small Planet* (Friends of The Earth Ballantine, New York, 1971) pp. 4–11.
3. Although one might think that killing a being is obviously the ultimate wrong one can do to it, I think that the infliction of suffering is a clearer indication of speciesism because it might be argued that at least part of what is wrong with killing a human is that most humans are conscious of their existence over time, and have desires and purposes that extend into the future—see, for instance, M. Tooley, "Abortion and Infanticide," *Philosophy and Public Affairs,* vol. 2, no. 1 (1972). Of course, if one took this view one would have to hold —as Tooley does—that killing a human infant or mental defective is not in itself wrong, and is less serious than killing certain higher mammals that probably do have a sense of their own existence over time.
4. Ruth Harrison, *Animal Machines* (Stuart, London, 1964). This book provides an eye-opening account of intensive farming methods for those unfamiliar with the subject.

MORALITY AND TASTE

Milton Friedman

The purchaser of bread does not know whether it was made from wheat grown by a white man or a Negro, by a Christian or a Jew. In consequence, the producer of wheat is in a position to use resources as effectively as he can, regardless of what the attitudes of the community may be toward the color, the religion, or other characteristics of the people he hires. Furthermore, and perhaps more important, there is an

From *Capitalism and Freedom* by Milton Friedman, pp. 109–115. Corpyright © 1967 by the University of Chicago Press. Reprinted by permission of the publisher.

economic incentive in a free market to separate economic efficiency from other characteristics of the individual. A businessman or an entrepreneur who expresses preferences in his business activities that are not related to productive efficiency is at a disadvantage compared to other individuals who do not. Such an individual is in effect imposing higher costs on himself than are other individuals who do not have such preferences. Hence, in a free market they will tend to drive him out.

This same phenomenon is of much wider scope. It is often taken for granted that the person who discriminates against others because of their race, religion, color, or whatever, incurs no costs by doing so but simply imposes costs on others. This view is on a par with the very similar fallacy that a country does not hurt itself by imposing tariffs on the products of other countries.[1] Both are equally wrong. The man who objects to buying from or working alongside a Negro, for example, thereby limits his range of choice. He will generally have to pay a higher price for what he buys or receive a lower return for his work. Or, put the other way, those of us who regard color of skin or religion as irrelevant can buy some things more cheaply as a result.

As these comments perhaps suggest, there are real problems in defining and interpreting discrimination. The man who exercises discrimination pays a price for doing so. He is, as it were, "buying" what he regards as a "product." It is hard to see that discrimination can have any meaning other than a "taste" of others that one does not share. We do not regard it as "discrimination"—or at least not in the same invidious sense—if an individual is willing to pay a higher price to listen to one singer than to another, although we do if he is willing to pay a higher price to have services rendered to him by a person of one color than by a person of another. The difference between the two cases is that in the one case we share the taste, and in the other case we do not. Is there any difference in principle between the taste that leads a householder to prefer an attractive servant to an ugly one and the taste that leads another to prefer a Negro to a white or a white to a Negro, except that we sympathize and agree with the one taste and may not with the other? I do not mean to say that all tastes are equally good. On the contrary, I believe strongly that the color of a man's skin or the religion of his parents is, by itself, no reason to treat him differently; that a man should be judged by what he is and what he does and not by these external characteristics. I deplore what seem to me the prejudice and narrowness of outlook of those whose tastes differ from mine in this respect and I think the less of them for it. But in a society based on free discussion, the appropriate recourse is for me to seek to persuade them that their tastes are bad and that they should change their views and their behavior, not to use coercive power to enforce my tastes and my attitudes on others.

FAIR EMPLOYMENT PRACTICES LEGISLATION

Fair employment practice commissions that have the task of preventing "discrimination" in employment by reason of race, color, or religion have been established in a number of states. Such legislation clearly involves interference with the freedom of individuals to enter into voluntary contracts with one another. It subjects any such contract to approval or disapproval by the state. Thus it is directly an interference with freedom of the kind that we would object to in most other contexts. Moreover, as is true with most other interferences with freedom, the individuals subjected to the law may well not be those whose actions even the proponents of the law wish to control.

For example, consider a situation in which there are grocery stores serving a neighborhood inhabited by people who have a strong aversion to being waited on by Negro clerks. Suppose one of the grocery stores has a vacancy for a clerk and the first applicant qualified in other respects happens to be a Negro. Let us suppose that as a result of the law the store is required to hire him. The effect of this action will be to reduce the business done by this store and to impose losses on the owner. If the preference of the community is strong enough, it may even cause the store to close. When the owner of the store hires white clerks in preference to Negroes in the absence of the law, he may not be expressing any preference or prejudice or taste of his own. He may simply be transmitting the tastes of the community. He is, as it were, producing the services for the consumers that the consumers are willing to pay for. Nonetheless, he is harmed, and indeed may be the only one harmed appreciably, by a law which prohibits him from engaging in this activity, that is, prohibits him from pandering to the tastes of the community for having a white rather than a Negro clerk. The consumers, whose preferences the law is intended to curb, will be affected substantially only to the extent that the number of stores is limited and hence they must pay higher prices because one store has gone out of business. This analysis can be generalized. In a very large fraction of cases, employers are transmitting the preference of either their customers or their other employees when they adopt employment policies that treat factors irrelevant to technical physical productivity as relevant to employment. Indeed, employers typically have an incentive, as noted earlier, to try to find ways of getting around the preferences of their consumers or of their employees if such preferences impose higher costs upon them.

The proponents of FEPC argue that interference with the freedom of individuals to enter into contracts with one another with respect to employment is justified because the individual who refuses to hire a Negro instead of a white, when both are equally qualified in terms of physical productive capacity, is harming others, namely, the particular color or religious group whose employment opportunity is limited in the process. This argument involves a serious confusion between two very different kinds of harm. One kind is the positive harm that one individual does another by physical force, or by forcing him to enter into a contract without his consent. An obvious example is the man who hits another over the head with a blackjack. . . . The second kind is the negative harm that occurs when two individuals are unable to find mutually acceptable contracts, as when I am unwilling to buy something that someone wants to sell me and therefore make him worse off than he would be if I bought the item. If the community at large has a preference for blues singers rather than for opera singers, they are certainly increasing the economic well-being of the first relative to the second. If a potential blues singer can find employment and a potential opera singer cannot, this simply means that the blues singer is rendering services which the community regards as worth paying for whereas the potential opera singer is not. The potential opera singer is "harmed" by the community's taste. He would be better off and the blues singer "harmed" if the tastes were the reverse. Clearly, this kind of harm does not involve any involuntary exchange or an imposition of costs or granting of benefits to third parties. There is a strong case for using government to prevent one person from imposing positive harm, which is to say, to prevent coercion. There is no case whatsoever for using government to avoid the negative kind of "harm." On the contrary, such government intervention reduces freedom and limits voluntary co-operation.

FEPC legislation involves the acceptance of a principle that proponents would find abhorrent in almost every other application. If it is appropriate for the state to say that individuals may not discriminate in employment because of color or race or religion, then it is equally appropriate for the state, provided a majority can be found to vote that way, to say that individuals must discriminate in employment on the basis of color, race or religion. The Hitler Nuremberg laws and the laws in the Southern states imposing special disabilities upon Negroes are both examples of laws similar in principle to FEPC. Opponents of such laws who are in favor of FEPC cannot argue that there is anything wrong with them in principle, that they involve a kind of state action that ought not to be permitted. They can only argue that the particular criteria used are irrelevant. They can only seek to persuade other men that they should use other criteria instead of these.

If one takes a broad sweep of history and looks at the kind of things that the majority will be persuaded of if each individual case is to be decided on its merits rather than as part of a general principle, there can be little doubt that the effect of a widespread acceptance of the appropriateness of government action in this area would be extremely undesirable, even from the point of view of those who at the moment favor FEPC. If, at the moment, the proponents of FEPC are in a position to make their views effective, it is only because of a constitutional and federal situation in which a regional majority in one part of the country may be in a position to impose its views on a majority in another part of the country.

As a general rule, any minority that counts on specific majority action to defend its interests is short-sighted in the extreme. Acceptance of a general self-denying ordinance applying to a class of cases may inhibit specific majorities from exploiting specific minorities. In the absence of such a self-denying ordinance, majorities can surely be counted on to use their power to give effect to their preferences, or if you will, prejudices, not to protect minorities from the prejudices of majorities.

To put the matter in another and perhaps more striking way, consider an individual who believes that the present pattern of tastes is undesirable and who believes that Negroes have less opportunity than he would like to see them have. Suppose he puts his beliefs into practice by always choosing the Negro applicant for a job whenever there are a number of applicants more or less equally qualified in other respects. Under present circumstances should he be prevented from doing so? Clearly the logic of the FEPC is that he should be.

The counterpart to fair employment in the area where these principles have perhaps been worked out more than any other, namely, the area of speech, is "fair speech" rather than free speech. In this respect the position of the American Civil Liberties Union seems utterly contradictory. It favors both free speech and fair employment laws. One way to state the justification for free speech is that we do not believe that it is desirable that momentary majorities decide what at any moment shall be regarded as appropriate speech. We want a free market in ideas, so that ideas get a chance to win majority or near-unanimous acceptance, even if initially held only by a few. Precisely the same considerations apply to employment or more generally to the market for goods and services. Is it any more desirable that momentary majorities decide what characteristics are relevant to employment than what speech is appropriate? Indeed, can a free market in ideas long be maintained if a free market in goods and services is destroyed? The ACLU will fight to the death to protect the right of a racist to preach on a street corner the doctrine of racial segregation. But it will favor putting him in jail if he acts on his principles by refusing to hire a Negro for a particular job.

As already stressed, the appropriate recourse of those of us who believe that a particular criterion such as color is irrelevant is to persuade our fellows to be of like mind, not to use the coercive power of the state to force them to act in accordance with our principles. Of all groups, the ACLU should be the first both to recognize and proclaim that this is so.

Note

1. In a brilliant and penetrating analysis of some economic issues involved in discrimination, Gary Becker demonstrates that the problem of discrimination is almost identical in its logical structure with that of foreign trade and tariffs. See G. S. Becker, *The Economics of Discrimination* (Chicago: University of Chicago Press, 1957).

FEDERAL FOOD, DRUG, AND COSMETIC ACT
FOOD ADDITIVES AMENDMENT OF 1958

AN ACT

To protect the public health by amending the Federal Food, Drug, and Cosmetic Act to prohibit the use in food of additives which have not been adequately tested to establish their safety.

Be it enacted by the Senate and House of Representatives of the United States of America in Congress assembled, That this Act may be cited as the "Food Additives Amendment of 1958."

SEC. 2. Section 201, as amended, of the Federal Food, Drug, and Cosmetic Act is further amended by adding at the end of such section the following new paragraphs:

"(s) The term 'food additive' means any substance the intended use of which results or may reasonably be expected to result, directly or indirectly, in its becoming a component or otherwise affecting the characteristics of any food (including any substance intended for use in producing, manufacturing, packing, processing, preparing, treating, packaging, transporting, or holding food; and including any source of radiation intended for any such use), if such substance is not generally recognized, among experts qualified by scientific training and experience to evaluate its safety, as having been adequately shown through scientific procedures (or, in the case of a substance used in food prior to January 1, 1958, through either scientific procedures or experience based on common use in food) to be safe under the conditions of its intended use; except that such term does not include—

"(1) a pesticide chemical in or on a raw agricultural commodity; or

"(2) a pesticide chemical to the extent that it is intended for use or is used in the production, storage, or transportation of any raw agricultural commodity; or

"(3) any substance used in accordance with a sanction or approval granted prior to the enactment of this paragraph pursuant to this Act, the Poultry Products Inspection Act (21 U.S.C. 451 and the following) or the Meat Inspection Act of March 4, 1907 (34 Stat. 1260), as amended and extended (21 U.S.C. 71 and the following).

"(t) The term 'safe,' as used in paragraph (s) of this section and in section 409, has reference to the health of man or animal.". . .

"Petition To Establish Safety

"(b) (1) Any person may, with respect to any intended use of a food additive, file with the Secretary a petition proposing the issuance of a regulation prescribing the conditions under which such additive may be safely used.

"(2) Such petition shall, in addition to any explanatory or supporting data, contain—

"(A) the name and all pertinent information concerning such food additive, including, where available, its chemical identity and composition;

"(B) a statement of the conditions of the proposed use of such additive, including all directions, recommendations, and suggestions proposed for the use of such additive, and including specimens of its proposed labeling;

"(C) all relevant data bearing on the physical or other technical effect such additive is intended to produce, and the quantity of such additive required to produce such effect;

"(D) a description of practicable methods for determining the quantity of such additive in or on food, and any substance formed in or on food, because of its use; and

"(E) full reports of investigations made with respect to the safety for use of such additive, including full information as to the methods and controls used in conducting such investigations.

"(3) Upon request of the Secretary, the petitioner shall furnish (or, if the petitioner is not the manufacturer of such additive, the petitioner shall have the manufacturer of such additive furnish, without disclosure to the petitioner) a full description of the methods used in, and the facilities and controls used for, the production of such additive.

"(4) Upon request of the Secretary, the petitioner shall furnish samples of the food additive involved, or articles used as components thereof, and of the food in or on which the additive is proposed to be used.

"(5) Notice of the regulation proposed by the petitioner shall be published in general terms by the Secretary within thirty days after filing.

"Action on the Petition

"(c) (1) The Secretary shall—

"(A) by order establish a regulation (whether or not in accord with that proposed by the petitioner) prescribing, with respect to one or more proposed uses of the food additive involved, the conditions under which such additive may be safely used (including, but not limited to, specifications as to the particular food or classes of food in or in which such additive may be used, the maximum quantity which may be used or permitted to remain in or on such food, the manner in which such additive may be added to or used in or on such food, and any directions or other labeling or packaging requirements for such additive deemed necessary by him to assure the safety of such use), and shall notify the petitioner of such order and the reasons for such action; or

"(B) by order deny the petition, and shall notify the petitioner of such order and of the reasons for such action.

"(2) The order required by paragraph (1) (A) or (B) of this subsection shall be issued within ninety days after the date of filing of the petition, except that the Secretary may (prior to such ninetieth day), by written notice to the petitioner, extend such ninety-day period to such time (not more than one hundred and eighty days after the date of filing of the petition) as the Secretary deems necessary to enable him to study and investigate the petition.

"(3) No such regulation shall issue if a fair evaluation of the data before the Secretary—

"(A) fails to establish that the proposed use of the food additive, under the conditions of use to be specified in the regulation, will be safe: *Provided,* That no additive shall be deemed to be safe if it is found to induce cancer when ingested by man or animal, or if it is found, after tests which are appropriate for the evaluation of the safety of food additives, to induce cancer in man or animal; or

"(B) shows that the proposed use of the additive would promote deception of the consumer in violation of this Act or would otherwise result in adulteration or in misbranding of food within the meaning of this Act.

"(4) If, in the judgment of the Secretary, based upon a fair evaluation of the data before him, a tolerance limitation is required in order to assure that the proposed use of an additive will be safe, the Secretary—

"(A) shall not fix such tolerance limitation at a level higher than he finds to be reasonably required to accomplish the physical or other technical effect for which such additive is intended; and

"(B) shall not establish a regulation for such proposed use if he finds upon a fair evaluation of the data before him that such data do not establish that such use would accomplish the intended physical or other technical effect.

"(5) In determining, for the purposes of this section, whether a proposed use of a food additive is safe, the Secretary shall consider among other relevant factors—

"(A) the probable consumption of the additive and of any substance formed in or on food because of the use of the additive;

"(B) the cumulative effect of such additive in the diet of man or animals, taking into account any chemically or pharmacologically related substance or substances in such diet; and

"(C) safety factors which in the opinion of experts qualified by scientific training and experience to evaluate the safety of food additives are generally recognized as appropriate for the use of animal experimentation data.

"Regulation Issued on Secretary's Initiative

"(d) The Secretary may at any time, upon his own initiative, propose the issuance of a regulation prescribing, with respect to any particular use of a food additive, the conditions under which such additive may be safely used, and the reasons therefor. After the thirtieth day following publication of such a proposal, the Secretary may by order establish a regulation based upon the proposal."

OF ACCEPTABLE RISK

William W. Lowrance

Few headlines are so alarming, perplexing, and personal in their implications as those concerning safety. Frightening stories jolt our early morning complacency so frequently that we wonder whether things can really be *that* bad. We are disturbed by what sometimes appear to be haphazard and irresponsible regulatory actions, and we can't help being suspicious of all the assaults on our freedoms and our pocketbooks made in the name of safety. We hardly know which cries of "Wolf!" to respond to; but we dare not forget that even in the fairy tale, the wolf really did come.

The issues: X-rays, cosmetics, DDT, lead, pharmaceuticals, toys, saccharin, intrauterine contraceptive devices, power lawn mowers, air pollutants, noise. . . .

The questions: How do we determine how hazardous these things are? Why is it that cyclamates one day dominate the market as the principal calorie-cutting sweetener in millions of cans of diet drinks, only to be banned the next day because there is a "very slight chance" they may cause cancer? Why is it that one group of eminent experts says that medical X-rays (or food preservatives, or contraceptive pills) are safe and ought to be used more widely, while another group of authorities, equally reputable, urges that exposure to the same things should be restricted because they are unsafe? At what point do debates such as that over DDT stop being scientific and objective and start being political and subjective? How can anyone gauge the public's willingness to accept risks? Why must there be these endless controversies over such things as lead, whose effects on health have been known in detail for years? Are people being irresponsible, or is there something about these problems that just naturally spawns confusion? Just what sort of a decisionmaking tool is this notion of "safety"? . . .

The Nature of Safety Decisions

Much of the widespread confusion about the nature of safety decisions would be dispelled if the meaning of the term *safety* were clarified. For a concept so deeply rooted in both technical and popular usage, safety has remained dismayingly ill-defined.

We will define safety as a judgment of the acceptability of risk, and risk, in turn, as a measure of the probability and severity of harm to human health.

A thing is safe if its risks are judged to be acceptable.

By its preciseness and connotative power this definition contrasts sharply with simplistic dictionary definitions that have "safe" meaning something like "free from risk." Nothing can be absolutely free of risk. One can't think of anything that isn't, under some circumstances, able to cause harm. Because nothing can be absolutely free of risk, nothing can be said to be absolutely safe. There are degrees of risk, and consequently there are degrees of safety.

Notice that this definition emphasizes the relativity and judgmental nature of the concept of safety. It also implies that two very different activities are required for determining how safe things are: *measuring risk,* an objective but probabilistic pursuit; and *judging the acceptability of that risk (judging safety),* a matter of personal and social value judgment. . . .

Failure to appreciate how safety determinations resolve into the two discrete activities is at the root of many misunderstandings. In one of the most common instances, it gives rise to the false expectation that scientists can *measure* whether something is safe. They cannot, of course, because the methods of the physical and biological sciences can assess only the probabilities and consequences of events, not their value to people. Scientists are prepared principally to measure risks. Deciding whether people, with all their peculiarities of need, taste, tolerance, and adventurousness, might be or should be willing to bear the estimated risks is a value judgment that scientists are little better qualified to make than anyone else. Technical people such as engineers, scientists, and physicians do venture such judgments when they design an automobile or power saw, advise the government about the safety of food colorings, or prescribe an antibiotic. And social scientists, such as market researchers, poll people's attitudes toward taking certain risks. Often, though, risks are weighed by a nonscientist consumer, manufacturer, or political official: a consumer purchases a power lawn mower, a manufacturer decides whether to incorporate a safeguarding feature in one of his products, or a legislator takes a stand on automotive pollution control. Our point is not to criticize any of these actions, but rather to urge that they be recognized for what they are.

Safety is obviously a highly relative attribute that can change from time to time and be judged differently in different contexts. Knowledge of risks evolves, and so do our personal and social standards of acceptability. Our decision whether to cross a street is different on different days, depending on whether it is raining, for instance, or whether we are carrying a heavy load of groceries, or whether we are already late for an appointment. A power saw that is safe for an adult may not be safe in the hands of a child. Partly because we have discovered adverse health effects we didn't know about earlier, and partly because more sensitive techniques are now available, X-ray doses thought safe forty years ago are now deemed intolerably risky. DDT is essentially banned from most uses in the United States, where we have access to and can afford more costly alternatives, are not so much exposed to tropical diseases, and can afford to be concerned about even a slight risk of cancer—but in contrast, DDT is the pesticide of choice in many tropical, less wealthy countries where every scrap of food has to be protected from insect predators, and where malaria and other diseases carried by DDT-susceptible insects are more imminent threats to life than the remote possibility of cancer.

Gauging risk is a matter of probabilities. A risk estimate can assess the overall chance that an untoward event will occur, but it is powerless to predict any specific event. From various evidence we can determine the likelihood that an automobile part will break and cause an accident; but we cannot predict *which* individual automobile will be the unlucky one or *when* the part will fail. By surveying large numbers of women we can estimate the general risk of uterine infection for users of intrauterine contraceptive devices, but we are helpless to predict which particular women will suffer that infection in the future. The great advantage of thinking in terms of probabilities is that it enables us to make broad comparisons among different hazardous circumstances. Risk is not an unfamiliar concept; it is involved at least implicitly in activities ranging from finance to romance.

In recent years safety decisions have been accorded increasing importance. New products, many of novel design, are being put on the market faster than society can test them all thoroughly for hazard. As we have become more aware of the interdependence of the parts of our environment we have tried to learn to anticipate the consequences that a change in one sector, such as agricultural pest control, will have on other sectors, such as the health of the ocean environment. The rights granted to workers are changing; a person no longer has to perform his job strictly at his own peril. Safety has become important in marketing consumer products. As people become less vulnerable to diseases and other natural hazards, the risks from manmade hazards gain importance. As we come to understand the causes of illness and injury, we worry about adverse effects, such as some genetic effects, that we weren't even aware of until a few years ago. The growth of the scale of human events has dwarfed the ability of individuals to estimate, appraise, and reduce their own risks. For all these reasons, the rational and centralized determination of safety has been gaining importance.

The public's expectation is that science and technology can and should get us out of some of the problems they got us into in the first place. From the laboratory and the factory and the agency comes the reply: Yes, much can be done to learn more and to keep us safer, and much will be done; but each aspect of the work has its costs, and society will have to decide what it wants to pay for and make the required commitment of resources.

In attempting to steer among the pitfalls we have devised for ourselves, we continually have to seek a proper balance between the comprehensive, rigorous, rational approaches that seem so essential, and the subjective, less quantifiable but not necessarily less valid approaches characteristic of political and social confrontations with the unknown. Just as the public and its political leaders must avoid irrationality, technical people must avoid illegitimate pretensions to authority. Failure to blend the several approaches satisfactorily will weaken our defenses against these unprecedented threats and will weaken the humanistic cause as well.

Judging Safety

. . . Safety is not measured. *Risks* are measured. Only when those risks are weighed on the balance of social values can safety be judged: *a thing is safe if its attendant risks are judged to be acceptable.*

Determining safety, then, involves two extremely different kinds of activities; . . .

> *Measuring risk*—measuring the probability and severity of harm—is an empirical, scientific activity;
>
> *Judging safety*—judging the acceptability of risks—is a normative, political activity.

Although the difference between the two would seem obvious, it is all too often forgotten, ignored, or obscured. This failing is often the cause of the disputes that hit the front pages.

We advocate use of this particular definition for many reasons. It encompasses the other, more specialized, definitions. By employing the word "acceptable" it emphasizes that safety decisions are relativistic and judgmental. It immediately elicits the crucial questions, "Acceptable in whose view?" and "Acceptable in what terms?" and "Acceptable for whom?" Further, it avoids all implication that safety is an intrinsic, absolute, measurable property of things.

In the following four examples, risk-measuring activity is described in Roman type, and safety-judging in italics.

> • Shopping for a lawn-mower gasoline can, a man compares cans having explosion-proof "safety closures" with ones having ordinary lids. The safety cans cost a good deal more, but, bearing the seal of an independent testing laboratory, they are certified as less hazardous than other designs. *Put on guard by recent newspaper warnings about fuel can explosions, he judges the ordinary cans to be too risky for his family, despite their greater convenience and lower cost. He buys a safety can.*

• A legislature asks questions about seat belts: How effective are they? Will people wear them? What reduction in injuries can be expected from seat belts? How much do they cost? Can manufacturers make them available in all new cars? *How much does society value that injury reduction? Are the belts an acceptable solution? Should they be required by law?*

• A scientific advisory committee is charged by the government with recommending radiation exposure standards. The committee reviews all the animal experiments, the occupational medical record, the epidemiological surveys of physicians and patients exposed to X-rays, and the studies of the survivors of the Nagasaki and Hiroshima explosions. It inventories the modes of exposure; it reviews present radiation standards, including those of other nations and international organizations; and it examines the practical possibility of reducing exposures. *It weighs all the risks, costs, and benefits, and then decides that the allowed exposure has been unacceptably high; it recommends that because the intensity of some major sources, such as medical X-rays, can be reduced at reasonable cost and with little loss of effectiveness, the standards should be made more restrictive.*

• Over a three-year period, William Ruckelshaus, administrator of the Environmental Protection Agency, considered many different petitions from the various interested parties before acting on his agency's inquiry into the use of DDT. Finally, in 1972, he ruled that the scientific evidence led him to conclude that DDT is "an uncontrollable, durable chemical that persists in the aquatic and terrestrial environments" and "collects in the food chain," and that although the evidence regarding human tumorogenicity and other long-term effects was inconclusive, there was little doubt that DDT has serious ecological effects. Ruckelshaus reviewed the benefits of DDT in the protection of cotton and other crops and affirmed that other equally effective pesticides were available. *Summing the arguments, then, he ruled that "the long-range risks of continued use of DDT for use on cotton and most other crops is unacceptable and outweighs any benefits. . . ."*[1]

The notion of acceptability is pervasive, although it is seldom given explicit emphasis (emphasis is supplied typographically in the following examples). In a report on the accident risks from nuclear power plants:

> While the study has presented the estimated risks from nuclear power plant accidents and compared them with other risks that exist in our society, it has made no judgment on the *acceptability* of nuclear risks. Although the study believes nuclear accident risks are very small, the judgment as to what level of risk society should *accept* is a broader one than can be made here.[2]

And in the title of a food supply report:

> A report on current ethical considerations in the determination of *acceptable* risk with regard to food and food additives.[3]

In heading down the slopes a skier attests that he accepts the risks; at a later stage of his life he may reject those very same risks because of changes in his awareness, his physical fragility, or his responsibilities to family or firm. While one woman may accept the side effects of oral contraceptives because she doesn't want to risk pregnancy, another woman may so fear the pill that she judges a diaphragm to be a more acceptable compromise among the several risks. Even though he is fully aware of the mangled fingers, chronic coughs, or damaged eyes or ears of those around him, a worker may accept those risks rather than endure the daily nuisance and tedium of blade guards, respirators, goggles, or ear protectors; but his employer, for reasons of cost, paternalism, or government requirement, may find this risky behavior unacceptable.

The elusive character of the word *acceptable* led a report on congressional radiation protection hearings to offer some guidance in "untangling the language of the record":

> "Acceptable" is used to mean such different things as (a) a conscious decision perhaps based upon some balancing of good and bad or progress and risk, (b) a decision implying a comparison, possibly subjective, with hazards from other causes, these latter being "acceptable" in turn in one of the senses given here, or perhaps just historically and possibly unconsciously, (c) the passive but substantive fact that nothing has been done to eliminate or curtail the thing being deemed "acceptable."[4]

Acceptance may be just a passive, or even stoical, continuance of historical momentum, as when people accept their lot at a dangerous traditional trade or continue to live near a volcano. Acceptance may persist because no alternatives are seen, as in the case of automobiles and many other technological hazards. Acceptance may result from ignorance or misperception of risk: variations on "I didn't know the gun was loaded" and "It won't happen to me" show up in every area. Acceptance may be simply acquiescence in a majority decision, such as a referendum-based decision on fluoridation, or in a decision by some governing elite, as with the average person's tacit approval of most public standards. Acceptance may even be an expression of preference for modern but known risks over perhaps smaller but less well understood risks, as with preference for coal- and oil-fired power plants over nuclear plants. Later parts of this chapter will deal further with these points. For now, it is important to appreciate that such decisions may or may not be—and are certainly not necessarily—fair, just, consistent, efficient, or rational.

There is a great deal of overlap between the two decisionmaking domains implied by our definition of safety. Scientists, engineers, and medical people are called upon by political officials to judge the desirability of certain courses for society. Panels of scientists recommend exposure limits. Physicians prescribe medicines and diets. Engineers design dams, television sets, toasters, and airplanes. All of these decisions are heavily, even if only implicitly, value-laden.

On the other hand, by adopting particular risk data in their deliberations, political and judiciary agents at least implicitly rule on the correctness of measurements. The business of determining risk must often be settled operationally in hearings or other political deliberations, because the day-to-day management of society can't always wait for scientists to complete their cautious, precise determinations, which may take years. Congressional committees and regulatory agencies conduct hearings and issue rulings on the risks of food additives and air pollutants. Courts rule on the dangers of DDT. Risk and its acceptability are weighed by both manufacturers and consumers in the push-and-pull of the marketplace.

Between the two activities—measuring risk and judging safety—lies a discomforting no-man's-land . . . or every-man's-land. Scientists on the fringe of the political arena, attempting to avoid charges of elitism, are looking for more objective ways to appraise society's willingness to accept various risks. At the same time, political officials confronted by scientifically controversial "facts" that never seem to gain the clarity promised by textbooks are exploring the possibilities of advisory assistance, fact-finding hearings, and formal technology assessments.

Guides to Acceptability

"Reasonableness." This is by far the most commonly cited and most unimpeachable principle in safety judgments. For instance, the legislative charter of the Consumer Product Safety Commission directs it to "reduce unreasonable risk of injury" associated with consumer goods.[5] Panels of experts frequently invoke a "rule of reason" in rendering advice. The concept of reasonableness pervades economic analyses of hazard reduction and the structures of legal liability.

Unfortunately, reference to reasonableness is in a sense a phantom citation. It provides little specific guidance for public decisionmakers, for whom reasonableness is presumably a requirement for staying in office. Not surprisingly, the Consumer Product Safety Act does not venture to define reasonableness. As guidance, the Safety Commission quotes the description given by the final report of its progenitor, the National Commission on Product Safety:

> Risks of bodily harm to users are not unreasonable when consumers understand that risks exist, can appraise their probability and severity, know how to cope with them, and voluntarily accept them to get benefits that could not be obtained in less risky ways. When there is a risk of this character, consumers have reasonable opportunity to protect themselves; and public authorities should hesitate to substitute their value judgments about the desirability of the risk for those of the consumers who choose to incur it.
> But preventable risk is not reasonable
> (a) when consumers do not know that it exists; or
> (b) when, though aware of it, consumers are unable to estimate its frequency and severity; or
> (c) when consumers do not know how to cope with it, and hence are likely to incur harm unnecessarily; or
> (d) when risk is unnecessary in . . . that it could be reduced or eliminated at a cost in money or in the performance of the product that consumers would willingly incur if they knew the facts and were given the choice.[6]

The point of safety judgments is indeed to decide what is reasonable; it's just that any rational decision will have to be made on more substantive bases, such as the following, which are in a sense criteria for reasonableness.

Custom of usage. The Food and Drug Administration has designated hundreds of food additives as "generally recognized as safe" (GRAS). The GRAS list, established in 1958, includes such substances as table salt, vitamin A , glycerin, and baking powder, whose long use has earned them wide and generally unquestioned acceptance.[7] Being classified as GRAS exempts those substances from having to pass certain premarket clearances. From time to time this sanction is challenged, but most critics of the GRAS list have argued not so much that it should be abandoned as that individual items should be subjected to periodic review. In 1969, following its decision to ban the popular artificial sweetener cyclamate (until then GRAS), the Food and Drug Administration initiated a full review of the GRAS list. That review is still in progress, and "so far nothing has been found to lead to any further bans similar to the one on cyclamate."[8]

Prevailing professional practice. Long established as the criterion for physicians' clinical practice, this principle is increasingly being invoked in evaluating the protection that engineers, designers, and manufacturers provide their clients. Buildings are said to conform to the "prevailing local standards." Toys are "of a common design." X-ray machines are operated "at normal intensities." In many instances the wisdom of such deference to convention can be questioned. The underlying assumption is that if a thing has been in common use it must be okay, since any adverse effects would have become evident, and that a thing sanctioned by custom is safer than one not tested at all.

Best available practice, highest practicable protection, and lowest practicable exposure. Air and water quality regulations have stipulated that polluters control their emissions by the "best available means." So have noise abatement laws. Obviously, although such a requirement does provide the public regulator with a vague rationale, he must still exercise judgment over what constitutes "best" practice for every individual case and what economic factors should be considered in defining "practicable." Hardware for pollution control or noise abatement may exist, but only at a cost that many allege to be prohibitive; is it to be considered "available"?

Degree of necessity or benefit. This consideration was explicit in a statement from the 1969 White House Conference on Food, Nutrition and Health, which recommended that

> no additional chemicals should be permitted in or on foods unless they have been shown with reasonable certainty to be safe on the basis of the best scientific procedures available for the evaluation of safety and meet one or more of the following criteria:
> 1. They have been shown by appropriate tests to be significantly less toxic than food additives currently employed for the same purpose.
> 2. They significantly improve the quality or acceptability of the food.
> 3. Their use results in a significant increase in the food supply.
> 4. They improve the nutritive value of food.
> 5. Their use results in a decrease in the cost of food to the consumer.[9]

Similarly, the Environmental Mutagen Society has said:

> Given a reasonable calculation of the genetic hazard posed by an environmental mutagen, it then becomes necessary to consider how acceptable such a risk will be to the population at large. The guiding principle in all cases should be that no risk whatsoever is acceptable when the mutagenic compound presents no clear benefits, or when an alternative nonmutagenic compound is available.[10]

The Delaney principle.   This principle, part of an amendment to the Food and Drug Act introduced in 1958 by Congressman James J. Delaney, requires that "no [food] additive shall be deemed to be safe if it is found . . . after tests which are appropriate for the evaluation of the safety of food additives to induce cancer in man or animal."[11]

Seemingly of the best intention—for who would wish to add proven carcinogens to anyone's food?—and seemingly a sharp decision tool for a regulator ("if it causes cancer, ban it"), this bold amendment has been controversial from the beginning. Because of the extraordinarily difficult problems of assessing carcinogenicity, as we described earlier, it is extremely difficult for either scientists or political officials to decide what "appropriate tests" are and what evidence suffices to prove that an agent can "induce cancer." Far from resolving the regulatory problem, the amendment has in some ways compounded it. The principle was intended to be an absolute, highly discriminating criterion, an aid to decisionmaking. But the Food and Drug Administration has used it as the explicit basis for decisions to ban fully registered products on only two occasions, both involving compounds used in food packaging materials. Nevertheless, the Delaney principle has served continually as a guide in many decisions even outside the area of foods. Its very existence, and the well-understood intentions behind it, are strong deterrents to risky actions. Indeed, some would like to see it extended to govern not only carcinogens but mutagens and teratogens as well; legislation to that effect has been pending in the Congress, and petitions opposing and supporting such legislation are being circulated among scientists. Consumerist James Turner has stated that:

> The loose collection of organizations and individuals generally called the "consumer movement" in the United States tends to believe that the principle of social policy embodied in the Delaney Clause is the best way to deal with these slower acting and less direct causes of death and chronic sickness. In general they are also highly skeptical that any better principle for dealing with the chemical threat to man can be found.[12]

Others, such as a panel of the President's Science Advisory Committee, have objected that the clause nullifies case-by-case judgments of risks, costs, and benefits:

> The rigid stipulation of the Delaney Clause, springing from presently inadequate biological knowledge, places the administrator in a very difficult interpretative position. He is not allowed, for example, to weigh any known benefits to human health, no matter how large, against the possible risks of cancer production, no matter how small.[13]

Some people object to singling out carcinogenic food additives for this special attention, which is not given to agents possibly causing liver disease, brain damage, or other serious disabilities. The debate continues. As scientists perfect techniques allowing detection of ever tinier amounts of chemicals, the viability of the Delaney principle will be challenged further. An impasse seems avoidable. Even now there are chemicals widely present in our food that are both detectable (using special techniques not necessarily employed on a routine basis) and carcinogenic (in some large dosage, under some conditions, to some particular test animal), but which are allowed to remain there by license of administrative oversight or bureaucratic definition as not being food additives or by invocation of a side-stepping "rule of reason."[14]

"No detectable adverse effect."   Although such a principle is applied frequently in our everyday lives, and although it has a certain operational value, it is a weak criterion which may amount to little more than an admission of uncertainty or ignorance. Many hazards now recognized, such as moderate levels of X-rays or asbestos or vinyl chloride, could at an earlier time have been said to have "no detectable adverse effect."

"Toxicologically insignificant levels."   On occasion, guidelines have been proposed under which toxicologically insignificant levels would be defined administratively for certain classes of food substances: chemicals which have been in sustained commercial production without evidence of toxicological hazard; pesticide degradation products occurring at very low levels; or chemicals about which toxicological information is lacking but which possess certain chemical structural features. This has been defended as a practical approach, but it is open to criticism as being quite arbitrary. One scientific panel has said that the concept of toxicologically insignificant dose levels, "of dubious merit in any life science, has absolutely no validity in the field of carcinogenesis" and has proposed alternative ways of establishing a "socially acceptable level of risk."[15]

The threshold principle.   If it can be proven that there is indeed a level of exposure below which no adverse effect occurs, subthreshold exposures might be considered safe. But determining whether there really is a threshold, for the especially vulnerable as well as for the average populace, is usually a nearly impossible task. As we mentioned earlier, for loud noises there are clearly thresholds of annoyance, pain, and ear damage. But whether there are thresholds for effects of radiation, chemical carcinogens, and mutagens has never been firmly established. . . .

On Being, and Being Held, Responsible

Anyone who has read to this point has surely become so concerned about issues of responsibility that further introduction to this section is unnecessary. Every sector of society has its ethical problems. We will focus on those concerning scientists and other technical people, for the most part limiting ourselves to those concerning issues of personal safety.

In essence, the issue is posed by the following questions. Should technically trained people be expected to bear any social responsibilities different from those borne by others? Why? What are the unique obligations? And further, can all the obligations be met simply by individuals working alone, or are there in addition some responsibilities requiring technical people to act collectively?

Most discussions of these questions are not very useful: either they harangue the reader about how technology has sent the world to the brink of oblivion, without admitting to their scapegoating or suggesting a way back from the brink; or else they preach a benign sermon reducing ethics to moral goodness, and merely plead with people to be virtuous. We will try to avoid these extremes. Our approach will be to describe briefly what society's expectations are, show that they form a general pattern of obligations that both scientists and nonscientists recognize and that scientists seem to accept in principle, point out that this responsibility is based on a tacit but real compact between the technical professions and society, and argue that this compact is fairly workable as long as it is enforced and renegotiated to keep up with the needs of the times.

The public does have special expectations of technical people. "I don't know anything about building materials, but I would certainly expect anyone who designs a hospital, nursing home, or school to make it fireproof." "If scientists learn that a food additive or drug is harmful, it is unethical for them not to warn the public." "It is wrong for a research chemist or engineer to develop a manufacturing process that will expose workers to conditions that, for health reasons, the researcher himself wouldn't tolerate." "A designer or engineer who designs or approves a dangerous toy or appliance should be drummed out of the profession." Such opinions are widespread among both technical and nontechnical people. They fall into several different categories, as we will show.

[Since this (selection) has emphasized that value judgments should be labelled as such, the author feels bound to state that the following is strictly his personal opinion; nonetheless, he believes that it is widely shared.]

Scientists, engineers, designers, architects, physicians, public health experts, and other technically trained people *do* have special responsibilities to the rest of society with respect to personal safety. Some principal kinds of risks which ought to be taken upon the conscience of the technical community are:

1. Technically complex risks whose intricacies are comprehensible only to highly trained people;

2. Risks that can be significantly reduced by applying new technology or by improving the application of existing technology;

3. Risks constituting public problems whose technical components need to be distinguished explicitly from their social and political components so that responsibilities are assigned properly;

4. Technological intrusions on personal freedom made in the pursuit of safety; and

5. Risks whose possible consequences appear so grave or irreversible that prudence dictates the urging of extreme caution, even before the risks are known precisely.

Notice that we have said that these problems *should be taken as matters of conscience* by the technical community. Whether the verb describing the action should be *protecting,* or *watching over,* or *looking out for,* or *issuing a warning,* depends on the situation. The specific response might be doing an experiment, raising an issue before a professional society, blowing the whistle on an employer, exerting political leverage, or aiding a legislator or administrator in untangling the parts of a public issue. We will mention some examples of the above categories; a single problem often belongs to several of them.

1. *Technically complex risks whose intricacies are comprehensible only to highly trained people.* The complexities of deciding whether chemicals are carcinogenic, or of evaluating the design of such large structures as bridges, dams, tunnels, and aircraft, obviously leave such problems squarely in the province of those with advanced training and experience. And this goes beyond "You made it; you worry about it"; technical people must also be relied upon to predict the consequences of natural disasters and other such hazards.

2. *Risks that can be significantly reduced by applying new technology or by improving the application of existing technology.* Here we think of aircraft landing guidance systems, tidal wave warning devices, vaccines against disease, and occupational protective measures. In most cases only technical people can envision the possibilities.

3. *Risk constituting public problems whose technical components need to be distinguished explicitly from their social and political components so that responsibilities are assigned properly.* Scientists need to point out over and over that although developing nuclear power is a technical matter, as is the development of solar power, deciding how much of what kind of commitment to make to each of the two programs is a thoroughly hybrid scientific-political issue. They then need to stay involved as the tasks are "factored apart"; otherwise, politicians may overlook some issues that are obvious only to science, or scientists may find themselves having to make social decisions under illegitimate pretenses.

4. *Technological intrusions on personal freedom made in the pursuit of safety.* This category includes the responsibility of researchers to protect their experimental subjects, with respect not only to their physical health but to their emotional well-being and personal liberty as well. It might conceivably also include warning of some of the subtle intrusions on freedom implied by certain government decisions, such as requirements that all school children submit to genetic screening.

5. *Risks whose possible consequences appear so grave or irreversible that prudence dictates the urging of extreme caution, even before the risks are known precisely.* Wearing the prophet's cape is itself a risky business. Unless it is done with care, not only is the specific prophecy ignored, but the prophet loses his credibility. Nevertheless, scientists are counted upon to issue warnings about especially insidious hazards, to prescribe safeguards, and to raise public awareness of the danger. Some scientists are now doing this with

radioactive waste problems—particularly with the toxic and exceedingly long-lived material, plutonium—and with the upper-atmospheric ozone problem. In the latter case, for instance, even if the effects of freons, SST exhausts, and so forth eventually turn out not to be serious threats (it is too early to tell), it will not have been wrong to investigate—indeed, because of the extraordinary potential gravity of the risks it would be irresponsible *not* to see that they get appraised.

These are but a few of the social responsibilities of scientists, but they are among the most readily identified and agreed upon. There are others: obligations to frame risk and safety issues in proper relation to factors of equity, cost, efficacy, and so on, and obligations to interpret new findings for the lay public. There are also attitudinal and procedural responsibilities such as defending against suppression, misinterpretation, and falsification of data, and preserving the distinction between factual and valuational decisions. In all of these tasks nonscientists can be enlisted for reinforcement. But scientists must often be depended upon to take the initiative.

These responsibilities have several deep origins. Basically they arise, in congruence with all major moral philosophies, from the conviction that every person has a general responsibility for the well-being of his fellow men. Reflecting this, the common law has held through the centuries that anyone who becomes aware of the possibility of danger has a responsibility to warn those at risk. But we are obliged to push further and ask whether, in this age of cultural specialization, there isn't more to the issue —for if we don't press, we may be left simply making vague exhortations to virtue.

When we examine what society expects, we find that it does look to the technical community for warning, guidance, and protection, in the kinds of situations we have described and in others as well. Highly trained people are definitely seen as having special status. Given this, a key to developing a compelling ethical argument, and to understanding why the lay public feels as it does, seems to reside in the notion of professionalism.

Over the years a tacit but nonetheless real compact has developed. Society *invests in* the training and professional development of scientists and other technical people. It invests heavily; substantial public subsidy of one form or another goes to virtually every college, university, medical school, field station, and research facility in the United States. By and large the professions are left free to govern themselves, control admission to membership, choose their direction of research, enforce the quality of work, and direct the allocation of public funds within their subject area.

Concomitantly, society *invests with* the professions and their institutions certain trusts, among them a trust that the professions will watch over the well-being of society, including its safety. As Berkeley sociologist William Kornhauser has expressed it, "Professional responsibility is based on the belief that the power conferred by expertise entails a fiduciary relationship to society."[16] This "fiduciary relationship," or what we have called a tacit compact, is what gives rise to the ethical "oughts."

Within this compact, the professions develop two kinds of obligations. The first is an ethics governing maintenance of the profession; it consists of a set of restraints mutually agreed to by peers, and it shades into being an etiquette. The second is a commitment to the service of society as well as to individual clients. This commitment usually grows slowly. By stepping into gaps during crises, or by deliberately staking out pieces of social territory, the profession comes to be responsible for special matters. For example, geneticists have not only dispassionately studied our chromosomes as objects of scientific curiosity, but, slowly and by subtle stages, they have come to be guardians of this genetic treasure as well. In part, this guardianship is self-appointed. It is appreciated and it is rarely contested. Because this particular compact seems to work—that is, geneticists get their support and freedom, and society gets protection for its genes—society now *expects* geneticists, as a matter of their ethical responsibility, to continue their watch for mutagenic menaces. And in general geneticists seem to accept the responsibility. Similar expectations are held in many areas. The obligations go far beyond the duties for which people draw their salaries, and the seriousness of some of the possible errors of omission exceeds anything people can be held legally liable for.

From time to time, the compact is modified. Someone, perhaps an outsider, perhaps a member of the profession, levels a charge of irresponsibility or corruption. In response, the profession purges itself of charlatans or revises its code of practice, or the public withdraws its support or stiffens its licensing requirements for admission to the profession. Such "clean house, or else we'll clean it for you" challenges are currently being laid, for instance, against researchers who are thought to be taking unethical advantage of research subjects and against industrial scientists who have allegedly suppressed data about carcinogens in their factories.

The professions not only face inward and enforce their codes, but they also face outward to support and defend members who meet resistance in discharging their obligations. On occasion, an employer may interpret a professional's act of conscience as an act of disloyalty or worse, and harass him or threaten to fire or sue. The principal recourse for the repressed professional may be to retreat to the sanctuary of the guildhall (the metaphor is apt; the high guilds, such as the goldsmiths', set an effective and honorable precedent). In several recent instances, professional societies have provided legal defense and supportive publicity for members who were suffering unduly for "blowing the whistle" on what they believed were unconscionable situations.[17] Many professional societies now have ethics committees to review these matters in general and to prepare for contingencies. A society may choose not to defend its members' particular stands, but rather to defend their right to issue warnings and take stands without recrimination. A society may be able to advise its members on the most reasonable ways to exert influence. And a society may take the lead in converting an accusatory confrontation into a more broadly based assessment.

As this century has careened along it has brought an increasing need for a collective shouldering of responsibility. The one-to-one personal relationships that once governed ethical conduct have been supplanted by more diffuse ones involving many intermediaries. Industrial scientists plan their research by committee. Engineers who design tunnels and dams interact with their ultimate public clients only indirectly, through managers, attorneys, and the officials who supervise public contracts. Physicians may still carry the wand of Aesculapius, but they do so in the context of one of the nation's largest businesses. Two sorts of diffuseness enlarge the collective dimension. First, the cliency is expanding, often in the interest of social justice: a national health care system that intends to reach every citizen has quite different ethical dimensions from a free-market private physician system. And second, as we confront hazards that are more diffuse, we often realize that *nobody* has considered that the problem was specifically his concern: there is no International Agency for the Supervision of the Ozone Layer.

We try to manage these problems by government action, building in mechanisms of accountability where possible; and we test the justice of specific actions in the courts, as when people feel that they are being unfairly denied medical care. Beyond that, and usually leading it, we have to depend on action by communities of scholars and coteries of professionals—hence the obligations we listed earlier.

Two current cases exemplify some of the difficulties. Three engineers in California, backed to a limited extent by several engineering societies, have pressed suit against the Bay Area Rapid Transit (BART) system for firing them after they publicly protested that the automatic train control systems their companies were developing for BART were inadequate and not up to the best professional standards with regard to passenger safety. The dispute raises complex questions about how great the risks really were, whether they should have been considered acceptable, how engineers should play their roles, how corporations should handle dissension, and what the professional societies should do.[18] In another case, an international group of biologists has voluntarily convened itself to discuss whether and how to control certain genetics experiments that would have bizarre, disastrous consequences if they ran amok.[19]

There is little precedent for either case, so it is not surprising that neither has been handled with assurance. In the BART case, the engineering societies were not well prepared to act and could muster only limited support. Perhaps for lack of experience and guidance, the three engineers party to the suit were not able to pursue the case through the courts to completion; the case has reportedly had to be settled out of court, thus setting only weak legal precedent. In the genetic experiments case, the scientists involved continue to suffer the anguish of not even being able to reach a firm consensus on the issue, and they are hard pressed to take any action other than to issue stern pronouncements, plead for prudence, and cross their collective fingers that researchers will be careful.

We have developed the above arguments because we believe they are important. They are by no means the sole guide to action. There can be no substitute for honesty, courage, sacrifice, and the other manifestations of high morality. Nor should legal and other sanctions fail to be applied: enforceable building codes can be adopted to supplement voluntary action; duties can be made a matter of contractual responsibility; and falsification of records is cause for lawsuit. There are many obligations in addition to ethical ones. The ethical ones are of a special sort, though, and urgently deserve to be developed.

The great questions of responsibility will remain with us. Is simply providing information or issuing warnings a sufficient response, or ought those with the knowledge do more? How is responsibility passed up through administrative and managerial hierarchies? In what sense is tacit acquiescence in a misleading scheme irresponsible (as when corporate scientists who know better say nothing when their company makes false claims for its products or evades pollution control laws)? To what extent should those who generate scientific and technological innovations be responsible for their subsequent application?

Notes

1. U.S. Environmental Protection Agency, "Consolidated DDT hearings," *37 Federal Register,* 13369–13376 (July 7, 1972).
2. U.S. Atomic Energy Commission, "An assessment of accident risks in U.S. commercial nuclear power plants," AEC no. WASH-1400, summary volume p. 7 (September 1974).
3. Citizens' Commission on Science, Law and the Food Supply (March 25, 1974).
4. U.S. Congress, Joint Committee on Atomic Energy, "Radiation protection criteria and standards: Their basis and use," Summary-analysis of hearings May 24–25 and June 1–3, 1960.
5. Consumer Product Safety Act, *Public Law 82-573* (1972).
6. National Commission on Product Safety, *Final Report,* 11 (1970).
7. *21 U.S. Code of Federal Regulations,* 121.101 (subpart B).
8. Alan T. Spiher, Jr., "Food ingredient review: where it stands now," *FDA Consumer,* 23–26 (June 1974).
9. *White House Conference on Food, Nutrition and Health, Final Report,* 130 (1970).
10. Environmental Mutagen Society, committee 17, "Environmental mutagenic hazards," *Science 187,* 503–514 (1975).
11. *21 U.S. Code of Federal Regulations* 409 (c)(3)(A); section 512 (d)(1)(H) extends the principle to animal-growth-promoting feed additives, and section 706 (b)(5)(B) to food colorings.
12. James Turner, "Consumer views of the Delaney Amendment," in *Hearings before the House Agriculture—Environmental, and Consumer Protection Committee, Part 8, 225* (May 6, 1974).
13. President's Science Advisory Committee, Panel on Chemicals and Health, *Chemicals and Health,* 11 (1973).
14. Arguments have appeared in *Preventive Medicine 2,* 123–170 (1973), a special issue devoted to the Delaney Clause; in the President's Science Advisory

Committee, *Chemicals and Health* (1973); in National Academy of Sciences/ National Research Council, *How Safe is Safe? The Design of Policy on Drugs and Food Additives* (1974); and in the Food and Drug Administration, "Study of the Delaney clause and other anti-cancer clauses," *Hearings before the House Subcommittee on Agriculture—Environmental and Consumer Protection, Part 8* (May 6, 1974).

15. National Academy of Sciences/National Research Council, Food Protection Committee, *Guidelines for estimating toxicologically insignificant levels of chemicals in food* (1969); Ad Hoc Committee on the Evaluation of Low Levels of Environmental Chemical Carcinogens, "Evaluation of environmental carcinogens, Report to the Surgeon General, U.S. Public Health Service," in the *Congressional Record,* E952–958 (February 9, 1972).

16. William Kornhauser, *Scientists in Industry,* 1 (University of California Press, Berkeley, 1962).

17. Ralph Nader *et al.,* editors *Whistle Blowing: The Report of the Conference on Professional Responsibility* (Bantam, New York, 1971).

18. Gordon D. Friedlander, *IEEE Spectrum 11,* 69–76 (October 1974); Gordon D. Friedlander, "Fixing BART," *IEEE Spectrum* 12, 43–45 (February 1975).

19. Nicholas Wade, "Genetics: Conference sets strict controls to replace moratorium," *Science 187,* 931–935 (1975); Stuart Auerbach, "And man created risks," *Washington Post* (March 9, 1975).

SUGGESTED SUPPLEMENTARY READINGS

BENNIGSON, LAWRENCE A., and ARNOLD I. BENNIGSON. "Product Liability: Manufacturers Beware!" *Harvard Business Review,* May-June 1974.

CASEY, WILLIAM J. "Corporate Responsibility as Seen from the SEC." *Business and Society Review,* 1 (Spring 1972).

DRUCKER, PETER F. "The Shame of Marketing." *Marketing Communications,* August 1960.

GOBLE, ROSS L., and ROY T. SHAW. *Controversy and Dialogue in Marketing.* Englewood Cliffs, N.J.: Prentice-Hall, 1975.

HETHERINGTON, J. A. C. "Fact and Legal Theory: Shareholders, Managers, and Corporate Responsibility." *Stanford Law Review,* 21 (January 1969).

KENNEDY, ROGER G. "Portfolio Decisions and Social Responsibility." In *Social Responsibility and Accountability,* ed. Jules Backman. New York: New York University Press, 1975.

LONGSTRETH, BEVIS, and DAVID H. ROSENBLOOM. *Corporate Social Responsibility and the Institutional Investor: A Report to the Ford Foundation.* New York: Praeger Publishers, 1973.

LOWRANCE, WILLIAM W. *Of Acceptable Risk: Science and the Determination of Safety.* Los Altos, Calif.: William Kaufmann, Inc., 1976.

"The Movement for Corporate Responsibility." *Economic Priorities Report,* 2 (April/May 1971).

NARVESON, JAN. "Animal Rights." *Canadian Journal of Philosophy,* 7 (March 1977).

National Commission on Product Safety. *Final Report Presented to the President and Congress.* Washington, D.C.: U.S. Government Printing Office, June 1970.

POWERS, CHARLES W., ed. *People/Profits: The Ethics of Investments.* New York: Council on Religion and International Affairs, 1972.

————. *Social Responsibility and Investments.* New York: Abington Press, 1971.

ROSENBERG, LARRY J. *Marketing.* Englewood Cliffs, N.J.: Prentice-Hall, 1977.

SIMON, JOHN G., CHARLES POWERS, and JON P. GUNNEMANN. *The Ethical Investor.* New Haven, Conn.: Yale University Press, 1972.

SINGER, PETER. *Animal Liberation: A New Ethics for Our Treatment of Animals.* New York: A New York Review Book, 1975.

STEINER, GEORGE A. *Business and Society* (2nd ed.), Chapter 15. New York: Random House, 1975.

Chapter *7*

ETHICAL ISSUES
IN ADVERTISING

case 1: The Firestone Tire and Rubber Case

The "Stop 25 Per Cent Quicker" ad read as follows:

> Year after year, more races are won on Firestone tires than on any other kind.
> But we're not racing just to win. We're in it to learn, too. And what we learn on the track goes into building safer tires for your car.
> Like the original Super Sports Wide Oval tire.
> It came straight out of Firestone racing research.
> It's built nearly two inches wider than regular tires. To corner better, run cooler, stop 25 per cent quicker.
> Before we sell a single tire, each new Firestone design is thoroughly tested on indoor test equipment, on our test track and in rigorous day-to-day driving conditions.
> Firestone tires are custom-built and personally inspected for an extra margin of safety. So that when you buy a Firestone tire—no matter how much or how little you pay—you get a safe tire.[1]

Between 1967 and 1968, Firestone Tire and Rubber ran a series of ads which were challenged by the Federal Trade Commission on the grounds that the ads were deceptive in a way that endangered human life and safety. Although the Commission had specific criticisms for each ad, the "Stop 25 Per Cent Quicker" ad can serve as an accurate illustration of most of the Commission's criticisms. The Commission argued first that contrary to the implications of Firestone advertising, Firestone could not truthfully claim that every tire is "custom-built and personally inspected" in any way that could guarantee each and every tire to be free of defects. Second, Firestone testing procedures, particularly the tests for stopping, were not made over a wide variety of conditions. There were two different widths of tires tested on a wet, smooth, concrete surface. All tests were run on the same day under the same load and with the same level of tire inflation pressure. Third, the Commission argued that the general tone of the ad lulled the consumer into a sense of false security. To counteract this tendency, the Commission argued that Firestone's ads should indicate to the consumer, "that the safety of any tire is affected by conditions of use, such as inflation pressure, vehicle weight, or other operating conditions."[2]

The Firestone Company challenged the FTC on all points, although Firestone ultimately lost in court. Firestone argued that they did in fact use the best quality control techniques known and that the vast majority of people never interpreted the ad as a guarantee of *absolute* safety. In defense of their testing procedures, Firestone contended that the conditions used were genuinely hazardous. There was no point in testing on a dry surface. Besides, it could be argued that performance would be even better on dry surfaces than on wet ones. Firestone had nothing but scorn for the requirement that ads contain explicit mention of the common-sense conditions that affect tire safety. The company said, "The Commission has reached the absurd conclusion that a tire cannot be advertised as safe . . . unless the advertisements also include a warning that air must be put in the tire. . . ."[3]

Notes

1. *FTC* vs. *Firestone,* 481 F 2d 246 (1973), p. 249
2. *Ibid.* p. 248.
3. "Firestone to Fight FTC on Ad Charges." *Wall Street Journal,* October 9, 1972, p. 9.

case 2: What Does "List Price" Mean?

Giant Food, Inc. is a supermarket chain, which sells housewares and appliances in some of its stores. Its advertising in the Washington, D.C. area sometimes appeared in the form:

Sunbeam Mixmaster	$24.00—Manufacturer List Price $37.95
Regina Twin Brush Waxer	$25.47—Manufacturer List $66

The advertisements also contained the following note at the bottom of each page.

> The manufacturer's list prices referred to in this advertisement are inserted to assist you in identification of the products and to allow you to compare accurately the selling prices offered here and elsewhere. The use of the term manufacturer's list, or similar terminology in our advertising, is not to imply that Giant has ever sold the advertised product at such list prices, or that the products are being offered for sale generally in the area at such list prices. Many reputable national brand manufacturers issue to retailers, from time to time, suggested retail list prices that are intended to afford reasonable profits to all retailers based upon their traditional costs of marketing. Giant's employment of self-service supermarket techniques enables it usually to sell below suggested list prices. Consumers, however, have come to recognize most brand merchandise by the list prices, rather than model numbers, consequently Giant includes these manufacturer's list prices so that you may make simple, intelligent comparisons between our selling prices and those of others.

According to buyers from three companies in the Washington area, their stores never sold at the list prices advertised by Giant. Thus where Giant had advertised a Sunbeam appliance as selling for $13.97 with a list of $21, the three stores charged the following prices for the same item: $16.49, $14.97 and $13.49.

Giant contended that at least some stores in the Washington area had advertised the product for sale at the manufacturer's list price. Furthermore, Giant's comparison shoppers had discovered stores which actually sold the advertised products at the list price. In addition the manufacturers themselves had used these list prices in *Life, Look,* and *McCall's.*

The Federal Trade Commission claimed that despite the note inserted by Giant, the term *manufacturer's list price* meant that this was the price at which the item was usually and customarily sold in that area.

The matter was taken to the U.S. Court of Appeals of the District of Columbia, which had to decide whether the FTC has the right—when an advertisement has two meanings, one of which is deceptive—to demand the termination of such advertising. The court was also expected to rule on whether the insertion itself tended to reinforce the deception.

From Thomas Garrett, Raymond C. Baumhart, Theodore Purcell, and Perry Roets, eds. *Cases in Business Ethics.* Copyright © 1968 by Appleton-Century Crofts, New York. Reprinted by permission of Prentice-Hall, Inc.

INTRODUCTION

Of all business activities, advertising is perhaps the one that is most frequently criticized. In this chapter, some of the most serious criticisms will be discussed. We begin with the charge that advertising is deceptive —that it is little more than a socially condoned form of lying. Everyone agrees that lying is wrong under most circumstances and hence that advertisements which actually lie are usually and probably always immoral. However, there is far less agreement on what constitutes a lie. A work of drama or fiction is not a lie. An honest mistake is not a lie. What about a "white lie"? What about exaggeration or the withholding of information? In the first selection, Arnold Isenberg examines these issues about lying, with particular focus on the intention of the speaker.

In "Advertising as a Philosophical System," Jules Henry argues that words like "truth" have a particular meaning for advertisers. Truth for them means "what sells," and thus ads are not literally *true.* However, are the claims of advertisers more like poetic utterances and harmless exaggerations than like deceitful lies? Henry seems to think that most ads are more like harmless exaggerations. However, he draws the line when advertisers try to "sell" health products or other items of fundamental importance to human health and welfare. Who cares whether one lipstick *really* makes one more beautiful than another? People do care, however, which medicine is more effective. Henry thinks there must be some rules for determining when exaggerations in advertisements are permissible and when an advertisement must present the literal truth.

Burton Leiser would expand our concern with deception beyond advertisements that "sell" health products or other items directly affecting human welfare. However, Leiser does not substitute other criteria for Henry's. Rather, he provides a catalogue of the kinds of deception that occur. He objects to deception because it interferes with rational economic decision-making and hence is costly to the consumer. In so doing, he thinks advertising is undermining the utilitarian results that business practice allegedly brings. Suppose Leiser's contention that misleading advertising distorts rational economic choice is correct. What kinds of people are being misled? This issue arises in the Firestone Tire and Rubber case. *Most* people did not construe the Firestone ads as guaranteeing absolute safety, but about 15 percent did. It is the responsibility of the Federal Trade Commission to determine when an advertisement is misleading or deceptive. Would the FTC be unreasonable to insist that Firestone explicitly mention that the safety of its tires depends on putting air in them or on putting the right amount of air in them? The two legal cases, *FTC* v. *Colgate-Palmolive Co.* and *FTC* v. *Sterling Drug, Inc.,* illustrate the difficulties in establishing deception. In the Colgate-Palmolive case the FTC decision was upheld, but in the Sterling Drug case the FTC was overruled. What criteria can the FTC use to establish deception?

In practice, regulatory agencies that grapple with these questions appeal to two competing standards—the reasonable consumer standard and the ignorant consumer standard. Ivan Preston describes the history behind the use of these two standards by the FTC and provides some analysis of the strengths and weaknesses of them. A decision as to which standard is appropriate has important implications for whether ads should be viewed as inherently deceptive or simply given to harmless exaggeration.

One classic defense of American business practice is that it gives the public what it wants: In the American free enterprise system the consumer is king, and the market responds to consumer demands. This response to consumer demand allegedly represents one of the chief strengths of the market economies over collectivist economies. In the latter economies, consumption patterns are severely constrained by government bureaucrats. In a competitive free enterprise economy, freedom of consumer choice is presumably protected.

Critics of advertising point out that the very effectiveness of advertising destroys the alleged benefits of consumer sovereignty. Contrary to the official myth, the market does not respond to consumer demand; rather it creates demand through advertising. Selections from John Kenneth Galbraith and David Braybrooke develop this theme. Both believe that this creation of demand through advertising has harmful effects. Central to Galbraith's argument is the distinction between privately produced and marketed goods and services and publicly rendered services. Publicly rendered services include most education, police and fire protection, public transit, and state parks, to name but a few. Galbraith argues that we are extremely rich in privately produced goods and tragically poor in publicly rendered services. Such an imbalance in private and public goods is harmful because public and private goods are symbiotic. For example, a transportation system is composed of both private and public elements which must be of uniform quality if the goals of safety and efficiency are to be achieved. Only an absurdly ill-coordinated society has excellent automobiles and poor highways. On traditional economic arguments, Galbraith's critics would argue that even if there is an imbalance between private goods and public services, this decision is the result of the free choice of individual consumers. Even if society is poor in terms of public goods, by what right does Galbraith substitute his judgment for the democratic judgment expressed in the market?

Galbraith has anticipated this line of reply. The argument of Galbraith's critics relies on the assumption that the wants of consumers originate with them. But Galbraith believes he has shown that assumption to be false. His challenge to the advocacy of consumer sovereignty is expanded in David Braybrooke's article. Braybrooke provides six reasons why business corporations cannot claim that they merely give society what it wants. Indeed, not only do business corporations not give society what it wants, but they actually subvert wants in ways that, although beneficial to the corporation, are harmful to the consumer. Automobile safety serves as Braybrooke's chief illustration.

The conclusions reached by Galbraith and Braybrooke have not gone unchallenged. Arguments such as Galbraith's are based on a distinction between basic needs and nonbasic needs. A need is a basic need in his categorization if it is a biological need necessary for survival or physical health. All other needs are not basic and are culturally influenced. In a stinging critique of Galbraith's views, Friedrich von Hayek is quite willing to accept Galbraith's distinction between different levels of need, but is quite unwilling to accept the conclusions Galbraith draws from this distinction. For example, von Hayek argues that it is not true that culturally induced needs are of comparatively little value. If that were true, the products of music, painting, and literature would be of little value. Moreover, even though nonbasic needs may not originate with the consumer, that fact does not show that such needs were not freely adopted. When a student develops the need to hear Beethoven rather than popular music, has his or her music teacher forced this need upon him or her? Surely not! Von Hayek argues: Consumers are of necessity influenced, but to be influenced is not to be *unduly* influenced and therefore unfree.

As one reads Galbraith, Braybrooke, and von Hayek, it seems that the underlying dispute centers on an old philosophical issue—the conditions for human freedom. Both Galbraith and Braybrooke think that some advertising is coercive and hence undermines human freedom and consumer sovereignty. Von Hayek, on the other hand, agrees that advertising influences consumers but denies that it coerces or unduly influences.

The philosophic tradition has distinguished two kinds of freedom— negative freedom and positive freedom. Negative freedom is simply the absence of coercion or undue influence by other human beings. Most of the freedoms enumerated in the Bill of Rights are negative freedoms. They protect certain individual activities from the coercive power of agents of the state. Positive freedom, on the other hand, is a broader concept; it includes not only the absence of coercion by other human beings but also freedom from internal restraints such as ignorance and lack of ability. Positive freedom thus includes self-mastery. On this view, one cannot be genuinely free if one is under the sway of compulsive desires or overwhelmed by depression. Nor is one free if one has no available alternatives. In summary, a person has negative freedom if he or she is not coerced or unduly influenced by others, and a person has positive freedom to do something if he or she has the ability to do that thing, has the opportunity to do it, has a genuine alternative, and is not forced by others to make the decision.

If advertising endangers freedom, it cannot pose dangers to negative freedom, since no advertiser coerces another to do something he or she does not want to do. Hence, the threat from advertising must be to positive freedom. The critics of advertising point out that some advertising diminishes genuine consumer choice. It also plays on ignorance and molds desires in such a way that one's self-mastery is undermined. If the critics are right, some advertising represents an assault on positive freedom.

However, the contentions of critics of advertising do not go unchallenged. The difficulty centers on the notion of self-mastery. Who is to say when a person is master of his or her fate? Either the individual decides, or the decision is made by some other authority. Suppose that, as a result of advertising, a person purchases consumer goods at the expense of an adequate savings account for the future? If the purchaser indicates that the decision represents what he or she genuinely wants to do, on what basis can an outsider deny that the decision was freely made? Suppose one buys the toothpaste on the basis that it gives your mouth sex appeal. One might disagree with the *reason* that person had for buying the toothpaste, but surely the decision was free.

Stanley Benn's concluding article grapples with the problem of how one can legitimately say that some advertising interferes with a person's freedom. Benn's first point is that advertising and propaganda raise difficulties for either of the two traditional definitions of freedom. Benn is not convinced by the critics who claim that much advertising undermines positive freedom. He thinks that most advertising would not interfere with the purchaser's freedom of choice, on either definition of freedom. What could be disturbing is the *grounds* on which the choice is made. Benn argues that what is needed is a distinction between legitimate and illegitimate influence. For him the key is whether the persuasion is directed toward human beings as rational autonomous agents. Rational persuasion certainly passes this test, and Benn thinks some nonrational persuasion does as well. He then suggests that we not only analyze the persuasion but take a look at the person on the receiving end. What can we reasonably expect of him or her? Benn seems to endorse the reasonable consumer model discussed above. He says we cannot protect men and women from their own carelessness. However, like Galbraith and Braybrooke, he does think advertising can subvert consumer choice; it can influence people to choose contrary to their own interests (contrary to what they need). Benn concludes with the provocative, but undeveloped, suggestion that nonrational persuasion is illegitimate when it influences people to choose on grounds that reflect a corrupt understanding of human nature. Benn is making an implicit appeal to the Platonic-Aristotelian tradition discussed in Chapter 1. There are choices that enhance human nature and choices that degrade it. Nonrational persuasion directed toward the latter is illegitimate. If Benn is right, a fair amount of advertising is morally suspect.

N.E.B.

OPINION IN FEDERAL TRADE COMMISSION v. COLGATE-PALMOLIVE CO. ET AL.

Chief Justice Earl Warren

The basic question before us is whether it is a deceptive trade practice, prohibited by § 5 of the Federal Trade Commission Act, to represent falsely that a televised test, experiment, or demonstration provides a viewer with visual proof of a product claim, regardless of whether the product claim is itself true.

The case arises out of an attempt by respondent Colgate-Palmolive Company to prove to the television public that its shaving cream, "Rapid Shave," outshaves them all. Respondent Ted Bates & Company, Inc., an advertising agency, prepared for Colgate three one-minute commercials designed to show that Rapid Shave could soften even the toughness of sandpaper. Each of the commercials contained the same "sandpaper test." The announcer informed the audience that, "To prove RAPID SHAVE'S super-moisturizing power, we put it right from the can onto this tough, dry sandpaper. It was apply . . . soak . . . and off in a stroke." While the announcer was speaking, Rapid Shave was applied to a substance that appeared to be sandpaper, and immediately thereafter a razor was shown shaving the substance clean.

The Federal Trade Commission issued a complaint against respondents Colgate and Bates charging that the commercials were false and deceptive. The evidence before the hearing examiner disclosed that sandpaper of the type depicted in the commercials could not be shaved immediately following the application of Rapid Shave, but required a substantial soaking period of approximately 80 minutes. The evidence also showed that the substance resembling sandpaper was in fact a simulated prop, or "mock-up," made of plexiglass to which sand had been applied. However, the examiner found that Rapid Shave could shave sandpaper, even though not in the short time represented by the commercials, and that if real sandpaper had been used in the commercials the inadequacies of television transmission would have made it appear to viewers to be nothing more than plain, colored paper. The examiner dismissed the complaint because neither misrepresentation—concerning the actual moistening time or the identity of the shaved substance—was in his opinion a material one that would mislead the public.

The Commission, in an opinion dated December 29, 1961, reversed the hearing examiner. It found that since Rapid Shave could not shave sandpaper within the time depicted in the commercials, respondents had misrepresented the product's moisturizing power. Moreover, the Com-

U.S. Reports 380 U.S. 374, 85 S. Ct. 1035, 13 L Ed. 2nd 904, pp 374–378, 385–394.

mission found that the undisclosed use of a plexiglass substitute for sandpaper was an additional material misrepresentation that was a deceptive act separate and distinct from the misrepresentation concerning Rapid Shave's underlying qualities. Even if the sandpaper could be shaved just as depicted in the commercials, the Commission found that viewers had been misled into believing they had seen it done with their own eyes. As a result of these findings the Commission entered a cease-and-desist order against the respondents.

An appeal was taken to the Court of Appeals for the First Circuit which rendered an opinion on November 20, 1962. That court sustained the Commission's conclusion that respondents had misrepresented the qualities of Rapid Shave, but it would not accept the Commission's order forbidding the future use of undisclosed simulations in television commercials. It set aside the Commission's order and directed that a new order be entered. On May 7, 1963, the Commission, over the protest of respondents, issued a new order narrowing and clarifying its original order to comply with the court's mandate. The Court of Appeals again found unsatisfactory that portion of the order dealing with simulated props and refused to enforce it. We granted certiorari, 377 U.S. 942, to consider this aspect of the case and do not have before us any question concerning the misrepresentation that Rapid Shave could shave sandpaper immediately after application, that being conceded. . . .

We are not concerned in this case with the clear misrepresentation in the commercials concerning the speed with which Rapid Shave could shave sandpaper, since the Court of Appeals upheld the Commission's finding on that matter and the respondents have not challenged the finding here. We granted certiorari to consider the Commission's conclusion that even if an advertiser has himself conducted a test, experiment or demonstration which he honestly believes will prove a certain product claim, he may not convey to television viewers the false impression that they are seeing the test, experiment or demonstration for themselves, when they are not because of the undisclosed use of mock-ups.

We accept the Commission's determination that the commercials involved in this case contained three representations to the public: (1) that sandpaper could be shaved by Rapid Shave; (2) that an experiment had been conducted which verified this claim; and (3) that the viewer was seeing this experiment for himself. Respondents admit that the first two representations were made, but deny that the third was. The Commission, however, found to the contrary, and, since this is a matter of fact resting on an inference that could reasonably be drawn from the commercials themselves, the Commission's finding should be sustained. For the purposes of our review, we can assume that the first two representations were true; the focus of our consideration is on the third, which was clearly false. The parties agree that § 5 prohibits the intentional misrepresentation of any fact which would constitute a material factor in a purchaser's decision whether to buy. They differ, however, in their conception of what "facts" constitute a "material factor" in a purchaser's decision to buy. Respondents submit, in effect, that the only material facts are those which deal with the substantive qualities of a product.[1] The Commission, on the other hand, submits that the misrepresentation of *any* fact so long as it materially induces a purchaser's decision to buy is a deception prohibited by § 5.

The Commission's interpretation of what is a deceptive practice seems more in line with the decided cases than that of respondents. This Court said in *Federal Trade Comm'n* v. *Algoma Lumber Co.*, 291 U.S. 67, 78: "[T]he public is entitled to get what it chooses, though the choice may be dictated by caprice or by fashion or perhaps by ignorance." It has long been considered a deceptive practice to state falsely that a product ordinarily sells for an inflated price but that it is being offered at a special reduced price, even if the offered price represents the actual value of the product and the purchaser is receiving his money's worth.[2] Applying respondents' arguments to these cases, it would appear that so long as buyers paid no more than the product was actually worth and the product contained the qualities advertised, the misstatement of an inflated original price was immaterial.

It has also been held a violation of § 5 for a seller to misrepresent to the public that he is in a certain line of business, even though the misstatement in no way affects the qualities of the product. As was said in *Federal Trade Comm'n* v. *Royal Milling Co.*, 288 U.S. 212, 216:

> If consumers or dealers prefer to purchase a given article because it was made by a particular manufacturer or class of manufacturers, they have a right to do so, and this right cannot be satisfied by imposing upon them an exactly similar article, or one equally as good, but having a different origin.

The courts of appeals have applied this reasoning to the merchandising of reprocessed products that are as good as new, without a disclosure that they are in fact reprocessed. And it has also been held that it is a deceptive practice to misappropriate the trade name of another.

Respondents claim that all these cases are irrelevant to our decision because they involve misrepresentations related to the product itself and not merely to the manner in which an advertising message is communicated. This distinction misses the mark for two reasons. In the first place, the present case is not concerned with a mode of communication, but with a misrepresentation that viewers have objective proof of a seller's product claim over and above the seller's word. Secondly, all of the above cases, like the present case, deal with methods designed to get a consumer to purchase a product, not with whether the product, when purchased, will perform up to expectations. We find an especially strong similarity between the present case and those cases in which a seller induces the public to purchase an arguably good product by misrepresenting his line of business, by concealing the fact that the product is reprocessed, or by misappropriating another's trademark. In each the seller has used a misrepresentation to break down what he regards to be an annoying or irrational habit of the buying public—the preference for particular manufacturers or known brands regardless of a product's actual qualities, the prejudice against reprocessed goods, and the desire for verificaton of a product claim. In each case the seller reasons that when the habit is broken the buyer will be satisfied with the performance of the product he receives. Yet, a misrepresentation has been used to break the habit and, as was stated in *Algoma Lumber,* a misrepresentation for such an end is not permitted.

We need not limit ourselves to the cases already mentioned because there are other situations which also illustrate the correctness of the Commission's finding in the present case. It is generally accepted that it is a deceptive practice to state falsely that a product has received a testimonial from a respected source. In addition, the Commission has consistently acted to prevent sellers from falsely stating that their product claims have been "certified." We find these situations to be indistinguishable from the present case. We can assume that in each the underlying product claim is true and in each the seller actually conducted an experiment sufficient to prove to himself the truth of the claim. But in each the seller has told the public that it could rely on something other than his word concerning both the truth of the claim and the validity of his experiment. We find it an immaterial difference that in one case the viewer is told to rely on the word of a celebrity or authority he respects, in another on the word of a testing agency, and in the present case on his own perception of an undisclosed simulation.

Respondents again insist that the present case is not like any of the above, but is more like a case in which a celebrity or independent testing agency has in fact submitted a written verification of an experiment actually observed, but, because of the inability of the camera to transmit accurately an impression of the paper on which the testimonial is written, the seller reproduces it on another substance so that it can be seen by the viewing audience. This analogy ignores the finding of the Commission that in the present case the seller misrepresented to the public that it was being given objective proof of a product claim. In respondents' hypothetical the objective proof of the product claim that is offered, the word of the celebrity or agency that the experiment was actually conducted, does exist; while in the case before us the objective proof offered, the viewer's own perception of an actual experiment, does not exist. Thus, in respondents' hypothetical, unlike the present case, the use of the undisclosed mock-up does not conflict with the seller's claim that there is objective proof.

We agree with the Commission, therefore, that the undisclosed use of plexiglass in the present commercials was a material deceptive practice, independent and separate from the other misrepresentation found. We find unpersuasive respondents' other objections to this conclusion. Respondents claim that it will be impractical to inform the viewing public that it is not seeing an actual test, experiment or demonstration, but we think it inconceivable that the ingenious advertising world will be unable, if it so desires, to conform to the Commission's insistence that the public be not misinformed. If, however, it becomes impossible or impractical to show simulated demonstrations on television in a truthful manner, this indicates that television is not a medium that lends itself to this type of commercial, not that the commercial must survive at all costs. Similarly unpersuasive is respondents' objection that the Commission's decision discriminates against sellers whose product claims cannot be "verified" on television without the use of simulations. All methods of advertising do not equally favor every seller. If the inherent limitations of a method do not permit its use in the way a seller desires, the seller cannot by material misrepresentation compensate for those limitations.

Respondents also claim that the Commission reached out to decide a question not properly before it and has presented this Court with an abstract question. They argue that since the commercials in the present case misrepresented the time element involved in shaving sandpaper, this Court should not consider the additional misrepresentation that the public had objective proof of the seller's claim. As we have already said, these misrepresentations are separate and distinct, and we fail to see why respondents should be sheltered from a cease-and-desist order with respect to one deceptive practice merely because they also engaged in another.

Respondents finally object to what they consider to be the absence of an adequate record to sustain the Commission's finding. It is true that in its initial stages the case was concerned more with the misrepresentation about the product's underlying qualities than with the misrepresentation that objective proof was being given. Nevertheless, both misrepresentations were in the case from the beginning, and respondents were never prejudicially misled into believing that the second question was not being considered. Nor was it necessary for the Commission to conduct a survey of the viewing public before it could determine that the commercials had a tendency to mislead, for when the Commission finds deception it is also authorized, within the bounds of reason, to infer that the deception will constitute a material factor in a purchaser's decision to buy. See *Federal Trade Comm'n* v. *Raladam Co.,* 316 U.S. 149, 152. We find the record in this case sufficient to support the Commission's findings.

We turn our attention now to the order issued by the Commission. . . . The Court of Appeals has criticized the reference in the Commission's order to "test, experiment or demonstration" as not capable of practical interpretation. It could find no difference between the Rapid Shave commercial and a commercial which extolled the goodness of ice cream while giving viewers a picture of a scoop of mashed potatoes appearing to be ice cream. We do not understand this difficulty. In the ice cream case the mashed potato prop is not being used for additional proof of the product claim, while the purpose of the Rapid Shave commercial is to give the viewer objective proof of the claims made. If in the ice cream hypothetical the focus of the commercial becomes the undisclosed potato prop and the viewer is invited, explicitly or by implication, to see for himself the truth of the claims about the ice cream's rich texture and full color, and perhaps compare it to a "rival product," then the commercial has become similar to the one now before us. Clearly, however, a commercial which depicts happy actors delightedly eating ice cream that is in fact mashed potatoes or drinking a product appearing to be coffee but which is in fact some other substance is not covered by the present order.

The crucial terms of the present order—"test, experiment or demonstration . . . represented . . . as actual proof of a claim"—are as specific as the circumstances will permit. If respondents in their subsequent commercials attempt to come as close to the line of misrepresentation as the Commission's order permits, they may without specifically intending to do so cross into the area proscribed by this order. However, it does not seem "unfair to require that one who deliberately goes perilously close to an area of proscribed conduct shall take the risk that he may cross the line." *Boyce Motor Lines, Inc.* v. *United States,* 342 U.S. 337, 340. In commercials where the emphasis is on the seller's word, and not on the viewer's own perception, the respondents need not fear that an undisclosed use of props is prohibited by the present order. On the other hand, when the commercial not only makes a claim, but also invites the viewer to rely on his own perception for demonstrative proof of the claim, the respondents will be aware that the use of undisclosed props in strategic places might be a material deception. We believe that respondents will have no difficulty applying the Commission's order to the vast majority of their contemplated future commercials. If, however, a situation arises in which respondents are sincerely unable to determine whether a proposed course of action would violate the present order, they can, by complying with the Commission's rules, oblige the Commission to give them definitive advice as to whether their proposed action, if pursued, would constitute compliance with the order.

Notes

1. Brief for Respondent Colgate, p. 16: "What [the buyer] is interested in is whether the actual product he buys will look and perform the way it appeared on his television set." *Id.,* at 17: "[A] buyer's real concern is with the truth of the substantive claims or promises made to him, not with the means used to make them." *Id.,* at 20: "[T]he Commission's error was to confuse the substantive claim made for a product with the means by which such claim was conveyed."

   Brief for Respondent Bates, pp. 2–3: "If the viewer or reader of the advertisement buys the product, and it will do exactly what the portrayal in the advertisement asserts it will do, can there be any unlawful misrepresentation?" *Id.,* at 13–14: "What induces the buyer to purchase is the claim that the product will perform as represented in the portrayed test. That is the material claim." *Id.,* at 25: "It is not a representation in any way relating to the product or to its purchase, so that even if the strained suggestion that there is such an implied representation were realistic, the representation plainly would be immaterial."

2. *Federal Trade Comm'n* v. *Standard Education Society,* 302 U.S. 112, 115–117; *Kalwajtys* v. *Federal Trade Comm'n,* 237 F. 2d 654, 656 (C. A. 7th Cir. 1956), cert. denied, 352 U.S. 1025.

OPINION IN FEDERAL TRADE COMMISSION
v. STERLING DRUG, INC.

Judge Irving R. Kaufman

The Federal Trade Commission, appellant here, instituted an action in the District Court for the Southern District of New York praying for a temporary injunction designed to prevent the dissemination of what the Commission alleged it had reason to believe was false and misleading advertising. Judge Dawson denied the injunction. . . .

I

The controversy has its roots in the December 29, 1962 issue of the *Journal of the American Medical Association,* which carried an article written by two physicians and a medical statistician,[1] titled "A Comparative Study of Five Proprietary Analgesic Compounds." The article analyzed the results of a study made of the efficacy as well as the unhappy after-effects of certain pain-relieving drugs, sold in pharmacies and supermarkets throughout the nation. These five were Bayer Aspirin, St. Joseph's Aspirin, Bufferin (aspirin with buffering agent), and two of the so-called "combination of ingredients" tablets, Anacin and Excedrin. Also used in the experiment, as a form of control, was a placebo, the name given a harmless non-medicinal substance administered in the form of a pill for those pill-poppers whose ailment is without organic origin and whose pain seems to be relieved by following the ritual of downing a tablet irrespective of size, shape, or content which the user believes has qualities of medicinal value; the placebo utilized by the three researchers was composed of lactose, or milk sugar, and a conventional cornstarch binder. After investigating the efficacy of the five analgesic agents as pain relievers, the study noted, "The data failed to show any statistically significant difference among any of the drugs (that is, excluding the placebo) at any of the check points [fifteen minutes through four hours] . . . [T]here are no important differences among the compounds studied in rapidity of onset, degree, or duration of analgesia." Fifteen minutes after the drugs were administered, so-called "pain-relief scores" were computed, and Bayer earned a score of 0.94, while the next most effective drug at that point in time, Excedrin, earned a score of 0.90; the others were rated at 0.76 and lower. The chart on which these figures appeared indicated that the "standard error of mean," or the margin of statistical accuracy of the study, was 0.124. Upon investigating the incidence of stomach upset after the administration of the five drugs as well as the placebo, the

The Federal Reporter 317 Fed 669, pp. 370–378 edited.

researchers came to this conclusion: "Excedrin and Anacin form a group for which the incidence of upset stomach is significantly greater than is the incidence after Bayer Aspirin, St. Joseph's Aspirin, Bufferin, or the placebo. The rates of upset stomach associated with these last 4 treatments are not significantly different, one from the other." The accompanying table revealed that of the 829 doses taken of Bayer Aspirin, there were nine episodes of upset stomach, a rate of 1.1%; the placebo was administered in 833 cases, and caused stomach upset but seven times, a rate of 0.8%. The article concluded by stating, "This study was supported by a grant from the Federal Trade Commission, Washington, D.C."[2]

It is not difficult to understand the heartwarming reception this article received in the upper echelons of Sterling and its Madison Avenue colleagues; no sooner were the results of the study published in the *Journal of the American Medical Association* when Sterling Drug and its advertising agencies decided to make the most of them. This decision, we may fairly assume, did not surprise Sterling's competitors. The public had long been saturated with various claims proved by the study to be of doubtful validity. One of the products had boasted in its advertisements that it "works twice as fast as aspirin," and "protects you against the stomach distress you can get from aspirin alone"; another, that it "does not upset the stomach" and "is better than aspirin"; and yet another, that it is "50% stronger than aspirin." Believing that the Judgment Day has finally arrived and seeking to counteract the many years of hard-sell by what it now believed to be the hard facts, Sterling and its co-defendants prepared and disseminated advertising of which the following, appearing in *Life* Magazine and numerous newspapers throughout the country, is representative:

GOVERNMENT-SUPPORTED MEDICAL TEAM COMPARES BAYER ASPIRIN AND FOUR OTHER POPULAR PAIN RELIEVERS.

FINDINGS REPORTED IN THE HIGHLY AUTHORITATIVE JOURNAL OF THE AMERICAN MEDICAL ASSOCIATION REVEAL THAT THE HIGHER PRICED COMBINATION-OF-INGREDIENTS PAIN RELIEVERS UPSET THE STOMACH WITH SIGNIFICANTLY GREATER FREQUENCY THAN ANY OF THE OTHER PRODUCTS TESTED, WHILE BAYER ASPIRIN BRINGS RELIEF THAT IS AS FAST, AS STRONG, AND AS GENTLE TO THE STOMACH AS YOU CAN GET.

This important new medical study, supported by a grant from the federal government, was undertaken to compare the stomach-upsetting effects, the speed of relief, and the amount of relief offered by five leading pain relievers, including Bayer Aspirin, aspirin with buffering, and combination-of-ingredients products. Here is a summary of the findings.

UPSET STOMACH

According to this report, the higher priced combination-of-ingredients products upset the stomach with significantly greater frequency than any of the other products tested, while Bayer Aspirin, taken as directed, is as gentle to the stomach as a plain sugar pill.

SPEED AND STRENGTH

The study shows that there is no significant difference among the products tested in rapidity of onset, strength, or duration of relief. Nonetheless, it is interesting to note that within just fifteen minutes, Bayer Aspirin had a somewhat higher pain relief score than any of the other products.

PRICE

As unreasonable as it may seem, the products which are most likely to upset the stomach—that is, the combination-of-ingredients products—actually cost substantially more than Bayer Aspirin. The fact is that these products, as well as the buffered product, cost up to 75% more than Bayer Aspirin.

II

In a proceeding such as this, the burden was upon the Commission, in seeking its temporary injunction against the advertising, to show that it had "reason to believe" that the advertisements were false and misleading, and that the injunction during the pendency of administrative proceedings which the Commission initiated against Sterling Drug in January 1963 "would be to the interest of the public."

The Commission alleged and sought to prove that the appellees' advertisements falsely represented, directly and by implication: (a) that the findings of the medical research team were endorsed and approved by the United States Government; (b) that the publication of the article in the *Journal of the American Medical Association* is evidence of endorsement and approval thereof by the association and the medical profession; (c) that the research team found that Bayer Aspirin is not upsetting to the stomach and is as gentle thereto as a sugar pill; (d) that the research team found that Bayer Aspirin, after fifteen minutes following administration, affords a higher degree of pain relief than any other product tested. An injunction was alleged to be in the public interest, since the consuming public would otherwise unwarrantedly rely upon the advertising to their "irreparable injury," and since competitors of Sterling Drug might be encouraged to engage in similar advertising tactics in order to maintain competitive standing.

The legal principles to be applied here are quite clear. The central purpose of the provisions of the Federal Trade Commission Act under discussion is in effect to abolish the rule of *caveat emptor* which traditionally defined rights and responsibilities in the world of commerce. That rule can no longer be relied upon as a means of rewarding fraud and deception, *Federal Trade Commission* v. *Standard Education Society,* 302 U.S. 112, 116, 58 S.Ct. 113, 82 L.Ed. 141 (1937), and has been replaced by a rule which gives to the consumer the right to rely upon representations of facts as the truth, *Goodman* v. *Federal Trade Commission,* 244 F.2d 584, 603 (9th Cir., 1957). In order best to implement the prophylactic purpose of the statute, it has been consistently held that advertising falls within its proscription not only when there is proof of actual deception but also

when the representations made have a capacity or tendency to deceive,
i.e., when there is a likelihood or fair probability that the reader will be
misled. . . . For the same reason, proof of intention to deceive is not
requisite to a finding of violation of the statute, *Gimbel Bros., Inc.* v. *Federal
Trade Commission,* 116 F.2d 578 (2d Cir., 1941); since the purpose of the
statute is not to punish the wrongdoer but to protect the public, the
cardinal factor is the probable effect which the advertiser's handiwork will
have upon the eye and mind of the reader. It is therefore necessary in
these cases to consider the advertisement in its entirety and not to engage
in disputatious dissection. The entire mosaic should be viewed rather
than each tile separately. "[T]he buying public does not ordinarily carefully study or weigh each word in an advertisement. The ultimate impression upon the mind of the reader arises from the sum total of not only
what is said but also of all that is reasonably implied." [*Aronberg* v. *Federal
Trade Commission,* 132 F.2d 165, 167 (7th Cir., 1942).]

Unlike that abiding faith which the law has in the "reasonable man,"
it has very little faith indeed in the intellectual acuity of the "ordinary
purchaser" who is the object of the advertising campaign.

> The general public has been defined as "that vast multitude which includes
> the ignorant, and unthinking and the credulous, who, in making purchases,
> do not stop to analyze but too often are governed by appearances and
> general impressions." The average purchaser has been variously character-
> ized as not "straight thinking," subject to "impressions," uneducated, and
> grossly misinformed; he is influenced by prejudice and superstition; and he
> wishfully believes in miracles, allegedly the result of progress in science. . . .
> The language of the ordinary purchaser is casual and unaffected. He is not
> an "expert in grammatical construction" or an "educated analytical reader"
> and, therefore, he does not normally subject every word in the advertise-
> ment to careful study.

[Callman, Unfair Competition and Trademarks § 19.2(a) (1), at 341–44
(1950), and the cases there cited.][3]
It is well established that advertising need not be literally false in order
to fall within the proscription of the act. Gone for the most part, fortunately, are the days when the advertiser was so lacking in subtlety as to
represent his nostrum as superlative for "arthritis, rheumatism, neu-
ralgia, sciatica, lumbago, gout, coronary thrombosis, brittle bones, bad
teeth, malfunctioning glands, infected tonsils, infected appendix, gall
stones, neuritis, underweight, constipation, indigestion, lack of energy,
lack of vitality, lack of ambition and inability to sleep. . . ." See *Federal
Trade Commission* v. *National Health Aids, Inc.,* 108 F.Supp. 340, 342 (D.Md.
1952). The courts are no longer content to insist simply upon the "most
literal truthfulness," *Moretrench Corp.* v. *Federal Trade Commission,* 127 F.2d
792 at 795, for we have increasingly come to recognize that "Advertisements as a whole may be completely misleading although every sentence
separately considered is literally true. This may be because things are
omitted that should be said, or because advertisements are composed or

purposefully printed in such way as to mislead." . . . There are two obvious methods of employing a true statement so as to convey a false impression: one is the half truth, where the statement is removed from its context and the nondisclosure of its context renders the statement misleading, see *P. Lorillard Co.* v. *Federal Trade Commission,* 186 F.2d 52, 58 (4th Cir., 1950); a second is the ambiguity, where the statement in context has two or more commonly understood meanings, one of which is deceptive.

III

The Federal Trade Commission asserts here that the vice of the Bayer advertisement is of these types. It concedes that none of the statements made therein is literally false, but it contends that the half-truths and ambiguities of the advertisement give it "reason to believe" that our hypothetical, sub-intelligent, less-than-careful reader will be misled thereby. Thus, we are told that the reference in large type to a "Government-Supported Medical Team" gives the misleading impression that the United States Government endorsed or approved the findings of the research team. Surely the fact that the word "supported" might have alternative dictionary definitions of "endorsed" or "approved" is not alone sufficient to show reason to believe that the ordinary reader will probably construe the word in this manner. Most words *do* have alternative dictionary definitions; if that in itself were a sufficient legal criterion, few advertisements would survive. Here, no impression is conveyed that the *product itself* has its source in or is being endorsed by the Government; for this reason, the cases cited by the Commission are inapt. If the reader of the advertisement believes that the Government in some way vouched for the soundness of the study's conclusions, then this impression would have also been conveyed had the advertisement "told the whole story," relating in full detail the extent of the Commission's participation: it selected the research team, supported the study with a grant, and authorized the publication of the report. The capsulized expression "Government-Supported" can not, therefore, be characterized as misleading. The Commission indicated to us upon argument that it would have been equally unhappy had the advertisement stated that the medical team was "Government-Financed" or "Government-Subsidized." But surely the concise statement of an established fact, immediately thereafter expanded—"This important new medical study, supported by a grant from the federal government . . ."—cannot fairly be proscribed by the Commission; the alternatives are complete omission of the admittedly true statement or long-winded qualification and picayune circumlocution, neither of which we believe was in the contemplation of Congress.

The Commission's attack upon the use of the phrase "Findings reported in the highly authoritative *Journal of the American Medical Association,*" as misleadingly connoting endorsement and approval, is similarly unfounded, for much the same reasons already discussed. To assert that the ordinary reader would conclude from the use of the word "authoritative" that the study was endorsed by the *Journal* and the Association is to attribute to him not only a careless and imperceptive mind but also a propensity for unbounded flights of fancy. This we are not yet prepared to do. If the reader's natural reaction is to think that the study, because of publication in the *Journal,* is likely to be accurate, intelligent, and well-documented, then the reaction is wholly justified, and one which the advertiser has every reason to expect and to seek to inculcate. We, as judges, know that an article on the law which has survived the rigorous selection and editing process of one of the major law publications is most probably more reliable and more thoroughly researched than the report of a recent trial or judicial decision carried in the *Podunk Daily Journal.* But we hardly think that there is "reason to believe" that either we or the lay observer would tend to construe the views expressed in the article as having secured the wholehearted endorsement and approval of the "authoritative" periodical in which it appears.[4]

The Commission's third objection deals with the probable vulnerability of the ordinary reader to Bayer's representations concerning stomach upset. We pass without comment the Commission's claim that the Bayer advertisement represented that no other available analgesic product was more gentle to the stomach; clearly, any comparative statements made in the advertisement could only be understood to refer to the four other products tested. More seriously pressed upon us is the claim that the reader will be deceived by the statement that "Bayer Aspirin, taken as directed, is as gentle to the stomach as a plain sugar pill." "Sugar pill," we are told, is misleading terminology; the advertisement should have used the word "placebo." Again, we are confronted by a simple problem of communication. For how can we expect our hypothetically slow-witted reader to react when he reads that "Bayer Aspirin is as gentle to the stomach as a placebo"! Most likely, he will either read on, completely unaware of the significance of the statement, or impatiently turn the page. Perhaps he will turn to his neighbor, and in response to a request for a definition of the troublesome word be greeted with the plausible query, "A *what?*" (This assumes that the reader will have been able to muster the correct pronounciation of the word.) But, all this aside, the pill used as a control in this case was indeed constituted of milk sugar, and the use of the term "sugar pill" was neither inaccurate nor misleading.

The Commission next shifts its focus to the words "as gentle as," alleging that it has reason to believe that the reader will conclude that Bayer is not in the slightest bit harmful to the stomach; this can be rectified, we are told, by stating that Bayer is "no more upsetting" than the placebo, which did in fact cause a very minor degree of stomach upset. Unlike the standard of the average reader which the Commission avidly endorses throughout these proceedings, it here would have us believe that he is linguistically and syntactically sensitive to the difference between the phrases "as gentle as" and "no more upsetting than." We do not find that the Commission has reason to believe that this will be the case, and we therefore reject its contentions.

Finally, the Commission attacks the manner in which the Bayer advertisement treated the results of the study on speed and effectiveness of pain relief. As we understand the Commission's argument, no objection is taken to the statement that "The study shows that there is no significant difference among the products tested in rapidity of onset, strength, or duration of relief." Indeed, no objection can properly be taken, for the statement reproduces almost verbatim one of the conclusions enumerated in the article. It is thought, however, that the advertisement improperly represents greater short-run pain relief with Bayer Aspirin by stating that "Nonetheless, it is interesting to note that within just fifteen minutes, Bayer Aspirin had a somewhat higher pain relief score than any of the other products." As we have seen, the statement is literally true, for Bayer's "score" after fifteen minutes was 0.94 while its closest competitor at that time interval was rated 0.90. The fact that the margin of accuracy of that scoring system was 0.124—meaning that the second-place drug might fare as well as or better than Bayer over the long run of statistical tests—does not detract from the fact that on this particular test, Bayer apparently fared better than any other product in relieving pain within fifteen minutes after its administration. It is true that a close examination of the statistical chart drawn up by the three investigators reveals that they thought the difference between all of the drugs at that time interval not to be "significantly different." But that is precisely what the Bayer advertisement stated in the sentence preceding its excursion into the specifics of the pain-relief scores. We cannot, therefore, conclude that Judge Dawson clearly erred in finding that the Commission failed properly to carry its statutory burden of proof, however slim that burden might be. Not even the Commission contends that in a proceeding under section 13(a) the judge is merely a rubber stamp, stripped of the power to exercise independent judgment on the issue of the Commission's "reason to believe."

The Commission relies heavily, especially as to the pain-relief aspects of its case, upon *P. Lorillard Co.* v. *Federal Trade Commission,* 186 F.2d 52 (4th Cir., 1950). There, *Reader's Digest* sponsored a scientific study of the major cigarettes, investigating the relative quantities of nicotine, tars, and resins. It accompanied its conclusions with a chart which revealed that, although Old Gold cigarettes ranked lowest in these deleterious substances, the quantitative differences between the brands were insignificant and would have no effect in reducing physiological harm to the smoker. The tenor of the study is revealed by its cheery words to the smoker "who need no longer worry as to which cigarette can most effectively nail down his coffin. For one nail is just about as good as another." Old Gold trumpeted its dubious success, claiming that it was found lowest in nicotine, tars, and resins, and predicting that the reader upon examining the results of the study would say "From now on, my cigarette is Old Gold." The Court quite properly upheld a cease-and-desist order issued by the Commission. An examination of that case shows that it is completely distinguishable in at least two obvious and significant respects. Although the statements made by Old Gold were at best literally true, they were used in the advertisement to convey an impression diametrically opposed to that intended by the writer of the article. As the Court noted, "The company proceeded to advertise this difference as though it had received a citation for public service instead of a castigation from the *Reader's Digest.*" 186 F.2d at 57. Moreover, as to the specifics of brand-comparison, it was found that anyone reading the advertisement would gain "the very definite impression that Old Gold cigarettes were less irritating to the throat and less harmful than other leading brands of cigarettes. . . . The truth was exactly the opposite." 186 F.2d at 58. In the instant case, Sterling Drug can in no sense be said to have conveyed a misleading impression as to either the spirit[5] or the specifics of the article published in the *Journal of the American Medical Association.*

Notes

1. Dr. DeKornfeld was then chief of the department of anesthesiology, Baltimore City Hospitals. Dr. Lasagna was affiliated with Johns Hopkins School of Medicine. Mr. Frazier was director of the Bureau of Biostatistics, Baltimore City Health Department.
2. We find support in the record for the article's statement regarding the Commission's involvement in the study. For in January 1963, the Chairman of the Federal Trade Commission appeared before a special committee of the Senate, and testified, in response to the question "I understand that the Aspirin study was financed at least in part by a Federal Trade Commission grant. Is that so?" that "[W]e had these tests made, sir . . . we paid for the study. We obtained and entered into a contract to get that study made."
3. See Federal Trade Commission v. Standard Education Society, 302 U.S. 112, 116, 58 S.Ct. 113, 82 L.Ed. 141 (1937); Exposition Press, Inc. v. Federal Trade Commission, 295 F.2d 869, 872 (2d Cir., 1961), cert. denied. 370 U.S. 917, 82 S.Ct. 1554, 8 L.Ed.2d 497 (1962); Niresk Industries, Inc. v. Federal Trade Commission, 278 F.2d 337, 342 (7th Cir.), cert. denied, 364 U.S. 883, 81 S.Ct. 173, 5 L. Ed.2d 104 (1960); Book-of-the-Month Club, Inc. v. Federal Trade Commission, 202 F.2d 486 (2d Cir., 1953); Moretrench Corp. v. Federal Trade Commission, 127 F.2d 792, 795 (2d Cir., 1942); Charles of the Ritz Distributors Corp. v. Federal Trade Commission, supra; Florence Mfg. Co. v. J. C. Dowd & Co., 178 F. 73, 75 (2d Cir., 1910); Handler, "The Control of False Advertising under the Wheeler-Lea Act," 6 *Law & Contemp. Prob. 91, 98* (1939).
4. It is interesting to note that the American Medical Association, contemporaneously with the publication of the issue of the *Journal* in which the findings appeared, transmitted a press release throughout the country which called attention to the study, the fact of its publication in the *Journal,* and a detailed summary of its findings. Subsequently, the AMA issued another press release,

claiming that certain current advertising had been misinterpreted as statements of AMA endorsement of Bayer Aspirin. We note, however, that the
press release, although disclaiming endorsement of the product itself, did not
question either the findings of the article or the responsibility of the AMA in
publishing them.
5. The Commission makes no contention here that the allegedly misleading
advertising will cause or induce physical harm.

CONDITIONS FOR LYING

Arnold Isenberg

In the following analysis of the lie, I shall keep to those points that have
some connection with issues in ethics.

A lie is a statement made by one who does not believe it with the
intention that someone else shall be led to believe it.

This definition leaves open the possibility that a person should be
lying, even though he says what is true: for example, a man who does not
know that his watch is one hour slow says, "It is ten o'clock," thinking
that it is nine. He gives what he thinks is the wrong time; but it happens
to be the right time. The dictionary definition—"a falsehood uttered or
acted for the purpose of deception"—rules out this awkward possibility
but has, I believe, other things the matter with it. Any short definition will
leave some queer possibilities open. The differences among customary
definitions are not very material for the ethics of lying.

The essential parts of the lie, according to our definition, are three. (1)
A statement—and we may or may not wish to divide this again into two
parts, a proposition and an utterance. (2) A disbelief or a lack of belief
on the part of the speaker. (3) An intention on the part of the speaker.
Since (1) and (2) are obvious, I shall elaborate only on (3).

The intention is essential. If the speaker does not intend to make
someone believe what he himself does not believe, he is not lying. Examples: (a) A *mistaken* utterance is not as such a lie. (b) The deliberate
utterance of a statement that the speaker *knows* to be false need not be
a lie. "There is a camel in my closet." This is not a lie if the person
addressed is one whom the speaker believes intelligent and informed. (c)
Poets do not often lie, even when they say what they know is false; for they
do not often wish or expect to be believed. Plato, who tries to show that

From "Deontology and the Ethics of Lying" by Arnold Isenberg, in *Philosophy and
Phenomenological Research*, vol. 24, no. 3, March 1964. Reprinted by permission.

poetry is false, if not mendacious, touches only on what is relatively credible in Homer and the other poets; not on any of the real whoppers which Lucian was to list later on—one-eyed giants, caves of the winds, men turned into swine. These were not "dangerous" untruths; for they would not be believed.

Since the author of the lie wants to be believed, he will have some opinions beforehand about the people he is speaking to and will shape his lie accordingly. This means that the element of intention interlocks, causally, if not logically, with the other two elements in the lie, as they do with each other. For example, the liar will not only have reason for not believing his own words, but will have some opinion as to their "inherent credibility," that is, their plausibility relative to the general information that he thinks is available to the members of his audience. If the listener is believed to be very foolish or very ignorant, the inherent credibility of the lie need not be great. And since, among the supposed grounds of the listener's credence, there is a certain opinion about the speaker and the likelihood of his telling the truth, there will enter into the speaker's intention an opinion about *that* opinion: he will reckon upon what he believes to be the other man's opinion of him.

Thus there appears another, decidedly complex element which, though it may not belong to the definition of the lie, is always present: a set of estimates by the speaker, apart from his main opinion of the statement he makes, of the existing evidence for that statement, the probability of the statement upon various portions of that evidence, the listener's mentality and cognitive situation. Liars, dupes, and cognitive situations are of many different kinds; and so the combinations of elements within the lie can be very numerous.

Now, what *is* the liar's intention? I believe we have to say that what is common to every lie is the wish to make someone believe something— the same motive that so often prompts us to tell the truth. We should beware of ascribing a stronger intention to the liar, e.g., the "wish to deceive." One can lie without wishing to deceive. A man who tells a creditor that he has no money on his person wants the other to believe what he says, not to be mistaken in what he is led to believe: it might suit this man very well, in fact, if he *had* no money just then and could say so truthfully. On the other hand, it can be the liar's intention to produce an *erroneous* belief—for example, about a future point of attack in time of war. But the "wish to deceive" is stronger still. That phrase implies that deception is the end and suggests, therefore, that a man would look about at random for a false story to perpetrate upon others. Such a motive, or something like it, is to be found in the April Fool's Day joke, where the joker indeed does not care what it is that he gets the other to believe, so long as it is false—for he wishes "to deceive." If there were a devil who enjoyed the thought of our being in perpetual error, he would be regularly governed by a will to deceive. But it is obvious that we should be letting too many people off if we said that no one is a liar who does not wish to deceive.

A liar, if successful, does deceive. And if he is unsuccessful, the observer will naturally be tempted to say that he was "trying to deceive." But that is only an example of a common mistake which, though not serious in ordinary speech, is fatal to the precise analysis of motives. Some general class to which either the object or the result of an action belongs is made to sound like the object of the action. If A wants to get the upper hand of B and C, we say he desires power; and that is objectionable, because there may well exist for some men a general object, power, which is different from the generalized description of a number of objects.

But though deception is not always the liar's aim, it cannot very well be absent from his consciousness. He knows that if his lie succeeds, the victim will be deceived. For not only does he not *believe* what he says; but in saying it, he is naturally aware of the proposition and therefore aware of his own opinion. And since he knows too what his intention is, he knows that he is trying to make someone believe what *he* thinks false or doubtful. (The name for this state of mind is "duplicity.") Therefore, even though he is not *trying* to deceive, he is *willing* that his action should deceive.

Since there is bound to be a considerable vagueness in our conception of the lie, there will be many doubtful cases. (i) If the *statement* is very vague, it can hardly be the subject of a definite lie. A celebrated case, formerly pending in the courts, turned upon the question whether a man can lie in saying that he did not "follow the Communist line." But there are vaguer statements still; and though we could accuse their authors of some kind of imposture, we could not accuse them of lying. Besides, the usage of the word "lie" restricts the subject of the lie to questions of information in a fairly narrow sense; it does not permit us to speak of lying about matters of theory. Suppose that a scientist, who is to be the referee in a bet on the laws of motion, has been bribed to distort the truth. I do not think we would say he was lying; but if he were supposed to be reporting scientific *opinion* about the laws of motion, we should call it a lie. Yet usage is capricious; and if an adult were to tell a child that the world was full of demons, without believing it himself, we should probably call that a lie. Other types of statement could be mentioned which can only questionably figure in lies. (ii) *Belief* and *disbelief* are strong or weak and also vary in a good many other ways. If a speaker thinks it very probable that a proposition, p, is true but intentionally communicates to another a degree of confidence slightly greater than his own, the question of mendacity may well be doubtful. (iii) And the *intention* may be strong or weak, definite or indefinite. The large and irregular fringe which surrounds the concept of intention is, as a matter of fact, the source of most of our uncertainties in judging the veracity of others. An advertiser who "boosts" his product beyond its merits, knowing that everyone expects him to exaggerate and that no one will believe what he says, is probably not to be called a liar. But an advertiser who makes a false claim for his product in the hope that, though *most* will not believe him, *some* people may, is a liar. And an advertiser who makes exorbitant claims in the hope of creating, through suggestion, a partial or subconscious belief in the consumer is a borderline liar.

ADVERTISING AS A PHILOSOPHICAL SYSTEM

Jules Henry

Advertising is an expression of an irrational economy that has depended for survival on a fantastically high standard of living incorporated into the American mind as a moral imperative. Yet a moral imperative cannot of itself give direction; there must be some institution or agency to constantly direct and redirect the mind and emotions to it. This function is served for the high-rising living standard by advertising which, day and night, with increasing pressure reminds us of what there is to buy; and if money accumulates for one instant in our bank accounts, advertising reminds us that it must be spent and tells us how to do it. As a quasi-moral institution advertising, like any other basic cultural institution anywhere, must have a philosophy and a method of thinking. The purpose of this [article] is to demonstrate the character of advertising thought, and to show how it relates to other aspects of our culture. In order to make this relationship manifest at the outset I have dubbed this method of thought *pecuniary philosophy*.

THE PROBLEM

Since the problem of truth is central to all philosophy, the reader is asked to ask himself, while perusing the following advertising, "Is it literally true that . . ."

> . . . everybody's talking about the new *Starfire* [automobile]?

> . . . *Alpine* cigarettes "put the men in menthol smoking"?

> . . . a woman in *Distinction* foundations is so beautiful that all other women want to kill her?

> . . . *Hudson's Bay Scotch* "is scotch for the men among men"?

> . . . if one buys clothes at Whitehouse and Hardy his wardrobe will have "the confident look of a totally well-dressed man"?

> . . . *Old Spice* accessories are "the finest grooming aides a man can use"?

> . . . *7 Crown* whiskey "holds within its icy depths a world of summertime"?

> . . . "A man needs *Jockey* support" because *Jockey* briefs "give a man the feeling of security and protection he needs"?

> . . . one will "get the smoothest, safest ride of your life on tires of *Butyl*"?

> . . . the new *Pal Premium Injector* blade "takes the friction out of shaving" because it "rides on liquid ball bearings"?

> . . . *Pango Peach* color by Revlon comes "from east of the sun . . . west of the moon where each tomorrow dawns" . . . is "succulent on your lips" and

"sizzling on your finger tips (And on your toes, goodness knows)" and so will be one's "adventure in paradise"?

. . . if a woman gives in to her "divine restlessness" and paints up her eyelids with *The Look* her eyes will become "jungle green . . . glittery gold . . . flirty eyes, tiger eyes"?

. . . a "new ingredient" in *Max Factor Toiletries* "separates the men from the boys"?

. . . when the Confederate General Basil Duke arrived in New York at the end of the Civil War "*Old Crow* [whiskey] quite naturally would be served"?

. . . *Bayer* aspirin provides "the fastest, most gentle to the stomach relief you can get from pain"?

Are these statements, bits of advertising copy, true or false? Are they merely "harmless exaggeration or puffing"[1] as the Federal Trade Commission calls it? Are they simply para-poetic hyperboles—exotic fruits of Madison Avenue creativity? Perhaps they are fragments of a new language, expressing a revolutionary pecuniary truth that derives authority from a phantasmic advertising universe. In the following pages I try to get some clarity on this difficult and murky matter by teasing out of the language of advertising some of the components of pecuniary philosophy I perceive there.

Pecuniary Pseudo-Truth. No sane American would think that literally everybody is "talking about the new *Starfire,*" that Alpine cigarettes literally "put the men in menthol smoking" or that a woman wearing a *Distinction* foundation garment becomes so beautiful that her sisters literally want to kill her. Since he will not take these burblings literally, he will not call them lies, even though they are all manifestly untrue. Ergo, a new kind of truth has emerged—*pecuniary pseudo-truth*—which may be defined as a false statement made as if it were true, but not intended to be believed. No proof is offered for a pecuniary pseudo-truth, and no one looks for it. Its proof is that it sells merchandise; if it does not, it is false.

Para-Poetic Hyperbole. 7 *Crown* whiskey's fantasies of icy depths, Revlon's rhapsodies on *Pango Peach, The Look's* word pictures of alluring eyes, and similar poesies are called para-poetic hyperbole because they are something like poetry, with high-flown figures of speech, though they are not poetry. Note, however, that they are also pecuniary pseudo-truths because nobody is expected to believe them.

Pecuniary Logic. When we read the advertisements for *Butyl* and *Old Crow* it begins to look as if *Butyl* and *Old Crow* really *want* us to believe, for they try to prove that what they say is true. *Butyl,* for example, asserts that "major tire marketers . . . are now bringing you tires made of this remarkable material"; and *Old Crow* says that the reason it "would quite naturally be served" to General Duke in New York was because he "esteemed it 'the most famous [whiskey] ever made in Kentucky.'" When one is asked to accept the literal message of a product on the basis of shadowy evidence, I dub it *pecuniary logic.* In other words, pecuniary logic is a proof that is not a proof but is intended to be so for commercial purposes.

There is nothing basically novel in pecuniary logic, for most people use it at times in their everyday life. What business has done is adopt one of the commoner elements of folk thought and use it for selling products to people who think this way all the time. This kind of thinking—which accepts proof that is not proof—is an *essential* intellectual factor in our economy, for if people were careful thinkers it would be difficult to sell anything. From this it follows that in order for our economy to continue in its present form people must learn to be fuzzy-minded and impulsive, for if they were clear-headed and deliberate they would rarely put their hands in their pockets; or if they did, they would leave them there. If we were all logicians the economy could not survive, and herein lies a terrifying paradox, for *in order to exist economically as we are we must try by might and main to remain stupid. . . .*

PITFALLS TO PECUNIARY PHILOSOPHY

Like all philosophies pecuniary philosophy has its limitations. The central issue in the viability of philosophies is the truth they assume and what they try to explain. Every philosophy must work in its own backyard, so to speak; that is why Buddhism, for example, has no place in a physics laboratory or logical empiricism in a Buddhist temple. When one philosophy "encroaches" on the "territory" of another's universe it runs into difficulties. Now pecuniary philosophy may be satisfactory for selling cosmetics or whiskey but when it tries to "sell" health or any other form of human welfare it becomes vulnerable to attack by the more traditional logical methods. At such a point the question, "Does aspirin *really* provide the fastest relief for pain, and is its effect on the digestive tract literally gentler than that of any other pain-killer?" cannot be answered by a logic whose only test is whether the product sells, but must be answered by the more traditional truth-logic. Pecuniary philosophy has two problems here. In the first place, human suffering is at issue; in the second place, terms like "relief," "fast," and "gentle" have specific, identifiable physiological referents, and physiology is the province of true scientific research and discovery. Each has its own sphere, and traditional logic and science are as inappropriate for selling nail polish in American culture as pecuniary reasoning is for selling medicine. When medicine is to be sold the canons of traditional reasoning must be respected; when one is selling whiskey or electric razors "folk-think" and pecuniary logic will, perhaps, serve. Put another way, government, with the connivance of the people, permits the exploitation of wooly-mindedness up to a certain point, in the interests of maintaining an irrational economy; but this cannot be allowed if it results in obvious physical suffering, since the right to seek, without trammel or deceit, relief from physical anguish, has become an inviolable value of the American people. . . .

Every culture creates philosophy out of its own needs, and ours has produced traditional philosophers based on truths verifiable by some primordial objective or supernatural criteria, and another, pecuniary philosophy, derived from an irrational need to sell. The heart of truth in our traditional philosophies was God or His equivalent, such as an identifiable empirical reality. The heart of truth in pecuniary philosophy is contained in the following three postulates:

> Truth is what sells.
> Truth is what you want people to believe.
> Truth is that which is not legally false.

The first two postulates are clear, but the third probably requires a little explaining and a good example. A report in *Science* on the marketing practices of the *Encyclopaedia Britannica* is just what we need at this point.

> One of the tasks of the Federal Trade Commission, according to the Encyclopaedia Britannica, is to order business organizations to stop using deceptive advertising when such organizations are found to be so engaged. A few weeks ago Encyclopaedia Britannica, Inc., was ordered by the Federal Trade Commission to stop using advertising that misrepresents its regular prices as reduced prices available for a limited time only. . . .
> Some of the company's sales practices are ingenious. The FTC shows, for example, how the prospective customer, once he has gained the impression that he is being offered the Encyclopaedia and accessories at reduced prices, is led to believe that the purported reduced prices are good only for a limited time. This is done by two kinds of statements, each one being true enough if regarded separately.
> The first kind of statement, which appears in written material, says such things as "This offer is necessarily subject to withdrawal without notice."[2]

Science explains that the second kind of statement is made by the salesman when he applies pressure to the prospective customer by telling him he will not return. The Federal Trade Commission, in enjoining the *Encyclopaedia Britannica* from using this kind of sales technique, argued that the first statement plus the second created the impression in the customer's mind that if he does not buy now he will lose the opportunity to buy at what he has been given to think is a reduced price. Actually, *Science* points out, it is not a reduced price, for the price has not changed since 1949. Since it is literally true that a business has the right to raise prices without advance notice, the *Britannica* advertisement is not legally false, even though it reads like a warning that prices will go up soon. I have coined the term *legally innocent prevarication* to cover all statements which, though not legally untrue, misrepresent by implication. . . .

WHAT'S TO BE DONE?

What shall we do? The ideal might seem to be to resocialize all these men, but this is obviously impossible. Ideally we should send them all to a "truth school" where, under the direction of wise and benevolent philosophers of the old tradition, they would have classes in (1) the difference between pecuniary and traditional truth; (2) the nature of values and their social function; (3) the nature of human dignity: problems of human feelings and why they should not be exploited; the importance of shame, female and other; problems in human degradation (self and other). It is unlikely, however, that such retraining would accomplish much. Furthermore, advertising is self-selective, so that youngsters with a traditional ethical sense avoid it; as late as September 20, 1961 Thomas B. Adams, president of the Campbell-Ewald Company, a big Detroit agency, was " 'shocked' at the degree to which promising young men were shunning the advertising profession because they believed it 'dishonorable.' "[3] Those that do not believe it dishonorable can only be young people perfectly socialized to the corrupt system, who will enthusiastically practice the pecuniary ethic of legal innocence. Thus the dishonesties and distortions of advertising are bound to be self-renewing. The most we can expect in the long run, therefore, is some diminution of unlawfulness, some sparking up of the campaigns in order to eliminate dullness and repetition, and more elaborate and whimsical art work—for example, a larger, cuter and more intensely *green* green giant advertising Green Giant vegetables; better looking, more tastefully dressed women occupying more space in advertisements for cosmetics; more realistic and more carefully color-photographed children poring over encyclopedias, et cetera.

Spontaneous moral regeneration is thus impossible for advertising because it does not know what the problem is and is self-selective in recruitment of personnel. Furthermore, since business competition will grow more intense (projected expenditures for advertising are about $25 billion by 1970), the chances of self-regulation are illusory. In view of the increasing competition and the expanding operations of advertising, greatly increased budgets of the FDA, FTC, and FCC should be countermoves against advertising's strong inherent tendency to misrepresent. Federal regulatory agencies, however, find it difficult to deal effectively with anything but legal dishonesty. It seems possible, however, to set up, within the FCC a division, the function of which would be perusal of the *non-legal* aspects of the commercial uses of the mass media. If such a unit were to take a project a year or a subject matter a year—toys, women's magazines, cosmetics—and publish its findings, it would have a tremendous effect on advertising through exercising a moral force, bringing the attention of the public to the nature of the corrosive influence. Such publication would be a kind of textbook of clean advertising practice which, over the years, might gradually re-educate the older generation of advertising men while providing fundamental principles to younger personnel. It would have the further effect, through naming agencies and products, of keeping the young job-seeking generation out of companies responsible for copy that is nauseating, insulting, or merely legally innocent.

Notes

1. An expression used by the Federal Trade Commission in dismissing a complaint against a company for using extreme methods in its advertising.
2. From "The Company They Keep," J. Turner, *Science,* Vol. 134, p. 75, 14 July 1961. Copyright 1961 by the American Association for the Advancement of Science.
3. *New York Times,* September 20, 1961.

DECEPTIVE PRACTICES IN ADVERTISING

Burton Leiser

This paper is deliberately designed to point out some of the problems that arise as a result of the advertising industry's failure to develop meaningful ethical guidelines for its members' use. While considerable attention is devoted to such well-known and frequently discussed practices as deception, fraud, and the like, some issues that are not so frequently discussed are raised as well. . . .

MISLEADING STATEMENTS OR CONTEXTS

Campbell's Soups concocted a television commercial that showed a thick, creamy mixture that the announcer suggested was Campbell's vegetable soup. Federal investigators, intrigued by the fact that the soup shown in the commercial was much thicker than any Campbell's vegetable soup they had ever seen, discovered that the bowl shown in the commercial had been filled with marbles to make it appear to be thicker than it really was and to make it seem to contain more vegetables than it did. Max Factor promoted a wave-setting lotion, Natural Wave, by showing how a drinking straw soaked in the lotion curled up. The FTC pointed out, however, that it did not logically follow that human hair would react as drinking straws did. The implication left in the viewer's mind, therefore, was false, because, in fact, straight hair did not curl after being soaked in Natural Wave. . . .

Misleading words and phrases, particularly when those words and phrases have special technical meanings, are often employed to create false impressions in the minds of persons who are not familiar with the jargon of particular businesses. And ordinary language may be used in such a way as to suggest to the uninitiated that certain conditions exist which do not in fact exist at all. For example, in describing insurance coverage, the terms *all, full, complete, comprehensive, unlimited, up to, as high as,* and the like can be extremely deceptive. "This policy will pay your hospital and surgical bills" suggests (though it does not *literally* say) that *all* of the hospital and surgical bills of the insured will be paid; and "This policy will replace your income" suggests that *all* of a person's income will be replaced if he becomes disabled—when in fact, only a very small portion of his bills or his income will be paid or replaced. The use of several synonymous terms (e.g., to describe the same condition or disease) may suggest to the uninitiated that he is buying much broader

Adapted from *Liberty, Justice and Morals* by Burton M. Leiser. Copyright © 1973 by Burton M. Leiser. Reprinted by permission of the author and of Macmillan Publishing Co., Inc.

coverage than is in fact the case. Offering a "family" contract suggests to the unwary that each member of his family will receive equal coverage—the coverage that is announced in bold type—when in fact, his spouse and/or his children will receive substantially less coverage than the policyholder will.

When an ad says that a given policy "pays full coverage," it does not mean what it seems to mean. It *seems* to say that it will pay the full costs of (e.g.) the policyholder's hospitalization and doctor bills. But it *really* says that it will pay as much as the policy stipulates that it will pay—that is, it pays as much as you contract for, not as much as you may have to pay. (In other words, it utters a meaningless, uninformative tautology which the consumer misinterprets.)

An ad that proclaims that "This policy pays $10,000 for hospital room and board expenses" may not make it clear that there is a daily limit, a maximum time limit, and complete exclusion of all hospital expenses.

Most potential insurance buyers are unaware of the fact that "noncancellable" and "guaranteed renewable" are technical terms which have very definite meanings within the insurance industry that may not mean anything like what the layman thinks they mean. A noncancellable policy is one which the insured has the right to keep in force by timely payment of premiums until at least age 50, or, if the policy is issued after age 44, for at least five years after the date of issue. The insurer may not unilaterally change any provision of the policy while it is in force. But it does *not* guarantee the insured that he will be able to keep the policy in force *after* he reaches age 50 (or after five years)—though he might very well suppose that that is what it means.[1]

Similarly, "guaranteed renewable" means that the insured has the right to keep his policy in force by timely premium payments until at least age 50 or, if he purchases the policy after age 44, for five years from the date of issue, and that insurer may not unilaterally change any provision of the policy, but that the insurer may change the premium rates by classes.[2]

The use of such terms is misleading unless the ad makes it clear that the insured does *not* have the option of renewing his policy indefinitely.

Similarly, advertising "Eligible—ages 18 to 65" suggests that if a person buys the policy, he will be covered until he reaches age 65—when in fact, what is meant is that anyone who is under 65 may *purchase* the policy —but the policy itself may not be renewed by the insurer.

Life insurance ads often read, "This policy is flexible and can be changed as your needs change—you may convert it to permanent life insurance," or "This policy (ANNUAL PREMIUM, ONLY $————) is flexible and can be changed to fit your needs—you may convert it to permanent life insurance." Such ads don't even *suggest* that conversion will entail payment of much higher rates based upon the insured's age at the time of conversion.

The same is true of policies that are advertised as offering "generous loan privileges at low interest rates." Nowhere is it made clear that the policy has no loan or cash value for several years, or that the "low"

interest rates may not be low at all relative to bank rates that might prevail
at the time the loan might be made.

One of the most misleading mail order insurance ads was described in
FTC Consumer Bulletin No. 1. The ad said:

> "Maximum Policy Benefits. For Hospital Care $5,000. For Death Natural
> Cause $10,000. For Accidental Death $20,000. . . . this big Family Plan for
> only $6.25 monthly."

In fact, the policy was written in such a way that the insurer was not
obliged to pay more than $500 in any one year for any one person. Only
$2,000 was payable for each death by natural causes and $4,000 for
accidental death. Any full benefits did not accrue until after the policy had
been in effect for a considerable period of time. . . .

The land promoter who sends a glossy pamphlet advertising his
"retirement city" in Arizona may not make a single false statement in the
entire pamphlet. But by filling it with beautiful color photographs of
swimming pools, golf links, and lush vegetation, none of which exist
within 100 miles of the land he is selling, he leads his prospects to believe
that certain features exist within the area which do *not* exist. Thus, without uttering or printing a single false statement, he is able to lead his
prospects to believe what he knows is not true. . . .

In none of these cases could one say that false statements were made.
Strictly speaking, these advertisers are not guilty of lying to the public,
if *lying* is defined as the deliberate utterance of an untrue statement. For,
taken literally, none of the statements made in these advertisements is
untrue. But the messages of the ads are misleading. Because of the
pictorial matter in them, the reader or viewer makes inferences that are
false; and the advertiser juxtaposes those pictures with the narrative in
such a way that false inferences *will* be made. It is through those false
inferences that he expects to earn enough money to pay for the ad and
to have something left over for himself.

FALSE CLAIMS OF NEED

Part of the American scheme of things seems to be the creation of
needs, the introduction of a conviction into the minds of people that they
ought to have something that they had never needed before, often because it had never existed before. Not only Americans, but people the
world over today feel that certain items that would have been regarded
as luxuries by their grandparents—or even by themselves a few years ago
—are necessities today. Yesterday's luxury has become today's necessity.
Electric refrigerators, hair driers, canned foods, soup mixes, and instant
potatoes are considered by many to be necessities, though the "need" for
some of them has been created. The automobile is probably the most
outstanding example of a product whose increasing use has in fact
created a genuine need for itself by driving all the competition—including not only the horse, but passenger railroads and commuter bus services—out of business. Cosmetics of all kinds are generally regarded by

American women as being quite necessary, though women in other countries, including some very advanced nations, feel no particular compulsion about using them, and some American women are now beginning to question the necessity of using them as well. The need for razor blades was created some years ago by clever advertising by the Gillette Company, which convinced men that they were "cleaner" and more attractive if they were "clean-shaven" than if they wore beards or long sideburns. Many members of a new generation have not only called these premises into question, but have acted upon the assumption that it is not necessary to shave in order to be attractive. . . .

Observing that the proprietary drug industry spends an average of 14 percent of its gross dollar volume on advertising, as compared to 6 percent for tobacco, 9 percent for candy, and 3 percent for food, the pharmacists conclude that the drug advertisers are first coaxing, cajoling, and convincing the people into thinking that they are ill, and then persuading them to purchase something that is supposedly designed to cure their illness. How else, they ask, can the enormous expenditures on advertising be justified? It isn't necessary to persuade people that they are hungry and therefore need to eat, after all. Incidentally, in 1970, $382 million were spent on this kind of advertising for a gross business of $2.6 billion—a business which grows by $100 million per year.

Not the least of the problems being exacerbated by the drug industry through its many advertising campaigns is the feeling, among young and old alike, that pills offer a magical solution to virtually all of life's problems—"Fast, fast, fast," as one ad goes. According to the pharmacists, "bombarding the young mind with the 'pill for every ill' philosophy is reaping its grim harvest as these children grow into adolescence and begin seeking their kicks in their own drug world."[3]

THE EXPLOITATION OF ILLUSIONS

Closely related to misleading pictures and statements is the use made by manufacturers and advertisers of illusions in selling their goods. This is best illustrated by the use merchandisers make of certain optical illusions in their choice of packaging. Cereal boxes would be much more stable, less apt to spill over, if they were short and squat. But the packaging experts at Kellogg's, General Foods, and General Mills know that if housewives are given the choice between two boxes of cereal, one short and squat and the other tall and narrow, they will almost invariably choose the tall and narrow box, *even if it contains less cereal and costs more.* Most housewives judge by the outward appearance of the box and do not look for the net weight and attempt to calculate the price per ounce (a project that is virtually impossible anyway, unless one is equipped with a slide rule). Two lines of equal length, one horizontal and the other vertical, do not *appear* to be of equal length. The vertical line always appears to be longer. Tall boxes appear to be larger than short ones, and the housewife doing her shopping thinks she is getting more in the tall box than she would be getting if she were to purchase the short box.

Bottles follow the same principle. Shampoos, for example, are packaged in tall, narrow bottles—often with the waist pinched to make them even taller—to give the illusion of quantity. Some jars and bottles are manufactured with inner compartments, or double glass walls, so that the actual quantity of goods in the container is much less than it appears to be. Fruit and other goods are canned in large quantities of syrup, and cookies, nuts, and other dry foods are packed in tins or cartons that are stuffed with cardboard—allegedly to prevent breakage, but more realistically to reduce the quantity of goods in the package while giving the customer the illusion that he is purchasing more than is actually to be found in the package.

Manufacturers argue that these stuffings are necessary to prevent breakage, that there is a certain amount of "settling" in some products that results in their packages being a third empty when they reach the consumer, and that their machines have been designed in any case to fill the packages by weight so that the customer always receives an honest measure, regardless of the size or shape of the package. But these explanations do not explain the hiss of air that escapes from my toothpaste tube when I open it (the tube seemed full and firm until then, but turns out to have been full of air); and it does not explain the manufacturers' aversion to standardized weights and their vigorous battle against requirements that the net weight be printed boldly and prominently on the front of the package. Until recent legislation was passed, the net weight of many products was printed in obscure corners of the packages, in microscopic type, and in a color that was just two shades lighter than the background color of the package (e.g., red against a dark red background) so that it was almost impossible for the normal shopper to find out how much merchandise was contained in the package.

However, the producer and the manufacturer may have legitimate excuses for some of these practices. A relatively small macaroni company, for example, may produce a number of different products, in different shapes and with a variety of densities. By standardizing all of its packages by *dimensions* rather than by *weight,* it is able to purchase packages and cases in great quantities and to save considerable money both for itself and, one would hope, for its customers. If it were required to standardize its packages by *weight,* it would have to invest a considerable amount of money in new plant and equipment, and the time during which its plant and equipment were standing idle would be increased significantly, thus raising its costs and, eventually, the cost to the consumer.[4] If standardized packaging were suddenly legislated into existence, it is conceivable that a number of smaller firms would be forced out of business because of their inability to absorb the added costs, and that the giant corporations would be bequeathed an even larger share of the total market than they now have. Still, none of these considerations should apply to a requirement that all packages bear, in clear and unmistakable type, a true and unambiguous statement of the nature of their contents and their weight.

Merchants and producers have many ways of concealing truth from the customers—not by lying to them, but simply by not telling them facts that are relevant to the question of whether they ought to purchase a particular product or whether they are receiving full value for their money. A particularly good example of this is the great ham scandal that broke into the open a few years ago. Major packers, including Swift, Armour, and others, were selling ham that was advertised as being particularly juicy. The consumer was not told, however, that the hams were specially salted and that hypodermic syringes were used to inject large quantities of water into them. The "juice" was nothing but water that evaporated away during cooking, leaving a ham some 40 percent smaller than the one that had been put into the oven. The housewife purchasing such a ham had no advance warning that she was purchasing water for the price of ham, unless she knew that the words *artificial ham* that were printed in small letters on the seal of the package meant that that was the case. Even that small warning, if it can be called such, was added only because of pressure brought to bear against the packers by the FTC. And there was no publicity to arouse the consumer to the special meaning of that odd term, *artificial ham.* [5]

Probably the most common deception of this sort is price deception, the technique some high-pressure salesmen use to sell their goods by grossly inflating their prices to two, three, and even four times their real worth. Again, there may be no "untruth" in what they say; but they conceal the important fact that the same product, or one nearly identical to it, can be purchased for far less at a department or appliance store. It is not the business of salesmen and businessmen to send their clients to their competitors, but it is certainly unethical for them to fail to tell their customers that they are not getting full value for their money.

A common form of deception involves a company advertising a product as if the product were on sale at a reduced price, when in fact, the product is never sold at the so-called original or regular price. This sometimes hurts the little man, as it did in the case of *FTC* v. *Mary Carter Paint Company,* in which a small paint manufacturer advertised: "Buy 1 gallon for $6.98 and get a second gallon free." The company claimed that it used this method to compete with national companies who normally sold similar paint at $6.98 per gallon. It feared that if it sold paint at half price, the public would think that its product was inferior. It therefore used the "one gallon free" device to achieve the same result. The FTC found that the practice was deceptive, since the paint in question was *never* sold at $6.98 per gallon, and the Supreme Court upheld the FTC's decision.

Encyclopedia and book salesmen are notorious for their deceptive practices. Almost everyone has had an encyclopedia salesman come to the door misrepresenting himself as an agent for the school board, or as a person taking a public opinion survey, or as a representative of some "educational" organization. And we are all familiar with the gimmick used by them, in which they claim that they are "placing"—they never "sell" anything, of course—encyclopedias or "earning programs" in homes at no cost whatever to the lucky recipient. It is all part of their advertising or public relations program, they say. "All we ask is that you give us five or ten references, and that you allow us to use your name. In addition, there will be a small monthly service charge for the ten-year extension service, or the ten-year research service," which will allegedly make a scholar out of your son or daughter and guarantee him or her a place in law school *(FTC* v. *Standard Education Society)*. . . .

Perhaps it may be put as follows: A burglar or a thief may be heavily fined or sent to jail for many months for stealing a relatively small amount of money or valuables from a single person. But a salesman who cheats hundreds of people out of equal sums of money that total, in the aggregate, hundreds of thousands of dollars, is immune to prosecution, and may, in fact, be one of the community's most respected citizens. If Armour and Swift and other large corporations can bilk their customers out of enormous sums of money and do it with impunity, why, one might ask, should the petty thief be subjected to such severe penalties for his activities? He may plead that he desperately needs the money he derives from his dishonest activities, but that excuse would hardly be credible if it was uttered by corporate executives.

TESTIMONIALS

Too many "testimonials" are phony. By now, most people probably know that the people who offer testimonials on TV and in printed ads are paid for their services, and they must suspect that there isn't an ounce of sincerity in them. They must rightly believe that the so-called testimonials are written by admen, and not by the people who read them. But it is reasonable to assume that there are still some unsuspecting, gullible, and naive people who believe that the people who speak to them from their TV screens are honest and are persuaded by what they hear. At least the admen must think so, for otherwise it would be difficult to understand why they would continue to use this ancient device.

When football and basketball stars promote foods, their expertise in home economics ought at least to be brought into question by those who watch their ads. Pearl Bailey is a fine singer, but her singing ability is irrelevant to her ability to judge kitchen ranges. ("There's just two cooks allowed in Pearl's kitchen, me and this handsome devil by White-Westinghouse. Me, I've been filling hungry mouths with my scrumptious cooking . . . since most of you were making mud pies. So any assistant that Pearl lets in has got to be real able." [Two-page ad in *Better Homes and Gardens,* November 1976. Notice the deliberately poor grammar.]) Even worse are the actors and models who are posed in white coats and stethoscopes, or are dressed in dark business suits and filmed in hospital corridors or seated behind huge desks in book-lined studies, suggesting that they are physicians, lawyers, or high-paid executives; or in laboratories, suggesting that they are distinguished scientists or engineers. Far from reporting information derived from their own expert appraisal of the facts, they merely mouth the words prepared for them by advertising men —in deep voices and with profound conviction—sometimes seeming to read from beautifully bound "reports" prepared by the same advertising men. . . .

OUR DECEPTIVE LANGUAGE

Equivocation was recognized by Aristotle as one of the most deceptive of all logical tricks. The ambiguity of language makes man's most valuable instrument subject to distortion so that it may be used to take advantage of unsuspecting persons who are not familiar with the ways in which seemingly precise terms can actually be used to make considerable profit for those who know how to use them to mean what they want them to mean.

One might suppose that mathematical terms would be the most precise and unambiguous of all, and that "8 percent of $1,200" would mean the same thing everywhere and at all times. But it is easy to show that this seemingly innocent expression, "8 percent of $1,200," can have a number of meanings, and the precise meaning conferred upon that expression can make a considerable difference to the person who borrows $1,200 for one year at what is said to be 8 percent interest.

Though there are many variations, the following three will serve to illustrate the point.

The 8 Percent Loan

Suppose you go to a bank or a finance company and ask for a loan of $1,200. After all the necessary formalities have been completed, you are told that your credit is good, and that the loan will be made "at 8 percent interest." This might mean any of the following things:

1. You are given $1,200 by the banker, and, at the end of each month or whenever you make your payments, you pay interest on the outstanding balance at the rate of 8 percent per year, or .08/12 per month. You will then pay a total of $1,252 and have the use of an average of $650 of the bank's money through the twelve-month period during which you are paying it back, for a true interest rate of 8.05 per cent.

2. Eight percent of the total amount of your loan is deducted from the amount given to you when you make the loan. That is, you pay your interest in advance, and then repay the loan in monthly installments. Suppose that you intend to make the loan for one year. Ninety-six dollars will be deducted from the sum given to you, and you then pay the bank $1,200 in monthly installments. Under these circumstances, because you start off with only $1,104 and repay a part of it each month, you would have the use of an average of $554 of the bank's money throughout the loan period. The interest of $96 constitutes 17.3 percent of this amount.

3. Your interest is added to the total amount of the loan you make, and

then you pay that amount to the bank in equal installments. Thus, your loan is for the amount of $1,296, but you receive $1,200 cash, and repay the loan in monthly installments of $1,296/12 or $108 per month. Because the average amount of the bank's money in use by the borrower is only $530, he pays a true interest rate of 18.1 percent on his loan.

When the bank or finance company adds "service charges" and insurance charges, the rate can climb considerably higher still. Your friendly neighborhood banker, despite his reputation for honesty in financial affairs, is not above using such verbal trickery to make you believe that you're receiving the prime rate on your loan, when in reality, you're paying two or three times as much for your loan as a wealthy businessman pays for his. A true 8 percent loan on $1,200 would permit the borrower to take $1,200 and keep it for the time agreed—say, one year. At the end of that time, he would return the principal ($1,200) and pay the interest ($96). He would have had the use of the full amount for the full time. When you pay the interest in advance, or have it added to or deducted from the amount of money you receive on the face amount of the loan, you pay considerably more for your use of the money, for you start returning the money to the lender at the end of one month and continue to return it to him throughout the period of the loan, though you have paid interest on it as if you had been able to keep it throughout the period of the loan. The money you have had in your hands during the full period of the loan is not the $1,200 you borrowed, but about half as much—for you must average it out over the number of months that you have been returning it. Thus, in real terms, the money you hold is half as much as you think, and your interest rate is doubled or trebled. Such practices have become more difficult since the United States government passed its truth-in-lending law, but many consumers still don't know how to tell a good loan from a bad one.

A FINAL WORD ON ADVERTISING

Advertising has an important and constructive role to play in the life of the nation. It is not true that all advertising men are unscrupulous or that all businessmen are concerned only with selling, no matter what the cost to the customers. Nor is it true that advertisements are necessarily misleading or fraudulent.

David Ogilvy, one of the most successful advertising executives in the United States, is the creator of such successful advertising images as Schweppes's Commander Whitehead and Hathaway Shirt's man with the eye patch.[6] In his discussion of techniques for building a successful advertising campaign, he says:

> Give the Facts. Very few advertisements contain enough factual information to sell the product. There is a ludicrous tradition among copywriters that consumers aren't interested in facts. Nothing could be farther from the truth. Study the copy in the Sears, Roebuck catalogue; it sells a billion dollars' worth of merchandise every year by giving *facts*. In my Rolls-Royce

advertisements I gave nothing but facts. No adjectives, no "gracious living."

The consumer isn't a moron; she is your wife. You insult her intelligence if you assume that a mere slogan and a few vapid adjectives will persuade her to buy anything. She wants all the information you can give her.[7]

And he adds the following bit of advice that bears directly on our subject:

You wouldn't tell lies to your own wife. Don't tell them to mine. Do as you would be done by.

If you tell lies about a product, you will be found out—either by the Government, which will prosecute you, or by the consumer, who will punish you by not buying your product a second time.

Good products can be sold by *honest* advertising. If you don't think the product is good, you have no business to be advertising it. If you tell lies, or weasel, you do your client a disservice, you increase your load of guilt, and you fan the flames of public resentment against the whole business of advertising. . . .[8]

Some 2,000 years ago there was a debate between the scholars of two great academies as to whether it was proper to praise the beauty of an ugly bride. According to one faction, the principle that one should refrain from uttering any falsehood required that the honest man refrain from praising the ugly bride. The other group, however, insisted that principles of kindness should prevail and that even if one had to lie, one was obliged to add to the newlyweds' happiness rather than to detract from it. They went on to say that in a matter of far less moment to a man than his marriage, the principle of kindness should take precedence, so that if a person had made a bad bargain at the market, one should not rub it in by telling him so.[9] If they were here to participate in a discussion on the issue presently under consideration, it is not hard to imagine what they might say:

Thousands of men and women are too poor to afford foreign travel, or large and flashy automobiles, or Hathaway shirts, or expensive liquors, or costly cosmetics. What useful purpose is served by dangling these luxuries before their eyes? To some, perhaps, the enticing display of such luxuries may serve as an incentive, spurring them on to greater achievement so that they too may enjoy what their more affluent neighbors take for granted. But to many, and perhaps to most, the display may arouse feelings of frustration, anger, and hurt. "Why," they may ask, "are we unable to have all of these things, when so many others do? Why can we not give our children what those ads show other people giving their children? Why can we not share the happiness that is depicted here?" Before a man is married, it might be appropriate to point out some of his fiancee's faults; but at the wedding, when it's obviously too late, it's unkind to dwell on them. For those who cannot afford the luxuries—and they are luxuries, whatever Ogilvy may say—offered in advertisements that are often directed *specifically at them,* it is cruel to hurt them by offering them what they cannot buy, or to seduce them with false promises of happiness or prestige or success into neglecting their primary obligations in order to seek the fantasy world portrayed in advertisements.

Everyone wants a beautiful bride, I suppose, and it may be good that the working classes no longer desire to live Spartan lives, if they ever did. But some men learn to live very happily with women whose proportions are not even close to those that are currently considered to be the standard of beauty, and it is wrong to jeopardize their happiness by constantly reminding them of that fact; and it would be infinitely worse to parade well-proportioned beauties before them and to urge them to switch. No one is married to a life of poverty. But some people, unable to escape from such a life themselves, have made the adjustment and have found that it is possible to be happy and respectable even on a severely limited income. Is it right to parade the latest fashions in "good living" before their eyes at every opportunity, urging them to buy them *"Now, while our limited supply lasts!"*? Men who have been seduced into discontentment over their wives have been known to commit murder. So have some who have been seduced into dissatisfaction with their style of life. Some of the latter may be partially attributable to advertising.

This is not to say that all advertising is bad; but even when the message is not distorted, those who use the mass media to disseminate it should do so with some sense of social and public responsibility. It is far worse, though, when the message is distorted. And even David Ogilvy, for all his insistence on honesty in advertising, admits that he is "continuously guilty of *suppressio veri* (the suppression of the truth). Surely it is asking too much to expect the advertiser to describe the shortcomings of his product. One must be forgiven for putting one's best foot forward."[10] So the consumer is *not* to be told all the relevant information; he is *not* to be given all the facts that would be of assistance in making a reasonable decision about a given purchase. In particular, he will *not* be told about the weaknesses of a product, about its shock hazards, for example, if it is an electrical appliance; about the danger it poses to the consumer's health if it is a cleaning fluid; about the danger it poses to his life if it is an automobile tire that is not built to sustain the heavy loads of today's automobile at turnpike speeds; or, if one carries the doctrine to its final conclusion, about the possibly harmful side effects of a new drug that is advertised to the medical profession. Telling the truth combined with *"suppressio veri"* is *not* telling the truth. It is *not* asking too much of the advertiser to reveal such facts when they are known to him, and he should *not* be forgiven for "putting his best foot forward" at his customer's expense.

Notes

1. Cf. Richard L. Ismond, *Insurance Advertising: Ethics and Law* (New York: Roberts Publishing Company, 1968), pp. 101ff.
2. *Ibid.*, pp. 103ff.
3. Statement by American Pharmaceutical Association presented to National Commission on Marijuana and Drug Abuse, reprinted in *ACT,* Appendix M, p. 5.

4. See "The Consumer," an address by Lloyd E. Skinner, president of the Skinner Macaroni Company, in *Vital Speeches of the Day,* vol. 33 (January 1, 1967), pp. 189ff., reprinted in Grant S. McClellan, "The Reference Shelf," vol. 40, no. 3, *The Consuming Public* (New York: H. W. Wilson Company, 1968), pp. 143ff. He explains that his company produces some nineteen or twenty different kinds of macaroni products, all packaged in the same containers. If his firm were required to standardize by weight, rather than by volume, he would have to invest $86,000 in new machinery over the $300,000 investment in packaging machinery that he already has, as well as $100,000 in new plant facilities to accommodate the new machines. As opposed to the 90 percent operating time of the packaging machinery that he had at the time, the new machinery would have been operating only 40 to 50 percent of the time, according to his estimates. This would have resulted in an increase of 1 to 2 cents per package in the cost of producing macaroni.
5. Cf. *Consumer Reports,* March and August 1961, follow-up reports April and August 1962.
6. The firm is Ogilvy, Benson, and Mather.
7. David Ogilvy, *Confessions of an Advertising Man* (New York: Atheneum, 1963), pp. 95f.
8. *Ibid.,* p. 99.
9. Babylonian Talmud, *Ketuvot,* p. 17a. The academies were those that went under the names of Shammai and Hillel, respectively. The "debate" was not comparable to the kind of oratory contest that might be staged by college debating teams. It was a serious discussion on matters of legal and moral principle.
10. Ogilvy, *Confessions,* pp. 158f.

REASONABLE CONSUMER OR IGNORANT CONSUMER?
How the FTC Decides

Ivan L. Preston

Introduction

Is the Federal Trade Commission obligated to protect only reasonable, sensible, intelligent consumers who conduct themselves carefully in the marketplace? Or must it also protect ignorant consumers who conduct themselves carelessly?

Since its origin in 1914, the Commission has varied its answer to these questions. It has committed itself at all times to prohibit sellers' claims

From *Journal of Consumer Affairs,* vol. 8, no. 2, Winter 1974. Reprinted by permission.

which would deceive reasonable people, but has undergone changes of direction on whether to ban claims which would deceive only ignorant people. At times it has acted on behalf of the latter by invoking the "ignorant man standard."[1] At other times it has been ordered by courts to ignore these people and invoke the "reasonable man standard." In still other cases it has chosen voluntarily to protect certain ignorant persons but not others.

The significance of the issue is that the FTC will rule against the fewest types of sellers' claims under the reasonable man standard, and against the most under the ignorant man standard. The latter guideline therefore means, in the eyes of many, the greatest protection for the consuming public. Some consumerists may feel, in fact, that such a standard should be mandatory on the grounds that a flat prohibition is needed against all sellers' deceptions which would deceive anyone at all.

The FTC, however, works under a constraint which makes it necessary to temper its allegiance to the ignorant man standard. The constraint is that the Commission may proceed legally only in response to substantial public interest.[2] Over the years the Commissioners have been sensitive to the argument that there is no public interest in prohibiting messages which would deceive only a small number of terribly careless, stupid or naive people. To explain the compelling nature of this argument, I would like to describe a deception of that sort.

AN EXAMPLE

In my hometown of Pittsburgh, Pennsylvania, there appears each Christmas-time a brand of beer called Olde Frothingslosh. This quaint item is nothing but Pittsburgh Brewing Company's regular Iron City Beer in its holiday costume, decked out with a specially designed label to provide a few laughs. The label identifies the product as "the pale stale ale for the pale stale male," and there is similar wit appended, all strictly nonsense. One of the best is a line saying that Olde Frothingslosh is the only beer in which the foam is on the bottom.

A customer bought some Olde Frothingslosh to amuse friends at a party and was disturbed to find the claim was nothing but a *big lie:* the foam was right up there on top where it always is! She wanted her money back from the beer distributor, couldn't get it, and went to a lawyer with the intention of bringing suit. The true story ended right there because the lawyer advised her there was no chance of success. The reasonable man (woman! person!) standard would be applied to her suit, and her reliance on the belief about the foam would be judged unreasonable.

Had the ignorant man standard applied she would possibly have succeeded, which illustrates the difference the choice of standards makes. It also illustrates the essential weakness, in conjunction with definite strengths, possessed by a legal standard which sets out to protect everybody from everything. Many of the resulting prohibitions would eliminate only infinitesimal amounts of deception.

There are other reasons, too, for the FTC's cautious attitude toward the ignorant man standard. A pragmatic point is that the Commission does not have the resources to prosecute all cases [2; 3, p. 1082; 4, p. 494],* therefore those which are investigated might better be ones which endanger greater numbers of people. Another problem is that an extreme concern for the ignorant could lead to repression of much communication content useful to consumers, and could lead as well to possible violation of the First Amendment's freedom of speech guarantee [4, pp. 462–465; 3, pp. 1027–1038; 8].

Probably the most important objection to the ignorant man standard is that the reasonable man standard was traditional in the common law which preceded the development of the FTC in 1914. The common law held that to avoid being negligent a person must act as a reasonable person would act under like circumstances.[3] Mention of the reasonable or prudent person first appeared in an English case of 1837,[4] and has been in widespread use since.

In many of its applications the reasonable man concept has been applied to the defendant; did he, for example, act negligently in causing an accident which injured the plaintiff? In the law of misrepresentation, however, the concept is applied to the plaintiff, the deceived consumer. He brings a suit against the deceptive seller, and the question is whether he is guilty of contributory negligence which the deceiver may use as a defense. The rules require the plaintiff to assert and show that he relied upon the false representation, and that the damages he suffered were a result of such reliance. In addition, he must show that his reliance was justified—that is, his reliance must pass the test of the conduct of a reasonable man. He may not claim to have relied on a statement which sensible and prudent people would recognize as preposterous. If he does, he is guilty of contributory negligence which the deceiver may use as a reason for having the suit dismissed.[5]

This rule usually does not apply in the case of a fraudulent misrepresentation, where the deceiver consciously knows the representation was false and deliberately seeks to deceive with it. If that is shown, the person deceived is entitled to rely without having to justify the action as reasonable conduct.[6] But where the deceit is not intentional (or not so proved!) the reasonable man standard applies and the seller's falsity will not amount legally to deception where it is felt that the buyer should have known better than to rely on it. Various types of sellers' statements thereby escape legal liability under the reasonable man standard, beginning with those such as the Olde Frothingslosh claim which are physically impossible and therefore presumed obviously false. Also included are the exaggerations and superlatives called puffery—"The Greatest Show on Earth" [5, 6] and the claims that psycho-social values are present in products—"Ultra-Brite gives your mouth sex appeal" [4, pp. 439–450].

*Bracketed numbers refer to References on page 495.

At the time the FTC was created, the only specific law on these matters was the common law just described. The FTC Act stated nothing explicitly about what persons the Commission was authorized to protect; it said only that proceedings must be in the interest of the public. The most obvious procedure therefore would have been to follow the common law precedents and embrace the reasonable man standard. Instead, the FTC did the unexpected and flaunted the reasonable man standard in many of its early cases. Neither that concept nor a replacement standard were discussed explicitly, but numerous early cases show that the Commission was applying an ignorant man standard or a close approximation of it. In 1919 it ordered a manufacturer to stop advertising that its automobile batteries would "last forever."[7] One might assume that no reasonable person even in that year would have relied upon this claim literally, especially when the same ads offered a service by which "the purchaser pays 50 cents per month and is entitled to a new battery as soon as the old one is worn out." The FTC saw the latter phrase, however, as confirming the falsity and deceptiveness rather than the sheer frivolousness of "last forever." The case indicates that the Commission was developing a policy of stopping deceptions which would deceive only a minority.[8]

The switch to the ignorant man standard appeared questionable legally; precedent did not support it. But before we describe the eventual court considerations of this matter, we should acknowledge that there was much argument against the reasonable man standard in common sense if not in law. The legal conception of the buyer who failed to be reasonable in the marketplace was that of a person who made a stupid purchase through his own fault—he should have known better. It was this conception with which common sense could disagree. Some so-called stupid choices may be made not through carelessness but through the impossibility of obtaining and assessing information even when great caution and intelligence are applied. The world of goods and services was once simple, but has become terribly technical. Many poor choices were being made by persons who *couldn't* have known better.

These problems might have been incorporated into the reasonable man standard by adjusting that standard to the realities of the market. Consider a store scene in which a product was available at six cans for a dollar while one can was 16 cents. In considering whether a reasonable person would be deceived, the law might have taken into account that many people are slow at arithmetic, and that the bustle of a market and the need to make many other choices in the same few minutes rendered it unlikely they would fully use the mathematical capacity they possessed. The competence assumed of a "reasonable person" might have been reduced accordingly, and the traditional standard, altered in this way, might still have been applied.

Something bordering the opposite actually occurred in legal actions. The reasonable man came to be regarded as a *better* than average person, as someone who was never negligent and who therefore was entirely fictitious outside the courtroom.[9] He was "an ideal creature. . . . The factor controlling the judgment of [his] conduct is not what *is,* but *what ought to be*" [1]. The law, apparently, had created an unreasonable conception of the reasonable man.

It was this problem the FTC sought to correct. We do not know, because the point was not discussed as such, whether the Commission regarded its new conception as a move to the ignorant man standard or as a re-definition of the reasonable man standard by the method described above. But the practical effect was the same in either case—the Commission moved toward protecting the public from deceptions which regulators previously had ignored because they did not harm the fictitiously reasonable man.

COURT INTERPRETATIONS

Considerations of the reasonable and ignorant man standards eventually were made explicit through the intervention of appeals court decisions into FTC affairs. In 1924 the Commission outlawed a sales method which offered an encyclopedia "free" provided a purchaser paid $49 for two supplementary updating services.[10] The seller appealed and won a reversal on the grounds that no deception was involved.[11] "It is conceivable," the opinion stated, "that a very stupid person might be misled by this method of selling books, yet measured by ordinary standards of trade and by ordinary standards of the intelligence of traders, we cannot discover that it amounts to an unfair method of competition. . . ."

The FTC did not adopt the reasonable man standard as a result of this ruling; its subsequent activities reflected instead a posture of resistance.[12] When it stubbornly invoked a similar restraint against a different encyclopedia company[13] it was again reversed by an appeals court.[14] Circuit Judge Learned Hand was most adamant in declaring that

> . . . a community which sells for profit must not be ridden on so short a rein that it can only move at a walk. We cannot take seriously the suggestion that a man who is buying a set of books and a ten years' extension service, will be fatuous enough to be misled by the mere statement that the first are given away, and that he is paying only for the second. Nor can we conceive how he could be damaged were he to suppose that that was true. Such trivial niceties are too impalpable for practical affairs, they are will-o'-the wisps which divert attention from substantial evils.[15]

This time, however, the FTC took the case to the U.S. Supreme Court, where a new justice delivering his first opinion told Learned Hand that the encyclopedia decision *was* a substantial evil. Hugo Black's opinion in *FTC* v. *Standard Education* of 1937[16] restored the Commission's use of the ignorant man standard:

> The fact that a false statement may be obviously false to those who are trained and experienced does not change its character, nor take away its power to deceive others less experienced. There is no duty resting upon a citizen to suspect the honesty of those with whom he transacts business.

> Laws are made to protect the trusting as well as the suspicious. The best element of business has long since decided that honesty should govern competitive enterprises, and that the rule of *caveat emptor* should not be relied upon to reward fraud and deception.

Though Black mentioned the name of neither standard, his words suggest he was rejecting the reasonable man standard rather than proposing merely to adjust it. It was his words, above all, which led to the concept of an "ignorant man standard" for the FTC in place of what went before.

Just how *Standard Education* was supported by precedent is a curious question. Justice Black's opinion cited none. It affirmed that the sales method not merely had deceptive capacity but clearly deceived many persons,[17] and it also stated that the deception was committed knowingly and deliberately.[18] This suggests the Supreme Court was invoking the common law notion that the reasonable man standard should not apply in case of deliberate deception. Something left unclarified, however, is what significance such a ruling should have for an agency such as FTC which routinely did not make findings of deliberate deception. Deliberate intent to deceive undoubtedly occurs in many cases where no one can prove it. The whole advantage of FTC procedure, in comparison with what went before, was that it could rule sellers' messages out of the marketplace *without* bothering with the traditional requirement of having to prove intent. What was the advantage, then, of obtaining the right to use the ignorant man standard only in conjunction with proven intent to deceive?

The result, strangely, was that the FTC, on the basis of *Standard Education,* began applying the ignorant man standard liberally without regard for determining intent, and in some cases without regard for the fact that intent to deceive was almost surely absent. The appeals courts, also via *Standard Education,* approved this procedure. The trend was thoroughly questionable but was pursued decisively, particularly by the Second Circuit Court of Appeals, the one which *Standard Education* had reversed. In *General Motors* v. *FTC,*[19] involving a "6% time payment plan" which actually charged 11½% interest, the Second Circuit's Judge Augustus Hand concluded:

> It may be there was no intention to mislead and that only the careless or the incompetent could be misled. But if the Commission, having discretion to deal with these matters, thinks it best to insist upon a form of advertising clear enough so that, in the words of the prophet Isaiah, "wayfaring men, though fools, shall not err therein," it is not for the courts to revise their judgment.

The influence of the *Standard Education* reversal was unmistakable on the one Hand—and on the other Hand as well. When Judge Learned Hand considered an appeal to the Second Circuit of the Commission's finding of deception in an admittedly untrue claim that "one Moretrench wellpoint is as good as any five others," he said:

It is extremely hard to believe that any buyers of such machinery could be misled by anything which was patently no more than the exuberant enthusiasm of a satisfied customer, but in such matters we understand that we are to insist upon the most literal truthfulness. *Federal Trade Commission* v. *Standard Education Society*. . . .[20]

It was clear that the Second Circuit's Hands were tied. Substitution of the ignorant man standard for the reasonable man standard proceeded in additional Second Circuit cases,[21] and in others as well.[22] Under these liberal interpretations the FTC appeared during most of the 1940's to be knocking down right and left every advertising claim it thought had the slightest chance of deceiving even the most ignorant person. There was a good bit of unchecked exuberance in this spree,[23] reaching an extreme when Clairol was forbidden to say that its dye will "color hair permanently."[24] The FTC thought the public would take this as a claim that all the hair a person grows for the rest of her life will emerge in the Clairol color. That expectation was based on the testimony of a single witness who said she thought somebody might think that—although she added that *she* wouldn't.

On Clairol's appeal the Second Circuit said it couldn't imagine *anybody* believing the claim, but in accordance with *Standard Education* it said it had to support the FTC.[25] No hint was offered that the Clairol claim was used with intent to deceive, and no acknowledgment was made by the Second Circuit that *Standard Education* might have been intended by the Supreme Court to apply only where such intent was evident. We may speculate that if the Olde Frothingslosh matter had been appealed to the Second Circuit in the same year as the Clairol case, 1944, the purchaser might have recovered damages because the beer's foam wasn't on the bottom!

RETURN TO THE REASONABLE MAN STANDARD

We have now seen the development of a strong emphasis on the ignorant man standard. The next task is to describe how this emphasis came to be diluted, a matter which involved additional curious events. One of the arbitrary facts of life in U.S. law is that the various Circuit Courts of Appeal are sometimes inconsistent in their rulings. They need not take each other's decisions into account, so a case may be decided differently in one than in another. The Second Circuit was the one reversed by *Standard Education,* and we have seen that this court in subsequent cases applied the ignorant man standard assiduously. This included the prohibition of puffery in *Moretrench,* even though puffery had traditionally been called non-deceptive. With its long-standing immunity, puffery might have been expected to resist the courts even if nothing else did, but under the ignorant man standard the Second Circuit moved to eliminate this kind of falsity along with everything else.

But the time came, in 1946, when a puffery case was appealed to the Seventh Circuit rather than the Second, and the difference was significant. *Carlay*[26] involved a claim that Ayds candy mints make weight-reducing easy, which FTC said was false. On appeal the Seventh Circuit,[27] which had tended earlier to object to the ignorant man standard,[28] said the claim of "easy" was "mere puffing or dealer's talk upon which no charge of misrepresentation can be based." The court cited previous non-FTC cases which had allowed puffery, and completely ignored the cases stemming from Justice Black and the Second Circuit, which would have supported the FTC's outlawing of "easy."

As a result the FTC had a contradiction on its hands. The Second Circuit told it to protect the ignorant man; the Seventh Circuit told it to permit puffery which could deceive the ignorant man. The contradiction might have been resolved by the Supreme Court, but was never considered there. The FTC's resolution was to allow puffery thereafter, which tended to dilute the ignorant man standard.

An example of the dilution occurred in *Bristol-Myers,*[29] in which the Commission issued a complaint against the "Smile of Beauty" phrase used by Ipana tooth paste. Apparently it felt the line amounted to a claim that Ipana would straighten out people's crooked teeth.[30] The complaint was issued in 1942, about the same time as the Clairol *(Gelb)* case and prior to *Carlay* which legitimized puffery. But the final decision was made in 1949, post-*Carlay,* and produced a change of mind in which the Commission decided that "the reference to beautification of the smile was mere puffery, unlikely, because of its generality and widely variant meanings, to deceive anyone factually."

The trend away from the extreme ignorant man standard had begun, but only slightly. Cases followed in which the FTC retained a strong protective stance on behalf of ignorant consumers.[31] But in 1963 the FTC finally commented that the standard could be carried too far. *Heinz W. Kirchner*[32] was a case about an inflatable device to help a person stay afloat and learn to swim. Called Swim-Ezy, it was worn under the swimming suit and was advertised as being invisible. It was not invisible, but the FTC found it to be "inconspicuous," and ruled that that was all the claim of invisibility would mean to the public:

> The possibility that some persons might believe Swim-Ezy is, not merely inconspicuous, but wholly invisible or bodiless, seems to us too far-fetched to warrant intervention.

But what about the few persons who would accept this far-fetched belief? The Commission made clear it no longer intended to protect such ignorant persons:

> True ... the Commission's responsibility is to prevent deception of the gullible and credulous, as well as the cautious and knowledgeable. .... This principle loses its validity, however, if it is applied uncritically or pushed to an absurd extreme. An advertiser cannot be charged with liability in respect of every conceivable misconception, however outlandish, to which his representations might be subject among the foolish or feeble-minded. .... A representation does not become "false and deceptive" merely because it will be unreasonably misunderstood by an insignificant and unrepresentative segment of the class of persons to whom the representation is addressed.

That is the position the FTC has followed since. It holds no longer to the strict ignorant man standard by which it would protect everyone from everything which may deceive them.[33] It would rule out consideration, for example, of the Olde Frothingslosh claim which apparently fooled only one stray individual. Perhaps we may call the new stance a modified ignorant man standard which protects only those cases of foolishness which are committed by significant numbers of people.

Some observers may protest that any behaviors which are customary for a substantial portion of the population shouldn't be called "ignorant." They might rather call the new stance a modified reasonable man standard in which what is reasonable has been equated more closely than before with what is average or typical.[34] Whatever the name, however, the FTC's present position appears to remain closer to the spirit and practice of the strict ignorant man standard of the 1940's than to the reasonable man standard of tradition.[35]

Notes

1. "Ignorant man standard" is my own term, which I feel is correctly blunt. The terms "credulous man standard" and "lowest standard of intelligence," which lack semantic punch, have been used elsewhere: see [4, pp. 458–462; 7, pp. 2–3, 30–34].
2. FTC Act, #5(b), 15 *U. S. C.* #45(b); [4, pp. 483–487]; See also [3].
3. *Restatement of Torts (Second)*, Section 283 (1965). Section 283A states that a child must act as would a reasonable person of like age, intelligence, and experience under like circumstances.
4. *Vaughan* v. *Menlove*, 3 Bing. N.C. 468, 132 Eng. Rep. 490 (1837). For other cases and references see Reporter's Notes to Section 283 in *Restatement of Torts (Second) Appendix.*
5. The terminology "contributory negligence" is not always used, but the idea of denying recovery for unreasonable reliance on misrepresentations is based on that concept; William L. Prosser, *Torts,* 4th ed., p. 717 (1971).
6. Prosser, *ibid.,* p. 716.
7. *FTC* v. *Universal Battery,* 2 FTC 95 (1919).
8. See also *FTC* v. *A. A. Berry,* 2 FTC 427 (1920); *FTC* v. *Alben-Harley,* 4 FTC 31 (1921); *FTC* v. *Williams Soap,* 6 FTC 107 (1923); *Alfred Peats,* 8 FTC 366 (1925).
9. #283, *Restatement of Torts (Second),* comment c.
10. *John C. Winston,* 8 FTC 177 (1924).
11. *John C. Winston* v. *FTC,* 3 F.2d 961 (3rd Cir., 1925).
12. *Nugrape,* 9 FTC 20 (1925); *Ostermoor,* 10 FTC 45 (1926), but set aside, *Ostermoor* v. *FTC,* 16 F.2d 962 (2d Cir., 1927); *William F. Schied,* 10 FTC 85 (1926); *Good Grape,* 10 FTC 99 (1926); *Hobart Bradstreet,* 11 FTC 174 (1927); *Frank P. Snyder,* 11 FTC 390 (1927); *Dr. Eagan,* 11 FTC 436 (1927); *Berkey & Gay Furniture,* 12 FTC 227 (1928), but set aside, *Berkey & Gay Furniture* v. *FTC,* 42 F.2d 427 (6th Cir., 1930); *Northam-Warren,* 15 FTC 389 (1931), but set aside, *Northam-Warren* v. *FTC,* 59 F.2d 196 (2d Cir., 1932); *Fairyfoot,* 20 FTC 40 (1934), affirmed in *Fairyfoot* v. *FTC,* 80 F.2d 684 (7th Cir., 1935).
13. *Standard Education Society,* 16 FTC 1 (1931).
14. *FTC* v. *Standard Education Society,* 86 F.2d 692 (2d Cir., 1936).

15. *Ibid.*

16. 302 U.S. 112, 58 S.C. 113 (1937).

17. *Ibid.*, p. 117.

18. "It was clearly the practice of respondents through their agents, in accordance with a well matured plan, to mislead customers . . ." *Ibid.*, p. 116.

19. 114 F.2d 33 (2d Cir., 1940).

20. *Moretrench* v. *FTC*, 127 F.2d 792 (2d Cir., 1942). Turning to another literally untrue Moretrench claim, that its product had an advantage to which "contractors all over the world testify," Hand stated, "It is again hard to imagine how anyone reading it could have understood it as more than puffing; yet for the reasons we have just given, if the Commission saw fit to take notice of it, we may not interfere." This was the same judge who once had rejected similar claims on the grounds that "There are some kinds of talk which no man takes seriously, and if he does he suffers from his credulity. . . . Neither party usually believes what the seller says about his opinions, and each knows it. Such statements, like the claims of campaign managers before election, are rather designed to allay the suspicion which would attend their absence than to be understood as having any relationship to objective truth." *Vulcan Metals* v. *Simmons*, 248 F. 853 (2d Cir., 1918).

21. *Charles of the Ritz* v. *FTC*, 143 F.2d 676 (2d Cir., 1944); *Gelb* v. *FTC*, 144 F.2d 580 (2d Cir., 1944).

22. *D.D.D.* v. *FTC*, 125 F.2d 679 (7th Cir., 1942); *Aronberg* v. *FTC*, 132 F.2d 165, (7th Cir., 1942); *Gulf Oil* v. *FTC*, 150 F.2d 106 (5th Cir., 1945); *Parker Pen* v. *FTC*, 159 F.2d 509 (7th Cir., 1946). In the latter case the FTC's role was said to be to "protect the casual, one might say the negligent, reader, as well as the vigilant and more intelligent. . . ." A much-used quote, cited in *Aronberg* and *Gulf Oil*, above, and in *Gelb, op. cit.*, was from *Florence* v. *Dowd*, 178 F. 73 (2d Cir., 1910): "The law is not made for the protection of experts, but for the public—that vast multitude which includes the ignorant, the unthinking, and the credulous, who, in making purchases, do not stop to analyze, but are governed by appearances and general impressions." This was a pre-FTC case with evidence of deliberate deception.

23. *Charles of the Ritz, op. cit.*

24. *Gelb*, 33 FTC 1450 (1941).

25. *Gelb* v. *FTC, op. cit.* "There is no dispute that it imparts a permanent coloration to the hair to which it is applied, but the commission found that it has 'no effect upon new hair,' and hence concluded that the representation as to permanence was misleading. It seems scarcely possible that any user of the preparation could be so credulous as to suppose that hair not yet grown out would be colored by an application of the preparation to the head. But the commission has construed the advertisement as so representing it. . . . Since the Act is for the protection of the trusting as well as the suspicious, as stated in *Federal Trade Commission* v. *Standard Education Society* . . . we think the order must be sustained on this point."

26. 39 FTC 357 (1944).

27. *Carlay* v. *FTC* 153 F.2d 493 (1946).

28. *Allen B. Wrisley* v. *FTC*, 113 F.2d 437 (7th Cir., 1940); also later in *Buchsbaum* v. *FTC*, 160 F.2d 121 (7th Cir., 1947).

29. 46 FTC 162 (1949).

30. "The beauty of human teeth depends primarily upon their conformation, color, arrangement in the mouth and other natural physical features, and teeth which do not possess these natural qualities will not be rendered beautiful by the use of Ipana tooth paste." *Ibid.*

teeth which do not possess these natural qualities will not be rendered beautiful by the use of Ipana tooth paste." *Ibid.*
31. *Lorillard* v. *FTC*, 186 F.2d 52 (4th Cir., 1950); *Goodman* v. *FTC*, 244 F.2d 584 (9th Cir., 1957); *FTC* v. *Sewell*, 353 U.S. 969 (1957); *Exposition Press* v. *FTC*, 295 F.2d 869 (2d Cir., 1961); *Colgate* v. *FTC*, 310 F.2d 89 (1st Cir., 1962); *Giant Food* v. *FTC*, 322 F.2d 977 (D.C. Cir., 1963).
32. 63 FTC 1282 (1963).
33. In *Papercraft*, 63 FTC 1965, 1997 (1963), Commissioner MacIntyre protested that the retreat from the extreme ignorant man position was unfortunate. The majority opinion had withdrawn from protecting the "foolish or feeble-minded," and MacIntyre dissented: "Should this observation be construed as a retreat from our long-held position that the public as a whole is entitled to protection, including even 'the ignorant, the unthinking, and the credulous,' then the result may well be confusion."
34. [7, p. 31].
35. "It might be said that the test of consumer competence generally employed by the Commission appears to approximate the least sophisticated level of understanding possessed by any substantial portion of the class of persons to whom the advertisement is addressed." Personal correspondence to Peter B. Turk from Gale T. Miller, law clerk, Bureau of Consumer Protection, Federal Trade Commission, December 6 (1971). The "class of persons" assumed in the present article is that of adults. Special consideration for representations made to children (see footnote 3) was recognized in *FTC* v. *Keppel*, 291 U.S. 304, 54 S.C. 423 (1934). As for other groups, Miller wrote, "It is the position of the staff that advertising geared towards other special audiences, such as the ghetto dweller, the elderly, and the handicapped, might also be subjected to a more rigorous test than is applied to advertisements addressed to the public at large."

References

BOHLEN, FRANCIS H. "Mixed Questions of Law and Fact." *University of Pennsylvania Law Review*, vol. 72, 1923, pp. 111–122.

COX, E. F., R. C. FELLMETH, and JOHN E. SCHULZ. *Nader's Raiders: Report on the Federal Trade Commission*, 1969.

"Developments in the Law—Deceptive Advertising." *Harvard Law Review*, vol. 80, 1967, pp. 1005–1163.

MILLSTEIN, I. M. "The Federal Trade Commission and False Advertising." *Columbia Law Review*, vol. 64, 1964, pp. 439–499.

PRESTON, IVAN L. "Why Use False Puffery?" *The New York Times*, Feb. 25, 1973, business section, p. 17.

PRESTON, I. L., and RALPH H. JOHNSON. "Puffery—A Problem the FTC Didn't Want (And May Try to Eliminate)." *Journalism Quarterly*, vol. 49, Autumn 1972, pp. 558–568.

Truth In Advertising: A Symposium of the Toronto School of Theology, Toronto, Canada, 1972.

TURK, PETER B. "Justice Hugo Black and Advertising: The Stepchild of the First Amendment," in Teeter and Gray, eds, *For Freedom of Expression:* Essays in Honor of Hugo L. Black, in press.

THE DEPENDENCE EFFECT

John Kenneth Galbraith

The theory of consumer demand, as it is now widely accepted, is based on two broad propositions, neither of them quite explicit but both extremely important for the present value system of economists. The first is that the urgency of wants does not diminish appreciably as more of them are satisfied or, to put the matter more precisely, to the extent that this happens it is not demonstrable and not a matter of any interest to economists or for economic policy. When man has satisfied his physical needs, then psychologically grounded desires take over. These can never be satisfied or, in any case, no progress can be proved. The concept of satiation has very little standing in economics. It is neither useful nor scientific to speculate on the comparative cravings of the stomach and the mind.

The second proposition is that wants originate in the personality of the consumer or, in any case, that they are given data for the economist. The latter's task is merely to seek their satisfaction. He has no need to inquire how these wants are formed. His function is sufficiently fulfilled by maximizing the goods that supply the wants. . . .

The notion that wants do not become less urgent the more amply the individual is supplied is broadly repugnant to common sense. It is something to be believed only by those who wish to believe. Yet the conventional wisdom must be tackled on its own terrain. Intertemporal comparisons of an individual's state of mind do rest on doubtful grounds. Who can say for sure that the deprivation which afflicts him with hunger is more painful than the deprivation which afflicts him with envy of his neighbour's new car? In the time that has passed since he was poor his soul may have become subject to a new and deeper searing. And where a society is concerned, comparisons between marginal satisfactions when it is poor and those when it is affluent will involve not only the same individual at different times but different individuals at different times. The scholar who wishes to believe that with increasing affluence there is no reduction in the urgency of desires and goods is not without points for debate. However plausible the case against him, it cannot be proved. In the defence of the conventional wisdom this amounts almost to invulnerability.

However, there is a flaw in the case. If the individual's wants are to be urgent they must be original with himself. They cannot be urgent if they must be contrived for him. And above all they must not be contrived by

Excerpted from *The Affluent Society*, Third Edition, Revised by John Kenneth Galbraith. Copyright © 1958, 1969, 1976. Reprinted by permission of the publisher, Houghton Mifflin Company, and Andre Deutsch.

the process of production by which they are satisfied. For this means that the whole case for the urgency of production, based on the urgency of wants, falls to the ground. One cannot defend production as satisfying wants if that production creates the wants.

Were it so that a man on arising each morning was assailed by demons which instilled in him a passion sometimes for silk shirts, sometimes for kitchenware, sometimes for chamber-pots, and sometimes for orange squash, there would be every reason to applaud the effort to find the goods, however odd, that quenched this flame. But should it be that his passion was the result of his first having cultivated the demons, and should it also be that his effort to allay it stirred the demons to ever greater and greater effort, there would be question as to how rational was his solution. Unless restrained by conventional attitudes, he might wonder if the solution lay with more goods or fewer demons.

So it is that if production creates the wants it seeks to satisfy, or if the wants emerge *pari passu* with the production, then the urgency of the wants can no longer be used to defend the urgency of the production. Production only fills a void that it has itself created. . . .

The even more direct link between production and wants is provided by the institutions of modern advertising and salesmanship. These cannot be reconciled with the notion of independently determined desires, for their central function is to create desires—to bring into being wants that previously did not exist.[1] This is accomplished by the producer of the goods or at his behest. A broad empirical relationship exists between what is spent on production of consumers' goods and what is spent in synthesizing the desires for that production. A new consumer product must be introduced with a suitable advertising campaign to arouse an interest in it. The path for an expansion of output must be paved by a suitable expansion in the advertising budget. Outlays for the manufacturing of a product are not more important in the strategy of modern business enterprise than outlays for the manufacturing of demand for the product. None of this is novel. All would be regarded as elementary by the most retarded student in the nation's most primitive school of business administration. The cost of this want formation is formidable. In 1956 total advertising expenditure—though, as noted, not all of it may be assigned to the synthesis of wants—amounted to about ten thousand million dollars. For some years it had been increasing at a rate in excess of a thousand million dollars a year. Obviously, such outlays must be integrated with the theory of consumer demand. They are too big to be ignored.

But such integration means recognizing that wants are dependent on production. It accords to the producer the function both of making the goods and of making the desires for them. It recognizes that production, not only passively through emulation, but actively through advertising and related activities, creates the wants it seeks to satisfy.

The businessman and the lay reader will be puzzled over the emphasis which I give to a seemingly obvious point. The point is indeed obvious. But it is one which, to a singular degree, economists have resisted. They have sensed, as the layman does not, the damage to established ideas which lurks in these relationships. As a result, incredibly, they have closed their eyes (and ears) to the most obtrusive of all economic phenomena, namely modern want creation.

This is not to say that the evidence affirming the dependence of wants on advertising has been entirely ignored. It is one reason why advertising has so long been regarded with such uneasiness by economists. Here is something which cannot be accommodated easily to existing theory. More pervious scholars have speculated on the urgency of desires which are so obviously the fruit of such expensively contrived campaigns for popular attention. Is a new breakfast cereal or detergent so much wanted if so much must be spent to compel in the consumer the sense of want? But there has been little tendency to go on to examine the implications of this for the theory of consumer demand and even less for the importance of production and productive efficiency. These have remained sacrosanct. More often the uneasiness has been manifested in a general disapproval of advertising and advertising men, leading to the occasional suggestion that they shouldn't exist. Such suggestions have usually been ill received.

And so the notion of independently determined wants still survives. In the face of all the forces of modern salesmanship it still rules, almost undefiled, in the textbooks. And it still remains the economist's mission —and on few matters is the pedagogy so firm—to seek unquestioningly the means for filling these wants. This being so, production remains of prime urgency. We have here, perhaps, the ultimate triumph of the conventional wisdom in its resistance to the evidence of the eyes. To equal it one must imagine a humanitarian who was long ago persuaded of the grievous shortage of hospital facilities in the town. He continues to importune the passers-by for money for more beds and refuses to notice that the town doctor is deftly knocking over pedestrians with his car to keep up the occupancy.

And in unravelling the complex we should always be careful not to overlook the obvious. The fact that wants can be synthesized by advertising, catalysed by salesmanship, and shaped by the discreet manipulations of the persuaders shows that they are not very urgent. A man who is hungry need never be told of his need for food. If he is inspired by his appetite, he is immune to the influence of Messrs. Batten, Barton, Durstine and Osborn. The latter are effective only with those who are so far removed from physical want that they do not already know what they want. In this state alone men are open to persuasion.

The general conclusion of these pages is of such importance for this essay that it had perhaps best be put with some formality. As a society becomes increasingly affluent, wants are increasingly created by the process by which they are satisfied. This may operate passively. Increases in consumption, the counterpart of increases in production, act by suggestion or emulation to create wants. Or producers may proceed actively to create wants through advertising and salesmanship. Wants thus come to depend on output. In technical terms it can no longer be assumed that welfare is greater at an all-round higher level of production than at a lower one. It may be the same. The higher level of production has, merely, a higher level of want creation necessitating a higher level of want satisfaction. There will be frequent occasion to refer to the way wants depend on the process by which they are satisfied. It will be convenient to call it the Dependence Effect. . . .

The final problem of the productive society is what it produces. This manifests itself in an implacable tendency to provide an opulent supply of some things and a niggardly yield of others. This disparity carries to the point where it is a cause of social discomfort and social unhealth. The line which divides our area of wealth from our area of poverty is roughly that which divides privately produced and marketed goods and services from publicly rendered services. Our wealth in the first is not only in startling contrast with the meagreness of the latter, but our wealth in privately produced goods is, to a marked degree, the cause of crisis in the supply of public services. For we have failed to see the importance, indeed the urgent need, of maintaining a balance between the two.

This disparity between our flow of private and public goods and services is no matter of subjective judgment. On the contrary, it is the source of the most extensive comment which only stops short of the direct contrast being made here. In the years following World War II, the papers of any major city—those of New York were an excellent example —told daily of the shortages and shortcomings in the elementary municipal and metropolitan services. The schools were old and overcrowded. The police force was under strength and underpaid. The parks and playgrounds were insufficient. Streets and empty lots were filthy, and the sanitation staff was underequipped and in need of men. Access to the city by those who work there was uncertain and painful and becoming more so. Internal transportation was overcrowded, unhealthful, and dirty. So was the air. Parking on the streets had to be prohibited, and there was no space elsewhere. These deficiencies were not in new and novel services but in old and established ones. Cities have long swept their streets, helped their people move around, educated them, kept order, and provided horse rails for vehicles which sought to pause. That their residents should have a non-toxic supply of air suggests no revolutionary dalliance with socialism.

The contrast was and remains evident not alone to those who read. The family which takes its mauve and cerise, air-conditioned, power-steered, and power-braked car out for a tour passes through cities that are badly paved, made hideous by litter, blighted buildings, billboards, and posts for wires that should long since have been put underground. They pass on into a countryside that has been rendered largely invisible by commercial art. (The goods which the latter advertise have an absolute priority in our value system. Such aesthetic considerations as a view of the countryside accordingly come second. On such matters we are consistent.) They picnic on exquisitely packaged food from a portable icebox by a polluted stream and go on to spend the night at a park which is a menace to public health and morals. Just before dozing off on an air-mattress, beneath a nylon tent, amid the stench of decaying refuse, they may reflect vaguely on the curious unevenness of their blessings. Is this, indeed, the American genius? . . .

The case for social balance has, so far, been put negatively. Failure to keep public services in minimal relation to private production and use of goods is a cause of social disorder or impairs economic performance. The matter may now be put affirmatively. By failing to exploit the opportunity to expand public production we are missing opportunities for enjoyment which otherwise we might have had. Presumably a community can be as well rewarded by buying better schools or better parks as by buying bigger cars. By concentrating on the latter rather than the former it is failing to maximize its satisfactions. As with schools in the community, so with public services over the country at large. It is scarcely sensible that we should satisfy our wants in private goods with reckless abundance, while in the case of public goods, on the evidence of the eye, we practice extreme self-denial. So, far from systematically exploiting the opportunities to derive use and pleasure from these services, we do not supply what would keep us out of trouble.

The conventional wisdom holds that the community, large or small, makes a decision as to how much it will devote to its public services. This decision is arrived at by democratic process. Subject to the imperfections and uncertainties of democracy, people decide how much of their private income and goods they will surrender in order to have public services of which they are in greater need. Thus there is a balance, however rough, in the enjoyments to be had from private goods and services and those rendered by public authority.

It will be obvious, however, that this view depends on the notion of independently determined consumer wants. In such a world one could with some reason defend the doctrine that the consumer, as a voter, makes an independent choice between public and private goods. But given the dependence effect—given that consumer wants are created by the process by which they are satisfied—the consumer makes no such choice. He is subject to the forces of advertising and emulation by which production creates its own demand. Advertising operates exclusively, and emulation mainly, on behalf of privately produced goods and services.[2] Since management and emulative effects operate on behalf of private production, public services will have an inherent tendency to lag behind. Car demand which is expensively synthesized will inevitably have a much larger claim on income than parks or public health or even roads where no such influence operates. The engines of mass communication, in their highest state of development, assail the eyes and ears of the community on behalf of more beer but not of more schools. Even in the conventional wisdom it will scarcely be contended that this leads to an equal choice between the two.

The competition is especially unequal for new products and services. Every corner of the public psyche is canvassed by some of the nation's most talented citizens to see if the desire for some merchantable product can be cultivated. No similar process operates on behalf of the non-merchantable services of the state. Indeed, while we take the cultivation of new private wants for granted we would be measurably shocked to see it applied to public services. The scientist or engineer or advertising man who devotes himself to developing a new carburetor, cleanser, or depilatory for which the public recognizes no need and will feel none until an advertising campaign arouses it, is one of the valued members of our society. A politician or a public servant who dreams up a new public service is a wastrel. Few public offences are more reprehensible.

So much for the influences which operate on the decision between public and private production. The calm decision between public and private consumption pictured by the conventional wisdom is, in fact, a remarkable example of the error which arises from viewing social behaviour out of context. The inherent tendency will always be for public services to fall behind private production. We have here the first of the causes of social imbalance.

Notes

1. Advertising is not a simple phenomenon. It is also important in competitive strategy and want creation is, ordinarily, a complementary result of efforts to shift the demand curve of the individual firm at the expense of others or (less importantly, I think) to change its shape by increasing the degree of product differentiation. Some of the failure of economists to identify advertising with want creation may be attributed to the undue attention that its use in purely competitive strategy has attracted. It should be noted, however, that the competitive manipulation of consumer desire is only possible, at least on any appreciable scale, when such need is not strongly felt.
2. Emulation does operate between communities. A new school or a new highway in one community does exert pressure on others to remain abreast. However, as compared with the pervasive effects of emulation in extending the demand for privately produced consumer's goods there will be agreement, I think, that this intercommunity effect is probably small.

SKEPTICISM OF WANTS, AND CERTAIN SUBVERSIVE EFFECTS OF CORPORATIONS ON AMERICAN VALUES

David Braybrooke

What is being charged is the creation of untoward effects in fields where there are insufficient external controls, whether these are controls established by new legal assignments of responsibility or other sorts of controls (such as more vigorous competition). The point about irresponsibility is thus, in fact, not really a charge at all, but an index designating a problem. The charges against corporation leaders are, properly speaking, that some of them, some of the time, pretend no problem exists, and that (by this and other means) they obstruct efforts to deal with the problem.

I wish to focus my comments on one particular—familiar and deplorably effective—device used by corporation management, their public-relations experts, and other apologists to keep up the pretense that no problem exists. This is the device of saying, "We only give the public what it wants." In the manner of ordinary language philosophy, I want to examine this statement very literally and deliberately. This examination, though it will begin with what may seem to be petty details, will fairly quickly bring us to matters of deep concern about economic judgments. It will also, by the way, justify at least in part the provocative suggestion contained in my title. Corporations do subvert American values, very extensively, in important ways, though I do not mean to suggest that everything any corporation does amounts to such subversion, or that all corporations do so all of the time. Corporations also, no doubt, do much good; but since they spend night and day singing their own praises, the praises need not be repeated here.

At first sight, the statement, made on behalf of the corporations, "We only give the public what it wants," may be taken for an excuse. But I think no one—especially not those putting the statement forward—would want to hold that it is an excuse when they take a second look at it. For to be an excuse, the statement would have to be relevant in a certain way to the actions or policies being excused. It is a necessary condition of its being relevant in this way that there be something objectionable about those actions or policies—else why do they need an excuse? I think spokesmen for the corporations would be unwilling to grant that (barring occasional imperfections) there is something objectionable about what

From *Human Values and Economic Policy,* ed. Sidney Hook. Copyright © 1967 by New York University Press, New York. Reprinted by permission of the publisher.

they produce and sell. But suppose it is insisted that there is. Then the statement, "We only give the public what it wants," would fulfill one condition of being an excuse; but it would immediately fail others. For by its very meaning, the statement could not be accepted as an excuse; we in fact clearly rule it out as a way of excusing people from supplying objectionable commodities. It is no excuse for the drug-peddler to say that his customers wanted the drugs; for the mail-order antitank merchant to say that he only gave the safecrackers what they wanted; for the manufacturer of defective automobiles to say that the public wanted them. One does not excuse oneself from contributing to evil by saying that other people wanted the contribution.

If it is not an excuse, the statement, "We only give the public what it wants," may still be regarded as a device for escaping blame, now not as a device for diminishing it or transferring it to someone else, but as one for preventing questions about blame or praise from arising. I think it does this by, on this interpretation, presupposing that the transactions at issue fall within the free moral competence of the customers to choose what they want; and by implying that the goods that the customers receive are those that they have, within this competence, expressed themselves as wanting.

So interpreted, the statement is a very effective one. It calls into play not only our generalized feelings in favor of personal liberty and against interfering with other people's choices, even trivial ones, but also the refined scruples of economists about respecting other people's preferences, and the theory of market optima in which these scruples are assumed. It is no drawback to the effectiveness of the statement, furthermore, that so interpreted it seems to be substantially true. Most things bought in the United States are chosen within the free moral competence of the customers to choose; and the customers do receive what within that competence they express themselves as wanting.

Moreover, are not the customers who express these wants the ultimate authorities on what those wants are? If a person, N, says, given a choice of x, y, or z, "I want z," it follows that he does want z (in the sense of "want" that corresponds to the philosophical term "desire") provided that, knowing the language, he speaks sincerely and provided that the name or description represented by "z" accurately designates what N intends it to designate. Philosophers have thought that these provisos suffice to guarantee the truth of certain first-person statements; indeed, they have thought that the first proviso, about speaking sincerely, knowing the language, suffices; and they have called such statements "logically incorrigible." Thus "I am in pain" is regarded as logically incorrigible; and "I want," taken as expressing an inner experience or feeling, may be thought to be on somewhat the same footing.

There may seem to be nothing more to be said. Very likely, the spokesmen for the corporations would gratefully join us in believing that there is nothing more to be said; our ideas (and their ideas) about personal liberty and consumer sovereignty, as well perhaps as some awareness of the philosophical point just made, cooperate in silencing us. But we all know lots more to say, of which we need only be reminded. N's statement, "I want z," made under the provisos mentioned, and given a suitable time coordinate, will properly be recorded as true, and the record will stand; but this doesn't mean that his statement is very happily called "incorrigible." By its very use of the concept of want, it invites criticism; and it is corrigible, as first-person statements about pain and (in suitable circumstances) about seeing afterimages are not. It is corrigible by being superseded, as N revises his view of what he wants. Without implying that he did not want z at the time, N will now, on revision, say that he was *mistaken* in wanting it. Thus "I want z" assimilates to "I believe p" rather than to "I am in pain."

The dimensions of criticism that might lead to revisions of want-statements support six reasons for thinking that the claim made by the corporations, "We only give the public what it wants," is in respect to one or another of its implications much less than fully warranted. I shall now canvass these reasons.

In the first place, the evidence about consumers getting what they want may be indeterminate; the evidence to decide crucial questions of economic policy all too often is. The automobile companies have said that car-buyers did not want safety, when safety features were offered them. But, I wonder, how conclusive was their evidence on this point? Does it rule out what in the eyes of the consumers themselves would have been misjudgments of what they wanted? Was the information about safety as widely distributed, and as effectively communicated, as other information about the cars being offered? If N did not know the presence of all three alternatives, x, y, and z, or did not know of certain properties of these alternatives, or failed to apply certain principles to which he himself subscribes, but whose relevance then escaped him, N's statement, "I want z," is ripe for revision. Now, this consideration would be effective even if all consumers had been unanimous in expressing themselves as wanting cars other than those with the safety features; but it is of interest to inquire whether there was not in fact a sizable proportion of consumers who did then want the cars with the safety features, perhaps a proportion large enough to cover the costs of producing such cars, if the consumers making it up had been reached with information and offers. One might note, furthermore, that there are other ways in which the evidence about consumers not wanting safety features may be defective. How did the cars with these new features compare with other cars on other points? Was there agreement between companies and the public on what features of cars are most important for safety?

Rather than branch out, however, into such general skeptical considerations, healthy as they are, let us return to the particular subject of wants. The second reason for distrusting the statement by the corporations, "We only give the public what it wants," is that the corporations have had a good deal to do with instilling these wants in the public; they have done enough, one would think, to destroy any implication depending on those wants being spontaneously the consumers' own. The automobile companies have shaped the public's ideas about safety, and hence the wants related to safety: negatively, by suppressing information about the dangers of the cars that they produce; and positively, by extolling speed, and selling cars on the basis of power. Half a century of dilation on speed, power, and thrills have fostered and intensified wants that now seem questionable to many; and those who have the wants, without now questioning them, might be brought to revise them by perceiving the interested part that the automobile companies have played in instilling them. When N discovers that he was more under someone else's influence than he thought, he has a good reason for reconsidering his statement, "I want z."

The automobile companies and the advertising that they have paid for have operated to subvert the American value of safety. A third reason for refusing to agree to all the implications of the statement, "We only give the public what it wants," consists in the extent to which this subversion has been carried through the whole field of American values. The subversion affects not only safety—which we profess to cherish, and mean to, but which the automobile companies connive with us in undermining—but all sorts of other values, in many insidious ways. American business spends a great deal of time and energy confusing the public about values, and thus deliberately produces the sort of misjudgment about x, y, and z that will lead N to revise his expression when he detects his mistake. I shall mention just two further illustrations. There is, specifically, the systematic abuse of sexual interests, so that people have their wants for automobiles and all sorts of other things seriously mixed up with their sexual desires. The automobile companies (though certainly not these alone) have strenuously assisted in mixing us up about sex, making it more urgent, but also more diffuse, and commonly misdirected. More generally, I might mention the besetting clamor about goods and gadgets, which all the corporations join in generating. How often do members of the public get a chance to think quietly in a sustained way about what they might want out of life? Do they ever have time to reflect that perhaps they want too many things already and could well do without wanting still more?

In the fourth place, the claim "We only give the public what it wants" is suspect because the corporations not only assist in confusing the public about what it might want; they also obstruct institutional remedies for the lack of information that leads N and his fellow consumers into misjudgments about wants. A simpleminded man might ask, if the corporations were devoted to the public interest (as they so continually and profusely profess), would they not press for greatly enlarged facilities, public or private, but at any rate disinterested (and known to be so), for consumers' research? For public standards of quality? For trade fairs giving prizes for honest workmanship? Perhaps the corporations have objections to the relevance and thoroughness of the particular tests used by going consumers' research organizations; but such objections do not explain why the corporations resist disinterested tests of any kind, by any institutions with the capacity to do more thorough research than consumers can do for themselves. How shameful to find, besides the automobile companies dragging their feet about safety standards, the tire companies doing the same thing; the grocers and packagers objecting to truth-in-packaging; the credit firms protesting against truth-in-lending. If corporations wonder why they do not attract idealistic young men fresh from college, they need only consider the impression that such conduct makes on people outside the corporations.

One must remark, fifth, carrying forward an observation of Professor Kaysen's, that corporations often have a considerable amount of discretion respecting innovation,[1] and hence respecting the variety of products that they offer the public. In the automobile industry, with its high concentration and high barriers to entry, the variety of products is especially subject to arbitrary limitation on the producers' side. But from the fact that given a choice between x, y, and z, N expresses himself as wanting z, nothing can be inferred about his wants for u, v, w, goods that were not offered him. Many consumers might prefer very different cars—if they are never produced, so that consumers never have a chance to see them or to try them out, how can it be known that they are not wanted? It is true, one could say of *any* industry that there might be some other products that the industry is not now offering the public, but that the public would prefer to anything that is being offered. But I do not believe the fact that this could always be said makes it sometimes entirely trivial to say it. Saying it is not trivial as a reminder of the limitations on what can be inferred about wants from the wants expressed in the face of some limited set of alternatives. In the case of the automobiles offered the public, moreover, it is not nature, or even the market, that determines what shall figure in the set of alternatives. The very corporations that affect to be doing no more than responding to the wants of the public determine what range of wants shall be expressed. Furthermore, the alternative products that have not been introduced can be significantly specified—for example, the various backward-seating safety cars.

The sixth and last reason that I shall mention for distrusting the statement by the corporations, "We only give the public what it wants," lies in the existence, or possible existence, of wants that consumers may have but can satisfy only by concerted action, not in the market. Historic cases in point are legislation for safety in factories or legislation against child labor (in which consumers have been joined by conscientious producers, unable to risk independent self-restraint). I do not think that the allowances economists make for third-party costs or neighborhood effects suffice for wants respecting concerted action. For such wants may range even beyond the examples just given, to wants regarding the overall structure and development of the economy. One might well think, because of the resources that it uses up, the pressures that it creates, ranging from conspicuous consumption to the destruction of urban amenities, the automobile industry is much too large for the country to keep going, much less continue expanding. Rising to another sort of choice, between R, S, and T, N may express himself as wanting an alternative that would either entail not choosing z or preclude choosing between x, y, and z at all. So many people might, confronted with such a choice, want to have the automobile industry reduced in size; but such a choice could hardly be effective unless it were not a market choice, but a political one, offering the possibility of concerted action.

My six reasons are (I think) so obvious, once stated, and so compelling, that it might well be asked, how could any of them be overlooked? Now, if they are overlooked in some connections, they are of course frequently mentioned in others, though not perhaps all at once. All of them, I am sure, have often been mentioned by economists. Indeed, what is correct in the way that I have stated the reasons may depend on the teaching of economists; the mistakes are my own contribution. Yet I believe, for all the familiarity with which economists will greet the six reasons, one of the effects of economic teaching has been to divert attention from them, and so to open the way for general unthinking acquiescence in the corporations' contention, "We only give the public what it wants." The trouble is that the core of economic teaching is the fascinating idea of the free, self-regulating market—which I join Professors Arrow and Boulding and Friedman in admiring as one of the most beautiful thoughts ever to occur to man. The six reasons are all distressing qualifications to the application of the market idea. I conjecture that economists are happier refining the idea by expressing it in elegant models than entangling themselves with the qualifications that must be entered to it. Moreover, the qualifications that economists do elaborate are mainly qualifications on the supply side of the market—monopoly in its various degrees. Finally, economists have backed steadily away from the criticism of wants, first, by renouncing Benthamite utility, which was both intersubjective and normative; next by discarding the notion of subjective satisfaction—the pleasure, however perverse, that the consumer might realize from the goods that he bought; and lately, I gather, by abandoning in favor of "revealed preference" even subjective expectations of satisfaction.

These tendencies on the part of economists, combined with the incautious simplifications of their students, lead to the statement, "We only give the public what it wants," frequently, I think, being taken at face value. Dare I suggest that sometimes even economists let it slip by without protesting? The wants at issue are identified with the wants *assumed* by the economist as expressed within his models, defining the demand side of the market. But one of the most important observations to make about wants actually observed is that they are not to be taken for granted; they require examination and invite criticism. What people want is even in their own eyes always contingent on the circumstances in which their expressions of wants have been called for.[2]

Notes

1. Carl Kaysen, "The Corporation: How Much Power? What Scope?" in *The Corporation in Modern Society*, Edward S. Mason, ed., (Cambridge, Mass.: Harvard University Press, 1959), p. 93.

2. This study was written while I enjoyed a research appointment in the Department of Philosophy, University of Pittsburgh, to work on the values-study project supported by the Carnegie Corporation of New York and IBM. My aims in the study will perhaps be fully appreciated only if I publicly recall that the comment was prepared for delivery a few weeks after *The New York Times Magazine* had published an attack on contemporary American philosophy for discussing trivial questions of language rather than offering religious inspiration (or some robust substitute for inspiration). I set out to demonstrate that minute questions about language may quickly lead to important questions of social policy, and that answers to the one may crucially affect answers to the other.

THE NON SEQUITUR *OF THE "DEPENDENCE EFFECT"*

F. A. von Hayek

For well over a hundred years the critics of the free enterprise system have resorted to the argument that if production were only organized rationally, there would be no economic problem. Rather than face the problem which scarcity creates, socialist reformers have tended to deny that scarcity existed. Ever since the Saint-Simonians their contention has been that the problem of production has been solved and only the problem of distribution remains. However absurd this contention must appear to us with respect to the time when it was first advanced, it still has some persuasive power when repeated with reference to the present.

The latest form of this old contention is expounded in *The Affluent Society* by Professor J. K. Galbraith. He attempts to demonstrate that in our affluent society the important private needs are already satisfied and the urgent need is therefore no longer a further expansion of the output of commodities but an increase of those services which are supplied (and presumably can be supplied only) by government. Though this book has been extensively discussed since its publication in 1958, its central thesis still requires some further examination.

I believe the author would agree that his argument turns upon the "Dependence Effect" explained in Chapter XI of the book. The argument of this chapter starts from the assertion that a great part of the wants which are still unsatisfied in modern society are not wants which would

From *Southern Economic Journal*, April 1961. Reprinted by permission.

be experienced spontaneously by the individual if left to himself, but are wants which are created by the process by which they are satisfied. It is then represented as self-evident that for this reason such wants cannot be urgent or important. This crucial conclusion appears to be a complete *non sequitur* and it would seem that with it the whole argument of the book collapses.

The first part of the argument is of course perfectly true: we would not desire any of the amenities of civilization—or even of the most primitive culture—if we did not live in a society in which others provide them. The innate wants are probably confined to food, shelter, and sex. All the rest we learn to desire because we see others enjoying various things. To say that a desire is not important because it is not innate is to say that the whole cultural achievement of man is not important.

This cultural origin of practically all the needs of civilized life must of course not be confused with the fact that there are some desires which aim, not as a satisfaction derived directly from the use of an object, but only from the status which its consumption is expected to confer. In a passage which Professor Galbraith quotes (p. 118), Lord Keynes seems to treat the latter sort of Veblenesque conspicuous consumption as the only alternative "to those needs which are absolute in the sense that we feel them whatever the situation of our fellow human beings may be." If the latter phrase is interpreted to exclude all the needs for goods which are felt only because these goods are known to be produced, these two Keynesian classes describe of course only extreme types of wants, but disregard the overwhelming majority of goods on which civilized life rests. Very few needs indeed are "absolute" in the sense that they are independent of social environment or of the example of others, and that their satisfaction is an indispensable condition for the preservation of the individual or of the species. Most needs which make us act are needs for things which only civilization teaches us to exist at all, and these things are wanted by us because they produce feelings or emotions which we would not know if it were not for our cultural inheritance. Are not in this sense probably all our esthetic feelings "acquired tastes"?

How complete a *non sequitur* Professor Galbraith's conclusion represents is seen most clearly if we apply the argument to any product of the arts, be it music, painting, or literature. If the fact that people would not feel the need for something if it were not produced did prove that such products are of small value, all those highest products of human endeavor would be of small value. Professor Galbraith's argument could be easily employed, without any change of the essential terms, to demonstrate the worthlessness of literature or any other form of art. Surely an individual's want for literature is not original with himself in the sense that he would experience it if literature were not produced. Does this then mean that the production of literature cannot be defended as satisfying a want because it is only the production which provokes the demand? In this, as in the case of all cultural needs, it is unquestionably, in Professor Galbraith's words, "the process of satisfying the wants that creates the wants." There have never been "independently determined desires for"

literature before literature has been produced and books certainly do not
serve the "simple mode of enjoyment which requires no previous conditioning of the consumer" (p. 217). Clearly my taste for the novels of Jane
Austen or Anthony Trollope or C. P. Snow is not "original with myself."
But is it not rather absurd to conclude from this that it is less important
than, say, the need for education? Public education indeed seems to
regard it as one of its tasks to instill a taste for literature in the young and
even employs producers of literature for that purpose. Is this want creation by the producer reprehensible? Or does the fact that some of the
pupils may possess a taste for poetry only because of the efforts of their
teachers prove that since "it does not arise in spontaneous consumer
need and the demand would not exist were it not contrived, its utility or
urgency, ex contrivance, is zero?"

The appearance that the conclusions follow from the admitted facts is
made possible by an obscurity of the wording of the argument with
respect to which it is difficult to know whether the author is himself the
victim of a confusion or whether he skillfully uses ambiguous terms to
make the conclusion appear plausible. The obscurity concerns the implied assertion that the wants of the consumers are determined by the
producers. Professor Galbraith avoids in this connection any terms as
crude and definite as "determine." The expressions he employs, such as
that wants are "dependent on" or the "fruits of" production, or that
"production creates the wants" do, of course, suggest determination but
avoid saying so in plain terms. After what has already been said it is of
course obvious that the knowledge of what is being produced is one of
the many factors on which it depends what people will want. It would
scarcely be an exaggeration to say that contemporary man, in all fields
where he has not yet formed firm habits, tends to find out what he wants
by looking at what his neighbours do and at various displays of goods
(physical or in catalogues or advertisements) and then choosing what he
likes best.

In this sense the tastes of man, as is also true of his opinions and beliefs
and indeed much of his personality, are shaped in a great measure by his
cultural environment. But though in some contexts it would perhaps be
legitimate to express this by a phrase like "production creates the wants,"
the circumstances mentioned would clearly not justify the contention that
particular producers can deliberately determine the wants of particular
consumers. The efforts of all producers will certainly be directed towards
that end; but how far any individual producer will succeed will depend
not only on what he does but also on what the others do and on a great
many other influences operating upon the consumer. The joint but un-
coordinated efforts of the producers merely create one element of the
environment by which the wants of the consumers are shaped. It is because each individual producer thinks that the consumers can be persuaded to like his products that he endeavours to influence them. But
though this effort is part of the influences which shape consumers' tastes,
no producer can in any real sense "determine" them. This, however, is
clearly implied in such statements as that wants are "both passively and

deliberately the fruits of the process by which they are satisfied" (p. 124). If the producer could in fact deliberately determine what the consumers will want, Professor Galbraith's conclusions would have some validity. But though this is skillfully suggested, it is nowhere made credible, and could hardly be made credible because it is not true. Though the range of choice open to the consumers is the joint result of, among other things, the efforts of all producers who vie with each other in making their respective products appear more attractive than those of their competitors, every particular consumer still has the choice between all those different offers.

A fuller examination of this process would, of course, have to consider how, after the efforts of some producers have actually swayed some consumers, it becomes the example of the various consumers thus persuaded which will influence the remaining consumers. This can be mentioned here only to emphasize that even if each consumer were exposed to pressure of only one producer, the harmful effects which are apprehended from this would soon be offset by the much more powerful example of his fellows. It is of course fashionable to treat this influence of the example of others (or, what comes to the same things, the learning from the experience made by others) as if it amounted all to an attempt of keeping up with the Joneses and for that reason was to be regarded as detrimental. It seems to me that not only the importance of this factor is usually greatly exaggerated but also that it is not really relevant to Professor Galbraith's main thesis. But it might be worthwhile briefly to ask what, assuming that some expenditure were actually determined solely by a desire of keeping up with the Joneses, that would really prove? At least in Europe we used to be familiar with a type of persons who often denied themselves even enough food in order to maintain an appearance of respectability or gentility in dress and style of life. We may regard this as a misguided effort, but surely it would not prove that the income of such persons was larger than they knew how to use wisely. That the appearance of success, or wealth, may to some people seem more important than many other needs, does in no way prove that the needs they sacrifice to the former are unimportant. In the same way, even though people are often persuaded to spend unwisely, this surely is no evidence that they do not still have important unsatisfied needs.

Professor Galbraith's attempt to give an apparent scientific proof for the contention that the need for the production of more commodities has greatly decreased seems to me to have broken down completely. With it goes the claim to have produced a valid argument which justifies the use of coercion to make people employ their income for those purposes of which he approves. It is not to be denied that there is some originality in this latest version of the old socialist argument. For over a hundred years we have been exhorted to embrace socialism because it would give us more goods. Since it has so lamentably failed to achieve this where it has been tried, we are now urged to adopt it because more goods after all are not important. The aim is still progressively to increase the share of the resources whose use is determined by political authority and the coercion of any dissenting minority. It is not surprising, therefore, that Professor Galbraith's thesis has been most enthusiastically received by the intellectuals of the British Labour Party where his influence bids fair to displace that of the late Lord Keynes. It is more curious that in this country it is not recognized as an outright socialist argument and often seems to appeal to people on the opposite end of the political spectrum. But this is probably only another instance of the familiar fact that on these matters the extremes frequently meet.

FREEDOM AND PERSUASION

Stanley I. Benn

I

Some time in the fifties, everyone became conscious of the menace of the hidden persuaders. Whether as commercial advertisers or as political propagandists, they formed, it was said, an invisible power elite, corrupting taste and manipulating opinion for private gain or sectional power. We learnt with alarm that having the sense of choosing freely was no guarantee that one really had a free choice; choices could be rigged by skillful operators who could make us want what they or their clients wanted us to want.

This scandal of our age seems to have been exaggerated. It is now the fashion to take a more sober view of the claims of the persuasion industry and its supporting "motivational research." Propaganda and advertising, we are assured, can shape beliefs and attitudes only within limits; people resist suggestions that run counter to their basic personality characteristics. So a film intended to counter a prejudice may actually reinforce it. Though authoritarian personalities can be readily switched from fascism to communism, they make poor liberals. "Brain-washing" is effective only with alienated and anomic individuals—and its effects even on them are relatively short-lived once they leave the reinforcing environment.

All the same, although mass persuasive techniques are less successful in changing attitudes than the alarmists would have us suppose, they seem to be very effective in reinforcing already existing tendencies to change. Furthermore, all the research done so far has been on "campaign effects" i.e., on the kind of short-term effects which are typically the goals of publicity and advertising; little is known as yet of the long-term effects

From *The Australasian Journal of Philosophy,* vol. 45, December 1967. Reprinted by permission.

of mass persuasive influences. Besides, the reassurances that have been given amount only to saying that not much progress has been made so far. As yet, our minds cannot readily be made up for us unless we are initially indifferent (as, for instance, between one kind of soap and another, or, maybe, between one brand of authoritarianism and another); altering basic attitudes is very much more difficult. Propaganda may "boomerang"; human personality is not infinitely plastic; psychologists have much to learn about the formation of human attitudes, and propagandists about how to manipulate them. In much the same way one might have been assured at the end of the last century that fear of aerial warfare was fantastic—pioneers had barely succeeded in getting a heavier-than-air machine off the ground. For the fact remains that there are interested people who are spending a great deal to find out what makes a man believe and behave as he does, and who clearly live in hope that out of it will come more efficient ways of influencing both. Discovering why primitive techniques have only limited effectiveness is the first step to more effective ones.

My intention here, however, is not to assess the claims of the persuasion industry, but rather to examine what the expressions of alarm that these claims evoke presuppose about freedom and the social interactions of aims and influences, and to gain from this an insight into certain liberal ways of thinking about politics and society. . . .

. . . The classic discussions of political obligation have all been concerned with what constitutes a good reason for requiring a man to put aside his own wishes or opinions and to act instead in accordance with someone else's. The problem presented by propagandists, advertisers and public relations experts is quite different. They aim not at overruling contrary intentions by threats of coercion but, by persuasion, to create a willing—if possible an enthusiastic—accord. They seek to avoid or dissolve conflict, not to overrule it. . . .

. . . But liberalism has never taken much notice of how men come to want what they do want—or rather, the traditional target for liberal critics like Milton, Jefferson, and Mill, has been censorship, the monopolistic control of the supply of ideas, not the techniques used to persuade people to adopt some ideas rather than others. Pinning their faith to human rationality, they believed that to drive out error truth needed no special privilege beyond the opportunity to be heard; the shoddy tricks of those who exploited credulity could not survive exposure to rational criticism. This faith never faced the challenge that there might be non-rational techniques for persuading a person to believe certain things or to adopt certain desired attitudes—that is, techniques for inducing him to want to do or be something that someone else had decided upon, even though arguments and evidence to the contrary remained fully accessible. Would the classical liberals have said that a person who was able to do what he wanted without interference, but whose preferences had been shaped by such techniques, was free because he was "left to do or be what he wanted to do or be, without interference by other persons"?

The classical liberals might have objected that the techniques of persuasion that modern liberals fear do in fact "interfere"—not, certainly, with a man's doing what he wants to do, but with his freely *deciding* what he wants to do. But making this move commits the liberal to some way of distinguishing forms of persuasion that interfere from those that do not. For in defining social and political freedom, the liberal relies on a conception of a free market in ideas, a conception which actually presupposes that men will attempt to influence one another's beliefs. Accordingly, he must allow that there are some ways at least of getting people to change their minds that are not in his sense interferences. . . .

II

The liberal emphasis on rationality may suggest that the distinction sought for, between persuasion that is consistent with autonomy and persuasion that is not, would be the distinction between rational and non-rational persuasion. This distinction can indeed be made, and, as I hope to show, can be useful, but it will not take us the whole way we have to go. Persuasion is rational in so far as the persuasiveness lies in the substance of the arguments rather than in the manner of presentation, the authority of the persuader, or some other special relationship by virtue of which one party is particularly susceptible to suggestions from the other. Rational persuasion, in short, is impersonal, in the sense that it is the argument not the person that persuades—the same argument advanced by anyone else would be as effective. Of course, not any kind of reason will do. To give as a reason the injury you will do to me if I reject your suggestions is to threaten me, not to use rational persuasion. However, some neutral or disinterested person with no control over your behaviour would be using rational persuasion if *he* warned me of what you would do to me if I disobeyed you. The distinctive feature of rational persuasion is that it invites and responds to criticism. The would-be persuader is committed to changing his opinion too if the persuadee gives sufficient reasons for rejecting it. Rational persuasion is therefore essentially a dialogue between equals. Although the man who warns me of the probable consequences of what I am doing may be trying to stop me doing it, and perhaps succeeds, he is not acting inconsistently with my autonomy; for though I might have preferred to remain ignorant of the inconvenient facts—or even to have gone on disregarding what I already really knew—still, he has not made my mind up for me, but, on the contrary, has made it more possible for me to make a rational decision for myself. Indeed, by offering reasons why I should make one decision rather than another, so far from abusing my rational autonomy he recognizes and respects it. It was because the liberal classics took this as the paradigm of persuasion that they never felt the necessity for defining the relation between persuasion and power.

I said above that persuasion is rational *in so far as* it seeks to convince by giving reasons, and consequently in so far as it is impersonal. This is not to say that we can distinguish sharply between the case of pure rational persuasion and others. Most cases combine rational and non-rational elements; any argument, however good, can be spoilt by bad presentation, and its effect heightened by fitting eloquence. Still, we can envisage a case of successful persuasion in which the persuader is so distasteful to the persuadee, his presentation so graceless and his whole demeanour so repellent, that almost anyone else could have done it better. Unless the persuadee is over-compensating for his personal dislike, we shall have to attribute the persuader's success entirely to the rational merits of his argument.

The possibility of distinguishing rational and non-rational persuasion does not imply, however, that an instance of persuasion is an invasion of personal freedom or autonomy precisely to the extent that it involves non-rational elements, like appeals to emotion or prejudice. The pretty girl in the tooth paste advertisement may be captivating, but do her charms really make slaves of us? While, therefore, we can confidently say that rational persuasion is consistent with freedom, we still have to distinguish among different forms of non-rational persuasion those that are not.

A is not unfree merely because his conduct is influenced (i.e., affected) by someone else's actions or communications of some kind other than rational arguments. Suppose, for instance, that he confides in B a plan from which he has great hopes; B, while offering no criticism, treats it scornfully; A, discouraged, gives up. Should we say that A's freedom had been infringed? Has B interfered with A, because B's non-rational influence upon A has put him off? Or should we not rather say that A must have been unusually weak-minded to be put off so easily?

This example suggests that whether a man is really master of himself or whether he is being interfered with, does not depend solely on the kind of influence another man exerts, nor on its actual effects; it depends *also* on whether it would be reasonable to expect him, in the given conditions, to withstand influence of that kind.

I suggested earlier that to say that a man was not free to do what he would certainly be punished for doing is not to say that no one, faced with the same consequence, has ever chosen to do such a thing, but rather that the choice is not one we could reasonably expect a man to make. Similarly a temptation or a provocation is not irresistible merely because someone has in fact failed to resist it; but neither is the fact that someone has resisted it proof that it is not irresistible. A temptation is said to be irresistible only if a man *could not reasonably be expected* to resist it, even though others might actually have resisted it in the past.

These are instances of a class of judgements which cannot be satisfactorily elucidated without using some standard of "the normal man." Judgements about freedom, influence, power, and interference are, I believe, of the same class. What does it mean to say that a man does not withstand an influence? It is not simply that he falls in with what is proposed. For the idea of withstanding it suggests some inner source of strength, some kind of disposition, interest, or motive for not falling in with it. It is not merely that the influence fails in its intent, but that it fails on account of something about the patient, not simply on account of the ineptitude of the agent. Consider the following dialogue:

CUSTOMER: I want a cake of soap, please.
SHOPKEEPER: Which brand?
CUSTOMER: Which do you recommend?
SHOPKEEPER: *Pongo.* (Aside) It's no different from any of the others,
and I make a quarter cent more profit per bar.
CUSTOMER: Very well, I'll take *Pongo.*

Clearly, he could have said no. But why should he have done so? To say
that he failed to withstand the suggestion seems to presuppose, what is
not the case in this example, that he had some contrary interest or disposition, that he knew, for instance, that he was allergic to *Pongo.* Even then,
one would not say that the grocer's influence was irresistible. For any
other customer in his place would have said: "No, not that one—I'm
allergic to it."

Bribery raises similar issues. If A asks B for a service in return for a
sum of money, there is no reason *prima facie* why B should be expected
to refuse the offer; and if B accepts it, we should not say that he failed
to withstand or resist it. If, however, he accepts, having an interest that
could provide a counter-motive, or a duty, e.g., as a public official, not
to do what A asks, one could properly say that he did not resist. Furthermore, if we wanted to plead irresistible temptation in his defence, we
should have to argue that no one under the exceptional conditions in
which B was placed (whatever they may have been) could *reasonably be
expected* to resist. That a man has been provided with a counter-motive is
not enough to make it impossible for him to do his duty, though it may
sufficiently explain why he did not do it. In the absence of exceptional
conditions, attempting to corrupt him does not deprive him of free
choice. On the contrary, his freedom is an indispensable condition for his
being held responsible should he give in to the temptation. Similarly one
cannot plead by way of excuse that a man has been subject to non-rational
persuasive influence, unless one can also maintain that no one, despite
an interest counter to the suggestion, could reasonably have been expected not to fall in with it.

The problem for the liberal, then, is to establish tests by which to
identify non-rational influences that a person could not reasonably be
expected to resist, supposing that he has some interest in doing so. One
such test is whether the patient can be aware of what is happening to him.
For if one cannot know that an attempt is being made to manipulate one's
preferences, and if one has no way of distinguishing a manipulated preference, one cannot be on one's guard against it. Subliminal suggestion
would probably prove objectionable by this test (though there appear to
be subconscious censors operating even here to inhibit out-of-character
responses). An extension of the same principle would cover propaganda,
supported and protected by censorship. For supposing the subject to
have some initial disposition, presumed interest, or duty not to accept it,
an apparently well-supported suggestion in the complete absence of any
counter-evidence might fairly be called irresistible. Beyond these rather
obvious criteria we should have to rely on the results of psychological

research. If we want to discuss whether protection from mass persuasive techniques is necessary or even desirable, we must first have some idea of the kinds of influence that a person of normal firmness of purpose and with normal interests could reasonably be expected to withstand in a given situation. Moreover, there may be classes of persons, like children, who are peculiarly vulnerable to particular techniques, or to suggestions of particular kinds; principles of protection may very possibly have to use different norms for different purposes. Information like this is as important to the defenders of freedom as it is to the manipulators, and may well be among the fruits of psychologists' investigations into the effectiveness of advertising and propaganda techniques.

III

To what extent can such criteria for distinguishing forms of persuasion inconsistent with freedom suggest moral criteria for the use and control of persuasion and manipulative techniques? The liberal presupposition that every man has a right not to be interfered with unless he is doing something that itself interferes with the freedom or well-being of someone else, applies as much to the persuader as to the persuadee. Unless a form of persuasion itself interferes with the freedom or interests either of the persuadee or someone else, to interfere with it would be an invasion of the rights of the persuader. On the other hand, the persuadee can properly claim as a condition for *his* freedom, that he be protected from hidden manipulation aimed at political or economic exploitation. From these considerations we can elicit, in the first place, criteria for any advertising or propaganda that is designed to promote the interests of the persuaders. We can say, provisionally, that there is no ground for objecting to such influences if they do not infringe the freedom of the persuadee, and constitute no threat to the interests of anyone else. It is up to the persuadee to determine whether his own interests would be served or impaired by letting himself fall in with what is suggested to him. It is not consistent, in other words, with liberal presuppositions about human nature and its characteristic excellence that he should be protected from every kind of influence that might lead him to do things against his own interests. If men allow themselves to be exploited, through lack of reasonable caution or of the exercise of normal critical judgement, they have only themselves to blame. As rational and autonomous beings, they are responsible within reason for safeguarding their own interests—*caveat emptor* applies to ideas and tastes as well as to goods. There is a case, of course, for protection against misrepresentation of both ideas and goods. But this is not to protect the consumer against freely choosing what is damaging to his own interests; it is rather that in determining where his interest lies he shall not be deliberately and unfairly deceived by a lack of information he cannot remedy or by false information that he cannot reasonably be expected to check. Lying newspapers are at least as objectionable as false statements of the weight of soap powder in a King Size packet. Though there may be no objection to manufacturers attracting customers by putting small amounts of soap in large packets, the consumer who wants to make a reasoned choice between brands is entitled to know the weight of soap he is buying without the inconvenience of carrying his own scales or insisting on having the alternative packages weighed before he decides. Of far greater importance is his right to be told the truth in news reports, on which he has to base rational judgements on public affairs, and which he simply cannot confirm for himself. Of course, insisting that newspapers tell the truth is far more problematic and politically hazardous than insisting on the truth about soap powders. Since governments are interested parties there are no doubt good reasons for leaving it to the reader to check one against the other.

Applying the criteria to techniques which, designed to get under the consumer's guard, may be incompatible with his autonomy, is rather more complicated. A practice which simply exploits the consumer (or the voter) presents no theoretical difficulty; if it is both an infringement of the consumer's freedom and an attack on his interest, it is indefensible. But how firmly can the liberal turn down a plea that a manipulative technique is being used in the general interest, or in the interests of the individual himself? *Pace* Mill, it is difficult to sustain unqualified the doctrine that "the sole end for which mankind are warranted, individually or collectively, in interfering with the liberty of action of any of their number, is self-protection" and that "his own good . . . is not a sufficient warrant."[1] Mill's equivocation in the matter of the unsafe bridge[2] is evidence of his own uneasiness; and one can have legitimate doubts about his plea that poisons and dangerous drugs be freely available without medical prescription. What kind of an interest, however, would justify interference for a man's own good?

Consider a possible advertiser's argument that, by persuading a consumer to want G (which the consumer can afford and the manufacturer can supply) he makes it possible for the former to satisfy his wants; moreover, creating a want he can also satisfy, he is acting in the consumer's own interests by maximizing his satisfactions. (If this be a man of straw, this particular kind of straw can still be illuminating.)

The argument would be mistaken, in my view, firstly in identifying the consumer's wants with his interests. Tobacco manufacturers who by advertising create tobacco consumers, may cultivate their customers' wants but are questionably serving their interests. And this is not because the experience might not be "really satisfying." For once the habit is formed smoking undoubtedly satisfies a craving, and deprivation is so unpleasant that many smokers accept the risk of lung cancer rather than give it up. One has to recognize that people often want what is conspicuously bad for them, and that what satisfies their desires may not be in their interests. Suppose, however, the desire were for something reasonably harmless; what value would we attach to satisfying it, once it were seen as the deliberate creation of someone else? If the advertiser succeeds in producing a mass demand for a product that no one wanted before, is his product valuable and his activity worthwhile, simply because it now meets a demand? Or are we entitled to look critically at the sorts of things that men are encouraged to demand, and to decide that some demands may be unworthy of satisfaction?

Writers in the empirical, liberal tradition, and most notably, of course, writers in the utilitarian tradition, have been inclined to treat as a reason in favour of any performance or provision whatsoever that someone wanted it. Though this reason might be overridden in a given instance by other people's wishes, or by the expectation of harmful consequences, these would weigh as reasons against doing something that would still have been intrinsically worth doing simply as satisfying a desire. Moreover, if the thing were not done, there would be a presumption in favour of saying that the person desiring it had been deprived of a satisfaction, that the result had been to his disadvantage, and that he would have been better off had he got what he wanted. So *ceteris paribus* a world in which many desires were satisfied would seem to be a better world than one in which fewer were satisfied, whether because some remained unsatisfied or because people had fewer desires.

Though this view is persuasive when stated generally, I have difficulty in extending this presumption in favour of satisfying desires to desires demonstrably contrived by someone else, especially if contrived for his own purposes. That is not to say that no contrived desire would ever be worth satisfying; one might properly claim that some kind of experience for which one had induced a desire in someone else, for whatever purpose, was worth having, and that he would consequently be better off if his desire for it were satisfied. But this would be to recognize a distinction between experiences which were worth having, for which the corresponding desires would be worth satisfying, and those which were not. This is quite different from allowing a residual kind of worth in the satisfaction of any desire, simply as such and irrespective of its object.

It might be objected, as a general negative reason for satisfying desires, that a desire unsatisfied is a source of suffering. Certainly, if a drug addict had no hope of cure, what he suffered from his unsatisfied desire would be a strong reason, perhaps sufficient reason, for satisfying it. It is surely a mistake, however, to assimilate all desires to cravings; to be disappointed is not necessarily to suffer, or, at any rate, to suffer in the same sense in which deprived addicts suffer. Furthermore, there is something repugnant about saying that, in a case of deliberate torturing a saving factor in an otherwise totally deplorable situation is that the sadistic desires of the torturer have been satisfied. Malicious satisfaction makes a situation worse, not better.

The view I am challenging depends for its persuasiveness in part on a meaning shift in the word "satisfaction." I may get satisfaction from contemplating a picture or reading a novel, but this is not necessarily because a desire to look at a picture has been satisfied. On the other hand, if I desire X and get X my desire is satisfied but it may give me no satisfaction. I may discover that what I wanted was not worth having. And this may not be because I was misinformed about the nature of the thing; I may have got precisely what I desired and expected, yet still be no better off for having it. The quality of the life into which it enters may be no better for it—it may have no function in my life, and add nothing to me as a person. My wanting it may have been factitious, in the sense that the desire arose from no integral tendency in my nature, no search for a mode of expression, no recognizable need. I could have set my heart on almost anything else, or on nothing at all, and have been no worse off. Now, if my desires were simply the contrivance of persuaders, they might very well be like this. In that case one would be led to ask whether the mere fact of a desire could really be a reason for satisfying it or whether what gives value to the satisfaction of a desire is the quality of the life of which it forms a part and in which it has a function. Satisfying a desire would be valuable then if it sustained or made possible a valuable kind of life. To say this is to reject the argument that in creating the wants he can satisfy the advertiser (or the manipulator of mass emotion in politics or religion) is necessarily acting in the interests of his public. What their interests are depends now on some objective assessment of what constitutes excellence in human beings, not on what they happen, for whatever reason, to want. If this is true, advertising that presents consumption as a self-justifying activity, that attributes value to things, rather than to what they do to and for a person, is essentially corrupting in that it promotes a misconception of the nature of man. Misunderstanding what we are, we are misled about the nature of the enterprize in which as men we are engaged.

This does not mean that we ought to repudiate the cautious liberal approach to protection "in one's own interests." For everything depends on what one takes to be the characteristic human excellences. The liberal concept of man, as sustained by Kant and Mill, places at the top of the list a man's capacity for making responsible choices among alternative ways of life, for striving no matter how mistakenly or unsuccessfully to make of himself something worthy of his own respect. This is a creative enterprise calling for experiment, intelligent self-appraisal, and criticism. Consequently, it cannot be fostered by denying men the opportunity to make false starts and to learn from experience. Men have an overriding interest in liberty itself.

This account of human interests suggests an important qualification to my earlier provisional statement, that there was no ground for objecting to persuasion that did not infringe the freedom of the persuadee, and constituted no threat to the interests of anyone else, since it was for him to determine whether his own interests would be served or impaired by falling in with it. For we can now suggest a case for protecting a man from any influence, irresistible or not, which if successful would lead to a condition like drug addiction in which his ability to make further rational choices would be permanently and irremediably impaired. For though the mode of persuasion might not itself be an interference, nevertheless, if successful, it would impair freedom, understood as rational self-mastery.

I do not expect everyone to agree on the application of this criterion, on whether, for instance, it would rule out advertising by cigarette manufacturers, or advertising of the type mentioned earlier, which corrupts by promoting the worship of consumption for its own sake. It is arguable, on the one hand, that advertisements of this latter kind are not, taken severally, irresistible, nor would responding to them irremediably impair the individual's capacity for discovering for himself what kinds of things are valuable and why. Indeed, the very opposite might be the case. On the other hand, the cumulative influence of an environment filled with a variety of advertisements all with the same underlying message hidden by its very ubiquity may be more closely analogous to influences like subliminal suggestions that one cannot directly perceive than to a straightforward appeal to emotions.

The same basic principles on which I have relied for criteria justifying protection from persuasion also provide criteria for the use of irresistible manipulative techniques. Just as the sole ground for protecting a man from an influence which is not irresistible is that he should not risk impairing his capacity for choosing rationally and for making critical appraisals of his own experience and achievements; so the justification for manipulation must be that he is suffering from some impediment or handicap, which inhibits such activities, and which he could not remedy by his own efforts. This would justify, for instance, the use in psychotherapy of hypnosis and "truth-drugs"; for the aim of the treatment is not to dominate nor to mould the patient, but to restore his capacity for making his own rational appraisals of his environment, and for deciding for himself what would be his appropriate adjustment to it. Here again one has to rely heavily on conceptions of normality; for to be handicapped is to lack capacities that a man normally enjoys.

I have said that these criteria are not easy to apply, and there would be plenty of argument about any particular application. Nevertheless since we are bound to make decisions of this kind, it is well that we should be conscious of what we are about in making them.

Notes

1. John Stuart Mill, *On Liberty,* Everyman Edition (New York: E. B. Dutton Company, 1910), pp. 72–73.
2. *Ibid.,* pp. 151–152

SUGGESTED SUPPLEMENTARY READINGS

Bok, Sissela. *Lying: Moral Choice in Public and Private Life.* New York: Pantheon Books, 1978.

Clasen, Earl A. "Marketing Ethics and the Consumer." *Harvard Business Review,* January–February 1967.

Finn, David. "Struggle for Ethics in Public Relations." *Harvard Business Review,* January–February 1959.

Fried, Charles. *Right and Wrong,* Chapter 3. Cambridge, Mass.: Harvard University Press, 1978.

Gardner, David M. "Deception in Advertising: A Conceptual Approach." *Journal of Marketing,* 39 (January 1975).

Hentoff, Nat. "Would You Run This Ad?" *Business and Society Review,* 14 (Summer 1975).

Keane, John G. "On Professionalism in Advertising." *Journal of Advertising,* Fall 1974.

Lucas, John T., and Richard Gurman. *Truth in Advertising.* New York: American Management Association, 1972.

Millum, Trevor. *Images of Woman: Advertising in Women's Magazines.* Totowa, N.J.: Rowman and Littlefield, 1975.

Murphy, Pat, and Ben M. Enis. "Let's Hear the Case Against Brand X." *Business and Society Review,* 12 (Winter 1974–75).

Packard, Vance. *The Hidden Persuaders.* New York: Pocket Books, 1957.

Phillip, Nelson. "Advertising and Ethics." In *Ethics, Free Enterprise and Public Policy: Original Essays on Moral Issues In Business,* ed. Richard T. DeGeorge and Joseph A. Pichler. New York: Oxford University Press, 1978.

Preston, Ivan L. *The Great American Blow-up: Puffery in Advertising and Selling.* Madison: University of Wisconsin Press, 1975.

Reilly, John H., Jr. "A Welfare Critique of Advertising." *American Journal of Economics and Sociology,* 31 (July 1972).

Sandage, C. H., and Vernon Fryburger. *Advertising Theory and Practice* (9th ed.). Homewood, Ill.: Richard D. Irwin, Inc., 1975.

Steiner, George A. *Business and Society* (2nd ed.), Chapter 15. New York: Random House, 1975.

Stuart, Frederick, ed. *Consumer Protection from Deceptive Advertising.* Hempstead, N.Y.: Hofstra University, 1974.

Chapter ***8***

ENVIRONMENTAL
RESPONSIBILITY

case 1: The Tocks Island Dam Case

Between 1962 and 1975 a protracted controversy erupted over whether or not to build a dam in the remote regions of Tocks Island, New Jersey. The dam was designed to provide flood control, an additional water supply, a new electrical source, and a recreation center. On the other hand, it would have destroyed some local communities, ecological systems, and natural beauty. Opposition emerged between business and allied state interests in promoting economic growth (and recreational facilities) and the interests of environmentalists in preserving nature against further destruction. Terrible floods and severe drought had preceded plans for the dam and were responsible for the initial commission to build the dam. In 1962 the project was expected to cost $98 million, but by 1975 the projected figure moved to $400 million. Originally environmental groups favored the project, because it would limit growth in the area and would provide a recreation area run by the conservation-minded National Park Service. However, after cost/benefit studies were completed, environmentalists, governors, senators, and congressmen turned against the project for environmental reasons. It appeared that the dam would encourage heavy industrial and residential development, as well as tourism (9.4 million visitors annually was the projected figure). While this outcome would be extremely good for business in the area, for water and power companies, and for the growth of tourist facilities, there also would be ineliminable traffic congestion, waste disposal problems, lake eutrophication, damage to fisheries, the destruction of the last free-flowing river in

523

the Eastern United States, the destruction of several forms of aquatic life in the area, and the flooding of a picturesque and historical valley. Although it was clearly demonstrated that business in the region would be spurred, that the community's tax base would be increased, and that the economic benefits outdistanced the economic costs, the project was eventually voted down by the states immediately affected by its construction. New York, New Jersey, and Delaware voted against the project, while Pennsylvania voted in favor of it.

case 2: The Velsicol Chemical Corporation Case

On December 24, 1975, the administrator of the Environmental Protection Agency of the United States Government, Russell E. Train, issued an order suspending some uses of the pesticides heptachlor and chlordane. A Federal act seemed to give him authority to do so, but both the Secretary of the Department of Agriculture and the manufacturer of the pesticides, Velsicol Chemical Corporation, joined hands in asking for a public hearing on the decision. Train and the EPA adduced considerable evidence to indicate that these pesticides, which were widely used in the environment to control pests, produced cancer in laboratory animals. Testing on laboratory animals was the sole basis for the inference that the pesticides posed a cancer threat to humans, although it also was conclusively demonstrated that residues of the chemical were widely present in the human diet and in the human tissues of those exposed. Velsicol Chemical stood to lose a substantial amount of money unless existing stocks could be sold, and the EPA administrator did allow them to sell limited stock for use on corn pests (for a short period of time). The Environmental Defense Fund felt strongly that no sale should be permitted whatsoever, and sought an injunction against continued sale. During the course of the public hearing, Velsicol argued both that its product should not be suspended unless the governmental agency could demonstrate that it is unsafe, and that any other finding would be a drastic departure from past federal policy. However, both the agency and the judge argued that *the burden of proof is on the company;* i.e., the company must be able to prove that its product is safe. Since most issues about environmental and human safety turn on a demonstration of either safety or hazardousness, this burden-of-proof argument was strongly contested in the hearing. The judge found in favor of the agency largely because he believed the animal tests demonstrated a "substantial likelihood" of serious harm to humans. [Note: At the press deadline for this book EPA was considering backing down on this suspension ruling.]

INTRODUCTION

Everyone is familiar with the struggle between environmentalists and certain business interests. This battle has not emerged simply because we now *know* more than we used to know about ecosystems and the environmental sciences in general. The struggle has emerged because human life, animal life, and plant life are threatened in various ways by our use of the environment. On the other hand, certain business interests are equally threatened by policies and laws that protect the environment against further encroachment. Classic conflicts between public and private interests have resulted from this struggle. For example, there have been attempts to show (and government officials now believe it has been demonstrated) that fluorocarbons in aerosol spray cans sufficiently damage the earth's ozone shield that serious repercussions may follow from continued use: e.g., possible melting of polar ice caps, flooding of cities along the world's coasts, and radioactive contamination. The food industry has also been accused of raping the land by failing to balance its high-level methods of food production with the land's actual lower-level capacity to produce. The timber industry has been accused of deforestation without replenishment. And pollution of various descriptions has been laid at the door of the bottle and can industries, plastics industries, the chemical industry, and the oil industry.

In this chapter these problems of environmental safety and protection, as balanced against the interests of business, will concern us. In particular, the following problems will be discussed: (1) What sort of framework of ethical principles is needed to attack these environmental issues? And does this framework grant *rights* either to citizens, corporations, or natural objects? (2) What balancing considerations between business and public interests can be validly institutionalized as public policies? (3) What are the facts about the extent of the environmental crisis, and how do these facts bear on moral problems and questions of industry responsibility? The first question asks whether a unique and new commitment to the environment needs to be made through what has been called a special "environmental ethic," or whether the general moral principles outlined in Chapter 1 of this book (liberty, justice, utility, the public interest, etc.) will suffice, if fairly applied. The second question raises the issue of how costs and benefits are to be balanced in making policy and how ethical principles might themselves limit the use of cost/benefit schemes. Especially important is whether it is justified to balance social goals such as a clean environment against *business* interests, instead of using some other means to achieve the same goals. The third question asks not only for the facts, but for an account of how the crises have been created by business interests, by questionable public policies, and by an inadequate ethical framework.

RELEVANT ETHICAL PRINCIPLES

Those who promote a radically new environmental ethic argue that there is a special problem produced by overpowering habits and background beliefs prevalent in Western culture. For example, there are religious beliefs about nature which inform the attitudes of many persons. According to some religious teachings human beings alone have intrinsic value; the rest of nature is inferior and is to be used for human enjoyment and betterment. From this view, humans are not conceived so much as a part of the ecosystem as external to it. Those who believe differently point out that such beliefs run deep in Western culture and will be difficult to eliminate short of overturning the entire religious tradition. Hence they call for a new environmental ethic.

Others disagree with this protective approach. They argue that we need to view the environment in a different way only to the extent that doing so would improve our quality of life and continued existence, now and in the future. That is, they argue that environmental concerns are valid only to the extent that they improve the human situation, and not because animals and plants have some sort of rights. This approach emphasizes the freedom of businesses to continue a heavy use of the environment, subject to limitations only insofar as they harm other individuals in society by this use of the environment.

The articles in this chapter by Neil Chamberlain, Nicholas Rescher, and John Passmore all use some variant of this latter argument. Chamberlain argues that stronger environmental controls than (roughly) those now operative "would require a larger sacrifice of immediate pleasures and preferences than the public is willing to make." Passmore looks to the welfare of future generations and ponders our present obligations to those generations. He contends that many uncertainties attend such speculation and that we are obliged to be extremely cautious with natural resources (e.g., coal) only if there is a reasonable certainty that future generations will require them. He goes on to argue that although we should be prepared to make some sacrifices for the sake of environmental quality, we ought not to make so many sacrifices that they would seriously impair our cultural heritage or business activity (as, for example, would occur by not producing gasoline or electricity). Large sacrifices, he contends, would do more serious damage to future generations than would a heavy present use of the environment.

In a separate article, William T. Blackstone takes a substantially different view. He asks whether a livable environment is merely a *desirable* outcome or one to which all persons have a *right*. After developing a theory of human rights, he argues that we do have a right to a livable environment because it is a necessary condition of human flourishing. He also contends that this moral right should be made a legal right (compatible with some qualifications in presently operative property rights). Blackstone urges his program because he thinks "we cannot expect private business to provide solutions to the multiple pollution problems for which they themselves are responsible." He explicitly argues against the self-regulation proposals advanced in some quarters: "We are deluding ourselves if we think that private business can function as its own pollution police." Blackstone then offers a series of arguments that focus on the incompatibility of the notions of economic profit and altruistic interest in a clean environment.

A counter to Blackstone's views is found in the article by Rescher. He argues that even though attempts to clean up the environment are noble, "the environment has had it and . . . we simply cannot 'go home again' to 'the good old days' of environmental purity." Rescher argues that typical economic and business solutions to problems of scarcity through the appeal to higher production will not help resolve this problem; but he contends that both economically and socially we will have to learn to live with scarce environmental goods and will have to scale down our expectations for the quality of life accordingly. In effect, Rescher seems to be calling for a cost/benefit assessment of the situation, and it seems clear from his projections that business will not suffer from what he calls a "cool realistic" analysis.

"EXTREME" POSITIONS AND THE QUESTION OF BALANCING COMPETING INTERESTS

Other individuals take a starkly different view from all those thus far mentioned. They are upset about the idea that nature should be protected only because it is in our own interest that it be protected. This general problem about ethics and business recurs repeatedly throughout this book: to justify something as in one's own interest is quite different from justifying a position on grounds that moral duties and rights demand a certain action. (This problem was explored in Chapter 1 as the problem of egoism.) In the present case, those who support a strong environmental ethic—e.g., Christopher D. Stone in the present chapter —do so because they believe we have certain kinds of obligations to nature, or at least to the animals in it, not to destroy the ecosystem. From this perspective there are valuable entities in nature quite independent of nature's relation to us, and it is important to protect those values by appropriate environmental policies. Because business interests are in conflict with these values, business's values take second place to the values found inherent in nature. It does not follow from such a view that the value of the environment outweighs all human values, but only that it can outweigh the interests of the *business* community. As we saw in Chapter 6 and shall see again in this chapter, at the root of much of this discussion is the philosophical claim that we cannot justify our "exploitation" of animals and other parts of the human environment on any rational philosophical basis, because it is a mere human prejudice that leads us to believe we are justified in doing so.

Some writers, including both Christopher Stone (in a famous article included in this chapter) and Supreme Court Justice William O. Douglas (in his equally famous *Sierra Club* Dissent), have argued that in various ways plants and animals—and perhaps even other natural objects such as oceans and trees—should be given legal standing. Only this maneuver, they argue, will provide natural objects with sufficient environmental status to protect them. While these natural entities cannot initiate court action, others could institute such actions on their behalf—just as guardians now do for children, the comatose, and the retarded. These natural objects could then be defended against the actions of corporations. Corporations will sometimes *win*, because they have some clear rights to use the environment; but if these entities themselves have rights, corporations cannot use environmental entities in any way they please, and this conclusion is Stone's larger objective. Moreover, in his view these objects would have stricter legal standing than would corporations, which are mere legal "fictions." Natural objects, he argues, would themselves have rights that are based on their needs and interests: those who support this point of view argue that these needs and interests generate moral obligations to these entities, and this moral basis supplies the grounds for the grant of legal rights.

Stone admits that this proposal is "bound to sound odd or frightening or laughable" to some, but he thinks this psychological reaction occurs only because we already categorize natural entities as "things" rather than as "bearers of rights." He is calling, then, for an environmental liberation that parallels the "black liberation" and "women's liberation" movements that have resulted in expanded rights for blacks and women. The radically revisionary conclusions to which Stone is led are challenged, in the final selection in this chapter, by Joel Feinberg. This difficult but penetrating article serves to synthesize many of the arguments found throughout the chapter. Feinberg begins with a careful analysis of the nature of rights. He argues that only entities capable of having *interests* can have rights—and therefore vegetables, trees, etc. cannot have rights. However, Feinberg argues that both animals in the environment and future generations of persons can be meaningfully said to have rights. These rights include the moral requirement that we of the present generation must protect the environment in order to protect their interests. Insofar, then, as business practices would leave us with a "garbage heap" in the future, these practices deserve moral condemnation.

These issues also bear on the problem of social and political control over industry. Many believe that severe curbs on industry and severe judicial penalties provide the only viable ways to protect the environment, while others believe that the filing of environmental impact statements and other currently employed practices will be sufficient. Still others believe that there is now a severe overregulation or underregulation in the face of the actual problem. Almost everyone believes that there will in the future be some loss of the liberty to use property as businesses see fit. Like all important values, some liberties must be balanced against other liberties. The heart of the environmental problem is the way in

which the balancing is to be done, and especially which role considerations of justice, rights, and liberty (in the form of the free market so
important to business) are themselves to be protected.

In the opening selection in this chapter, these balancing considerations are pondered by Judge Robert Merhige in his ruling in the celebrated Kepone case (*U.S.A.* v. *Allied Chemical Corporation*). Judge Merhige
argues that while Allied Chemical has been "a good corporate citizen,"
in this case the corporation appears to have intentionally violated fair and
equitable laws erected to protect the environment. In the case, Allied and
five of its employees were indicted on 153 charges of conspiracy to
defraud the Environmental Protection Agency and the Army Corps of
Engineers in their efforts to enforce water pollution control laws. Allied
denied all charges, saying the indictments displayed an "extreme reaction" by public officials. However, Allied pleaded *nolo contendere* (no contest to the charges). Judge Merhige fined Allied $13.2 million, but later
reduced the fine to $5 million because Allied put $8 million into a fund
set up to relieve suffering that resulted from its pollution. This fine is the
largest ever imposed in an environmental case, but the indictments were
also the most ever returned in a single environmental case. Judge Merhige's fine was originally set at the maximum. In his ruling he argues the
utilitarian thesis that corporations will "think several times before anything such as this happens again." But he also argues what would be
construed by many in the business community as an unacceptable
nonutilitarian thesis: "I don't think that commercial products or the
making of profits are as important as the God-given resources of our
country." He then goes on to advance the striking thesis that we are all
collectively responsible for what happened in this case because we tolerate too much environmental pollution in contemporary society. This
important judicial ruling, as we might expect, has been severely criticized
by representatives of the business community.

A second court opinion included in this chapter is actually a composite
of two opinions in a single case (*Reserve Mining Company* v. *United States*),
both delivered by Judge Myron Bright, but on separate occasions. This
case occurred during a critical transitional phase of American environmental law. Roughly prior to this case, the courts had held that the
burden of proof in showing hazardous environmental conditions rested
on the government, rather than there being a burden on industry to
prove that the effects of its discharges are nonhazardous. Several cases
in the mid-Seventies, including this one, indicate a change of view in the
courts (a changing "environmental ethic"): they began to hold that the
burden of proof was on industry rather than on the government. There
appears to be some sympathy in Judge Bright's first opinion (on June 4,
1974) that the government must prove that a hazardous condition prevails, whereas in his second opinion he seems to take the view that the
identical evidence proves that a public health hazard exists and hence that
the burden is on industry to take positive steps to end the pollution. Still,
the matter of proof is not quite this simple. The larger thesis spanning
these two opinions is that the burden of proof is always heavier on the

government if it seeks an injunction to stop an industry from producing its products on grounds of pollution. The burden is lighter on the government when it seeks only to force industry to reduce the amount of its discharge, thereby cleaning up the environment but without stopping production. This approach by courts is now a familiar one, and its general framework is utilitarian: industry's pollution must be justified on a cost/benefit basis. If it costs the community more than it profits the community, then the company must either cease production or improve the quality of its environmental discharges. However, if it benefits the community more than it places the community at risk, then the balance of justification tips in the direction of industry.

PROBLEMS OF FACTUAL EVIDENCE
AND INDUSTRY RESPONSIBILITY

Problems of judicial and agency rulings are touched on at several points in this chapter. In the aforementioned article by Chamberlain , for example, it is argued that governmental and judicial regulation are inevitable. However, he argues strongly for self-regulation and responsible cooperation in order that external interventions be kept at a minimum. In other quarters, governmental regulation of business through environmental control is even more strongly resisted. Opponents of regulation argue: (1) that there are inadequate statistics and predictions about energy resources and their destruction or depletion; (2) that there are presently no acceptable cost/benefit studies to show that governmental regulation serves the public interest more than it hurts; (3) that we have yet to understand how government can aid in balancing the public interest against private interests better than private interests themselves; and (4) that the problem of the environment is a problem created not only by business but also by public facilities (such as inadequate sewage treatment) and by poor government planning. Opponents also point to the need for greater education about the environment and larger incentives to clean it up (as contrasted to regulation). And finally opponents attempt to provide facts to favor unfettered or only mildly fettered business control: facts to show, for example, that far from there being a food shortage created by poor agricultural land use, there is excellent land use and enough land to give us food to feed twice the number of persons now on the earth. These arguments, if correct in their premises, lead inescapably to the conclusion that voluntary controls and incentives alone should control business. But are the factual and ethical claims used in these arguments correct?

T.L.B.

RULING IN UNITED STATES OF AMERICA v. ALLIED CHEMICAL CORPORATION

Judge Robert R. Merhige, Jr.

I think my view of pollution of the environment is well known. The environment does truly, and I don't want to burden you with a bunch of clichés, belong to every single person in this country, every single citizen, from the lowest to the highest.

I think you also know, because you have all been before me on criminal cases, that my initial view in every criminal case is to look for ways to temper justice with mercy. I think that is what the law contemplates. I want to be sure that my feelings on pollution are not so strong that I neglect the element of mercy.

I am reasonably familiar with the legislative history of the acts that are involved in this case. I have had to study them, not only in connection with this case, but with regard to several others we have had and several that are coming. I am satisfied that we, as a nation, are dedicated to clean water, unpolluted waters. I also recognize that the commercial factors become involved, politics gets involved, and I am not critical of any of them. They all have their place, but this is not the place.

Long ago I came to the conclusion that Congress intended, and properly so, that when matters come to a court the responsibility, the heat, no matter how you phrase it, will fall on the Court. There isn't anything wrong with that. That is the way it is supposed to be. It never has disturbed me. Courts are not to be concerned with matters politic. Our responsibility is to law, and the law alone.

How do you deal with a corporation which is, as all are—as you pointed out, Mr. Janus—made up of people? How do you deal with a corporation that has been a good corporate citizen? The pre-sentence report shows that this corporation has been that.

Nevertheless, I disagree with the defendants' position that all of this was so innocently done, or inadvertently done. I think it was done because of what it considered to be business necessities, and money took the forefront.

Now, I believe, hope, and have reason to believe that Allied, of all the corporations in the country, in light of this case, is going to think several times before anything such as this happens again. I think they are going to go the extra mile to see that it doesn't. That is not only good, but I think it is necessary as well.

They say sentencing is for punishment, deterrence, and retribution. I have never been very good at the retributional aspect of it.

Oct. 5, 1976 U.S. District Court, Eastern Div. of Va., Richmond Division.

531

I do think that deterrence is important. We can't start any sooner. Today is really the first day of the rest of our country's national life. I don't think that commercial products or the making of profits are as important as the God-given resources of our country.

I also recognize in one sense that all of us are responsible for what happened, because we have either affirmatively or through indifference permitted things like this to happen. You know, we drive down the street and see smoke belching from a smokestack. We see garbage being thrown into our rivers. We think it is terrible, but unless we are personally affected, that is the extent of our action.

I hope after this sentence, that every corporate official, every corporate employee that has any reason to think that pollution is going on, will think, "If I don't do something about it now, I am apt to be out of a job tomorrow." I want the officials to be concerned when they see it.

Allied knew it was polluting the waters. As Mr. Justice Rehnquist said, "Polluters do so at their own risk." Yes, admittedly, there was a great deal of bureaucratic dealings. Actually, I came away from the case the other day in which Allied was acquitted, as they should have been, with the feeling that the only ones who really cared were some young man in the State Water Control Board, his immediate superior who kept after him to bug Life Science, and the State Health Department.

All right, what do we do? How do we do it? How do you temper mercy with justice in a case like this?

A plea of nolo was tendered. As you know, I give no credit for pleas of guilty or nolo just as I don't punish people for pleading not guilty. It is a constitutional right. I refuse to put a price on constitutional rights.

But this was a corporation who admittedly could have been no worse off, I suspect, with a plea of not guilty. I am satisfied that it would have been found guilty, or they wouldn't have plead nolo. The lawyers are too good.

I am satisfied the nolo plea has enured to Allied's benefit, because it made me consider a manner in which justice could indeed be tempered with mercy. I have concluded this:

On Counts 1 through 456, as to each count, the defendant will pay unto the United States of America a fine of $2,500. As to Counts 457 to 940, the defendant will pay as to each count a fine of $25,000. That is the maximum.

I am going to enter an order which will give the defendant a period of ninety days to pay the respective fines.

As you know, I said when the plea was accepted, that I would hope there would be some way that the fines that obviously would be forthcoming could be used to benefit those who directly were hurt. We have all been hurt, but I mean those who have been directly hurt. I believe I previously suggested the State. I am satisfied, however, that this cannot be done under the law.

TWO OPINIONS IN RESERVE MINING CO. v. UNITED STATES

Circuit Judge Myron H. Bright

OPINION I (JUNE 4, 1974)

Reserve Mining Company is a jointly owned subsidiary of Armco Steel Corporation and Republic Steel Corporation which mines low-grade iron ore, called "taconite," near Babbitt, Minnesota. The taconite is shipped by rail to Reserve's "beneficiating" plant at Silver Bay, Minnesota, on the north shore of Lake Superior, where it is concentrated into "pellets" containing some 65 percent iron ore. The process involves crushing the taconite into fine granules, separating out the metallic iron with huge magnets, and flushing the residue into Lake Superior. Approximately 67,000 tons of this waste product, known as "tailings," are daily discharged into the lake.

The use of Lake Superior for this purpose was originally authorized by the State of Minnesota in 1947, and Reserve commenced operations in 1955. In granting this permit to Reserve, the State of Minnesota accepted Reserve's theory that the weight and velocity of the discharge would insure that the tailings would be deposited at a depth of approximately 900 feet in the "great trough" area of the lake, located offshore from Reserve's facility. The permit provides that:

> [T]ailings shall not be discharged . . . so as to result in any material adverse effects on fish life or public water supplies or in any other material unlawful pollution of the waters of the lake. . . .

Until June 8, 1973, the case was essentially a water pollution abatement case, but on that date the focus of the controversy shifted to the public health impact of Reserve's discharge of asbestiform particles into the air and water. Hearings on a motion for preliminary injunction were consolidated with the trial on the merits, and on April 20, 1974, after 139 days of trial extending over a nine month period and after hearing more than 100 witnesses and examining over 1,600 exhibits, Judge Miles Lord of the United States District Court for the District of Minnesota entered an order closing Reserve's Silver Bay facility. In an abbreviated memorandum opinion, Judge Lord held that Reserve's water discharge violated federal water pollution laws and that its air emissions violated state air pollution regulations, and that both were common law nuisances. Most importantly to the question now before this court, Judge Lord concluded in Findings 9 and 10 of his opinion that:

498 F. 2d 1073 (1974) and 514 Federal Reporter, 2nd Series, 492 (1975).

9. The discharge into the air substantially endangers the health of the people of Silver Bay and surrounding communities as far away as the eastern shore of Wisconsin.

10. The discharge into the water substantially endangers the health of the people who procured their drinking water from the western arm of Lake Superior, including the communities of Silver Bay, Beaver Bay, Two Harbors, Cloquet, Duluth [Minnesota], and Superior, Wisconsin.

Defendants Reserve, Armco, and Republic noticed their appeal to this court and moved for a stay of the district court's injunction pending the appeal. Judge Lord denied this request and Reserve applied to us for a stay. . . .

. . . The question now before us is whether, considering all facts and circumstances, the injunction order should be stayed pending Reserve's appeal. We grant the stay subject to certain conditions and limitations as stated herein.

Although there is no dispute that significant amounts of waste tailings are discharged into the water and dust is discharged into the air by Reserve, the parties vigorously contest the precise nature of the discharge, its biological effects, and, particularly with respect to the waters of Lake Superior, its ultimate destination. Plaintiffs contend that the mineral cummingtonite-grunerite, which Reserve admits to be a major component of its taconite wastes and a member of the mineral family known as amphiboles, is substantially identical in morphology (or shape and form) and similar in chemistry to amosite asbestos, a fibrous mineral which has been found, in certain occupational settings, to be carcinogenic. The plaintiffs further argue that the mineral fibers discharged represent a serious health threat, since they are present in the air of Silver Bay and surrounding communities and, by way of dispersion throughout Lake Superior, in the drinking water of Duluth and other communities drawing water from the lake. . . .

The suggestion that particles of the cummingtonite-grunerite in Reserve's discharges are the equivalent of amosite asbestos raised an immediate health issue, since inhalation of amosite asbestos at occupational levels of exposure is a demonstrated health hazard resulting in asbestosis and various forms of cancer. However, the proof of a health hazard requires more than the mere fact of discharge; the discharge of an agent hazardous in one circumstance must be linked to some present or future likelihood of disease under the prevailing circumstances. An extraordinary amount of testimony was received on these issues. . . .

The theory by which plaintiffs argue that the discharges present a substantial danger is founded largely upon epidemiological studies of asbestos workers occupationally exposed to and inhaling high levels of asbestos dust. A study by Dr. Selikoff of workers at a New Jersey asbestos manufacturing plant demonstrated that occupational exposure to amosite asbestos poses a hazard of increased incidence of asbestosis and various forms of cancer. Similar studies in other occupational contexts leave no doubt that asbestos, at sufficiently high dosages, is injurious to health. However, in order to draw the conclusion that environmental exposure to Reserve's discharges presents a health threat in the instant case, it must be shown either that the circumstances of exposure are at least comparable to those in occupational settings, or, alternatively, that the occupational studies establish certain principles of asbestos-disease pathology which may be applied to predicting the occurrence of such disease in altered circumstances.

Initially, it must be observed that environmental exposure from Reserve's discharges into air and water is simply not comparable to that typical of occupational settings. The occupational studies involve direct exposure to and inhalation of asbestos dust in high concentrations and in confined spaces. This pattern of exposure cannot be equated with the discharge into the outside air of relatively low levels of asbestos fibers. . . .

. . . In order to make a prediction, based on the occupational studies, as to the likelihood of disease at lower levels of exposure, at least two key findings must be made. First, an attempt must be made to determine, with some precision, what that lower level of exposure is. Second, that lower level of exposure must be applied to the known pathology of asbestos-induced disease, i.e., it must be determined whether the level of exposure is safe or unsafe.

Unfortunately, the testimony of Dr. Arnold Brown[1] indicates that neither of these key determinations can be made. Dr. Brown testified that, with respect to both air and water, the level of fibers is not readily susceptible of measurement. This results from the relatively imprecise state of counting techniques and the wide margins of error which necessarily result, and is reflected in the widely divergent sample counts received by the court. . . .

Even assuming that one could avoid imprecision and uncertainty in measuring the number of fibers at low levels, there remains vast uncertainty as to the medical consequences of low levels of exposure to asbestos fibers. . . .

. . . In commenting on the statement, "This suggests that there are levels of asbestos exposure that will not be associated with any detectable risk," Dr. Brown stated:

> As a generalization, yes, I agree to that. But I must reiterate my view that I do not know what that level is. . . .

A fair review of this impartial testimony by the court's own witnesses —to which we necessarily must give great weight at this interim stage of review—clearly suggests that the discharges by Reserve can be characterized only as presenting an unquantifiable risk, i.e., a health risk which either may be negligible or may be significant, but with any significance as yet based on unknowns. This conclusion is simply a logical deduction from the following facts: (1) that fiber levels are not at occupational levels; (2) that the low levels present cannot be expressed or measured as a health risk; and (3) that, in any event, threshold values and dose-response relationships are undetermined. In other words, it is not known what the level of fiber exposure is, other than that it is relatively low, and it is not known what level of exposure is safe or unsafe. Finally, no basis exists, save a theoretical one, for assuming that drinking water, otherwise pure but containing asbestos-like particles, is dangerous to health. . . .

Considering all of the above, we think one conclusion is evident: although Reserve's discharges represent a possible medical danger, they have not in this case been proven to amount to a health hazard. The discharges may or may not result in detrimental health effects, but, for the present, that is simply unknown. . . .

Our stay of the injunction rests upon the good faith preparation and implementation of an acceptable plan. Therefore, we grant a 70-day stay upon these conditions:

1. Reserve's plans shall be promptly submitted to plaintiff-states and to the United States for review and recommendations by appropriate agencies concerned with environmental and health protection. Such plan shall be filed with the district court and submitted to all plaintiffs in no event later than 25 days from the filing of this order.
2. Plaintiffs shall then have an additional 20 days within which to file their comments on such plan.
3. The district court shall consider Reserve's plan and any recommendations made by the United States and plaintiff-states and make a recommendation, within 15 days following submission of plaintiffs' comments, whether or not a stay of the injunction should be continued pending the appeal.
4. Based on these plans, comments, and recommendations, this court will then review the status of its stay order within the time remaining.

OPINION II (APRIL 8, 1975)

On June 4, 1974, [this] court issued an opinion granting Reserve a 70-day stay of the injunction. *Reserve Mining Co.* v. *United States*, 498 F.2d 1073 (8th Cir. 1974). The court conditioned the stay upon Reserve taking prompt steps to abate its air and water discharges, and provided for further proceedings to review whether Reserve had proceeded with the good faith preparation and implementation of an acceptable plan. . . .

The initial, crucial question for our evaluation and resolution focuses upon the alleged hazard to public health attributable to Reserve's discharges into the air and water. . . .

In this preliminary review, we did not view the evidence as supporting a finding of substantial danger. We noted numerous uncertainties in plaintiff's theory of harm which controlled our assessment, particularly the uncertainty as to present levels of exposure and the difficulty in attempting to quantify those uncertain levels in terms of a demonstrable health hazard. . . .

We reached no preliminary decision on whether the facts justified a less stringent abatement order.

As will be evident from the discussion that follows, we adhere to our preliminary assessment that the evidence is insufficient to support the kind of demonstrable danger to the public health that would justify the immediate closing of Reserve's operations. We now address the basic question of whether the discharges pose any risk to public health and, if so, whether the risk is one which is legally cognizable. . . .

As we noted in our stay opinion, much of the scientific knowledge regarding asbestos disease pathology derives from epidemiological studies of asbestos workers occupationally exposed to and inhaling high levels of asbestos dust. Studies of workers naturally exposed to asbestos dust have shown "excess" cancer deaths and a significant incidence of asbestosis. The principal excess cancers are cancer of the lung, the pleura (mesothelioma) and gastrointestinal tract ("gi" cancer).

Studies conducted by Dr. Irving Selikoff, plaintiffs' principal medical witness, illustrated these disease effects. Dr. Selikoff investigated the disease experience of asbestos insulation workers in the New York-New Jersey area, asbestos insulation workers nationwide, and workers in a New Jersey plant manufacturing amosite asbestos. Generally, all three groups showed excess cancer deaths among the exposed populations. . . .

Several principles of asbestos-related disease pathology emerge from these occupational studies. One principle relates to the so-called 20-year rule, meaning that there is a latent period of cancer development of at least 20 years. [A.10:284–285.] Another basic principle is the importance of initial exposure, demonstrated by significant increases in the incidence of cancer even among asbestos manufacturing workers employed for less than three months (although the incidence of disease does increase upon longer exposure). [A.10:279–280.] Finally, these studies indicate that threshold values and dose-response relationships, although probably operative with respect to asbestos-induced cancer, are not quantifiable on the basis of existing data. [A.10:280, 317–319.]

Additionally, some studies implicate asbestos as a possible pathogenic agent in circumstances of exposure less severe than occupational levels. For example, several studies indicate that mesothelioma, a rare but particularly lethal cancer frequently associated with asbestos exposure, has been found in persons experiencing a low level of asbestos exposure.

Plaintiffs' hypothesis that Reserve's air emissions represent a significant threat to the public health touches numerous scientific disciplines, and an overall evaluation demands broad scientific understanding. We think it significant that Dr. Brown, an impartial witness whose court-appointed task was to address the health issue in its entirety, joined with plaintiffs' witnesses in viewing as reasonable the hypothesis that Reserve's discharges present a threat to public health. Although, as we noted in our stay opinion, Dr. Brown found the evidence insufficient to make a scientific probability statement as to whether adverse health consequences would in fact ensue, he expressed a public health concern over the continued long-term emission of fibers into the air. . . .

The . . . discussion of the evidence demonstrates that the medical and scientific conclusions here in dispute clearly lie "on the frontiers of scientific knowledge." . . .

As we have demonstrated, Reserve's air and water discharges pose a danger to the public health and justify judicial action of a preventive nature.

In fashioning relief in a case such as this involving a possibility of future harm, a court should strike a proper balance between the benefits conferred and the hazards created by Reserve's facility.

Reserve must be given a reasonable opportunity and a reasonable time to construct facilities to accomplish an abatement of its pollution of air and water and the health risk created thereby. In this way, hardship to employees and great economic loss incident to an immediate plant closing may be avoided. . . .

We cannot ignore, however, the potential for harm in Reserve's discharges. This potential imparts a degree of urgency to this case that would otherwise be absent from an environmental suit in which ecological pollution alone were proved. Thus, any authorization of Reserve to continue operations during conversion of its facilities to abate the pollution must be circumscribed by realistic time limitations. Accordingly, we direct that the injunction order be modified as follows.

A. The Discharge into Water

Reserve shall be given a reasonable time to stop discharging its wastes into Lake Superior. A reasonable time includes the time necessary for Minnesota to act on Reserve's present application to dispose of its tailings at Milepost 7. . . .

Upon receiving a permit from the State of Minnesota, Reserve must utilize every reasonable effort to expedite the construction of new facilities. . . .

B. Air Emissions

Pending final action by Minnesota on the present permit application, Reserve must promptly take all steps necessary to comply with Minnesota law applicable to its air emissions. . . .

We wish to make it clear that we view the air emission as presenting a hazard of greater significance than the water discharge. Accordingly, pending a determination of whether Reserve will be allowed to construct an on-land disposal site or will close its operations, Reserve must immediately proceed with the planning and implementation of such emission controls as may be reasonably and practically effectuated under the circumstances. . . .

Finally, this court deems it appropriate to suggest that the national interest now calls upon Minnesota and Reserve to exercise a zeal equivalent to that displayed in this litigation to arrive at an appropriate location for an on-land disposal site for Reserve's tailings and thus permit an important segment of the national steel industry, employing several thousand people, to continue in production. As we have already noted, we believe this controversy can be resolved in a manner that will purify the air and water without destroying jobs.

The existing injunction is modified in the respects stated herein.

Note

1. Dr. Brown, a research pathologist associated with the Mayo Clinic of Rochester, Minnesota, served the court both in the capacity of a technical advisor and that of an impartial witness.

CORPORATIONS AND
THE PHYSICAL ENVIRONMENT

Neil W. Chamberlain

The centrality of consumption as a social value is splendidly displayed in the matter of environmental quality. Public alarms over pollution and resource exhaustion lead to legislative controls and regulatory actions. These can be modulated, "within reason," with incremental effects on the environment. But if they begin to bite, in the sense of threatening consumption through higher prices and taxes, industry can count on a reduction in the alarm level. Not only industry's ox but society's own horsepower is being gored. Industry's responsibility to the environment is thus limited by society's conception of the good life—a conception that . . . can be traced back ultimately to values inculcated by the corporate system itself.

No single corporation—whatever its size or however socially sensitive its management—can break out of this institutionalized constraint.

THE DARK UNDERSIDE OF ECONOMIC GROWTH

Concern for the conservation of natural resources has a long history. Originating in aesthetic revulsion at the commercial despoliation of natural resources such as timberlands, scenic areas, and animal life, it eventually extended also to outcries against the unrestricted and wasteful exploitation of land and fossil fuels. Concern with pollution also has a long history. It early expressed itself in abhorrence of the concentration of smoke in Europe's growing cities and the fetid atmosphere of the "Satanic mills" of the industrial revolution. This latter, however, was viewed as a matter of entrepreneurial greed, a kind of class conflict rather than a general social disaster.

Present fears concerning depletion and pollution are more widespread, embracing imminent dangers both to life as we know it and to life itself. They are expressed in picturesque concepts such as "spaceship earth," which views the planet as a vessel in space, whose stock of provisions are all there is to sustain whatever the number of passengers, and so both provisions and number of passengers must be managed carefully. Others have described ours as a "throughput economy," which mines the earth for the materials out of which it fashions articles of consumption for temporary enjoyment; these, once used, are thrown back on the earth as though it were a dumpheap. The "mines" become exhausted and the dumpheap grows.

Let us agree at the outset that the problems of depletion and pollution are basically the same in that both involve the using up of natural resources. Pollution uses up air and water, just as extraction uses up minerals. Pollution reduces people to using air and water of inferior quality, just as mineral extraction drives producers to lower-grade ores. Presumably the producer bears the cost in the latter case but not in the former, but in both cases it is the consumer who ultimately pays, either a money cost or a real cost, and in any event this distinction is one that could conceivably be erased by appropriate forms of taxation on the producer, a subject with which we shall deal later. Production that takes place without pollution may nevertheless involve depletion, by dispersing scarce natural resources, but that distinction too, if important, could presumably be met by some form of "recovery" tax or regulation. The antipollution movement is founded on the "discovery" that air and water are natural resources that should not be squandered as though they were unlimited in quantity. They are now appreciated as scarce resources requiring economic use like any other resource. Thus, whether our discussion deals with one or the other, it relates to both. . . .

GOVERNMENT RESPONSE TO ENVIRONMENTAL CONCERNS

As concern for the environment spread from a handful of conservationists to a more general public, the federal government reacted with legislation to curb pollution. But how does a government go about such a task, when "the problem" has scarcely been defined and means of combating it are in a trial-and-error stage? The consumer-protection movement offers something of a model. Modest legislation takes a few hesitant steps forward. Thus in 1955 the Public Health Service was authorized to conduct limited research on air pollution and to offer technical assistance to state and local governments. The Clean Air Act of 1963 moved a little further by providing grants to the states to establish and maintain air-pollution control agencies and by authorizing federal authorities to initiate proceedings against interstate polluters. A 1965 amendment to this act for the first time recognized automobile exhaust as a contributor to unclean air and empowered the Secretary of Health, Education, and Welfare to set emission standards. This was followed by the Air Quality Act of 1967, which retained the provisions of the preceding legislation, but also called for collaboration of federal and state governments and major industrial corporations in setting standards for the most seriously polluted regions....

In 1970 the Environmental Protection Agency (EPA) was established under administrative reorganization procedure, bringing together the water-quality office lodged in the Department of the Interior, the air-pollution control group in the Department of Health, Education, and Welfare, the pesticide control function then in the Department of Agriculture, and nuclear-radiation control previously under the jurisdiction of the Atomic Energy Commission. The new agency was mandated to conduct research, and to set and enforce standards with respect to air, water, and solid-waste pollution....

If public awareness of environmental decay is recent, government response has been relatively quick and extensive. Indeed, the Nixon Administration by 1972 had moved to the position that Congress was overreacting and that such measures as the Water Pollution Control bill (enacted later that same year), which required total elimination of all effluent discharges into the nation's waterways by 1985, are wasteful, if not capricious. The Chairman of the Council on Environmental Quality has pointed out that the cost of pollution control, too, has an exponential aspect, so that removal of the last 1 percent of contaminant may cost as much as the removal of the first 99 percent. "Zero discharge" may thus be a goal that diverts substantial resources away from other more badly needed public works to an unnecessarily finicky scrubbing of air and water. In any event, we are safe in concluding that once the public had recognized pollution as a problem, the political authorities vied with one another in doing "something," piling laws on administrative agencies and legislative amendments on regulatory orders.

BUSINESS REACTION

Could anything be more predictable than the response of business to this flurry of political activity? ... The first reaction is defensive and bitter: business is being made a scapegoat for society's own failings; politicians are pandering to a panicky public; the cleanup demanded will bankrupt many companies and increase the public's cost of living more than it realizes. After this initial irritation, business professionalism reasserts itself: the public-relations offices take over with the soothing message that industry is busily coping with an admittedly serious problem. Millions of dollars are being spent on the research needed to take effective action, even as billions are being spent to improve old equipment and develop new equipment in line with what is already known. This is the period when resistance to remedial action shades over into acceptance of the inevitability of some action, but this is accompanied by pressures for making standards "practical" and the time period for their enforcement "reasonable."

This reaction pattern is wholly understandable. It suggests that at least in some respects the Supreme Court was not too far afield in picturing the corporation as human. When, within the space of a decade, a cause takes on the dimensions of a crusade, with industry assuming the role of the infidels, what else but a defensive reaction can be expected? With pollution controls entailing costs running into literally unknown but clearly massive sums loosely spoken of as the "ransom" that would be legislatively demanded of business to permit it freedom to operate, how else could business feel but victimized, at least in the first fresh shock of recognition that the contest was "for real"?

The instinct to fight back, with whatever arguments come to hand, is surely understandable. Thus one leading businessman informed—mistakenly—a college audience that "U.S. Department of Commerce figures show that 219 plants last year were forced to shut down because of environmental pressures."[1] As a House-Senate conference committee pondered legislation to set strict limits on automobile pollution emissions in 1975, the executive vice president of Ford Motor Company, urging a specially called meeting of principal Ford suppliers and dealers to initiate a telegram campaign to their Washington representatives, "went so far as to claim that the bill 'could prevent continued production of automobiles after January 1, 1975.' "[2] The president of a steel company, speaking before a group of university economists, emphasized the adverse effects of ill-advised pollution control legislation: "The thrust for an improved environment has caused many of us in the steel industry to close and/or drastically alter plant operations; . . . shifted vital funds away from essential revenue producing activities, including research and development; increased the competitive advantage of foreign competitors; placed an additional annual operating cost burden on our industry of about $412 million."[3]

A sanitation engineering consultant, speaking of Detroit's costly and largely "wasted" efforts to control discharges into Lake Erie, drew more lurid conclusions: "This excessive expenditure diverts funds from other environmental blights in Detroit such as crime on the streets, ghettos, malnutrition, and the needs of education. Can Detroit afford to have such a warped concept of environmental priorities? Why can't a child be as important as a fish?"[4] Such costly public ventures into pollution control obviously increase business taxes and provide undesirable examples of what might be expected of business itself. A suspicious business partisan might conclude and feel justified in suggesting to others that there are "efforts afoot, avowedly to control the quality of the environment but more accurately to control industrial operations and the American way of life."[5]

Business's counterattack has included undercover efforts to "defuse" the public. A "news" item describing the movement against leaded gasoline as "misleading and irrelevant" asserted that no evidence existed that lead in the atmosphere poses a health hazard. *Natural History,* a magazine published by New York's American Museum of Natural History, traced the story to *Editor's Digest,* a division of Planned Communications Services, Inc., "a company that writes and distributes stories to small-circulation newspapers on behalf of corporate and industrial clients. This story, it turns out, originated with the Lead Industries Association. . . ."[6]

Corporate leadership is, on the whole, too sophisticated to rely solely on opposition when a problem has been shown to be real and demand for its solution has generated a popular following, however misguided. One time-tested device is to join the opposition in calling for a "common" effort. "We" have erred, but "we" can make up for our folly. Again Atlantic Richfield Company, employing reproductions of contemporary art to illustrate its "cultural" concern, offers what might paradoxically be referred to as a "good" example:

> The ideal: Seas that are permanently protected from man's abuse.
> The real: Thoughtlessly, man spews waste into the world's oceans. From the air, from the stream, from ships, all of it from ourselves.
> We must find new and better ways to guard our waters from ourselves. Our solutions must be swift. They must be creative and mature. For tomorrow the waters of the world will inherit what we do today.
> Throughout the world, man must learn to function without fouling the oceans—and the air and earth that adjoin them. Until then, we cannot protect the environment in which life began—and on which our lives still depend.[7]

In place of such soothing syrup, the steel industry prefers the language of hard cash: "Our industry has put its money where its mouth is. Companies producing about 98% of the nation's iron and steel spent slightly over $735 million between '66 and '71. In '71, they spent $161.5 million, equal to 10.3% of our total capital expenditures . . . the largest of any industry and twice the average for all manufacturing. Last year, environmental control spending accounted for about 20% of net profits. An additional 12% of initial construction costs, or $142,000,000 a year, must be spent annually to keep equipment working."[8]

But communicating with the public is not enough in a situation where the stakes are so high. The real objective is to help mold the legislation which cannot be avoided. Industry finds itself, willy-nilly, engaged in a bargaining process with politicians over the shape of pollution-control laws that will satisfy the public. The politicians can ignore neither the interests of large-scale industry, which after all exercises enormous, if not dominant, influence over the very structure and functioning of the American society,[9] nor the wishes and interests of their popular constituencies, whose votes must return them to office. Bargaining is something at which both politicians and industrialists have long been adept.

The passage of the Air Quality Act of 1967 nicely illustrates this process. Although the whole story of such an event can never be reassembled, it appears that the White House was more interested in the political than the pollution effect of endorsing *national* emission standards and actually offered little support for its own bill when introduced into the Senate. Industry lobbyists, at first alarmed over the bill's stringent provisions, became reassured during the course of informal meetings with staff members of the Air and Water Pollution Subcommittee of the Public Works Committee. In these discussions details were hashed out over such issues as how *regional* criteria would work, timetables for coordinating state standards, whether the federal government should be given powers to subpoena company records and monitor industry emissions. . . .

Controls over industry there are, and there will be more, but any which pose a threat to continuity of the corporate system as we know it are likely to be curbed not by the government's "knuckling under" to blatant industry demands, but simply by tempering the regulatory process. This can be done through jurisdictional ambiguities, budgetary curtailment, concessions to other competing political objectives, uncertainties in standard setting, and weakness in enforcement.

ACCEPTABILITY OF LIMITED PROGRESS

These limitations on the legislative and administrative protection of the environment do not mean that public interest will be slighted and the public's will thwarted. On the contrary, such incremental measures as are forthcoming to alleviate, in whatever degree, the discomforts of pollution will probably be sufficient to satisfy public pressures. This is because any more effective environmental controls would require a larger sacrifice of immediate pleasures and preferences than the public is willing to make.

When the costs of achieving more stringent standards of air and water purity drastically affect the prices of consumer goods, we can expect public resistance to the higher standards. We have already noted the contribution made by divided political objectives to less effective pollution control. In the kind of consumption-oriented society that we encountered in the preceding chapter, consumer goods and clean environment become seriously competing objectives. If, as has been estimated, the standards for automobile emissions now set for 1976 will add between $390 and $425 to the price of a car, we may confidently anticipate an outcry by the automobile-buying public. I concur with René Dubos when he says: "We would like to improve our polluted and cluttered environments, but we like gadgets and economic prosperity even more. In fact, values such as political power and gross national income so dominate our collective lives that we shall undertake the social and technological reforms essential for environmental control only if we are forced into action by some disaster."[10]

This consumption-mindedness of the American public goes beyond a desire for more goods. It is linked to a way or style of life that those goods make possible. It is thus not only the price increase that irritates car buyers, but the fact that even present emission controls increase fuel consumption and reduce engine performance. One consequence has been that some car owners have had emission controls disconnected. The manager of the auto-diagnostic clinic of the Missouri Automobile Club reported that one-fourth of the late-model cars going through his clinic had their emission controls tampered with. A Detroit automobile mechanic says that thirty of the forty automobile tune-ups he does every month involve modifications of the control system.[11]

The former head of EPA had no illusions about the unpopularity of actions necessary for effective pollution control if these begin to affect people's private lives. It has been popular to talk about "changing life styles," he observed, "but when someone finds out that means bicycling or carpooling to work, or going home at a different time, he may not be for it."[12] Nor do the politicians have any illusions on this score. When the iconoclast Admiral Hyman G. Rickover testified at House hearings on the prospects of a national energy shortage, he suggested the desirability of banning "nonessential" air conditioners and putting a high tax on such "luxuries" as clothes driers. A congressman thereupon "observed with undisguised disdain that the admiral had never run for office. 'What do you think we can do and still stay in office?' " he asked. John B. Connally, then Secretary of the Treasury and a former governor of Texas, advised the House committee that he too "was too much of a pragmatist" to embrace the Rickover program. He could live without air conditioning but would "hate to give it up." People can "save a tremendous amount of energy just by going around and turning off a few lights," Mr. Connally counseled reassuringly.[13]

Ambivalence over priorities in establishing political objectives ripens into profound disagreement between the disadvantaged minorities and the more advantaged majority within the general public. Blacks and Latins, large numbers of whom have suffered from lack of social amenities in matters of housing, health, education, and employment, often believe that the billions of dollars of expenditures that they hear advocated for clean air and water should be redirected into improving their general way of life. Appeals of the conservationists to save the marshlands near urban areas or the Everglades of Florida sound like an almost callous disregard for more fundamental reforms needed in the ghettos. It is not that the ghetto residents do not suffer from bad air and bad water; if anything, they are more the victims than the suburban whites. The polluted beaches characteristic of most large cities deprive black children of desirable recreation far more than they adversely affect white children who have access to less polluted waters of remoter areas, not to mention backyard swimming pools. Nevertheless, to blacks fighting against what often appears as a hopeless existence, pollution control emerges as a political objective rather far down the list. Consumption is more important than environment.

As one black leader put the matter: "We suffer from pollution as much as anyone, but we're not the beneficiaries of the affluence that produced the pollution."[14] For the government to institute stricter controls over industry, an action that causes the latter to pass along higher costs in the form of higher prices, thus appears to shut the blacks off from any opportunity of achieving the material advancement that they seek. It would be as though the government had capriciously increased the cost of the goods they buy by 10 or 20 percent at the very time it professed to be seeking to improve their standard of living.

Blacks and Latins are not the only groups who see their economic interests jeopardized by the campaign to clean up the environment. Workers whose jobs appear threatened by new pollution standards have often joined in opposition. The previously cited example of community persecution of a citizen group that secured a court order against the Blackwell, Oklahoma, zinc smelter of American Metal Climax has numerous counterparts. The 1972 National Conference on Strip Mining, meeting in Kentucky to pass a resolution urging abolition of this form of coal extraction, was harassed by some hundred strip miners from neighboring counties, wearing their work clothes and hard hats decorated with stickers proclaiming "I Dig Coal" and "Coal Puts Bread on My Table." " 'I think you can understand the feelings of the men,' said Paul Patton, the young president of the Kentucky Elkhorn Company, who is a leading spokesman for the smaller operations. 'These people [the conferees] have the emotions of idealism, but my men have the emotions of their livelihood, which is a lot stronger.' "[15]

Although a number of national unions have adopted positions favorable to environmental protection, local union leaders often find themselves placed in an ambiguous position when the employment of their members seems to be the price of a cleaner environment.

> A United Steelworkers local in El Paso lobbied hard and successfully in the city council recently to help an American Smelting & Refining Co. plant to obtain more time in which to bring its air-cleanup equipment up to par; many of the plant's 1,000 employees faced possible layoffs.
>
> Representatives of the Teamsters Union, Glass Bottle Blowers Association and Steelworkers helped in September to stymie efforts by New Jersey legislators to impose restrictions on nonreturnable containers; there were warnings that up to 30,000 jobs were threatened.
>
> Local 1 of the United Papermakers and Paperworkers in Holyoke, Mass., has replaced its customary fall job-safety campaign with a drive "to save jobs by halting the ecology steamroller." Union officials contend a local paper company had to abolish more than 150 jobs this year because of the "excessive cost of a pollution-control system. . . ."
>
> A Maine labor representative arguing for a new oil refinery along the state's picturesque coast maintains, "We can't trade off the welfare of human beings for the sake of scenery. . . ."
>
> United Auto Workers President Leonard Woodcock recently told a congressional subcommittee that "their economic circumstances require them to think first of jobs, paychecks and bread on the table. . . ."
>
> Even A. F. Grospiron, president of the Oil, Chemical and Atomic Workers, which has taken a tougher antipollution stand than most unions, warns: "We will oppose those theoretical environmentalists who would make air and water pure without regard to whether or not people have food on their tables."[16]

Nor has management failed to perceive the advantage of encouraging closer collaboration with organized labor in opposition to more stringent environmental legislation or administrative regulation. "One of the things industry and labor have to do is get together to protect ourselves from these ecology groups that have one-track minds," one manager comments.[17] Corporate officials have also played on labor's fears and self-interest by pointing out that costly pollution standards required by the U.S. government, but not matched by foreign governments, would put American industry at a competitive disadvantage and thus would cause further loss of employment. The same argument has been used in support of federal assistance to industrial research and development and to such industry projects as the supersonic transport plane, which has been condemned by numerous scientists for both known and potential adverse environmental effects. The president's special consultant on technology asserted that the United States "needed" the program to stay competitive in technology with foreign countries.[18]

The consumer culture is too closely allied with corporate interests to subordinate the latter to ecological considerations. The dominant role of the corporation in American society derives from its ability to satisfy a mass-consumption appetite, not from its contribution to an unpolluted environment. Thus, when the Bay Area Rapid Transit was proposed for the San Francisco area, it was hailed as the answer to air pollution and traffic congestion, by substituting mass transit for the rising tide of private automobiles, and as the means for opening up a wider geographical range of jobs for blacks confined to the ghettos. "But in spite of such possible advantages, it was not ecology or job access, but the potential profits from land development and the rejuvenation of downtown San Francisco that prompted a group of influential businessmen to provide the push necessary to bring a transit system to the Bay Area. . . . Nurtured more by vested interests than by a desire of Bay Area residents to find an alternative to the automobile, BART was built without a long-range commitment to shift the emphasis to public transportation in the Bay Area. Thus highway construction continues. And the region could end up with the harmful side effects of both mass transit and the automobile."[19]

Corporate profit-mindedness is of course directly related to the nation's consumption. By hallowed tradition, the former is identified as the reward for superior performance in the service of the latter, in the supply of public needs and wants. [M]anufactured products—especially, but not only, drugs—are often put on the market before their long-run effects on people or on the environment can be established. The purpose may be profit, but the justification lies in not keeping from a waiting public products that produce immediate gratification.

Within the prevalent American culture there is thus a coalescing of interest in improving environmental quality only within bounds that do not basically threaten the more basic consumption objective. Corporation executives who have been most responsible for nurturing that focal value; workers—organized and unorganized—whose position in the consumer culture depends on the continuity of their employment and the buying power of their wages; disadvantaged minorities who aspire to catch up with the material success that they have so far been denied; and government officials who depend for their office on performing satisfactorily a brokerage function between dominant interests and a mass electorate—all these unite in insisting that the admitted problem of protecting the environment be met by incremental measures that do not rock the economic boat. The result may be modest improvement over time, or it may be simply to slow the rate of deterioration. . . .

CONCLUSION

What can we say, then, about the social responsibilities of the individual large corporation in the matter of environmental protection, given the present corporate system?

Those who argue for the Social Responsibility Thesis must face the fact that while some costs of pollution control can be assimilated as general expenses of doing business, competitors, stockholders, and employees collectively place limits on that amount. Such expenditures are viewed by management as "nonproductive," and hence something to be held down. What is not required by law becomes a marginal item, to be indulged in in years of high profit, but giving way to cost reduction and profit maintenance in the lean years.

Those who argue for the Social Engineering Thesis have a larger vision. Athelstan Spilhaus, former president of the American Association for the Advancement of Science, speaks eloquently for this view: "In the next industrial revolution, industry must close the loop back from the user to the factory. If American industrial genius can mass-assemble and mass-distribute, why cannot the same genius mass-collect, mass-disassemble, and massively reuse the materials? If American industry takes upon itself to close this loop, then the original design of the articles would facilitate their return and remaking. If, on the other hand, we continue to have the private sector make things, and the public sector dispose of them, designs for reuse will not easily come about."[20]

Unfortunately, such a vision cannot be pursued by any individual corporation. It would require a more concerted effort, with a grant to some corporations of powers comparable to state planning agencies. At the same time, other corporations would have to be denied the discretion to continue activities deemed incompatible with the recycling on which Spilhaus's "industrial revolution" depends. Obviously what would be involved here would be massive industrial reorganization, not simply something that American industry could "take upon itself."

In the last analysis, then, we are driven back upon the Limited Responsibility Thesis. Henry Ford II phrases it nicely: "In fact, there are severe limits to what business can do, entirely by itself, to solve environmental problems. The reason is that in the absence of appropriate government regulation, there is only a limited market for the main solutions to environmental problems. Few consumers, for example, will pay much for lower vehicle emissions unless their choices are limited by government regulation. Business lives and dies in the market, and no company can survive if it voluntarily assumes pollution control costs far out of line with those of its competitors."[21]

Once again we conclude that however pervasive is the influence of corporate values in American society, the power of any single corporation, however large, is limited. It is caught within the system of relationships it has helped to weave, subject to constraints that, by channeling and concentrating its activities, have given it the freedom to grow great, but that likewise limit its freedom to move in other directions.

Notes

1. *The New York Times,* June 4, 1972. Subsequently a Department of Commerce employee denied that any such figure had been released and suggested that the speaker had taken his statistic from a business-news syndicate that had misinterpreted a federal study.
2. *Business Week,* December 5, 1970.
3. Reynold C. MacDonald, "Steel and the Environment: Today," an address before the Steel Industry Seminar, University of Chicago, June 14, 1972.
4. John E. Kinney, "Economic Effects of Ecological Efforts," Earhart Foundation Lecture, University of Detroit, March 30, 1971.
5. *Ibid.*
6. *Natural History,* December 1971, p. 6.
7. From a series of advertisements, this one appearing in *Intellectual Digest,* June 1972, p. 48.
8. MacDonald, "Steel and the Environment: Today."
9. As I have delineated in *The Place of Business in America's Future: A Study in Social Values* (New York: Basic Books, 1973).
10. René Dubos, *Reason Awake* (New York: Columbia University Press, 1970), pp. 193–194.
11. *Wall Street Journal,* June 22, 1972. In most states there is nothing illegal about this operation; only automobile manufacturers and dealers are covered by federal law.
12. William D. Ruckelshaus, quoted in *Business Week,* August 21, 1971, p. 58.
13. *The New York Times,* April 23, 1972.
14. James Spain, urban affairs director of Allied Chemical Corp. and president of the Association for the Integration of Management, quoted in "To Blacks, Ecology is Irrelevant," *Business Week,* November 14, 1970, p. 49.
15. *The New York Times,* June 19, 1972.
16. *Wall Street Journal,* November 19, 1971. Not all local union leaders have allowed fear of unemployment to blunt their demands for pollution control.
17. Walter Sherman, vice president of the Flambeau Paper Co., quoted in the *Wall Street Journal,* November 19, 1971.
18. William G. Magruder, quoted in *The New York Times,* May 23, 1972.
19. Robert J. Bazell, "Rapid Transit: A Real Alternative to the Auto for the Bay Area?" *Science* CLXXI (March 19, 1971), 1125, 1128.
20. Athelstan Spilhaus, "The Next Industrial Revolution," *The Conference Board Record,* February 1970, p. 39.
21. Henry Ford II, in an address before the annual convention of Sigma Delta Chi, professional journalistic society, Chicago, Illinois, November 13, 1970.

ETHICS AND ECOLOGY

William T. Blackstone

Much has been said about the right to a decent or livable environment. In his 22 January 1970 state of the union address, President Nixon stated: "The great question of the seventies is, shall we surrender to our surroundings, or shall we make our peace with Nature and begin to make the reparations for the damage we have done to our air, our land, and our water? . . . Clean air, clean water, open spaces—these would once again be the birthright of every American; if we act now, they can be." It seems, though, that the use of the term *right* by President Nixon, under the rubric of a "birthright" to a decent environment, is not a strict sense of the term. That is, he does not use this term to indicate that one has or should have either a legal right or a moral right to a decent environment. Rather he is pointing to the fact that in the past our environmental resources have been so abundant that all Americans did in fact inherit a livable environment, and it would be *desirable* that this state of affairs again be the case. Pollution and the exploitation of our environment is precluding this kind of inheritance.

Few would challenge the desirability of such a state of affairs or of such a "birthright." What we want to ask is whether the right to a decent environment can or ought to be considered a right in a stricter sense, either in a legal or moral sense. In contrast to a merely desirable state of affairs, a right entails a correlative duty or obligation on the part of someone or some group to accord one a certain mode of treatment or to act in a certain way.[1] Desirable states of affairs do not entail such correlative duties or obligations.

THE RIGHT TO A LIVABLE ENVIRONMENT AS A HUMAN RIGHT

Let us first ask whether the right to a livable environment can properly be considered to be a human right. For the purposes of this paper, however, I want to avoid raising the more general question of whether there are any human rights at all. Some philosophers do deny that any human rights exist.[2] In two recent papers I have argued that human rights do exist (even though such rights may properly be overridden on occasion by other morally relevant reasons) and that they are universal and inalienable (although the actual exercise of such rights on a given occasion is alienable).[3] My argument for the existence of universal human rights rests, in the final analysis, on a theory of what it means to be human, which specifies the capacities for rationality and freedom as essential, and on the fact that there are no relevant grounds for excluding any human from the opportunity to develop and fulfill his capacities (rationality and freedom) as a human. This is not to deny that there are criteria which justify according human rights in quite different ways or with quite different modes of treatment for different persons, depending upon the nature and degree of such capacities and the existing historical and environmental circumstances.

If the right to a livable environment were seen as a basic and inalienable human right, this could be a valuable tool (both inside and outside of legalistic frameworks) for solving some of our environmental problems, both on a national and on an international basis. Are there any philosophical and conceptual difficulties in treating this right as an inalienable human right? Traditionally we have not looked upon the right to a decent environment as a human right or as an inalienable right. Rather, inalienable human or natural rights have been conceived in somewhat different terms; equality, liberty, happiness, life, and property. However, might it not be possible to view the right to a livable environment as being entailed by, or as constitutive of, these basic human or natural rights recognized in our political tradition? If human rights, in other words, are those rights which each human possesses in virtue of the fact that he is human and in virtue of the fact that those rights are essential in permitting him to live a human life (that is, in permitting him to fulfill his capacities as a rational and free being), then might not the right to a decent environment be properly categorized as such a human right? Might it not be conceived as a right which has emerged as a result of changing environmental conditions and the impact of those conditions on the very possibility of human life and on the possibility of the realization of other rights such as liberty and equality? Let us explore how this might be the case.

Given man's great and increasing ability to manipulate the environment, and the devastating effect this is having, it is plain that new social institutions and new regulative agencies and procedures must be initiated on both national and international levels to make sure that the manipulation is in the public interest. It will be necessary, in other words, to restrict or stop some practices and the freedom to engage in those practices. Some look upon such additional state planning, whether national or international, as unnecessary further intrusion on man's freedom. Freedom is, of course, one of our basic values, and few would deny that excessive state control of human action is to be avoided. But such restrictions on individual freedom now appear to be necessary in the interest of overall human welfare and the rights and freedoms of *all* men. Even John Locke with his stress on freedom as an inalienable right recognized that this right must be construed so that it is consistent with the equal right to freedom of others. The whole point of the state is to restrict unlicensed freedom and to provide the conditions for equality of rights for all. Thus it seems to be perfectly consistent with Locke's view and, in general, with the views of the founding fathers of this country to restrict certain rights or freedoms when it can be shown that such restriction is necessary to insure the equal rights of others. If this is so, it has very important implications for the rights to freedom and to property. These rights, perhaps properly seen as inalienable (though this is a controversial philosophical question), are not properly seen as unlimited or unrestricted. When values which we hold dear conflict (for example, individual or group freedom and the freedom of all, individual or group rights and the rights of all, and individual or group welfare and the welfare of the general public) something has to give; some priority must be established. In the case of the abuse and waste of environmental resources, less individual freedom and fewer individual rights for the sake of greater public welfare and equality of rights seem justified. What in the past had been properly regarded as freedoms and rights (given what seemed to be unlimited natural resources and no serious pollution problems) can no longer be so construed, at least not without additional restrictions. We must recognize both the need for such restrictions and the fact that none of our rights can be realized without a livable environment. Both public welfare and equality of rights now require that natural resources not be used simply according to the whim and caprice of individuals or simply for personal profit. This is not to say that all property rights must be denied and that the state must own all productive property, as the Marxist argues. It is to insist that those rights be qualified or restricted in the light of new ecological data and in the interest of the freedom, rights, and welfare of all.

The answer then to the question, Is the right to a livable environment a human right? is yes. Each person has this right *qua* being human and because a livable environment is essential for one to fulfill his human capacities. And given the danger to our environment today and hence the danger to the very possibility of human existence, access to a livable environment must be conceived as a right which imposes upon everyone a correlative moral obligation to respect.

THE RIGHT TO A LIVABLE ENVIRONMENT AS A LEGAL RIGHT

If the right to a decent environment is to be treated as a legal right, then obviously what is required is some sort of legal framework which gives this right a legal status. Such legal frameworks have been proposed. Sen. Gaylord Nelson, originator of Earth Day, recently proposed a Constitutional Amendment guaranteeing every American an inalienable right to a decent environment.[4] Others want to formulate an entire "environmental bill of rights" to assist in solving our pollution problems. Such a bill of rights or a constitutional revision would provide a legal framework for the enforcement of certain policies bearing on environmental issues. It would also involve the concept of "legal responsibility" for acts which violate those rights. Such legal responsibility is beginning to be enforced in the United States. President Nixon on 23 December 1970 signed an executive order requiring industries to obtain federal permits before dumping pollutants. He issued the order not under the authority of new legislation but under the Refuse Act of 1899, which was originally designed to control discharges in connection with dredging and water construction operations but now has been broadened by Supreme Court decisions to cover pollution resulting from industrial operations. (The extension of this act is similar to my suggestion above, namely, the extension of the constitutional rights to equality, liberty, and property to include the right to a livable environment.)

Others propose that the right to a decent environment also be a cardinal tenet of international law. Pollution is not merely a national problem but an international one. The population of the entire world is affected by it, and a body of international law, which includes the right to a decent environment and the accompanying policies to save and preserve our environmental resources, would be an even more effective tool than such a framework at the national level. Of course, one does not have to be reminded of the problems involved in establishing international law and in eliciting obedience to it. Conflicts between nations are still settled more by force than by law or persuasion. The record of the United Nations attests to this fact. In the case of international conflict over environmental interests and the use of the environment, the possibility of international legal resolution, at least at this stage of history, is somewhat remote; for the body of enforceable international law on this topic is meager indeed. This is not to deny that this is the direction in which we should (and must) move.

A good case can be made for the view that not all moral or human rights should be legal rights and that not all moral rules should be legal rules. It may be argued that any society which covers the whole spectrum of man's activities with legally enforceable rules minimizes his freedom and approaches totalitarianism. There is this danger. But just as we argued that certain traditional rights and freedoms are properly restricted in order to insure the equal rights and welfare of all, so also it can plausibly be argued that the human right to a livable environment should become a legal one in order to assure that it is properly respected. Given the magnitude of the present dangers to the environment and to the welfare of all humans, and the ingrained habits and rules, or lack of rules, which permit continued waste, pollution, and destruction of our environmental resources, the legalized status of the right to a livable environment seems both desirable and necessary.

Such a legal right would provide a tool for pressing environmental transgressions in the courts. At the present the right to a livable environment, even if recognized as a human right, is not generally recognized as a legal one. One cannot sue individuals or corporations for polluting the environment, if the pollution harms equally every member of a community. One can sue such individuals or corporations if they damage one's private property but not if they damage the public environment. It is true that public officials have a legal standing in cases of generalized pollution, but unfortunately they have done little to exercise that standing.

Since public officials are failing to take steps to protect the environment, Joseph Sax, professor of law at the University of Michigan, argues that the right to take environmental disputes to court must be obtained as a right of private citizens: "The No. 1 legal priority of those concerned with environmental protection now is that the old restraints of the public nuisance doctrine and other archaic rules be rooted out of the law and be replaced with the recognition of every citizen's opportunity to enforce at law the right to a decent environment."[5] Sax himself drafted a model environmental law which was presented to the Michigan legislature, which "empowered any person or organization to sue any private or public body and to obtain a court order restraining conduct that is likely to pollute, impair, or destroy the air, water, or other material resources or the public trust therein."[6] This bill has now become law, and a similar bill is pending in the U.S. Congress, having been introduced by Senators McGovern and Hart and Representative Udall. I concur with Sax that this law, which provides an enforceable right to a decent environment and which places the burden of proof on a polluter or would-be polluter to show that his action affecting the environment is consistent with public health and welfare, "offers the promise of a dramatic legal break-through in the effort to protect environmental quality."[7] Although it may add to the clogged conditions of the courts, it should also have the effect of encouraging careful planning of activities which affect the environment.

The history of government, in this country and elsewhere, has been that of the gradual demise of a laissez-faire philosophy of government. Few deny that there are areas of our lives where government should not and must not intrude. In fact, what we mean by a totalitarian government is one which exceeds its proper bounds and attempts to control nearly all human activities. But in some areas of human life, it has been seen that the "keep-government-out-of-it" attitude just will not work. The entire quality of life in a society is determined by the availability and distribution of goods and services in such vital areas as education, housing, medical treatment, legal treatment, and so on. In the field of education, for example, we have seen the need for compulsory education and, more recently, for unitary school systems in order to provide equality of educational opportunity. . . .

In the same way, it is essential that government step in to prevent the potentially dire consequences of industrial pollution and the waste of environmental resources. Such government regulations need not mean the death of the free enterprise system. The right to private property can be made compatible with the right to a livable environment, for if uniform antipollution laws were applied to all industries, then both competition and private ownership could surely continue. But they would continue within a quite different set of rules and attitudes toward the environment. This extension of government would not be equivalent to totalitarianism.

In fact it is necessary to insure equality of rights and freedom, which is essential to a democracy.

ECOLOGY AND ECONOMIC RIGHTS

We suggested above that it is necessary to qualify or restrict economic or property rights in the light of new ecological data and in the interest of the freedom, rights, and welfare of all. In part, this suggested restriction is predicated on the assumption that we cannot expect private business to provide solutions to the multiple pollution problems for which they themselves are responsible. Some companies have taken measures to limit the polluting effect of their operations, and this is an important move. But we are deluding ourselves if we think that private business can function as its own pollution police. This is so for several reasons: the primary objective of private business is economic profit. Stockholders do not ask of a company, "Have you polluted the environment and lowered the quality of the environment for the general public and for future generations?" Rather they ask, "How high is the annual dividend and how much higher is it than the year before?" One can hardly expect organizations whose basic norm is economic profit to be concerned in any great depth with the long-range effects of their operations upon society and future generations or concerned with the hidden cost of their operations in terms of environmental quality to society as a whole. Second, within a free enterprise system companies compete to produce what the public wants at the lowest possible cost. Such competition would preclude the spending of adequate funds to prevent environmental pollution, since this would add tremendously to the cost of the product— unless all other companies would also conform to such antipollution policies. But in a free enterprise economy such policies are not likely to be self-imposed by businessmen. Third, the basic response of the free enterprise system to our economic problems is that we must have greater economic growth or an increase in gross national product. But such growth many ecologists look upon with great alarm, for it can have devastating long-range effects upon our environment. Many of the products of uncontrolled growth are based on artificial needs and actually detract from, rather than contribute to, the quality of our lives. A stationary economy, some economists and ecologists suggest, may well be best for the quality of man's environment and of his life in the long run. Higher GNP does not automatically result in an increase in social well-being, and it should not be used as a measuring rod for assessing economic welfare. This becomes clear when one realizes that the GNP

> aggregates the dollar value of all goods and services produced—the cigarettes as well as the medical treatment of lung cancer, the petroleum from offshore wells as well as the detergents required to clean up after oil spills, the electrical energy produced and the medical and cleaning bills resulting from the air-pollution fuel used for generating the electricity. The GNP

allows no deduction for negative production, such as lives lost from unsafe cars or environmental destruction perpetrated by telephone, electric and gas utilities, lumber companies, and speculative builders.[8]

To many persons, of course, this kind of talk is not only blasphemy but subversive. This is especially true when it is extended in the direction of additional controls over corporate capitalism. (Some ecologists and economists go further and challenge whether corporate capitalism can accommodate a stationary state and still retain its major features.)[9] The fact of the matter is that the ecological attitude forces one to reconsider a host of values which have been held dear in the past, and it forces one to reconsider the appropriateness of the social and economic systems which embodied and implemented those values. Given the crisis of our environment, there must be certain fundamental changes in attitudes toward nature, man's use of nature, and man himself. Such changes in attitudes undoubtedly will have far-reaching implications for the institutions of private property and private enterprise and the values embodied in these institutions. Given that crisis we can no longer look upon water and air as free commodities to be exploited at will. Nor can the private ownership of land be seen as a lease to use that land in any way which conforms merely to the personal desires of the owner. In other words, the environmental crisis is forcing us to challenge what had in the past been taken to be certain basic rights of man or at least to restrict those rights. And it is forcing us to challenge institutions which embodied those rights. . . .

ETHICS AND TECHNOLOGY

I have been discussing the relationship of ecology to ethics and to a theory of rights. Up to this point I have not specifically discussed the relation of technology to ethics, although it is plain that technology and its development is responsible for most of our pollution problems. This topic deserves separate treatment, but I do want to briefly relate it to the thesis of this work.

It is well known that new technology sometimes complicates our ethical lives and our ethical decisions. Whether the invention is the wheel or a contraceptive pill, new technology always opens up new possibilities for human relationships and for society, for good and ill. The pill, for example, is revolutionizing sexual morality, for its use can preclude many of the bad consequences normally attendant upon premarital intercourse. *Some* of the strongest arguments against premarital sex have been shot down by this bit of technology (though certainly not all of them). The fact that the use of the pill can prevent unwanted pregnancy does not make premarital sexual intercourse morally right, nor does it make it wrong. The pill is morally neutral, but its existence does change in part the moral base of the decision to engage in premarital sex. In the same way, technology at least in principle can be neutral—neither necessarily good nor bad in its impact on other aspects of the environment. Unfortunately, much of it is bad—very bad. But technology can be meshed with an ecological attitude to the benefit of man and his environment.

I am not suggesting that the answer to technology which has bad environmental effects is necessarily more technology. We tend too readily to assume that new technological developments will always solve man's problems. But this is simply not the case. One technological innovation often seems to breed a half-dozen additional ones which themselves create more environmental problems. We certainly do not solve pollution problems, for example, by changing from power plants fueled by coal to power plants fueled by nuclear energy, if radioactive waste from the latter is worse than pollution from the former. Perhaps part of the answer to pollution problems is less technology. There is surely no real hope of returning to nature (whatever that means) or of stopping *all* technological and scientific development, as some advocate. Even if it could be done, this would be too extreme a move. The answer is not to stop technology, but to guide it toward proper ends, and to set up standards of antipollution to which all technological devices must conform. Technology has been and can be used to destroy and pollute an environment, but it can also be used to save and beautify it.

Notes

1. This is a dogmatic assertion in this context. I am aware that some philosophers deny that rights and duties are correlative. Strictly interpreted this correlativity thesis is false, I believe. There are duties for which there are no correlative rights. But space does not permit discussion of this question here.
2. See Kai Nielsen's "Scepticism and Human Rights," *Monist,* 52, no. 4 (1968): 571–594.
3. See my "Equality and Human Rights," *Monist,* 52, no. 4 (1968): 616–639; and my "Human Rights and Human Dignity," in Laszlo and Gotesky, eds., *Human Dignity.*
4. *Newsweek,* 4 May 1970, p. 26.
5. Joseph Sax, "Environment in The Courtroom," *Saturday Review,* 3 October 1970, p. 56.
6. *Ibid.*
7. *Ibid.*
8. See Melville J. Ulmer, "More Than Marxist," *New Republic,* 26 December 1970, p. 14.
9. See Murdock and Connell, "All about Ecology," *Center Magazine,* 3, no. 1 (January–February 1970): 63.

THE ENVIRONMENTAL CRISIS AND
THE QUALITY OF LIFE

Nicholas Rescher

INTRODUCTION

Most of us tend to think of the environmental crisis as resulting from "too much"—too much pollution, wastage, pesticide, and so forth. But from the economists' angle the problem is one of *scarcity:* too little clean air, pure water, recreationally usable land, safe fruit. The answer traditional among welfare economists to problems of scarcity is based singlemindedly on the leading idea of *production.* But alas the things which the environmental crisis leaves in too short supply—fresh air, clean rivers, unpolluted beaches, and the like are not things to which the standard, traditional concept of the production of goods and services—or anything like it—will be applicable. The project of *producing* another planet earth to live on after we have used this one up is unfortunately unfeasible.

For reasons such as this, various economists—Kenneth Boulding most prominent among them—have urged a broadening of economic horizons and redeployment of concern. Economics is to deal not just narrowly with the production and consumption of goods and services but broadly with the maintenance of a quality of life. Such a reorientation of welfare economics has profound consequences. It once again renders relevant to economics the traditional concerns of the philosopher with matters of norms and values, of ideology and the rational structure of social appraisal.

It is from this philosophical vantage point—not ignoring the concerns of the economist and sociologist and social psychologist but seeking to transcend the bounds of their disciplinary bailiwicks—that I should like to consider the impact of the environmental crisis.

Most of the discussions of the environmental crisis in which I have been a participant or witness are basically exercises in social uplift. The lesson is driven home that if only we are good and behave ourselves everything will come out just fine. To adopt more stringent legislation of control, to subject grasping enterprise to social pressure, to adopt better social values and attitudes, to espouse the program and ideology of planned parenthood or women's lib, to hand the control of affairs over to those who are younger and purer of heart . . . so runs the gamut of remedies which their respective advocates would have us adopt and which, once adopted, will—so we are told—put everything to rights. Throughout this stance there runs the fundamentally activistic optimism

From *Philosophy and Environmental Crisis,* ed. William T. Blackstone. Copyright © 1974 by University of Georgia Press, Athens. Reprinted by permission of the publisher.

of the American experience: virtue will be rewarded; and by the end of the sixth reel, the good guys will be riding off into the glorious sunset.

My aim is to dash some cold water on all this. I want to propose the deeply pessimistic suggestion that, crudely speaking, the environment has had it and that we simply cannot "go home again" to "the good old days" of environmental purity. We all know of the futile laments caused by the demise of the feudal order by such thinkers as Thomas More or the ruralistic yearnings voiced by the romantics in the early days of the Industrial Revolution. Historical retrospect may well cast the present spate of hand-wringing over environmental deterioration as an essentially analogous—right-minded but utterly futile—penchant for the easier, simpler ways of bygone days. Actually even to think of the problem as an environmental crisis is tendentious. Crises are by definition transitory phenomena: they point toward a moment of decision for life or death, not toward a stable condition of things. The very terminology indicates an unwillingness to face the prospect of a serious environmental degradation as a permanent reality, an ongoing "fact of life."

To take this view goes deep against the grain, and I have little hope of persuading many people of its correctness. I certainly do not like it myself. But perhaps it could be granted—at least for the sake of discussion—that the view might be correct. Granting this hypothesis, let us explore its implications.

First let me be clearer about the hypothesis itself. I am not saying that environmental activism is futile—that man cannot by dint of energy and effort manage to clean up this or that environmental mess. What I am saying is that we may simply be unable to solve the environmental crisis as a whole: that once this or that form of noxiousness is expelled from one door some other equally bad version comes in by another. My hypothesis in short is that the environmental crisis may well be incurable. It just may be something that we cannot solve but have to learn to live with.

This hypothesis is surely not altogether unrealistic and fanciful. Basically the environmental mess is a product of the conspiration of three forces: (1) high population densities, (2) high levels of personal consumption, and (3) a messy technology of production. Can one even realistically expect that any of these can really be eliminated? Not the population crunch surely. As the character remarked in a recent "Peanuts" cartoon: "Everybody says there are too many of us, but nobody wants to leave." So much for population. Moreover, lots of people everywhere in the world are clamoring for affluence and a place on the high-consumption bandwagon, and pitifully few are jumping off. . . .

THE ESCALATION OF EXPECTATIONS

The concept of social *progress* is deeply, almost irremovably, impressed on the American consciousness. And this is so not just in the remote past but very much in our own day. Take just the most recent period since World War II. Consider the marked signs of progress:

1. The increase of life expectancy (at birth) from sixty-three years in 1940 to seventy years in 1965.
2. The rise of per capita personal income from $1,810 in 1950 to $2,542 in 1965 (in constant [1958] dollars).
3. The increase in education represented by a rise in school enrollments from 44 percent of the five-to-thirty-four-year-old group in 1950 to 60 percent in 1965.
4. The growth of social welfare expenditures from $88 per capita in 1945 to $360 per capita in 1965 (in constant [1958] dollars).

Taken together, these statistics bring into focus the steady and significant improvement in the provisions for individual comfort and social welfare that has taken place in the United States since World War II. If the progress-oriented thesis that increased physical well-being brings increased happiness were correct, one would certainly expect Americans to be substantially happier today than ever before. This expectation is not realized. In fact, the available evidence all points the reverse way....

... We are facing ... an escalation of expectations, a raising of the levels of expectations with corresponding increased aspirations in the demands people make upon the circumstances and conditions of their lives. With respect to the requisites of happiness, we are in the midst of a revolution of rising expectations, a revolution that affects not only the man at the bottom, but operates throughout, to the very top of the heap.

This supposition of an escalation of expectations regarding the quality of life, and correspondingly of aspirations regarding the requisites of happiness, finds striking confirmation in the fact that despite the impressive signs that people think of themselves as less happy than their predecessors of a generation or so ago, they would be quite unwilling to contemplate a return to what we hear spoken of (usually cynically) as the good old days....

... This sort of perception of unhappiness has a surprising twist to it. It indicates a deep faith in progress—a progression of steady improvement in the circumstances of life, however little we may actually savor this improvement in terms of increased happiness.

SOME IDEOLOGICAL VICTIMS

Let us now return in the light of these considerations to my initial hypothesis. If in the continued unfolding an ongoing environmental crisis occurs, various conceptions integral to the American social ideology will have to go by the board: in particular the conceptions of material progress, of technological omnipotence, and of millennial orientation.

Material Progress. ... A parting of the ways with the concept of progress will not come easy to us. It's going to take a lot of doing to accustom us to the idea that things are on balance to get worse or at any rate no better as concerns the quality of life in this nation. (And once we are persuaded of this, there may be vast social and political repercussions in terms of personal frustration and social unrest.) The conception of a deescalation of expectations, of settling for less than we've been accustomed to, is

something Americans are not prepared for. We have had little preparatory background for accepting the realization that in some key aspects in
the quality of life the best days may be behind us. I myself very much
doubt that we are going to take kindly to the idea. The British have made
a pretty good show of having to haul down the flag of empire. You will,
I hope, forgive me for evincing skepticism about our ability to show
equally good grace when the time comes to run down our banner embla-
zoned with "Standard of Living."

Technological Omnipotence. The conception of get-it-done confidence,
virtually of technological omnipotence, runs deep in the American character. We incline to the idea that, as a people, we can do anything we set
our mind to. In a frontier nation there was little tendency toward a serious
recognition of limits of any sort. The concept of finite resources, the
reality of opportunity costs, the necessity for *choice* in the allocation of
effort and the inescapable prospect of unpleasant consequences of
choices (negative externalities) are newcomers to American thinking.
This era of economic awareness and recognition of the realities of cost-
benefit analysis is so recent it has hardly trickled down to the popular
level.

The course of our historical experience has not really prepared us to
face the realities of finiteness and incapacity. We expect government to
"handle things"—not only the foreign wars, economic crises, and social
disorders of historical experience, but now the environmental crises as
well. The idea that our scientific technology and the social technology of
our political institutions may be utterly inadequate to the task does not
really dawn on us. If and when it finally does, you may be sure that the
fur will fly.

Millennial Hankerings. Americans have manifested more millennial
hankerings than perhaps any other people since the days when apocalyp-
tic thinking was in fashion. The idea that a solution to our problems lies
somehow just around the corner is deeply ingrained in our consciousness. Nobody knows the themes to which people resonate better than
politicians. And from Woodrow Wilson's Fourteen Points to Franklin
Roosevelt's New Deal to the quality-of-life rhetoric of Lyndon Johnson's
campaign the fundamentally millennial nature of our political rhetoric is
clear. "Buy our program, accept our policies, and everything in the country will be just about perfect." That is how the politicians talk, and they
do so because that is what people yearn to hear. We can accept deprivation now as long as we feel assured that prosperity lies just around the
corner. No political campaign is complete without substantial pandering
to our millennial yearnings through assurances that if only we put the
right set of men in office all our troubles will vanish and we can all live
happily ever after. We as a nation have yet to learn the unpleasant lesson
that such pie-in-the-sky thinking is a luxury we can no longer afford.

The ideological consequences of the demise of a faith in progress,
technological omnipotence, and the millennial orientation will clearly be
profound. The result cannot but be a radically altered ideology, a wholly
new American outlook. What will this be? All too temptingly it may be

a leap to the opposite extreme: to hopelessness, despondency, discouragement—the sense of impotence and *après nous le déluge.* I am afraid that such an era of disillusionment may well be the natural consequence of the presently popular rhetoric of the environmental crisis. And the American people do not have a particularly good record for sensible action in a time of disappointed expectations. Our basic weakness is a rather nonstandard problem of morale: a failure not of nerve but of patience.

Yet such a result—despair and disillusionment—seems to me wholly unwarranted. It is realism not hopelessness that provides the proper remedy for overconfidence. Let us by all means carry on the struggle to "save the environment" by all feasible steps. But let us not entertain misguided expectations about the prospects of success—expectations whose probable disappointment cannot but result in despondency, recrimination, and the tempting resort to the dire political measures that are natural to gravely disillusioned people.

The stance I see as necessary is not one of fatalistic resignation but of carrying on the good fight to save the environment—but doing so in fully realistic awareness that we are carrying on a limited war in which an actual victory may well lie beyond our grasp. It has taken an extraordinarily difficult struggle for us to arrive at a limited war perspective in international relations under the inexorable pressure of the political and technological facts of our times. And we have not even begun to move toward the corresponding mentality in the sphere of social problems and domestic difficulties. Yet just this—as I see it—is one of the crucial sociotechnological imperatives of our day.

CONCLUSION

The time has come for summing up. The conception that the quality of life—currently under threat by the environmental crisis—represents simply another one of those binds for which the welfare economists' classic prescription of "producing oneself out of it" seems to me profoundly misguided. In my discussion I have set before you the hypothesis of the environmental crisis as not really a crisis at all, but the inauguration of a permanent condition of things.

I have tried to argue that one of the main implications of this is a reversal of the ongoing escalation of expectations that is and long has been rife among Americans. In various crucial respects regarding the quality of life we just may have to settle for less. I have maintained that this development will exact from Americans a great price in terms of ideological revisionism. In particular, it will demand as victims our inclination to progressivism, our Promethean faith in man's technological omnipotence, and our penchant for millennial thinking. What is needed in the face of the environmental crises at this point, as I see it, may well be not a magisterial confidence that things can be put right, but a large dose of cool realism tempered with stoic resignation. We had better get used to the idea that we may have to scale down our expectations and learn to settle for less in point of standard of living and quality of life.

This conclusion will very likely strike many as a repulsive instance of "gloom and doom" thinking. This would be quite wrong. The moral, as I see it, is at worst one of gloom without doom. Man is a being of enormous adaptability, resiliency, and power. He has learned to survive and make the best of it under some extremely difficult and unpleasant conditions. By all means, let us do everything we can to save the environment. But if we do not do a very good job of it—and I for one do not think we will—it is not necessarily the end of the world. Let us not sell man short. We have been in some unpleasant circumstances before and have managed to cope.

SHOULD TREES HAVE STANDING?—
TOWARD LEGAL RIGHTS FOR
NATURAL OBJECTS

Christopher D. Stone

Throughout legal history, each successive extension of rights to some new entity has been, theretofore, a bit unthinkable. We are inclined to suppose the rightlessness of rightless "things" to be a decree of Nature, not a legal convention acting in support of some status quo. It is thus that we defer considering the choices involved in all their moral, social, and economic dimensions. And so the United States Supreme Court could straight-facedly tell us in *Dred Scott* that Blacks had been denied the rights of citizenship "as a subordinate and inferior class of beings, who had been subjugated by the dominant race. . . ."[1] In the nineteenth century, the highest court in California explained that Chinese had not the right to testify against white men in criminal matters because they were "a race of people whom nature has marked as inferior, and who are incapable of progress or intellectual development beyond a certain point . . . between whom and ourselves nature has placed an impassable difference."[2] The popular conception of the Jew in the 13th Century contributed to a law which treated them as "men *ferae naturae,* protected by a quasi-forest law. Like the roe and the deer, they form an order apart."[3] Recall, too, that it was not so long ago that the foetus was "like the roe and the deer." In an early suit attempting to establish a wrongful death action on behalf of a negligently killed foetus (now widely accepted practice), Holmes, then

From *Southern California Law Review,* vol. 45 (1972) pp. 453–460, 463–464, 480–481, 486–487. Reprinted by permission.

on the Massachusetts Supreme Court, seems to have thought it simply inconceivable "that a man might owe a civil duty and incur a conditional prospective liability in tort to one not yet in being."[4] The first woman in Wisconsin who thought she might have a right to practice law was told that she did not, in the following terms:

> The law of nature destines and qualifies the female sex for the bearing and nurture of the children of our race and for the custody of the homes of the world. . . . [A]ll life-long callings of women, inconsistent with these radical and sacred duties of their sex, as is the profession of the law, are departures from the order of nature; and when voluntary, treason against it. . . . The peculiar qualities of womanhood, its gentle graces, its quick sensibility, its tender susceptibility, its purity, its delicacy, its emotional impulses, its subordination of hard reason to sympathetic feeling, are surely not qualifications for forensic strife. Nature has tempered woman as little for the juridical conflicts of the court room, as for the physical conflicts of the battle field. . . .[5]

The fact is, that each time there is a movement to confer rights onto some new "entity," the proposal is bound to sound odd or frightening or laughable. This is partly because until the rightless thing receives its rights, we cannot see it as anything but a *thing* for the use of "us"—those who are holding rights at the time. In this vein, what is striking about the Wisconsin case above is that the court, for all its talk about women, so clearly was never able to see women as they are (and might become). All it could see was the popular "idealized" version of *an object it needed.* Such is the way the slave South looked upon the Black. There is something of a seamless web involved: there will be resistance to giving the thing "rights" until it can be seen and valued for itself; yet, it is hard to see it and value it for itself until we can bring ourselves to give it "rights"— which is almost inevitably going to sound inconceivable to a large group of people.

The reason for this little discourse on the unthinkable, the reader must know by now, if only from the title of the paper. I am quite seriously proposing that we give legal rights to forests, oceans, rivers and other so-called "natural objects" in the environment—indeed, to the natural environment as a whole.

As strange as such a notion may sound, it is neither fanciful nor devoid of operational content. In fact, I do not think it would be a misdescription of recent developments in the law to say that we are already on the verge of assigning some such rights, although we have not faced up to what we are doing in those particular terms. We should do so now, and begin to explore the implications such a notion would hold.

TOWARD RIGHTS FOR THE ENVIRONMENT

Now, to say that the natural environment should have rights is not to say anything as silly as that no one should be allowed to cut down a tree. We say human beings have rights, but—at least as of the time of this writing—they can be executed. Corporations have rights, but they cannot plead the fifth amendment; *In re Gault* gave 15-year-olds certain rights in juvenile proceedings, but it did not give them the right to vote. Thus, to say that the environment should have rights is not to say that it should have every right we can imagine, or even the same body of rights as human beings have. Nor is it to say that everything in the environment should have the same rights as every other thing in the environment.

But for a thing to be *a holder of legal rights,* something more is needed than that some authoritative body will review the actions and processes of those who threaten it. As I shall use the term, "holder of legal rights," each of three additional criteria must be satisfied. All three, one will observe, go towards making a thing *count* jurally—to have a legally recognized worth and dignity in its own right, and not merely to serve as a means to benefit "us" (whoever the contemporary group of rights-holders may be). They are, first, that the thing can institute legal actions *at its behest;* second, that in determining the granting of legal relief, the court must take *injury to it* into account; and, third, that relief must run to the *benefit of it.*

The Rightlessness of Natural Objects at Common Law

Consider, for example, the common law's posture toward the pollution of a stream. True, courts have always been able, in some circumstances, to issue orders that will stop the pollution. . . . But the stream itself is fundamentally rightless, with implications that deserve careful reconsideration.

The first sense in which the stream is not a rights-holder has to do with standing. The stream itself has none. So far as the common law is concerned, there is in general no way to challenge the polluter's actions save at the behest of a lower riparian—another human being—able to show an invasion of *his* rights. This conception of the riparian as the holder of the right to bring suit has more than theoretical interest. The lower riparians may simply not care about the pollution. They themselves may be polluting, and not wish to stir up legal waters. They may be economically dependent on their polluting neighbor. And, of course, when they discount the value of winning by the costs of bringing suit and the chances of success, the action may not seem worth undertaking. . . .

The second sense in which the common law denies "rights" to natural objects has to do with the way in which the merits are decided in those cases in which someone is competent and willing to establish standing. At its more primitive levels, the system protected the "rights" of the property owning human with minimal weighing of any values: *"Cujus est solum, ejus est usque ad coelum et ad infernos."* Today we have come more and more to make balances—but only such as will adjust the economic best interests of identifiable humans.

. . . None of the natural objects, whether held in common or situated on private land, has any of the three criteria of a rights-holder. They have no standing in their own right; their unique damages do not count in determining outcome; and they are not the beneficiaries of awards. In such fashion, these objects have traditionally been regarded by the common law, and even by all but the most recent legislation, as objects for man to conquer and master and use—in such a way as the law once looked upon "man's" relationships to African Negroes. Even where special measures have been taken to conserve them, as by seasons on game and limits on timber cutting, the dominant motive has been to conserve them *for us* —for the greatest good of the greatest number of human beings. Conservationists, so far as I am aware, are generally reluctant to maintain otherwise. As the name implies, they want to conserve and guarantee *our* consumption and *our* enjoyment of these other living things. In their own right, natural objects have counted for little, in law as in popular movements. . . .

As I mentioned at the outset, however, the rightlessness of the natural environment can and should change; it already shows some signs of doing so.

Toward Having Standing in Its Own Right

It is not inevitable, nor is it wise, that natural objects should have no rights to seek redress in their own behalf. It is no answer to say that streams and forests cannot have standing because streams and forests cannot speak. Corporations cannot speak either; nor can states, estates, infants, incompetents, municipalities or universities. Lawyers speak for them, as they customarily do for the ordinary citizen with legal problems. One ought, I think, to handle the legal problems of natural objects as one does the problems of legal incompetents—human beings who have become vegetable. If a human being shows signs of becoming senile and has affairs that he is de jure incompetent to manage, those concerned with his well being make such a showing to the court, and someone is designated by the court with the authority to manage the incompetent's affairs. The guardian (or "conservator" or "committee"—the terminology varies) then represents the incompetent in his legal affairs. Courts make similar appointments when a corporation has become "incompetent"—they appoint a trustee in bankruptcy or reorganization to oversee its affairs and speak for it in court when that becomes necessary.

On a parity of reasoning, we should have a system in which, when a friend of a natural object perceives it to be endangered, he can apply to a court for the creation of a guardianship. . . .

. . . One reason for making the environment itself the beneficiary of a judgment is to prevent it from being "sold out" in a negotiation among private litigants who agree not to enforce rights that have been established among themselves. Protection from this will be advanced by making the natural object a party to an injunctive settlement. Even more importantly, we should make it a beneficiary of money awards. . . .

The idea of assessing damages as best we can and placing them in a trust fund is far more realistic than a hope that a total "freeze" can be put on the environmental status quo. Nature is a continuous theatre in which things and species (eventually man) are destined to enter and exit. In the meantime, co-existence of man and his environment means that *each* is going to have to compromise for the better of both. Some pollution of streams, for example, will probably be inevitable for some time. Instead of setting an unrealizable goal of enjoining absolutely the discharge of all such pollutants, the trust fund concept would (a) help assure that pollution would occur only in those instances where the social need for the pollutant's product (via his present method of production) was so high as to enable the polluter to cover *all* homocentric costs, plus some estimated costs to the environment *per se,* and (b) would be a corpus for preserving monies, if necessary, while the technology developed to a point where repairing the damaged portion of the environment was feasible. Such a fund might even finance the requisite research and development.

I do not doubt that other senses in which the environment might have rights will come to mind, and, as I explain more fully below, would be more apt to come to mind if only we should speak in terms of their having rights, albeit vaguely at first. "Rights" might well lie in unanticipated areas. It would seem, for example, that Chief Justice Warren was only stating the obvious when he observed in *Reynolds* v. *Sims* that "legislators represent people, not trees or acres." Yet, could not a case be made for a system of apportionment which *did* take into account the wildlife of an area? It strikes me as a poor idea that Alaska should have no more congressmen than Rhode Island primarily *because there are in Alaska all those trees and acres, those waterfalls and forests.* I am not saying anything as silly as that we ought to overrule *Baker* v. *Carr* and retreat from one man-one vote to a system of one man-or-tree one vote. Nor am I even taking the position that we ought to count each acre, as we once counted each slave, as three-fifths of a man. But I am suggesting that there is nothing unthinkable about, and there might on balance even be a prevailing case to be made for, an electoral apportionment that made some systematic effort to allow for the representative "rights" of non-human life. And if a case can be made for that, which I offer here mainly for purpose of illustration, I suspect that a society that grew concerned enough about the environment to make it a holder of rights would be able to find quite a number of "rights" to have waiting for it when it got to court.

Notes

1. Dred Scott v. Sandford, 60 U.S. (19 How.) 396, 404–5 (1856).
2. People v. Hall, 4 Cal. 399, 405 (1854).
3. Schechter, "The Rightlessness of Mediaeval English Jewry," 45 *Jewish Q. Rev.,* 121, 135 (1954) quoting from M. Bateson, *Medieval England,* 139 (1904).
4. Dietrich v. Inhabitants of Northampton, 138 Mass. 14, 16 (1884).
5. *In re* Goddell, 39 Wisc. 232, 245 (1875).

THE RIGHTS OF ANIMALS AND UNBORN GENERATIONS

Joel Feinberg

Every philosophical paper must begin with an unproved assumption. Mine is the assumption that there will still be a world five hundred years from now, and that it will contain human beings who are very much like us. We have it within our power now, clearly, to affect the lives of these creatures for better or worse by contributing to the conservation or corruption of the environment in which they must live. I shall assume furthermore that it is psychologically possible for us to care about our remote descendants, that many of us in fact do care, and indeed that we ought to care. My main concern then will be to show that it makes sense to speak of the rights of unborn generations against us, and that given the moral judgment that we ought to conserve our environmental inheritance for them, and its grounds, we might well say that future generations *do* have rights correlative to our present duties toward them. Protecting our environment now is also a matter of elementary prudence, and insofar as we do it for the next generation already here in the persons of our children, it is a matter of love. But from the perspective of our remote descendants it is basically a matter of justice, of respect for their rights. My main concern here will be to examine the concept of a right to better understand how that can be.

THE PROBLEM

To have a right is to have a claim[1] *to* something and *against* someone, the recognition of which is called for by legal rules or, in the case of moral rights, by the principles of an enlightened conscience. In the familiar cases of rights, the claimant is a competent adult human being, and the claimee is an officeholder in an institution or else a private individual, in either case, another competent adult human being. Normal adult human beings, then, are obviously the sorts of beings of whom rights can meaningfully be predicated. Everyone would agree to that, even extreme misanthropes who deny that anyone in fact has rights. On the other hand, it is absurd to say that rocks can have rights, not because rocks are morally inferior things unworthy of rights (that statement makes no sense either), but because rocks belong to a category of entities of whom rights cannot be meaningfully predicated. That is not to say that there are no circumstances in which we ought to treat rocks carefully, but only that the rocks

From *Philosophy and Environmental Crisis,* ed. William T. Blackstone. Copyright © 1974 by University of Georgia Press, Athens. Reprinted by permission of the publisher.

themselves cannot validly claim good treatment from us. In between the clear cases of rocks and normal human beings, however, is a spectrum of less obvious cases, including some bewildering borderline ones. Is it meaningful or conceptually possible to ascribe rights to our dead ancestors? to individual animals? to whole species of animals? to plants? to idiots and madmen? to fetuses? to generations yet unborn? Until we know how to settle these puzzling cases, we cannot claim fully to grasp the concept of a right, or to know the shape of its logical boundaries.

One way to approach these riddles is to turn one's attention first to the most familiar and unproblematic instances of rights, note their most salient characteristics, and then compare the borderline cases with them, measuring as closely as possible the points of similarity and difference. In the end, the way we classify the borderline cases may depend on whether we are more impressed with the similarities or the differences between them and the cases in which we have the most confidence.

It will be useful to consider the problem of individual animals first because their case is the one that has already been debated with the most thoroughness by philosophers so that the dialectic of claim and rejoinder has now unfolded to the point where disputants can get to the end game quickly and isolate the crucial point at issue. When we understand precisely what *is* at issue in the debate over animal rights, I think we will have the key to the solution of all the other riddles about rights.

Individual Animals

Almost all modern writers agree that we ought to be kind to animals, but that is quite another thing from holding that animals can claim kind treatment from us as their due. Statutes making cruelty to animals a crime are now very common, and these, of course, impose legal duties on people not to mistreat animals; but that still leaves open the question whether the animals, as beneficiaries of those duties, possess rights correlative to them. We may very well have duties *regarding* animals that are not at the same time duties *to* animals, just as we may have duties regarding rocks, or buildings, or lawns, that are not duties *to* the rocks, buildings, or lawns. Some legal writers have taken the still more extreme position that animals themselves are not even the directly intended beneficiaries of statutes prohibiting cruelty to animals. During the nineteenth century, for example, it was commonly said that such statutes were designed to protect human beings by preventing the growth of cruel habits that could later threaten human beings with harm too. Prof. Louis B. Schwartz finds the rationale of the cruelty-to-animals prohibition in its protection of animal lovers from affronts to their sensibilities. "It is not the mistreated dog who is the ultimate object of concern," he writes. "Our concern is for the feelings of other human beings, a large proportion of whom, although accustomed to the slaughter of animals for food, readily identify themselves with a tortured dog or horse and respond with great sensitivity to its sufferings."[2] This seems to me to be factitious. How much more natural it is to say with John Chipman Gray that the true purpose of cruelty-to-animals statutes is "to preserve the dumb brutes from suffering."[3] The very people whose sensibilities are invoked in the alternative explanation, a group that no doubt now includes most of us, are precisely those who would insist that the protection belongs primarily to the animals themselves, not merely to their own tender feelings. Indeed, it would be difficult even to account for the existence of such feelings in the absence of a belief that the animals deserve the protection in their own right and for their own sakes.

Even if we allow, as I think we must, that animals are the intended direct beneficiaries of legislation forbidding cruelty to animals, it does not follow directly that animals have legal rights, and Gray himself, for one,[4] refused to draw this further inference. Animals cannot have rights, he thought, for the same reason they cannot have duties, namely, that they are not genuine "moral agents." Now, it is relatively easy to see why animals cannot have duties, and this matter is largely beyond controversy. Animals cannot be "reasoned with" or instructed in their responsibilities; they are inflexible and unadaptable to future contingencies; they are subject to fits of instinctive passion which they are incapable of repressing or controlling, postponing or sublimating. Hence, they cannot enter into contractual agreements, or make promises; they cannot be trusted; and they cannot (except within very narrow limits and for purposes of conditioning) be blamed for what would be called "moral failures" in a human being. They are therefore incapable of being moral subjects, of acting rightly or wrongly in the moral sense, of having, discharging, or breeching duties and obligations.

But what is there about the intellectual incompetence of animals (which admittedly disqualifies them for duties) that makes them logically unsuitable for rights? The most common reply to this question is that animals are incapable of *claiming* rights on their own. They cannot make motion, on their own, to courts to have their claims recognized or enforced; they cannot initiate, on their own, any kind of legal proceedings; nor are they capable of even understanding when their rights are being violated, of distinguishing harm from wrongful injury, and responding with indignation and an outraged sense of justice instead of mere anger or fear.

No one can deny any of these allegations, but to the claim that they are the grounds for disqualification of rights of animals, philosophers on the other side of this controversy have made convincing rejoinders. It is simply not true, says W. D. Lamont,[5] that the ability to understand what a right is and the ability to set legal machinery in motion by one's own initiative are necessary for the possession of rights. If that were the case, then neither human idiots nor wee babies would have any legal rights at all. Yet it is manifest that both of these classes of intellectual incompetents have legal rights recognized and easily enforced by the courts. Children and idiots start legal proceedings, not on their own direct initiative, but rather through the actions of proxies or attorneys who are empowered to speak in their names. If there is no conceptual absurdity

VEGETABLES

It is clear that we ought not to mistreat certain plants, and indeed there are rules and regulations imposing duties on persons not to misbehave in respect to certain members of the vegetable kingdom. It is forbidden, for example, to pick wildflowers in the mountainous tundra areas of national parks, or to endanger trees by starting fires in dry forest areas. Members of Congress introduce bills designed, as they say, to "protect" rare redwood trees from commercial pillage. Given this background, it is surprising that no one[7] speaks of plants as having rights. Plants, after all, are not "mere things"; they are vital objects with inherited biological propensities determining their natural growth. Moreover, we do say that certain conditions are "good" or "bad" for plants, thereby suggesting that plants, unlike rocks, are capable of having a "good." (This is a case, however, where "what we say" should not be taken seriously: we also say that certain kinds of paint are good or bad for the internal walls of a house, and this does not commit us to a conception of walls as beings possessed of a good or welfare of their own.) Finally, we are capable of feeling a kind of affection for particular plants, though we rarely personalize them, as we do in the case of animals, by giving them proper names.

Still, all are agreed that plants are not the kinds of beings that can have rights. Plants are never plausibly understood to be the direct intended beneficiaries of rules designed to "protect" them. We wish to keep redwood groves in existence for the sake of human beings who can enjoy their serene beauty, and for the sake of generations of human beings yet unborn. Trees are not the sorts of beings who have their "own sakes," despite the fact that they have biological propensities. Having no conscious wants or goals of their own, trees cannot know satisfaction or frustration, pleasure or pain. Hence, there is no possibility of kind or cruel treatment of trees. In these morally crucial respects, trees differ from the higher species of animals.

Yet trees are not mere things like rocks. They grow and develop according to the laws of their own nature. Aristotle and Aquinas both took trees to have their own "natural ends." Why then do I deny them the status of beings with interests of their own? The reason is that an interest, however the concept is finally to be analyzed, presupposes at least rudimentary cognitive equipment. Interests are compounded out of *desires* and *aims,* both of which presuppose something like *belief,* or cognitive awareness. . . .

WHOLE SPECIES

The topic of whole species, whether of plants or animals, can be treated in much the same way as that of individual plants. A whole collection, as such, cannot have beliefs, expectations, wants, or desires, and can flourish or languish only in the human interest-related sense in which individual plants thrive and decay. Individual elephants can have interests, but the species elephant cannot. Even where individual elephants are not granted rights, human beings may have an interest—economic, scientific or sentimental—in keeping the species from dying out, and *that* interest may be protected in various ways by law. But that is quite another matter from recognizing a right to survival belonging to the species itself. Still, the preservation of a whole species may quite properly seem to be a morally more important matter than the preservation of an individual animal. Individual animals can have rights but it is implausible to ascribe to them a right to life on the human model. Nor do we normally have duties to keep individual animals alive or even to abstain from killing them provided we do it humanely and nonwantonly in the promotion of legitimate human interests. On the other hand, we do have duties to protect threatened species, not duties to the species themselves as such, but rather duties to future human beings, duties derived from our house-keeping role as temporary inhabitants of this planet. . . .

FUTURE GENERATIONS

We have it in our power now to make the world a much less pleasant place for our descendants than the world we inherited from our ancestors. We can continue to proliferate in ever greater numbers, using up fertile soil at an even greater rate, dumping our wastes into rivers, lakes, and oceans, cutting down our forests, and polluting the atmosphere with noxious gases. All thoughtful people agree that we ought not to do these things. Most would say that we have a duty not to do these things, meaning not merely that conservation is morally required (as opposed to merely desirable) but also that it is something due our descendants, something to be done for their sakes. Surely we owe it to future generations to pass on a world that is not a used up garbage heap. Our remote descendants are not yet present to claim a livable world as their right, but there are plenty of proxies to speak now in their behalf. These spokesmen, far from being mere custodians, are genuine representatives of future interests.

Why then deny that the human beings of the future have rights which can be claimed against us now in their behalf? Some are inclined to deny them present rights out of a fear of falling into obscure metaphysics, by granting rights to remote and unidentifiable beings who are not yet even in existence. Our unborn great-great-grandchildren are in some sense "potential" persons, but they are far more remotely potential, it may seem, than fetuses. This, however, is not the real difficulty. Unborn generations are more remotely potential than fetuses in one sense, but not in another. A much greater period of time with a far greater number of causally necessary and important events must pass before their potentiality can be actualized, it is true; but our collective posterity is just as certain to come into existence "in the normal course of events" as is any given fetus now in its mother's womb. In that sense the existence of the distant human future is no more remotely potential than that of a particular child already on its way.

The real difficulty is not that we doubt whether our descendants will ever be actual, but rather that we don't know who they will be. It is not their temporal remoteness that troubles us so much as their indeterminacy—their present facelessness and namelessness. Five centuries from now men and women will be living where we live now. Any given one of them will have an interest in living space, fertile soil, fresh air, and the like, but that arbitrarily selected one has no other qualities we can presently envision very clearly. We don't even know who his parents, grandparents, or great-grandparents are, or even whether he is related to us. Still, whoever these human beings may turn out to be, and whatever they might reasonably be expected to be like, they will have interests that we can affect, for better or worse, right now. That much we can and do know about them. The identity of the owners of these interests is now necessarily obscure, but the fact of their interest-ownership is crystal clear, and that is all that is necessary to certify the coherence of present talk about their rights. We can tell, sometimes, that shadowy forms in the spatial distance belong to human beings, though we know not who or how many they are; and this imposes a duty on us not to throw bombs, for example, in their direction. In like manner, the vagueness of the human future does not weaken its claim on us in light of the nearly certain knowledge that it will, after all, be human.

Doubts about the existence of a right to be born transfer neatly to the question of a similar right to come into existence ascribed to future generations. The rights that future generations certainly have against us are contingent rights: the interests they are sure to have when they come into being (assuming of course that they will come into being) cry out for protection from invasions that can take place now. Yet there are no actual interests, presently existent, that future generations, presently nonexistent, have now. Hence, there is no actual interest that they have in simply coming into being, and I am at a loss to think of any other reason for claiming that they have a right to come into existence (though there may well be such a reason). Suppose then that all human beings at a given time voluntarily form a compact never again to produce children, thus leading within a few decades to the end of our species. This of course is a wildly improbable hypothetical example but a rather crucial one for the position I have been tentatively considering. And we can imagine, say, that the whole world is converted to a strange ascetic religion which absolutely requires sexual abstinence for everyone. Would this arrangement violate the rights of anyone? No one can complain on behalf of presently nonexistent future generations that their future interests which give them a contingent right of protection have been violated since they will never come into existence to be wronged. My inclination then is to conclude that the suicide of our species would be deplorable, lamentable, and a deeply moving tragedy, but that it would violate no one's rights. Indeed if, contrary to fact, all human beings could ever agree to such a thing, that very agreement would be a symptom of our species' biological unsuitability for survival anyway.

For several centuries now human beings have run roughshod over the lands of our planet, just as if the animals who do live there and the generations of humans who will live there had no claims on them whatever. Philosophers have not helped matters by arguing that animals and future generations are not the kinds of beings who can have rights now, that they don't presently qualify for membership, even "auxiliary membership," in our moral community. I have tried in this essay to dispel the conceptual confusions that make such conclusions possible. To acknowledge their rights is the very least we can do for members of endangered species (including our own). But that is something.

Notes

1. I shall leave the concept of a claim unanalyzed here, but for a detailed discussion, see my "The Nature and Value of Rights," *Journal of Value Inquiry*, 4 (Winter 1971): 263–277.
2. Louis B. Schwartz, "Morals, Offenses and the Model Penal Code," *Columbia Law Review*, 63 (1963): 673.
3. John Chipman Gray, *The Nature and Sources of the Law*, 2d ed. (Boston: Beacon Press, 1963), p. 43.
4. And W. D. Ross for another. See *The Right and the Good* (Oxford: Clarendon Press, 1930), app. 1, pp. 48–56.
5. W. D. Lamont, *Principles of Moral Judgment* (Oxford: Clarendon Press, 1946), pp. 83–85.
6. Cf. H. J. McCloskey, "Rights," *Philosophical Quarterly*, 15 (1965): 121, 124.
7. Outside of Samuel Butler's *Erewhon.*

POLLUTION, CONSERVATION, AND POSTERITY

John Passmore

The conservationist programme confronts us with a fundamental moral issue: ought we to pay any attention to the needs of posterity? To answer this question affirmatively is to make two assumptions: first, that

Excerpt from *Man's Responsibility for Nature* by John Passmore is reprinted with the permission of Charles Scribner's Sons, New York and Duckworth & Co., Ltd., London. Copyright © 1974 John Passmore.

posterity will suffer unless we do so; secondly that if it will suffer, it is our duty so to act as to prevent or mitigate its sufferings. Both assumptions can be, and have been, denied. To accept them does not, of course, do anything to solve the problem of conservation, but to reject them is to deny that there is any such problem, to deny that our society would be a better one—morally better—if it were to halt the rate at which it is at present exhausting its resources. Or it is to deny this, at least, in so far as the arguments in favour of slowing-down are purely conservationist in character—ignoring for the moment, that is, such facts as that the lowering of the consumption-rate is one way of reducing the incidence of pollution and that a high rate of consumption of metals and fossil fuels makes it impossible to preserve untouched the wildernesses in which they are so often located.

To begin with the assumption that posterity will suffer unless we alter our ways, it is still often suggested that, on the contrary, posterity can safely be left to look after itself, provided only that science and technology continue to flourish. This optimistic interpretation of the situation comes especially from economists and from nuclear physicists. . . . If these scientists, these economists, are right, there simply is no "problem of conservation."

Very many scientists, of course, take the opposite view, especially if they are biologists. Expert committees set up by such scientific bodies as the American National Academy of Sciences have, in fact, been prepared to commit themselves to definite estimates of the dates at which this resource or that will be exhausted. This is always, however, on certain assumptions. It makes a considerable difference whether one supposes or denies that rates of consumption will continue to increase exponentially as they have done since 1960; it makes a very great—in many cases an overwhelming—difference whether one supposes or denies that substitutes will be discovered for our major resources. The Academy's extrapolations are best read as a *reductio ad absurdum* of the supposition that our present patterns of resource consumption can continue even over the next century.

The possibility that substitutes will be discovered introduces a note of uncertainty into the whole discussion, an uncertainty which cannot be simply set aside as irrelevant to our moral and political decisions about conservation, which it inevitably and properly influences. At the moment, for example, the prospect of developing a fuel-cell to serve as a substitute for petrol is anything but bright; confident predictions that by 1972 nuclear fusion would be available as an energy source have proved to be unrealistic. But who can say what the situation will be in twenty years time? The now commonplace comparison of earth to a space-ship is thus far misleading: the space-ship astronaut does not have the facilities to invent new techniques, nor can he fundamentally modify his habits of consumption. Any adequate extrapolation would also have to extrapolate technological advances. But by the nature of the case—although technologists have a bad habit of trying to persuade us otherwise—we cannot be at all certain when and whether those advances will take place, or what form they will assume, especially when, unlike the moonshots, they involve fundamental technological innovations such as the containing of nuclear fusion within a magnetic field.

No doubt, the space-ship analogy is justified as a protest against the pronouncements of nineteenth-century rhetoricians that the earth's resources are "limitless" or "boundless." (It was often supposed, one must recall, that oil was being produced underground as fast as it was being consumed.) Fuel-cells, nuclear fusion reactors, machinery for harnessing solar energy all have to be built out of materials, including, as often as not, extremely rare metals. Men can learn to substitute one source of energy or one metallic alloy for another, the more plentiful for the less plentiful. But that is the most they can do. They cannot harness energy without machines, without radiating heat, without creating wastes. Nor can they safely presume that no source of energy, no metal, is indispensable; there is nothing either in the structure of nature or in the structure of human intelligence to ensure that new resources will *always* be available to replace old resources. Think how dependent we still are on the crops our remote agriculture-creating forefathers chose to cultivate; we have not found substitutes for wheat, or barley, or oats, or rice. Nor have we domesticated new animals as beasts of burden. So, quite properly, the conservationist points out.

The uncertainties, however, remain. We can be confident that some day our society will run out of resources, but we do not know when it will do so or what resources it will continue to demand. The Premier of Queensland recently swept aside the protests of conservationists by arguing that Queensland's oil and coal resources should be fully utilised now, since posterity may have no need for them. This is not a wholly irrational attitude. One can readily see the force of an argument which would run thus: we are entitled, given the uncertainty of the future, wholly to ignore the interests of posterity, a posterity whose very existence is hypothetical —granted the possibility of a nuclear disaster—and whose needs, except for such fundamentals as air and water, we cannot possibly anticipate. . . .

We are called upon not to waste those resources our successors will certainly need. But we ought not to act, out of concern for posterity's survival, in ways which are likely to destroy the civilised ideals we hope posterity will share with us. We should try so to act that our successors will not be wholly without electricity, but we need not, should not, close down our civilisation merely in the hope that a remote posterity will have some hope of surviving. . . .

But what sort of sacrifices ought we to make? It follows from what I have already said that we ought not to be prepared, in the supposed interests of posterity, to surrender our loves or the freedom which makes their exercise possible, to give up art, or philosophy, or science, or personal relationships, in order to conserve resources for posterity. Posterity will need our loves as much as we need them; it needs chains of love running to and through it. . . . Those who urge us to surrender our freedom and to abandon our loves so that posterity can enjoy a "true freedom" and a "true love" ought never to be trusted. No doubt, as individuals, we might sometimes have to sacrifice our freedom or certain of our loves. But only to ensure their maintenance and development by others. And this is true, I should argue, even if they can be maintained only at the cost of human suffering—although there is in fact no evidence to suggest that we shall save posterity from suffering by surrendering our freedoms.

The surrender of forms of enjoyment is a different matter. What we would be called upon to do, at this level, is to reduce the consumption of certain goods—those which depend on raw materials which cannot be effectively recycled—and to recycle whenever that is possible, even although the costs of doing so would involve the sacrifice of other goods. That is the kind of sacrifice we ought to be prepared to make, if there is a real risk that it is essential for the continued existence of a posterity able to carry on the activities we love. . . .

Intent on maximising their profits, particular industries will certainly do what they can to prevent or to render ineffective anti-pollution legislation, just as they opposed laws laying down minimum sanitary or safety measures in factories. In so far as they restrict themselves to argument, one might even say that it is their *responsibility* to oppose; if a society is to arrive at the optimal situation at which pollution is reduced to a tolerable level at the minimum cost, someone needs to emphasise the costs, as distinct from the benefits, of anti-pollution measures. (It is not inhumanly complacent to be content with a "tolerable level" of pollution; to demand that the Thames or the Rhine be drinkable without filtration would be, at least in my judgment, totally absurd.) . . .

The corporation, too, is a powerful and permanent institution; anti-pollution campaigns depend on the energy and zeal of a few energetic people, often enthusiasts who have not the patience to conduct a long campaign. The corporations often lose the initial battles but win the war. It would be wrong to be either complacent or cynical about the outcome of anti-pollution campaigns. The prospects are at their worst when corporations and trade unions share the opposition. Particular battles will certainly be lost. But at least democratic societies provide mechanisms of protest and agitation which are wholly absent in any of their actual alternatives. And can we even imagine a society so constituted that within it no anti-pollution battle could ever be lost? (Not to raise the further question whether there is any ground whatever for believing that such a society, were it imaginable, would in fact arise out of the flames of our present society.)

Political resistance to anti-pollution programmes, it is worth observing in this context, does not only come from "big corporations." The history of aborted anti-pollution measures in the United States—as told in James Ridgeway's *The Politics of Ecology*—is basically a tale of political manoeuvres, of battles between the Federal Government and the States, between Congress and the White House, of the influence exerted by government agencies, especially the Corps of Army Engineers. Such power conflicts are not confined to democracies; as so often, the striking thing about the United States is the degree to which conflicts are there made public which in other societies are successfully concealed behind closed doors. The disappearance of large corporations, then, would not necessarily bring with it the death of all opposition to anti-pollution measures: conflicts between government agencies can be quite as significant as conflicts between reformers and corporations, a National Electricity Board quite as given to polluting as a private corporation.

SUGGESTED SUPPLEMENTARY READINGS

ACKERMAN, ROBERT W. *The Social Challenge to Business.* Cambridge, Mass.: Harvard University Press, 1975.

BARBOUR, IAN G., ed. *Western Man and Environmental Ethics.* Reading, Mass.: Addison-Wesley Publishing Co., 1973.

BLACKSTONE, WILLIAM T., ed. *Philosophy and Environmental Crisis.* Athens: University of Georgia Press, 1974.

COMMONER, BARRY. *The Closing Circle.* New York: Alfred A. Knopf, 1971.

DUBOS, RENÉ, and BARBARA WARD. *Only One Earth.* New York: W. W. Norton and Co., 1972.

JACOBY, NEIL H. *Corporate Power and Social Responsibility,* Chapter 10. New York: Macmillan Publishing Co., 1973.

KAPP, K. WILLIAM. *The Social Costs of Private Enterprise.* New York: Schocken Books, 1971.

NEW YORK ACADEMY OF SCIENCES. *Public Policy Toward Environment 1973: A Review and Appraisal. Annals of the New York Academy of Sciences,* 216 (May 1973).

PASSMORE, JOHN. *Man's Responsibility for Nature.* New York: Charles Scribner's Sons, 1974.

————. "Removing the Rubbish." *Encounter,* April 1974.

ROLSTON, HOLMES. "Is There an Ecologic Ethic?" *Ethics,* 85 (January 1975).

ROUTLEY, VAL."Critical Notice: Passmore's *Man's Responsibility for Nature." Australasian Journal of Philosophy,* 53 (August 1975).

SAGOFF, MARK. "On Preserving the Natural Environment." *The Yale Law Journal,* 84 (December 1974).

SAYRE, KENNETH, ed. *Values in the Electric Power Industry.* Notre Dame, Ind.: University of Notre Dame Press, 1977.

SCHUMAKER, E. F. *Small Is Beautiful.* New York: Harper and Row, 1973.

TRIBE, LAWRENCE. "Ways Not to Think About Plastic Trees." *The Yale Law Journal,* 83 (1974).

WHITE, LYNN. "The Historical Roots of Our Ecologic Crisis." *Science,* 155 (March 10, 1967).

Chapter 9

PREFERENTIAL HIRING AND REVERSE DISCRIMINATION

case 1: The A. T. & T. Settlement Case

In January 1971 the Equal Employment Opportunity Commission (EEOC) brought charges of discrimination (to the Federal Communications Commission) against American Telephone and Telegraph Co. (A. T. & T.) on grounds of discrimination in hiring and promotion. A. T. & T. denied the charges and adduced statistics showing (1) that 12.4 percent of its work force was from minority groups, (2) that while only 2.9 percent of its management positions were held by minorities, 9.3 percent of those recently promoted were from minority groups, (3) that women constituted 55.5 percent of all employees and 33.5 percent of the management and professional staff, etc. Meanwhile, women workers became upset over a contract negotiated by their own union that apparently offered better pay for craft jobs that were held mostly by men. Women's salaries would have been set at roughly 65 percent of those for men (by the women's calculations). While union and management began negotiations, the EEOC pressed charges.

A. T. & T. produced 100,000 pages of documents and statistical arguments intended to prove its innocence, and the EEOC filed 30,000 pages of counterargument. The EEOC not only supported the women's charges of economic discrimination, but argued that sex stereotyping was prevalent in hiring and promotion. They argued that the company was set up to funnel women into operators' jobs and men into management positions. A. T. & T. argued that what it did was no different than airlines' practices of training stewardesses and pilots and adduced statistics to prove its point. The EEOC in turn used statistics to show that 99.9 percent of all operators were female, only 1.1 percent of (more highly paid) craft workers were female, etc. Meanwhile, at least one other government office (the GSA) expressed disagreement with the EEOC position, finding an equal employment plan submitted by A. T. & T. highly favorable.

Eventually A. T. & T. settled with the EEOC out of court. Though complicated, the main provision was that A. T. & T. would pay lump sums of money totaling $15 million to 13,000 of its female and 2,000 of its male employees who had suffered discrimination and would grant $23 million in pay increases to 36,000 workers who had suffered from job discrimination (plus a commitment of $25–35 million over another five-year period). The Bell System further agreed to alter its patterns of hiring and to set goals and timetables to upgrade female and minority employees. However, Bell never formally admitted that it was guilty of any charges brought by the EEOC.

case 2:   The Teamsters—T.I.M.E. Case

In 1977 a case reached the United States Supreme Court that had been brought by the government against both an employer (T.I.M.E.—D.C.) and the Teamsters Union, which represented the company's employees. The government argued that there existed a pattern of discrimination in hiring blacks and Spanish-surnamed persons and that the union seniority system perpetuated the effects of past discrimination in hiring, assignment, and promotion. The government argued that these minorities were consistently assigned to lower-paying positions and consistently never promoted to higher-paying positions. The charge was that a "pattern or practice" of discrimination existed in the recruitment, hiring, transferring, and promoting of its minority employees. The union and the employer both denied this charge.

The case for or against a finding of discriminatory treatment turned on whether statistical differences in the employment of groups were "racially premised." The government bore the burden of proof and thus was required to show that the company's standard operating procedure was to discriminate. The government argued as follows: They contended that the company hired 5 percent blacks and 4 percent Spanish-surnamed persons, but placed only 0.4 percent of blacks and 0.3 percent of Spanish-surnamed persons in the higher-paying positions. All of the blacks had been hired after the issue was taken to court, and no black had ever been employed on a regular basis by the company until 1969. (Action in this case began as early as 1970.) The government also gave evidence of 40 instances of discrimination, largely by the testimony of those allegedly discriminated against. These were usually cases where requests by minority members to be hired or advanced were simply ignored.

The company argued in response that the government's entire case was based on statistical findings and hearsay, and that these alone are never sufficient to establish a "pattern or practice of discrimination." The Supreme Court held, however, that the government's statistics were a valid and sufficient indicator of discriminatory practices and found against the union and the employer.

INTRODUCTION

In recent years government policies that are intended to ensure fairer opportunities for women and minority groups have provoked sustained controversy. Target goals, timetables, and quotas seem to many citizens not merely to be preferential treatment but actually to discriminate against more talented applicants who are excluded yet would be hired or accepted on their merits were it not for the preferential advancement of others. Such government policies are said to create a situation of "reverse discrimination." By balancing or compensating for past discrimination against persons on the basis of (morally irrelevant) characteristics such as race, sex, nationality, and religion, these policies now require discrimination in favor of such persons and therefore against the members of other previously favored classes. These policies seem unfairly discriminatory to some because they violate basic principles of justice and equal protection. Others believe this conclusion to be incorrect for a variety of reasons. In this chapter we will study whether some compulsory government policies and even some policies voluntarily adopted by private industry would result in preferential treatment of persons and, if so, whether such policies are appropriate and justifiable.

Several articles in this chapter—those by Keith Davis and Robert Blomstrom, Jules Cohn, Sidney Hook, and J. Stanley Pottinger—address the issues that have emerged from recent congressional, executive, and judicial determinations. These issues include the moral and legal responsibilities of business to eradicate discrimination, and the problem of whether there should be hiring quotas. The responsibilities of business and the problems in its present hiring practices are addressed by Davis and Blomstrom and by Cohn, while Hook and Pottinger address issues of the role and responsibilities of the federal government. It gradually becomes apparent in these articles that most of the contemporary controversy about hiring centers on (1) affirmative action programs and (2) programs that might result in reverse discrimination. It is sometimes said in popular literature that "affirmative action" is synonymous with "reverse discrimination," but this equation of meaning is probably mistaken, as we shall now see.

AFFIRMATIVE ACTION AND REVERSE DISCRIMINATION

"Affirmative action" basically means the taking of positive steps to hire persons from groups previously discriminated against in educational and employment situations. Passive nondiscrimination, as Davis and Blomstrom characterize it, is not sufficient to qualify as affirmative action. Federal requirements at a minimum impose on business the responsibility to advertise jobs fairly and to seek out members of those groups discriminated against in the past for employment. As Pottinger and Hook discuss, the projected means for the fulfillment of these responsibilities are called employment *goals*. A "goal" in this context is a targeted employment outcome (intended to eliminate discrimination) that is planned by an institution (probably after consultation with government officials). A goal is commonly distinguished from a *quota,* which is construed in this context as a hard and fast figure or proportion—usually expressed in percentages. Goals and quotas sound to many ears like the same thing, and it is often difficult to know which an author has in mind. However, one fact seems clear: there is a crucial *symbolic* difference between the two. Goals have come largely to symbolize federally mandated or negotiated targets and timetables, whereas quotas have come largely to symbolize policies resulting in reverse discrimination. But what is "reverse discrimination" and how does it differ from both "affirmative action" and "preferential hiring"?

Writers on the subject of reverse discrimination often use the term "reverse discrimination" in different ways. At a minimum this term means discrimination by one person or set of persons P_1 against another set of persons P_2, where P_2 formerly had discriminated against P_1. Some also assert or assume that, by definition, reverse discrimination occurs only as a result of policies involving *blanket* preferential treatment on the basis of sex or race for whole groups of persons who are members of those classes. Yet this understanding of reverse discrimination is questionable on at least two counts. First, properties other than race or sex may be used—religion or nationality, for example. Second, and more importantly, there is no reason why (by definition) a policy of compensation resulting in a reversal of discrimination must apply in blanket fashion to whole groups rather than more restrictedly to a limited number of individuals who are members of those groups. Suppose an industry-wide preferential policy were adopted that competitively advantaged the job applications of all blacks earning less than $10,000 per year (and which discriminated against competitive whites earning equivalent amounts) but did not advantage blacks who earned more than that figure. This policy would certainly qualify as reverse discrimination (based on race), but the *entire* racial group would not have been given blanket preferential treatment.

This issue is important because it is often said that affluent women and minority group members would be advantaged, and disadvantaged poor whites or males would be discriminated against, by preferential hiring policies. Some authors have seemed to favor this possible outcome: "The mere fact of a person's being black in the United States is a sufficient reason for providing compensatory techniques even though that person may in some ways appear fortunate in his personal background."[1] But this is a particular *moral* thesis about the justifiability of reverse discrimination. It does not explicate necessary features of the term's *meaning*. Hence, one can advocate even radical policies of compensation resulting in reverse discrimination and at the same time advocate nonblanket, perhaps highly restrictive policies of preferential treatment. This issue, though without this conclusion, is discussed in Robert Simon's critique of Judith Thomson in this chapter.

We can now summarize the basic outlines of the concept of reverse discrimination as follows: reverse discrimination is a discriminatory action or practice based on a (normally) morally irrelevant property; policies resulting in reverse discrimination may also apply to individual persons and/or groups and need not involve unqualified blanket preferential treatment; and, finally, any morally irrelevant property could be used—not simply race and sex.

It should also be noted that *both* minimal affirmative action programs *and* policies possibly productive of reverse discrimination involve what is referred to as "preferential hiring." This notion refers to hiring that gives preference in recruitment and ranking to women, minority groups, and others previously discriminated against. This preference can be practiced either by the use of goals or quotas, or merely by choosing blacks, women, etc. whenever their credentials are *equal* to those of other candidates. However, "preferential hiring" carries connotations for some persons of reverse discrimination or at least of quotas. Accordingly, one should be careful to understand the term's exact use in any document or article in which it appears. This warning should be observed in the case of the two articles by Thomson and Simon in this chapter, both of which explicitly discuss preferential hiring.

MORAL ISSUES IN PREFERENTIAL POLICIES

We sometimes think that a severe injustice has been done to a *group* of persons. Naturally we wish to restore the balance of justice by compensating them for their loss. The *principle of compensatory justice* says that whenever an injustice has been committed, just compensation or reparation is owed the injured parties. It is now a widespread view that minority groups discriminated against in the past, including women, blacks, North American Indians, and French Canadians, should be recompensed for these injustices by compensatory policies such as affirmative action or equal opportunity programs. Whatever one may think of this proposal, it is not difficult to understand why this view is espoused. For years deliberate barriers or quotas were placed on opportunities for blacks, women, and other groups to participate in some of society's most desirable institutions (universities, business, law, etc.). In addition, even when barriers were formally dropped matters often did not improve. Inequalities, many came to think, are rooted in early training in public schools or in unfair testing. They further charged that our systems of screening and promotion discriminate not intentionally *against* certain groups so much as unintentionally *in favor of* other groups. All of these factors have conspired to produce a range of government programs, all of which are in effect compensatory measures.

Because of this history of discrimination and its persistence, it is widely believed that we could restore the balance of justice by making it easier for previously discriminated-against groups to obtain admission to educational institutions and job interviews. Presumably, special programs also avoid the problem of mere *token* approval of more equal distribution. This system seems clearly, however, to involve an extensive network of preferential treatments, and many have asked the following question about it: If quotas or social policies require that, for example, a woman or a black be given preference over a white man otherwise better qualified (i.e., if the circumstances had been anonymous the white man would have been selected), is this an acceptable instance of compensatory justice or is it a pure and simple case of treating the white man unjustly? In answer to this question it has been argued in various ways by some that such practices of preferential treatment are (a) just, (b) unjust, or (c) not just but permitted by principles other than our concepts of justice and equality.

a. Those who claim that such compensatory measures are just, or perhaps required by justice, argue that the past lives in the present: the victims of past discrimination against blacks are still handicapped or discriminated against, while the families of past slave owners are still being unduly enriched by inheritance laws. Those who have inherited wealth which was accumulated by iniquitous practices do not have as much right to the wealth, it is argued, as do the sons of slaves, who at least have a right of compensation. In the case of women it is argued that culture equips them with a lack of self-confidence, prejudicially excludes them from much of the work force, and treats them as a low-paid auxiliary labor unit. Hence only extraordinarily independent women can be expected to compete even psychologically with males. Sometimes a slightly stronger argument is advanced: compensation is fair even if some inequalities cannot be removed by offering the best available training measures. The compensation is said to be fair simply because it is *owed* to those who in the past suffered unjust treatment. As Judith Thomson argues in this chapter, we may think veterans are owed preferential treatment because of their service and sacrifice to country, and thus we may similarly think blacks and women are owed preferential treatment because of their economic sacrifices, systematic incapacitation, and consequent personal and group losses.

b. Those who claim that compensatory measures are unjust argue variously that no criteria exist for measuring compensation, that the extent of discrimination is now minor (insufficiently broad to justify preferential treatment), and that none of those actually harmed in previous eras is available now to be compensated. Instead of providing compensation, they argue, we should continue to guide justice by strict equality and merit, while attacking the roots of discrimination. Also, some now successful but once underprivileged minority groups argue that their long struggle for equality is jeopardized by programs of "favoritism" to blacks and women. Their view is that they either will suffer unfairly, having already suffered enough, or else will not suffer only because they too will be compensated for past oppressions. Is it not absurd, they say, to suggest that *all* past oppressed groups—blacks and women being only two among a great many—should receive compensatory reparations? Are we not compounding initial injustices with a vastly complicated system of further injustices? Some of these arguments are carefully developed in the articles below by Robert Simon and William Blackstone.

c. The third possible view is that some strong compensatory measures are *not just,* because they violate principles of justice, and yet *are justifiable* by appeal to principles other than justice. This view is argued in this chapter by Tom Beauchamp. Because his argument is a straightforward attempt to justify reverse discriminatory policies in general, we may now shift to this topic.

THE MORAL PROBLEM OF REVERSE DISCRIMINATION

Among those writers who would permit policies of reverse discrimination, a fairly standard approach is taken: They attempt to justify reverse discrimination by showing that under certain conditions compensation owed for *past* wrongs justifies (for varying reasons) *present* policies productive of reverse discrimination. Judith Thomson takes one form of this approach in this chapter. By contrast, Beauchamp argues that because of past wrongs to classes of persons, we have special and strong obligations to see that these wrongs do not continue. His argument differs from Thomson's and the more usual ones based on compensatory justice because he holds that reverse discrimination is permitted and even required in order that we might eliminate *present* discriminatory practices against classes of persons. He adduces factual evidence for his claim of present, continuing discrimination, and this evidence in turn is supposed to support his claim that reverse discrimination is sometimes justified. Beauchamp's larger ethical contention is that because these larger social conditions prevail, policies producing reverse discrimination are justified. These policies are morally *permitted* because they are social measures necessary for the protection of those harmed by invidious social attitudes and selection procedures. This argument—in the language of the first chapter of this book—is a utilitarian argument. In the final selection in this chapter William T. Blackstone argues against utilitarian justifications of reverse discrimination, on grounds that principles of justice override the principle of utility. Blackstone and Beauchamp thus come into direct controversy over a fundamental issue in ethical theory: utilitarian versus nonutilitarian justifications.

Blackstone and many other opponents of policies that might result in reverse discrimination argue that reverse discrimination violates fundamental and overriding principles of justice. It is argued in this literature that since reverse discriminatory policies create injustices, they cannot be justified. The most widely argued thesis is that policies productive of reverse discrimination violate the equality of persons by discriminating for or against a group, thus favoring them with special privileges and damaging the rule of law by replacing it with power struggles. Other reasons proposed as supplementary to this primary argument include the following: (1) Some who are innocent of and not responsible for the past invidious discrimination pay the price (e.g., qualified young white males); but this treatment is discriminatory because such persons are penalized solely on the basis of their race. (2) Male members of minority groups such as Poles, Irish, and Italians—themselves discriminated against in the past—will bear a heavy and unfair burden of the cost of compensating women and minority groups such as blacks. (3) Many members of the *class* selected for preferential treatment will have never themselves been unjustly treated and will not deserve preferential policies. (4) There are some relevant differences between the sexes which justify differential expectations and treatment (men are naturally better at some things, women at others). (5) Compensation can be provided to *individuals* treated unfairly in the past without resort to reverse discrimination, which is the result of blanket treatment for groups. The last reason (5) is presumably not only a reason against reverse discrimination, but an alternative *policy,* as well.

As indicated by the two cases of discrimination in hiring placed just prior to this introduction and by the court cases included as early selections in this chapter, the problem of preferential hiring remains a troublesome and surprisingly complicated issue.

T.L.B.

Note

1. Graham Hughes, "Reparations for Blacks?" *New York University Law Review,* 43 (December 1968), 1073.

OPINION IN GRIGGS v. DUKE POWER CO.

Chief Justice Warren Burger

We granted the writ in this case to resolve the question whether an employer is prohibited by the Civil Rights Act of 1964, Title VII, from requiring a high school education or passing of a standardized general intelligence test as a condition of employment in or transfer to jobs when (a) neither standard is shown to be significantly related to successful job performance, (b) both requirements operate to disqualify Negroes at a substantially higher rate than white applicants, and (c) the jobs in question formerly had been filled only by white employees as part of a long-standing practice of giving preference to whites.

Congress provided, in Title VII of the Civil Rights Act of 1964, for class actions for enforcement of provisions of the Act and this proceeding was brought by a group of incumbent Negro employees against Duke Power Company. All the petitioners are employed at the Company's Dan River Steam Station, a power generating facility located at Draper, North Carolina. At the time this action was instituted, the Company had 95 employees at the Dan River Station, 14 of whom were Negroes; 13 of these are petitioners here.

The District Court found that prior to July 2, 1965, the effective date of the Civil Rights Act of 1964, the Company openly discriminated on the basis of race in the hiring and assigning of employees at its Dan River plant. The plant was organized into five operating departments: (1) Labor, (2) Coal Handling, (3) Operations, (4) Maintenance, and (5) Laboratory and Test. Negroes were employed only in the Labor Department, where the highest paying jobs paid less than the lowest paying jobs in the other four "operating" departments, in which only whites were employed. Promotions were normally made within each department on the basis of job seniority. Transferees into a department usually began in the lowest position.

In 1955 the Company instituted a policy of requiring a high school education for initial assignment to any department except Labor, and for transfer from the Coal Handling to any "inside" department (Operations, Maintenance, or Laboratory). When the Company abandoned its policy of restricting Negroes to the Labor Department in 1965, completion of high school also was made a prerequisite to transfer from Labor to any other department. From the time the high school requirement was instituted to the time of trial, however, white employees hired before the time of the high school education requirement continued to perform satisfactorily and achieve promotions in the "operating" departments. Findings on this score are not challenged.

The Company added a further requirement for new employees on July

401 US 424 (1970).

2, 1965, the date on which Title VII became effective. To qualify for placement in any but the Labor Department it became necessary to register satisfactory scores on two professionally prepared aptitude tests, as well as to have a high school education. Completion of high school alone continued to render employees eligible for transfer to the four desirable departments from which Negroes had been excluded if the incumbent had been employed prior to the time of the new requirement. In September 1965 the Company began to permit incumbent employees who lacked a high school education to qualify for transfer from Labor or Coal Handling to an "inside" job by passing two tests—the Wonderlic Personnel Test, which purports to measure general intelligence, and the Bennett Mechanical Comprehension Test. Neither was directed or intended to measure the ability to learn to perform a particular job or category of jobs. The requisite scores used for both initial hiring and transfer approximated the national median for high school graduates. . . .

The objective of Congress in the enactment of Title VII is plain from the language of the statute. It was to achieve equality of employment opportunities and remove barriers that have operated in the past to favor an identifiable group of white employees over other employees. Under the Act, practices, procedures, or tests neutral on their face, and even neutral in terms of intent, cannot be maintained if they operate to "freeze" the status quo of prior discriminatory employment practices.

The Court of Appeals' opinion, and the partial dissent, agreed that, on the record in the present case, "whites register far better on the Company's alternative requirements" than Negroes. This consequence would appear to be directly traceable to race. Basic intelligence must have the means of articulation to manifest itself fairly in a testing process. Because they are Negroes, petitioners have long received inferior education in segregated schools and this Court expressly recognized these differences in *Gaston County* v. *United States*, 395 U. S. 285 (1969). . . . Congress did not intend by Title VII, however, to guarantee a job to every person regardless of qualifications. In short, the Act does not command that any person be hired simply because he was formerly the subject of discrimination, or because he is a member of a minority group. Discriminatory preference for any group, minority or majority, is precisely and only what Congress has proscribed. What is required by Congress is the removal of artificial, arbitrary, and unnecessary barriers to employment when the barriers operate invidiously to discriminate on the basis of racial or other impermissible classification.

. . . The Act proscribes not only overt discrimination but also practices that are fair in form, but discriminatory in operation. The touchstone is business necessity. If an employment practice which operates to exclude Negroes cannot be shown to be related to job performance, the practice is prohibited.

On the record before us, neither the high school completion requirement nor the general intelligence test is shown to bear a demonstrable relationship to successful performance of the jobs for which it was used. Both were adopted, as the Court of Appeals noted, without meaningful study of their relationship to job-performance ability. Rather, a vice president of the Company testified, the requirements were instituted on the Company's judgment that they generally would improve the overall quality of the work force.

The evidence, however, shows that employees who have not completed high school or taken the tests have continued to perform satisfactorily and make progress in departments for which the high school and test criteria are now used. The promotion record of present employees who would not be able to meet the new criteria thus suggests the possibility that the requirements may not be needed even for the limited purpose of preserving the avowed policy of advancement within the Company. . . .

The Court of Appeals held that the Company had adopted the diploma and test requirements without any "intention to discriminate against Negro employees." We do not suggest that either the District Court or the Court of Appeals erred in examining the employer's intent; but good intent or absence of discriminatory intent does not redeem employment procedures or testing mechanisms that operate as "built-in headwinds" for minority groups and are unrelated to measuring job capability.

The Company's lack of discriminatory intent is suggested by special efforts to help the undereducated employees through Company financing of two-thirds the cost of tuition for high school training. But Congress directed the thrust of the Act to the *consequences* of employment practices, not simply the motivation. More than that, Congress has placed on the employer the burden of showing that any given requirement must have a manifest relationship to the employment in question.

The facts of this case demonstrate the inadequacy of broad and general testing devices as well as the infirmity of using diplomas or degrees as fixed measures of capability. History is filled with examples of men and women who rendered highly effective performance without the conventional badges of accomplishment in terms of certificates, diplomas, or degrees. Diplomas and tests are useful servants, but Congress has mandated the commonsense proposition that they are not to become masters of reality.

The Company contends that its general intelligence tests are specifically permitted by § 703 (h) of the Act. That section authorizes the use of "any professionally developed ability test" that is not "designed, intended *or used* to discriminate because of race. . . ." [Emphasis added.]

The Equal Employment Opportunity Commission, having enforcement responsibility, has issued guidelines interpreting § 703 (h) to permit only the use of job-related tests. . . .

Nothing in the Act precludes the use of testing or measuring procedures; obviously they are useful. What Congress has forbidden is giving these devices and mechanisms controlling force unless they are demonstrably a reasonable measure of job performance. Congress has not commanded that the less qualified be preferred over the better qualified simply because of minority origins. Far from disparaging job qualifications as such, Congress has made such qualifications the controlling factor, so that race, religion, nationality, and sex become irrelevant. What

Congress has commanded is that any tests used must measure the person for the job and not the person in the abstract.

The judgment of the Court of Appeals is, as to that portion of the judgment appealed from, reversed.

OPINION IN MCDONALD v. SANTA FE TRAIL TRANSPORTATION CO.

Justice Thurgood Marshall

Petitioners L. N. McDonald and Raymond L. Laird brought this action in the United States District Court for the Southern District of Texas seeking relief against Santa Fe Trail Transportation Co. (Santa Fe) and International Brotherhood of Teamsters Local 988 . . . , which represented Santa Fe's Houston employees, for alleged violations of the Civil Rights Act of 1866, 42 U.S.C. § 1981, and of Title VII of the Civil Rights Act of 1964, 42 U. S. C. § 2000e *et seq.,* in connection with their discharge from Santa Fe's employment. . . . We must decide, first, whether a complaint alleging that white employees charged with misappropriating property from their employer were dismissed from employment, while a black employee similarly charged was not dismissed, states a claim under Title VII. Second, we must decide whether § 1981, which provides that "[a]ll persons . . . shall have the same right . . . to make and enforce contracts . . . as is enjoyed by white citizens . . ." affords protection from racial discrimination in private employment to white persons as well as nonwhites. . . .

I

. . . On September 26, 1970, petitioners, both white, and Charles Jackson, a Negro employee of Santa Fe, were jointly and severally charged with misappropriating 60 one-gallon cans of antifreeze which was part of a shipment Santa Fe was carrying for one of its customers. Six days later, petitioners were fired by Santa Fe, while Jackson was retained. A grievance was promptly filed with Local 988, pursuant to the collective-bargaining agreement between the two respondents, but grievance proceedings secured no relief. The following April, then, complaints were filed with the Equal Employment Opportunity Commission (EEOC)

US 75–260.

charging that Santa Fe had discriminated against both petitioners on the basis of their race in firing them, and that Local 988 had discriminated against McDonald on the basis of his race in failing properly to represent his interests in the grievance proceedings, all in violation of Title VII of the Civil Rights Act of 1964. Agency process proved equally unavailing for petitioners, however, and the EEOC notified them in July 1971 of their right under the Act to initiate a civil action in district court within 30 days. This suit followed, petitioners joining their § 1981 claim to their Title VII allegations.

Respondents moved to dismiss the complaint. . . .

II

Title VII of the Civil Rights Act of 1964 prohibits the discharge of "any individual" because of "such individual's race," § 703 (a)(1), 42 U.S.C. § 2000e–2 (a)(1). Its terms are not limited to discrimination against members of any particular race. Thus, although we were not there confronted with racial discrimination against whites, we described the Act in *Griggs* v. *Duke Power Co.,* 401 U. S. 424, 431 (1971), as prohibiting "[d]iscriminatory preference for *any* [racial] group, *minority* or *majority*" [emphasis added]. Similarly the EEOC, whose interpretations are entitled to great deference, *Griggs* v. *Duke Power Co.,* 401 U.S., at 433–434, has consistently interpreted Title VII to proscribe racial discrimination in private employment against whites on the same terms as racial discrimination against non-whites, holding that to proceed otherwise would

> "constitute a dereliction of the Congressional mandate to eliminate all practices which operate to disadvantage the employment opportunities of any group protected by Title VII, including Caucasians." [EEOC Decision No. 74–31, 7 FEP 1326, 1238, CCH EEOC Decisions ¶ 6406, p. 4084 (1973).]

This conclusion is in accord with uncontradicted legislative history to the effect that Title VII was intended to "cover all white men and white women and all Americans," 110 Cong. Rec. 2579 (remarks of Rep. Celler) (1969), and create an "obligation not to discriminate against whites," *id.,* at 7218 (memorandum of Sen. Clark). See also *id.,* at 7213 (memorandum of Sens. Clark and Case); *id.,* at 8912 (remarks of Sen. Williams). We therefore hold today that Title VII prohibits racial discrimination against the white petitioners in this case upon the same standards as would be applicable were they Negroes and Jackson white. . . .

. . . While Santa Fe may decide that participation in a theft of cargo may render an employee unqualified for employment, this criterion must be "applied, alike to members of all races," and Title VII is violated if, as petitioners alleged, it was not.

. . . The Act prohibits *all* racial discrimination in employment, without exception for any group of particular employees, and while crime or other misconduct may be a legitimate basis for discharge, it is hardly one for racial discrimination. . . .

... The same reasons which prohibit an employer from discriminating on the basis of race among the culpable employees apply equally to the Union; and whatever factors the mechanisms of compromise may legitimately take into account in mitigating discipline of some employees, under Title VII race may not be among them.

Thus, we conclude that the District Court erred in dismissing both petitioners' Title VII claims against Santa Fe, and petitioner McDonald's Title VII claim against Local 988.

BUSINESS, MINORITIES, AND LESS-ADVANTAGED PERSONS

Keith Davis
Robert L. Blomstrom

THE BUSINESS ROLE UNDER CIVIL RIGHTS LEGISLATION

Few would disagree with a social objective of achieving equal opportunity for all Americans. And indeed, equal opportunity became a firm national objective during the 1960s. In few other instances has the concept of functionalism been so clearly applied to a major social problem. Clearly the role of government was to establish objectives, formulate policies, and provide support which would enable business and other social institutions to achieve the objectives. It was equally clear that actual achievement of objectives lay not with government but with other social institutions that controlled opportunities for equality. Business, government, labor, and various nonprofit organizations controlled job opportunities; school systems controlled educational opportunities; city councils and other municipal agencies controlled housing opportunities, and so on. Since this [article] is about business, emphasis in our discussion will be on equal opportunity for jobs, although business can and does affect opportunities for the less-advantaged in other areas such as housing.

In its efforts to end discrimination in employment, government has relied on two major programs. One program was established by Title VII of the Civil Rights Act of 1964, which forbids discrimination on the basis of race, color, religion, sex, or national origin. The act also established the Equal Employment Opportunity Commission (EEOC), which, since 1972, has had the power to sue to bring about compliance. The other major federal program concerns businesses that contract with government and the special obligations imposed on them. This program originated under President Roosevelt in 1941, when, by executive order, he outlawed racial discrimination by defense contractors. Subsequent executive orders by other Presidents have broadened the coverage until now it affects every division of every company with a government contract of $10,000 or more. About 250,000 companies employing about one-third of the United States labor force are covered by the executive orders.[1] Compliance with these executive orders is the responsibility of the Department of Labor and is accomplished through the Office of Federal Contract Compliance (OFCC).

Thus, federal legislation has imposed upon business responsibilities to eliminate discrimination and equalize employment opportunities for all regardless of sex, race, religion, color, or national origin. It has imposed upon business a requirement for "affirmative action," that is, setting goals to eliminate discrimination and timetables for achieving those goals. Companies have responded in several ways. Some companies have adapted a posture of *passive nondiscrimination,* under which all decisions about hiring and promotion are made without regard to race or sex. This posture focuses on the present and future and does not consider the past. It does little to overcome past discrimination which leaves many potential employees unaware of present opportunities. Another approach to ending discrimination is *affirmative action.* Under this approach companies make every effort to ensure that employment opportunities are highly visible and to seek minorities for employment. While this approach enlarges the number of applicants, hiring and promotion decisions most often are made on the basis of qualifications for the job. A third approach is *affirmative action combined with preferential hiring,* which not only tries to expand the number of people from whom to choose, but also gives preference to women and minority groups in hiring and promotion. A fourth approach is to *establish hard quotas.* Unlike affirmative action with preferential hiring, which does not establish any particular numbers of disadvantaged who must be hired and/or promoted, hard quotas establish specific numbers or proportions which must be hired.

The Question of Employment Quotas

Two major questions concerning hiring of the less-advantaged have become troublesome for businessmen. One question is: Whatever became of merit? The second question is: Which posture toward employing the less-advantaged does government really want us to take? Each question is related to the other. Most government officials interpret civil rights legislation to mean nondiscrimination with affirmative action. However, in spite of the wording of the law there are many people in the United States today who favor preferential hiring and/or hard quotas, and they argue persuasively at times. One argument for establishing minority hiring quotas is that past discrimination against minorities and women entitles them to hiring and promotion advantages now.

A second argument admits that in an ideal world the only just method for hiring and promotion would be merit. However, in the real world of today, the criteria that make up merit are systematically denied to large portions of the population. Merit, as the word is generally defined, cannot be attained unless all have equal educational opportunities and equal opportunities to be hired. Merit cannot be attained unless cultural bias is removed from qualifying tests for employment.

Another argument for quotas is that traditionally hiring and promotion decisions are not made on the basis of objective and proven methods for assessing an applicant's qualifications. Hiring decisions of many employers are made on subjective and unproven criteria; thus racial and sexist stereotypes are created which exclude minorities and women regardless of their actual qualifications.

Yet another argument is that while progress has been made, discrimination still exists. For continued progress, minimum standards must be set, and when a minimum standard has been set, this is the same as setting a quota. Conversely, if no standards are set, there is not likely to be any more progress.

A Case Against Minority Employment Quotas

On the other side of the coin are the arguments opposing the establishment of hard quotas for minority hiring. One argument is simply that quotas are illegal. Civil rights legislation clearly forbids discrimination on the basis of membership in a group.

A second argument against quotas is that they promote hiring of less-qualified persons over those who are better qualified. A person should progress in life on ability, not appearance. In spite of the language of the law, quotas force employers to focus on color or sex rather than upon how well a person is qualified for the job.

Another argument against quotas is that they cause reverse discrimination. Quotas encourage discrimination in favor of minority groups, and it is impossible to discriminate *for* one group without discriminating *against* one or more other groups. Thus, the very nature of quotas produces discrimination against nonminority groups. Discrimination against some should not be remedied in our society by discriminating against others. A corollary to this argument is the question: If it is proper to establish quotas for blacks and women, why not do the same for Armenians, Orientals, and all the other groups who might be thought of as minority groups? And what about employees who because of religious beliefs do not work on Saturday or Sunday?

Another argument is that quotas are demeaning and paternalistic. The practice of hiring less-qualified minority-group members to meet a quota is likely to put a stamp of "less-qualified" on all members of that group. There is likely to be a question of the real abilities of all regardless of how well qualified individuals may be. This question is likely to be asked by white job applicants, customers, and the minority-group member himself.

A further argument is that quotas sometimes are construed as maximums rather than minimums, thus limiting opportunities for minorities. Quotas are sometimes viewed as ceilings above which minority proportions should not or need not go, rather than floors upon which greater opportunities for minorities should be built. However, when quotas are used, ceilings need to be applied, because if a quota for one group is exceeded, then it encroaches on some other minority's quota or the majority's quota.

Who are the Hard-Core Unemployed?

Discrimination, lack of education, and lack of industrial experience have created a large group of people who are known as the hard-core unemployed. They are poor, and they are unemployed. They find it difficult to qualify for most jobs and have given up the idea that "the system" can offer them any opportunities. The National Alliance of Businessmen has developed a profile of the hard-core unemployed, and while the profile may not fit all people who are classified as hard-core, those who are so classified meet most of the criteria. According to the NAB definition, a person classified as hard-core unemployed has never received intensive skill training and has been unemployed for at least eighteen months. His parents were unskilled. He has seen a physician only once in his life and needs eyeglasses and dental work. He is married with three children. He has no transportation. He has a sixth-grade education, a tested third-grade reading level, and a tested fourth-grade level in mathematics. He has had some contact with the law and has spent at least thirty days in jail.[2]

The term "hard-core unemployed" is often equated with the term "ethnic minority," thus implying that all hard-core unemployed are members of ethnic minority groups, and their plight has been emphasized by civil rights legislation and by publicity. However, there are also large numbers of hard-core unemployed who are white. For example, there are many white former farm workers now living in city slums who have no skills to offer a modern industrial society. Furthermore, there are large numbers of whites living in city ghettos who, for a variety of reasons, simply have never had the chance to obtain employable skills. There are also those who are classified as hard-core because of limited mental or motor ability.

The Challenge of Providing Jobs

Persons who have the characteristics outlined above are almost certainly prohibited from qualifying for meaningful employment, because they do not meet traditional hiring criteria which have been established by business and they have no skills to offer employers. Thus they have remained trapped in ghettos of the cities or isolated in rural areas with few options open to them for maintaining life and decency. As a result there has developed a large group of people who have been chronically unemployed and who have been viewed by business as unemployable.

In 1967 when Clifford Alexander accepted the chairmanship of the Equal Employment Opportunity Commission, he commented that jobs were at the heart of three-quarters of the ghetto problems.[3] Also during the 1960s dozens of new organizations were added to those that were already established and pressing for greater opportunities for less-advantaged persons.[4] Society's challenge to business was loud and clear—rethink hiring practices and change those practices in whatever ways are necessary to provide equal opportunities for high-paying and responsible jobs to all persons. While progress in hiring minorities perhaps has not been as fast or as great as some social critics would like, business has risen to the challenge and has made remarkable progress in a short time. Perhaps one of the most effective programs to bring the hard-core unemployed into the work force has been the one established by the National Alliance of Businessmen (NAB). This program has consisted of a partnership effort between business and government to attack the social problem. The NAB *Employers Digest* describes the program as follows: "Its implementation combines government resources with business know-how. Its goal is to find permanent jobs for the hard-core poor in the nation's largest cities and summer employment for in-school youth from the inner city."[5]

Aside from the challenges to society in general which have been raised by the social mandate of equal employment opportunity, many hard challenges have been posed to business. In a variety of ways these challenges have forced business to rethink "the way things have always been done." What, for example, are the responsibilities of business in recruiting, hiring, and training hard-core unemployed? These subjects will be discussed in the next sections.

Recruiting

For many people the search for a job is not difficult. They know how to locate job opportunities; they know how to go to the company employment office to apply; they know how to fill out forms; and they expect to be hired if no one else is better qualified. For the most part the hard-core unemployed do not have this knowledge, and for a variety of reasons they simply do not apply for jobs.

First, experience has taught the hard-core unemployed that because of their lack of marketable skills, low education levels, police records, and a history of rejection because of discrimination, the chances of obtaining a meaningful job are very remote. Second, when they do apply, they are often frustrated by complex application blanks and other forms they are required to fill out. Third, and perhaps more subtle, is that the decor of the personnel office and the formality of personnel often so intimidate hard-core applicants that they walk out or refuse to enter. Finally, most jobs are located long distances from where the hard-core live, thus requiring a long trip by public transportation to the employment office. Often the person is broke and cannot make the trip; or if he does have the money, he is reluctant to spend it on a venture he expects to result in failure.

The message for business has been that if the hard-core unemployed will not come to you, then you better find ways of going to them. The challenge is to find better ways to reach them. One life insurance executive assistant advised: "Take a card table under your arm and your own folding chair. Go into the black barber shops of the ghettos. Set up your own employment office right there. Since you can't be in all the shops, enlist the barbers as your recruiters."[6]

Not all businesses can or want to "take a card table to the barber shop." Most have preferred to work actively through various government and/or community agencies, depending on the agencies to do the actual recruiting; however, most major companies also have developed some off-premises hiring arrangements.

Hiring Practices

Locating hard-core unemployed who want to work and convincing them that jobs are really available to them is only the first step. Many preemployment screening and selection devices used by business have come under close scrutiny by the EEOC in recent years, because the devices themselves often discriminate against the hard-core unemployed and against minority groups in general. One example is the use of arrest records. The EEOC and the courts have held that, in general, the use of arrest records to disqualify persons from employment is discriminatory because blacks have been more commonly arrested than whites. Consider the case of John Smith.[7]

> John Smith was convicted of assault and robbery. When he was released from prison, the one thing he wanted to do was "go straight." But this was not easy. He tried construction work without success because with his record he could not get into the union. He could not sing with a group as he once had done because he could not get a cabaret license to sing where alcoholic beverages were served. And he could not even practice the trade he had learned in prison—barbering. The state would not issue barber licenses to those with prison records. . . .

Other hiring practices that tend to discriminate against the less-advantaged are the formal requirements of many preemployment forms and the use of tests as screening devices. Hiring the hard-core unemployed simply does not fit traditional hiring patterns. A person from the ranks of the hard-core unemployed, for example, may not be able to complete successfully an application blank. First of all, because of reading ability, he may not understand the questions. And second, he may not know or be able to recall much traditional information such as social security number, date of last employment, previous employment, or salary on last job. For these reasons some employers have simplified application blanks for the hard-core unemployed. Others have chosen not to simplify forms but rather have a trained personnel person help the applicant fill out the form to the extent that information is available.

Another hiring practice that has caused serious problems in hiring hard-core unemployed is the practice of using tests as screening devices. The whole area of preemployment testing, and especially psychological testing, has come under critical scrutiny. There is little argument that testing is a valuable instrument in predicting success of job applicants and in identifying training needs. The real problem lies with the tests themselves and questions of validity and reliability. So far as the EEOC is concerned, the burden of proof is on users of tests to prove that the tests measure traits or abilities that are truly critical to successful job performance.

One problem is that many tests are culturally biased—that is, tests which may be valid for one ethnic group may not be valid for other ethnic groups. Because the hard-core unemployed are usually culturally disadvantaged, they are often ill equipped to take tests. Low levels of education may make it very difficult to read and understand questions or to write satisfactory answers. Furthermore, they may have a psychological block against taking tests because from experience they have learned to fear all tests that determine whether or not a person gets a job.

Another problem is that tests used by employers sometimes eliminate all but those who are overqualified for a job. That is, standards of performance required by the tests are often much higher than standards of performance actually required by the job. Thus, many who could perform the job if given the opportunity are needlessly eliminated.

Training

What are the responsibilities of business to train the hard-core unemployed? Should business-conducted training programs go beyond the usual in-house orientation and on-the-job training? If so, how far? Should business be expected to assume responsibilities for education and training that normally occur in the school and family? The main reason why the hard-core unemployed remain unemployed is that the educational and training process has somehow passed them by. In our society, we expect that people will in the normal course of growing up receive education in academic and social skills through the schools and the family, and will therefore be prepared to enter the world of work at a reasonable age. For many of the hard-core unemployed, this process has broken down or simply has not occurred. This means that if a member of the hard-core unemployed group is to become a productive member of the work force, he must somehow be helped to recover lost ground. Experience has shown that offering a job is not enough. In order to perform their jobs properly, some hard-core unemployed will need training in one or more areas such as face-to-face communication, speaking, listening, reading, writing, simple arithmetic, job-related vocabulary, customer relations, and other basic social and business-related skills such as promptness and personal reliability.

Business has accepted the challenge of training hard-core unemployed, and while some programs have not succeeded, many have. And, as business learns from experience how to develop and implement hard-core training, the rate of success is increasing. . . .

EMPLOYING THE UNDEREMPLOYED

Not all those who have been discriminated against in employment opportunities are hard-core unemployed. Indeed many have been capable, well-trained individuals who have not been able to find jobs consistent with their skills and capabilities because of stereotyped social attitudes concerning race or sex. Discrimination has resulted not so much from unilateral business practice as from business decisions and practices which have been shaped and encouraged by attitudes of society as a whole. Business practices have been a mirror of overall social attitudes. On the other hand, business, for the most part, is where job opportunities are. Therefore, because business is a major social institution, it faces the challenge created by changing social attitudes—attitudes which demand that those who have been discriminated against in the past now be assured that they can compete for jobs solely on merits of their talents and abilities.

Significant strides have been made in bringing minority groups, especially blacks, into business at all levels. Passage of civil rights legislation and subsequent government efforts to enforce the laws triggered a rush to hire minorities. But minorities continue to insist that while business has made a good start, it has much further to go. They complain that blacks and other minorities still are not being given equal opportunities because they are, for the most part, kept out of the main managerial stream that leads to promotion. Many blacks, they argue, were brought in merely to demonstrate compliance with the law, even though there may not have been a specific job which could utilize their talents. A second argument is that minority managers have been most often assigned to special staff jobs dealing with minority-group problems—jobs such as urban affairs, community relations, recruitment of minority employees, and special minority markets. These arguments seem to be substantiated to some degree. At least there are few minority persons in high-level executive positions in major companies. To demonstrate this point, one black executive reported his experience in the Harvard Business School's advanced management program.[8]

> There were guys in the class from about 125 U.S. corporations, and they didn't want to believe that blacks weren't making great progress in major companies. But when the three blacks in the class asked them what blacks their companies had in meaningful jobs, they had to say none. Each thought his company was probably an exception.

Business argues that there are very few minority persons who are really qualified at this time to assume high-level positions of responsibility. Because of historical cultural isolation from the world of big business, people from minority groups often have not had parents, relatives, or close friends who could help them understand and relate to the corporate world. Furthermore, business argues, there is no such thing as an instant corporate president. Movement through the ranks, which provides experience and maturity required by top jobs, takes time. Most minority persons have not had time to make that climb.

What most members of minority groups want is an opportunity to move into the promotion stream and be allowed to succeed or fail on the basis of their performance in the same way that nonminority persons are allowed to succeed or fail. The challenge to business is to make *genuine* promotional opportunities open to all.

Notes

1. Daniel Seligman, "How Equal Opportunity Turned into Employment Quotas," *Fortune,* March 1973, p. 162.
2. Lawrence A. Johnson, *Employing the Hard-Core Unemployed* (New York: American Management Association, 1969), pp. 31–33.
3. "Jobs Are the Heart of the Problem—An Interview with Clifford Alexander," *The MBA,* February 1971, p. 7.
4. A partial list of organizations may be found in Robert S. Benson and Harold Wolman, eds., *Counterbudget* (New York: Praeger Publishers, 1971), pp. xxvii and xxix.
5. *Employers Digest,* Washington: National Alliance of Businessmen, n.d., p. 2.
6. Johnson, *op. cit.* p. 55.
7. Richard Shaffer, "Erasing the Past," *Wall Street Journal* (Midwest edition), Nov. 13, 1973, p. 1.
8. Ernest Holsendolph, "Black Executives in a Nearly All-White World," *Fortune,* September 1972, p. 142.

AFFIRMATIVE ACTION PROGRAMS:
Their Organizational Impact in the Corporate World

Jules Cohn

The federal affirmative action (AA) program for hiring and upgrading blacks, Puerto Ricans, other minorities, and women in accordance with number goals and timetables, will have some important, albeit unintended, organizational consequences. To critics of the corporate world, the potential gains from the general thrust of the AA approach are clear; quantitative goals encourage renewed efforts by employers, and timetables serve as yardsticks for the measurement and evaluation of these efforts. To female and minority job applicants, the AA program assures that employer practices will be scrutinized by government agencies and that government pressure can be brought to bear to insure that job applications receive nondiscriminatory consideration.

In addition to the above contributions, however, AA programs may produce negative consequences that were not anticipated by their proponents. And, because they have been busily occupied with negotiating goals and establishing timetables, many corporate executives have not yet had time to consider these negative consequences. However, as company AA programs get underway, these negative aspects will become evident to employers, job applicants, and corporate critics. For the past 18 months, I have been able to study the negotiation and development of AA programs by several major corporations. Accordingly, the comments and speculations that follow are based in part on firsthand observation.

Affirmative action programs, once the process for setting them up has begun, may have some of the following effects on corporate organization: (1) a redefinition of the personnel function; (2) tensions and strains among employees, and between employees and managers; (3) reduced productivity; and (4) changes in corporate organization and structure.

REDEFINITION OF THE PERSONNEL FUNCTION

Quite plainly, the AA concept makes inevitable a redefinition of the corporate personnel function. Until now, personnel work has centered on the need to find, screen, and test able candidates, determine where to place them, and develop practices that will help retain them. Salary scales, fringe benefits, and procedures for advancement have also been the charge of personnel officers. In recent years, a new issue has received the attention of personnel departments: nonmaterial ways to motivate or to "humanize" (the word now in vogue) work. AA also represents an expansion of function, because it introduces a new emphasis—doing all of the above, while paying special attention to women and other minority groups.

A new dimension is thereby added to personnel work. The personnel officer is asked to identify employees and potential employees by the racial and sexual groups into which they fit. Policy must be formulated in accordance with these classifications. Personnel officers are, in effect, asked to be agents of society's newest priorities as well as of their companies.

Personnel executives who are sensitive about their responsibilities and thoughtful about their tasks could well be troubled by this new dimension of their work. How, for example, will they relate individual merit to racial and sexual factors when it comes to filling a vacancy? Their problems will be complex, their decisions controversial. Therefore, their work can no longer be dismissed as it was in the past as passive and clerical in nature;

on the contrary, it will be discretionary, and more a focal point of public attention under the pressures brought by AA programs.

Employee relations with a company will be affected by the new AA programs. In some companies, negative effects are already being felt. As the new goals and timetables are announced, employees wonder how their hopes and plans for advancement will be affected by a corporate commitment to allot a specified number of jobs to women, blacks, and Spanish-surnamed Americans. The employee who doesn't fit into the new "protected" groups may feel, on the one hand, that it is about time, that the company should do more to provide the opportunities to people hitherto left out in the cold. But, on the other hand, he may also very naturally feel concern about his own ability to advance or to get a fair hearing when he wants to transfer.

Companies that added new jobs to their organizational charts a few years ago so that minority group members who felt they were being discriminated against would have a department to take their grievances to will probably have to consider creating still another new post to receive and mediate complaints from nonminority group members. The racial and ethnic conflicts among employees that occupied personnel executives in recent years, when minority group members, particularly the disadvantaged, were being hired, will resume. The techniques that were applied to deal with them, such as special training programs for supervisors, orientation sessions, and incentive programs, may once again be needed as new problems arise between white and black, or male and female employees. Personnel executives will have to explain the nuances of the new programs to employees and be prepared to answer tough questions about them.

The new AA programs may have other unintended and unwelcome effects: They may, albeit indirectly, reduce productivity. Employers will have to take on a lot of new paperwork. Supervisors, for example, will have to fill out forms and file reports on recruiting, hiring, and advancement of employees. More paperwork means more time, and more man (or woman) power. Master files have to be augmented, computers newly programmed, and new sets of instructions for recordkeeping devised and disseminated.

The added paperwork is only one aspect of the problem, however. Productivity may also be affected, particularly at the outset, by the array of attitudes with which employees greet the announcement of AA programs. Large companies, in particular, where news of changes or new direction in personnel practices must be transmitted through layers of management and through regional and local offices, may find considerable amounts of confusion among their employees. Therefore, time will have to be set aside for explanations, orientations, and interpretations. Confusion may be a minor attitudinal problem. Some employees will protest; others will scrutinize the AA program and discern ambiguities that demand clarification. "What are *my* rights?" they will ask. "How does this affect me?"

Moreover, their supervisors may feel torn between alternatives: recruiting, hiring, and advancing employees on racial or sexual grounds, on the one hand, or on grounds of ability, on the other. It will not always be easy to find the right resolution of these alternatives.

Will AA goals and timetables be given first priority in filling, say, a key slot on the assembly line? Or will production goals come first? How can the two priorities be balanced? At what level will these questions be answered—in headquarters, in the offices of personnel executives, or by the assembly line foreman? How these questions are answered will surely affect productivity, along with the time- and manpower-consuming process of finding the answers.

CHANGES IN ORGANIZATION AND STRUCTURE

The poverty programs of the 1960's and many of the social welfare programs launched during the New Deal often had as their major beneficiaries the social welfare professionals assigned to implement them, rather than their official clientele groups. Similarly, AA programs could potentially be more helpful to the careers of personnel officials than to minority group members or women. Because of the AA program, a new corporate title has already been created in some organizations: every large company's personnel department has designated at least one manager as the person in charge of developing and administering the new programs. His (her) task usually involves negotiating the details of the AA program with federal officials and interpreting the program to line managers.

Although the AA program job is not an easy one, it will provide a career opportunity for personnel executives by offering "exposure" to a man (or woman) who wants to be noticed by top management, as well as the prospect of introductions to federal officials.

The problems that go with affirmative action, however, are many. Negotiations over AA goals and timetables are usually complicated and delicate and may seem to continue endlessly as corporate and government officials haggle over numbers and dates. Job titles and work assignments throughout the country usually need to be defined in minute details in order to complete an AA program. Some jobs need to be redefined or created. Goals for women in jobs formerly filled exclusively by men need to be developed. The government's notions about what these goals should be are often different from the ideas of the AA officer's superiors, or his (her) colleagues. Thus, the government may ask that ten percent of all outside repair jobs be set aside for women in a utilities company, but colleagues on the line may (perhaps mistakenly) feel that ten percent is too high a number—unrealistic and unattainable.

In short, the AA manager will have to negotiate between the company's notions and needs, on the one hand, and those of the government, on the other. In one large company that I have been observing, these negotiations have already taken ten full months and have involved an AA group of six personnel executives and a government team of the same number. In addition, other executives and bureaucrats have dropped in and out of the negotiations, from time to time, as advisers.

The new job of AA officer will not be fun. One newly appointed AA officer said:

> My children are egging me on to press for more blacks in our southern departments. At the same time, my boss is pressuring me to develop conservative projections, for he's concerned about keeping smooth relationships with the field organizations. But the government bureaucrats are on the same side as my kids. As to my own conscience, I waver between feeling guilty in the office with my colleagues. I guess you could say that I'm not going to be able to satisfy anybody in this job, least of all myself. No matter what I do, I'm wrong.

The AA officer's job resembles that of the urban affairs officer. Each is paid to be an in-house gadfly, but such gadflies function under obvious constraints. They can lobby within the company, up to a point, and can try to persuade, push, convince, and cajole. But, unless they are granted sufficient power by employers, they cannot alone decide what the company's position will be, what goals and timetables it will seek to establish. If anything, the AA officer is destined to be even more uncomfortable than his urban affairs counterpart, whose job was created in an atmosphere of similar social pressures only a few years ago. He or she is the link between the company and the government (usually represented by the General Services Administration or the Office of Federal Contract Compliance in the Labor Department). Even if the AA officer is able to keep his (her) cool, he (she) may be seated across the bargaining table from ideologists. Even if he (she) has made every effort to push the company forward toward a progressive program, there is always the risk of being attacked by outside adversaries as a "front man" or "puppet."

CONCLUSIONS

Some steps can be taken to lessen the seriousness of the above problems. Although the AA program concept will inevitably raise the issues, the alert corporate management will have opportunities to resolve some of these issues. Probably the most important requirement is *planning*.

The sad fact is that many companies add the AA job to the organizational chart too quickly. The pressure to develop AA programs was steady and strong, and action had to be taken before an organizational plan could be developed. But now there is time to think through the implications of the new job, its responsibilities, and the problems that are associated with it. What kind of person seems best for it? To whom should this person report? What kind of support will he (she) require in order to do an effective job?

Developing appropriate and effective means for communicating the details of the new AAP to employees will also be useful. Orientation programs that are thorough and that allow ample time for employee questions should be scheduled. As open an atmosphere as possible for these meetings will also help; if employees are encouraged to express their anxieties and raise their questions, personnel executives will be able to provide assurances and clarify confusion.

Some problems will not be cleared up by orientation sessions, however, or by putting the AA job in the right spot on the organizational chart. But these problems flow from the basic issue of social policy raised by the affirmative action approach. Now that government agencies have the right to scrutinize the decision-making process with regard to hiring, refusing to hire, promoting or refusing to promote, or, as in the case of the universities, reappointing or refusing to reappoint personnel, the issue goes beyond personnel matters. How to achieve social justice is the issue. Everybody wants justice, but there are disagreements about how to assure it, or even what it is. Years of discrimination against blacks, women, Jews, and other minority group members were in part the result of an unspoken (even sometimes, unwitting) gentlemen's agreement about what constituted fairness, and where and when it was applicable: Fairness simply didn't apply to these groups according to the gentlemen's agreement. Otherwise—within the boundaries drawn by prejudice—issues were decided on the merits: For example, which white Anglo male is most competent?

The question now is whether or not the merits or a potential new unfairness will prevail. In other words, there is the risk that a new kind of gentlemen's agreement will be implemented by corporate personnel who, under pressure to meet AA goals and timetables, will—with good intentions—make their choices on the basis of racial, ethnic, and sexual biases, just as they were doing a few years ago.

DISCRIMINATION, COLOR BLINDNESS, AND THE QUOTA SYSTEM

Sidney Hook

Every humane and fair-minded person must approve of the presidential executive order of 1965, which forbade discrimination with respect to race, religion, national origin or sex by any organization or group that receives financial support from the government in the course of fulfilling

From *Measure*, no. 30, (Summer 1974). Reprinted by permission of the author and University Centers for Rational Alternatives.

its contractual obligations with it. The difficulties in enforcing this order flow not from its ethical motivation and intent, but in establishing the criteria of evidence that discrimination has been practiced. Very rarely are the inequities explicitly expressed in the provisions guiding or regulating employment. They must be inferred. But they cannot be correctly inferred from the actual figures of employment independently of the *availability* of different minority groups, their *willingness* to accept employment, and the objective *qualifications* of those able and willing to apply. To be sure, the bigoted and prejudiced can distort these considerations in order to cover up flagrant discriminatory practices. But only the foolish and unperceptive will dismiss these considerations as irrelevant and assume that reference to them is an obvious sign of prejudice.

There is, unfortunately, evidence that some foolish and unperceptive persons in the Office of Civil Rights of the Department of Health, Education, and Welfare are disregarding these considerations and mechanically inferring from the actual figures of academic employment in institutions of higher learning the existence of discriminatory practices. What is worse, they are threatening to cancel federal financial support, without which many universities cannot survive, unless, within a certain period of time, the proportion of members of minorities on the teaching and research staff of universities approximate their proportion in the general population. Further, with respect to women, since it is manifestly absurd to expect that universities be staffed in an equal sexual ratio in all departments, the presence of discrimination against them is to be inferred if the composition of the teaching and research staffs does not correspond to the proportion of *applicants*—independently of the qualifications of the applicants.

In the light of this evidence, a persuasive case can be made that those who have issued these guidelines and ultimata to universities, whether they are male or female, black or white, Catholic, Jewish, or Protestant are unqualified for the offices they hold and therefore unable to properly enforce the presidential executive order. For they are guilty of fostering the very racialism and discrimination an executive order was issued to correct and forestall.

It is not hard to demonstrate the utter absurdity of the directives issued by the Office of Civil Rights of the Department of Health, Education, and Welfare. I shall use two simple instances. A few years ago, it was established that more than 80 percent of the captains of tugboats in the New York Harbor were Swedish. None were black. None were Jewish. And this in a community in which blacks and Jews outnumbered Swedes by more than a hundred to one. If one were to construe these figures along the lines laid down by the office of Civil Rights of HEW, this would be presumptive proof of crass discrimination against Negroes and Jews. But it is nothing of the sort. Negroes and Jews, for complex reasons we need not here explore, have never been interested in navigating tugboats. They have not applied for the positions. They have therefore never been rejected.

The faculties of many Negro colleges are overwhelmingly black out of all proportion to their numbers in the country, state, or even local community. It would be a grim jest therefore to tax them with discriminatory practices. Until recently, they have been pathetically eager to employ qualified white teachers, but they have been unable to attract them.

The fact that HEW makes a distinction between women and minorities, judging sexual discrimination not by simple proportion of women teachers and researchers in universities to their proportion in the general population, but only to their proportion among *applicants,* shows that it has a dim understanding of the relevant issue. There are obviously various occupational fields—military, mining, aeronautical, and so forth, for which women have, until now, shown little inclination. Neither the school nor the department can be faulted for the scarcity of female applications. But the main point is this: no matter how many applicants there are for a post, whether they are male or female, the only relevant criterion is whether or not they are qualified. Only when there is antecedent determination that the applicants, with respect to the job or post specifications are equally or even roughly equally qualified, and there is a marked and continued disparity in the relative numbers employed, is there legitimate ground for suspicion and inquiry.

The effect of the ultimata to universities to hire blacks and women under threat of losing crucial financial support is to compel them to hire *unqualified* Negroes and women, and to discriminate *against* qualified nonblacks and men. This is just as much a manifestation of racism, even if originally unintended, as the racism the original presidential directive was designed to correct. Intelligent, self-respecting Negroes and women would scorn such preferential treatment. The consequences of imposing any criterion other than that of qualified talent on our educational establishments are sure to be disastrous on the quest for new knowledge and truth as well as subversive of the democratic ethos. Its logic points to the introduction of a quota system, of the notorious *numerus clausus* of repressive regimes of the past. If blacks are to be hired merely on the basis of their color and women merely on the basis of their sex, because they are *under*represented in the faculties of our universities, before long the demand will be made that Jews or men should be fired or dismissed or not hired as Jews or men, no matter how well qualified, because they are *over*represented in our faculties.

The universities should not yield to the illiberal ultimata of the Office of Civil Rights of HEW. There is sufficient work for it to do in enforcing the presidential directive in areas where minorities are obviously qualified and are obviously suffering from unfair discrimination. It undoubtedly is true, as some members of UCRA who have long been active in the field of civil rights have long pointed out, that some educational institutions or their departments have been guilty of obvious religious and racial discrimination. The evidence of this was flagrant and open and required no elaborate questionnaires to establish. The Office of Civil Rights could cooperate with the Department of Justice here. Currently, its activities in the field of higher education are not only wasting time, effort, and the taxpayer's money but debasing educational standards as well. It is bringing confusion and conflict into an area where, prior to its intervention, the issues were well understood and where voluntary efforts to hire qualified women and members of minorities were being made with increasing success.

THE DRIVE TOWARD EQUALITY

J. Stanley Pottinger

About two years ago, a previously unnoticed executive order prohibiting employment discrimination by federal contractors (which includes most universities) was discovered by women's organizations and minority groups on a few East Coast campuses. Soon afterwards, the volume of formal complaints of sex and race employment discrimination in institutions of higher education rose sharply, and the Office for Civil Rights began constructing a systematic program of enforcement. During the early stages of this process, as the office struggled to define law and policy and to obtain staff, the attention and support of women's and civil-rights groups increased, while the higher-education establishment remained unruffled.

When the office made its presence on campuses felt, however—by deferring payment of some twenty-three million dollars in federal contracts to various universities pending compliance with the order—it began to raise the academic community's eyebrows. Today a significant and vocal segment of that community is actively challenging HEW's enforcement of Executive Order 11246 and the policies upon which it is based.

The reasons for this challenge are, as one might expect, more complex than the current dialogue on the subject would suggest. But every crusade must have its simplistic side—a galvanizing symbol, a bogeyman, a rallying cry. The word *quotas* serves these rhetorical purposes in the present case. Since quotas are not required or permitted by the executive order, they are for the most part a phony issue, but very much an issue nevertheless.

To understand the quotas issue one must first understand what the executive order is all about. In attempting to deal with employment inequities, Executive Order 11246 embodies two concepts: nondiscrimination and affirmative action.

Nondiscrimination means the elimination of all existing discriminatory treatment of present and potential employees. University officials are

From *Change*, 4, no. 8, Oct. 1972. Reprinted with permission from Educational Change, Inc., New Rochelle, New York.

required under this concept to ensure that their employment policies do not, if followed as stated, operate to the detriment of any persons on grounds of race, color, religion, sex, or national origin. Typically, this means eliminating officially sanctioned quotas restricting women and minorities, antinepotism policies that operate to deny equal opportunities to women, recruitment procedures that tend exclusively to reach white males, and the like. In addition, the university must examine the practices of its decision-makers to ensure that nondiscriminatory policies are in fact implemented in a nondiscriminatory way. This may require warning or firing personnel who, for example, reject women's applications not on the basis of merit, but (as we have found) with a cursory note that "we have enough of these" or "sorry but we have filled our women's quota"—despite the fact that quotas or discriminatory policies are not official policy.

1

The concept of affirmative action requires more than mere neutrality on race and sex. It requires the university to determine whether it has failed to recruit, employ, and promote women and minorities commensurate with their availability, even if this failure cannot be traced to specific acts of discrimination by university officials. Where women and minorities are not represented on a university's rolls, despite their availability (that is, where they are "underutilized") the university has an obligation to initiate affirmative efforts to recruit and hire them. The premise of this obligation is that systemic forms of exclusion, inattention, and discrimination cannot be remedied in any meaningful way, in any reasonable length of time, simply by ensuring a future benign neutrality with regard to race and sex. This would perpetuate indefinitely the grossest inequities of past discrimination. Thus there must be some form of positive action, along with a schedule for how such actions are to take place, and an honest appraisal of what the plan is likely to yield—an appraisal that the regulations call a "goal."

It is at this point that the issue of "quotas" rears its ugly head. What is a quota, and what is wrong with it? What is a goal, and what is right about it?

Historically, hiring quotas have been rigid numerical ceilings on the number of persons of a given racial, ethnic, religious, or sex group who could be employed by (or admitted to) an academic institution. If quotas were required or permitted by the executive order, they would operate as levels of employment that must be fulfilled if the university is to remain eligible for federal contracts.

Some critics have assumed that the government is arguing that rigid numerical requirements would not constitute quotas under the executive order since, unlike traditional quotas, they would operate in favor of minorities and women rather than against them. But obviously, where the number of jobs is finite, as is true in all universities, a numerical requirement in favor of any group becomes by definition a restrictive ceiling or quota for all others. No one in the government is making an argument that any requirements in the form of quotas—for or against a defined class—are legitimate.

Once it is assumed that quotas are required, of course, there is no end to the horrors and hysteria that can be generated. University officials, it is said, will be obliged to hire regardless of merit or capability. Standards of excellence will crumble. Existing faculty will be fired and replaced wholesale. And if there are not enough qualified women engineers to fill the Engineering Department's quota, never mind; the positions will be filled with female home-economics teachers (a favorite stereotype), and don't blame the university if the country's next suspension bridge looks like a plate of spaghetti. If there are not enough black surgeons to teach surgery, no matter; they'll be hired anyway, and when scores of hapless patients (hopefully Office for Civil Rights personnel) are left bleeding on the table, don't come to the universities for so much as a Band-Aid. If there are not enough qualified Chicano professors of Latin and Greek to fill their quotas, Latin and Greek can be dropped from the curriculum, and don't blame the universities for the fall of Western civilization.

2

Perhaps those charges would be worthy of debate if quotas were required. But they are not. Department of Labor guidelines state that goals "may not be rigid and inflexible quotas that must be met." HEW directives reflect the same policy. Furthermore, the executive order is a *presidential* directive, and the President's prohibition of quotas is clear: "With respect to . . . Affirmative Action programs, I agree that numerical goals, although an important and useful tool to measure progress which remedies the effect of past discrimination, must not be allowed to be applied in such a fashion as to, in fact, result in the imposition of quotas. . . ."

What is required by the executive order is evidence of good faith and a positive effort to recruit and hire women and minorities. Since the road to exclusive white male faculties is paved with good intentions, however, we ask for something more than the mere promise of good behavior. Universities are required to commit themselves to defined, specific steps that will bring the university into contact with qualified women and minorities and that will ensure that in the selection process they will be judged fairly on the basis of their capabilities. Universities are also required to make an honest prediction of what these efforts are likely to yield over a given period of time, assuming that the availability of women and minorities is accurately approximated, and assuming that the procedures for recruitment and selection are actually followed.

This predictive aspect of affirmative action could be called any number of things: "level of expectancy"; "honest guesses"; "targets." They happen to be called "goals." The important point is not the term, but how it functions. Unlike quotas, goals are not the sole measure of a contractor's compliance. Good-faith efforts and adherence to procedures that are likely to yield results remain the test of compliance. A university, in other words, would be required to make precisely the same level of effort, set and adhere to the same procedures, and take the same steps to correct the lack of women and minorities resulting from former exclusion, even if goals and timetables did not exist at all.

If goals are not designed to warp affirmative action toward quotas, what is the purpose of requiring them at all? There are two reasons:

First, since a university cannot predict employment results in the form of goals without first analyzing its deficiencies and determining what steps are likely to remedy them, the setting of goals serves as an inducement to lay the analytical foundation necessary to guarantee nondiscrimination and the affirmative efforts required by the executive order.

Second, goals serve as one way of measuring a university's level of effort, even if not the only way. If a university falls short of its goals at the end of a given period, that failure in itself does not require a conclusion of noncompliance (as would be the case if quotas were in use). It does, however, signal to the university that something has gone awry, and that reasons for the failure should be examined. If it appears, for example, that the cause for failure was not a lack of defined effort or adherence to fair procedures, then we regard compliance to have taken place. Perhaps the university's original goals were unrealistically high in light of later job-market conditions. Or perhaps it faced an unforeseen contraction of its employment positions, or similar conditions beyond its control. On the other hand, if the failure to reach goals was clearly a failure to abide by the affirmative-action program set by the university, compliance is an issue, and a hearing is likely to ensue.

3

Once it is understood that there is nothing in the executive order that requires quotas, it should be equally clear that there is nothing that requires their undesirable side-effects either. White males or other allegedly "overrepresented" groups should not be fired in order to permit goal fulfillment; indeed, to do so would constitute a violation of law. Standards of performance and qualifications that are not themselves discriminatory need not be abandoned nor compromised in order to hire unqualified women and minorities. (The argument frequently advanced by university officials that there are virtually no qualified women and minorities simply does not stand up, particularly when advanced by universities that have failed even to canvass the market.) Nothing in the affirmative-action concept infringes on "academic freedom" or the university's right to teach, research, or publish whatever it wishes, in whatever forum it desires—whether the classroom, the laboratory, the campus, the press, or elsewhere.

If goals are not quotas, and quotas really are not required, why the current fuss and confusion?

The Office for Civil Rights must share some of the blame for not getting the distinction between quotas and goals firmly and early implanted in the higher-education community. But such efforts have not been lacking in the last year. The distinction has been drawn repeatedly in press releases, speeches, letters to editors, articles, compliance reviews, and negotiations. Indeed, the effort has been so substantial that a cynical observer might be inclined to conclude that at least some of the academic community, priding itself as it does on careful research and the intellectual ability to comprehend important distinctions, hears us loud and clear but simply doesn't want to understand. At any rate, comprehensive guidelines are presently in draft form and, when issued, should resolve the quota controversy once and for all.

Some critics object to goals, not because they fail to understand how they differ from quotas, nor because they secretly want to throttle effort-oriented affirmative action. They object to the use of goals because of their fear that sound conceptual distinctions will be lost, and in actual practice, goals will be used as quotas, regardless of the law.

In confirmation of this fear, such evidence as a university official's letter is cited (but not condoned) by John Bunzel, the distinguished president of California State University at San Jose.

No one would agree more quickly than I that any form of "Affirmative Action-with-a-vengeance" is an outrageous and illegal form of reverse bias. I am not ready to agree, however, that blame for this petulant behavior must be laid to goals, or that valid distinctions between goals and quotas are too elusive for university officials to follow if they are sharply interested in equal opportunity.

More than once, we have discovered that what appears to be reverse discrimination born of a confusion about quotas is really nothing more than avoidance of a decision on the merits. A white male, like the person who received the letter quoted by Dr. Bunzel, is told that he was the "top candidate" for the job, when in fact that is not the truth. The personnel officer, lacking the fortitude to reject the applicant honestly, and shaking his head in mock sympathetic disgust, conveniently delivers the bad news as "federally required reverse discrimination."

But even if some employment decision-makers engage in reverse discrimination out of an honest mistake about what is required, the concept of goals should not be abandoned by way of overreaction, at least not while so many questions remain unanswered. When reverse discrimination is discovered on the campus, why should the academic community immediately assume that the federal government is the villain? The Office for Civil Rights is remote from the actual hiring process, and rightly so, while the university department head is right where the action is. The scant efforts by top university officials to correct abuses or to educate their colleagues to the real issues at stake in carrying out affirmative action cast doubt on the credibility of their protestations.

One also needs to ask just how widespread reverse discrimination really is. Evidence suggests that there may be some loosening of high-school academic achievement scores with regard to the admission of disadvantaged students to undergraduate colleges. The merits of this policy aside, it has nothing to do with *employment* standards under the executive order, and there is no clear evidence that goals or affirmative-action requirements are prompting widespread abuses in the employment processes.

But even if the problem is widespread, or likely to become so, assuming that goals are the problem still misses the point. If, as our critics seem to imply, numbers of faculty and administrators are truly incapable of understanding and adhering to the distinction between a goal and a quota, or willfully commit reverse discrimination, are we ready to believe that these people will behave differently if goals are removed? To make the point that goals cannot operate in the real world without becoming quotas, critics must characterize university officials generally as ignorant, as spiteful, as unconcerned about merit, or as weaklings ready to collapse in the face of supposed whispered directions "from upstairs" to hire unqualified women and minorities because that is the easiest way to ensure a flow of federal dollars. It is an unconscionable argument and an unfair condemnation of the academics' intelligence and integrity.

4

There is yet another fear: even if goals are not converted to quotas by university officials, they may be by the government. As a prominent newspaper editor said recently, "The distinction between goals and quotas may be sound today, but how do we know that in the future a different Director of Civil Rights will not tack goals to the university door and proclaim them to be quotas?" The short answer is that we don't know. No one can guarantee today that tomorrow's government officials will never exceed the bounds of good policy or legitimate discretion. This possibility exists in virtually every government program, but we also enjoy adequate due process safeguards in the courts, as well as a consistent vigilance by the Congress and the president.

PREFERENTIAL HIRING

Judith Jarvis Thomson

Many people are inclined to think preferential hiring an obvious injustice.[1] I should have said "feel" rather than "think": it seems to me the matter has not been carefully thought out, and that what is in question, really, is a gut reaction.

Judith Jarvis Thomson, "Preferential Hiring," *Philosophy & Public Affairs* 2, no. 4 (Summer 1973). Copyright © 1973 by Princeton University Press. Excerpts reprinted by permission.

I am going to deal with only a very limited range of preferential hirings: that is, I am concerned with cases in which several candidates present themselves for a job, in which the hiring officer finds, on examination, that all are equally qualified to hold that job, and he then straightway declares for the black, or for the woman, because he or she *is* a black or a woman. And I shall talk only of hiring decisions in the universities, partly because I am most familiar with them, partly because it is in the universities that the most vocal and articulate opposition to preferential hiring is now heard—not surprisingly, perhaps, since no one is more vocal and articulate than a university professor who feels deprived of his rights.

I suspect that some people may say, Oh well, in *that* kind of case it's all right, what we object to is preferring the less qualified to the better qualified. Or again, What we object to is refusing even to consider the qualifications of white males. I shall say nothing at all about these things. I think that the argument I shall give for saying that preferential hiring is not unjust in the cases I do concentrate on can also be appealed to to justify it outside that range of cases. But I won't draw any conclusions about cases outside it. Many people do have that gut reaction I mentioned against preferential hiring in *any* degree or form; and it seems to me worthwhile bringing out that there is good reason to think they are wrong to have it. Nothing I say will be in the slightest degree novel or original. It will, I hope, be enough to set the relevant issues out clearly.

I

But first, something should be said about qualifications.

I said I would consider only cases in which the several candidates who present themselves for the job are equally qualified to hold it; and there plainly are difficulties in the way of saying precisely how this is to be established, and even what is to be established. Strictly academic qualifications seem at a first glance to be relatively straightforward: the hiring officer must see if the candidates have done equally well in courses (both courses they took, and any they taught), and if they are recommended equally strongly by their teachers, and if the work they submit for consideration is equally good. There is no denying that even these things are less easy to establish than first appears: for example, you may have a suspicion that Professor Smith is given to exaggeration, and that his "great student" is in fact less strong than Professor Jones's "good student"—but do you *know* that this is so? But there is a more serious difficulty still: as blacks and women have been saying, strictly academic indicators may themselves be skewed by prejudice. My impression is that women, white and black, may possibly suffer more from this than black males. A black male who is discouraged or down-graded for being black is discouraged or down-graded out of dislike, repulsion, a desire to avoid contact; and I suspect that there are very few teachers nowadays who allow themselves to feel such things, or, if they do feel them, to act on them. A woman who is discouraged or down-graded for being a woman is not discouraged or down-graded out of dislike, but out of a conviction she is not serious. . . .

II

. . . Suppose two candidates for a civil service job have equally good test scores, but that there is only one job available. We could decide between them by coin-tossing. But in fact we do allow for declaring for A straightway, where A is a veteran, and B is not.[2] It may be that B is a nonveteran through no fault of his own: perhaps he was refused induction for flat feet, or a heart murmur. That is, those things in virtue of which B is a nonveteran may be things which it was no more in his power to control or change than it is in anyone's power to control or change the color of his skin. Yet the fact is that B is not a veteran and A is. On the assumption that the veteran has served his country, the country owes him something. And it seems plain that giving him preference is a not unjust way in which part of that debt of gratitude can be paid.

And now, . . . we should turn to those debts which are incurred by one who wrongs another. It is here we find what seems to me the most powerful argument for the conclusion that the preferential hiring of blacks and women is not unjust.

I obviously cannot claim any novelty for this argument: it's a very familiar one. Indeed, not merely is it familiar, but so are a battery of objections to it. It may be granted that if we have wronged A, we owe him something: we should make amends, we should compensate him for the wrong done him. It may even be granted that if we have wronged A, we must make amends, that justice requires it, and that a failure to make amends is not merely callousness, but injustice. But (a) are the young blacks and women who are amongst the current applicants for university jobs amongst the blacks and women who were wronged? To turn to particular cases, it might happen that the black applicant is middle class, the son of professionals, and has had the very best in private schooling; or that the woman applicant is plainly the product of feminist upbringing and encouragement. Is it proper, much less required, that the black or woman be given preference over a white male who grew up in poverty, and has to make his own way and earn his encouragements? Again, (b), did we, the current members of the community, wrong any blacks or women? Lots of people once did; but then isn't it for them to do the compensating? That is, if they're still alive. For presumably nobody now alive owned any slaves, and perhaps nobody now alive voted against women's suffrage. And (c) what if the white male applicant for the job has never in any degree wronged any blacks or women? If so, *he* doesn't owe any debts to them, so why should *he* make amends to them?

These objections seem to me quite wrong-headed.

Obviously the situation for blacks and women is better than it was a hundred and fifty, fifty, twenty-five years ago. But it is absurd to suppose that the young blacks and women now of an age to apply for jobs have not been wronged. Large-scale, blatant, overt wrongs have presumably disappeared; but it is only within the last twenty-five years (perhaps the last ten years in the case of women) that it has become at all widely agreed in this country that blacks and women must be recognized as having, not merely this or that particular right normally recognized as belonging to white males, but all of the rights and respect which go with full membership in the community. Even young blacks and women have lived through down-grading for being black or female: they have not merely not been given that very equal chance at the benefits generated by what the community owns which is so firmly insisted on for white males, they have not until lately even been felt to have a right to it.

And even those who were not themselves down-graded for being black or female have suffered the consequences of the down-grading of other blacks and women: lack of self-confidence, and lack of self-respect. For where a community accepts that a person's being black, or being a woman, are right and proper grounds for denying that person full membership in the community, it can hardly be supposed that any but the most extraordinarily independent black or woman will escape self-doubt. All but the most extraordinarily independent of them have had to work harder—if only against self-doubt—than all but the most deprived white males, in the competition for a place amongst the best qualified.

If any black or woman has been unjustly deprived of what he or she has a right to, then of course justice does call for making amends. But what of the blacks and women who haven't actually been deprived of what they have a right to, but only made to suffer the consequences of injustice to other blacks and women? *Perhaps* justice doesn't require making amends to them as well; but common decency certainly does. To fail, at the very least, to make what counts as public apology to all, and to take positive steps to show that it is sincerely meant, is, if not injustice, then anyway a fault at least as serious as ingratitude.

Opting for a policy of preferential hiring may of course mean that some black or woman is preferred to some white male who as a matter of fact has had a harder life than the black or woman. But so may opting for a policy of veterans' preference mean that a healthy, unscarred, middle class veteran is preferred to a poor, struggling, scarred, nonveteran. Indeed, opting for a policy of settling who gets the job by having all equally qualified candidates draw straws may also mean that in a given case the candidate with the hardest life loses out. Opting for any policy other than hard-life preference may have this result.

I have no objection to anyone's arguing that it is precisely hard-life preference that we ought to opt for. If all, or anyway all of the equally qualified, have a right to an equal chance, then the argument would have to draw attention to something sufficiently powerful to override that right. But perhaps this could be done along the lines I followed in the case of blacks and women: perhaps it could be successfully argued that we have wronged those who have had hard lives, and therefore owe it to them to make amends. And then we should have in more extreme form a difficulty already present: how are these preferences to be ranked? shall we place the hard-lifers ahead of blacks? both ahead of women? and what about veterans? I leave these questions aside. My concern has been only to show that the white male applicant's right to an equal chance does not make it unjust to opt for a policy under which blacks and women are given preference. That a white male with a specially hard history may lose out under this policy cannot possibly be any objection to it, in the absence of a showing that hard-life preference is not unjust, and, more important, takes priority over preference for blacks and women.

Lastly, it should be stressed that to opt for such a policy is not to make the young white male applicants themselves make amends for any wrongs done to blacks and women. Under such a policy, no one is asked to give up a job which is already his; the job for which the white male competes isn't his, but is the community's, and it is the hiring officer who gives it to the black or woman in the community's name. Of course the white male is asked to give up his equal chance at the job. But that is not something he pays to the black or woman by way of making amends; it is something the community takes away from him in order that *it* may make amends.

Still, the community does impose a burden on him: it is able to make amends for its wrongs only by taking something away from him, something which, after all, we are supposing he has a right to. And why should *he* pay the cost of the community's amends-making?

If there were some appropriate way in which the community could make amends to its blacks and women, some way which did not require depriving anyone of anything he has a right to, then that would be the best course of action for it to take. Or if there were anyway some way in which the costs could be shared by everyone, and not imposed entirely on the young white male job applicants, then that would be, if not best, then anyway better than opting for a policy of preferential hiring. But in fact the nature of the wrongs done is such as to make jobs the best and most suitable form of compensation. What blacks and women were denied was full membership in the community; and nothing can more appropriately make amends for that wrong than precisely what will make them feel they now finally have it. And that means jobs. Financial compensation (the cost of which could be shared equally) slips through the fingers; having a job, and discovering you do it well, yield—perhaps better than anything else—that very self-respect which blacks and women have had to do without.

But of course choosing this way of making amends means that the costs are imposed on the young white male applicants who are turned away. And so it should be noticed that it is not entirely inappropriate that those applicants should pay the costs. No doubt few, if any, have themselves, individually, done any wrongs to blacks and women. But they have profited from the wrongs the community did. Many may actually have been direct beneficiaries of policies which excluded or down-graded blacks and women—perhaps in school admissions, perhaps in access to financial aid, perhaps elsewhere; and even those who did not directly benefit in this way had, at any rate, the advantage in the competition which comes of confidence in one's full membership, and of one's rights being recognized as a matter of course.

Of course it isn't only the young white male applicant for a university job who has benefited from the exclusion of blacks and women: the older white male, now comfortably tenured, also benefited, and many defenders of preferential hiring feel that he should be asked to share the costs. Well, presumably we can't demand that he give up his job, or share it. But it seems to me in place to expect the occupants of comfortable professorial chairs to contribute in some way, to make some form of return to the young white male who bears the cost, and is turned away. It will have been plain that I find the outcry now heard against preferential hiring in the universities objectionable; it would also be objectionable that those of us who are now securely situated should placidly defend it, with no more than a sigh of regret for the young white male who pays for it.

III

One final word: "discrimination." I am inclined to think we so use it that if anyone is convicted of discriminating against blacks, women, white males, or what have you, then he is thereby convicted of acting unjustly. If so, and if I am right in thinking that preferential hiring in the restricted range of cases we have been looking at is *not* unjust, then we have two options: (a) we can simply reply that to opt for a policy of preferential hiring in those cases is not to opt for a policy of discriminating against white males, or (b) we can hope to get usage changed—e.g., by trying to get people to allow that there is discriminating against and discriminating against, and that some is unjust, but some is not.

Best of all, however, would be for that phrase to be avoided altogether. It's at best a blunt tool: there are all sorts of nice moral discriminations [*sic*] which one is unable to make while occupied with it. And that bluntness itself fits it to do harm: blacks and women are hardly likely to see through to what precisely is owed them while they are being accused of welcoming what is unjust.

Notes

1. This essay is an expanded version of a talk given at the Conference on the Liberation of Female Persons, held at North Carolina State University at Raleigh, on March 26–28, 1973, under a grant from the S & H Foundation. I am indebted to James Thomson and the members of the Society for Ethical and Legal Philosophy for criticism of an earlier draft.
2. To the best of my knowledge, the analogy between veterans' preference and the preferential hiring of blacks has been mentioned in print only by Edward T. Chase, in a Letter to the Editor, *Commentary,* February 1973.

Robert Simon

Judith Jarvis Thomson has recently defended preferential hiring of women and black persons in universities.[1] She restricts her defense of the assignment of preference to only those cases where candidates from preferred groups and their white male competitors are equally qualified, although she suggests that her argument can be extended to cover cases where the qualifications are unequal as well. The argument in question is compensatory; it is because of pervasive patterns of unjust discrimination against black persons and women that justice, or at least common decency, requires that amends be made.

While Thomson's analysis surely clarifies many of the issues at stake, I find it seriously incomplete. I will argue that even if her claim that compensation is due victims of social injustice is correct (as I think it is), it is questionable nevertheless whether preferential hiring is an acceptable method of distributing such compensation. This is so, even if, as Thomson argues, compensatory claims override the right of the white male applicant to equal consideration from the appointing officer. For implementation of preferential hiring policies may involve claims, perhaps even claims of right, other than the above right of the white male applicant. In the case of the claims I have in mind, the best that can be said is that where preferential hiring is concerned, they are arbitrarily ignored. If so, and if such claims are themselves warranted, then preferential hiring, while *perhaps* not unjust, is open to far more serious question than Thomson acknowledges.

A familiar objection to special treatment for blacks and women is that, if such a practice is justified, other victims of injustice or misfortune ought to receive special treatment too. While arguing that virtually all women and black persons have been harmed, either directly or indirectly, by discrimination, Thomson acknowledges that in any particular case, a white male may have been victimized to a greater extent than have the blacks or women with which he is competing. However, she denies that other victims of injustice or misfortune ought automatically to have priority over blacks and women where distribution of compensation is concerned. Just as veterans receive preference with respect to employment

Robert Simon, "Preferential Hiring: A Reply to Judith Jarvis Thomson," *Philosophy & Public Affairs* 3, no. 3 (Spring 1974). Copyright © 1974 by Princeton University Press. Excerpts reprinted by permission.

in the civil service, as payment for the service they have performed for society, so can blacks and women legitimately be given preference in university hiring, in payment of the debt owed them. And just as the former policy can justify hiring a veteran who in fact had an easy time of it over a nonveteran who made great sacrifices for the public good, so too can the latter policy justify hiring a relatively undeprived member of a preferred group over a more disadvantaged member of a nonpreferred group.

But surely if the reason for giving a particular veteran preference is that he performed a service for his country, that same preference must be given to anyone who performed a similar service. Likewise, if the reason for giving preference to a black person or to a woman is that the recipient has been injured due to an unjust practice, then preference must be given to anyone who has been similarly injured. So, it appears, there can be no relevant *group* to which compensation ought to be made, other than that made up of and only of those who have been injured or victimized.[2] Although, as Thomson claims, all blacks and women may be members of that latter group, they deserve compensation *qua* victim and not *qua* black person or woman.

There are at least two possible replies that can be made to this sort of objection. First, it might be agreed that anyone injured in the same way as blacks or women ought to receive compensation. But then, "same way" is characterized so narrowly that it applies to no one except blacks and women. While there is nothing logically objectionable about such a reply, it may nevertheless be morally objectionable. For it implies that a non-black male who has been terribly injured by a social injustice has less of a claim to compensation than a black or woman who has only been minimally injured. And this implication may be morally unacceptable.

A more plausible line of response may involve shifting our attention from compensation of individuals to collective compensation of groups.[3] Once this shift is made, it can be acknowledged that as individuals, some white males may have stronger compensatory claims than blacks or women. But as compensation is owed the group, it is group claims that must be weighed, not individual ones. And surely, at the group level, the claims of black persons and women to compensation are among the strongest there are.

Suppose we grant that certain groups, including those specified by Thomson, are owed collective compensation. What should be noted is that the conclusion of concern here—that preferential hiring policies are acceptable instruments for compensating groups—does not directly follow. To derive such a conclusion validly, one would have to provide additional premises specifying the relation between collective compensation to groups and distribution of that compensation to individual members. For it does not follow from the fact that some group members are compensated that the group is compensated. Thus, if through a computer error, every member of the American Philosophical Association was asked to pay additional taxes, then if the government provided compensation for this error, it would not follow that it had compensated the Association. Rather it would have compensated each member *qua* individual. So what is required, where preferential hiring is concerned, are plausible premises showing how the preferential award of jobs to group members counts as collective compensation for the group.

Thomson provides no such additional premises. Moreover, there is good reason to think that if any such premises were provided, they would count against preferential hiring as an instrument of collective compensation. This is because although compensation is owed to the group, preferential hiring policies award compensation to an arbitrarily selected segment of the group; namely, those who have the ability and qualifications to be seriously considered for the jobs available. Surely, it is far more plausible to think that collective compensation ought to be equally available to all group members, or at least to all kinds of group members.[4] The claim that although compensation is owed collectively to a group, only a special sort of group member is eligible to receive it, while perhaps not incoherent, certainly ought to be rejected as arbitrary, at least in the absence of an argument to the contrary.

Accordingly, the proponent of preferential hiring faces the following dilemma. Either compensation is to be made on an individual basis, in which case the fact that one is black or a woman is irrelevant to whether one ought to receive special treatment, or it is made on a group basis, in which case it is far from clear that preferential hiring policies are acceptable compensatory instruments. Until this dilemma is resolved, assuming it can be resolved at all, the compensatory argument for preferential hiring is seriously incomplete at a crucial point.

Notes

1. Judith Jarvis Thomson, "Preferential Hiring," *Philosophy & Public Affairs* 2, no. 4 (Summer 1973), 364–384. All further page references to this article will be made within the text.
2. This point also has been argued for recently by J. L. Cowen, "Inverse Discrimination," *Analysis* 33, no. I (1972), 10–12.
3. Such a position has been defended by Paul Taylor, in his "Reverse Discrimination and Compensatory Justice," *Analysis* 33, no. 4 (1973), 177–182.
4. Taylor would apparently agree, *ibid.,* 180.

THE JUSTIFICATION OF
REVERSE DISCRIMINATION IN HIRING

Tom L. Beauchamp

In recent years government policies intended to ensure fairer employment and educational opportunities for women and minority groups have engendered alarm. Although I shall in this paper argue in support of enlightened versions of these policies, I nonetheless think there is much to be said for the opposition arguments. In general I would argue that the world of business is now overregulated by the federal government, and I therefore hesitate to support an extension of the regulative arm of government into the arena of hiring and firing. Moreover, policies that would eventuate in reverse discrimination in present North American society have a heavy presumption against them, for both justice-regarding and utilitarian reasons: The introduction of such preferential treatment on a large scale could well produce a series of injustices, economic advantages to some who do not deserve them, protracted court battles, jockeying for favored position by other minorities, congressional lobbying by power groups, a lowering of admission and work standards in vital institutions, reduced social and economic efficiency, increased racial hostility, and continued suspicion that well-placed women and minority group members received their positions purely on the basis of quotas. Conjointly these reasons constitute a powerful case against the enactment of policies productive of reverse discrimination in hiring.

I find these reasons against allowing reverse discrimination to occur both thoughtful and tempting, and I want to concede from the outset that policies of reverse discrimination can create serious and perhaps even tragic injustices. One must be careful, however, not to draw an overzealous conclusion from this admission. Those who argue that reverse discrimination creates injustices often say that, because of the injustice, such policies are *unjust*. I think by this use of "unjust" they generally mean "not justified" (rather than "not sanctioned by justice"). But a policy can create and even perpetuate injustices, as violations of the principle of formal equality, and yet be justified by other reasons. It would be an injustice in this sense to fire either one of two assistant professors with exactly similar professional credentials, while retaining the other of the two; yet the financial condition of the university or compensation owed the person retained might provide compelling reasons which justify the

Adapted from "The Justification of Reverse Discrimination" by Tom L. Beauchamp, in *Social Justice and Preferential Treatment*, ed. Blackstone and Heslep. Copyright © 1977 by University of Georgia Press, Athens. Reprinted by permission of the publisher.

action. The first reason supporting the dismissal is utilitarian in character, and the other derives from the principle of compensatory justice. This shows both that there can be conflicts between different justice-regarding reasons and also that violations of the principle of formal equality are not in themselves sufficient to render an action unjustifiable.

A proper conclusion, then—and one which I accept—is that all discrimination, including reverse discrimination, is prima facie immoral, because a basic principle of justice creates a prima facie duty to abstain from such treatment of persons. But no absolute duty is created come what may, for we might have conflicting duties of sufficient weight to justify such injustices. The latter is the larger thesis I wish to defend: Considerations of compensatory justice and utility are conjointly of sufficient weight in contemporary society to neutralize and overcome the quite proper presumption of immorality in the case of some policies productive of reverse discrimination.

I

It is difficult to avoid accepting two important claims: (a) that the law ought never to sanction any discriminatory practices (whether plain old unadorned discrimination or reverse discrimination), and (b) that such practices can be eradicated by bringing the full weight of the law down on those who engage in discriminatory practices. The first claim is a moral one, the second a factual one. I contend in this section that it is unrealistic to believe, as *b* suggests, that in contemporary society discriminatory practices *can* be eradicated by legal measures which do not permit reverse discrimination. And because they cannot be eradicated, I think we ought to relax our otherwise unimpeachably sound reservations (as recorded in *a* and discussed in the first section) against allowing any discriminatory practices whatever.

My argument is motivated by the belief that racial, sexual, and no doubt other forms of discrimination are not antique relics but are living patterns which continue to warp selection and ranking procedures. In my view the difference between the present and the past is that discriminatory treatment is today less widespread and considerably less blatant. But its reduction has produced apathy; its subtleness has made it less visible and considerably more difficult to detect. Largely because of the reduced visibility of racism and sexism, I suggest, reverse discrimination now strikes us as all too harsh and unfair. After all, quotas and preferential treatment have no appeal if one assumes a just, primarily non-discriminatory society. Since the presence or absence of seriously discriminatory conditions in our society is a factual matter, empirical evidence must be adduced to show that the set of discriminatory attitudes and selection procedures I have alleged to exist do in fact exist. The data I shall mention derive primarily from historical, linguistic, sociological, and legal sources.

Statistical Evidence

Statistical imbalances in employment and admission are often discounted because so many variables can be hypothesized to explain why, for non-discriminatory reasons, an imbalance exists. We can all think of plausible non-discriminatory reasons why 22% of Harvard's graduate students in 1969 were women but its tenured Arts and Sciences Faculty in the Graduate School consisted of 411 males and 0 females.[1] But sometimes we are able to discover evidence which supports the claim that skewed statistics are the result of discrimination. Quantities of such discriminatory findings, in turn, raise serious questions about the real reasons for suspicious statistics in those cases where we have *not* been able to determine these reasons—perhaps because they are so subtle and unnoticed. I shall discuss each factor in turn: (a) statistics which constitute prima facie but indecisive evidence of discrimination; (b) findings concerning discriminatory reasons for some of these statistics; and (c) cases where the discrimination is probably undetectable because of its subtleness, and yet the statistical evidence is overwhelming.

a. A massive body of statistics constituting prima facie evidence of discrimination has been assembled in recent years. Here is a tiny but diverse fragment of some of these statistical findings.[2] (1) Women college teachers with identical credentials in terms of publications and experience are promoted at almost exactly one-half the rate of their male counterparts. (2) In the United States women graduates of medical schools in 1965 stood at 7%, as compared with 36% in Germany. The gap in the number of women physicians was similar. (3) Of 3,000 leading law firms surveyed in 1957 only 32 reported a woman partner, and even these women were paid much less (increasingly so for every year of employment) than their male counterparts. (4) 40% of the white-collar positions in the United States are presently held by women, but only 10% of the management positions are held by women, and their pay again is significantly less (70% of clerical workers are women). (5) 8,000 workers were employed in May 1967 in the construction of BART (Bay Area Rapid Transit), but not a single electrician, ironworker, or plumber was black. (6) In the population as a whole in the United States, 3 out of 7 employees hold white-collar positions, but only 1 of 7 blacks holds such a position, and these latter jobs are clustered in professions which have the fewest jobs to offer in top-paying positions. (7) In the well-known A. T. & T. case, this massive conglomerate signed a settlement giving tens of millions of dollars to women and minority employees. A. T. & T. capitulated to this settlement based on impressive statistics indicating discriminatory treatment. [See Case 1 in this chapter.]

b. I concede that such statistics are far from decisive indicators of discrimination. But when further evidence concerning the reasons for the statistics is uncovered, they are put in a perspective affording them greater power—clinching power in my view. Consider (3)—the statistics on the lack of women lawyers. A survey of Harvard Law School alumnae in 1970 provided evidence about male lawyers' attitudes.[3] It showed that business and legal firms do not generally expect the women they hire to become lawyers, that they believe women cannot become good litigators, and that they believe only limited numbers of women should be hired since clients generally prefer male lawyers. Surveys of women applicants for legal positions indicate they are frequently either told that a woman will not be hired, or are warned that "senior partners" will likely object, or are told that women will be hired to do only probate, trust, and estate work. (Other statistics confirm that these are the sorts of tasks dominantly given to women.) Consider also (5)—a particular but typical case of hiring in non-white-collar positions. Innumerable studies have shown that most of these positions are filled by word-of-mouth recruitment policies conducted by all-white interviewers (usually all-male as well). In a number of decisions of the Equal Employment Opportunity Commission, it has been shown that the interviewers have racially biased attitudes and that the applications of blacks and women are systematically handled in unusual ways, such as never even being filed. So serious and consistent have such violations been that the EEOC has publicly stated its belief that word-of-mouth recruitment policies without demonstrable supplementary and simultaneous recruitment in minority group communities is in itself a "prima facie violation of Title VII."[4] Gertrude Ezorsky has argued, convincingly I believe, that this pattern of "special ties" is no less present in professional white collar hiring, which is neither less discriminatory nor more sensitive to hiring strictly on the basis of merit.[5]

c. Consider, finally, (1)—statistics pertaining to the treatment of women college teachers. The Carnegie Commission and others have assembled statistical evidence to show that in even the most favorable construal of relevant variables, women teachers have been discriminated against in hiring, tenuring, and ranking. But instead of summarizing this mountain of material, I wish here to take a particular case in order to illustrate the difficulty in determining, on the basis of statistics and similar empirical data, whether discrimination is occurring even where courts have been forced to find satisfactory evidence of discrimination. In December 1974 a decision was reached by the Commission against Discrimination of the Executive Department of the State of Massachusetts regarding a case at Smith College where the two complainants were women who were denied tenure and dismissed by the English Department.[6] The women claimed sex discrimination and based their case on the following: (1) Women at the full professor level in the college declined from 54% in 1958 to 21% in 1972, and in the English department from 57% in 1960 to 11% in 1972. These statistics compare unfavorably at all levels with Mt. Holyoke's, a comparable institution (since both have an all female student body and are located in Western Massachusetts). (2) Thirteen of the department's fifteen associate and full professorships at Smith belonged to men. (3) The two tenured women had obtained tenure under "distinctly peculiar experiences," including a stipulation that one be only part-time and that the other not be promoted when given tenure.

(4) The department's faculty members conceded that tenure standards were applied subjectively, were vague, and lacked the kind of precision which would avoid discriminatory application. (5) The women denied tenure were at no time given advance warning that their work was deficient. Rather, they were given favorable evaluations of their teaching and were encouraged to believe they would receive tenure. (6) Some stated reasons for the dismissals were later demonstrated to be rationalizations, and one letter from a senior member to the tenure and promotion committee contradicted his own appraisal of teaching ability filed with the department. (7) The court accepted expert testimony that any deficiencies in the women candidates were also found in male candidates promoted and given tenure during this same period, and that the women's positive credentials were at least as good as the men's.

The commissioner's opinion found that "the Complainants properly used statistics to demonstrate that the Respondents' practices operate with a discriminatory effect." Citing *Parham* v. *Southwestern Bell Telephone Co.,*[7] the commissioner argued that "in such cases extreme statistics may establish discrimination as a matter of law, without additional supportive evidence." But in this case the commissioner found abundant additional evidence in the form of "the historical absence of women," "word-of-mouth recruitment policies" which operate discriminatorily, and a number of "subtle and not so subtle, societal patterns" existing at Smith.[8] On December 30, 1974 the commissioner ordered the two women reinstated with tenure and ordered the department to submit an affirmative action program within 60 days.

This case is interesting because there is little in the way of clinching proof that the members of the English Department actually held discriminatory attitudes. Yet so consistent a pattern of *apparently* discriminatory treatment must be regarded, according to this decision, as *de facto* discrimination. The commissioner's ruling and other laws are quite explicit that "intent or lack thereof is of no consequence." If a procedure constitutes discriminatory treatment, then the parties discriminated against must be recompensed. Here we have a case where irresistible statistics and other sociological evidence of "social exclusion" and "subtle societal patterns" provide convincing evidence that strong, court backed measures must be taken because nothing short of such measures is sufficiently strong to overcome the discriminatory pattern, as the Respondents' testimony in the case verifies.[9]

Some understanding of the attitudes underlying the statistical evidence thus far surveyed can be gained by consideration of some linguistic evidence now to be mentioned. It further supports the charge of widespread discrimination in the case of women and of the difficulty in changing discriminatory attitudes.

Linguistic Evidence

Robert Baker has assembled some impressive linguistic evidence which indicates that our language is male-slanted, perhaps male chauvinistic, and that language about women relates something of fundamental importance concerning the males' most fundamental conceptions of women.[10] Baker argues that as the term "boy" once expressed a paternalistic and dominating attitude toward blacks (and was replaced in our conceptual structure because of this denigrating association), so are there other English terms which serve similar functions in regard to women (but are not replaced because not considered by men as in need of replacement). Baker assembles evidence both from the language itself and from surveys of users of the language to show the following.

The term "woman" is broadly substitutable for and frequently interchanged in English sentences such as "Who is that _____ over there?" by terms such as those in the following divisions:

A. Neutral Categories	B. Animal Categories	C. Plaything Categories	D. Gender Categories	E. Sexual Categories
lady	chick	babe	skirt	snatch
gal	bird	doll	hem	cunt
girl	fox	cuddly		ass
broad	vixen	thing		twat
(sister)	filly			piece
	bitch			lay
				pussy

Baker notes that (1) while there are differences in the frequency of usage, all of these terms are standard enough to be recognizable at least by most male users of the language; (2) women do not typically identify themselves in sexual categories; and (3) typically only males use the non-neutral categories (B-E). He takes this to be evidence—and I agree—that the male conception of women differs significantly from the female conception and that the categories used by the male in classifying women are "prima facie denigrating." He then argues that it is clearly and not merely prima facie denigrating when categories such as C and E are used, as they are either derived from playboy male images or are outright vulgarities. Baker argues that it is most likely that B and D are similarly used in denigrating ways. His arguments center on the metaphorical associations of these terms, but the evidence cannot be further pursued here.

Although Baker does not remark that women do not have a similar language for men, it seems to me important to notice this fact. Generally, any negative categories used by women to refer to men are as frequently or more frequently used by men to apply to women. This asymmetrical relation does not hold, of course, for the language used by whites and blacks for denigrating reference. This fact perhaps says something about how blacks have caught onto the impact of the language as a tool of denigrating identification in a way women have yet to do, at least in equal numbers. It may also say something about the image of submissiveness which many women still bear about themselves—an image blacks are no longer willing to accept.

Baker concludes from his linguistic studies that "sexual discrimination permeates our conceptual structure. Such discrimination is clearly inimical to any movement toward sexual egalitarianism and virtually defeats its purpose at the outset."[11] His conclusion may somewhat overreach his premises, but when combined with the corroborating statistical evidence previously adduced, it seems apt. Linguistic dispositions lead us to categorize persons and events in discriminatory ways which are sometimes glaringly obvious to the categorized but accepted as "objective" by the categorizer. My contention, derived from Baker's and to be supported as we proceed, is that cautious, good faith movements toward egalitarianism such as affirmative action guidelines *cannot* succeed short of fundamental conceptual and ethical revisions. And since the probability of such revisions approximates zero (because discriminatory attitudes are covertly embedded in language and cultural habit), radical expedients are required to bring about the desired egalitarian results, expedients which may result in reverse discrimination.

Conclusions

Irving Thalberg has argued, correctly I believe, that the gravest contemporary problems with racism stem from its "protectively camouflaged" status, which he calls "visceral." Thalberg skillfully points to a number of attitudes held by those whites normally classified as unprejudiced which indicate that racism still colors their conception of social facts.[12] My alliance with such a position ought to be obvious by now. But my overall intentions and conclusions are somewhat different. I hold that because of the peculiarly concealed nature of the protective camouflage under which sexism and racism have so long thrived, it is not a reasonable expectation that the lightweight programs now administered under the heading of affirmative action will succeed in overcoming discriminatory treatment. I turn now directly to this topic.

II

The rawest nerve of the social and political controversy concerning reverse discrimination is exposed by the following question: What government policies are permissible and required in order to bring about a society where equal treatment of persons is the rule rather than the exception? Fair-minded opponents of any government policy which might produce reverse discrimination—Carl Cohen and William Blackstone, for example—seem to me to oppose them largely because and perhaps only because of their *factual belief* that present government policies not causing reverse discrimination will, if seriously and sincerely pursued, prove sufficient to achieve the goal of equal consideration of persons.

Once again a significant factual disagreement has emerged: what means are not only fair but also sufficient? I must again support my contentions by adducing factual data to show that my pessimism is sustained by the weight of the evidence. The evidence cited here comes from government data concerning affirmative action programs. I shall discuss the affirmative action program in order to show that on the basis of present government guidelines (which, to my knowledge, are the best either in law or proposed as law by those who oppose reverse discrimination), discriminatory business as usual will surely prevail.

Affirmative Action

I begin with a sample of the affirmative action guidelines, as understood by those who administer them. I use the example of HEW guidelines for educational institutions receiving federal financial aid. These guidelines are not radically different from those directed at hiring practices throughout the world of business. Specifically, these guidelines cover three areas: admission, treatment of students, and employment. A sample of the sorts of requirements universities are under includes: (1) They may not advertise vacant positions as open only to or preferentially to a particular race or sex, except where sex is a legitimate occupational requirement. (2) The university sets standards and criteria for employment, but if these effectively work to exclude women or minorities as a class, the university must justify the job requirements. (3) An institution may not set different standards of admission for one sex, race, etc. (4) There must be active recruitment where there is an underrepresentation of women and minorities, as gauged by the availability of qualified members of these classes. However, the relevant government officials have from time to time made it clear that (1) quotas are unacceptable, either for admission or employment, though target goals and timetables intended to correct deficiencies are acceptable and to be encouraged. (2) A university is never under any obligation to dilute legitimate standards, and hence there is no conflict with merit hiring. (3) Reserving positions for members of a minority group (and presumably for the female sex) is "an outrageous and illegal form of reverse bias" (as one former director of the program wrote).[13] By affirmative action requirements I mean this latter interpretation and nothing stronger (though I have given only a sample set of qualifications, of course).

The question I am currently asking is whether these guidelines, assuming they will be vigorously pursued, can reasonably be expected to bring about their goal, which is the social circumstance of non-discriminatory treatment of persons. If they *are* strong enough, then Cohen, Blackstone, and others are right: Reverse discrimination is not under such circumstances justified. Unfortunately the statistical and linguistic evidence previously adduced indicates otherwise. The *Smith College* case is paradigmatic of the concealed yet serious discrimination which occurs through the network of subtle distortions, old-boy procedures, and prejudices we have accumulated. Only when the statistics become egregiously out of proportion is action taken or a finding of mistreatment possible. And that is one reason why it seems unlikely that substantial progress can be made, in any realistic sense of "can," by current government measures not productive of reverse discrimination. According to Peter Holmes, once the Director of HEW's Office for Civil Rights and in charge of interpreting affirmative action guidelines: "It has been our policy that it is the institutions' responsibility to determine non-discriminatory qualifications in the first instance, and that such qualifications, in conjunction with other affirmative action steps, should yield results."[14] This is the received HEW view, but the last sentence contains an ambiguous use of the word "should." If the "should" in this statement is a moral "should," none will disagree. But if it is an empirical, predictive "should," as I take Mr. Holmes to intend, we are back to the core of the difficulty. I now turn to a consideration of how deficient such affirmative action steps have proven to be.

Government Data

The January 1975 Report of the United States Commission on Civil Rights contains a section on "compliance reviews" of various universities. These are government assessments of university compliance with Executive Orders pertaining to affirmative action plans. The report contains a stern indictment of the Higher Education Division (HED) of HEW—the division in charge of overseeing all HEW civil rights enforcement activities in the area of higher education. It concludes that "HED has, in large part, failed to follow the procedures required of compliance agencies under the Executive order regulations."[15] But more interesting than this mere failure to enforce the law is the report's discussion of how very difficult it is to obtain compliance even when there is a routine attempt to enforce the law. The Commission reviewed four major campuses in the United States (Harvard, University of Michigan, University of Washington, Berkeley). They concluded that there is a pattern of inadequate compliance reviews, inordinate delays, and inexcusable failures to take enforcement action where there were clear violations of the Executive order regulations.[16]

Consider the example of the "case history of compliance contacts" at the University of California at Berkeley. According to HED's own staff a "conciliation agreement" with this university "is now being used as a model for compliance activities with other campuses." When the Office for Civil Rights of HEW determined to investigate Berkeley (April 1971), after several complaints, including a class action sex discrimination complaint, the university refused to permit access to its personnel files and refused to permit the interviewing of faculty members without an administrator present. Both refusals are, as the report points out, "direct violations of the Executive order's equal opportunity clause," under which Berkeley held contracts. Despite this clear violation of the law, no enforcement action was taken. A year and one-half later, after negotiations and more complaints, the university was instructed to develop a written affirmative action plan to correct "documented deficiencies" of "pervasive discrimination." The plan was to include target goals and timetables wherever job underutilization had been identified.[17]

In January 1973 the university, in a letter from Chancellor Albert H. Bowker, submitted a draft affirmative action plan which was judged "totally unacceptable." Throughout 1973 Berkeley received "extensive technical assistance" from the government to aid it in developing a better plan. No such plan emerged, and OCR at the end of the year began to question "the university's commitment to comply with the executive order." The university submitted other unacceptable plans, and finally in March 1974 "a conciliation agreement was reached." However, "the document suffered from such extreme vagueness that, as of August 1974, the university and OCR were in substantial disagreement on the meaning of a number of its provisions," and "the agreement specifically violated OFCC regulations in a number of ways." These violations are extensive and serious, and the report characterizes one part as "outrageous." Four years after this "model" compliance case began, it was unresolved and no enforcement proceedings had been taken against the university. The report concludes: "In its Title VI reviews of colleges and universities, HEW routinely finds noncompliance, but it almost never imposes sanctions; instead HEW responds by making vague recommendations. Moreover, HEW does not routinely require the submission of progress reports or conduct sufficient followup to determine if its recommendations have been followed."

III

No one could be happy about the conclusions I have reached or about the depressing and disturbing facts on which they are based. But I do take it to be a *factual* and not an *evaluative* conclusion both (1) that the camouflaged attitudes I have discussed exist and affect the social position of minority groups and women and (2) that they will in all likelihood continue to have this influence. It is, of course, an evaluative conclusion that we are morally permitted and even required to remedy this situation by the imposition of quotas, target goals, and timetables. But anyone who accepts my *interpretation* of the facts bears a heavy burden of moral argument to show that we ought not to use such means to that end upon which I take it we all agree, viz., the equal consideration of persons irrespective of race, sex, religion, or nationality.

By way of conclusion, it is important to set my arguments in the framework of a distinction between real reverse discrimination and merely apparent reverse discrimination. My evidence demonstrates present, ongoing barriers to the removal of discriminatory practices. My contentions set the stage for showing that *because* of the existence of what Thalberg calls "visceral racism," and because of visceral sexism as well, there will be many occasions on which we can only avoid inevitable discrimination by policies productive of reverse discrimination. Sometimes, however, persons will be hired or admitted—on a quota basis, for example—who appear to be displacing better applicants, but the appearance is the result of visceral discriminatory perceptions of the person's qualifications. In this case there will certainly appear to the visceral racist or sexist to be reverse discrimination, and this impression will be reinforced by knowledge that quotas were used; yet the allegation of reverse discrimination will be a mistaken one. On other occasions there will be genuine reverse discrimination, and on many occasions it will be impossible to determine whether or not this consequence is occurring. The evidence I have adduced is, of course, intended to support the contention that real and not merely apparent reverse discrimination is justified. But it is justified only as a means to the end of ensuring genuinely non-discriminatory treatment of all persons.

Notes

1. From "Statement of Dr. Bernice Sandler," *Discrimination Against Women: Congressional Hearings on Equal Rights in Education and Employment,* ed. Catharine R. Stimpson (New York: R. R. Bowker Company, 1973), pp. 61, 415. Hereafter *Discrimination Against Women.*
2. All of the statistics and quotations cited are taken from the compilations of data in the following sources: (1) Kenneth M. Davidson, Ruth B. Ginsburg, and Herma H. Kay, eds., *Sex-Based Discrimination: Text, Cases, and Materials* (Minneapolis: West Publishing Company, 1974), esp. Ch. 3. Hereafter *Sex-Based Discrimination.* (2) *Discrimination Against Women,* esp. pp. 397–441 and 449–502. (3) Alfred W. Blumrosen, *Black Employment and the Law* (New Brunswick, N.J.: Rutgers University Press, 1971), esp. pp. 107, 122f. (4) *The Federal Civil Rights Enforcement Effort—1971,* A Report of the United States Commission on Civil Rights.
3. *Discrimination Against Women,* pp. 505f.
4. *Sex-Based Discrimination,* p. 516.
5. "The Fight Over University Women," *The New York Review of Books,* May 16, 1974, pp. 32–39.
6. *Maurianne Adams and Mary Schroeder* v. *Smith College,* Massachusetts Commission Against Discrimination, Nos. 72-S-53, 72-S-54 (December 30, 1974). Hereafter *The Smith College Case.*
7. 433 F.2d 421, 426 (8 Cir. 1970).
8. *The Smith College Case,* pp. 23, 26.
9. *Ibid.,* pp. 26f.
10. Robert Baker, " 'Pricks' and 'Chicks': A Plea for Persons," in Richard Wasserstrom, ed., *Today's Moral Problems* (New York: Macmillan Publishing Company, 1975), pp. 152–170.
11. *Ibid.,* p. 170.
12. "Visceral Racism," *The Monist,* 56 (1972), 43–63, and reprinted in Wasserstrom.
13. J. Stanley Pottinger, "Race, Sex, and Jobs: The Drive Towards Equality," *Change Magazine,* 4 (Oct. 1972), 24–29.
14. Peter E. Holmes, "HEW Guidelines and 'Affirmative Action,' " *The Washington Post,* Feb. 15, 1975.
15. *The Federal Civil Rights Enforcement Effort—1974,* 3: 276.
16. *Ibid.,* p. 281.
17. *Ibid.,* all subsequent references are from pp. 281–286.

REVERSE DISCRIMINATION AND COMPENSATORY JUSTICE

William T. Blackstone

Is reverse discrimination justified as a policy of compensation or of preferential treatment for women and racial minorities? That is, given the fact that women and racial minorities have been invidiously discriminated against in the past on the basis of the irrelevant characteristics of race and sex—are we now justified in discriminating in their favor on the basis of the same characteristics? This is a central ethical and legal question today, and it is one which is quite unresolved. Philosophers, jurists, legal scholars, and the man-in-the-street line up on both sides of this issue. These differences are plainly reflected (in the Supreme Court's majority opinion and Justice Douglas's dissent) in *DeFunis* v. *Odegaard.*[1] . . .

I will argue that reverse discrimination is improper on both moral and constitutional grounds, though I focus more on moral grounds. However, I do this with considerable ambivalence, even "existential guilt." Several reasons lie behind that ambivalence. First, there are moral and constitutional arguments on both sides. The ethical waters are very muddy and I simply argue that the balance of the arguments are against a policy of reverse discrimination.[2] My ambivalence is further due not only to the fact that traditional racism is still a much larger problem than that of reverse discrimination but also because I am sympathetic to the *goals* of those who strongly believe that reverse discrimination as a policy is the means to overcome the debilitating effects of past injustice. Compensation and remedy are most definitely required both by the facts and by our value commitments. But I do not think that reverse discrimination is the proper means of remedy or compensation. . . .

I

Let us now turn to the possibility of a utilitarian justification of reverse discrimination and to the possible conflict of justice-regarding reasons and those of social utility on this issue. The category of morally relevant reasons is broader, in my opinion, than reasons related to the norm of justice. It is broader than those related to the norm of utility. Also it seems to me that the norms of justice and utility are not reducible one to the other. We cannot argue these points of ethical theory here. But, if these assumptions are correct, then it is at least possible to morally justify injustice or invidious discrimination in some contexts. A case would have to be made that such injustice, though regrettable, will produce the best consequences for society and that this fact is an overriding or weightier moral reason than the temporary injustice. Some arguments for reverse discrimination have taken this line. Professor Thomas Nagel argues that such discrimination is justifiable as long as it is "clearly contributing to the eradication of great social evils."[3] . . .

Another example of what I would call a utilitarian argument for reverse discrimination was recently set forth by Congressman Andrew Young of Georgia. Speaking specifically of reverse discrimination in the context of education, he stated: "While that may give minorities a little edge in some instances, and you may run into the danger of what we now commonly call reverse discrimination, I think the educational system needs this. Society needs this as much as the people we are trying to help . . . a society working toward affirmative action and inclusiveness is going to be a stronger and more relevant society than one that accepts the limited concepts of objectivity. . . . I would admit that it is perhaps an individual injustice. But it might be necessary in order to overcome an historic group injustice or series of group injustices."[4] Congressman Young's basic justifying grounds for reverse discrimination, which he recognizes as individual injustice, are the results which he thinks it will produce: a stronger and more relevant education system and society, and one which is more just overall. His argument may involve pitting some justice-regarding reasons (the right of women and racial minorities to be compensated for past injustices) against others (the right of the majority to the uniform application of the same standards of merit to all). But a major thrust of his argument also seems to be utilitarian.

Just as there are justice-regarding arguments on both sides of the issue of reverse discrimination, so also there are utilitarian arguments on both sides. In a nutshell, the utilitarian argument in favor runs like this: Our society contains large groups of persons who suffer from past institutionalized injustice. As a result, the possibilities of social discord and disorder are high indeed. If short-term reverse discrimination were to be effective in overcoming the effects of past institutionalized injustice and if this policy could alleviate the causes of disorder and bring a higher quality of life to millions of persons, then society as a whole would benefit.

There are moments in which I am nearly convinced by this argument, but the conclusion that such a policy would have negative utility on the whole wins out. For although reverse discrimination might appear to have the effect of getting more persons who have been disadvantaged by past inequities into the mainstream quicker, that is, into jobs, schools, and practices from which they have been excluded, the cost would be invidious discrimination against majority group members of society. I do not think that majority members of society would find this acceptable, i.e., the disadvantaging of themselves for past inequities which they did not control and for which they are not responsible. If such policies were put into effect by government, I would predict wholesale rejection or noncooperation, the result of which would be negative not only for those who have suffered past inequities but also for the justice-regarding institutions of society. Claims and counter-claims would obviously be raised by other ethnic or racial minorities—by Chinese, Chicanos, American Indians, Puerto Ricans—and by orphans, illegitimate children, ghetto residents, and so on. Literally thousands of types or groups could, on similar grounds as blacks or women, claim that reverse discrimination is justified on their behalf. What would happen if government attempted policies of reverse discrimination for all such groups? It would mean the arbitrary exclusion or discrimination against all others relative to a given purpose and a given group. Such a policy would itself create an injustice for which those newly excluded persons could then, themselves, properly claim the need for reverse discrimination to offset the injustice to them. The circle is plainly a vicious one. Such policies are simply self-destructive. In place of the ideal of equality and distributive justice based on relevant criteria, we would be left with the special pleading of self-interested power groups, groups who gear criteria for the distribution of goods, services, and opportunities to their special needs and situations, primarily. Such policies would be those of special privilege, not the appeal to objective criteria which apply to all.[5] They would lead to social chaos, not social justice.

Furthermore, in cases in which reverse discrimination results in a lowering of quality, the consequences for society, indeed for minority victims of injustice for which reverse discrimination is designed to help, may be quite bad. It is no easy matter to calculate this, but the recent report sponsored by the Carnegie Commission on Higher Education points to such deleterious consequences.[6] If the quality of instruction in higher education, for example, is lowered through a policy of primary attention to race or sex as opposed to ability and training, everyone—including victims of past injustice—suffers. Even if such policies are clearly seen as temporary with quite definite deadlines for termination, I am sceptical about their utilitarian value. . . .

II

The inappropriateness of reverse discrimination, both on utilitarian and justice-regarding grounds, in no way means that compensation for past injustices is inappropriate. It does not mean that those who have suffered past injustices and who have been disadvantaged by them are not entitled to compensation or that they have no moral right to remedy. It may be difficult in different contexts to translate that moral right to remedy into practice or into legislation. When has a disadvantaged person or group been compensated enough? What sort of allocation of resources will compensate without creating additional inequities or deleterious consequences? There is no easy answer to these questions. Decisions must be made in particular contexts. Furthermore, it may be the case that the effects of past injustices are so severe (poverty, malnutrition, and the denial of educational opportunities) that genuine compensation —the balancing of the scales—is impossible. The effects of malnutrition or the lack of education are often non-reversible (and would be so even under a policy of reverse discrimination). This is one of the tragedies of injustice. But if reverse discrimination is inappropriate as a means of compensation and if (as I have argued) it is unjust to make persons who are not responsible for the suffering and disadvantaging of others to suffer for those past injuries, then other means must be employed unless overriding moral considerations of another type (utilitarian) can be clearly demonstrated. That compensation must take a form which is consistent with our constitutional principles and with reasonable principles of justice. Now it seems to me that the Federal Government's Equal Opportunity and Affirmative Action Programs are consistent with these principles, that they are not only not committed to reverse discrimination but rather absolutely forbid it.[7] However, it also seems to me that some officials authorized or required to implement these compensatory efforts have resorted to reverse discrimination and hence have violated the basic principles of justice embodied in these programs. I now want to argue both of these points: first, that these federal programs reject reverse discrimination in their basic principles; secondly, that some implementers of these programs have violated their own principles.

Obviously our country has not always been committed constitutionally to equality. We need no review of our social and political heritage to document this. But with the Fourteenth Amendment, equality as a principle was given constitutional status. Subsequently, social, political, and legal practices changed radically and they will continue to do so. The Fourteenth Amendment declares that states are forbidden to deny any person life, liberty, or property without due process of law or to deny to any person the equal protection of the laws. In my opinion the principles of the Equal Opportunity and Affirmative Action Programs reflect faithfully this constitutional commitment. I am more familiar with those programs as reflected in universities. In this context they require that employers "recruit, hire, train, and promote persons in all job classifications without regard to race, color, religion, sex or national origin, except where sex is a bona fide occupational qualification."[8] They state explicitly that "goals may not be rigid and inflexible quotas which must be met, but must be targets reasonably attainable by means of good faith effort."[9] They require the active recruitment of women and racial minorities where they are "underutilized," this being defined as a context in which there are "fewer minorities or women in a particular job classification than would reasonably be expected by their availability."[10] This is sometimes difficult to determine; but some relevant facts do exist and hence the meaning of a "good faith" effort is not entirely fluid. In any event the Affirmative Action Program in universities requires that "goals, timetables and affirmative action commitment, must be designed to correct any identifiable deficiencies," with separate goals and timetables for minorities and women.[11] It recognizes that there has been blatant discrimination against women and racial minorities in universities and elsewhere, and it assumes that there are "identifiable deficiencies." But it does not require that blacks be employed because they are black or women employed because they are women; that is, it does not require reverse discrimination with rigid quotas to correct the past. It requires a good faith effort in the present based on data on the availability of qualified women and racial minorities in various disciplines and other relevant facts. (Similar requirements hold, of course, for non-academic employment at colleges and universities.) It does not mandate the hiring of the unqualified or a lowering of standards; it mandates only equality of opportunity for all which, given the history of discrimination against women and racial minorities, requires affirmative action in recruitment.

Now if this affirmative action in recruitment, which is not only consistent with but required by our commitment to equality and social justice, is translated into rigid quotas and reverse discrimination by those who implement equal opportunity and affirmative action programs in the effort to get results immediately—and there is no doubt in my mind that this has occurred—then such action violates the principles of those programs.

This violation—this inconsistency of principle and practice—occurs, it seems to me, when employers hire with *priority emphasis* on race, sex, or minority-group status. This move effectively eliminates others from the competition. It is like pretending that everyone is in the game from the beginning while all the while certain persons are systematically excluded. This is exactly what happened recently when a judge declared that a certain quota or number of women were to be employed by a given agency regardless of their qualifications for the job,[12] when some public school officials fired a white coach in order to hire a black one,[13] when a DeFunis is excluded from law school on racial grounds, and when colleges or universities announce that normal academic openings will give preference to female candidates or those from racial minorities.

If reverse discrimination is prohibited by our constitutional and ethical commitments, what means of remedy and compensation are available? Obviously, those means which are consistent with those commitments. Our commitments assure the right to remedy to those who have been treated unjustly, but our government has not done enough to bring this right to meaningful fruition in practice. Sound progress has been made in recent years, especially since the Equal Employment Opportunity Act of 1972 and the establishment of the Equal Employment Opportunities Commission. This Act and other laws have extended anti-discrimination protection to over 60% of the population.[14] The Commission is now authorized to enforce anti-discrimination orders in court and, according to one report, it has negotiated out-of-court settlements which brought 44,000 minority workers over 46 million dollars in back-pay.[15] Undoubtedly this merely scratches the surface. But now the framework exists for translating the right to remedy into practice, not just for sloughing off race and sex as irrelevant criteria of differential treatment but other irrelevant criteria as well—age, religion, the size of hips (I am thinking of airline stewardesses), the length of nose, and so on.

Adequate remedy to overcome the sins of the past, not to speak of the present, would require the expenditure of vast sums for compensatory programs for those disadvantaged by past injustice in order to assure equal access. Such programs should be racially and sexually neutral, benefiting the disadvantaged of *whatever sex or race.* Such neutral compensatory programs would have a high proportion of blacks and other minorities as recipients, for they as members of these groups suffer more from the injustices of the past. But the basis of the compensation would be that fact, not sex or race. Neutral compensatory policies have definite theoretical and practical advantages in contrast to policies of reverse discrimination: Theoretical advantages, in that they are consistent with our basic constitutional and ethical commitments whereas reverse discrimination is not; practical advantages, in that their consistency, indeed their requirement by our constitutional and ethical commitments, means that they can marshall united support in overcoming inequalities whereas reverse discrimination, in my opinion, can not.

Notes

1. 94 S.Ct. 1704 (1974).
2. I hasten to add a qualification—more ambivalence!—resulting from discussion with Tom Beauchamp of Georgetown University. In cases of extreme recalcitrance to equal employment by certain institutions or businesses some quota requirement (reverse discrimination) may be justified. I regard this as distinct from a general policy of reverse discrimination.
3. "Equal Treatment and Compensatory Discrimination," *Philosophy and Public Affairs,* 2 (Summer 1974).
4. *The Atlanta Journal and Constitution,* Sept. 22, 1974, p. 20-A.
5. For similar arguments see Lisa Newton, "Reverse Discrimination as Unjustified," *Ethics,* 83 (1973).
6. Richard A. Lester, *Antibias Regulation of Universities* (New York, 1974); discussed in *Newsweek,* July 15, 1974, p. 78.
7. See The Civil Rights Act of 1964, especially Title VII (which created the Equal Employment Opportunity Commission), amended by The Equal Employment Opportunity Act of 1972, found in *ABC's of The Equal Employment Opportunity Act,* prepared by the Editorial Staff of The Bureau of National Affairs, Inc., 1972. Affirmative Action Programs came into existence with Executive Order 11246. Requirements for affirmative action are found in the rules and regulations 41-CFR Part 60-2, Order #4 (Affirmative Action Programs) generally known as Executive Order #4 and Revised Order #4 41-CFR 60-2 B. For discussion see Paul Brownstein, "Affirmative Action Programs," in *Equal Employment Opportunities Compliance,* Practising Law Institute, New York City (1972), pp. 73–111.
8. See Brownstein, "Affirmative Action Programs" and, for example, *The University of Georgia Affirmative Action Plan,* Athens, Ga., 1973–74, viii, pp. 133, 67.
9. Brownstein and *The University of Georgia Affirmative Action Plan,* Athens, Ga., 1973–74, p. 71.
10. *Ibid.,* p. 69.
11. *Ibid.,* p. 71.
12. See the *Atlanta Journal and Constitution,* June 9, 1974, p. 26-D.
13. See *Atlanta Constitution,* June 7, 1974, p. 13-B.
14. *Newsweek,* June 17, 1974, p. 75.
15. *Ibid.,* p. 75.

SUGGESTED SUPPLEMENTARY READINGS

BAYLES, MICHAEL. "Compensatory Reverse Discrimination in Hiring." *Social Theory and Practice,* 2, no. 3 (1971–72).

BEAUCHAMP, TOM L., ed. *Ethics and Public Policy,* Chapter 1. Englewood Cliffs, N.J.: Prentice-Hall, 1975.

BLACKSTONE, WILLIAM T., and ROBERT HESLEP, eds. *Social Justice and Preferential Treatment.* Athens: University of Georgia Press, 1977.

BLUMENROSEN, ALFRED. "Strangers in Paradise: *Griggs* v. *Duke Power Co.* and the Concept of Employment Discrimination." *Michigan Law Review,* 71 (1975).

BOWIE, NORMAN E., and ROBERT L. SIMON. *The Individual and the Political Order,* Chapter 9. Englewood Cliffs, N.J.: Prentice-Hall, 1977.

COHEN, MARSHALL, THOMAS NAGEL, and THOMAS SCANLON, eds. *Equality and Preferential Treatment.* Princeton, N.J.: Princeton University Press, 1977.

"Constitutionality of Remedial Minority Preferences in Employment." *Minnesota Law Review,* 56 (1972).

GLAZER, NATHAN. *Affirmative Discrimination: Ethnic Inequality and Public Policy.* New York: Basic Books, 1975.

GOLDMAN, ALAN. "Justice and Hiring by Competence." *American Philosophical Quarterly,* January 1977.

GROSS, BARRY R. *Reverse Discrimination.* Buffalo, N.Y.: Prometheus Books, 1977.

HUGHES, GRAHAM. "The Right to Special Treatment." In *The Rights of Americans,* ed. Norman Dorsen. New York: Pantheon Books, 1971.

KATZNER, LOUIS. "Is the Favoring of Women and Blacks in Employment and Educational Opportunities Justified?" In *Philosophy of Law,* ed. Joel Feinberg and Hyman Gross. Belmont, Calif.: Wadsworth-Dickenson, 1975.

NAGEL, THOMAS. "Equal Treatment and Compensatory Discrimination." *Philosophy and Public Affairs,* 2 (Summer 1973).

NEWTON, LISA. "Reverse Discrimination as Unjustified." *Ethics,* 83 (1973).

SETHI, S. PRAKASH. *Business Corporations and the Black Man.* Scranton, Penn.: Chandler Publishing Co., 1970.

SHER, GEORGE. "Justifying Reverse Discrimination in Employment." *Philosophy and Public Affairs,* 4, no. 2 (Winter 1975).

Thalberg, Irving. "Reverse Discrimination and the Future." *Philosophical Forum,* V (1973–74).

"What Do You People Want?" *Harvard Business Review,* March–April 1969.